Germany since 1815

Related titles from Palgrave Macmillan

A. J. Nicholls, *Weimar and the Rise of Hitler*

Pól O'Dochartaigh, *Germany since 1945*

James Reallack, *Germany in the Age of Kaiser Wilhelm II*

Matthew S. Seligmann, *Germany from Reich to Republic, 1871–1918*

Peter H. Wilson, *From Reich to Revolution*

Germany since 1815

A Nation Forged and Renewed

David G. Williamson

First published 2005 by
PALGRAVE MACMILLAN
Houndmills, Basingstoke, Hampshire RG21 6XS and
175 Fifth Avenue, New York, N.Y. 10010
Companies and representatives throughout the world

PALGRAVE MACMILLAN is the global academic imprint of the Palgrave Macmillan
division of St. Martin's Press, LLC and of Palgrave Macmillan Ltd. Macmillan® is a
registered trademark in the United States, United Kingdom and other countries.
Palgrave is a registered trademark in the European Union and other countries.

ISBN 0–333–92094–5 hardback
ISBN 0–333–92095–3 paperback

This book is printed on paper suitable for recycling and made from fully
managed and sustained forest sources.

A catalogue record for this book is available from the British Library.

Library of Congress Cataloging-in-Publication Data
Williamson, D. G.
   Germany since 1815 : a nation forged and renewed / David G. Williamson.
       p. cm.
   Includes bibliographical references and index.
   ISBN 0-333–92094–5 (cloth) – ISBN 0-333-92095-3 (pbk.)
       1. Germany–History–1789-1900. 2. Germany–History–20th century. I. Title.

DD203 .W48 2004
943.08–dc22   200405001

10 9 8 7 6 5 4 3 2 1
14 13 12 11 10 09 08 07 06 05

Printed in China

To Sue, a loyal, loving and very patient friend

Contents

List of Illustrations

List of Maps

Preface

German history is an important component in so many history syllabuses at both schools and universities. Germany has, after all, had a profound impact on European, American and indeed world history in the twentieth century. Not only did the two great German wars of the twentieth century accelerate the collapse of the European colonial empires, but the vacuum that the defeat of Hitler created in central Europe led to the long Cold War and the division of the European continent until 1990. Both the threat of Soviet expansion and the need to contain a revived (albeit for the time being only a West) German state also led to western European integration with its immense, and as yet unfinished, consequences for the traditional structure of Europe's nation states. It is not surprising then that historians have paid so much attention to the 'course of German history' in the nineteenth and twentieth centuries.

The object of this book is to provide for students, and indeed all who are interested in this period, a concise and up-to-date study of German history since 1815, which combines the key facts of the period with analysis and wider reference to crucial historical debates. The book is divided into four main chronological parts: 1815–70, 1871–1918, 1918–45 and 1945–90, which includes a final section analysing the first years of the new Berlin Republic. Each chapter starts with an introduction outlining its major themes and a series of questions that indicate the main topics that are addressed in the chapter. Focus boxes and notes in the margin help elucidate points made in the text by providing background information or summaries of historiographical debates, while a timeline at the beginning of each chapter provides a guide to the key dates of the relevant material covered in the chapter. The text is comprehensively cross-referenced so that readers can explore the origins and consequences of events they are studying, as well as being reminded of the remarkable longevity of some issues in German history. In places bullet points are used to help readers grasp simply and speedily key developments of complex events, while in part six of the book there is a collection of documents, which both provides a basis for further discussion and helps readers understand more fully issues referred to in the main text. At the end of the book there is a critical bibliography of books in English on this period of German history, which is divided into chronological sections and enables readers to explore issues raised in this study in greater depth. There is also a glossary fully explaining the technical terms used in the text.

As the main focus of this book is on the German state or 'Germany', domestic Austrian politics are only touched upon where they are relevant to this history.

DAVID G. WILLIAMSON

Acknowledgements

The author and publishers wish to thank the following for permission to use copyright material.

Berg Publishers, for the statistical extract 'Productivity in the FRG. 1951–1959' from Alan Kramer, *The West German Economy, 1945–1955*, p. 206; reproduced courtesy of Berg Publishers.

Bundesbildstelle Berlin, for the post-1945 photographs © copyright Bundesbildstelle Berlin.

Oxford University Press, for the statistical extract 'Dollar Quotations for the Mark, 1914–23' from Gordon Craig, *Germany 1866–1945*, p. 450; reproduced with permission of Oxford University Press.

Sempringham Publishing for supplying the (copyright-free) image of the Kaiser from the cover of *New Perspective*, March 1999.

The Imperial War Museum, for an aerial view of the Krupp plant (ref: Q81743); an SPD rally in the early 1900s (ref: Q81737); Bismarck, the elder statesman (ref: Q81829); a French cartoon commenting on Bismarck's attempts to keep France and Russia apart in the 1880s (ref: Q81754); Hitler in 1936 (ref: HU5239); men of the German labour service marching (ref: NYP68056); all images reproduced with permission of the trustees of the Imperial War Museum, London.

The Royal Collection, for *Clemens Lothar Wenzel, Prince Metternich* by Sir Thomas Lawrence, and *The Congress of Vienna* by Jean Baptiste Isabey; both pictures reproduced courtesy of The Royal Collection © 2004, Her Majesty Queen Elizabeth II.

Walter de Gruyter GmbH & Co. KG, for the statistical extract 'National Election Results in the Weimar Republic in Percentages' from Thomas Childers, 'Inflation, Stabilization and Political Realignment in Germany 1924 to 1928', in G. D. Feldman, et al. (eds), *The German Inflation Reconsidered: A Preliminary Balance* (1982); reproduced courtesy of Walter de Gruyter GmbH & Co. KG.

Every effort has been made to trace the copyright holders, but if any have been inadvertently overlooked, the publishers will be pleased to make the necessary arrangements at the first opportunity.

Maps

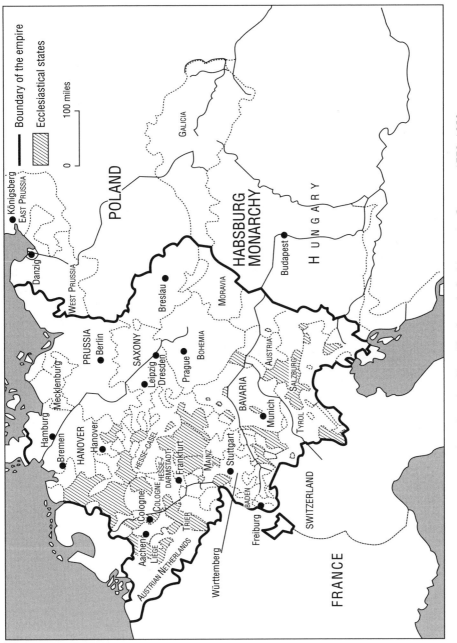

Map 1 Germany in 1789 (adapted from Brendan Sims, *The Struggle for Mastery in Germany, 1779–1850*, Macmillan, 1998, p. ix)

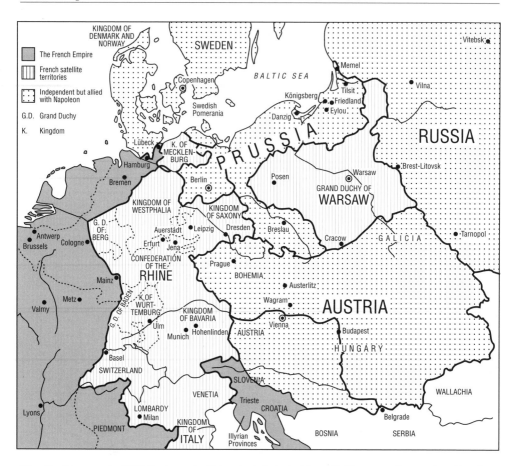

Map 2   Germany in 1810: the impact of Napoleon (adapted from D. Thomson, *Europe since Napoleon*, Longman, 1951, p. 47)

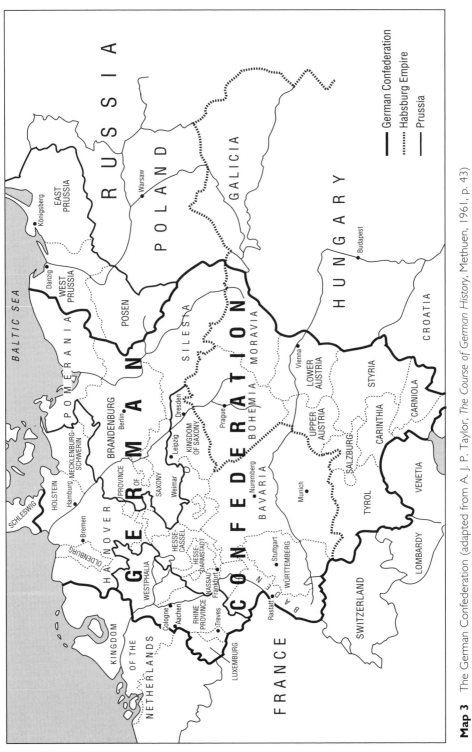

Map 3   The German Confederation (adapted from A. J. P. Taylor, *The Course of German History*, Methuen, 1961, p. 43)

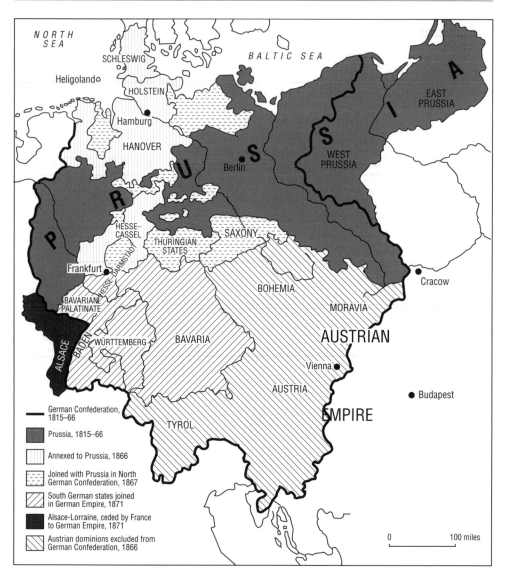

Map 4   The unification of *Kleindeutschland* (adapted from D. Thomson, *Europe since Napoleon*, Longman, 1951, p. 283)

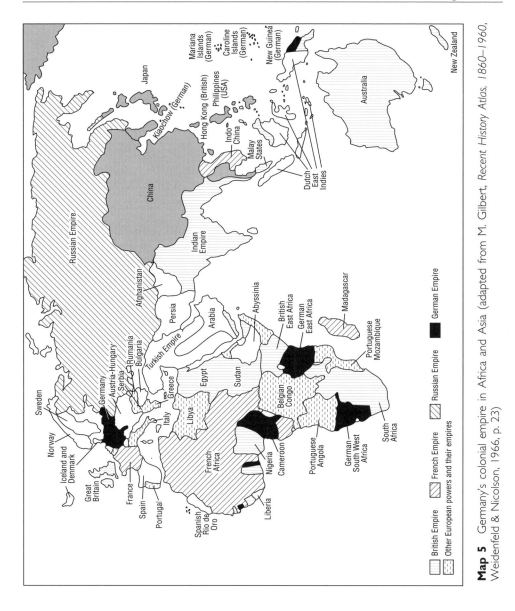

Map 5 Germany's colonial empire in Africa and Asia (adapted from M. Gilbert, *Recent History Atlas, 1860–1960*, Weidenfeld & Nicolson, 1966, p. 23)

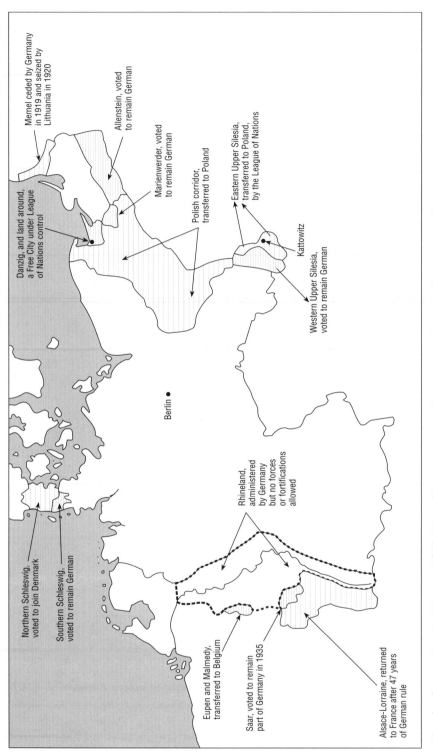

Map 6   Germany's territorial losses, 1919 (adapted from map in *New Perspective*, vol. 5, no. 2, December 1919)

Memel ceded by Germany in 1919 and seized by Lithuania in 1920

Allenstein, voted to remain German

Marienwerder, voted to remain German

Polish corridor, transferred to Poland

Danzig, and land around, a Free City under League of Nations control

Eastern Upper Silesia, transferred to Poland, by the League of Nations

Kattowitz

Western Upper Silesia, voted to remain German

Berlin ●

Northern Schleswig, voted to join Denmark

Southern Schleswig, voted to remain German

Rhineland, administered by Germany but no forces or fortifications allowed

Eupen and Malmedy, transferred to Belgium

Saar, voted to remain part of Germany in 1935

Alsace-Lorraine, returned to France after 47 years of German rule

Map 7 Nazi Germany at its fullest extent, 1942 (adapted from D. G. Williamson, *The Third Reich*, 3rd edition, Pearson, 2002, Map 3)

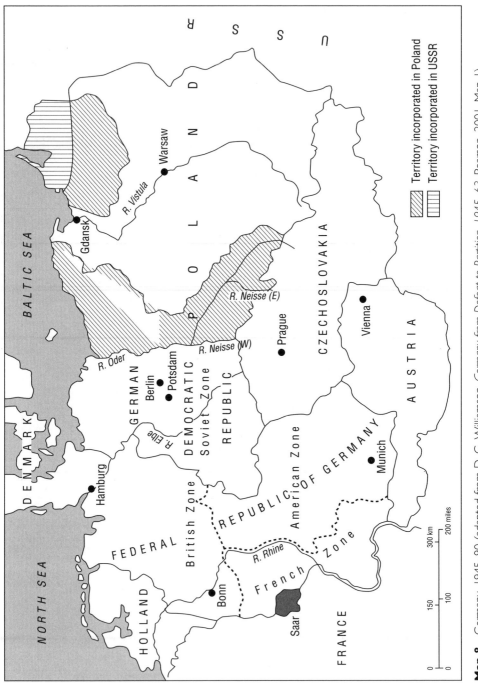

Map 8 Germany, 1945–90 (adapted from D. G. Williamson, *Germany from Defeat to Partition, 1945–63*, Pearson, 2001, Map 1)

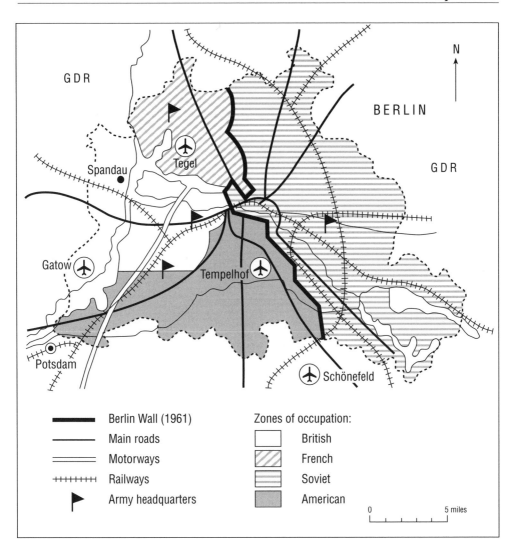

Map 9 Berlin 1945–90 (adapted from D. G. Williamson, *Germany from Defeat to Partition, 1945–63*, Pearson, 2001, Map 2)

Part One

Germany Unified, 1815–70

1 Germany Recast: The French Revolutionary Wars and the Vienna Settlement, 1789–1815

TIMELINE

1789 Start of French Revolution
1799 Napoleon comes to power as First Consul
1803 France annexes left bank of the Rhine
1805 Bavaria and Württemberg become kingdoms
France defeats Russia and Austria at Austerlitz
1806 End of Holy Roman Empire
France defeats Prussia at Jena and Auerstädt
Rhineland Confederation formed
1807 Treaty at Tilsit
Prussia reduced to a rump state and loses territory to Grand Duchy of Warsaw and Kingdom of Westphalia
Stein appointed first minister and embarks on reform programme
1808 Stein dismissed as a result of French pressure
1809 New Anglo-Austrian alliance against France
Austria defeated at Wagram
1812 French invasion of Russia and subsequent retreat
1813 *Mar.* Prussia declares war on France
Aug. Austria joins war against France
Oct. French armies defeated at Battle of Leipzig
1814 Napoleon abdicates
Congress of Vienna convened
1815 Napoleon's final defeat at Battle of Waterloo
German Confederation set up

Introduction: Germany on the eve of the French Revolution

The philosopher, Gottfried Wilhelm Leibniz, observed in the early eighteenth century that 'Germany is the centre of Europe . . . the battlefield on which the struggle for mastery in Europe is fought.'[1] Its ethnic core spread from the left bank of the Rhine to the great European plain in the east and from Denmark across the Alps to the Tyrol. 'Germany' was no compact nation state like France or Great Britain, protected by relatively well-defined geographical barriers. Germans indeed had considerable problems in trying to define what Germany in practice meant. Goethe and Schiller, for instance, coined the much-quoted epigram: 'Germany? But where is it? I don't know how to find such a country.'[2]

On the eve of the French revolution 'Germany' presented a fragmented picture of regions divided not only by formidable physical barriers but

Johann Wolfgang von Goethe, 1749–1832, and **Friedrich von Schiller, 1759–1805**: playwrights, poets and writers, who represent the peak of German literary classicism

See Map 1

also by a great variety of dialects and cultural differences. Along the borders of German-speaking Europe there were areas of mixed settlements, but even beyond these there were small German-speaking communities in the Balkans and Russia, and along the Baltic coast. Numerous Polish and German settlements straddled both sides of the Polish–German linguistic frontier. The political boundaries of German Europe were equally confusing: 'Small states, free cities, ecclesiastical territories, and semi-autonomous estates were scattered across the political landscape in bewildering profusion.'[3] Many of these states were further subdivided by internal ecclesiastical, legal and fiscal boundaries.

Up to a point these fragmented states found a degree of political expression in the Holy Roman Empire of the German Nation, which was, as David Blackbourn has succinctly put it, 'a product of historical accretion, loosely draped over an array of independent, highly diverse territories'.[4] The Holy Roman Emperor was a shadowy figure elected by the rulers of the eight largest German states. The Empire, which consisted of over eighteen hundred different territories, was not an organization capable of waging war or welding the German states into an effective entity. Its aim was 'not to clarify and dominate but rather to order and balance fragmented institutions and multiple loyalties'.[5]

There were two rival centres of potential hegemony in the Reich: Austria and Prussia. Neither was a compact nation state and both had territory outside the Reich. Austria was a large disparate empire, the territories of which included the Archduchy of Austria, Styria, Carinthia and Carniola, the Bohemian and Hungarian crown lands, as well as the Austrian Netherlands, Lombardy, Mantua and Galicia, while Prussia was

See Map 1

composed of a series of territories which sprawled across central and northern Germany. Their rivalry, which erupted into two European wars in the middle of the eighteenth century, shook the Empire, yet in the final analysis neither state was thinking of replacing it with a unified German state. Consequently, despite its contradictions and weaknesses, the Empire remained an element of stability in central Europe, and, in words which find an echo in the Europe of the European Union, the Swiss Jurist, Johannes von Müller, observed that it made Germany 'free through fragmentation'.[6]

The political fragmentation of the Holy Roman Empire was both strengthened by and reflected in the economic and communications infrastructures of central Europe. Roads were impassable in winter, while physical dangers still impeded the easy transport of goods on the rivers. There was no common German currency, uniform commercial code or recognized national economic capital. Above all, the mass of tolls and tariffs stifled any large-scale inter-German trade. Consequently, apart from a few major trading cities such as Hamburg or Frankfurt, economic activity was mostly of a local or regional character.

A. J. P. Taylor argued sweepingly that the German people had 'been for more than a thousand years, unmistakably a people'.[7] This is a view that the great German scholar, Johann Gottfried Herder, took. He argued that in practice there was a German fatherland, which was defined not territorially but by the idea of a German *Volk*, a community formed by language and culture. Certainly the Germans were united by a common language, although they spoke this in many different dialects, which were not always comprehensible to other Germans, and by the last quarter of the eighteenth century there was a real German literary culture facilitated by networks of publishers, the new periodicals, reading societies and libraries. To quote James Sheehan, 'threads made up of printed pages and personal connections linked people from Strassburg to Riga, from Hamburg to Vienna'.[8] Yet this was essentially a literary culture that involved only a small, educated élite in Germany. It did not touch the great majority of Germans, whose culture was local and traditionally based on their villages, churches and market towns. Thus it is more accurate to argue that Germany possessed 'a national culture in aspiration, but never, and certainly not before 1800 in actuality'.[9]

> **Johann Gottfried von Herder, 1774–1803**: court preacher at Weimar, teacher, theologian, philosopher and philologist

As elsewhere in Europe, life in the German states for the great mass of the people was hard and precarious, and usually only half a particular generation reached their late twenties. Society throughout the Reich was organized into 'orders' or 'estates' rather than classes: nobles, clergy, burghers, craftsmen, peasants. These estates were all subject to different laws and regulations depending on the estate they were in. Eighty per cent of the German population worked on the land, and was still legally subject to their lords. On the east of the Elbe in Prussia, the lord of the manor, or Junker exercised direct control over his peasants, who, in exchange for the land they cultivated, had to offer labour services in cash or kind. In the west and south, labour services had often been commuted into cash payment, although the lords remained the legal owners of the land and still had hunting rights. The towns, too, were organized into a corporate structure under which their population was divided into the 'patriciate' (the ruling mercantile elite),[10] master craftsmen and journeymen, all of whom were organized into craft guilds.

> The term **Junker** comes from the German *Jungherr*, which applied to sons of the Prussian landed gentry serving as officer cadets. Later the term came to describe the Prussian landowners, with large estates east of the Elbe, many of whom served in the Prussian bureaucracy or army

Eighteenth-century German Europe was full of paradoxes. In many ways it was a society with a relatively backward economy and small parochial states. On the other hand, it had writers and philosophers of the very first rank. While the Reich seemed stable, 'profound changes were taking place within [its] political shell'.[11] Prussia had joined Austria as a European great power and the German princes were gradually centralizing and subordinating the nobility, the churches, the guilds and the estates to their will. They were helped in this task by highly competent and uncorrupt officials, who were determined to be a force for enlightened reform. To contemporaries this process did not necessarily entail the liquidation of the Reich. It was, however, to be the French Revolution that was to sweep it away and ultimately bring about the reordering of German-speaking Europe.

Key issues

- Why did Germany's fate depend on the European balance of power?
- What impact did Napoleon have on Germany?
- What was the nature of German nationalism in the period 1790–1815?
- Did Prussia lead a German 'national uprising' as such against Napoleon?
- Why was the German Confederation rather than a united German state formed?

The impact of the French Revolution

The fate of Germany, as will be seen in subsequent chapters, depended essentially on the European balance of power. For most of the eighteenth century, France and Russia were anxious to maintain the Empire as an organization sufficiently strong to defend itself, but incapable of dominating Europe. The French Revolution shattered this balance and led to radical changes in Germany. Its initial impact triggered unrest in the Rhineland and in Saxony in 1789–90, but the real clash between revolutionary France and the Empire came when the French Assembly abolished the feudal privileges of the Imperial nobility and the diocesan rights of the German bishops in Alsace. In 1791 Austria and Prussia, motivated not least by the prospect of annexations in the west, issued the declaration of Pillnitz, which committed the two states to defending the principle of hereditary monarchy against revolutionary threats. In April 1792 France responded by declaring war on the two powers. After the decisive defeats of the alliance at Valmy and Fleurus, the French invasion of the Empire opened the way to a radical reordering of Germany:

These privileges derived from the medieval manorial system whereby a peasant held land from his lord in exchange for services both in cash and kind

See Document 1

- Prussia, more interested in asserting its claims in Poland, dropped out of the war in 1795 and accepted the French occupation of the Rhineland. In exchange for this, it was promised compensation on the right bank of the Rhine. Here a precedent was set for linking French annexations with compensation at the expense of the Holy Roman Empire.
- After Austria was forced to make peace with the French in 1797, subsequent negotiations at Rastatt between France and representatives of the Holy Roman Empire led to one of the most radical territorial reorganizations in European history. The middle-sized states of Bavaria, Württemberg, Baden and Saxony were given the basic shape they were to possess until their incorporation into the Bismarckian Reich in 1866–70. Their consolidation was achieved at the expense of the Imperial cities and the ecclesiastical territories, which were drastically reduced in number. The implementation of these terms was briefly delayed by the outbreak of war again in 1799, but with the defeat of Austrian forces at Marengo and Hohenlinden they were incorporated into the Treaty of Lunéville in 1801.

- In 1805 the Austrians, in alliance with Britain and Russia, made yet another unsuccessful attempt to liberate Europe, but this came to an abrupt end with the French occupation of Vienna and the defeat of Austro-Russian forces at Austerlitz in November 1805. The western states of the old Empire increasingly looked to Paris for leadership. The Archbishop–Elector of Regensburg–Aschaffenburg, Karl von Dalberg, tried to persuade Napoleon to accept the Imperial crown, arguing that the southern and western states would be better-off linked to France than in an Empire controlled by Austria and Prussia. Napoleon rejected this idea, dissolved the Empire and set up the Confederation of the Rhine in July–August 1806 as a buffer between France and its potential enemies in the East.

- Napoleon was given the opportunity to complete his reorganization of Germany when Prussia belatedly came into the war in August 1806 only to have its armies destroyed at Jena and Auerstädt in October. Once Napoleon had defeated the Russians at Friedland the following June, the tsar had little alternative but to accept French plans for compelling Prussia to cede both its territory west of the Elbe as well as its Polish possessions. The Prussian state was reduced to a rump of four provinces, which was occupied by French soldiers, and it was also forced to pay a large war indemnity, while its army was reduced to a mere 42,000 men.

> **Confederation**: a form of union of individual states in which the independence of each state is preserved. It contrasts with a **federation**, which insists on the supremacy of a common government

Reconstruction and reform, 1807–12

See Map 2

In the catastrophic period after the French victories of 1806–07, France was in effect the puppet master of Germany. Not only did Napoleon determine its organization, but all the states had to accept French economic policy and actively participate in the economic blockade of Britain. Yet it was also a period of radical reform for both rump Prussia and the new states that emerged within the Confederation.

Prussia

The reformers in Prussia, grouped around Barons Hardenberg, Gneisenau and Stein, were convinced that only a complete political transformation would enable Prussia to regain its strength and defeat the French. To survive, Prussia would have to base itself, to quote Gneisenau, on 'the triple alliance of arms, science and constitution'.[12] As a first step towards this, Stein began to create a structured, ministerial government to replace arbitrary rule by royal cronies. In November 1808 he successfully persuaded the king to agree to set up a central administration run by five ministers, each of whom would be responsible for a separate department. This then opened up the way for a series of important administrative reforms that went far to recast Prussia's administrative system for the next century. The country was divided up into

Key political figures in Prussia, 1807–14

Karl August von Hardenberg, 1750–1822, was state minister in the Prussian government and dismissed on Napoleon's orders in 1807. He returned to power as chancellor in 1810. His aims were internal reform and the restoration of Prussia as a great power. **August von Gneissenau, 1760–1831**, became a cult figure after his brilliant defence of Kolberg against the French and used his prestige to support the cause of reform. **Heinrich vom-und-zum Stein, 1757–1831**, became King Frederick William's chief minister in 1807, but was dismissed on Napoleon's insistence in 1808. He became the advisor on German policy to the Russian government and an advocate of a united Germany. **Frederick William III, 1770–1840**, whom Sheehan describes as 'at best an ordinary man, who found himself living in extraordinary times'[13] before 1806 attempted to acquire territory within the Empire by negotiating with the French, but this policy ended in ruins at Jena. He gave only half-hearted support to the reform party in Prussia and played a relatively minor part in the war and subsequent peace negotiations of 1813–15. Thereafter he increasingly became a reactionary and co-operated closely with Austria.

Regierungsbezirke: administrative districts

Kreise: literally circles, but the term is best translated as districts

Conscription: compulsory enlistment for military service

Landwehr: Reserve army or militia formed for all men between 17 and 60 years of age who were not serving in the army

administrative units, the Regierungsbezirke, and in 1812 the lower-tier organizations, the Kreise, were put firmly under state control, although two years later the Junkers forced a radical revision, which restored their powers at local level. By the Municipal Ordinance of 19 November 1808, the towns were given a system of municipal self-government, which enabled them, through elected councils, to determine taxes and expenditure. With the failure of the *Kreis* reforms in the countryside, the cities became, in nineteenth-century Prussia, beacons of reform. These administrative reforms were also coupled with attempts to create a free labour market and a competitive economic climate (see p. 34). The state also accepted the need to supervise the education of teachers and to inspect both the elementary and grammar schools and the universities. Education was, in the words of the Prussian education minister, Wilhelm von Humboldt, a 'practical need of the state'.[14]

Of crucial importance for the future were the military reforms. To survive, Prussia had to emulate the French and create a nation in arms. The key to military reform was universal conscription, but this could only be introduced once war broke out with France in February 1813. The regular army was drastically overhauled. A large number of its officers were dismissed, and from now on commissions could only be gained on merit. In March 1813 the concept of a 'people in arms' became a reality when the *Landwehr* was formed.

The Rhineland Confederation

In July 1806 the Confederation numbered 16 German states. In return for their loyalty and willingness to provide troops and money for the French war effort, the states were granted autonomy within the

Confederation, while the electors of Bavaria and Württemberg were made kings and the ruler of Baden was made a grand duke. By 1811 a further 23 territories joined the Confederation. Many contemporaries looked upon the Confederation as a new edition of the old Reich; others even saw it as the germ of a new Germany. There were plans for a diet to draw up and define its collective powers, but it never met. German, and indeed most European historians between the 1870s and the 1950s, on the other hand, tended to view the Confederation with its creation of several key, middle-sized states as part of the long-drawn-out process of building a united Germany, but in fact, as James Sheehan has pointed out, 'the creation of several medium sized, relatively well-integrated states, ready and willing to preserve their identity, did not make the formation of a nation state any easier'.[15]

Like Prussia, the states within the Confederation were faced with similar tasks of reorganization. The Grand Duchy of Berg, the Kingdom of Westphalia and the Grand Duchy of Frankfurt were deliberately intended by Napoleon to be model states and 'a bridgehead for the moral conquest of central Europe'.[16] Under Napoleon's brother, Jerome, Westphalia was given a constitution, a parliament elected on a narrow franchise, civil equality and religious liberty, yet in reality what counted was military power and bureaucratic control. Westphalia was virtually stripped bare to provide the French empire with money and mercenaries. In south Germany, Baden, Bavaria and Württemberg sought to integrate the land ceded to them by Napoleon into their core territory. Baden quadrupled in size, Württemberg doubled, while Bavaria had to absorb 80 territories which had previously been independent. This effectively created new states and forced the governments to adopt sweeping reforms over the next five years, which were both animated by the spirit of the enlightened absolutism of the late eighteenth century and tempered by the ideas of the French Revolution: unified and effective administrations were created, the hierarchy of feudal, religious and estate-based organizations was abolished and state control was established over education, taxation and military conscription. In sum, the reforms meant that 'for the first time, the individual experienced the direct influence of the state; they established the enormous power of the modern state to control lives'.[17] Only in Bavaria was a constitution introduced with a parliament elected on a narrow franchise, but this was never summoned. Collectively, however, these reforms strengthened the south German states and the potential of the 'third Germany'.

Napoleon's defeat

In May 1812 Napoleon ordered his German allies to attend a congress of princes in Dresden as a preliminary to the invasion of Russia. On 24–25 June his huge army, a third of which was made up of Germans, crossed the Niemen. Its destruction through disease and the skilful tactics of the

---

See Map 2

Diet: an assembly

Enlightened absolutism: the term used to describe the modernizing reforms carried out by many European eighteenth-century monarchs. These were inspired by the Enlightenment, but had no intention of widening political participation

Third Germany: term used to describe the medium-sized German states such as Bavaria and Württemberg, which wished to pursue a policy independent of both Austria and Prussia

Prince Clemens von Metternich (1773–1859)

Originally a Rhinelander, he became an Austrian diplomat. In 1809 he was appointed Austrian foreign minister . At first he hoped to come to terms with Napoleon and so avoid having to introduce radical reforms at home as Prussia had been compelled to do. In 1813 he joined the alliance against France, and a year later presided brilliantly over the Congress of Vienna (1814–15) where he witnessed the triumph of his conservative policies of monarchical restoration and defensive alliances against aggression and revolution. He became Austrian chancellor in 1821 and, until forced to resign in 1848, (see p. 000) used his formidable skills to defend the 1815 settlement.

Russians forced Napoleon to retreat. In December 1812, when Tsar (Emperor) Alexander I decided to turn the hitherto defensive war into a struggle for the liberation of Europe, the commander of the Prussian corps, General Yorck von Wartenburg, defied the orders of his king and concluded the Convention of Tauroggen with the Russians. Meanwhile, in East Prussia, Stein, who had earlier fled to Russia, set up a provincial assembly which conscripted troops and declared war on France. Frederick William initially hesitated, but was pressurized by the patriots to enter the war.

The subsequent war had 'aspects of a popular uprising'.[18] Conscription was made obligatory and special units of volunteers, the *Freikorps*, were formed. However, outside the provinces of rump Prussia in the states of the Confederation of the Rhine, the population remained loyal to Napoleon. The war had an ambiguous note. For the patriots, it was a war of the people for emancipation and freedom, while for Frederick William and Clemens von Metternich, the Austrian foreign minister, once Austria joined the war in August 1813, it was a struggle for dynastic rights and claims, balance of power and restoration. When the French forces were driven beyond the Rhine in late 1812, allied unity was threatened by divisions between the hawks and the doves. The former included the Tsar of Russia, Stein, most of the Prussian generals and nationalist intellectuals such as Ernst Arndt and Joseph Görres, who wanted to liberate the whole of Europe from Napoleon, while the latter, led by Metternich, hoped in the interests of the balance of power to stop at the Rhine and preserve Napoleonic France intact. Napoleon's rejection of Metternich's peace feelers, however, ensured that there was no option but the invasion of France, the occupation of Paris and ultimately his abdication in May 1814.

Did the French Revolution accelerate the formation of a German national consciousness?

At the end of the eighteenth century there was no single concept of German nationalism. Some German intellectuals identified Germany with the Empire, others, like the poets Klopstock, Hölderlin and Schiller, perceived Germany to be primarily a cultural nation defined by its literature and language.

At the start of the revolution the majority of German intellectuals welcomed the French Revolution as a blow for liberty, but the rise of Maximilien Robespierre and attempts to export the revolution by force alienated most of them. There was no uniform 'national' reaction against the French occupation. Some Germans looked to the Rhineland Confederation as a future nucleus for the 'German nation'. The more conservative-minded patriots, such as Friedrich Gentz, were drawn to Vienna, while others were attracted by appeals for an uprising of the German *Volk*, which were beginning to emanate from Berlin. For instance, the French occupation of Berlin in 1806 caused the philosopher, J. G. Fichte, to turn his back on France and, in a series of lectures entitled *Reden an die deutsche Nation* (*Addresses to the German Nation*), which he delivered in the Berlin Academy in the winter of 1807–08, to extol Germany's cultural mission and argue that patriotism was as valuable as cosmopolitanism. The theologian, Friedrich Schleiermacher, and the writer and man of letters, Ernst Arndt, began to call for the creation of a nation state. The latter, with his call for a single, monarchical German state with its own army, laws and parliament, anticipated the ideal of the nineteenth-century German liberals.

How much support was there in fact for these ideas? Much of the German population in the Rhineland Confederation remained loyal to the French, or at least lukewarm towards their liberators. The Prussian government did indeed attempt to harness the new wave of patriotism, but Frederick William was interested primarily in Prussian rather than German patriotism. As Sheehan has pointed out, '[t]he *Volk*'s role in its own "liberation" was, at best, a minor one. Napoleon was defeated by regular armies, not patriotic poets and quaintly attired gymnasts.'[19] In retrospect the *Freikorps* and the war of liberation became a powerful myth, which inspired later generations of nationalists, who lacked the liberalism of their predecessors. A mass of memoirs, stories, histories, pageants and paintings all portrayed the war of liberation as a seminal experience in German nationalism, but in reality 'this "birth myth" of the German nation was an artificial construct of nationalist ideology'.[20]

The Vienna Settlement

The territorial settlement in German Europe was anticipated by Metternich in the autumn of 1813 when he negotiated the Treaty of Ried, by which Bavaria agreed to join the coalition on the condition that its sovereignty and territorial possessions were guaranteed. In November and December similar treaties were signed with Württemberg, Hesse-Darmstadt, Baden, Nassau, Saxe-Coburg and

See Document 1

Volk: people sharing a common ethnic origin, language and culture, but not necessarily belonging to the same state

See Document 2

I   A sketch of the key figures at the Congress of Vienna by Jean Baptiste Isabey (1767–1855)
The Royal Collection © HM Queen Elizabeth II, RCIN 451893

Hesse-Kassel. This ensured essentially that the Napoleonic re-organization of southern Germany would remain intact and that the reorganization of Germany would not be pre-empted by a *fait accompli* carried out by the Prussian army, but instead arranged by the great powers at the coming peace conference.

When the allied powers assembled at Vienna in the autumn of 1814, the settlement of German Europe was one of the most complex problems confronting them. Their statesmen had not only to define the boundaries of the surviving German states, but also to achieve a balance between interstate co-operation and independence. Should there, for instance, be a federation, a confederation or a straight Prusso-Austrian hegemony? Stein, as early as the autumn of 1813, had made radical proposals for amalgamating the Rhineland Confederation states into a 'third Germany' which would be linked to Austria and Prussia. These ideas were then worked on by Wilhelm von Humboldt, the Prussian ambassador in Vienna. Hoping that a federal Germany would eventually evolve, he proposed first of all a voluntary confederation in which the states would create a joint defence force and then gradually co-ordinate their domestic policies. 'The firm, consistent, and unwavering agreement and friendship of Austria and Prussia' would form the essential 'cornerstone for this entire structure'.[21] Hardenberg, in his 41 Articles, put forward a draft constitution for an 'Eternal Confederation' which would be run by a committee of the larger German states under the joint direction of Austria and Prussia. He was in effect proposing joint Austro-Prussian control over the German states in return for Metternich's acceptance of Prussia as an equal partner within the Confederation. Inevitably the prospect of this dualism alarmed the *Mittelstaaten*, who desperately looked round for influential allies amongst the great powers.

At the congress the final decision over the future of Germany was left to the great powers, advised by the German Committee on which Austria, Prussia, Bavaria, Württemberg and Hanover were represented. Initially Metternich, Humboldt and Count Munster, the Hanoverian representative, produced a revised draft of the 41 Articles – the so-called 'twelve Articles' – which both considerably increased the powers of the larger states and gave Austria the presidency of the Confederation. Inevitably this met with bitter opposition from the smaller states, which threatened to paralyze the deliberations. The eruption of the Saxon–Polish dispute momentarily appeared to play into the hands of the Prussian patriots and the generals. When Metternich under Russian pressure withdrew his consent to a Prussian annexation of Saxony, the reformers in the army, Generals Boyen and Gneisenau, were ready to fight Austria and remodel Germany under Prussian hegemony, but they were forced to back down when Austria concluded a secret alliance with France and Britain in January 1815.

Napoleon's return from Elba put the whole peace settlement at risk and powerfully concentrated the minds of the German princes on the need for a compromise. The final details of the territorial and political settlement in Germany were rapidly agreed on in May 1815 and were confirmed in the Act of the German Confederation of 8 May 1815. Napoleon's defeat at Waterloo temporarily raised hopes among the Prussian patriots of a revised settlement. Arndt, for instance, argued that Prussia should 'use its strength to build and preserve honour, power and harmony'.[22] In the armistice and occupation negotiations after Waterloo, Blücher, the commander of the Prussian troops at the battle, and

The Saxon–Polish Issue

In 1806 Napoleon strengthened his influence in Saxony by turning it into a kingdom and appointing its new king the absentee ruler of Poland. When the French were driven from Germany, Prussia hoped to annex Saxony as compensation for her former Polish territory, which she was ready to cede to Russia. Initially both Metternich and Castlereagh, the British foreign minister, appeared to agree to the annexation, provided Prussia helped them block Russian ambitions in Poland, but, in response to furious complaints from Tsar Alexander, Austria had rapidly to back-pedal and withdraw the offer of Saxony. A compromise was reached in the New Year whereby the tsar received most of the Napoleonic Duchy of Warsaw, and Prussia was given only the northern half of Saxony and territories in the Rhineland and Westphalia as compensation.

See Maps 2 and 3

Gneissenau attempted to demand massive reparations and indemnities, which would have involved the surrender of Alsace-Lorraine, the Saar and Luxemburg. Castlereagh, Metternich and the Tsar came to the conclusion that the Prussian army was a potentially revolutionary force, but ultimately all it managed to achieve were a few minor boundary changes on the Belgian frontier and the transfer of the fortresses of Landau and Saarlouis to the German Confederation.

In the territorial settlement, which was confirmed in the second Peace of Paris in November, the map of German Europe was again redrawn:

See Map 3

- The 39 states, which survived the wreck of the Holy Roman Empire and the Rhineland Confederation, established the new German Confederation. Besides the territories of Austria and Prussia, which had previously been included in the Holy Roman Empire, the most important members were the kingdoms of Saxony, Bavaria, Hanover and Württemberg, and the Grand Duchies of Hessen and Baden. The great majority of members, including the four free cities of Lübeck, Frankfurt, Bremen and Hamburg, were small territorial units. Twenty-one member states had populations of under 100,000, and the smallest, Liechtenstein, had a population of barely more than 5000.
- Prussia emerged as the main beneficiary after absorbing northern Saxony, former Polish territory around Danzig, Swedish Pomerania and considerable territories in the Rhineland and Westphalia.
- Hanover, which remained tied to Britain, became a kingdom, while Bavaria received Ansbach, Bayreuth, Würzburg and Aschaffenburg. Baden and Württemberg gained little but survived the post-Napoleonic reorganization intact.

Austria annexed no German territory. Her main aim was the consolidation of her dynastic territories and new position in Italy. Within Germany itself, Metternich's policy was to rely on diplomacy rather than force in order to maintain Austrian hegemony. He intended to exploit the role allotted to Austria of president of the Diet, or federal assembly, to ensure that the Confederation did not evolve into a federal state.

Compared to the earlier proposals circulated, the Confederation was a relatively straightforward association or congress of 39 independent states and cities, with the intention of guaranteeing the external and internal security of its members. It possessed only one statutory institution, the Diet, which was composed of the ambassadors of the member states. This met, however, in plenary sessions only when there were important matters to consider, such as constitutional changes, which affected the whole Confederation. Any change in the constitution required unanimity and consequently even the smallest state enjoyed an effective veto. Normally it was envisaged that the Diet would meet in a smaller council (*Engerer Rat*) in which 17 votes were distributed amongst the 39 members. The larger states – Austria, Prussia, Bavaria, Saxony, Hanover and Württemberg, Baden, Electoral Hesse, the Grand Duchy of

Hesse, Denmark and the Netherlands – had one vote each, while the remaining votes were distributed amongst the other states. According to Article 11 of the *Bundesakt*, members were permitted to make alliances with other states as long as these were not aimed against the Confederation or any of its members. In the event of the Confederation going to war, the individual states would supply money and troops, and renounce the negotiation of any independent peace treaties, which only it could conclude.

Bundesakt: treaty creating the Confederation

See Document 3

Conclusion

The Germany of 1815 was very different from that of 1789. The old Holy Roman Empire contained over 1800 different states, cities and territories, while the new German Confederation had just 39. The balance of power within it was also very different. A fact of political life for most of the eighteenth century was Austro-Prussian rivalry. The German Confederation, on the other hand, was based on close Austro-Prussian political co-operation, which more or less survived until 1848. The 'third Germany' – the medium-sized states, particularly Bavaria – was strengthened by Metternich's acceptance of the Napoleonic settlement in southern Germany. In retrospect, Prussian–German historians have seen Napoleon as the midwife of a united Germany and his destruction of the Reich as acting as a catalyst for the emergence of German nationalism under Prussian leadership, which eventually resulted in the unification of Germany in 1871. Revisionist historians in the 1980s and 1990s have, however, reacted to this Prussocentric approach and argued that both the Empire and the Confederation had the potential to survive as viable solutions, which respected German diversity, while affording the individual states some degree of collective protection.

2 The Post-war Era 1815–47: Restoration and Change

Introduction

Like the Holy Roman Empire, the German Confederation was relegated to the 'historical lumber room'[1] by the nationalist school of historians, as it had little relevance for either nationalism or liberalism, the two most powerful ideologies in late nineteenth century Germany. Seen from the perspective of German unification, it appeared to be an entirely negative political structure, which merely retarded the apparently inevitable move to unification under Prussia. Yet the American historian, Enno Kraehe, in the 1950s and then, rather later, the West German historians, Werner Conze and Wolf Grüner, began to analyse the Confederation and its member states within the context of their times rather than through the distorting lenses of the Bismarckian Reich. The history of the German states within the Confederation was, as are most post-war eras, a complex mixture of modernization and restoration. Late twentieth-century historians were also more sympathetic to the potential of the Confederation as an 'intermediary body', which could balance the demands of 'the major

See Documents 3 and 4

German powers' for independence with the smaller states' need for security and protection'.[2]

The German Confederation

In 1815 there was no agreement amongst its members as to what the main purposes of the Confederation were. Prussians reformers, like Wilhelm von Humboldt, hoped it would develop into a federal state in which Prussia would play a key role, a view not shared by the smaller states for whom it was a way of protecting their independence, while to Metternich it was a piece in the jigsaw of his overall European policy, constructed to protect the interests of the Habsburg monarchy. In the immediate post-war years it soon became clear that the Confederation was an intensely conservative organization which would leave the sovereignty of the individual states intact wherever possible. No attempts, for instance, were made to draw up regulations on such complex issues as trade, transport and a single currency, and even the question of a common defence caused major problems.

Habsburg: the family name of the Austrian ruling house

This apparent betrayal of the national ideal led to protests by a small minority of students and intellectuals organized in the *Burschenschaft* movement. In March 1819, when Karl Sand, a theology student, assassinated August von Kotzebue, a playwright and a political agent employed by the Russian legation in Mannheim, Metternich skilfully exploited the alarm created by the incident to strengthen the conservative forces within the Confederation. He secured Frederick William's backing in August 1819 for a series of repressive laws aimed at the universities and the press. These were then approved by the representatives of the ten most conservative states at a special conference at Karlsbad, and presented as a *fait accompli* to the Diet of the Confederation, which met at Frankfurt in late September.

Burschenschaften: fraternities or clubs pedged to work for a united liberal Germany. The first *Burschenschaft* was formed at Jena in 1815 (see Documents 4 and 5)

The Karlsbad Decrees gave Metternich the opportunity to strengthen

The Karlsbad Decrees

Ironically the four Karlsbad Decrees strengthened the federal nature of the Confederation. The University Law dictated a code of conduct for both students and staff, which undermined the traditional autonomy of the universities and was to be enforced by the individual state governments. Similarly the Press Law compelled the states to reintroduce censorship and made their governments ultimately responsible for all the published material that appeared within their frontiers. Prussia had originally wanted a special federal tribunal, which would both have investigated and passed sentence on political radicals. However, it was persuaded by Metternich to accept a Central Federal Investigation Office at Mainz, which would eventually communicate its findings to the Diet, and so prompt the individual state governments to take action. Metternich did, however, make the 'astonishing concession'[3] that in a real emergency he would agree to setting up a federal court. Finally the Confederation was given the legal powers to intervene if one of the member states refused to carry out its instructions for implementing the decrees.

See Document 6

Schlussakte: Final Document

the Prussian conservatives, stifle demands for a federal constitution and cement Austro-Prussian co-operation. This new axis enabled Austria and Prussia to create a dualistic hegemony and dictate the agenda at the ministerial conferences held in Vienna 1819–20, which determined the final shape of the Confederation. After six months of negotiation, the Diet was presented with a revised constitution for the Confederation, the Vienna *Schlussakte*, which it had to accept without debate. The *Schlussakte* finally confirmed the conservative nature of the Confederation. In many ways the Confederation became, as Sheehan has argued, 'a kind of counter-revolutionary holding company through which Metternich could co-ordinate governmental action against his political enemies':[4]

- All mention of Jewish emancipation and religious freedom was dropped. Article 58 vetoed any acceptance by the princes of a constitution 'that would limit or hinder them in fulfilment of their duties to the Confederation'.[5]
- There was no supreme federal court but the Confederation did have the legal powers to adjudicate between states; Article 29 stressed that every German should have access to justice and was instrumental in gradually forcing the German states to set up their own supreme courts.
- While power remained firmly with the existing sovereigns, the Confederation was nevertheless invested with potentially far-ranging powers. Article 26, for instance, gave it the right to intervene in the affairs of the member states to maintain order.
- Militarily a similar balance was struck between the independence of the individual states and the needs of the Confederation. The War Constitution of 1821 made provision for the formation of a single,

2 A portrait of Clemens Lothar Wenzel, Prince Metternich, painted in London in 1814 by Sir Thomas Lawrence (1769–1830)

The Royal Collection © HM Queen Elizabeth II, RCIN 404948

united army in wartime under one commander, who would be chosen by the *Engerer Rat* (small committee of the Diet), but in peace these forces would remain under the command of their own rulers.

Over the next decade the Confederation gradually became what Metternich had intended. The weak and incompetent Austrian ambassador, von Buol-Schauenstein, was replaced in 1822 by the more formidable Count von Munch-Bellinghausen, whose purpose, as the British ambassador wrote, was to establish 'the sole and exclusive supremacy'[6] of Austria. Under his watchful eye, the debates and spontaneity of the earlier assembly sessions were curtailed. The Diet remained a congress of ambassadors and the publication of its minutes were kept to the barest minimum. His task was made much easier when, in May 1823, Metternich insisted that the liberally-inclined ambassadors of Hesse–Darmstadt, Kurhesse and Württemberg be dismissed for criticizing the reactionary policies of the three eastern powers – Russia, Austria and Prussia.

After 1824 the Confederation entered a period of calm, but this was interrupted in 1830 by the July Revolution in Paris and the popular revolts in Belgium and Luxemburg against Dutch rule, all of which increased political tension within the German states. Exacerbated by poor harvests, unrest broke out in Saxony, Brunswick, Hesse–Darmstadt and Hesse–Cassel, which forced the authorities to grant political constitutions in all four states. In the local parliaments (*Landtage*), especially in the south-west German states, the liberals became more assertive, and there was a flood of political pamphlets. The culmination of these protests was a mass meeting of 20,000 at Hambach castle near Neustadt in the Bavarian Palatinate in May 1832 (see p. 29) which galvanized the Confederation into taking further repressive measures. As in 1819, Austria and Prussia first of all reached agreement on a list of measures, the so-called Six Articles, and only then were the remaining governments consulted. These increased the power of the princes and the Confederation to muzzle liberal dissidents and ban political meetings. The abortive attack in Frankfurt in early 1833 by a small group of students, university lecturers and Polish refugees on the local barracks, gave the Confederation another chance to intervene in the internal affairs of a member state. It sanctioned the occupation of the city by federal troops under the command of an Austrian general and brushed off British and French criticism by emphasizing 'the inadmissibility of the interference of foreign powers in the internal affairs of the German Confederation'.[7]

For the rest of the decade Metternich continued his offensive against the revolutionary threat. In June 1833 the Confederation at last created a centralized Bureau of Political Investigation, which could itself set up tribunals to examine dissidents, and a year later security measures against dissidents were further tightened up in the Sixty Articles. Although the articles were secret and were never discussed by the Diet, the German states were committed by Article 60 to implementing the new agreement, as if it were a federal decree. Further decrees were issued between 1835 and 1836, aimed at curbing threats from revolutionary students and travelling journeymen and banning the circulation of works written by the authors of 'Young Germany' (see p. 31).

It cannot be denied that the Confederation was reactionary and oppressive, and had alienated the liberals and nationalists (see pp. 29–31). In that sense George Werner is correct that it became 'increasingly difficult to visualize the Diet serving as a vehicle for German unification',[8] but then, as Christopher Clark reminds us, 'it is important not

At the Congress of Vienna both Belgium and Luxemburg had been placed under Dutch rule

See Documents 6 and 7

Travelling journeymen: skilled craftsmen, who would travel in search of work

to overestimate the power and homogeneity of German nationalism as a political force during this period'.[9] More serious criticisms of the confederation were its evident military weakness in the crises of 1830–31 and 1840, and its failure to devise an effective customs union, both of which are explored below.

Tensions and rivalries between the German states

Interstate politics within the Confederation were dominated by the dual hegemony of Austria and Prussia. As long as these two states co-operated, their power could not be effectively challenged. The medium-sized southern states, Bavaria, Württemberg and Baden did attempt in 1817 to create an independent third force within the Confederation, the so-called German Triad. They had some success in forcing Austria and Prussia to modify their plans for a purely federal army which would have emphasized Austro-Prussian preponderance, but the inherent rivalries between these three states effectively prevented any possibility of a triadic federation being formed.

Dual hegemony: joint leadership

Austro-Prussian dual hegemony in the Confederation rested on an uneasy balance which was only workable as long as Austria could stop the Confederation from becoming a federal state, and Prussia had no ambitions to seize the leadership of Germany. In the longer term, however, a conflict seemed inevitable. Brendan Simms has argued that 'the new geopolitical configuration of central Europe after 1815 almost predetermined Prussia's victory in the struggle for mastery in Germany'. Austrian concentration on Germany was increasingly distracted by the political situation in Italy and the Balkans, and it was unable effectively to protect the smaller states in southern and western Germany from the threat of French aggression. Prussia, in contrast, had no ambitions outside Germany, and had a vital interest in defending the Rhine frontier and in creating a German customs union, which would knit together its eastern and western territories. In both these areas, as Simms points out, 'her narrow state interests increasingly converged not only with the German national movement, but also with the interests of the southern and western states of the Third Germany'.[10] This became clearer in the two international crises of 1830–32 and 1840.

Triadic federation: a federation composed of the three medium-sized German states. For Bavarian attitudes to federal interference, see Document 8

Customs union: a free trade area where no customs duties are levied

The consequences of the French July Revolution

The July revolution (see also p. 29) and the subsequent uprisings in Belgium, Poland and Italy directly threatened the Vienna settlement and appeared to herald the beginning of a new revolutionary era. Metternich signally failed to reassure either the Prussians or the South Germans. First he had called for an invasion of France despite the military weakness of the Confederation, then the diplomatic and military support he gave to the threatened Austrian satellite states in Italy appeared to make a major

European war inevitable. Indeed, it seemed to the South Germans that Metternich was deliberately provoking an anti-revolutionary crusade so that he could bring in Russia and the German Confederation to maintain the Austrian-dominated status quo in central Europe. Yet when the French-supported revolts broke out in Belgium and the Duchy of Luxemburg, which was a member of the Confederation, the weaknesses of the Austrian position became very clear. Distracted by Italy and paralysed by financial weakness, it was unable to give a decisive lead to the Confederation. Prussia, on the other hand, was quite ready to act. Not only did it force the Diet to discuss the Luxemburg issue, but it made impressive military preparations and committed itself to raising 160,000 troops. It was not surprising then that in the south German states the idea of economic and military co-operation with Prussia became increasingly attractive. King Ludwig of Bavaria wanted an alliance with Prussia that would provide protection against France and constrain Austria from dominating the Confederation. Württemberg cautiously supported this approach, while Baden was ready to go further still and encourage Prussia to take the lead in turning the Confederation into a more cohesive federation which would be able to harness German nationalism. In August 1831 Count Christian von Bernstorff, the Prussian foreign minister, arguing that Prussia, 'as the state that would have to bear the greatest burden in the event of federal war' should 'seize the initiative in all areas where successful leadership will lead to greater preparedness and security',[11] invited the south German states to send representatives to Berlin to begin negotiations on a military alliance. Two years later he even argued that Prussia's mission was to encourage 'the union of all German governments'.[12] However, under pressure from Metternich, Frederick William agreed to drop these potentially revolutionary ideas and replace Bernstorff with the more conservative Friedrich Ancillon, and for the time being the Prussian–Austrian special relationship was restored.

The Rhine Crisis of 1840

In 1840 events in France again appeared to threaten the German Confederation (see also p. 31). When the French government was forced by the other European powers to give up its support for the occupation of Syria by Mehemet Ali, the Pasha of Egypt, and ally of France, French public opinion perceived this to be an intolerable humiliation. In the subsequent explosion of frustrated nationalism, Paris sought compensation in the annexation of the left bank of the Rhine. Once again it was shown that only under Prussian direction would Germany be able to defend itself. Austria was both unable and unwilling to intervene against France, while Prussia actually mobilized 200,000 troops and made great efforts to put the western fortresses on a war footing . The threat of a revisionist France on the Rhine unleashed a surge of nationalist feeling throughout Germany, which looked to Prussia for leadership. It seriously weakened the idea of an independent 'third Germany', and began the slow and often interrupted process of convergence of the south German states on Berlin.

The *Zollverein*: an economic confederation?

In 1815 interstate trade in Germany was crippled by the lack of a customs union. Each state levied its own tariffs and excise duties. Merchants trading, for instance, between Berlin and Switzerland had to cope with ten sets of customs tariffs and transit dues. The negotiation of a German customs union should have been one of the first tasks of the Confederation. Article 19 of its Constitution actually committed the Diet to deliberating, at its first meeting 'upon the manner of regulating the commerce and navigation from one state to another'.[13] Essentially, however, political particularism and the widely divergent economies of the different states all ensured that no progress was made.

The only other alternative was for small groups of states to negotiate regional customs unions. Prussia was the first German state to begin this process. Since its western provinces were separated from its core territory in the east and it had a 7500 km customs boundary studded with small enclaves belonging to other states, Prussia had a vital interest in negotiating a larger free-trade area. In 1818 the Prussian government accordingly introduced a new and strictly enforced customs law, which was aimed at creating an integrated Prussian customs system and compelling the small states surrounded by Prussian territory to join. In 1819 Schwarzburg–Sonderhausen entered the Prussian customs system and set a precedent by which the other small enclaves joined over the next 12 years. By the mid-twenties, influential Prussian officials like Albrecht Eichhorn, the head of Prussian and customs affairs in the Foreign Ministry and Friedrich von Motz, the finance minister, were urging the creation of what could be called a 'separate confederation with regard to customs policy',[14] at least as far as northern and central Germany went. To achieve this, Prussia pursued a complex policy of pressure and concession towards her smaller neighbours. Its greatest success, which, in the words of Heinrich Treitschke, the nationalist historian, reverberated around the German states 'like a bombshell',[15] was to establish a bridgehead on the other side of the Main by persuading Hesse–Darmstadt in 1828 to join the

Zollverein: customs union – an area of free trade between the German states

See Document 9

Political particularism: the principle that each state should have the maximum independence within the German Confederation

See Map 3

Heinrich von Treitschke, 1834–96

As a young man, he had supported a Germany unified and led by Prussia. In 1871 he was appointed professor of history at Berlin University. He sat as a National Liberal in the Reichstag and became an ardent supporter of Bismarck and German imperialism. His major work was *The History of Germany in the Nineteenth Century*, in which he strongly criticized Austria and the south German states and took a consistently pro-Prussian line.

Prussian customs union with some remarkably generous concessions. The adhesion of Hesse–Darmstadt to the Prussian customs system made the new Bavarian-Württemberg union, which had been negotiated in January 1828, less viable and moved the King of Württemberg to remark that 'sooner or later we shall be forced to follow this example'.[16]

To block the further expansion of the Bavarian and Prussian customs unions, Hanover, Hesse-Cassel, Nassau, Saxony and some of the Thuringian states as well as Brunswick and Bremen, formed the Middle German Commercial Union (MGCU) in December 1828. Members had specifically to commit themselves not to join a rival union, while heavy transit dues on goods passing through MGCU from non-member states were levied, with the express intention of interrupting trade between the eastern and western provinces of Prussia. However, this had little impact on Prussia, as Friedrich von Motz, the finance minister, first managed to negotiate both the opening up of two trade routes between north and south Germany outside the control of the MGCU and in May 1829 a commercial treaty with the Bavarian-Württemberg union. Then the final

See Document 10

blow to the viability of the MGCU was delivered by the defection of Hesse-Cassel in 1831, which at last enabled Prussia to link up her western and eastern provinces. In March 1833 the Prussian-Hesse system formed a joint customs union with the Bavarian and Württemberg Union, which was joined almost immediately by Saxony. On New Year's Eve 1833, all toll restrictions within the union were dropped and the *Deutscher Zollverein* came into being. In 1835–36 Frankfurt, Nassau and Baden joined, followed in 1841–42 by Brunswick and Luxemburg, leaving only 11 states outside the union.

Metternich viewed these events with consternation. When the *Zollverein* Treaty was signed in 1833, he could only stand on the sidelines and warn the Emperor that 'within the large federal union' (*sic*) there was being created 'a smaller rival confederation . . . which all too quickly will become accustomed to following its own objectives with its own means'.[17] In 1841 he even urged Austria's entry into the *Zollverein*, but fear of Prussian economic competition and the divisive effects of excluding those Habsburg territories from entry which were not part of the Confederation ensured that nothing came of this initiative.

See Document 11

The customs union has 'long played an almost mythical role in explanations of Prussia's eventual rise to political and economic supremacy in Germany'.[18] Treitschke saw it as heralding the ultimate conflict between Austria and Prussia, which ended on the field of Königgrätz, while Wilhelm Roscher, a professor in political theory at Göttingen was convinced in the late 1860s that it was 'not only the most beneficial, but also the greatest event in German history between Waterloo and Königgrätz'. The view was largely echoed by post-1945 West German historians such as Helmut Böhme, who saw it as the economic blueprint for a united Germany.[19]

Current research is more sceptical about its long-term political and economic consequences (see pp. 36–7). Yet, even so, there is a danger of

The functioning of the *Zollverein*

The main organ of the *Zollverein* was the General Council, which met annually each time in a different member state, and was the body where the key decisions on customs tariffs were made. Each full member state had one vote (the Thuringian states had one vote between them, and Nassau and Frankfurt also shared a vote) and was represented by its own envoy, who was bound by instructions from his home government. Decisions could only be made through unanimity. Trade and shipping treaties with non-member states were in practice negotiated by Prussia on behalf of all the *Zollverein*'s members.

The individual states implemented the decisions taken by the General Council. Each state levied the agreed tariffs at their frontiers, but the sharing out of these funds between the member states was the responsibility of the Central Treasury of the *Zollverein* in Berlin, and was calculated on an annual basis. This revenue was welcomed by the state governments as it was independent of any parliamentary control. To check that its members were carrying out the instructions from the General Conference correctly, officials from one state would monitor their colleagues in another. Constitutionally these officials were employees of their own states, but gradually they evolved a loyalty to the *Zollverein*. Huber has called this 'a vivid example of institutional change, which inevitably takes place in a group of states tied together [economically]'.[20]

underplaying its importance. Nipperdey argues that between 1814 and 1848 it was 'the single outstanding event in all German politics'.[21] It did strengthen Prussian influence over the other German states, and contemporaries were certainly aware of its potential impact on Austro-Prussian relations, as it isolated Austria economically within the Confederation, but politically it did not forge a united Germany. In 1866 most of the smaller German states joined Austria against Prussia (see p. 75), and it was only military victory at Königgrätz that enabled Bismarck to destroy the Confederation and drive Austria from Germany.

Domestic politics in the German states, 1815–48

Despite their historic names, many of the German states in 1814 were virtually new constructions. Their governments were faced with the problem of both integrating often extensive new territories and establishing a new legitimacy for regimes sanctioned by the Vienna Conference. Prussia, for instance, had to unite her new Rhineland territories with her core lands east of the Elbe, while the southern states had to absorb the disparate territories with which they had been left after the collapse of Napoleon. Only through the intervention of the state could the new populations be assimilated and a new loyalty created. Only it could stand above the individual interest and weld cities and the dispossessed ruling classes, who had previously enjoyed independence in the now defunct Holy Roman Empire, into a cohesive whole. Thus every-

See Map 3

where the state had by necessity to become more bureaucratic, and increasingly it was civil servants rather than the nobility or princes who in effect ran the state and began to impose a uniform pattern on society. As Thomas Nipperdey observed, the state 'now burdened the citizen with three of the great obligations of the modern man: the universal obligation to pay taxes, compulsory school attendance, and obligatory military service'.[22]

Prussia

In 1815 Prussia, was in all but name, a new state. It consisted of an uneasy union of the old territories with a very disparate group of lands, comprising the Rhineland, Westphalia, Saxony, Swedish Pomerania and the province of Posen, all of which had diverse political, legal and social constitutions. How was this somewhat random collection of territories to be welded together into a whole? The reform movement, supported at first by Hardenberg, wanted to adopt a constitution with parliamentary representation, but this was opposed by the conservatives, who were gaining influence at the court. Hardenberg made an initial tactical mistake in delaying setting up a commission to consider the whole constitutional question until 1817, while the introduction of the Karlsbad Decrees (see p. 18) led to the king shelving the whole constitutional question. In the end, only the provinces were given assemblies but these were based on the traditional estates or orders, which were corporatively elected and organized (see below).

A key figure in Prussia's turn to a more authoritarian regime was Prince Ludwig von Sayn-Wittgenstein-Hohenstein, Frederick William's grand chamberlain. He was in close contact with Metternich, whose ideas, according to Thomas Stamm-Kuhlmann, he 'was able to implant . . . into the mind of the King of Prussia'[23]

The absence of a constitution in Prussia up to 1848 was ' a fact fundamental to the course of German history'.[24] Prussia wore a Janus face. On the one hand it was a modern administrative state, humanely and efficiently run, while, on the other hand, after the victory of the anti-reform party it was also 'the classic state of the restoration'.[25] Despite the lack of a parliamentary constitution, its administration nevertheless possessed some constitutional characteristics:

Oberpräsidenten: senior administrative officials

- The provinces were run by the *Oberpräsidenten*, who were granted by the government a considerable degree of independence and formed semi-federal units within the Prussian state. Primarily as citizens of Westphalia, Brandenburg or the Rhineland did the population find an identity within the Prussian state.

Regierungs-präsidenten: district presidents

- Most of the provincial administration was carried out at district level by the *Regierungspräsidenten*, who exercised their power on a collegiate basis. In other words, decisions were only taken on a unanimous basis after consultation with colleagues, which ensured discussion and compromise.

Staatsminis-terium: cabinet

Staatsrat: privy council

- The same principle functioned right at the centre of government. After Hardenberg's death in 1822, the *Staatsministerium* also became a collegiate body, which had to make decisions collectively. The *Staatsrat*, which was composed of the royal princes, ministers and senior civil

---

Die Landtage

These 'assemblies of the estates', or *Landtage*, were essentially feudal and backward-looking. They gave representation to the three traditional estates or classes: the nobility, the burghers (townsmen) and the peasantry. Deputies could only represent the estate to which they belonged. In the eastern provinces, the ratio of representation between the landowners (Junkers), the burghers and the peasants was roughly 3:2:1, but in the Rhineland and Westphalia it was 1:1:1.

---

servants, was able critically to discuss drafts of new laws and in many ways played a role similar to a senate or a revising chamber.

It was these characteristics that won Prussia the admiration of many German liberals. Yet the influence of the conservatives steadily strengthened during the 1820s and 1830s. Reform-minded civil servants were neutralized and in core Prussia, east of the Elbe, the special status and privileges of the Junkers, the Prussian landowners, was restored. They retained their tax privileges and were still able to appoint the local *Landrat* (local administrative official). In the new provincial *Landtage*, the government increased their influence at the expense of the middle classes and peasantry. The conservatives were also able to exploit the reaction caused by Kotzebue's murder (see p. 17) to weaken the *Landwehr* (see p. 8) and strengthen the regular army, on whose royalist loyalties the Crown could safely rely.

The other German states

In contrast to Prussia, Baden, Bavaria and Württemberg introduced constitutions to integrate their recently acquired territories and win the loyalty of their new citizens. In 1815 Baden was on the brink of dissolution, and power appeared to be devolving back into the hands of the magistrates, burghers and traditional noble estates. To weld the state together, the grand duke was persuaded by a group of reforming civil servants to accept the most 'modern' constitution in Germany. Its upper house was still dominated by the nobility, but its lower house, composed of 63 members, was elected by individuals who met the necessary property and tax qualifications. This was unique in Germany because the link between possession of the vote and social status was broken, and it had the potential to 'overturn social and political arrangements on all levels of society'.[26] It also contained a bill of rights which gave the population equal civil rights, equality of taxation and religious freedom.

The Bavarian and Württemberg monarchies also came to the conclusion that limited parliamentary constitutions would help integrate their new territories and populations. The Bavarian constitution, which was introduced in 1818, included a bill of rights, which promised to its citizens equality before the law, even though the nobility were still guaranteed certain privileges. The chamber of deputies was still chosen according to the old estate-based principles, in that there were five separate categories of voter, but it was also made clear that its duty was to represent the state as a whole rather than individual classes. In Württemberg, too, a constitution was used to buttress the power of the Crown and weaken the embittered mediatized nobility by creating an elected chamber in which they would be in a minority.

The power of the new south German parliaments was, of course, very limited. The Crown still controlled the composition of the ministries and was solely responsible for foreign and military affairs. Yet the elected chambers had to give their consent to new taxes and fiscal bills, and became increasingly skilled in opposing ministers who broke the constitution. In 1832, for instance, the Bavarian *Landtag* forced the king to dismiss his minister of the interior and withdraw a censorship decree. South Germany became an important testing ground for German liberalism as a whole and gave liberal deputies valuable experience in parliamentary opposition.

In the smaller central and north German states, which had not gained new territories, there was a greater continuity with the past. The four 'free cities' of Hamburg, Bremen, Lübeck and Frankfurt all re-established their former estate-based constitutions. Similarly, in both Mecklenburgs, Saxony and Hanover the old estate-based constitution remained in place, while the Electorate of Hesse returned to its pre-revolutionary system of absolutism. In Schleswig-Holstein the nobility attempted to defend themselves against the centralizing policies of the King of Denmark by demanding a constitution along estate-based lines. The king rejected this, but did temporarily ease up on his attempts to integrate the two duchies into Denmark (see p. 44).

> The mediatized nobility were the former imperial knights of the Holy Roman Empire, who lost their land, but not their titles, when the Empire was abolished in 1806

> **Estate-based constitutions**: constitutions based on the three traditional estates as in the east Elbian Prussian provinces (see p. 5)

The growing national context of the political debate

In an introductory essay in the first edition of the *Staatslexikon* (State Encyclopaedia) in 1834, Theodor Welcker, the liberal leader in Baden, argued that politics dominated people's thoughts and actions in a way that had not occurred before.[27] There were several reasons for this:

- the rapid growth in the publication of lexicons, periodicals and newspapers, as well as lectures and the foundation of social, literary and learned institutions, all of which extended the 'public sphere';
- the massive upheavals of the revolutionary and Napoleonic wars;
- the growth in the power and responsibilities of the state as tax collector, organizer of education and economic regulator;
- the creation of elected chambers, particularly in south Germany, which also provided for a forum where grand political concepts could be discussed.

The 1830s and 1840s witnessed not only the growing debate between nationalists, liberals and democrats on the one side and conservatives and reactionaries on the other, but also the emergence of socialism and political Catholicism.

Liberalism

Liberalism was 'a multiform, almost protean movement with conflicting tendencies and blurred boundaries'.[28] It was both a political movement, which aimed to create a constitutional state under the rule of law and a force for modernization, but there was little agreement over what modernization actually entailed. The Rhineland entrepreneurs favoured rapid industrial growth, but many of the south German liberals wanted only stability and the preservation of the status quo, which involved the protection of small firms, state regulations and no free trade between the German states. Liberalism was strongest in south Germany, where parliaments gave liberal politicians a platform for their views, in the Rhineland and Westphalia, the universities and the Landtage (provincial assemblies), but, in the Prussian territories east of the Elbe, liberals could also be found in local government.

The French revolution of 1830 strengthened liberalism in the Confederation. In Brunswick, Hesse–Cassel, Saxony and Hanover, local liberal leaders were able to use the disturbances and fear of the mob to persuade the rulers to grant constitutions. In the Palatinate, the journalist, Johann Wirth, set up the *Presseverein* (press union) as a pressure group to campaign for liberal ideals throughout German-speaking Europe. By 1832 it already had 5000 members and well over a hundred branches in Bavaria, and in May held a large-scale 'political festival' in the ruins of the old castle near Hambach, which inspired a series of similar meetings throughout Germany. Its organizers called for a united, liberal and democratic Germany, but more radical proposals to create a revolutionary committee to work towards unification were rejected as being too Utopian.

Although Metternich was able to restore order within the Confederation (see p. 20), the events of 1830–33 went some way to turning liberalism into a national movement. When in 1837 seven professors at Göttingen university were dismissed after refusing to swear an oath of loyalty to the new elector, Ernst August, Duke of Cumberland, after he had suspended the constitution of 1833, they became martyrs and heroes to liberals throughout Germany. By 1840 liberalism was becoming a popular movement and its division into a left and right wing was becoming discernible. Its left wing was increasingly pressing for a strong parliamentary system in which the state would of necessity bow to parliament, while right-wing liberals were more pragmatic and looked to the state as a potential ally against too disruptive a pace of economic and social change.

The Origins of liberalism: The word liberal was first used by those who supported the Spanish constitution in 1812. Liberalism was essentially about self-government and the freedom of the individual. It was thus opposed to both the old feudal, corporate society and the authoritarian state. The term can also be applied to the economic and social spheres where liberals wanted the minimum controls on individuals, business and industry

Protean: taking many forms

The inspiration for the *Hambacherfest* were the political banquets in France, where critics of the government met and listened to political speeches (see Document 7)

The democrats and socialists

To the Left of the liberals there emerged in the 1840s both the radical democrats and the early socialists. The radicals, led by members of the intelligentsia, such as Johann Jacoby from Königsberg, drew their strength from 'the little people, the dependent and downtrodden'.[29] In September 1847 the left wing of the Baden opposition met with similar groups from the neighbouring states at Offenburg and agreed on a programme which called for a people's militia, equal voting rights, educational opportunities for the poor, and an end to the 'disparity between the rich and poor'.

The first socialist organization, the 'League of the Just', was formed in 1836–37 to a great extent as a result of the efforts of Karl Schapper and Wilhelm Weitling, the former journeyman tailor. Their targets were the impoverished craftsmen (see p. 35) rather than the industrial workers, but they envisaged revolution and the creation of a new regime of equality. This pre-industrial socialism was bitterly criticized by Karl Marx, who, by drawing on the philosophy of Feuerbach and the Young Hegelians, produced a blueprint for revolution, which called upon the industrial proletariat to rise up and revolt. His Communist Manifesto of 1848 was way in advance of its times, as industrialization in Germany was still in its infancy and his supporters consisted mainly of intellectuals rather than workers.

See Document 12

The philosopher, Ludwig Feuerbach, freed Hegelianism from its spiritual dimension and thus opened the way for applying Hegel's theories to the material world. The implication of this was that man himself could create the ideal world on earth rather than waiting for the after-life

Nationalism

Nationalism belonged with liberalism 'like a pair together'.[30] It aimed to combine liberation from external control with internal self-government. After the War of Liberation, 1813–14, and the disappointments of the Vienna Settlement, the hopes and ambitions of the predominantly young members of the nationalist movement were furthered principally by the gymnastic societies and the *Burschenschaften* (see p. 17). The former had been founded by Friedrich Jahn in 1811. These set out deliberately to encourage a feeling of German identity and managed to win the loyalty of a whole generation of school and university students. By 1820 there were 150 different societies with 12,000 members. In many ways they were 'the prototype of a political party',[31] and pioneered rallies and mass public meetings as a new form of public event. The latter, which were formed at the universities to create a new pan-German ethos of friendship and honour, were nationalist and liberal in orientation. On 18–19th October 1817 the *Burschenschaften* held a rally at the Wartburg, which was attended by 500 students, and a year later the *Allgemeine Deutsche Burschenschaft* (the General German Fraternity) was set up as a pan-German student organization. Within the *Burschenschaften*, a radical wing developed led by Karl Follen, a lecturer at Giessen University, with the intention of creating a united republican Germany, by force if necessary.

Pan-German: all-German, stretching right across all the German states

See Documents 4 and 5

This first phase of nationalist agitation was brought to an end by the Karlsbad Decrees, but Metternich did not succeed in stamping out the nationalist message. In southern Germany, for example, where the repression was less severe, a considerable number of male choral groups were formed which met at large regional festivals where nationalist songs were sung with great enthusiasm. The revolutionary events of 1830 further encouraged a brief revival, but the Six Articles and the defeat of the Frankfurt 'insurrection' of 1833 (see p. 20) again forced the *Burschenschaften* and the other nationalist groups to camouflage their activities.

German nationalism was part of a powerful pan-European and even American movement. It was thus inspired and strengthened by both the example of the Greek uprising against the Turks in the 1820s and the revolt of 1830 in Russian Poland. The threat of a French invasion of the Rhineland in 1840 also triggered a large-scale nationalist reaction, the spirit of which was caught by Nikolaus Becker's Rhineland song, *Der deutsche Rhein*, which was sung to over two hundred different tunes throughout Germany. Similarly, the ongoing threat by the Danish Crown to integrate the Duchies of Schleswig into the Danish state (see p. 44) caused growing concern amongst the German nationalists. In July 1844 12,000 people flocked to the Schleswig-Holstein singing festival and the 'battle hymn', *Schleswig-Holstein meerumschlungen*, became as popular as the Rhineland song. By 1848 about two hundred and fifty thousand Germans were organized in various nationalist organizations. Thanks to the improvement in communications, the press and the increasingly frequent interregional festivals, nationalism's tentacles had spread throughout Germany.

Schleswig-Holstein meerumschlungen: Schleswig-Holstein, encircled by sea

The emergence of a national culture

Although there was no political consensus amongst the poets and writers during this period – Friedrich Schlegel, for instance, supported Metternich, while Görres was a Bavarian conservative – the Young German Movement, whose two most gifted writers were Heinrich Heine and Georg Büchner, believed passionately in a united liberal German state. Even after the intensified surveillance and censorship introduced by the Six Articles in 1832 (see p. 20), which drove Heine into exile, their works continued to be circulated clandestinely. Patriotic songs dominated choir festivals, but music and opera also assumed an increasingly national character, as can be seen, for example, in Richard Wagner's operas, *Rienzi* and *Tannhäuser*, composed in 1841 and 1845 respectively. It is also possible to see the beginning of the 'nationalization of culture', which became much more pronounced in the 1860s. The new subject of German philology, which was pioneered by Jacob Grimm, and the growing interest in German medieval history and the rediscovery of Germany's ancient legal traditions all reflected this. Monumental new architecture, memorials to great German heroes, and museums also increasingly expressed the idea of a German national and cultural identity.

Conservatism

The roots of German and European conservatism lay in the opposition to the enlightened absolutism of the eighteenth century, the principles of the French Revolution and the emerging liberalism of the post-war era. Initially it appeared that conservatism was doomed to remain a reactionary, anti-modernist movement totally opposed to the development of the modern state. Thanks, however, to the work of the right-wing philosopher, Friedrich von Stahl, a workable synthesis between traditional, estate-based, conservative ideas and the need to come to terms with the reality of the contemporary state was devised in the 1840s. On the one hand, Stahl stressed the existence in society of a 'preordained order beyond human will'[32] and a close relationship between Church and State. On the other hand, he recognized the need for a constitution and an elected parliament, but it would be a monarchical constitution, in which the Crown would determine policy, while parliament would be the legislature and guarantor of both the constitution and the legal rights of the subjects. This formula enabled the conservatives to escape from the cul-de-sac of total opposition to the modern state. Traditionally the conservatives had been opposed to nationalism. Yet there were now signs that these two enemies were drawing closer to each other. Joseph von Radowitz, the councillor and friend of Frederick William IV of Prussia, was beginning to argue that, to survive, the Prussian monarchy and state needed to accept the 'idea of nationality [which] was the most powerful force of the present time'.[33] Other thinkers, like Victor Huber, were putting forward programmes for social conservatism, which involved a state-controlled welfare policy and the setting up of co-operatives, which would give workers a chance of gaining property and running their own businesses.

Political Catholicism

After the French revolution, the Catholic Church became a fierce critic of the claims of the modern state and liberal individualism. As early as the 1830s, small groups of Catholic delegates began to join forces in the south German *Landtage*, but it was the arrest of the Archbishop of Cologne in 1838 by the Prussian authorities for opposing regulations on mixed marriages between Protestants and Catholics that acted as a catalyst for the development of Catholicism as a political force. Political Catholicism was in itself a coalition of forces. On the one hand, there were the conservatives, whose politics were a mixture of romanticism and conservatism. They regarded unquestioning faith in the institutions of the Catholic Church as the key to opposing the secular and reformist evils of the time. On the other hand, there were Catholics, mainly in the Rhineland, who supported liberal demands for individual freedom and a constitution, while there was also a growth in social Catholicism, which urged controls on *laissez-faire* capitalism, limits on property ownership and the guaran-

Laissez-faire capitalism: belief in a completely free economy and working conditions uncontrolled by the state

tee of full employment by the state. There was considerable tension between Catholicism and nationalism. The Catholic paper, *Historische-politische Blätter*, observed that there was 'a vastly more profound bond' between a Catholic German and a Catholic African than between the latter and a German atheist.[34] The Catholics also distrusted Prussia and instinctively looked to Catholic Vienna rather than to Protestant Berlin to take the lead in German affairs.

A Catholic faction was formed in the Prussian diet in 1852, but it was not until 13 December 1870 that the Catholic Centre party was founded at Reich level (see pp. 112–13).

Economic and social developments

Although the outlines of the old regime remained intact, in reality German society was 'shaken up and rearranged in the decades before 1848',[35] but the pace and impact of modernization was uneven. Large-scale capitalist landowners lived next to subsistence farmers, while, in the Rhineland, modern factories sprang up in areas where traditional craftsmen continued to sell their wares exclusively within their own villages.

Agriculture

In 1815 Germany was overwhelmingly an agricultural society with three-quarters of its population living in the countryside, and traditional agricultural methods were still very much the norm. Contemporary reformers were convinced that the emancipation of the peasantry from serfdom (see p. 5) was the vital precondition for the modernization of agriculture. In Prussia, peasant emancipation certainly proved to be 'a major step towards economic and social modernization',[36] as the large landowners were forced to adapt to a more capitalistic system. They expanded their estates by absorbing much of the land hitherto cultivated by the peasantry and were able to turn them into modern, capitalist concerns. Elsewhere, emancipation developed differently. In some areas like Mecklenburg, Hesse and Hanover, progress towards emancipation was much slower, while in Schleswig-Holstein and on the left bank of the Rhine, emancipation led to generally more favourable conditions for the peasantry. Amongst the peasants there were both winners and losers. On the whole, the peasants with medium-sized holdings, which had horses or oxen, were able to survive. Others, like the lease-holding peasants in Prussia, had to surrender some 32.4 per cent of their land to their former feudal lords as compensation for the abolition of their feudal obligations. The enclosure of common lands also hit the poorer peasantry a devastating blow, as it deprived them of their customary free grazing rights for their animals.

Although up to the early 1830s German agriculture suffered a series of crises and collapsing markets, which bankrupted many of the east Elbian Junkers, the productivity of German agriculture doubled between 1800 and 1850 thanks to the following developments:

Three-field system: the traditional medieval system of farming whereby farmers allowed one field to lie fallow for a season in order to rest it

- The old three-field system was slowly replaced by more intensive farming except in various backward areas like the Eifel and the Saar in the west. Gradually, farmers everywhere had to bow to the dictates of agricultural capitalism or else go bankrupt.
- Arable land increased by 20 per cent as common and waste land was increasing brought under the plough.
- The number of cattle was increased by 50 per cent.
- There was a steady improvement in agricultural implements, and, thanks to the work of Justus Liebig, professor of chemistry at Giessen University, the application of applied science to agriculture was beginning to result in the use of chemicals in German agriculture. By the 1840s potash was commonly used as fertilizer, and saltpetre, a vital ingredient in creating artificial fertilizers, was being imported from Chile.

Industry

The industrial revolution and its consequences determined the fate of the whole period covered by this book. It revolutionized production and the economy, and irrevocably changed German society, although, compared to Britain, the full impact on the German states of the industrial revolution was felt later. Germany did not form a single coherent market and lacked the abundant capital which Britain could draw on from her colonial trade, yet it did possess many of the essential preconditions for industrialization. There were a large number of skilled workers, a strong professional middle class and a strong social discipline reinforced by Christianity. The reforms introduced by Napoleon in the Rhineland Confederation and by Stein and Hardenberg in Prussia, as well as the emancipation of the peasantry, began to create a society more orientated towards personal liberty, property and social mobility. The Vienna Settlement also went some way towards simplifying the German political map.

In 1815 Britain was an economic colossus that dominated the world, and the German market was flooded with cheap British goods, which initially overwhelmed and came near to throttling local industries. Yet, as Wehler has argued,[37] this experience was not entirely negative. In the medium term it facilitated industrialization through the delivery of cheap, half-finished goods, and goaded the Germans into copying and eventually competing with British industrial techniques. Although the British government did everything it could to stop 'industrial espionage' and the export of modern machinery, thousand of Germans went to Britain to learn the secrets of industrialization. Gradually, the combination of British ideas and German skills laid the foundations of the German industrial revolution. The governments of the German states assisted in creating the basic conditions for industrialization by improving the communications network – roads, canals, railways and a *Zollverein*. Reform-minded civil servants also attempted to inculcate the

How was the early industrial revolution financed?

Although Germany was not as short of capital as historians originally believed, capital backing for industrial projects was much thinner than in either France or Britain. Joint-stock companies were formed to finance shipping and railway companies, but initially industrial projects were largely financed by capital from the entrepreneurs themselves and their families. It was only with the foundation of the first credit banks, the *Schaffhausen Bankverein* in 1848 and the *Diskonto-Gesellschaft* in 1851, that credit became more easily available to industrialists.

'entrepreneurial spirit' in the population by arranging trips abroad for up-and-coming technicians, organizing industrial exhibitions and generally encouraging a more *laissez-faire* economic climate by setting up chambers of commerce and industry.

Joint-stock companies: companies formed on the basis of capital which is jointly owned by a number of people

Unlike Britain, it was not the textile industry in Germany that led the industrial revolution. Although most of the cotton industry was powered by steam by the 1830s, the wool industry was much slower to adapt, and in 1850 only 50 per cent of its production was steam-driven, while the linen industry remained a pre-industrial cottage industry that was almost destroyed by British competition. Mechanization did not, however, halt the growth in the number of handweavers. In 1800, for instance, there were about three hundred and fifteen thousand weavers in Germany, while 50 years later this total had risen by nearly 70 per cent. The reason for this was largely because the abundance of cheap labour made cottage industries still just about economically viable.

The iron and coal industries began the process of technological modernization. First the puddling process for producing wrought iron was imported from England, and then in the 1830s rolling mills and coke-fired blast furnaces appeared. These innovations, which required a ready access to coal supplies, ensured that successful foundries had to move to the coal-mining regions of the Ruhr or Upper Silesia, or else to areas with good transport connections. This in turn, of course, stimulated the development of the coal industry. The construction of the railways enormously boosted production in both these two industries. The first 6-km stretch of railway was built between Nuremberg and Fürth in 1834. By 1840, 468 km of railway track had been laid in the German states and 473 in Austria. Ten years later this had risen to 5859 in the former area and only 1357 in the latter. The rapid pace of railway construction ensured that there was a growing demand for engines, tracks, iron and coal, even though at first much of the equipment was imported from England. Railways also meant that ore and coal would now potentially be available to factories anywhere in Germany. The railways increased the mobility of labour and enabled its concentration in large-scale plants.

3 A newly constructed stretch of railway track near Erlangen, Bavaria

Leipzige Illustrierte

The economic impact of the *Zollverein*

The economic impact of the customs union is as controversial as is its alleged contribution to German unity. Following Friedrich List's argument that without a protective tariff the Germans would be reduced to being economically dependent on Britain, a long tradition of historians (more recently, for example, Walther G. Hoffmann and H. Mottek) have argued that the creation of the *Zollverein* was a turning-point in German economic history because it created a tariff wall behind which German industry could modernize itself. The actual economic benefits of the customs union are, however, more difficult to quantify. Wehler stresses that it created a market of 30 million and enabled the infant German industries to enjoy the economies of scale, but he is somewhat vague as to whether the German industries actually did take advantage of this during the period 1840–60.[38] It is of course true that Germany's economic position did improve between those years. Yet, as Henderson has observed, 'it is easy to see a connection between the two. But it is a dangerous half-truth – an over simplification of a highly complicated situation – to say the one caused the other.'[39] Hans-Joachim Voth argues that Prussia's economy 'derived little benefit from it',[40] and points out that, while the potential for economic growth in Germany was high, in practice both its investment and GDP were disappointing. Between 1840 and 1860, for instance, its growth in GDP averaged 1.6 per cent, compared to 2.2 in

GDP: Gross Domestic Product

Britain and 4.7 in the USA. He also stresses that the customs union gener-
ated inter-German trade, at the cost of exports. However, the argument
over the economic impact of the *Zollverein* is inconclusive. Even Voth is
uncertain about whether the *Zollverein* really did provide economies of
scale which compensated for the other short-comings of the German
economy. Probably, as Sheehan has remarked, 'the best that can be said
is that the *Zollverein*, especially in combination with other phenomena,
such as railroad construction, helped to promote growth'.[41]

German society between old and new

Although superficially the years 1814–48 appeared to be a period of
restoration, in reality, like all post-war eras, they were a period of change.
Despite the preservation of the monarchical principle and with it the
whole apparatus of the courts and the nobility, a radical-social economic
transformation was taking place. In Prussia the Junkers only remained a
strong force thanks to their ability to modernize their estates. In southern Germany the nobility were strictly subject to the laws of the bureaucratic state, and while they were represented in the upper chambers of the
new parliament, they lost many of their original privileges. In Baden, for
instance, they lost both their exemption from taxation and their legal
privileges, while in Bavaria the traditional aristocracy was infiltrated by
rich merchants, middle-class landowners and Jewish bankers.

A new bourgeois society was struggling painfully to be born. The
emerging bourgeois elite was, however, very diverse. Businessmen and
industrialists were divided by regional, social and economic differences.
To the bourgeoisie also belonged the *Bildungsbürgertum*, composed of
civil servants, the intelligentsia and Protestant clergy. The civil servants,

*Bildungsbürger-
tum*: educated
bourgeoisie

Biedermeier culture and the role of women

The term *Biedermeier* was coined in the 1850s to describe the developing bourgeois culture
in the post-war period of 1815–48. The home was no longer a workshop but rather a refuge
from the world. The father of the family , a civil servant, teacher or businessman, worked
away from home, while the mother presided over the domestic scene. For the middle classes
the decline of the home as a production unit, where the women's contribution had been vital,
had the consequence of narrowing the range of the bourgeois woman's sphere of activities
and of limiting her to the role of homemaker. For the wives of peasants and artisans, the situation was, of course, different, as they continued to play a vital economic role in their
husbands' businesses. For bourgeois women wishing to escape from 'the private sphere',
there were chances of voluntary work in welfare organizations or as nurses trained, for
example, by the Rhenish-Westfalian Association of Deaconesses. A very few women, such as
Fanny Lewald (1811–89) or Louise Aston (1814–71), for example, who were both from prosperous, professional backgrounds, even had the courage to reject the marriage plans of their
parents or divorce their husbands and earn their own living and pursue their own interests.[42]

selected on the new meritocratic principle of educational achievement rather than birth, were in many ways the shock troops of the new order, yet ironically they too had evolved into an estate which extracted privileges from the governments they served.

The new bourgeois society was a society of individuals rather than estates and corporate bodies. The old control exercised by the feudal lords in the countryside and the guilds in the town was breaking down under the dual pressures of market-driven society and the demographic revolution. Some of the surplus population was able to find work in the new factories, or migrated to the cities, while others had no option but to work for lower rates in the traditional craft industries . By the 1830s mass poverty had become a major social problem, which contemporaries, using the English word, called *Pauperismus*. A large underclass had emerged, which could no longer be sustained by the traditional structures of society.

By the early 1840s, German society was becoming increasingly atomized and the individual alienated. How was it to be given a new basis of cohesion? Gradually, abstract ideas like the nation or the ideologies of political liberty and social equality as represented by liberalism or socialism became the focus for new loyalties. New types of organization, such as political and cultural clubs and associations, filled the gap left by the collapse of the old society. In the countryside, however, despite the inroads made by modern capitalist agriculture, the peasantry remained 'a latent conservative force',[43] increasingly hostile towards the cities, bureaucracy and liberal individualism After 1848 it was there that the forces of anti-modernism – the conservatives, particularists, local patriots, Catholics and royalists – were to find their chief support.

Demographic revolution: the immense changes caused by greater longevity of life and the increase in the population

See Document 12

Conclusion

Historians have had particular difficulty in attempting to characterize the years between 1814 and 1848. Some refer to it as a period of restoration; others by using the term *Vormärz*, or pre-March (1848), period, see it primarily as a mere interim period leading to the 1848 revolts. In this book, however, the term 'post-war era' is used, as the years 1814–48 were only in a very limited sense a period of restoration. The German Confederation based on the co-operation of Prussia and Austria was a very different structure from the old Holy Roman Empire, and the major German states had gone through a political and territorial transformation. To describe the years 1815–48 as the *Vormärz* period focuses attention on the growth of nationalism and the social discontents that fused together to cause the 1848 revolts, and thus runs the risk of distorting the history of the period. It was, as David Blackbourn has stressed, a period 'of transition, marked by ambiguous conflicting elements':[44] modern industry coexisted with the traditional craft industries and developing parliamentary politics in southern Germany, and mass nationalist and liberal demonstrations or 'festivals' coexisted with the survival of the traditional estates and the autocratic rule of the princes. As Heinrich Heine observed, Germany had turned into a 'hybrid creature . . . [t]hat is neither fish nor fowl'.[45]

3 Revolution and Reaction, 1847–58

TIMELINE

1845–46		Poor harvests create food crisis
1846	*July*	Christian III's 'open letter' triggers Schleswig-Holstein crisis
1847		Swiss civil war
		Meeting of United Diet in Berlin
1848	*25 Feb.*	Declaration of French Republic
	5 Mar.	Heidelberg Assembly demands a national parliament
	13 Mar.	Outbreak of revolution in Vienna
		Metternich flees
	18 Mar.	Uprising in Berlin
	21–22 Mar.	Frederick William IV promises political reforms and a parliament
	24 Mar.	Formation of provisional revolutionary government in response to Denmark's annexation of Schleswig
	29–30 Mar.	Camphausen–Hansemann ministry established in Berlin
	3 Apr.	Pre-parliament in session in Frankfurt
	12 Apr.	Outbreak of revolution in Baden
	27–30 Apr.	Fighting between republicans and royal troops in Mannheim
	1 May	Elections to German National Parliament in Frankfurt
	16 May	Emperor Ferdinand flees to Innsbruck
	18 May	National Assembly opens at Innsbruck
	22 May	Prussian National Assembly opens
	13 June	Prague bombarded by Windischgrätz
	20 June	Resignation of Camphausen government
	29 June	Archduke John elected Regent and head of provisional German government
	22 July	Austrian *Reichstag* opens
	26 Aug.	Armistice of Malmö
	21 Sept.	Outbreak of second revolution in Baden
	6 Oct.	Popular uprising in Vienna
	20 Oct.	Windischgrätz lays siege to the city
	8 Nov.	Prussian army forces Prussian *Landtag* to quit Berlin
	5 Dec.	Imposition of new Prussian constitution
1849	*4 Mar.*	Dissolution of Austrian diet
	3 Apr.	Frederick William rejects offer of imperial crown from Frankfurt delegation
	5 Apr.	Austria recalls delegates from National Assembly
	3 May	Outbreak of Saxon revolution
	7 May	Prussia rejects imperial constitution
	14 May	Prussian delegates recalled from Frankfurt
	19 May	Outbreak of third revolution
	31 May	Rump of Frankfurt National Assembly moves to Stuttgart
	18 June	Rump assembly dissolved by Württemberg troops
	28 June	Collapse of revolutionary government in Karlsruhe
1850	*Mar.*	Erfurt parliament
	Nov.	Prussia retreats over Hesse–Cassel affair
		Proclamation of Olmütz
1851		Confederation restored
1853		*Zollverein* renewed for 12 years
1854–56		Crimean War
1858		William appointed regent
1859		Franco-Piedmontese war against Austria

See Document 13

Key issues

- What were the causes of the revolution?
- Why did splits develop between the moderate liberals and democrats?
- How effective was the Frankfurt parliament?
- What problems did the Frankfurt liberals encounter in their attempts to create a united Germany?
- To what extent did the 1848 revolts lead to the emergence of modern, nationally-based parties?
- To what extent was the fate of the revolution decided in Berlin and Vienna?
- Why did the 1848 revolutions in Germany fail?
- Could the Radowitz Plan have succeeded?
- Can the years 1851–58 be called a 'period of restoration'?

Introduction: 1848 and the historians

A. J. P. Taylor observed that '1848 was the decisive year of German, and so of European History'.[1] Until recently most historians have stressed the essential failure of the 1848 revolutions. In the repressive atmosphere of the 1850s it was dismissed as a 'mad year' and a dangerous aberration. After the creation of a *Kleindeutschland* by Bismarck, historians contrasted his successful policy of blood and iron with the efforts of the theoretical chatterers in the Frankfurt parliament to unify Germany. At the very least, the events of 1848 were seen as a mere stage to 1871 and not worth study for their own sake. However, in 1919 the black, red and gold flag of the revolutionaries became the new flag of the Weimar Republic, while Theodor Heuss, a leading liberal and, later, President of the *Bundesrepublik* in 1949, advocated making the Frankfurt constitution the model for the new republican constitution (see pp. 171–2). Nevertheless, the majority of German historians continued to view the revolutions of 1848 with a hostility reinforced by their own experiences of the turmoil of November–December 1918 (see pp. 167–70). It was significant, for instance, that Veit Valentin's classic on the 1848 revolutions met with hostility from established scholars and its publication was delayed until 1930.[2] During the Third Reich the revolutions were interpreted as the first proper national uprising in German history, but one that, thanks to the intervention of foreign powers and the corroding influence of democracy and constitutionalism, was ignominiously aborted.

After 1949 the two successor states to the German Reich laid claims to the legacy of 1848. The FRG stressed the constitutional achievements of the revolution, while the GDR was primarily interested in the role of the peasants and workers. Slowly in the 1960s and 1970s, under the influence of the social sciences, West German historians began to synthesize all the

Modernization: much used by modern historians to describe the process of building a modern state with a constitutional government, an industrial, capitalist economy and an effective bureaucracy

diverse themes of the 1848–49 revolutions and put them into their European context. Increasingly the revolts are seen more as a complex crisis of modernization which witnessed the emergence of modern politics as well as attempts to forge a German nation. Wehler argues that, despite their failure, they did in fact transform German society and create the basis for a new kind of politics.[3]

The coming of the revolution

Although the speed with which the 1848 revolutions swept across central Europe in 1848 took some contemporaries by surprise, it had been clear for several years that the *ancien régime* was facing an imminent and possibly terminal crisis. Gustav Freytag, the writer and historian, later recalled 'how we lived then like people who feel under their feet the pressures of the earthquake'.[4] Explaining why the revolutions occurred on the scale they did inevitably runs the risk of simplifying a highly complex set of events.[5] Yet there are certain common patterns to the events, which the historian can trace and analyse. The revolts were more than just a delayed reaction to the agrarian crisis or a liberal backlash against the Prussian government or the Metternich regime. They constituted, in effect, a crisis of modernization where institutional, economic, social and political crises all converged.

Growing demands for German unity and constitutional change, 1846–48

Throughout German-speaking Europe there was a growing desire amongst the educated and propertied classes for the ending of censorship and increased political representation and power. The political experience its members had gained through clubs, associations and town councils put them in a strong position to exploit the fiscal crisis facing the governments of the German states in 1847–48 to demand political reform. In 1847 the Prussian government decided to build a railway linking its eastern and western provinces for both military and economic reasons.

Unable to raise the money privately, Frederick William IV rashly summoned a combined meeting of the provincial *Landtage* (see p. 26) to authorize loans. Inevitably, as Metternich had foreseen, this fuelled the liberals' demands for a state parliament and gave them an opportunity to seize initiatives, which were ' progressively to corrode absolute government until its final collapse the following year'.[6] They refused point-blank to grant the loan until a regular parliament had been convoked in Berlin, which the Crown was not ready to concede, and they also attempted to push the government into extending the anti-discriminatory Jewish legislation of 1812 to the whole kingdom as a symbolic act of liberalism. Similarly in Baden, the liberals used the government's need to

---

Frederick William IV, 1795–1861

Because of his interests in neo-gothic architecture and his old-fashioned political values, he was known as 'the romantic upon the throne'. Although he bitterly opposed constitutional reform, he quickly surrendered to the demands of the revolution in 1848, but by the autumn he was already moving to reverse these concessions. He refused to accept the Crown of a united Germany from the Frankfurt parliament but he did support plans by his foreign minister, Joseph Radowitz, for creating a Prussian-led Germany. He was forced by Austria to give this up in 1850 and agree to the restoration of the Confederation. Until 1858 he pursued a determinedly counter-revolutionary policy in Prussia, when he was incapacitated by illness and his brother, William I, became regent.

---

increase the military budget to extract political concessions, while, in Austria, Metternich was ultimately driven to calling an estates-general to gain sanction for new loans and taxes on 12 March 1848, a day before the outbreak of the revolution. As in France in 1789, the *ancien régime* in Germany had already been fatally weakened by the fiscal crisis before the political revolution broke.

Estates-general: A meeting of representatives of the estates or orders – not dissimilar to a parliament

By the autumn of 1847, political activity was increasingly assuming a more pan-German dimension that would make the calling of a national parliament a real possibility:

- The German Catholic Movement, which advocated institutional reform and religious toleration, had set up over two hundred regional organizations throughout Germany.
- The newspaper, the *Deutsche Zeitung*, which called for national unity, had a readership in both Prussia and south Germany.
- In the autumn of 1847, left-wing liberals in Baden and the neighbouring states met in Offenburg and insisted that Germans should have 'a fatherland and a voice in its affairs'.[7]
- A few weeks later a group of more moderate liberals met in Heppenheim to demand that the *Zollverein* should be given representative institutions so that it 'would become irresistibly attractive to other German states, and finally lead to the inclusion of the Austrian lands within the Confederation and thus found a true German power'.[8]

The impact of the Schleswig-Holstein and Swiss crises

In July 1846 Christian VIII of Denmark triggered a major crisis when he announced in his notorious 'open letter' that he was determined to tie Schleswig and possibly also areas of Holstein ever more tightly to Denmark, even if this meant ignoring the ancient law that succession to these duchies could only pass through the male line. These threats, as William Carr observed, made 1846 'a vintage year for German nationalism'. In the resulting uproar, according to the Prussian General von

The Schleswig-Holstein issue

The duchies were united by personal union, that is by rule of the Danish king, to Denmark. The Ripen Charter of 1460 guaranteed the 'eternal' unity of the two duchies, but Holstein was almost entirely German-speaking, whereas Schleswig had a large Danish peasant population, and nationalist Danes regarded it as an indissoluble part of Denmark. The situation was further complicated by different laws of succession applying to the duchies and Denmark. In Denmark the succession to the kingdom could pass through the female line, but in Holstein only through the male line, while in Schleswig the law of inheritance was unclear! Danish nationalists pressed their monarch to incorporate Schleswig into the Danish state. Christian VIII declared his intention of doing this, but it was his successor, Frederick VII, who attempted to carry out this policy in 1848 (see p. 53). Only Holstein belonged to the Confederation.

Radowitz, 'legitimists, liberals, radicals, Catholics, Protestants, dogmatists, rationalists, pantheists, Austrians, Prussians, Saxons, Franks, Swabians, all rose as one man'[9] to defend the independence of the ethnic Germans in the duchies. Wolfram Siemann has argued that this wave of nationalism marked the real beginning of the 1848 revolts. At the very least, it had a 'widespread politicizing impact' on the German nationalists and liberals.[10]

A year later the brief Swiss civil war had a similar impact on the democratic left wing of German liberalism and on the relatively small number of German republicans. Volunteers flocked from south-west Germany, and the defeat of the Swiss conservatives and the subsequent setting up of a liberal federation was visible evidence that the repressive system of 1815 could be overturned.

The agrarian and social-economic crises

Public sphere: the political world as opposed to the domestic world

The events in Schleswig-Holstein and Switzerland certainly enflamed 'the liberal nationalist public sphere',[11] but the 1848 revolutions were initially fuelled by agrarian unrest. From 1845 to the autumn of 1847, Germany, like the rest of Europe, suffered a series of bad harvests and was faced with what Hans-Ulrich Wehler called the last of the agrarian crises of 'the old type'. Prices inevitably started to rise and by 1847, when they reached their peak, the cost of food had risen between 90 and 130 per cent. The price of a bushel of rye, for instance, rose from 51 silver pennies in 1845 to 87 in 1847, while over the same period a bushel of wheat rose from 65 to 110.[12] The food shortages were exacerbated by speculators and the continuing export of wheat and use of scarce supplies of grain and potatoes for brandy and schnapps. Inevitably this drove up food prices and intensified the sufferings of the urban and rural poor, especially the handworkers desperately attempting to survive on low wages in overcrowded and fiercely competitive trades. This in turn depressed consumer demand and led to the contraction of industry. Domestic

By this he means that it was a crisis caused by the failure of the harvest in a largely pre-industrial society which was dependent on the food it grew

Bushel: a measure of capacity for corn, etc., equivalent to 36.4 litres

See p. 35 and Document 12

The situation in Switzerland

Since the Vienna Congress, the old ruling patrician class had consolidated its power in the majority of cantons. In opposition a reform party had emerged and demanded representative democracy, equality under the law and a proper constitution. In the 1840s the liberal-dominated canton of Aargau decided to dissolve the monasteries, a step which ran counter to the monastic guarantee in the Federal Pact of 1815. In response, in 1845 the seven Catholic cantons formed a military defence union, the *Sonderbund*. In the meantime, the anti-clericalist Radicals had won an absolute majority in the elections to the Swiss diet. When the *Sonderbund* refused to dissolve itself, civil war broke out in 1847, but it was rapidly defeated and in 1848 Switzerland was given a new federal constitution which established a more unified state with its capital in Bern.

depression coincided with a global financial crisis, which spread to Germany from Britain and America. By the end of 1847 the whole of the German banking and credit structure was in crisis. In most cities about 30 per cent of the population was only able to survive thanks to charity. Malnutrition also made the population vulnerable to typhus. In Silesia 5000 people died, while in East Prussia the total reached 40,000. From 1844 onwards an increasing number of popular protests, which took the form of riots or attacks on food convoys, took place. With the good harvest of 1847 the agrarian crisis began to abate, but it left a bitter legacy of institutional incompetence and reinforced the desire for change and reform.

The outbreak of the revolution

The spark that ignited the revolts in central Europe and indeed most of continental Europe was the Paris riots and the downfall of King Louis-Philippe. The news of it quickly crossed the Rhine and then spread through German Europe. Siemann has described the German revolution as presenting 'an image of a chain of local rebellions, all rapidly following and coinciding with one another'.[13] Its rapid spread was facilitated by the infectious optimism that a new era was dawning, the power of rumour, the lifting of press controls by the Confederation Diet, and above all by the new railways.

In reaction to the riots and the setting up of barricades in Paris, Louis-Philippe fled to England on 25 February

The revolts began in Baden, fanned out to the north and east and then paralysed Vienna and Berlin. On 27 February the storm broke with the Mannheim rally, which anticipated many similar gatherings throughout Germany. A petition, drawn up by the republican Gustav von Struve, was handed to the government in Karlsruhe. Its call for a people's army with elected officers, complete freedom of the press, trial by jury and the immediate summoning of a German parliament rapidly became known throughout Germany as the 'March Demands'. Similar demands were

4   The burning down of Waldenburg Castle in Silesia, April 1848
Leipzige Illustrierte

made in Hesse–Darmstadt, Nassau, Hanover, Württemberg, Bavaria, Saxony, Oldenburg and Brunswick, as well as in the Prussian provinces of the Rhineland and Silesia. In Munich the armoury was stormed, while in Cologne on 3 March a rally of 5000 inhabitants led by Andreas Gottschalk, a doctor and leading local Radical, demanded the arming of the population and the guarantee of work and welfare, although it was quickly broken up by Prussian troops.   Simultaneously a series of peasant revolts broke out in the impoverished and overpopulated areas of the Black Forest and the Bavarian Odenwald. The peasants were primarily interested in terminating the last of their feudal obligations, and the remaining rights of the mediatized princes and former imperial knights, who still controlled about a third of the state's territory. Once these were granted, they had no more interest in revolution and became an essentially conservative anti-revolutionary force over the next 18 months.

Initially the princes of the smaller German states hoped that Prussia and Austria would intervene to crush the revolts, but revolutions in both Vienna and Berlin made this impossible. Riots forced Metternich to resign on 13 March and two days later compelled the Emperor to

See Document 14

Mediatized Princes: Rulers of former states of the Holy Roman Empire whose land had been annexed by another state but who still retained some rights and titles

promise a constitution. In Berlin, mobs had been gathering and making demands similar to those advocated by Struve and Gottschalk. On 17 March Frederick William agreed to recall the United *Landtag* and grant a constitution. The following day, however, when troops fired into a peaceful crowd in front of the royal palace, a revolt broke out, which persuaded the king to order the army out of Berlin and appoint a transitional ministry composed of aristocratic and upper middle-class liberals.

See Document. 15

Institutionalization of the revolution and the growing tensions between Radicals and Moderates

With the appointment of the March ministries in Prussia, Austria and the other German states, the moderate liberals believed that the revolution was over, and that the time had come to consolidate their gains by drafting new constitutions at both local and national level, but it was not possible simply to turn off popular unrest like a tap. There was still hunger and poverty in both the large towns and the countryside and a volatile public mood , which led to continued agitation and the formation of pressure groups and political leagues. Inevitably a split began to develop between the moderate liberals and the democrats. In Saxony the two groups organized rival leagues, which rapidly came to symbolize the deep social, institutional and ideological cleavages dividing them. In Württemberg the left was contemptuous of the new government's call for peace and order so that the future constitution could be decided with 'reason and moderation'. One radical journalist observed that 'we no more want to be ruled by the liberal plutocrats than we did by the old reactionary system'.[14]

March ministries: the governments set up as a result of the revolutions in March

Plutocrats: members of the wealthy elite

In Baden increasing tension developed between the moderates and leftists. When the Radical journalist, Josef Fickler, was arrested, an uprising broke out amongst the peasants, journeymen, day-labourers and students in southern Baden, which became a test of strength between the leftists and the moderate liberals. The government appealed for military help from the Confederation, which sent a force of some 30,000 men, but Friedrich Hecker and Gustav von Struve, the leaders of the revolt, hoped to arm the population and persuade the federal troops to mutiny. Their decisive defeat at the Battle of Kandern on 20 April showed that this was an illusion, and indicated that the power of the revolutionaries was 'actually far more restricted than is usually assumed'.[15]

The Frankfurt parliament

Of vital importance for the course of the revolution was the meeting of 51 leading liberals and democrats held on 5 March at Heidelberg. Despite profound differences, it agreed to set up a committee of seven to summon 'a more complete assembly of trusted men from all German peoples',[16] which met at Frankfurt between 31 March and 3 April. This 'pre-parliament' regarded itself as the leading voice of the nation, even though it had not been officially sanctioned by either the states or the Confederation. The radical wing, led by Struve, attempted to transform the pre-parliament immediately into a revolutionary convention, which would claim legislative power and create a republic on American lines, but to the moderate majority these ideas were unacceptable. There was, however, agreement that there should be elections to a future constituent assembly. Theoretically the elections were to be held on the basis of universal manhood suffrage, but there were no instructions as to whether these elections were to be direct or indirect, and 'inexplicably'[17] the demand had found its way into print that only 'mature, independent' citizens could vote. The Confederation, which was still legally in existence, accepted these resolutions and simultaneously repealed all exceptional laws such as the Karlsbad Decrees, which had been passed since 1819 (see p. 17). Thus the way was opened up for the creation of a new constitution under the cover of legal continuity.

Each state interpreted the Frankfurt electoral guidelines as it wished. The majority of the German states set up a system in which the final choice of candidate was made by a college of electors. In some states there was a secret ballot, but in others it was public. Similarly, the term 'mature, independent' citizen was used by others to exclude those whose income was too low to be taxable. The elections produced a parliament of 812 delegates, the overwhelming majority of whom were from the professional classes. The single biggest group (436) were employed by the state governments as administrators, judicial officials or teachers and university lecturers. There were only 56 members representing the commercial middle classes, while only three small-scale farmers and four craftsmen were elected. Parties and associations were to develop over the year, but in May such groupings were only tentative and incoherent. The political nation still consisted of 'loose and informal groups of local notables, social and cultural organizations with latent political objectives, and a small, imperfectly defined national élite whose prominence rested on their reputation as publicists or state parliamentarians'.[18]

Although an overwhelming majority of the delegates could loosely be called liberals and were determined to create a united constitutional German state, there were, even at this early stage of the revolution, a number of ambiguities that would ultimately undermine the authority of the Frankfurt parliament:

- There was no consistent majority in Frankfurt that could achieve unanimity on key issues.
- Germany was not a unified nation state. There were in the individual states, especially Prussia and Austria, competing centres of power.
- The Frankfurt assembly had no money, administrative back-up or army under its control.

5   The introduction of Archduke John of Austria as Imperial Administrator in the Frankfurt Assembly in the Paulskirche, Frankfurt, 12 July 1848

Leipzige Illustrierte

- It was not clear where the boundaries of the new Germany should lie.
- Any unification of Germany would require international consent.

Parliamentary organization

Parliament sat in the Paulskirche, which was hardly a practical venue for a constituent assembly. Initially delegates were divided up into 15 sections, each responsible for a particular administrative task, such as electing a committee. Gradually parties did emerge, as it became obvious that like-thinking men needed to combine in support of their views. The parties, which took their name from the cafes and restaurants where the delegates met each evening, in the final analysis made the functioning of parliament viable, despite the verbose tendency of so many of their members. The left-wing groups were the most effective in relating to their voters. Through a series of congresses and such organizations as the Central March Association they began to construct solid bases of support in German society. Some deputies wrote reports on their activities for their constituents or articles for local newspapers, while voters

Paulskirche: St Paul's Church in Frankfurt

Party groupings at Frankfurt

Theoretically the Frankfurt parliament consisted of 812 delegates, but some of the non-German constituencies boycotted the elections. Within the first few weeks, the majority of delegates joined factions based on the restaurants or cafés where they could meet to discuss pressing issues. The groups were often fluid and at least a hundred delegates refused to identify with any of them, but gradually the bewildering mass of individual factions formed themselves into four main groups: right, centre-right, centre-left and left.

Party groupings in the Frankfurt National Assembly

Parties		Approximate Percentage of members
Café Milani	(right wing/conservative)	6
Casino, Landsberg and Augsburger Hof	(centre-right/Constitutional liberals)	34
Württemberger Hof and Westendhall	(centre-left/parliamentary liberals)	13
Deutscher Hof and Donnersberg	(left/ democratic)	15
Non-aligned		32

Source: W. Siemann, *Die Frankfurter Nationalversammlung 1848/9 zwischen democratischem Liberalismus und konservativer Reform*, Frankfurt, Lang, 1976, p. 27.

Central March Organization (*Zentralmärzverein*): In November 1848 deputies from the three left-wing factions, *Donnersberg, Deutscher Hof* and *Westendhall* formed this organization to defend what had been achieved by the revolution. Throughout Germany it issued press releases, organized rallies and demonstrations. By March 1849 it had about nine hundred and fifty local associations and 500,000 members

bombarded their representatives with petitions, declarations, etc. Clearly, huge strides were made in creating a modern parliament, but poor communications, the continued existence of the independent states and the ambiguity about the Frankfurt Parliament's powers ensured that institutionally it remained weak and uncertain.

'The Provisional Central Power' May–October 1848

Before creating a national executive, the Frankfurt Assembly had to establish its claim to superiority over the individual state parliaments. Inevitably this met with some hostility both from state governments which wished to safeguard their own particularist powers and from the conservative factions, particularly the *Café Milani* and *Landsberg* groups. Although on 19 May Franz Raveaux, a left-wing democrat, failed to win a majority for a motion asserting Frankfurt's superiority over the Prussian *Landtag*, he did secure a compromise resolution which stated that 'all regulations of individual parliaments which are not in agreement with its yet to be determined constitution will be considered valid only with reference to the latter [the constitution], regardless of current validity'.[19] This at least opened up the way for the creation of some sort of central government, but there was disagreement between the right and left about the form that this was to take. The former wanted the participation of the Austrian and Prussian Crowns, while the latter argued for a republican executive committee. Heinrich von Gagern, the Assembly's

Heinrich von Gagern, 1799–1880

After fighting at the Battle of Waterloo in 1815, he became a civil servant in Hesse-Darmstadt and was then elected as a Liberal deputy to the state's parliament. He played an active role in the Liberal opposition and in 1848 was elected to the National Assembly at Frankfurt. He was appointed head of the provisional government in December, but resigned when Frederick William IV refused the offer of the Crown of Germany. In 1870 he welcomed the Prussian-driven unification of Germany under Bismarck, although he enthusiastically backed the alliance between Prussia and Austria in 1879 (see pp. 129–30).

chairman, carried the day with a compromise proposing the Austrian Archduke John as *Reichsverweser* or Imperial Regent, who would be elected by the Assembly, but who would then appoint an independent executive. On 28 June 'the Provisional Central Power' was accordingly set up in the form of a small cabinet consisting of a minister–president and ministers of foreign affairs, the interior, finance, justice, trade and war.

How much power did this central authority really have? It had no means of raising taxation and was dependent on financial handouts from the individual states. It also lacked a civil service and above all an army. In an attempt to remedy this latter deficiency, the war minister, a former Prussian general, tried to insist that the armies of the individual states should pay homage to the Regent and wear the colours of the new Reich. The smaller states were ready to accept this but it was rejected by Prussia, Austria, Bavaria and Hanover.

Devising a constitution for a united Germany proved a lengthy business. The Frankfurt Parliament did not adopt a draft constitution drawn up by the Confederation, as this gave parliament too few powers. It therefore set up on 24 May the Constitutional Committee which took the fateful decision to start with the question of fundamental rights rather than with the complex task of drafting a constitution. The Frankfurt deputies have traditionally been accused of letting time slip away while discussing the abstruse principles of fundamental rights. It was, for instance, not until October 1848 that the Constitutional Committee began to grapple with the key questions of whether Austria should belong to Germany and who should be the head of state. On the other hand, the decision to begin with the question of fundamental rights can be defended. They were, after all, to quote Thomas Nipperdey, 'an elementary, emotional and popular reality; they were like the articles of the civilian faith and represented the very meaning of the constitutional state'.[20] In a sense they were the symbol of the revolution and would override the rights of the individual states. To start here was also a political decision because the question of fundamental rights represented an area of potential agreement between the factions in the Paulskirche. Those who wished to exclude Austria from a united Germany felt that they needed time before they could win majority backing for their ideas. Similarly there was also hope that a declaration of fundamental rights would go some way to appease the Radicals, who were pushing for far-reaching social changes.

The dominant group on the constitutional committees responsible for drafting the fundamental laws was the centre-right Cassino constitutional Liberals, but it also included two key left-wingers, Blum and Wiegand, from the left-wing Deutscher Hof. The final version contained 12 articles covering:

• the abolition of capital punishment and aristocratic privilege
• equality in appointment to public office
• religious freedom
• state supervision of education
• free elementary education
• admission of the public to parliamentary sessions
• state protection extended to every German citizen.

The 'German Question'

One of the most controversial issues debated at Frankfurt concerned what constituted the 'German nation'. Opinion was roughly divided between those who believed in self-determination and saw nationalism as an ideology of liberation for Germans and non-Germans alike, and those who primarily saw it in terms of the assertion of German self-interest and power. The general assumption of most of the delegates at the Paulskirche was that the territory of the German Confederation would serve as a basis for the new Germany, but this of course, as Wolfram Siemann has pointed out, 'was based on a pre-national construct which as a loose federation of princes and city republics, had incorporated constitutional hybrid relationships which ran counter to the nationality principle'.[21] The northern, eastern and southern borders of the Confederation followed the former frontiers of the Holy Roman Empire and did not mark a clear-cut ethnic divide. Germans were mixed up with Danes, Poles, Czechs, Slovaks, Slovenes, Croats, Italians and Dutch (see Map 3). So inevitably the process of creating a new German state would cause acute international and ethnic tension, as can be seen by the reaction of the Frankfurt parliament to the complex questions of nationality and territory.

Posen

In the pre-parliament a majority had voted for the re-creation of the Polish state, but in practice when confronted with a Polish uprising in the Prussian province of Posen in May 1848, the National Assembly supported the military measures taken against the rebels by Prussia, which firmly claimed that two-thirds of the province was composed of 'German Posen'. The *Realpolitik* of many liberals was given expression by

Wilhelm Jordan, a left-wing delegate from Prussia, who advocated a 'healthy national egoism' in the Polish question. He dismissed the views of the pro-Polish party as mere 'cosmopolitan liberalism' and argued that Germany's claims in Poland rested on its strength and the rights conquest.[22]

See Document. 16

South Tyrol

Logically the Paulskirche should have supported a motion in June put forward by five of the deputies requesting that the districts of Trent and Rovereto, which were settled mainly by Italians, should be separated from the German Confederation. The Democrats supported this idea, but shortly before the debate took place the Austrians reconquered Lombardy. The majority now rejected the motion and totally ignored the principle of national determination, which they so vehemently supported in Schleswig-Holstein, and agreed with the crude argument of an Austrian deputy: 'we own South Tyrol and we will keep it'.[23]

In April 1848, Piedmontese and other Italian forces had invaded Lombardy to assist the rebels against Austria. They were defeated in July 1848

Bohemia and Moravia

Here, too, the overwhelming majority in the *Paulskirche* assumed that both these provinces would belong to a future German state, despite the fact that 48 out of the 68 Bohemian deputies refused even to send their deputies to Frankfurt. While the majority were in favour of protecting the large Slav minorities in these provinces, there was a point-blank refusal to countenance the setting up of an independent Czech nation, and consequently Prince Windischgrätz's defeat of the Prague uprising in June 1848 was welcomed by the majority in Frankfurt, even though there were fears about the consequences of that victory for the liberal cause within Germany.

Limburg and Schleswig-Holstein

In both Limburg and Schleswig-Holstein, nation-making ran up against international reality. Limburg was a Dutch province and, in response to nationalist claims from Frankfurt, Britain, France and Russia made clear their support for the status quo. In March 1848 the German movement in Schleswig-Holstein countered renewed attempts by the Danish Crown to create a national and liberal constitution, which would also incorporate Schleswig into Denmark, by declaring an emergency and setting up a provisional state government. The Schleswig-Holstein issue had an explosive force that could unite both constitutional liberals and democrats and potentially radicalize the revolution. On 12 April the Confederation declared war on Denmark and sent in a force under the supreme command of the Prussian General Count von Wrangel which advanced as far as Jutland, but the Danish fleet was able to inflict considerable economic damage by blockading the Prussian coast. The

Provisional Central Power at Frankfurt took over the direction of the war and in the *Paulskirche* increasing demands were made for the construction of a German fleet as it was claimed that Germany was now a great power.

The conflict became a test case for the international standing of the new central government at Frankfurt. It could have led to a European war, in which conceivably German unity might have been forged, when Russia and Britain, who were the guarantors of Schleswig-Holstein under international law, vetoed the absorption of Schleswig into a united Germany. On 26 August the weakness of the Central Power in Frankfurt was painfully revealed when the Prussian government, partly as a result of Anglo-Russian pressure and partly as a consequence of the Danish blockade, unilaterally signed the Truce of Malmö with Denmark. Lacking an army, Frankfurt could not intervene and had little option but to accept the truce. This unleashed a storm of criticism and the government was forced to resign when the Frankfurt parliament voted by 238 to 221 to reject it. A new cabinet, which was based on a right–left coalition and opposed to the Malmö Truce, was appointed, only to fall apart when confronted with the divisive internal issues of constitution-making. Consequently, the Assembly had in the end no option but to vote in favour of the Truce on 16 September. This triggered renewed popular unrest right across Germany, including riots in Frankfurt itself, which shattered the national unity created by the Schleswig-Holstein crisis.

> Malmö provided for the withdrawal of both Prussian and Danish troops and the temporary administration of Schleswig-Holstein by a Prusso-Danish commission

Popular politics, spring–autumn 1848

The revolution of March 1848 unleashed political forces, which led not only to the founding of parties in Frankfurt, but to the emergence at local level of a large number of political associations representing a wide range of political views. A whole hierarchy of regional and district committees and congresses evolved with the ultimate aim of creating nationally-based parties and pressure groups. For instance, a congress of craftsmen's and tradesmen's representatives from all over Germany met in Frankfurt in July and set up an organization to lobby the Assembly for protective measures against the economic consequences of modern capitalism. A month later the Workers' Congress in Berlin decided to set up the General German Workers' Fraternity, which by the spring of 1849 had approximately fifteen thousand members. This attempted unsuccessfully to focus the attention of the Frankfurt parliament on the key questions of health insurance and the right to work. To the left of these groups was the Communist League, which attempted ineffectually to co-ordinate the emerging workers' societies into a national movement. There were, too, a large number of democratic and constitutional associations. In June the Democratic Association and Workers' Society of Marburg organized a congress in Frankfurt, which was attended by representatives from 89 other associations, to draft a programme for a national democratic party.

It then went on to set up in Berlin the first central party office in Germany. The Constitutional Liberals attempted to follow suit by forming the National Association in Kassel in September. The Catholic associations followed the same pattern. Pius Associations, which took their name from Pope Pius IX, were founded throughout Catholic Germany and, at a congress in Mainz in early October, their representatives came together to create a national organization. Even the Prussian Conservatives were forced to organize on an all-Prussian basis to defend the Crown and to strengthen their campaign to return to the status quo ante of 1847. In July 1848 Ernst Ludwig von Gerlach, a member of the Camarilla at the Prussian court created the Association for King and Fatherland, which was the first Conservative central party organization in Germany.

Camarilla: a group of reactionary politicians at the Prussian court

Political developments in Prussia and Austria

During 1848 the actual pace of political developments in each state varied, but the real nerve centres of the revolution were in Berlin and Vienna, and it was here that the fate of the revolutions in central Europe would ultimately be determined.

See Document. 17

Austria

In the spring of 1848 the Habsburg Empire seemed to be on the brink of disintegration. The government's attempts to appease both the non-German nationalities and the Liberals met with failure. On 11 May rioting by armed students and workers forced the government to extend the suffrage, and the emperor fled to Innsbruck for safety. At this stage, nationalism and liberalism seemed to be in the ascendant throughout the Empire. Yet over the next two months the *ancien régime* began to recover. First the Czech nationalists were defeated in Prague by General Windischgrätz in June, and then in July the Habsburg possessions in Italy were saved by General Radetzky's victory at Custoza. In October, however, a second revolution broke out in Vienna, when troops stationed there mutinied and refused to move against the Hungarians. Their defeat by General Windischgrätz was the decisive turning-point of the revolutions in central Europe and opened up the way for a new government in Austria, headed by Prinz Felix zu Schwarzenberg, to restore the independence and power of the Habsburg Empire as an alternative to a united *Grossdeutschland*.

Prussia

In the course of the summer of 1848, as the newly-elected Prussian *Landtag* debated the future of Prussia's constitution, the political forces of the right started to recover. At court Leopold von Gerlach and the

Prince Felix zu Schwarzenberg, 1800–52

After working in the Austrian diplomatic service, he was appointed Austrian Chancellor in December 1848. His policy was to defeat the revolution and re-establish a unified Habsburg state as a great power. He was, therefore, bitterly opposed to Prussian plans in 1849 for creating a Prussian-led German union, and played a major role in defeating them (see pp. 59–60). In 1851 he persuaded the emperor to abolish the Austrian constitution of 1849 and return to a system of absolutist rule.

Camarilla, began to turn the king against the revolution, while leading conservative landowners, including Otto von Bismarck (see p. 68) formed the League for the Protection of Landed Property. By the time the new constitution was drafted, the king, backed by the army and the conservatives, was in a position to stage a coup. On 2 November he dismissed the von Pfuel ministry, which was attempting to forge a compromise between the court and parliament, and appointed Count Brandenburg, a reliable, conservative soldier, as minister–president. A week later General von Wrangel occupied Berlin with 13,000 troops and ordered parliament to dissolve itself. A new constitution was decreed and elections took place in late January/early February 1849.

When it met in Berlin in August to draw up plans for defending their interests, it was called the Junker parliament

The new constitution was by no means reactionary. The upper house was chosen by restricted franchise but the lower house was elected by virtually all adult males

Frankfurt and the German Constitution

It was against the background of these events that the Frankfurt parliament began to consider the intricate question of a German constitution in October. It was clear that a united Germany would have to be a federal state. Its federal nature was an historic reality, but how in practice was the balance between Prussia, Austria and the rest of the new Reich to be secured?

- Should the small states be amalgamated as was to occur later in 1947 (see p. 284)?
- Alternatively could Prussia be weakened by turning it into a loosely knit structure of provinces?
- What should happen to Austria and its non-German territories?

*The **grossdeutsch** (greater German) solution would have included the German-speaking parts of the Habsburg monarchy. The **kleindeutsch** (small German) solution involved the exclusion of Austria and the creation of a predominantly Protestant, Prussian-dominated Germany – as was to happen in 1871 (see Ch. 4)*

Initially a clear majority of delegates in Frankfurt assumed that German Austria together with Bohemia would belong to the new German federal state, while the non-German parts of the Habsburg Empire (see Map 3) would be connected to the Reich by personal union. If the Austrian Empire had disintegrated, a *grossdeutsch* solution might have been possible, but once it was clear that the Empire would survive, it was increasingly appreciated that 'a state, and a major power at that could not remain a major power if one half of it was part of another major power'.[24] In November Schwarzenberg began to signal that he wished to see the whole Austrian Empire represented in a restored confederation.

Inevitably, therefore, the option of a *kleindeutsch* Germany began to gain ground, the focal point of which would be the Prussian state. By early January the Constitutional Committee had drafted plans for a federal Reich. Responsibility for the army, foreign relations, customs, coinage and postal services would all belong to the central Reich government. There was, however, still no consensus on how universal the franchise should be, the powers of the Crown or indeed on the place of Austria in the new state. On 13 January Heinrich von Gagern, the prime minister of the provisional central government managed to gain support in Frankfurt for a *kleindeutsch* Germany ruled by the royal house of Prussia but 'joined in a special relationship to a unified Habsburg Reich'. Ten days later this compromise solution fell apart when a coalition of *grossdeutsch* supporters and left-wingers defeated a motion to create a hereditary monarchy. In March 1849, when Schwarzenberg in the Kremsier Declaration finally ruled out Austrian participation in a united Germany, the moderate liberal *kleindeutsch* supporters had little option but to agree to a wider franchise bill and a stricter control on the Crown's powers of veto to secure enough democratic support to gain a small majority in favour of offering the position of hereditary emperor of the German Reich to Frederick William. This proposal gained the backing of 28 states but it was rejected out of hand by Austria, Prussia, Hanover, Saxony, Bavaria and Württemberg. Frederick William viewed the offer of the crown as a 'dog collar, with which they wish to lash me to the revolution of 1848'.[25]

See Document. 18

Kremsier Declaration

Although there would be no directly elected parliament, Schwarzenberg proposed an assembly attended by delegates from the individual state parliaments. The number of delegates each state could send would be calculated on the basis of its population, which would favour Austria with its total population of 38 million, as opposed to 32 million in the rest of the German states. While it could be argued that this proposal would ensure German hegemony in central south-east Europe, it was in the end rejected because the majority at Frankfurt wanted a German national state.

The defeat of the Revolution

By a small majority (190:180) the National Assembly decided to press on and set the date for elections to the new national parliament for 15 July. If Prussia refused to participate, the ruler of the next largest state represented in the new German upper chamber, the *Staatenhaus* would be invited to become the imperial governor. This attempt by the Assembly

It was planned that the new German constitution would consist of a lower chamber directly elected by the people (*Volkshaus*) and the *Staatenhaus* where representatives of the states would sit to speak over the heads of the state governments, directly to the people, was bitterly opposed by the *Reichsverweser*, Archduke John, on the grounds that it was both unconstitutional and would lead to civil war. In protest at his intervention, Heinrich von Gagern resigned and Archduke John then appointed a right-wing cabinet, which was almost immediately rejected by a damaging vote of no confidence. Increasingly the National Assembly pursued a more radical line, and called on the people to defend the new constitution. Prussia, Austria, Hanover and Baden retaliated by recalling their deputies. When the Prussian *Landtag* in Berlin recommended the acceptance of the new constitution, it was immediately dissolved. By 27 May only 103 left-of-centre delegates remained at Frankfurt. Three days later they moved to Stuttgart, where they announced the dismissal of Archduke John, and the appointment of a new government, but on 16 June the Stuttgart assembly was dissolved at bayonet point by Württemberg troops.

In Baden the Grand Duke accepted the constitution, but this did not prevent a revolt

The governments of the states which had rejected the constitution, were now faced with uprisings co-ordinated by the Central March Association (see p. 50). Uprisings took place in Silesia and the Rhineland, but these were easily crushed. In Saxony, Württemberg, the Bavarian Palatinate and Baden revolutionary forces were strong enough to force the governments on to the defensive. Compared, however, to March 1848, the revolutionaries were in a weak position. There was no supporting action from the peasantry, many of the middle classes were fearful of the new radicalism and the Prussian army was able to intervene first in Saxony and then in the Palatinate and Baden to defeat the revolutionaries. The fighting came to an end when the fortress of Rastatt in Baden surrendered to the Prussians (see Map 3).

Even though the 1848 revolts and the Frankfurt Parliament proved to be an invaluable school of politics for the German people, they had nevertheless failed to create a unified, liberal, federal Germany. The reasons for this are complex and overlapping:

- The initial easy successes of the revolts bred an over-confidence amongst the revolutionaries.
- The revolutionaries themselves were divided. The liberals and democrats failed to devise the necessary compromises that would have strengthened the revolution in the face of the counter-revolution.
- The polycentric nature of Germany made it more difficult for the Frankfurt regime to establish its ascendancy.
- The attempt to forge a *Grossdeutschland* wasted valuable time, as it was impractical to assume that a great power like Austria would in fact dismember itself to enter a purely German union.
- The ruling classes were much stronger than they looked. The armed forces stayed loyal and the bureaucracy and legal systems of the states continued to function throughout the revolutionary period.
- They were also able effectively to exploit the divisions amongst the revolutionaries by appeasing the peasantry and the handworkers (see

p. 61), playing on the ethnic fears of the Germans in the border lands and offering the bourgeoisie the prospect of security from revolutionary turmoil. As Hans-Ulrich Wehler has remarked, 'in this way the conservatives drove their wedges into the weak spot of the revolution'.[26]

The struggle to restore the Confederation

Although Frederick William had crushed the revolutions in Germany, he was not yet ready to abandon the model of a Prussian-led *Kleindeutschland*. Following advice from von Radowitz, he attempted to impose from above a conservative, *kleindeutsch*, national Germany – the so-called Prussian Union. In May, while Austria was still involved in military operations against the Hungarians and the Piedmontese, Prussia, Saxony, Hanover, Württemberg and Bavaria met to consider the new Radowitz Plan. The two southern states pulled out, but the three remaining states decided to support the Prussian initiative, and in June invited all the other German governments to take part and to draw up plans for an elected German parliament. However, with the defeat of the Hungarians in August 1849, Austria was able to organize an increasingly effective counter-offensive against the Radowitz Plan. Saxony and Hanover also withdrew from the Union and joined Bavaria and Württemberg to form an alliance with Austria, and in September, when Schwarzenberg summoned an assembly composed of the opponents of a Prussian-led *Kleindeutschland*, it was clear that Germany was now effectively divided into two hostile blocs. Initially this did not deter the Union states from holding elections for a constituent assembly based on the newly-introduced, Prussian, three-class voting system (see p. 61), which met at Erfurt in March 1850. The parliament was boycotted by the democratic left on the grounds that it was a mere camouflage for Prussian absolutism, but many of the Constitutional Liberals supported it in the hope that it would ultimately lead to German unity.

> Hungary had declared itself independent of Austria in April 1849, but, with help from Russia, Austria had forced it to capitulate at Vilagos on 13 August 1849

Yet with the renaissance of Austria as a great power, unity could only be achieved by war. Since the summer of 1849, tension had been growing between Austria and Prussia. The final crisis between the two powers was precipitated by domestic events in Hesse-Cassel. The ruler, Duke Frederick William, had replaced a liberal ministry with an ultra-reactionary government, and then, when confronted with opposition in the *Landtag* to his government's budget, had dissolved the *Landtag* and started to levy taxes illegally. He attempted to quell the resulting uproar from the liberals, the civil service and even the army by appealing to Schwarzenberg for help. Austria and its allies, diplomatically supported by Russia, were only too ready to intervene, as Hesse–Cassel was a strategically important state dominating Prussia's civilian and military roads to the west, whilst also providing direct links to Hanover and thence to Schleswig-Holstein. In early November 1850, Prussian and Austrian armies began to mobilize and converge on Hesse-Cassel. The Austrians were strengthened with units from Bavaria and Württemberg. Shots were actually exchanged between Prussian and Bavarian troops on 8 November.

See Document 19

The Prussians, however, facing the prospect of a war against Austria, the south German alliance and Russia, backed down, and agreed to the joint Austro-Prussian Proclamation of Olmütz on 29 November. By this, Prussia consented to demobilize its army, dissolve the Erfurt Union and discuss plans for reforming the Confederation at a second conference. Prussia had certainly suffered a serious diplomatic and political defeat at Olmütz, but not everything went Austria's way when this second conference met at Dresden in December. Prussia was able to block Schwarzenberg's proposals for integrating Austria's non-German territories into the Confederation, and, instead, the old Confederation of 1815 was revived. Nevertheless, as Schwarzenberg observed, ' a threadbare and worn coat is still better than no coat at all'.[27]

Reaction and restoration? German domestic politics, 1850–58

Although the 1850s were certainly a time of reaction, paradoxically the governments, like the Bonapartist regime, which was established in France in December 1851, often used strikingly modern policies to bolster their regimes. The great majority of the German states retained their constitutions, albeit heavily revised, which ultimately kept open the option for change. Many governments, particularly the Prussian government, displayed a new element of social realism, by which through judicious reforms and appeasement of each social class they attempted to gain a broadly-based consent or at least toleration of their quasi-authoritarian regimes.

Louis Napoleon, the nephew of Napoleon I, like Bismarck later (see p. 79), introduced universal manhood suffrage. Until the late 1860s the French Chamber had little power, and Napoleon consolidated his regime by appealing to the bourgeoisie, exploiting nationalism and appeasing the working classes with welfare reforms (see Document 20)

Although the exact course of reaction differed in each state, the German Confederation attempted to direct and guide it by setting up a special co-ordinating committee. The states were ordered to reverse the constitutional changes that had occurred in 1848 and to ensure that parliamentary procedure, the military oath of loyalty, the behaviour of the press and the voting system did not conflict with the monarchical principle. The Confederation sent out a constant stream of directives to the state governments and even dispatched commissioners to intervene directly in the domestic politics of Bremen and Frankfurt. Although in 1854 it promulgated a Press and Association Law for the whole Confederation, its preferred tactics were to manoeuvre the individual state governments into revoking the constitutional settlements of 1848–49, so that the subsequent opprobrium would fall on them. The state governments rolled back the constitutional achievements of 1848 through the imposition of new voting systems based on the Prussian model, and at election times they did not hesitate to intervene directly to influence the electorate. Workers' associations were suppressed, the civil service purged and the emphasis on teaching in schools was shifted to obedience and religion, while teacher training was carefully monitored.

In April 1849 Frederick William dissolved the Prussian *Landtag*, when its lower house voted to accept the new Reich constitution, which had just been drawn up in Frankfurt (see p. 57), and a month later he imposed the three-class voting system. After new elections, which were boycotted by the left, he promulgated a new constitution, which survived until 1918:

- The rights of the Crown were strengthened. It had the right of veto, and could issue emergency decrees and declare martial law.
- Control of the army was exercised by the royal military cabinet, which was responsible only to the king not to the war minister.
- In 1854 the upper house was reorganized so that effectively the majority of its members were hereditary members of the nobility.

As in the other German states, the Prussian press was muzzled, the civil service purged of liberals and educational policies exercised along conservative lines. Yet in many areas government policy pursued a Bonapartist rather than reactionary line. As under Louis Napoleon in France, there were attempts to reconcile the different classes to the loss of political liberty. The complete liberation of the peasants was confirmed, efforts were made to protect the craftsmen from hostile economic trends by restoring the authority of the guilds, and factory inspectors were appointed to enforce the implementation of health and security legislation.

The three-class voting system remained in place until 1918. The voters were not divided by estate or class, but by the amount of taxes they paid. In 1849, 4.7 per cent belonged to the first category, 12.6 to the second and 82.7 to the third. Each class accounted for a third of the electors, who in turn chose the actual delegates. The voting system did not necessarily guarantee a conservative majority. In the 1860s liberal majorities were regularly returned

The cushion of economic growth

The 1850s and 1860s were a period of accelerating economic growth which gradually brought to an end the 'scissor-effect of an expanding population and stagnant labour market'.[28] Economic growth also enabled the 'restoration' governments to balance their repressive political policies with more enlightened social reforms. The break-through of German industrialization occurred in the 1850s and 1860s. The Austrian economist, Carl von Czoernig, observed that the pace of change had been so rapid that 'conditions in 1847 seem much closer to 1758 than 1858'.[29] The volume of trade in both the *Zollverein* and Austria nearly doubled between 1851 and 1857. The creation of joint-stock companies, albeit not on a large scale, and the formation of modern investment banks helped sustain the momentum of economic growth up to the worldwide depression of 1857–59. This hit the Austrian economy severely, but the rest of German Europe escaped relatively lightly, and growth resumed again in 1860–61. Overall, the record of growth in the 1850s and 1860s was impressive, and by the 1860s the *Zollverein* had the largest railway

Scissor-effect: a widening gap comparable to the opening of a pair of scissors

network on the continent. The use of steam power in factories was becoming universal and pioneering steps were being taken towards mechanizing production. At the world exhibition of 1862, German machine tools were at least as good as their British competitors. Similarly, the output of the German textile industry, and coal and steel industries, increased dramatically over the period 1850 to 1865. Nevertheless the *Zollverein* economy still lagged behind Britain, the USA, France and Belgium. In 1860, Prussia's share of world manufacturing was only 5 per cent, as compared to Britain's 20 per cent and France's 8 per cent.[30] However, in the longer term the fact that Germany's most dynamic economic region, the Ruhr, lay within Prussian territory was to have, as James Sheehan has put it, 'profound political consequences'.[31]

See Document. 21

Austro-Prussian relations

The re-establishment of the Confederation did not mark a return to an unchallenged Austrian hegemony within Germany. At Frankfurt, co-operation between the two great German powers became increasingly difficult to maintain, as both, in the words of Bismarck (see p. 68), who was now the Prussian representative to the Confederation, were sucking 'the life blood' from each other. By this he meant that Austria needed to dominate the Confederation to protect its position as a great power, which would inevitably prevent Prussia from gaining its full potential within Germany. This fundamental clash of policies ensured that at Frankfurt Bismarck did everything he could to weaken Austria and block the development of a common policy. The latent antagonism between the two states became obvious in the negotiations to renew the *Zollverein* and the discussions on the foreign policy of the Confederation during the Crimean War and Franco-Piedmontese struggle against Austria in 1859.

See Document. 22

When the *Zollverein* treaty came up for renewal in 1853, the Austrians made a determined effort to join by proposing a new, central European, free-trade zone. The prospect was attractive to the south German states and Saxony, but opposed fiercely by Prussia, which did not want to forfeit its leadership of the *Zollverein*. Rudolf von Delbrück, a key official in the Prussian Ministry of Commerce, managed to strengthen Prussia's position within the *Zollverein* by offering Hanover and Oldenburg entry on very favourable terms. At first, as a means of putting pressure on Berlin, the pro-Austrian states threatened to form an independent customs union with Austria, but ultimately the pull of the Prussian economy was too powerful for them to resist. The Austrians were marginalized and had no option but to sign a 12-year trade agreement with Prussia and agreed not to raise the question of entry into the *Zollverein* until 1860.

The outbreak of the Crimean War led to further friction between the two powers. Austria, fearing Russian influence in the Balkans, refused to assist the Russian Empire against Britain and France. In early 1854

Prussia reluctantly signed a defensive treaty with Austria, but rejected an Austrian proposal to mobilize the Confederation's forces under Austrian supreme command in the case of a Russian invasion of the Balkans. At Frankfurt Bismarck was quick to exploit the fear of the smaller states that this would lead to war and the subsequent break-up of the Confederation to the great advantage of the French, by declaring that the Confederation would fight only to defend its own neutrality. He was thus able to imply that Prussia, unlike Austria, was a purely German state whose security interests were identical with the great majority of the states of the Confederation.

When war broke out between Austria and the Franco-Piedmont alliance in April 1859, Prussia again initially tried to remain neutral, but with the defeat of Austrian forces at Magenta and Solferino, Berlin abandoned this position and prepared to drive a hard bargain with Vienna. In exchange for military assistance, Prussia now insisted on equality with Austria within the Confederation, supreme command of forces on the Rhine and military and political hegemony in northern Germany. Austria, believing that the Confederation would inevitably be drawn into the struggle, was unwilling to make these concessions, but the matter was never put to the test. On 11 July France and Austria ended the war with the Armistice of Villafranca. Austria had suffered a heavy defeat in Italy and the loss of Lombardy, but had nevertheless prevented Prussia from strengthening its position within the Confederation.

> The Crimean War, 1854–56, was fought by Britain, Turkey, France and Piedmont against Russia to prevent the implementation of Russian plans for the partition of the Turkish Empire

> To drive Austria out of Italy, Napoleon and Cavour, the prime minister of Piedmont, had secretly planned at Plombières to provoke Austria into an attack on Lombardy

> **Hegemony:** leadership by one state over others

Conclusion

Was the 1848 Revolution the 'turning point that did not turn'? Certainly no united, liberal Germany was created and the final stages of the revolt were crushed on a scale and with a ruthlessness not seen since the Peasants' Revolt in 1525. On the other hand, the triumph of the conservatives did not lead to an unthinking return to the status quo. Even if they had not ultimately been successful, the 1848 revolts had given birth to a new politics. The liberals, the democrats and the conservatives had all organized on a national scale. The more far-sighted conservatives, who included Radowitz and eventually the young Otto von Bismarck, also realised that future governments of the right would have to harness nationalism and compensate both the masses and the bourgeoisie for the absence of political liberty by social reforms and economic prosperity. Thus it was no surprise that the 1850s witnessed the most determined intervention by the state in the social question until Bismarck's welfare reforms in the 1880s (see p. 115).

The economic, political and international climate in the 1850s was very different from that of the previous decades. The 1848 revolts had not led to the dramatic creation of a liberal Germany, but they had revealed the strength of nationalism and the potential for popular participation in politics, as well as confirming that a Prussian-led *Kleindeutschland* was the most likely, if not yet inevitable, formula for the united Germany of the future. The revolts also led to the introduction of a parliamentary constitution into Prussia, albeit one with a three-class franchise that grossly distorted the political power of the property-owning classes, but, as elections later in the decade were to show (see p. 66), did not rule out the possibility of liberal majorities and the potential for political change. Within the Confederation the events of 1849–50 also damaged the Austro-Prussian partnership which had dominated Germany since 1815. Although Prussia did return, to quote Marx, 'as a rueful sinner into the fold of the reconstituted diet of the Confederation',[32] its aims increasingly diverged from those of Austria.

4 *The Unification of Germany, 1858–71*

Introduction

The 13 years between 1858 and 1871 are a major watershed in German history. The Confederation was swept away. First Austria and then France were decisively defeated, and a *Kleindeutschland* emerged under Prussian leadership to become a major – perhaps the major – European power. The dream of the *kleindeutsch* Frankfurt liberals was at last realised. This was really a turning-point that turned! As far as domestic policies go, however, the picture is less clear. To the liberals it was axiomatic that unification and the liberalization of the constitution along Westminster lines went hand in hand. At first, in the optimistic times of the 'New Era' at the end of the 1850s, it seemed as if this might well be the case, but with the outbreak of the constitutional conflict and the appointment of the 'white revolutionary' Bismarck as Prussian minister-president, this apparently inevitable transition was called into question.

New Era, 1858–61: when William I became regent, he appointed a more liberal cabinet and raised hopes of a 'new era' or new start

White revolutionary: a right-wing as opposed to a left-wing (red) revolutionary

Key issues

- Why was the liberal revival during the 'New Era' so fragile?
- What was the significance of the Army Bill?
- How was Bismarck able to defeat the liberal opposition?
- How did the international situation favour Prussia in the early 1860s?
- To what extent had Austro-Prussian rivalry already become acute by the time of Bismarck's appointment as minister-president?
- How effective were the pressure groups: the *Nationalverein* and *Deutscher Reformverein*?
- What was the significance of the Schleswig-Holstein crisis and why did it ultimately lead to war between Prussia and Austria?
- How significant was Austria's failure to join the *Zollverein* in 1865?
- Why was Austria so rapidly defeated in 1866 and what were the consequences of Prussia's victory for Germany?
- Did the North German Confederation constitution represent a defeat for German liberalism?
- Was *Kleindeutsch* unity inevitable by 1869?
- Why did the war with France lead to the unification of Germany?

The constitutional conflict and Bismarck's appointment as minister-president

In October 1858 Crown Prince William was appointed regent when his brother was incapacitated by a severe stroke. Politically this was good news for the liberals. William had supported the Radowitz Plan and opposed Olmütz. He ignored the plans of his stricken brother to abolish the constitution and appointed a new cabinet of a moderately liberal persuasion. The reactionary Camarilla lost its authority, and, as the elections to the lower house in 1858 were no longer influenced by the government, the liberals were able to win a majority. By 1860 liberalism, despite its many divisions, dominated the political debate and set the tone in the Protestant churches, education, local government and business associa-

See Document 21

tions. 'It was almost a foregone conclusion that science and literature, students and all young people were liberals.'[1] Throughout Germany, wherever there were free elections, the liberals won majorities. However,

---

William I (1797–1888) was Frederick William IV's younger brother. He was a bitter enemy of the 1848 revolutionaries and highly critical of the Olmütz Proclamation (see p. 60). During the 1850s he came to accept the need for a constitution, but he was prepared to violate it to raise money to reform the army in 1861–62. He appointed Bismarck Minister–President to carry out this policy. Thereafter William supported him in his domestic and foreign policies until he died in 1888.

these successes were deceptive. Liberalism was not a mass movement, and it failed to reach out to the peasantry, the urban lower classes and the great majority of the Catholics. It was led by élites, and only become the dominant force in Prussian politics at a point when the masses were not yet mobilized. The liberals also seriously misinterpreted William's own politics. Their 'honeymoon' with him was 'based on illusory hopes and false premises,[2] as was to be shown in the bitter conflict that broke out over the reform of the army. The liberals believed passionately in integrating the army into society and making it subject to parliament, while the main thrust of the government's army reforms went in the opposite direction, and was intended to strengthen the grip of the professional officer corps and downgrade the role of the part-time *Landwehr*, or reserve army (see p. 8). This threatened the fundamental conception of a 'civilianized army' as represented by the *Landwehr*, which was as important to the liberals as 'the rights of man'.[3]

Initially the liberal leaders in the *Landtag* attempted to find a compromise, but von Roon, the war minister, supported by the ultra-conservative, Edwin von Manteuffel, who was hoping to persuade the regent to abolish the constitution, and if necessary launch a conservative counter-revolution, ruthlessly exploited the liberals' willingness to make provisional financial grants and pressed on with the military reorganization. With the foundation of the Progressive party in June 1861, the left-wing Liberals were able to mount a much more effective opposition against the Crown and widened the conflict by calling for a drastic reform of the constitution. After the election of December 1861, in which the

The details of the army bill

As a soldier, William wanted to modernize and expand the Prussian army, particularly in view of the way relations were deteriorating with Austria (see page 00). For 50 years the size of the Prussian army had not increased at all and only about a third of those eligible to serve were called up. When they had completed their service with the colours, they became reservists to the regular army for two years and thereafter joined the *Landwehr* for a further seven years. The officer corps was, however, both scornful of the part-time civilian officers of the *Landwehr* and suspicious of their political reliability. The war minister, Albrecht von Roon, consequently worked out the following plan for reform:

• The size of the standing army would virtually be doubled.
• The number of new recruits would be increased annually from 40,000 to 63,000.
• The period of active service would be set at three years.
• The *Landwehr* and the reserves would also be reorganized. The regular army would now be responsible for the first five years of the reserve service of the former conscripts, while the *Landwehr* would be allocated the remaining four years. The *Landwehr* would be deployed only at home and behind the front, and its officers would also gradually be replaced by professionals from the regular army.

The Progressive or left-wing liberal party was formed in June 1861

Progressives emerged as the largest group with 109 seats, the opposition began to subject the military budget to a painstaking analysis, so that it could draw attention to the funds illegally being transferred to the war ministry from other government departments. William retaliated by dismissing the 'New Era' government and appointing a conservative administration, but the subsequent elections in March 1862 again produced an overwhelming liberal majority. After further attempts to compromise were rejected by William, who, on the death of his brother, Frederick William IV, had now become king, the liberals were determined not only to reject the budget but also to force the king to appoint a liberal ministry. At first William was ready to abdicate rather than accept their demands, but, as a last throw, he turned to Bismarck who, in anticipation of this move, had been summoned to Berlin by von Roon.

The Bismarckian counter-revolution

Otto von Bismarck, 1815–98

Bismarck was born in 1815 into an old-established Junker family from Mark Brandenburg, but thanks to the social connections of his mother, Wilhelmina Mencken, whose father had been secretary to the royal cabinet, he was, as a boy, a frequent visitor to the Prussian royal household. After studying at Göttingen university, he entered the Prussian civil service, but soon gave it up and returned to farm the family estates at Schönhausen. He married Johanna von Puttkammer, and, partly as a result of her influence, renounced his religious scepticism and became a convinced Lutheran. He soon became bored with farming and entered politics, first of all in the United *Landtag* of 1847 (see p. 56), and then in the following year he made a reputation for himself as an ultra-Conservative Junker, royalist and counter-revolutionary. As a reward for his staunch support of the Crown, he joined the diplomatic service and served in Frankfurt, St Petersburg and Paris as Prussian minister and ambassador. At Frankfurt, Bismarck rapidly became critical (see p. 62) of Austria's attempt to dominate the Confederation and he consistently advised his government to use every opportunity to seize the leadership of Germany. Bismarck's ambition was to play a major political role in Berlin. His political ideology evolved from his diehard romantic defence of the old order, which made him seem to be 'a kind of Don Quixote of a feudal fantasy world'[4], to a realism which sought to deal with the world as it was and to mobilize German nationalism behind Prussia's efforts to seize the leadership of Germany.

Quixotic: the term comes from Cervantes's book *Don Quijote de la Mancha* and means a visionary, unworldly character pursuing impossible ideals

Bismarck dominated German politics and diplomacy for nearly three decades. Both the statesman and the Germany he created have been the subject of an immense volume of historical research . He has been both praised as a 'world historical figure' and depicted as the evil genius who set Germany on its special path or *Sonderweg* to the horrors of Third Reich. He is a towering figure in German history, who is very difficult to avoid, yet it is possible to fall into the trap of his hagiographers and credit him with almost superhuman skills that assume a 'marvellous march of events in which each stage seems to slip into its appointed place'.[5] In reality it is only in retrospect that his great successes seem to have been achieved so easily, and this emphasis on his apparently effortless successes 'slights his years of struggle when he was groping his way to solutions'.[6]

Bismarck initially hoped to resolve the constitutional crisis quickly before it impaired his freedom of action in foreign policy. He withdrew the budget proposals for 1863 and established contact with the more moderate wing of the Progressive Liberals, to whom he suggested that he would be able to persuade the king to compromise on the length of compulsory military service. When he addressed the budget committee of the *Landtag* on 30 September, he attempted in his notorious 'blood and iron speech' to signal that it was imperative that domestic harmony be restored as only power and military force could unite Germany. He intended to be conciliatory but, in Lothar Gall's words, he 'completely and utterly misjudged the situation',[7] and only succeeded in inflaming the situation still further, as the Liberals assumed that he was threatening a *coup d'état*. When the king stubbornly refused all compromise, Bismarck had no alternative, if he were to remain in power, but to bypass the *Landtag*. Consequently he encouraged the upper house to reject the amendments to the 1862 budget, and when the liberals protested, the *Landtag* was simply prorogued. Bismarck argued that this action was constitutionally defensible as a deadlock between the two houses created a 'constitutional hiatus',[8] which the government had every duty to fill. The battle between Bismarck and the Liberals resumed when parliament met again in January 1863 and for the next six months Bismarck was involved in a desperate fight for political survival, but by late summer he had established with the support of the Crown a virtual dictatorship. The civil service was purged, the press censored and municipal councils were banned from discussing politically sensitive subjects. Following the example of Napoleon III (see p. 60), Bismarck also played with the idea of advising the king to agree to a *coup d'état* and then holding a plebiscitary election based on universal franchise, which would mobilize the masses against the liberals. In May he held exploratory talks with Ferdinand Lassalle, the leader of the General Workers Union, and put before the cabinet a series of schemes for social reforms, which, if necessary, would enable him to draw up a programme designed to attract a mass electorate. However, on reflection, he decided to draw out the crisis until support for the liberals began to ebb away. Although it had a large majority in the *Landtag*, the liberal opposition was in reality much weaker than it seemed:

- The government controlled the civil service, could still collect taxes and above all enjoyed the complete loyalty of the army.
- The yield of the taxes steadily increased because Bismarck was fortunate to have come to power during an economic boom.

See Document 23

Landtag:: elected assembly of a German state

Prorogue: to suspend an assembly for a time without dissolving it and holding fresh elections

Plebiscitary election: one based on a single issue

- The opposition was composed of an unstable coalition of liberal factions, which found it difficult to co-operate with each other.
- The liberals had no mass backing. Their majorities in Prussia were the result of the three-class voting system which discriminated against the great mass of the electorate (see p. 61).

Nevertheless, despite the bitter conflict over the Army Bill, there was potentially considerable common ground between Bismarck and the liberals. Bismarck's economic policy met with their overwhelming support. His exclusion of Austria from the *Zollverein* (see p. 74) and the free-trade treaties with Britain, Belgium and Italy, for example, were all welcomed, as was the Mining Law of 24 June 1865, which established the freedom of exploration and exploitation. Similarly, the successful conclusion of the war against Denmark (see p. 73) also impressed many of the moderate and right-wing liberals. Yet, as William still refused to recognize parliament's powers over the military budget, the constitutional conflict dragged on into the early summer of 1866, and Bismarck remained unable to reconcile the bulk of the liberals.

The German question, 1859–63

Public opinion and German unity: the *Nationalverein* and the *Reformverein*

The greater political freedom of the 'new era' encouraged the formation of nationalist pressure groups. At the end of 1859 the German National Society (*Nationalverein*) was founded by Rudolf von Bennigsen, a liberal *Landtag* deputy in Hanover, Viktor von Unruh, the former president of the Prussian Assembly of 1848 and the democrat Hermann Schulze-Delitzsch. It was inspired by the Italian National Society and its members wanted an 'Italian-type solution' to German unity, which would involve the creation of a united Germany under Prussian leadership and the restoration of the *kleindeutsch* (see p. 57) constitution of 1849. Through agitation, propaganda and rallies it attempted to put pressure on the governments of the German states to work towards a *kleindeutsch* solution. Although it remained a pressure group with a membership of only 25,000 people, it did much to revive the debate on the German question. The society shrugged off arguments that its policies would lead to the Prussianization of Germany because it believed that the very process of unification would liberalize Prussia. However, once Bismarck came to power in Prussia, it was difficult for any liberal to support Prussia as a champion of German unity and the society steadily lost support, although after the defeat of Denmark in 1864, it began to revive.

The *kleindeutsch* policies advocated by the *Nationalverein* would inevitably lead to the division of Germany. To stop this, a wide cross-

The National Society was founded in Piedmont in 1856 and its aim was to raise support for a united Italy under the leadership of Piedmont

section of Catholic anti-Prussians, particularists and also *grossdeutsch* liberals and democrats came together and created the German Reform Society (*Deutscher Reformverein*). Its key attraction was its anti-Prussianism. It failed, however, to offer a positive programme for the creation of a *Grossdeutschland*, as it was split between those who wanted only to maintain the status quo and those who wanted a genuine *grossdeutsch* parliament.

Particularists: those believing that each state should have its own laws and government

Austro-Prussian rivalry and the reform of the Confederation

In both Berlin and Vienna, policies for the reform of the German Confederation were 'a confusion of plans, actions and counter actions, irritations and fluctuations'.[9] Nevertheless, broadly three main approaches can be identified:

1 Prussia hoped to achieve at the very least a dualistic hegemony with Austria. This would involve alternating the presidency of the Confederation between Vienna and Berlin and granting Prussia virtually a free hand north of the Main. In return, Prussia was ready to guarantee Austria's last possession in Italy – Venetia.

Hegemony: the leadership of one state over others

2 At times the Austrians were tempted by this guarantee, but essentially they wanted to hang on to their leading role in Germany. Their politics fluctuated between confrontation and dualistic co-operation. They did not trust Prussia and feared that such a compromise would only lead to further demands from Berlin.

3 There was opposition to both the Prussian and Austrian positions from the south German states. They wanted to strengthen the author-

---

The growing weakness of Austria

By the early 1860s Austria's position, both internationally and economically, had deteriorated to the advantage of Prussia:

- As a result of the Crimean war (see p. 63) the Austro-Russian axis, which had been of decisive importance in restoring Austria's position in Germany in 1850 (see p. 60), had collapsed.
- Austria had been seriously weakened by her loss of Lombardy in 1859 (see p. 63) and any chance of a Franco-Austrian rapprochement was ruled out by Napoleon's backing for Italian claims to her Venetian territory. The almost universal mistrust of Napoleon III also ensured that Europe was in a state, as Werner Mosse put it, of 'diplomatic disorientation'.[10] Both Britain and France welcomed the prospect of German unity under Prussia as a potential check to Russia and as a possible ally against the other.
- Prussia's economic and strategic position within Germany had also strengthened over the decade. It dominated the *Zollverein*, and by 1860 produced a greater tonnage of steel than France, Russia or Austria.

ity of the whole Confederation by standardizing its legal system and creating a parliament composed of delegates from the local *Landtage* without creating a Prussian–Austrian hegemony.

When it became clear by the summer of 1861 that no Austro-Prussian agreement was possible, the Prussian foreign minister, Albrecht von Bernstorff, revived the Radowitz Plan (see p. 59), the threat of which brought the medium-sized states, who dreaded Prussian domination, closer to Austria. In July 1863 Austria made one last attempt to seize the initiative in Germany and produced a complex plan for reform of the Confederation, which involved creating a directorate of ministers from the five largest states, an assembly of princes and a federal parliament elected from the state parliaments. The Austrians attempted to neutralize Bismarck's opposition by inviting the princes to a conference without first holding a ministerial meeting to prepare the agenda. Bismarck persuaded William to boycott the meeting and then played the nationalist card by proposing a central parliament elected by the 'entire [German] nation', which would inevitably maximize Prussian, as opposed to multiethnic Austrian, influence within the Confederation. This effectively killed the Austrian proposals, since, when it came to the point, the medium states were not ready to act without Prussia, as they feared the consequences of unchallenged Austrian domination for their own independence almost as much as they did Prussian hegemony. The eruption of the Schleswig-Holstein crisis in the winter of 1863-64 prevented Austria from resuming the initiative.

> By 1900 only about 35.5 per cent of the Austrian population was ethnically German

The Danish war and the Schleswig-Holstein question, 1863–65

> By the Treaty of London of 1852 the great powers confirmed that Schleswig and Holstein would remain under the Danish Crown and continue to enjoy their own local constitutions and not have a unitary constitution imposed upon them from Copenhagen. The succession of the female line would also apply both to Denmark *and* the duchies, which up to this point could only be inherited through the male line. The candidate from the male line, the Duke of Augustenburg, gave up his claims in exchange for financial compensation, and so cleared the way for the eventual succession of Christian IX (see pp. 53–4)

In March 1863 Frederick VII of Denmark, with the support of Sweden, decided to exploit the growing tension between Prussia and Austria and integrate Schleswig into a unitary Danish constitution. The crisis was heightened by Frederick's unexpected death in November. He was succeeded by Christian IX, who immediately confirmed the new constitution. This open violation of the London Treaty prompted the Duke of Augustenburg's son to claim the duchies and insist on their separation from Denmark. Augustenburg was backed everywhere by German liberals and nationalists. Within the Confederation the medium-sized states championed his claims as they welcomed the prospect of an independent Schleswig-Holstein joining the Confederation as a further counterweight to Austria and Prussia.

Bismarck had consistently argued that, unless the territories could be annexed by Prussia outright, Danish possession was preferable to their independence under Augustenburg, who would probably oppose Prussian interests in the Confederation. He was also wary of provoking Anglo-Russian intervention. Inevitably, however, this refusal to support Augustenburg made Bismarck even more unpopular with the liberals.

Initially both Austria and Prussia attempted, with only limited success, to moderate the Confederation's determination to come to the help of Augustenburg. The two powers agreed to the temporary occupation of Holstein by confederate troops – Saxons and Bavarians – in December. In January, however, when Augustenburg set up court unofficially at Kiel, Prussia and Austria themselves decided to occupy Schleswig in order to pre-empt a *fait accompli* by confederate troops. The Austro-Prussian alliance of 16 January 1864 cleverly yoked Austria to Prussia and committed both states to determining the future of the duchies by joint agreement. Bismarck's immediate aim was to avoid great-power intervention until Denmark had been decisively defeated. In March, when Britain proposed an international conference in London, he was able skilfully to delay its meeting until Prussian forces had decisively defeated the Danes at Düppel on 8 April. When the conference met two weeks later, the Danes, believing that they had the backing of the great powers, refused to restore the autonomy of Schleswig. This played into Bismarck's hands and enabled Austria and Prussia finally to repudiate the London Treaty of 1852 (see p. 73) and gain freedom of action. The British cabinet had no stomach for intervention and the Danes were left isolated. When the armistice expired on 26 June, they were defeated within days, and by the Treaty of Vienna, which was signed on 30 October, the Danish government agreed to hand over Holstein, Schleswig and Lauenburg to Prussia and Austria (see Map 4). For the time being, these territories were then put under joint military occupation, a situation which inevitably led to increasing friction.

Denmark's defeat confronted Austria with a difficult dilemma: should it do a deal with Berlin after all and recognize Prussian hegemony in North Germany in return for a guarantee of its possession of Venetia? At a meeting in Schönbrunn in August 1864 this alternative was discussed by Bismarck and the Austrian foreign minister, Count Rechberg. Provisional agreement was even reached that Prussia should receive the duchies in return for guaranteeing Venetia and helping with the reconquest of Lombardy. How genuine Bismarck was in offering this is hard to say. It may be that he was 'running full tilt after the conservative alliance'[11] but it is perhaps more likely that he was only attempting to secure continued Austrian co-operation by 'dangling once more, as so often in the past, the enticing possibility of such a bargain'.[12] The settlement was however rejected by both Franz Joseph who refused outright to cede the duchies to Prussia , and by William, who at that stage was still reluctant to ignore the legality of Augustenburg's claims.

Throughout the winter of 1864–65 the future of Schleswig-Holstein remained undecided. To thwart Prussian ambitions in the duchies, Austria now backed Augustenburg's claims, while Prussia would only recognize them provided the duchies in effect became a Prussian satellite. By the summer of 1865 it seemed that only force would decide their

The Battle of Düppel or Dybbol, February 1864: the Danes had evacuated the *Dannenvirke* defence line in the night of 5–6 February to Düppel in eastern Jutland. In the ensuing battle for Düppel the new professionalism of the Prussian army was seen for the first time. Prussia had a clear organizational and numerical superiority over the Danes. The recently acquired Dreyse rifles and artillery also proved their worth. Düppel finally fell on 18 April after a six-hour bombardment, the ferocity of which was not to be rivalled until the spring of 1915

future. The king and the Prussian Crown Council were ready to go to war. With the help of the Jewish financier, Gerson von Bleichröder, Bismarck, despite the refusal of the *Landtag* to vote funds, was able to raise sufficient sums of money for a one-year military campaign, but he still held back because he needed more time to neutralize France and win over his critics at home. In August, responding to an Austrian initiative, he accepted, after talks at Bad Gastein, a compromise solution. Lauenburg was to be purchased by Prussia and the administration of the Duchies to be divided: Schleswig was to be administered from Berlin and Holstein from Vienna, although legally joint sovereignty would remain intact. The Gastein Agreement, as Bismarck himself said, 'papered over the cracks' and bought time.

Joint sovereignty: joint power and control

Renewal of the *Zollverein*: Austria's economic Königgrätz?

Parallel to the Austro-Prussian diplomatic struggle over the future of the duchies ran the battle for economic control of the *Zollverein*. In 1853 further discussions on Austria's entry had been postponed for a seven-year period (see p. 62), but by 1860 it was already clear that any attempts by Austria to enter the *Zollverein* would once again meet with implacable Prussian hostility. The following year Berlin began negotiations for a free-trade treaty with France. Such an agreement would certainly be economically beneficial, but it would also serve an important political purpose, since it would effectively block Austria from joining the *Zollverein* because its industry was too weak to compete without protection against French imports. Despite intense pro-Austrian lobbying from the 'third Germany', Prussia and France signed the treaty in 1862.

When the *Zollverein*'s treaties came up for renewal in 1865, Austria demanded that the free-trade treaty should be scrapped, so that it could join the union. Again the 'third Germany' rallied to Austria, but in the final analysis it realized that the *Zollverein* was indispensable to its economic interests. Bismarck insisted that each member state would have to accept the Prussian–French Treaty *before* the *Zollverein* treaties could be renegotiated. The *kleindeutsch* liberals, the *Nationalverein*, the Congress of German Economists and the German Association of Trade and Commerce all put intense pressure on the governments of the German states to accept Prussia's demands. It was clear that realistically, as Lothar Gall has put it, the *Zollverein* already constituted 'so solid a network of interests that breaking out of it or dissolving it in favour of further combinations scarcely seemed a serious possibility any more'.[13] By October all the small and medium states had capitulated and on 16 May 1865 the *Zollverein* was renewed for a further 15 years.

Had Prussia inflicted an 'economic Königgrätz' on Austria? Thomas Nipperdey describes it as a 'preliminary round in the resolution of the German question'.[14] Yet if, as Hans-Joachim Voth, argues (see p. 36), the

The 'third Germany': the Germany of the middle-sized states, which wanted neither Prussian nor Austrian hegemony

The Battle of Königgrätz in June 1866 witnessed the decisive defeat of Austria by Prussia

Zollverein had relatively little economic importance, the battle for its control was 'simply another arena in which Austria and Prussia tested each other's resolve diplomatically'.[15] In itself, Austria's rebuff was not decisive. 'Economic preponderance', as Pflanze has stressed, 'did not lead necessarily to political domination'.[16] Indeed, Prussia's economic victory had the effect of strengthening the determination of Austria and her allies to defend their position even more tenaciously within the Confederation.

The defeat of Austria

Bad Gastein, not surprisingly, failed to improve Austro-Prussian relations. Throughout the winter of 1865–66 relations between Prussia and Austria continued to deteriorate. In Schleswig the Prussians systematically attempted to stamp out support for Augustenburg, while the Austrians pursued the opposite course in Holstein. By February 1866 the Prussian Crown Council agreed that war was inevitable. On 8 April, Bismarck, by holding out the promise of Austrian Venetia, concluded an offensive alliance with Italy for a period of three months. On the following day he challenged Austria head-on by proposing the reform of the German Confederation: the federal assembly would now become a proper national parliament for which every male German citizen would have the vote. This would, of course, effectively marginalize Austria with her much smaller ethnic German population, while enabling Prussia to appeal to German nationalism, but in fact this transparent manoeuvre merely alienated not only the medium-sized states that did not want Austria humiliated, but also many liberals who feared universal franchise and did not trust Bismarck an inch.

Throughout April and May the Austrian and Prussian armies began to mobilize, but still at this stage Bismarck did not totally close off all options for a settlement with Austria. He appeared to take seriously a proposal, which was made by the von der Gablenz brothers to divide Germany into Austrian and Prussian spheres of influence. He even had a plan drawn up which attempted to square the circle of an Austro-Prussian division of Germany along the Main and the election of a national parliament. Austria rejected this at the end of May, and then on 1 June unilaterally broke the Austro-Prussian Treaty of January 1864 by referring the whole Schleswig-Holstein issue to the Confederation. Prussia retaliated by invading Holstein and proposing a reform of the Confederation along *kleindeutsch* lines which would irrevocably exclude Austria. The Austrians appealed to the other members of the Confederation for support and secured French neutrality through a promise to cede Venetia to Italy. Baden, Bavaria, Württemberg, Hesse–Cassel and Hesse–Darmstadt, Saxony and Hanover all rallied to Austria, while only the small states and enclaves in northern Germany supported Prussia. Bismarck declared the Confederation dissolved and Prussian troops immediately occupied Saxony, Hanover and the Electorate of Hesse.

The von der Gablenz brothers: one, Anton, was a Prussian *Landtag* deputy, the other, Ludwig, was the Austrian commissioner in Holstein

Napoleon's attitude towards the German question

The opportunist policies of France remained a constant threat to Bismarck. Napoleon had two overriding aims: he wanted to complete the unification of Italy by handing Venetia to the Italians and to placate French nationalism in the event of a Prussian victory in Germany by gaining some concessions in the Rhineland, such as a buffer state under French protection, border changes along the Palatinate or even the outright annexation of the Saar. Clearly Napoleon did not want an Austro-Prussian understanding as that would have stymied his plans for Venetia and reorganizing central Europe. He therefore rather clumsily attempted to play Prussia off against Austria. Bismarck did not need a French alliance but her neutrality was indispensable. Both sides therefore attempted to exploit the situation: Bismarck hoped to escape paying a price for French neutrality but skilfully hinted, when he met Napoleon at Biarritz in October 1865, at the prospect of compensation in Luxemburg. Napoleon was careful to keep his options open between Austria and Prussia, even though he had persuaded the Italians to negotiate an agreement with Prussia. The diplomatic situation therefore remained fluid right up to the eve of war. Napoleon proposed a European conference to settle the German and Italian questions, but, luckily for Bismarck, the other great powers distrusted his motives. Then finally on 12 June France and Austria signed a secret agreement. Austria would surrender Venetia even if it defeated Prussia , and the balance of power in the Confederation would be tilted against Prussia, probably by creating an independent Rhineland state.

On the face of it, Bismarck seemed to be taking an enormous risk. Neither the liberals nor the conservatives supported the war. The former deeply distrusted Bismarck, while the latter disapproved of the humiliation of Austria and feared the consequences of revolutionary nationalism. To contemporaries a prolonged war involving foreign intervention ultimately leading to an Austrian victory seemed the most likely outcome. The Berlin Stock Exchange was even speculating on an Austrian victory!

To force a rapid conclusion, Bismarck was ready to bring pressure to bear on Austria by mobilizing the nationalism of the non-German peoples of the Habsburg Empire. Hungarian and Italian 'legions' were positioned in Silesia, and Garibaldi, the Italian veteran of the wars of unification, was given Prussian backing to move into Dalmatia. Plans were also drawn up to promise the Czechs an independent state. Yet none of these strategies was necessary. The war lasted seven weeks and ended in an overwhelming Prussian victory. By 29 June the armies of Hanover and Hesse had been eliminated, and on 3 July the Austrians themselves were defeated, although not annihilated, at Königgrätz (Sadowa), and by 18 July Prussian troops were only 19 km from the capital.

In many ways this was a victory of a modern army equipped by a rapidly industrializing state over a more backward power, which lacked the funds to modernize its armed forces. Although Austrian artillery had been reorganized after the defeat of 1859 (see p. 63), its troops lacked sufficient training, and the organizational and command structure of the army was still inadequate. The armies of the medium states were unco-ordinated and concerned with their own strategic interests. The Bavarians, for instance, did not come to the help of the Austrians in Bohemia. In contrast, the Prussian army was well-trained and equipped. General Helmut von Moltke, the Prussian chief of staff, was a soldier of genius, whose campaigns were based on rational and thorough planning. After the Danish war he had created a rail-road section in the General Staff and established district commands based on the railways. In 1866 he could use six trunk lines for mobilizing his troops, while the Austrians had only one. The Prussian army had also been fully equipped with the breech-loading needle gun, while the Austrians still used the old muzzle-loading rifles.

The diplomatic and political settlement

The very scale of the Prussian victory made it clear to Bismarck that he would have to end the war quickly or else face the danger of French inter-vention. Austria had appealed to Napoleon to mediate, and Bismarck with considerable difficulty managed to persuade the king, who wanted Vienna occupied, to accept French proposals for an armistice and agree on 26 July to the conclusion of the Preliminary Peace of Nikolsburg. In early August, somewhat belatedly responding to pressure from his advis-ers, Napoleon demanded the whole of the left bank of the Rhine up to Mainz. The scale of these demands destroyed his credibility as protector of south German independence, and made it easier for Bismarck to nego-tiate military treaties with the south German states, which agreed to place their armies firmly under the control of Berlin in wartime. Bismarck was then able to threaten Napoleon with the prospect of a nationalist war waged by the German nation under arms and force him to climb down.

On 23 August the provisional treaty was confirmed at Prague. Its terms were as follows:

- Austria was excluded from Germany and the old German Confederation was dissolved.
- North of the river Main, Prussia would have a free hand to form a new association of states – the North German Confederation.
- South of the river Main, the states would preserve their independence, but could form a southern confederation if they so wished.

See Document 24

On 20 September 1866 Prussia annexed Schleswig-Holstein, Hanover, Hesse-Cassel, Nassau and the city of Frankfurt. As a result of French pressure, Saxony escaped this fate, although it had to join the North German Confederation. In the autumn Bismarck also insisted that nego-tiations on the reform of the *Zollverein* should begin.

The North German Confederation

The Austrian defeat was a major turning-point in German history. It eliminated all possibility of a *grossdeutsch* solution and expelled Austria from the German political community after a period of nearly a thousand years. In 1866 the German Confederation was divided into not just two but three parts: the North German Confederation, the southern states and Austria (see Map 4). The Main line had, however, been breached by the military alliances between the North German Confederation and the southern states and of course by the *Zollverein*, which was in the process of reorganization. Bismarck, even if he had wanted to, could now no longer turn away from the German question. He had allied Prussia with the dynamic forces of nationalism and, until German *kleindeutsch* unification was completed, the situation in Germany would remain potentially unstable.

Main Line: The north-south divide formed by the river Main

The Indemnity Bill

The war also drastically changed the internal political situation in Prussia. In the Prussian *Landtag* elections, which were held on the day of Königgrätz, the liberals suffered heavily from rejecting Bismarck's war-expenditure programme and the conservatives made large gains. When the *Landtag* met in August 1866, the constitutional conflict was still unresolved, but, contrary to the wishes of the conservative die-hards, Bismarck did not scrap the constitution. In fact he persuaded the king to put before parliament an indemnity bill which would give retrospective approval to the government's expenditure on the armed forces over the previous four years. The bill caused an agonising debate on both the right and left, but in the end it was carried by an overwhelming majority of moderate conservatives and liberals on 3 September. In the course of the winter these divisions crystallized into two new political groupings: the Free Conservatives and the National Liberals, which were both ready to co-operate with Bismarck in creating a new Germany.

The constitution of the North German Confederation

The constitution, like almost everything Bismarck achieved, has never ceased to be the subject of considerable controversy. Was it, as C. Grant Robertson called it, 'the Königgrätz of liberalism in Germany' or did it in practice, as A. J. P. Taylor remarked, make North Germany 'a constitutional country'.[17] The key features of the constitution, which was in essence to be unchanged until 1918, were:

1 The *Praesidium*, or presidency, which was a post created for the King of Prussia. Nominally he was responsible for foreign affairs, the declaration of war and the dismissal of confederate officials. He was also supreme commander of the armed forces.

2 Initially Bismarck envisaged that a professional diplomat would be chancellor of the North German Confederation, whose main task would be to chair the *Bundesrat* (see below). He would receive instructions from Bismarck as minister–president of Prussia, but once its potential importance became clear, Bismarck filled the post himself, whilst still remaining minister–president in Prussia.

3 The *Bundesrat* was composed of representatives nominated by the governments of the member states who voted strictly according to their instructions. While all legislation had to be approved by both houses, constitutional changes needed a two-thirds majority which was impossible to secure without Prussian consent. To secure Prussia's position, Bismarck had allotted it a total of 17 out of 43 seats. This was reached by combining the votes possessed by Prussia and those of the states which it had annexed in the former Confederation Diet.

4 The *Reichstag*, as Pflanze has stressed, emphasized 'the fundamental dilemma of [Bismarck's] constitutional thinking'.[18] He wanted to use it as a potential check on the Crown, the federal states, the bureaucracy and the liberals without creating parliamentary government. He therefore took the key decision to introduce universal male franchise. Potentially this would enable him, like Napoleon III, to appeal over the heads of parliament to the people, but to discourage the formation of popular workers' and peasants' parties. There was to be no payment of parliamentary deputies. Initially there were also to be no annual budget provisions for parliamentary control of military expenditure or rights of interpellation. However, once the constituent assembly was elected on 12 February 1867, in which the National Liberals emerged as the largest party, Bismarck made several important concessions: legal immunity to deputies during parliamentary sessions; the right to interpellate; voting by secret ballot in general elections; and the crucial commitment to hold elections 60 days after the dissolution of parliament. Reluctantly Bismarck gave the *Reichstag* the right to approve the annual budget, but this did not give parliament complete control over the Confederation's finances. Most of its expenditure was earmarked for the military or 'iron' budget, as it was called. Initially Bismarck refused to make this dependent on a parliamentary vote, but in April when a complete deadlock had been reached with the *Reichstag*, which threatened the whole constitutional settlement, he did agree to a compromise that was facilitated by the war scare over Luxemburg (see below). The size of the army was fixed until 31 December 1871. Thereafter any further expansion bringing with it an increase in the budget would have to be approved by the *Reichstag*.

Interpellation: the right to subject ministers to parliamentary questioning

In practice the secret ballot did not become effective until proper ballot envelopes and voting booths were introduced in 1902

The constitution was at last approved by the *Reichstag* on 16 April 1867. Although Bismarck had protected both the Crown's and Prussia's power within the Confederation, whilst ensuring that his own position was almost impregnable, in many ways the constitution reflected the realities of German politics in 1867 and was a compromise between the forces of liberal-nationalism, democracy and Prussian conservatism. Lothar Gall has argued that it was 'much more a consumption of something for which the time was ripe than the manipulative creation of an individual'.[19]

Bismarck and southern Germany, 1867–70

Although the Treaty of Prague had confirmed Prussia's position north of the Main, the situation in Germany was still potentially unstable and dangerous. The southern states were divided and incapable of forming an independent confederation. Their economic and military ties with the German Confederation seemed to suggest, however, that their full absorption would only be a matter of time, but this was bitterly opposed by Napoleon, whose hostility had been strengthened by the humiliating outcome of the Luxemburg crisis. Taylor has argued that Bismarck 'had no clear aim after the victories of 1866 . . . he asked only to be left alone',[20] but he was acutely aware of the dangers of the power vacuum in the south, particularly after the Luxemburg crisis, and he developed a whole web of policies for gradually integrating the south by attempting to tighten its economic, military and political links with the north in such a way that an irresistible momentum towards national unity would be set up. The armies of the southern states were reorganized along Prussian lines and the *Zollverein* treaty was renegotiated. Its General Congress and the right of any member to veto a policy (see p. 25), were scrapped and replaced with a new council firmly under Prussian control and a popularly elected *Zollverein* parliament. In these elections Bismarck had expected that the National Liberals and their allies would sweep the

The Luxemburg crisis

This crisis has been described as 'the dress rehearsal for the crisis of 1870'.[21] Having failed to gain any concessions on the Rhine in August 1866, Napoleon put out feelers to buy Luxemburg. Although the duchy had been part of the German Confederation and had been garrisoned by Prussian troops since 1814, it had been awarded to Holland in 1815. Bismarck's reaction to the French initiative appears to have been opportunist. At first he seemed to encourage it; then when the news of the Franco-Dutch talks become public in March 1867, he turned against it. The French were convinced that he had led them into a trap. Certainly the crisis may have helped him achieve a settlement over the iron budget with the National Liberals (see above), but Bismarck had allied himself to the tiger of nationalism and, given the nationalist majority in the new *Reichstag*, he was not entirely a free agent. The Dutch were put under pressure to abandon plans for selling the duchy, but Bismarck also indicated that he would accept the mediation of the great powers. A compromise was eventually arranged whereby the Prussian garrison withdrew and the duchy was neutralized under great-power guarantee.

board in the southern states, but a large majority of the southern deputies was implacably hostile to any attempt to turn the economic union into a political one. The Democratic People's Party in Württemberg warned, for example, that entry into the North German Confederation would involve excessive taxation, conscription and 'keeping your mouth shut',[22] while in the Bavarian elections in November 1869 the Patriot party won the majority of seats. The evolutionary approach to German unity seemed to have failed completely.

The war with France

By early 1869 Bismarck was coming under increasing pressure in the *Reichstag* to complete unification. At the same time he was aware that a nationalist success would also help him gain parliamentary approval for the iron budget in two years' time. He needed, as Taylor remarked, 'to give Germany a new "dose" of national enthusiasm'.[23]

An opportunity to kick-start the German question arose unexpectedly when Queen Isabella of Spain was forced to abdicate in September 1868. To replace Isabella, the Spanish approached Prince Leopold, a member of the south German and Catholic branch of the Hohenzollerns. In June 1870, after Bismarck had exerted considerable pressure on him, despite reservations on the part of William I, he accepted. What was Bismarck intending? Did he underestimate the sharpness of the French reaction? This seems unlikely because he is on record as telling his agent in Madrid, Major Max von Versen, that he was in fact looking for 'complications'[24] with the French.

Bismarck had hoped that the Spanish parliament would ratify the agreement quickly, so that the French would be confronted with a *fait accompli*. However a mistake by a cypher clerk in the Prussian embassy in Madrid caused an unscheduled delay, during which the secret reached Paris. The explosion of anger in the press and the French Chamber prompted William to persuade Leopold to stand down. The French had achieved a resounding success, and Bismarck, convinced that Prussia had suffered a humiliation worse than Olmütz (see p. 60), actually thought of resigning, but he was saved by the French foreign minister's failure to recognize the extent of his victory, and his determination to force William to give written guarantees against a renewal of Leopold's candidacy. William, who was holidaying in his palace in Ems, refused the imperious demands of the ambassador, even though there was no question of Leopold changing his mind again, and sent Bismarck an account of his interview (the so-called Ems telegram). After checking with Moltke whether the army was ready to fight, Bismarck edited the telegram to give it a more aggressive 'spin', and released it to the press. In Paris it so infuriated the war party at court, in parliament and in the cabinet that Napoleon was driven to declare war on 15 July. Bismarck had certainly done much to provoke the war, but the French could have avoided it – at

6 Strassburg under Prussian fire, October 1870

Illustrated London News, 22 October 1870, p. 424

7   The King of Prussia arrives at Versailles, October 1870

Illustrated London News, 22 October 1870, p. 417

that point anyway – because the substance of their demands had already been offered. As William Halperin observed, the responsibility for war 'rests not on one side or the other but squarely on both'.[25]

As with Austria in 1866, France looked the more formidable adversary, but the Prussian army again triumphed, although the war lasted longer than Bismarck had expected. Once again, Moltke's organization and logistics were far superior to those of his opponents. He was able to move and sustain 700,000 to 800,000 troops over many hundreds of square miles. While the Prussians had superior artillery, the French army had better rifles and the *mitrailleuse*, a machine gun which fired 150 rounds a minute, but its troops were poorly led and organized. Thus the Prussians were able to inflict major defeats on the French at Sedan in September and Metz in October, and Paris itself was put under siege by the end of September.

As in 1864 and 1866, the international situation favoured Prussia and her south German allies. Napoleon had failed to create a triple alliance with Austria and Italy, despite a draft agreement in 1869, because the Italians refused to co-operate with the French until the French garrison, which had been protecting the Papacy in Rome since 1849, had been withdrawn. The Austrians, fearing an Italian attack on Trieste and Dalmatia, would not commit themselves to France until Italy was a firm member of the alliance. Bismarck also did all he could to localize the conflict. For instance, he skilfully defused the international crisis triggered by Russia's

Up to a point, public opinion and the army pushed Bismarck into demanding the annexation of Alsace-Lorraine, but he did see it as a vital strategic barrier against future French attacks against Germany. He showed little interest in the iron ore deposits in Lorraine. Initially the annexation fuelled the desire for French revenge, although in time it became less of an issue

unilateral repudiation of the clauses in the 1856 Paris treaty, which enforced the neutralization of the Black Sea after the end of the Crimean War. If that crisis had erupted into war, it would almost certainly have coalesced with the Franco-Prussian conflict. He was able to avoid this by proposing an international conference in London where a face-saving compromise for Britain and Russia was devised, and he stopped France from raising the issue of the war by securing agreement from the other powers to leave it off the agenda in return for his services as mediator.

Yet, despite these military and diplomatic advantages, the war dragged on longer than Bismarck wished. By December 1870 'the prestige of Sedan was dribbling away and with it all hope of securing a peace as cheap and successful as that which followed Sadowa'.[26] As soon as Paris fell in January, Bismarck seized the chance to end the fighting. On 25 January 1871 a three-week armistice was signed, which a month later was confirmed as a preliminary peace. The Germans extracted severe terms: Alsace and Lorraine, including the fortress of Metz, were annexed, and an indemnity was to be paid over four years, after which an army of occupation in the eastern provinces would be withdrawn. These terms were confirmed at the Treaty of Frankfurt in May 1871.

> Although Napoleon's regime collapsed after Sedan, the new republican government fought on unitl January 1871

The unification of Germany

Taylor has argued that Bismarck's decision to push the southern German states into union with the North German Confederation was really a result of the growing military uncertainties of the war, as he feared that the longer the struggle lasted, the greater the danger that they might conclude a separate peace with France. On the other hand, it seems more likely that Bismarck used the war as 'a sudden blessed opportunity'[27] to complete the unification of Germany. This is the interpretation that is most consistent with his policy towards the southern states since 1866.

Initially there was an upsurge of nationalist feeling throughout the south. Baden, Hesse-Darmstadt and Württemberg recognized that union with the North German Confederation was becoming inevitable, and even Bavaria agreed in principle that the status quo in Germany could no longer be preserved, but it wished to dissolve the existing North German Confederation and replace it with a much more loosely structured organization. By threatening Bavaria with economic and political isolation, Bismarck forced its government to adopt a more flexible policy. In separate negotiations with the southern states he was able to play them off against each other, although he had to make considerable concessions, which strengthened the power of the states in the new revised constitution:

- Before declaring war or taking action against a recalcitrant member state, the federal government now had to gain the approval of the *Bundesrat*.

- A vote of 14 , rather than, as originally, two-thirds of the *Bundesrat*, could now block any constitutional amendment, which meant that a combination of southern states such as Baden, Bavaria, Württemberg and Hesse could theoretically block any such amendment;
- Concessions were also made to Bavaria, Württemberg and Baden, authorizing local taxation and administration of the postal and telegraph systems, while Bavaria and Württemberg were permitted to maintain their own armies in peace-time.

See Document 25

The negotiations were successfully concluded by the end of November and King Ludwig of Bavaria was bribed by Bismarck to invite William to accept the title of emperor. By January 1871 the necessary enabling legislation had passed through both the north German *Reichstag* and the southern *Landtage*, and on 18 January 1871 the empire or Reich was proclaimed in the Hall of Mirrors at Versailles.

Conclusion

The decade 1860–70 was one of the most momentous in the history of Germany. It witnessed the final defeat of Austrian claims to lead the German states and the unification of *Kleindeutschland* under Prussian leadership. Was this the logical course of German history or, as John Breuilly has argued, 'was there nothing preordained about how it became a national state'.[28] Certainly in the 1780s Austria was the more dynamic power, and it was still capable after 1815 of dominating the German Confederation. Yet what Brendan Simms calls 'the geopolitical revolution of 1815' did 'cast Prussia in the role of first line of defence against France' (see p. 21),[29] and also made it potentially the strongest economic power in Germany with the possession of the Ruhr coalfields. By 1850 Prussia was in a more favourable position than Austria to harness the explosive powers of nationalism and benefit economically from industrialization. Of course that does not mean that even then the creation of the Prussian-led German Reich was preordained. It still took a man of Bismarck's genius and decisiveness to exploit the favourable international situation in the period 1865–70 caused by the isolation of France and the disintegration of the Holy Alliance in the Crimean War to unify Germany. To answer what would have happened if this 'brief window of opportunity'[30] had been missed, we can but move into the realms of virtual history and speculate.

Part Two

The Second Reich, 1871–1918

5 *Economic, Social and Cultural Transformation*

TIMELINE

1871–73	Boom fuelled, by the French indemnity and currency reform
1873	The Stock Exchange crash and beginning of the Great Depression
	The May Laws
1875	Foundation of the *Reichsbank*
1876	The Central Association of German Industrialists and League for Tax and Economic Reform founded
1878	Anti-Socialist Law
1879	General Protective Tariff introduced
1880	Industrial production sinks to the levels of 1872–73
1884	Accident Insurance Act
1889	Old-age pensions introduced
1890	Anti-Socialist Laws lapse
1892	Hauptmann's *Die Weber* performed
1893	Agrarian League formed as a response to cuts in the grain tariffs
1894	German Women's Association set up
1895	Great Depression ends
	Wilhelm Röntgen discovers x-rays
1898	Secessionists quit the German General Art Association
1908	Women given right to attend political meetings

Introduction

The economic transformation of modern Germany between 1870 and 1914 has been called, by Koppel S. Pinson, 'one of the most amazing chapters in the entire history of modern times'.[1] Even if there is an element of hyperbole in this assessment, few historians would in general disagree with him. Germany developed many of the characteristics of an advanced, modern industrial society: the norms of bourgeois culture became universally accepted, women slowly started to acquire equality, and the largest labour movement in Europe, the SPD, began the gradual process of integrating the new working classes into German society. Yet strong pre-industrial features still survived: the Prussian aristocracy, a large rural sector and a sizeable remnant of the traditional *Mittelstand*. The very speed of the industrial revolution also created an immense cultural upheaval, which artists and writers sought to interpret in revolutionary new ways in their work, but it also led to a backlash against industrialization and the creation of the anti-modernist *völkisch* movement.

SPD: The Social Democratic party of Germany formed in 1875

The *völkisch* ideology preached the creation and preservation of a traditional Germanic, national and above all racial community

89

- What were the causes of the Great Depression and what were its consequences?
- Was there an 'economic miracle' between 1896 and 1914?
- What was corporate capitalism and how significant was government economic intervention in the period 1879–1914?
- How 'modern' was Wilhelmine society?
- What were the minority groups in Imperial Germany? What forms of discrimination did they suffer?
- What progress did women make towards achieving equality?
- To what extent was there a 'revolution' in German culture?

Economic developments, 1871–1913

The *Gründerjahre* of 1871–73

The unification of Germany triggered a short-term speculative boom. Until 1873 the economy grew at a rate of nearly 5 per cent per annum, while as many ironworks and machine manufacturing companies were set up in the period 1871–75 as in the preceding 70 years. This spectacular expansion was facilitated by:

Until 1871 the German states had six independent currencies. Between 1871 and 1873 the Reich introduced the new mark currency, which was based on the gold standard

- the generous credit policies of the banks
- the liquid capital invested into the economy by the prompt payment of the French indemnity
- the inflationary effects of the currency reform of 1871, which added some 762,000,000 marks to the amount of free capital in the economy.

1871: 207 new joint-stock companies were floated for 758 million marks
1872: 479 for 1.5 billion marks
1873: 242 for 544 million marks

Unlike British banks, the German banks invested much of their capital in trade and industry. In 1872 in Prussia alone, 49 new banks were formed, amongst which were the two giants of the future, the *Dresdener Bank* and the *Deutsche Bank*. These channelled funds into the new joint-stock companies, the formation of which had been made easier by the law passed by the *Reichstag* in June 1870, but many of them lacked adequate financial backing and gambled on amassing short-term profits that would help them to build up adequate capital reserves. The easy availability of credit led to the setting up of large numbers of unsound companies, which went bankrupt when the stock market collapsed in the autumn of 1873.

The Great Depression 1873–96

At first a backlog of railroad projects kept the economy afloat, but by 1876 falling demand hit both the textile and the engineering industries.

The engineering firm, Borsig, for instance, produced 166 locomotives in 1875, but only 80 in 1876. There followed a long period of retarded or, at best, intermittent growth. It was not until 1880 that production achieved the levels of 1872–73, but it began to falter again between 1882 and 1886. Between the autumn of 1886 and the end of 1889 there was a strong recovery when net domestic product rose on average by 4 per cent per year, but in 1890 it again went into sharp decline. It was not until 1894 that the economy at last began to experience an upswing, which continued, apart from brief recessions in 1900–01 and in 1909, until 1913.

Although the severity of the Great Depression can be exaggerated, its economic and political impact was nevertheless considerable. Initially production was cut back, profits declined, the workforce was laid off, particularly in the engineering industries, and wages fell. In Berlin in 1879, for instance, 25 per cent of the industrial workers were unemployed. Only after 1880 did wages begin to creep upwards again. Inevitably once the boom broke, crisis management became the priority of the banks and industry. While before 1873 entrepreneurs were ready at least to pay lip-service to *laissez-faire*, the slump made them more than ready to seek protection from vicious competition in a contracting market. Cartels, or trusts, were founded, which fixed prices, working conditions and production, so that members would not undermine each other. In 1875 there had been only 8 cartels; by 1895 this number had increased to 143.

Laissez-faire economics: an economy based on free trade and the minimum of government interference

Politically, as Hans Rosenberg argued, the depression shifted 'the centre of gravity of political agitation . . . from issues of . . . national unification and constitutional reconstruction . . . to a crude emphasis on economic objectives'.[2] Both the industrialists and the great east Elbian estate-owners, who were facing severe competition from cheap foreign imports, founded highly effective pressure groups, which increasingly began to win the economic argument for the introduction of tariffs, and were an important factor in Bismarck's decision to abandon free trade in 1879 (see p. 113). Protective tariffs shielded the land-owning aristocracy from the destructive effects of economic competition. The perceived failure of liberal *laissez-faire* economics helped weaken political liberalism, which became associated by its critics with the excesses of free trade and Manchesterism. On the other hand, the depression galvanized the right and led to the creation of a more popularly-based conservative party, while it also played a part in bringing together the parties of the left to form the Social Democratic party (SPD) in 1875.

Protective tariffs: duties placed on imports to protect local industries and products

Manchesterism: *laissez-faire* practices as in nineteenth-century Britain

An 'economic miracle', 1896–1913

The German economy emerged from the depression both transformed and strengthened. In 1873 the consumer industry had still played the dominant role, but by the mid-nineties it was heavy industry which called the tune. Organized into cartels, closely linked to the banks and with its domestic markets protected by tariffs, it had survived the recession and

Cartel: A manu-
facturer's group set
up to control and
regulate produc-
tion and prices

was far stronger in 1895 than it had been in 1873. It was able to undercut its rivals abroad by selling at 40 per cent below the prices in the domestic market. Germany also made remarkable progress in developing the chemical, electrical and engineering industries, which were in the forefront of the second industrial revolution. At the turn of the century Germany's share in dyes accounted for 90 per cent of the world's production, while by the early 1900s it had also established a virtual world monopoly in chemicals, electrical goods and precision instruments. By 1910 the German mercantile fleet was the second largest in the world, and Germany had become the third largest creditor nation in the world. sixty per cent of its exports went to Britain, France and Russia, and the German economic penetration of Latin America, South Africa and the Ottoman Empire created what amounted to an informal empire. In the dangerously polarized world of 1914 this made German world trade a hostage to international events.

German foreign trade, 1872–1913 (in marks)

Year	Exports	Imports
1872	2,492,000,000	3,465,000,000
1880	2,977,000,000	2,844,000,000
1890	3,410,000,000	4,273,000,000
1900	4,475,000,000	6,043,000,000
1910	7,475,000,000	8,934,000,000
1913	10,097,000,000	10,770,000,000

Source: K. Pinson, *Modern Germany – Its History and Civilization*, New York, Macmillan, 1954, p. 229.

Corporate capitalism and government intervention, 1900–14

The trend towards concentration and cartelization continued right up to the war and beyond. For instance, by 1900 the ten largest coalmining companies produced 59 per cent of Germany's coal, while the five biggest dyestuff companies were responsible for 90 per cent of Germany's total output, and by 1905 there were 350 cartels, which attempted to guarantee economic stability for their members, so that businesses could rely on secure profits. In the years before 1914 the state became increasingly involved in economic policy. Here Hans-Ulrich Wehler sees 'the birth of a phenomenon of our own times' where 'under the prevailing system of state regulated capitalism political authority is chiefly legitimized by the government's concern to correct disturbances to economic growth so as to preserve the continuing stability of the economy and society'.[3] With the Reichsmark tied to the gold standard, the government could not devalue to help exports, but it could assist

8 An aerial view of the Krupp plant shortly before the First World War
Imperial War Museum, no. Q81737

through tariffs, and it was also able to subsidize shipping lines and reduce freight rates for export.

In 1890 serious disagreements between industry and agriculture about protection were beginning to surface. High prices for corn, which consequently drove up the cost of living for the working classes, coincided with the downturn in the economy between 1890 and 1894. The industrialists argued that if Germany lowered her agricultural tariffs, this would both bring down the price of food and persuade Russia and Austria–Hungary to reduce their industrial tariffs in return. The new chancellor, Caprivi, accepted these arguments, even though this would involve cutting the corn tariffs that bolstered the Junkers' economic and political position within the Reich. Despite fierce criticism from the agrarian pressure groups and the Conservative party, he went ahead and negotiated new trade treaties with Russia, Austria and Romania. This temporarily ruptured the alliance between heavy industry and the agrarians, but with the dismissal of Caprivi in 1894 (see p. 120) the common fear of Social Democracy brought the two sides together again. In 1902 the agriculture tariff was increased to a level higher than those set in 1887 after the heavy industrialists had been placated by the huge naval building programme (see p. 122). The heavy industrialists and the east Elbian landowners certainly received valuable assistance, but it would be a mistake to argue that the government totally subordinated its policy 'to coddle . . . the

General Leo von Caprivi, 1831–99

He fought with distinction in the wars of unification and over the next 20 years gained a reputation as a good administrator in the peacetime army. At the age of 60 he was appointed chancellor to replace Bismarck in 1890, but as a result of the Kaiser's campaign against the Socialists and reactionary domestic policy, he resigned in 1894 (see pp. 119–20).

large landowners'.[4] Many of their key demands, such as the proposal for a minimum price for imported grain, or the permanent cancellation of the construction of the *Mittelland* Canal, which they regarded as a highway for cheap imported grain were rejected.

A characteristic that all advanced economies shared in the years before 1914 was the emergence of pressure groups, which enjoyed close contacts with the government and the political parties. In Germany this development was particularly marked. The largest pressure group was the Agrarian League (see p. 119), and one of the most powerful was the heavy industrial Central Association, but these two groups by no means enjoyed a monopoly of influence. The Confederation of Industrialists represented the smaller firms, while the *Hansabund* was formed in 1909 as a union of commercial, exporting and shipping interests. Interest groups representing a wide spread of commercial and white-collar interests sprang up, which in 1911 were united under an umbrella organization, the Imperial German *Mittelstand* Confederation. In a period where economic issues were of increasing importance, these interest groups were able to influence public opinion, and make their views felt in the *Reichstag* through representatives in the parties closest to them or indeed directly at government level. In the long term, however, these activities helped 'to deform the parties' by turning them increasingly into the mouthpieces of economic pressure groups rather than broader coalitions of interests. The subsequent haggling that ensued both between and within the parties eventually helped create 'a powerful public distaste for the "system" – a reaction against deals and horse trading',[5] which was to have a negative impact on the Weimar Republic in the 1920s.

Pressure group: a group or association set up to further a particular interest by influencing government policy

The Central Association was formed in 1876 to campaign for the introduction of tariffs and then, after this was achieved in 1879, it widened its brief to address other political and economic matters of interest to industrialists

The Agrarian League, for example, gave support to candidates in the National Liberal, Centre and Conservative parties, while the Central Association financially backed 120 *Reichstag* candidates in 1912

Social change

Rapid economic growth transformed life and conditions for the majority of the German people. Not only did the German population increase by 60 per cent between 1870 and 1914, but by 1910 roughly two-thirds of the German population lived in urban areas. Berlin and the great cities of

Population shifts, 1871–1910

Year	Total population	Rural (%)	Urban (%)
1871	41,059,000	63.9	36.1
1880	45,234,000	58.6	41.4
1890	49,428,000	57.5	42.5
1900	56,367,000	45.6	54.4
1910	64,926,000	40.0	60.0

Source: K. Pinson, *Modern Germany – Its History and Civilization*, New York, Macmillan, 1954, p. 221.

western and central Germany acted as magnets for migrants from the rural east and south. Accelerating industrialization and urbanization created new classes and explosive pressures that threatened the Bismarckian political compromise.

The working class

The urban working class was not monolithic. Besides being composed of Germans from all over the Reich as well as immigrant Poles (see p. 99), there were also divisions between skilled and unskilled workers, and Catholics and Protestants. Nevertheless, the great majority shared the same formative experiences of urban life. They lived in overcrowded flats and rooms in working-class ghettos in the cities; most had experienced unemployment and continued to live under the shadow of sudden redundancy. The German industrial revolution did not, however, impose the crude sufferings of its British prototype. The introduction of social insurance by Bismarck in the 1880s (see p. 115), and the gradual extension of its provisions over the ensuing decades, the boom conditions for most of the period after 1895, and the slow but steady rise in wages created conditions far removed from the Manchester described by Engels in 1844. There was also the prospect of upward mobility. Labourers had the opportunity to become skilled workers, whose children in due course often managed to move into the lower middle classes (*Mittelstand*) and become white-collar workers.

See Document
26.1

Friedrich Engels
(1820–95) was,
with Karl Marx, the
joint founder of
Communism

9 A shanty town on the edge of Berlin, 1875

Leipzige Illustrierte

10   An SPD rally in the early 1900s

Imperial War Museum, no. Q81737

The trade unions and the SPD played an increasing role in creating a working-class consciousness in Germany. Blackbourn has called the labour movement 'a fixed point in a turning world, fostering a common identity and providing – through party press, unions, cooperatives – an opportunity for working men to exercise responsibility'.[6] By 1914 there were 3 million trade unionists, 85 per cent of whom were members of the left-wing, free trade unions. The SPD, the largest socialist party in the world, had nearly a million members to whom it was both an inspiration and a reassurance. In many ways the labour movement was a substitute religion and a way of life with its choral societies, cycling clubs, drama groups, etc., whilst also offering chances of improvement through educational courses and access to lending libraries.

The old and the new *Mittelstand*

The industrial revolution created a new middle class of white-collar employees in industry and commerce composed of foremen, clerks and petty officials. Between 1882 and 1887 their share of the workforce rose from 4.7 to 10.7 per cent. On the one hand they distanced themselves from the working classes and saw the monthly payment of their salaries and separate insurance schemes as signs of social superiority, but on the other they were critical of the apparent self-assumed superiority of the bourgeoisie and their claim to represent the nation.

Although the craft trades suffered in the depression, many managed to survive, and by 1907 the number of firms employing between one and five people still accounted for 31.2 per cent of those involved in manufacturing. Up to a point, industrialization created opportunities for small business to concentrate on specialized services. In the cutlery industry in Sölingen, for instance, small workshops produced high-quality cutlery. Others, however, were not so lucky. Tailors, shoemakers, many small shopkeepers and carpenters all had difficulties in making ends meet, and were faced with the constant threat of proletarianization. Competition from larger enterprises produced a widespread feeling of pessimism amongst the *Mittelstand* at the turn of the century, and numerous sectional organizations were set up to protect the rights of small businesses. Small businessmen and self-employed craftsmen were instinctively hostile to liberalism, which they frequently equated with 'Manchesterism' and 'Jewish capital', and had an ingrained belief that the state should support them in preserving their status.

> **Craft trades**: pre-industrial trades such as weaving, pottery, etc.

The bourgeoisie

In Wilhelmine Germany this class ran big business and staffed the professions, and its culture permeated society as a whole. It has been accused by a whole school of historians in both Germany and abroad of lacking 'a civic spirit',[7] of becoming feudalized and in effect through its spinelessness and failure to dominate politics, of allowing Germany by default to take its fatal *Sonderweg*. Usually these accusations are accompanied by comparisons with Britain. Yet, as British social historians have shown, the political role of the bourgeoisie in Britain, where the nobility remained influential for so long, can be exaggerated, while David Blackbourn and Geoff Eley have argued that the German bourgeoisie cannot so easily be branded as the guilty men of German history. There was, of course, intermarriage between the Prussian nobility and the grander bourgeoisie and a move by the more prosperous businessmen to buy estates from bankrupt Junkers, but this did not necessarily lead to their feudalization. After all, this pattern of intermarriage had been observable in England for centuries. The bourgeoisie in Germany certainly had a deep respect for the army and the reserve officer corps, and liked professional and academic titles and medals, but this did not, however, erode its core bourgeois philosophy: its belief in property, achievement, law and order, the importance of family, and rules of conduct governing personal behaviour. In fact, important bastions of former aristocratic power like the officer corps in the army, the consular corps in the diplomatic service, and the Reich and Prussian bureaucracies were being taken over by the bourgeoisie. Culturally the bourgeoisie dominated Germany. The rule of law, which enmeshed artisans, aristocrats, peasants, princes and workers, reflected bourgeois values. Zoos, museums, libraries and galleries, which were all open to the public, as well as spa resorts, the grand hotels, formal fashions, like evening dress,

> *Sonderweg*: 'special path' away from democracy towards authoritarianism and dictatorship

and fashionable restaurants were all part of the 'public sphere' created by the bourgeoisie. Blackbourn has even argued that 'the very success of a dynamic capitalist economy and a buoyant bourgeois society in Germany made political dominance in one sense less necessary'.[8]

The Junkers and peasants

The east Elbian Junkers (see p. 5) certainly exercised a power and influence far in excess of their numbers. The 1902 tariff laws protected their staple crops of rye and potatoes, while the law on entailed estates (*Fideikommis*) prevented the break-up of their family estates. 'Protection . . . became a system of direct subsidies to a privileged class who had managed to avoid the economic fight to death'.[9] Politically, too, the three-class voting system in Prussia enabled the estate-owners in the rural districts to maximize their strength (see p. 61), while nationally a less than secret voting system ensured that they could often influence their workers to vote for the Conservative party.

The success of the Junkers should not, however, divert attention from the other much larger sector of the German agrarian economy. Unlike its counterpart in Britain, German agriculture remained a powerful industry. In 1907 some 35 per cent of the economically active population still worked on the land. Almost three-quarters of the total cultivated area was in the hands of working farmers who owned anything between 25 and 50 acres. Up to a point it is possible to argue that the Junkers were supported at the expense of the rest of German agriculture in that grain tariffs hit dairy, poultry and pig farmers, who needed cheap, imported feed grain and fodder. Yet a large number of smaller farmers also benefited from protective duties on wine and imported horses and cattle, etc.

Superficially, German agriculture continued to prosper in the period 1870–1914. Overall food production doubled between 1870 and 1913. Agricultural colleges produced a new class of scientifically trained farm managers and farmers, which led directly to the introduction of improved seeds, crops and animal breeding, while the large east Elbian estates were becoming increasingly mechanized. Nevertheless, farmers were facing growing structural problems. Labour costs rose as millions quitted the land for industry (see p. 94) and the contribution of agriculture to GNP declined from 41 to 23 per cent between 1870 and 1913. German farming enjoyed an Indian summer of prosperity, but both at home and abroad the balance was shifting against it.

The minorities

In the late nineteenth century, tolerance of racial or cultural minorities was not a characteristic which the fiercely nationalist nations of Europe cultivated. Thanks to the social imperialism of Bismarck and his succes-

Only in 1903 did the ballot effectively become secret

Structural problems: fundamental problems which affected the very structure of the agricultural industry

Social imperialism: a term developed in the 1960s to describe efforts by Bismarck and his successors to unite a socially divided Germany by pursuing an imperialistic foreign policy which would appeal to all Germans as nationalists

sors, German unity was forged by reference to both external enemies and the ethnic and culturally alien 'enemy within'.

The Catholics

The Catholics were by far the largest minority in imperial Germany. In 1871, 36 per cent of the population was Catholic. In Bavaria, Baden, and Alsace-Lorraine as well as in West Prussia, Silesia, Posen and the Rhineland they were in the majority, but the Protestants dominated the Reich as a whole. The whole tradition of German liberalism was also essentially anti-Catholic and many of the leading liberals were sons of Protestant priests, and 'the historiography they learned at their mothers' knees depicted Luther as a national and liberal as well as a religious hero'.[10] Initially in 1870 German Catholics had welcomed the unification of Germany, but the outbreak of the *Kulturkampf* launched by the National Liberals and Bismarck rapidly alienated them and led them to be depicted as *Reichsfeinde* – or enemies of the state. The May Laws turned Prussia into a police state for the Catholics until they were repealed in the late 1880s. In the first four months of 1875, for instance, 241 clergy and 136 newspaper editors were fined or jailed.

> *Kulturkampf*: a struggle between cultures. A term used to describe Bismarck's conflict with the Catholic Church, 1871–87

See Document 29 and p. 112

The *Kulturkampf* was also a collision with the process of modernization (see p. 42). Under Pius IX the Catholic Church was profoundly anti-modern and opposed much of the core beliefs of liberalism. By and large, too, the majority of the Catholics lived in small towns and were less well-tuned to the new opportunities of the industrial society. Only in the early years of the new century did they begin to integrate with the rest of German society and Catholicism become 'more modern and less tightly knit', although in rural regions the parish priest still acted as a 'brake on modernity'.[11]

Poles, Danes and Alsatians

Nationalists perceived the Poles to be the main threat to the cohesion of the German state. According to the 1910 census there was a Polish population of over three million in Prussia's four eastern provinces, while nearly half a million Poles lived and worked in the Ruhr. Increasingly, however, the Ruhr coal companies sent agents to recruit Polish workers and gradually a 'chain migration'[12] pattern developed in which women and children followed the men. In 1905 nearly six hundred thousand foreigners, the majority of whom were Poles from the eastern provinces, worked in the Ruhr, the northern ports and the mines in Lorraine and central Germany. Their living conditions and treatment by employees was generally harsh. They were often housed in barracks and treated with hostility by their fellow German workers. Inevitably this pattern of east–west migration left the great estates in the east short of labour, which was remedied by recruiting seasonal labour from Russian and Austrian Poland.

> In 1815 the fourth partition of Poland took place between Austria, Prussia and Russia

Under Bismarck the Prussian government began a programme for Germanizing the eastern provinces. In 1886 the Royal Prussian Colonization Commission was set up to buy up bankrupt estates and settle German peasants on them. Over the next few years Polish was eliminated as a language of instruction in all primary schools, and all Prussian officials and conscripts of Polish origin were posted to western Germany where they could learn 'the blessings of German civilization'.[13] Bismarck and his successors underestimated the determination of the Poles to preserve their identity. They set up a Land Bank in 1889 to assist Polish farmers to buy land and pay their debts, and by 1914 'the nationalities were deadlocked in their competition for landowning primacy, neither one clearly winning or losing'.[14]

The other Slavic minorities in Germany had a less developed national consciousness:

- The Masurians, located mostly along the southern border of East Prussia, spoke a Polish dialect, but were Protestant and loyal to the Prussian state.
- The Kashubians in West Prussia were Catholic, but not ethnic Poles and had little interest in self-determination.
- There were, also, nearly 70,000 Slavic Sorbs in the Lausitz area between the Elbe and Oder and 121,345 Lithuanians in West Prussia (see Map 4).

In Northern Schleswig there were still 139,400 Danes, despite some emigration to the USA. As with the Polish areas in East Prussia, attempts were made to Germanize the province by insisting on the teaching in schools being conducted in German. The Danish minority fought back by publishing their own papers and setting up their own cultural organizations, rather as the Poles had done in the Ruhr. Gradually, however, the majority of Danish nationalists were absorbed in the mainstream parties, particularly the SPD. In the 1912 election the Nationalists polled a mere 5.5 per cent of the votes. In Alsace-Lorraine a similar process of Germanization took place, assisted by the emigration of many French speakers over the border into France. In 1875, 77 per cent of the population still spoke French, but by 1910 the total of German speakers had risen to 87 per cent.

The Jews

In 1815 the majority of Jews in Germany were pedlars, small traders and home-workers in cottage industries. A few were also dealers and money-lenders, and an even smaller number were *Hofjuden* (court Jews) like the Rothschilds. Yet by 1871, thanks to the continuing extension of civil rights and the increasing liberation of the economy from the guilds and restrictive practices, the Jews were able to become active in trade and industry and move into the professions. Increasingly important areas for middle-class Jewish employment were trade, catering, transport, insurance and textiles, while in the professions Jews made up 6 per cent of all doctors and 15 per cent of all lawyers in Germany. In 1895, 10 per cent of all university students were Jews, yet they had considerable difficulties in gaining posts in the civil service or university teaching. Not all German Jews, however, were middle class. There was still a significant minority, composed largely of immigrants from eastern Europe – in 1910 about 20,000 – who worked in mining, construction and manufacturing.

Although some Jews merged into the German population by inter-marriage, religious conversion and changing their names, the majority of German Jews wished to assimilate without giving up their religion, and increasingly saw themselves as 'German citizens of the Jewish faith'. Like most of their fellow-Germans, they saw religion and civic life as two distinct areas. Yet, despite their desire to embrace German culture, anti-Semitism became increasingly more strident in the *Kaiserreich*. The reasons for this were an explosive cocktail of economic jealousy, extreme nationalism and the emergence of the new *völkisch* (see p. 89) anti-modernist conservatism.

The Stock Exchange crash of 1873 by putting the spotlight on prominent Jewish bankers like the Rothschilds and Bleichröder, initially did much to fuel anti-Semitism. In 1878 the Jews were the subject of a more concentrated onslaught from Adolf Stoecker, a Lutheran pastor and court chaplain, whose Christian Social party became openly hostile to the Jews and accused them of being a 'people within a people'. Throughout the 1880s there were further attacks from pamphleteers like Wilhelm Marr and Otto Böckel. In the 1890s, immigration of eastern European Jews, whom Treitschke, the high-profile Berlin history professor (see p. 23), characterized as 'the multitudes of assiduous trouser selling youths from the inexhaustible cradle of Poland',[15] caused considerable concern and was one of the reasons why the anti-Semitic parties managed to win 16 seats in the *Reichstag* in the 1893 elections.

The tide of anti-Semitism did begin to ebb in the first decade of the new century, and the number of anti-Semitic deputies fell to seven in 1912, but the combination of racism and eugenics gave it a new twist. The

The emancipation of the Jews in Germany 1815–69

In 1820 there were 270,000 Jews living in what later became the German Reich, and a further 85,000 in the Austrian territories of the Confederation. By 1871 the former figures had increased to 512,000, and the latter to 200,000. It was only after 1850 that migration into the cities began. In Berlin, for instance, the Jewish population rose from 5645 in 1837 to 36,000 in 1866. In the French-occupied territories in the Rhineland Confederation, the Jews had been emancipated immediately, but elsewhere emancipation had been a long-drawn-out process. Jewish emancipation was finally completed in the 1860s. Jews received legal equality in Bavaria in 1861, Württemberg in 1861–64, Baden in 1862, Austria in 1867 and the North German Confederation in 1869.

popularizer of these ideas was Houston Stewart Chamberlain, who, in his two-volume *Foundations of the Nineteenth Century*, equated the 'superiority' of the German race to their racial purity. He argued that the real threat to this 'superiority' came from the Jews and created 'a dialectic between the two groups which Hitler would later copy'.[16]

Chamberlain, 1855–1927, was the son of an English admiral. He became a German citizen and a great admirer of the composer, Wagner, whose daughter he married

Although by 1914 the potentially lethal combination of racial hygienic ideals and anti-Semitism had been established, the imperial German state differed fundamentally from the Third Reich. It ultimately accepted that the Jews were German citizens. Indeed, as Richard Levy has pointed out, the 'state had proved its utter reliability by using troops to quell [the anti-Semitic] riots in Neustettin (1881), Xanten (1891) and Constance (1900) and by handing out stiff punishments to rioters'.[17] The young Jewish businessman and polymath, Walter Rathenau, argued with some exaggeration that the Jews 'as an alien secluded race in the middle of German life' were only saved from destruction by the power of the law 'holding in check all natural violence'.[18]

See p. 150 and Document. 27

The gypsies

The gypsies, who numbered a mere 2000 in 1900, were the smallest of the ethnic groups in Germany. Their traditional pre-industrial customs and itinerant life automatically alienated police and state authorities, who frequently referred to the 'gypsy plague'. They were subjected to harassment by philanthropic organizations and put under pressure by the state to abandon their nomadic life. It was, for instance, made obligatory for gypsy children to attend school in 1899. Also, great efforts were made to expel foreign gypsies, who frequently crossed over the Austrian and Russian frontiers into the Reich.

Women

Before the industrial revolution, women had worked in cottage industries, small workshops or on the land very much as the equals of men. Industrialization, however, did trigger an important change. It created many more jobs that did not require specific skills. These were for the most part given to women, who were paid less than men and whose promotion prospects remained very low indeed. Similarly, in offices and the new department stores women entered as secretaries or shop assistants with restricted career prospects. The large expansion in the size of the bourgeoisie and the managerial middle classes also created a great demand for female servants. Altogether in 1907 roughly 30 per cent of the total workforce was female.

Cottage industries: businesses and trades carried on at home

The great majority of women amongst the middle classes stayed at home in the 'private sphere', although in the case of artisans and shopkeepers, for example, wives might sometimes work behind the counter or do the accounts. The chief task of the wives of the bourgeoisie, however,

See Document. 26.2

was to run comparatively large households, supervise the servants and entertain for their husbands. Their domestic world was 'a world set apart from the virile ambiance of men, who engaged in business, gathered in clubs and smoke rooms, and occasionally even challenged each other to a duel'.[19]

It remained the norm for the majority of middle-class girls to prepare themselves for becoming young ladies and, eventually, wives and mothers, rather than embarking upon professional careers. Nevertheless, the big expansion in state education did open the doors to single women who wished to enter the teaching profession. By 1911 there were 24,000 women teachers, although they were paid far less than their male colleagues. Gradually, however, after 1890 an increasing but still small number of women began to sit the all-important *Abitur*, which was the basic qualification for university entrance. Saxony and Bavaria had allowed women to attend lectures even before the Reich had been founded. Only in the 1890s did the Prussian universities follow suit, and by 1905 some 1669 women were registered as 'auditors'. It was the southern universities, too, that first opened their doors to women as properly enrolled students. It was not until 1909 that the Prussian universities admitted women, but already by 1914 women made up 7 per cent of the total number of their students.

Right up to 1918 women were very much second-class citizens in Germany. Married women's rights to inherit property and decide the future of their children were strictly controlled by law, and in the event of divorce they lost most of their property. Neither could they vote in national elections, although in some states women with the right property qualifications were able to vote in local elections. Women were even banned from attending political meetings until 1908. This did not, however, mean that they had no collective voice in German life. The General German Association of Women had been founded before the unification of Germany and was committed to the cause of educating women. Specific professional associations for women teachers and commercial employees were founded, and in 1894 the German Women's Association (BDF) was set up, which acted as an umbrella organization for 70,000 members and 137 associations. Under the leadership of Marie Stritt, the BDF became more radical and feminist. Not only did it demand the vote, but it also claimed full legal equality for women within marriage, equal pay, educational opportunities, and abortion on demand.

In 1908 the Reich Law of Association at last gave women the right to attend political meetings and campaign politically. Paradoxically, after this concession a large number of traditionally-minded women joined the BDF. The German Evangelical Women's League, for instance, became affiliated to it, and immediately began a campaign against demands for legal abortion. Similarly, the female suffrage movement, which had originally been close to the SPD, moved closer to the National Liberals. By 1912 the BDF leadership adopted the argument that women were uniquely equipped to heal the bitter social divisions in Germany, and unite the nation into a national racial community – an attitude that was later to lead to a qualified acceptance of the Nazi regime in 1933.

Wilhelmine Culture: a bridge between the traditional and the new

In the early years of the empire, German culture was dominated by nationalist sentiments. Writers, musicians and artists all rallied to celebrate the unification of Germany. In the visual arts, for instance, there was a great demand for official portraits of German worthies and the depiction of great historical scenes. Anton von Werner's paintings of battles and ceremonies were particularly popular, and when he was made Director of the Royal Institute of Fine Arts in Berlin, he became the most influential artist in Germany. Conventional sculpture also enjoyed immense popularity, as there was an insatiable demand for monuments celebrating the unification of Germany and statues of Bismarck, the 'Iron Chancellor'. To Kaiser Wilhelm II the role of art was to 'elevate the people and to serve as a conservative stabilization of society'.[20]

For the most part, German fiction in the Bismarckian period also intended to be morally 'uplifting' and avoided contentious subjects, although a few writers like Theodor Fontane, Wilhelm Raabe and Max Kretzer did explore more profound issues. Historical novels were popular, as were novels and short stories set predominantly in Germany's rural backwaters.

By the early 1890s, however, German and indeed European culture had reached a turning-point. What Peter Gay has called a revolution 'transformed culture in all its branches. It utterly changed painting, sculpture and music . . . A very troop of masters compelled Western civilization to alter its angle of vision, and to adopt a new aesthetic sensibility, new philosophical style, a new mode of understanding social life and human nature'.[21] In Germany the manifestations of these changes soon became clear. The *Free Stage* theatre company, directed by Otto Brahm, had been set up by iconoclastic intellectuals like Theodor Wolff and Maximilian Harden. Brahm began to produce a series of naturalist plays such as Gerhardt Hauptmann's two plays, *Before Sunrise*, which dealt with alcoholism, immorality and cupidity, and *The Weavers*, a dramatized account of the sufferings of the handloom weavers in Silesia in 1844. A few years later Frank Wedekind was able to deal on the stage with hitherto taboo questions such as murder, masturbation, homosexuality and prostitution.

The art scene also experienced upheaval. In 1892 a group of 106 artists seceded from the local branch of the German General Art Association (*Allgemeine Deutsche Kunstgenossenschaft*) in Munich, and in Berlin Max Liebermann and Walther Leistikow formed the Group of Eleven so that they could exhibit modern art independently of the conservative art establishment. In 1897 when one of Leistikow's paint-

See Document 28

Theodor Storm (1817–88), who lived most of his life in Husum on the North Sea coast, was one of the leading writers of this genre with his tales set in north-west Germany

See Document 12

ings was rejected by the association's hanging committee in Berlin, the modernists, including Max Liebermann, Max Slevogt, Lovis Corinth and Käthe Kollwitz, all resigned, and in 1898 held an independent exhibition. In due course the Secessionists, as they called themselves, also broke into rival groups, the most famous of which were the *Blaue Reiter* and *Die Brücke*.

Literature and poetry ceased to give a uniform message. Some poets and writers like Stefan George advocated the retreat to the inner self, while others, like Thomas Mann in *Buddenbrooks*, explored the fragility of the bourgeois world, or else like his brother, Heinrich Mann, Carl Sternheim and Ludwig Thoma, the hypocrisy of Wilhelmine Germany. This message of increasing diversity and uncertainty was reinforced by contemporary science. The work of Heinrich Hertz on electric waves, Wihelm Röntgen on x-rays and Einstein's potentially revolutionary idea that radiation consisted of totally independent particles of energy destroyed the old ideas of a static universe and led to questioning whether there were actually any laws of nature. Like the writers and artists, scientists were coming to the conclusion that everything was relative.

The findings of the scientists were not widely understood by the general public. To the Kaiser and the traditional élite it was the changes in art and literature that were most threatening. Few opportunities were lost to denounce it as 'loathsome'[22] or un-German, and the authorities at the Kaiser's instigation attempted to stop the Secessionists' work being exhibited at the World Fair in St Louis, USA. The Kaiser and the traditionalists were, however, fighting a losing battle. The *Reichstag* condemned his meddling, and in the words of the SPD deputy, Paul Singer, declined 'to have a republic of the arts with William II at its head'.[23] Above all, two factors combined to defeat efforts by the establishment to suppress the modernist movement: the federal nature of Germany ensured that if pressure on an artist or director of an art gallery in Berlin, for example, became too intimidating, Munich, Stuttgart or Dresden might well be more accommodating and, similarly, playwrights could circumvent a ban on their work by having it performed privately.

See Document 28

Critics from the right

The fiercest critics of imperial Germany came from the right. By far the greatest, although most misunderstood, of these was Nietzsche. In his brilliant, colourful and pithy style he mocked the pretensions of Imperial Germany. As early as 1873 he warned that the great victories of 1870–71 were 'capable of converting our victory into a complete defeat: the defeat, even the death of German culture for the benefit of the German empire'.[24] He bitterly denounced the philistinism of Germany and the soulless process of mass education. Although Nietzsche himself was not a nationalist or anti-Semite, in the 1890s he became a cult figure of the

Friedrich Nietzche 1844–1900

Nietzsche was born in Prussia where his father was a Lutheran pastor. He had an enormous impact on psychology through Freud and Jung, on sociology through Max Weber and on literature and philosophy. He analysed the sickness of modern culture where religion had been replaced by materialism and the quest for pleasure, drawing the conclusion from this that God was 'dead'. To remedy this, he urged in Thus Spake Zaruthustra the creation of a new ruthless élite under a totally amoral leader or 'superman'. During his lifetime Nietzsche was not a fanatical nationalist or anti-Semite, but later his concept of the 'superman' was exploited by Fascism and Nazism.

new anti-modernist, *völkisch* ideology and was celebrated for his anti-modernism, cult of the heroic individual and 'aristocratic radicalism'.

The most influential member of this new ideology was Paul de Lagarde, who focused his attack on both the materialism and the creeping liberalism of the Bismarckian Reich. He argued that German society could only be revived by purging it of the Jews and liberalism, and by creating a new conservative nobility. Simultaneously he advocated German domination of central Europe. The anti-modernist message was further developed by Julius Langbehn in his book *Rembrandt Als Erzieher* (*Rembrandt as Educator*). Rembrandt was depicted as an ideal figure of a golden era, whose values would serve as a model for the new Germany. Collectively these romantic anti-modernist critics help spread the sort of mystical and exaggerated nationalism which Hitler was later to exploit.

Langbehn's influence was, for instance, evident in the emergence of the German Youth Movement, the *Wandervögel*, where groups of *Gymnasium* (high school) students sought to escape from the discipline of school and dullness of city life by walking and camping in the remote German countryside. For a time they even called their founder, Karl Fischer, the *Führer* and greeted him with cries of '*Heil!*'

Conclusion

The *Kaiserreich* is a paradoxical period in German history. In so many areas it witnessed the breakthrough to modernity. From being a late developer in the first industrial revolution, Germany became a pioneer of the second industrial revolution. Similarly, its artists, writers and scientists were busy setting the intellectual agenda for most of the rest of the twentieth century, while its workers had organized the largest and most effective socialist party in Europe. Bismarck had also laid the foundations for a welfare state, which other nations were to emulate years later. In many ways it was the most modern state in Europe, yet, as we shall explore in the next chapter, many historians argue that these achievements were to a great extent nullified by the 'basic mismatch between economic change on the one hand and developments in the political sphere on the other'.[25] It is these which will be explored in the next chapter.

6 *Domestic Politics from Bismarck to Bethmann Hollweg*

Introduction

Fritz Fischer's seminal work in 1961 on *Germany's Aims in the First World War*, which, he argued, were similar to those pursued later by Hitler, triggered a fierce debate on the nature of the Second Reich. Whereas traditional political history had stressed that Bismarck and his successors had pursued a primacy of diplomatic over domestic policy, the new generation of historians, such as Hans-Ulrich Wehler, Wolfgang Mommsen and Volker Berghahn, who had also been influenced by the growth of interest in social, economic and cultural history and the application of new sociological theories on modernization (see p. 193) from the United States and the *Annales* school in France, argued that it was domestic policy that really determined German foreign policy. The doyen of this 'new orthodoxy', Hans-Ulrich Wehler, using a structural approach to the period in his *German Empire, 1871–1918*, maintains that Bismarck and his successors were driven by fear of imminent revolution, and so embarked on a policy of Bonapartism and social imperialism in order

Structural approach: an approach which applies a structural analysis to history. This plays down the role of the individual and places more emphasis on the influence of the economy and other factors such as the political structure of a state

See Document 20 and p. 60

107

11   Bismarck, the elder statesman
Imperial War Museum, no. Q81829

both to divert public attention from the problems at home and to consolidate the position of the traditional ruling classes. He argues that Bismarck's deliberate decision to stop Germany from developing into a constitutional state through his skilful manipulation of the political parties, plebiscitary elections and negative integration tactics set Germany on a special path or *Sonderweg*, that ultimately led to the Third Reich. This view has, of course, been challenged both by the more conservative historians like Thomas Nipperdey, and by revisionists such as Manfred Rauh in Germany and Richard Evans, Geoff Eley and David Blackbourn in Britain.[1] Rauh believes that by 1914 the *Kaiserreich* was subject to a gradual but slow process of parliamentarization, while the British historians take issue with the whole question of the *Sonderweg*. Geoff Eley, for instance, argues that the structuralists are too centrist and

Prussian-orientated, and that a study of local politics and socio-cultural change modifies the standard picture of a people ruthlessly manipulated by Bismarck and the Prussian élites. In reality, he points out, the bourgeoisie dominated both the local politics of the cities and the culture and society of the Second Reich. Furthermore, he provocatively questions the *Sonderweg* theory by arguing that 'the very modernity'[2] of the Bismarckian state made further political reform for the time being unnecessary.

Key issues

- To what extent was the constitution of the Second Reich only workable while Wilhelm I lived and Bismarck was chancellor?
- Why was the 'liberal era' of 1871–78 so short-lived?
- Do the years 1878–79 mark the 'second foundation' of the Reich?
- What domestic problems did Bismarck face in the period 1880–90? How successful was he in solving them?
- What was Bismarck's political legacy? Did it leave his successors with virtually insoluble problems as far as domestic politics were concerned?
- How did German politics change in the 1890s?
- Is personal rule a meaningful concept?
- To what extent did a 'new politics' come into existence in the 1890s?
- Why did Bismarck's successors fail to establish the dominance Bismarck enjoyed for so long?
- Why did Germany not evolve into a constitutional monarchy over the period 1890–1914?
- To what extent was there a political crisis on the eve of the outbreak of the Great War?

The constitutional context

When the new German Reich was formed, the North German Confederation (see pp. 78–9) was merely adapted to absorb the south German states. It continued, as Wolfgang Mommsen has observed, to be a 'system of skirted decisions',[3] which protected the predominance of Prussia, while temporarily, at least, satisfying the National Liberals and appeasing the south German states. The Reich contained many of the characteristics of a parliamentary regime. It was a constitutional state with a parliament elected by universal franchise and vigorous political parties. On the other hand, as Matthew Seligmann and Roderick McLean have pointed out, 'such outward liberalism was . . . deceptive, the document upon which the whole legal framework rested was not a constitution in the normal sense of the word, but rather took the form of a treaty of 25 sovereign states for the ordering of their common affairs'.[4] This accounted for the structure of its upper house, the *Bundesrat* or federal council, where the federal states were represented by diplomats rather than politicians. A considerable amount of legislation was delegated to the state governments, whose existing and often conservative constitutions were not affected by unification. The constitution could theoretically still be abrogated by the sovereigns of the German states and consequently the recurring threats of a *coup d'état* made by Bismarck or Wilhelm II were in the final analysis quite possible and hung like the 'sword of Damocles over German political life'.[5]

Bismarck 'abhorred the idea of collective government'[6] and consequently no proper Reich cabinet existed. In 1867 he had set up a chancellor's office which, over the next decade, he expanded into eight separate Reich departments: the Foreign Office, the Treasury, the Interior Office, the Admiralty, Posts and Telegraphs, and the offices for Alsace-Lorraine, the railways and judicial affairs. These departments, however, never met as a cabinet, but were co-ordinated by a Reich Chancellery, headed by Rudolf Dellbrück, through which Bismarck communicated his instructions to all departments except for the Foreign Office, which reported directly to him. The real expression of German unity was the *Reichstag*, which represented the whole nation. It had the right to veto legislation, but it could not dissolve itself, propose legislation or force the chancellor to resign. Bismarck held the view that the *Reichstag* was a body which should react to events rather than initiate them. In other words, as he observed in 1884, 'it should . . . prevent bad laws from being passed . . . and the waste of public money; but it cannot govern'.[7] In practice, however, the power of the *Reichstag* turned out to be greater than Bismarck had envisaged, and with the emergence of mass parties like the Centre party and the SPD, he became increasingly afraid that it would develop into the dominant organ in the constitution.

Although Prussia controlled only 19 out of the 58 seats in the *Bundesrat*, and could theoretically be outvoted by a combination of the southern states, in reality its size, wealth and power placed it in a category of its own. The historian, Arthur Rosenberg, described the *Bundesrat* 'as the constitutional fig leaf of Prussian rule over the Empire',[8] as it disguised the reality of Prussian power in the Reich:

> **Centre party**: A Roman Catholic political party, which was founded in 1871 to defend Catholic interest in Germany

- The chancellor, as the Prussian minister-president, presided over the *Bundesrat*.
- Prussia provided most of the officials who worked in the new central agencies under Delbrück.
- The Reich was also dependent on Prussia financially since the central government had very limited powers of taxation and relied on grants from the federal state.
- Militarily Prussian hegemony was absolute; the Prussian General Staff took over the role of strategic planning for the German land forces and the Prussian minister of war was also the Reich minister for war.
- The head of the nation and president of the federation of German princes was the *Deutscher Kaiser* (German emperor), the King of

Prussia, whose formal powers remained considerable: he was theoretically in control of the nation's foreign policy; it was he who appointed the chancellor, the members of the Reich civil and foreign services; and he was also supreme commander of the armed forces.

In essence the new Reich could only function effectively if there was close co-operation between the Prussian and Reich administrations. In 1872 Bismarck briefly resigned his post as Prussian minister–president, but he quickly discovered that this led to such friction between the Reich and Prussia that he resumed it after only five months. As long as Bismarck remained chancellor, he was able to hold the federal structure of the Reich together, but the danger remained that a future German chancellor would be confronted by the conflicting pressures of a conservative Prussia where the three-class voting system ensured after 1878 a large conservative majority in the *Landtag*, and a more left-wing *Reichstag* voted in on universal franchise. As Wolfgang Mommsen has put it, 'As an assemblage of moderately progressive bourgeois parties took firmer shape in the Reichstag . . . so those in the conservative camp . . . grew steadily more disposed to take refuge in the Prussian redoubt and to use it as a base from which to forestall any reformist Imperial measures.'[9]

The Liberal era, 1871–78

A. J. P. Taylor observed that it was hard to judge whether between 1871 and 1877 'Bismarck or the National Liberals determined the character of German policy'.[10] Both they and to a lesser extent the Progressives were his natural allies and worked closely with him in the task of creating the necessary administrative and legal infrastructure for the new Reich. The Conservatives believed that Bismarck had become 'the lackey of Liberalism',[11] while the Centre party attracted those who remained sceptical about Prussian-led *Kleindeutschland* – the potential or actual *Reichsfeinde*: the South German Catholics, the Poles and the Alsatians.

The *Kulturkampf*

To the Liberals the Catholics were a potential Trojan horse in the new and predominantly Protestant Germany (see p. 99). Already in the 1860s a *Kulturkampf* had broken out in Baden with the Catholic Church over the control of elementary education. The Papacy had also contributed to the growing polarization between Protestants and Catholics by promulgating first in 1864 the *Syllabus Errorum*, which condemned the very doctrines liberals believed essential for a free society, and then in 1870, the doctrine of papal infallibility.

To what extent did Bismarck genuinely share the fears of his fellow-Protestants? In the autumn of 1870 when Italian troops had occupied

Reichsfeinde: literally enemies of the Reich, that is those Germans who were sceptical about the social and political structure of Bismarckian Germany

See Document 29

Rome, he had considered briefly the diplomatic advantages of offering the Pope refuge in Germany, but a year later he gave government support to the waging of a bitter *Kulturkampf* in Prussia. Why was this? The Bielefeld school of historiography argues that this was a classic example of Bismarck's technique of negative integration, whereby he hoped to unite the Protestant majority in Germany against the Catholic 'enemy' within, while deflecting the Liberals from pursuing awkward questions about the liberty of the individual and constitutional reform. Bismarck certainly exploited the political advantages of the *Kulturkampf*, but this underestimates both his very real concern that the Centre party would rally the *Reichsfeinde* and his hatred of Ludwig Windthorst, its courageous leader.

As education and religious affairs were the responsibilities of the states rather than of the Reich, the *Kulturkampf* was waged principally by the Prussian, Baden and Hesse governments. The most important elements in the Prussian *Kulturkampf* were the two May Laws of 1873 and 1874. In Prussia the May Law of 1873 extended state control over Catholic theological colleges, set up a Royal Tribunal for Ecclesiastical Affairs and allowed provincial governors to veto the appointment of parish priests. A year later further legislation sanctioned the confiscation of church properties and the imprisonment of recusant bishops. The Catholic lawyer and writer, Julius Bachem, admittedly with some exaggeration, compared the *Kulturkampf* to 'the Diocletian persecution' of the early Christians.[12] While these laws had unpleasant consequences for individual Catholics and strengthened Liberal support for the government, Bismarck failed to destroy the Centre party. The growth of the party was visible evidence that he had 'suffered the first significant defeat of his political career'. Windthorst successfully encouraged the Catholic voters to make the election 'a great plebiscite' against the *Kulturkampf*, and in 1874 won 91 seats.[13]

The decline of the Liberals and protectionism

The Stock Exchange crash of 1873 and the subsequent depression (see p. 90) slowly began to transform the political situation. As the liberals were closely identified with *laissez-faire*, free trade and industrialization, they were made 'to bear responsibility', as James Sheehan has

---

Ludwig Windthorst, 1812–91

A lawyer, who became minister of justice in the Hanoverian government; he was an opponent of *kleindeutsch* nationalism and leader of the Centre party until 1890. He attempted to create an alliance between German Catholics, the Polish, Danish and Alsatian ethnic minorities and the Hanoverians, who resented the annexation of the state by Prussia in 1866. He was a brilliant debater and could more than hold his own with Bismarck in the *Reichstag*.

observed, 'for what various groups did not like about the contemporary world'.[14]

The Depression also caused a crisis in the Reich's finances. The decline in industrial production led to a steep fall in tax receipts, which the central government received from the individual states, at the very time that the international crisis in the Balkans was erupting (see pp. 128–9). Bismarck initially hoped to open up new sources of revenue by nationalizing the highly profitable railway companies, but this was opposed by Bavaria, Saxony and Württemberg. Similarly, an increase in indirect taxation on tobacco, sugar and brandy was opposed by the Liberal parties as it would entail a lessening of parliamentary control. Inevitably, the failure of these plans made the possibility of raising money through tariffs more attractive to Bismarck, but he was also increasingly impressed by the economic arguments of the protectionists (see p. 91), and growing friction with Russia made him more ready to consider tariffs against Russian imported grain.

By late 1877 Bismarck had become converted to tariffs, but how was he to win a majority in the *Reichstag* for a bill introducing them? He first attempted to win over the National Liberals by offering their leader, Rudolf von Bennigsen, the position of Prussian minister of the interior. The manoeuvre failed when the National Liberals demanded two further seats in the cabinet, a request which he was not ready to grant. An alternative solution was to seek an early dissolution of the *Reichstag* and the election of a more manageable assembly in which a chastened National Liberal party, purged of its more radical members, would be ready to support tariffs. By moving over to a tariff policy, Bismarck would be able to win the support of the Conservative party and key interest groups in both agriculture and heavy industry. This alliance of 'rye and iron' would, he hoped, form 'the core of a new parliamentary coalition',[15] which would make him less dependent on the liberals.

On 11 May 1878 there was an attempted assassination of the Kaiser, which was at first thought to be a socialist plot. Bismarck immediately introduced an anti-socialist bill into the *Reichstag* with the intention of not only weakening the SPD but also of creating tension between the left and right wings of the National Liberal party. It was, however, overwhelmingly defeated in the *Reichstag*. Then a second assassination attempt on the Kaiser provided Bismarck with a marvellous chance to call a crisis election, which enabled the Conservatives to make considerable gains at the expense of the liberals. In return for limiting the initial period of the proposed anti-socialist law, which would ban socialist meetings and publications and empower the authorities to expel agitators from their homes, to two and a half years, the National Liberals, despite considerable reservations by their left wing, were now prepared to join the Conservatives in voting for the bill.

In the spring of 1879 Bismarck then asked the *Reichstag* to approve legislation for levying tariffs on iron, iron goods and grain, and indirect taxes on salt, coffee, tobacco and selected luxury goods. To get the bill

The first assassination was carried out by a half-crazed plumber's apprentice; the second one was attempted by a Doctor Karl Nobiling, an expert on soil and crop production, whose chief aim was self-publicity. See Document 30 for the Anti-Socialist Law

through the *Reichstag* he had to make a choice between the National Liberals and the Centre party. The National Liberals were prepared to support the bill only if the *Reichstag* could determine the salt tax and coffee duties annually, but Bismarck rejected this outright, as it would have entailed strengthening parliamentary control over the Reich's finances. He therefore had little option but to negotiate with the Centre. In the interests of the farming lobby in his own party, Windthorst was ready to back protection, but he was under pressure to indicate that this did not entail general support for Bismarck, the hated perpetrator of the *Kulturkampf.* Nor indeed did he wish to make the government more independent financially of the federal states. Bismarck, therefore, had no option but to accept a proposal from the Bavarian Centre deputy, Georg von Frankenstein, that only a fixed percentage of the income from the new duties would be allocated to the Reich, while the rest would go to the states, which would continue to make their annual budgetary contributions to the Reich. Consequently in July 1879 a Conservative–Centre majority, joined by 15 right-wing National Liberals, approved the bill. Ironically the Centre, as Windthorst remarked, had become the liquidator of the 'bankruptcy of the liberal Economy'.[16]

The 'second foundation' of the Reich

To historians like Helmut Böhme, who view Bismarck's policies 'through the lens of economic interest',[17] 1879 is a more important turning-point than 1871. Bismarck had in effect refounded the Reich, and set it on a conservative course. He had gained, as the French ambassador observed, 'one of the most substantial triumphs of his career'[18] and the long-term consequences of this were to influence the Reich until 1918:

• The new tariff policy marked a real shift to the right and brought together the alliance of 'iron and grain' that was to play a key role in German politics.
• It was the beginning of a policy that was to lead to further protectionist policies alienating Russia and arguably in the longer term running against Germany's true economic interests (see p. 129), which were increasingly dependent on exports and increasing world trade.

Bismarck had, however, failed to make the Reich financially independent of the German states, and, despite the temporary majority for tariffs, he lost control of the *Reichstag* until 1887. Bismarck's calculation that the National Liberals would split and that the majority would rally behind the government did not immediately work out. In 1880 the party did indeed split but in the 1881 election the breakaway group under Lasker, the Secessionists, won almost as many seats as the National Liberal party itself. Inevitably, the political realignments of 1878–80 strengthened the position of the Centre in the *Reichstag*, but Bismarck was not able to end the *Kulturkampf* immediately and turn the Centre into an ally. He did indeed attempt to make concessions on the May Laws but in July 1880 the Conservatives and National Liberals deleted key provisions, which would have allowed the Prussian government to pardon exiled bishops. Windthorst also skilfully blocked attempts by Bismarck to appeal to the right wing of his party by annually submitting to the *Landtag* a proposal for exempting the administration of the sacraments from criminal prosecution, which would have made the May Laws unenforceable. In the election of 1881 Bismarck suffered 'a striking defeat',[19] when over three-quarters of the newly-elected *Reichstag* was opposed to the government. For the next five years all Bismarck's bluster and threats could not hide the fact that he had lost control of the *Reichstag*. In 1990 Enno Kraehe observed that Bismarck's predicament reminded him 'less of an Iron Age Chancellor than [the then American President] George Bush facing a Democratic Congress on the defense budget'.[20]

Defending the fragile structure of the empire from corrosive change became a 'labour of Sisyphus',[21] which increasingly involved escalating attacks against the Social Democrats, 'Bonapartist' plebiscitary elections, imperialist diversions in Africa, and attempts to weaken the *Reichstag*. Bismarck sought to neutralize the Social Democrats both by renewing the Anti-Socialist Law, and by seeking to integrate the workers into a 'German national consensus based on the Prussian-German establishment'[22] through his pioneering welfare measures.

Corporatism: the process of integrating both workers and employers, organized in groups, into the administration and government of the state

Bismarck's social welfare programme

The scale of this programme is impressive. A. J. P. Taylor, for instance, argued that it was alone sufficient 'to establish his reputation as a constructive statesman, even if he had done nothing else'.[23] The Accident Insurance Bill of 1881 was closely based on proposals made by August Bebel, the leader of the SPD, in 1879. Initially Bismarck intended that the employers should pay two-thirds of the premiums and the employees a third, while the state would also make a considerable contribution. The state subsidy was of particular importance for he hoped to win over the working class with it. In the *Reichstag*, however, it was opposed by both the Centre and the National Liberals who voted against the state contribution, and the SPD itself, which was reluctant to accept reforms from the hated Bismarck. In 1883–84 the *Reichstag* did approve both a health insurance bill and an amended accident insurance bill, which had no state subsidies. Into the administration of both schemes Bismarck introduced a corporative element: health insurance was to be administered by local health committees which were elected by employers and workers, while the accident insurance scheme was organized by the employers, divided into groups according to industries. Bismarck hoped that these novel corporate associations would create the basis for a future body that could eventually replace the *Reichstag*, even if this had to be carried out by a coup d'état. In 1889 Bismarck completed his welfare legislation with the introduction of the old-age pension. Here there is clear evidence that Bismarck had been influenced by Napoleon III, as he told the *Reichstag* 'that the attachment of most Frenchmen to the government . . . is mainly connected with the fact that most Frenchmen are state pensioners'.[24]

Overall, however, Bismarck failed signally to prevent the steady rise of the SPD. In the 1884 election it managed to increase its seats to 24, which entitled it to regular representation on the *Reichstag* committees, and by 1890 30 SPD delegates sat in the *Reichstag*.

On the other hand, the apparently inexorable rise of the SPD did encourage the National Liberals to co-operate more closely with Bismarck and the Conservatives. In 1884 the south German National Liberals at a congress in Heidelberg unequivocally accepted Bismarck's welfare and tariff policies, and in the election of that year the Progressive vote markedly declined. Bismarck's expansionary policy in Africa and South East Asia (see pp. 131–3) also attracted the National Liberals and led to their close co-operation on the colonial question. Nevertheless, even though the underlying trend of the 1884 election was favourable, Bismarck still faced an unmanageable *Reichstag*, and by 1886 he was ready to seize any opportunity to dissolve it at an opportune moment. His chance came with the potentially dangerous combination of the Bulgarian crisis and the rise of Boulanger in France (see p. 133). Bismarck immediately brought forward the forward the *Septennat* and demanded a 10 per cent increase in the size of the army. When the Progressives and the Centre tried to reduce the period covered by the grant, Bismarck contemptuously dismissed their efforts to compromise and dissolved the *Reichstag* in January 1887. During the subsequent election campaign he did all he could to create an atmosphere of crisis, and his machinations were rewarded by the election of a parliament in which the electoral *Kartell* (bloc) composed of Free Conservatives, Conservatives and National Liberals won a clear majority, which enabled him to pass the *Septennat*. However, within the *Kartell* there were tensions between the National Liberals and Conservatives over tariffs. Neither did the National Liberals did give up their attempts to push Bismarck into making further constitutional concessions. In 1889 Bennigsen proposed the appointment of a Reich minister of finance responsible to the *Reichstag*. As a possible future alternative to the *Kartell*, Bismarck also worked for a rapprochement with the Centre, which became possible once the second ' Peace bill' in April 1887 ended the *Kulturkampf*.

Bismarck had persuaded the *Reichstag* to increase the military budget from five to seven years (the *Septennat*) in 1874

See Document 20

Bismarck's downfall

In March 1888 the old Kaiser died. If his heir, Crown Prince Frederick, had survived, it is likely that Bismarck would eventually have been replaced by a more liberal chancellor, although this would not have been easy, as Bismarck would have fought every inch of the way and would have skillfully rallied public opinion against Frederick. The Crown Prince was seen as an Anglophile 'hen-pecked husband',[25] dominated by his English wife, Victoria, who apparently wished to convert the Reich to Gladstonian liberalism. Bismarck had already skilfully turned Frederick's son William against him, but by the time Frederick came to

---

Wilhelm II, 1859–1941

Wilhelm was an unstable and neurotic figure, who suffered from rapid mood swings and may even have been mentally ill. His complex love–hate relationship with his English mother and Great Britain created considerable political problems. Partly to spite his parents he closely allied himself with Bismarck, and, according to the Crown Prince of Austria, his political opinions were the same as 'a dyed-in-the-wool Junker and reactionary'.[26] When he came to the throne in 1888, he was determined to re-establish the power of the Prussian monarchy and to rule in reality. By 1897 he had greatly increased his personal power at the expense of excluding genuinely independent-minded men from office.

---

the throne, he was suffering from terminal cancer and Bismarck had little to fear.

See Document 31

The accession of Wilhelm II was a turning-point in the history of the Second Reich. Initially Bismarck assumed that his advice would in the final analysis be accepted, but he rapidly found himself in serious disagreement with the new Kaiser over several major issues:

- Wilhelm intended to ease Bismarck slowly out of power and then appoint a man of his own choice, while Bismarck hoped to cling to power and eventually appoint his son, Herbert, thereby establishing a Bismarck 'dynasty'.
- The Kaiser was suspicious of ending the *Kulturkampf* and wished to see the existing *Kartell* with the National Liberals and Conservatives maintained.
- He also wished to enhance his independence of Bismarck by establishing himself as a progressive monarch, who could establish good relations with the workers. He thus received a delegation of striking miners from Ruhr coalfields in 1889.

Bismarck responded to these challenges to his power by attempting to conjure up a crisis that would make him indispensable to the Crown. In October, a few months before the next election, he introduced into the *Reichstag* a new Anti-Socialist Bill, which would not have to be renewed at regular intervals, as in the past, but would be permanent. When the opposition of the National Liberals to this threatened the unity of the *Kartell*, he rejected all requests from the Kaiser to accept a compromise. He calculated that the collapse of the *Kartell* would lead to an increase in the Social Democratic vote in the election, and that then the chastened National Liberals and propertied classes would turn to him for leadership. When, as predicted, the elections led to a strengthening of the Centre, the *Freisinnige Partei* (formerly the Progressive Liberals) and the SPD, Bismarck, intent on provoking a major crisis that would frighten the Kaiser into sanctioning a coup, planned to present the new *Reichstag* with the Anti-Socialist Law and a greatly increased military budget. As he waited for this crisis to mature, he took steps to tighten his grip on the Prussian cabinet by reviving the old Prussian cabinet order of 1852, which forbade ministers from being received by the Crown without consent of the prime minister. This threatened the Kaiser with the prospect of being isolated and led directly to him presenting Bismarck with the choice of either withdrawing the order or resigning. Bismarck, lacking any support in the *Reichstag*, resigned on 18 March 1890 and was replaced by General von Caprivi (see p. 93).

The new politics, 1890–1914

The 1890s witnessed the emergence of mass politics in Germany. Major issues such as imperialism, commercial and fiscal policies and the social question all helped mobilize large numbers of the peasantry and the working and middle classes, who had previously not participated in politics. The most dramatic evidence of growing mass participation in politics was the growth of the SPD (see p. 96), which by 1912 represented a third of the electorate. It was an effectively organized and centrally controlled 'people's party', which by 1914, as Sperber has shown,[27] also attracted bourgeois and secular Catholic votes. Its success was accompanied by a massive expansion of the free trade unions, which were affiliated to the SPD, to nearly three million members by 1913.

On the right, as a result of the growing crisis in the countryside (see p. 98), peasant radicalism was finding expression in the emergence of Peasant Leagues and the rise of anti-Semitic parties, which promised to rid the countryside of 'Junkers and Jews'. In 1893 the Agrarian League was founded ostensibly to oppose Caprivi's tariff policies, but it was also a successful attempt by the east Elbian aristocracy to channel and control popular agitation so that it did not challenge their own position. It was not, however, just a Junker pressure group; it was also 'a pressure group of a new kind',[28] that appealed to rural populism. In 1898 the league had enrolled 157,000 smallholders and 28,500 middle-sized farmers, as compared to just 1,500 large landowners.

See Document 32

Nationalist opinion was mobilized by a number of associations such as the Pan-German League, the Society for the Eastern Marches, the Army League and above all the Navy League, which had 331,000 supporters. As pressure groups, their aims were usually far in advance of the government's. The Pan-Germans wished, for instance, to incorporate Holland and Austria into Germany. These leagues sometimes co-operated with the government but were not controlled by them. Effectively they evolved into a strident nationalist opposition and helped create amongst their members a feeling of disillusionment with the government's policies.

The mushroom growth of these associations marked a growing politicization of ever-larger sections of the German people and changed 'the pattern of behaviour in the public sphere of German political life'.[29] How much direct influence did they in fact exert over the government? The

Agrarian League with its links with the Conservative party and a firm base in rural Germany played a key role in returning protectionist deputies, who by 1907 made up a third of the *Reichstag*. The influence of the Navy League, which was by far the most popular pressure group, was not so important at election times, but, as Margaret Anderson points out, 'by revealing the popularity of the imperialist variant of nationalism . . . it did suggest the reservoir of sentiment available for radicalization once international events enabled nationalism to trump other issues'.[30]

While the pressure groups were mobilizing public opinion from below, the constitution of 1867–71 remained unchanged. It had worked most effectively when the National Liberals had been the largest party in the *Reichstag* and had co-operated with Bismarck in the 1870s, and when Kaiser Wilhelm I had given his chancellor virtually a free hand. By 1890 these important preconditions for success had changed. Not only was the party composition of the *Reichstag* very different, but the new Kaiser was determined to take over the powers the constitution still ascribed to the crown (see p. 78). Willhelm attempted to be 'both Emperor and Chancellor in one', and his failure created a 'pyramid of power [that] no longer had a peak'.[31] Increasingly, ministers bypassed the chancellor to pursue their own policies.

General Leo von Caprivi and the New Course, 1890–94

The successor to Bismarck would under any conditions have faced a difficult task, but it was made even more challenging by Bismarck's implacable hostility. At first the new government stressed the continuity of its policies with the Bismarck era, but as early as April 1890 William was announcing a 'new course'. As far as Caprivi was concerned, this involved policies which would attract a broad coalition of support from all groups who put country before party. In his first speech to the *Reichstag* he announced that he would 'take the good from wherever and from whomsoever it may come'.[32] To ease the confrontational political climate which Bismarck had created, Caprivi launched the following initiatives:

- He attempted to create a more collegiate style of government and, in an attempt to delegate power and treat Prussia like the other German states, he gave the Prussian minister–presidency to Botho zu Eulenburg.
- Efforts were made to appease national minorities: in Alsace-Lorraine compulsory passport restrictions were dropped and in the eastern provinces the absolute ban on the use of Polish in schools was lifted.
- Similarly he hoped to win the goodwill of the working classes by enacting a series of safety laws regulating conditions in the workplace and prohibiting Sunday employment.
- More controversially he cut the tariffs on grain from 50 to 30 per cent,

which provided cheap food for the urban classes at the expense of agriculture.

These measures failed to win Caprivi's government any lasting support, as his policy of standing above the parties prevented him from building up an effective electoral alliance. Above all his tariff policy met with implacable opposition from the right wing of the Conservative party, and led to the foundation of the Agrarian League (see p. 118), which was supported by both Eulenburg, who rapidly became his bitter rival, and Johannes Miquel, the Prussian finance minister. By the middle of 1892 only the fear that his fall would bring back Bismarck kept him in place.

He also increasingly alienated the Kaiser. In 1893, for instance, he managed to persuade the *Reichstag* to increase the military budget by cutting conscription from three to two years and conceding its rights to debate the military budget every five rather than seven years, but to Wilhelm the price seemed too high. By the spring of 1894 the latter was persuaded to back Eulenburg's proposal to put a draconian bill aimed at combating 'revolutionary tendencies' before the *Reichstag*. Like Bismarck earlier, Eulenburg hoped that its rejection would give the necessary excuse to the government to suspend the constitution. Caprivi was highly critical of Eulenburg's machinations and could probably have hung on in office but, in face of the unremitting attacks from the right, he decided to use his resignation in October to force the Kaiser to get rid of Eulenburg at the same time.

Prince Hohenlohe, 1819–1901:
Hohenlohe was a Bavarian aristocrat who had, as a younger man, worked in the Prussian civil service. After the defeat of Bavaria in 1866, he became minister–president in Munich and attempted to Prussianize Bavaria. In 1873 he became German ambassador in Paris, and in 1885 the Prussian governor of Alsace-Lorraine

Wilhelm's 'personal rule' and Prince Chlodwig zu Hohenlohe-Schillingfürst, 1894–1900

The degree of Wilhelm's influence on the Reich government is the subject of considerable historical debate. Wolfgang Mommsen regards the term 'personal rule' as an exaggeration and argues that eventually it amounted to little more than 'muddling through with the existing system, while trying as far as possible to patch up cracks and weaknesses within the governing elite'. On the other John Röhl, Isabel Hull and Katherine Lerman[33] have shown that Wilhelm did manage to create a political system which revolved around him and was responsive to his personal wishes. Hohenlohe was appointed as a 'respectable figure head',[34] who would be easier to manipulate than his predecessors.

'Personal rule' did not imply an outright dictatorship by the Kaiser. His advisers, particularly Philipp zu Eulenburg-Hertefeld, were wary of his mercurial temperament and feared the consequences of a *coup d'état*, particularly as it might lead to the southern German states seceding from the union. Eulenburg observed, for instance: 'When William appears as an actual ruler, that is only his perfect right. The only question is whether the consequence can be endured in the long run.'[35] Although his govern-

12 Kaiser Wilhelm in 1900

New Perspective, March 1999, cover

ment had constantly to contend with the *Reichstag*, which blocked and mauled legislation, it is true to say that the Kaiser's will was the main force behind the Hohenlohe government:

- In the summer of 1887 it was he who decided to appoint Admiral von Tirpitz (see p. 139) to the state secretaryship at the Reich Navy Office, with a remit to build up a powerful German navy and Bülow to the Foreign Office to launch a new era of *Weltpolitik* (see p. 138).

Bülow entered the German Foreign Office in 1873 and 20 years later became ambassador in Rome

- Wilhelm was also the driving force in the government's efforts to weaken the SPD. Although Hohenlohe refused to go along with his demands for a coup, he did resurrect parts of Botho zu Eulenburg's bill (see above), but it was defeated on the floor of the *Reichstag*. A law designed to restrict trade union activities met a similar fate in August 1899.
- When the Prussian War Ministry proposed to modernize the Military Legal Code of 1845 by allowing court martials to be held in public, it met with Wilhelm's implacable opposition. Both the Prussian war minister and Reich foreign minister were dismissed for supporting this measure. Nevertheless in December 1898, as a result of persistent pressure from the Centre, the SPD and the Progressives, the reform was at last implemented.

For his last three years Hohenlohe was 'a pathetic figure – senile and excluded from policy making',[36] as well as being secretly dependent on financial handouts from the crown. Finally in October 1900 he was replaced by Count Bülow, who had been specially groomed by the Kaiser for the post of chancellor.

Bernhard von Bülow

Apart from Bismarck, Bülow was the ablest of Wilhelm's chancellors. He was, at least until 1905, trusted by him and, in most areas of government, allowed to use his discretion. Bülow regarded himself as Wilhelm's 'political chief of staff', whose task was to make personal rule function effectively, and he sought to maintain his influence with the monarch through 'the most byzantine forms of flattery'.[37] The key to success, he believed, was to create an alliance between the agrarian and industrial interests, and then 'reconcile, pacify, rally [and] unite' the population through a 'successful foreign policy'.[38] This was reinforced by the construction of a major battle fleet, which proved so popular that the government was able to exploit it 'as a principle means of secondary integration'.[39] To appease the agrarians and heavy industrialists, he avoided tackling such divisive subjects as tax reform and, after prolonged negotiations, increased the tariffs on grain and iron, while allowing most raw materials with the exception of timber to be imported freely. Nationally the tariff policy, which significantly increased the price of food, was unpopular, and in the election of 1903 Conservative losses and SPD gains led to a significant change in the party balance in the Reichstag, which resulted in the Centre enjoying a dominant position.

This policy was called *Sammlungspolitik* which means in German an attempt to collect together different groups and interests

From 1905 onwards, Bülow's system entered a protracted period of crisis, which ended in his dismissal in 1909. His government was badly shaken by the German diplomatic defeat over Morocco (see p. 140) and then by the savage attack by the left wing of the Centre party, supported by the SPD, on the German colonial administration in South West Africa, which was accused of brutality, corruption and incompetence. In

1907 Bülow's fortunes momentarily revived, when he fought a brilliant election, in which he persuaded the Liberal parties to co-operate with the Conservatives so that the domination of the Reichstag by an SPD–Centre 'Red–black' alliance could be avoided. Aided by considerable funds from finance and industry and with the support of the Pan-German and Navy League, he fought a brilliant campaign, which appealed to patriotism but studiously avoided reference to thorny domestic problems.

His success was short-lived and the new Conservative–Liberal bloc began rapidly to unravel when the Liberals attempted to exploit his dependence on them to demand reform of the Prussian franchise. The Conservatives in their turn ignored the financial plight of the Reich, which had witnessed a near doubling of the national debt since 1900, and again decided to vote against any form of income or property tax and even began to consider co-operation with the Centre party. It was, however, Bülow's handling of the *Daily Telegraph* affair in November 1908 which finally undermined his position with the Kaiser. The Kaiser had rashly agreed to have a conversation, which had taken place with Colonel Stuart Wortley after his state visit to Windsor, published in the *Daily Telegraph*. He had claimed, for instance, that he had thought up the military plan for defeating the Boers in the Anglo-Boer South African War of 1899–1902. Bülow was sent a draft of the interview but failed to read it. When it was published, it unleashed a storm of ridicule and anger in Germany, and momentarily united the parties in the *Reichstag* in demanding constitutional reform, which would diminish the royal prerogative. Briefly there was an opportunity to force the Kaiser to become a constitutional monarch, but the chance was lost, when the parties failed to keep a united front in the *Reichstag*. Instead, Bülow was able to get away with making the Kaiser promise to abide by the *existing* constitution. Wilhelm deeply resented the Chancellor's failure to spring to his defence, and once it was clear that Bülow was unable to get his bill for reforming the Reich's finances through the Reichstag, he had little option but to resign in June 1909. The *Daily Telegraph* affair and Bülow's resignation effectively ended the Kaiser's personal rule, although he still continued to intervene directly in military and foreign affairs.

See Document 33

Theobald von Bethmann Hollweg

Wilhelm's initial choices for successor ranged from General von der Goltz, who was the military adviser to the Sultan of Turkey, to Botho zu Eulenburg, the former Prussian minister–president, but in the end he was persuaded to appoint Bethmann Hollweg, the Reich secretary of state for the interior. Bethmann Hollweg's approach to government was essentially one of damage limitation rather than one of attempting to find root-and-branch solutions. He hoped to bring together the Liberals, Conservatives and the Centre to alleviate the main tensions in contemporary Germany, but this was not to be an easy task. His cautious

Bethmann Hollweg, 1856–1921, came from an eminent business family with a large estate in Brandenburg. He served in the Prussian civil service, becoming Prussian minister of the interior in 1905, and then in 1907 he became the Reich secretary of state for the interior

attempts to remove the worst abuses from the Prussian voting system (see p. 61) were regarded as too radical by the Conservatives and insufficiently radical by the National Liberals. Similarly, his efforts to reconcile the Poles by relaxing the full rigour of Bülow's Germanization policies, which had reversed Caprivi's more tolerant approach, met with violent opposition from the Conservatives and nationalist pressure groups without reconciling the Poles.

The election results of January 1912, in which the SPD became the single largest party in the *Reichstag* with 110 seats, merely exacerbated Bethmann's problems. Germany's humiliation in the second Moroccan crisis (see p. 142) infuriated the right, which bitterly attacked the government, while the SPD exploited rising food prices to attack the grain tariffs and the failure to introduce tax reform. This produced a complete deadlock in the *Reichstag* because mutual antipathy and suspicion still prevented the SDP and the Liberals from working together for any length of time.

The government was therefore 'forced more than ever to play for time, while doing what little it could to paper over the cracks in the Imperial fabric'.[40] Bethmann Hollweg thus attempted where possible to bypass the *Reichstag* and to stress that he stood above the quarrelling parties. Inevitably this made him more dependent on the Kaiser and the opinions of the bureaucrats, courtiers and generals who were close to him. Bethmann's weakness was illustrated by the crisis which blew up in the autumn of 1913, when a young lieutenant's insults to Alsatian recruits led to demonstrations in the town of Zabern in Alsace. The army overreacted

Impediments to SPD–Liberal co-operation

How possible was an alliance between the SPD and the Liberal parties in 1912? The SPD was an uneasy alliance between moderates or 'revisionists', who sought change constitutionally, and radicals, who were, theoretically at least, ready to wage a revolutionary struggle and thus opposed co-operation with the bourgeois parties. These two contradictory views were up to a point reconciled by (1) the Erfurt Programme of 1891, which combined an orthodox Marxist criticism of society with a set of moderate demands, which did not entail a revolution to implement, and (2) Karl Kautsky, who argued that, as capitalism was doomed and would inevitably collapse, a revolution as such was not needed. The moderates were greatly strengthened by the growth in the free trade unions (see p. 00), which in 1905 and 1906 actually managed to force the party to stop agitating for a political general strike. On communal health, housing and unemployment boards, town councils and provincial assemblies, as well as in the Baden *Landtag*, there were examples of co-operation between the SPD and the Liberal parties, but nationally it was possible only to achieve a fleeting co-operation. In 1912, for instance, the SPD voted with the National Liberals for measures which were intended to finance an expansion of the army because this would introduce the principle of taxing profits made from the increase in land value, but key groups in the National Liberals feared that they would have to pay for collaboration by agreeing to radical social reform and thus this co-operation remained exceptional.

and arrested the ringleaders. Privately Bethmann disapproved of its high-handedness, but, as the Kaiser supported the army, he was forced to defend it in the *Reichstag*, despite an overwhelming vote of no confidence. In a sense the Zabern affair was a 'lightning flash, which suddenly illuminated the horizon'.[41] It showed the fragility of Bethmann's government: it had no backing in the *Reichstag* and was dependent on an emperor, who was surrounded by a conservative military entourage which exaggerated the threat from the SPD and was preoccupied by Germany's increasing international isolation. It was, as we shall see, this 'siege mentality' that was to play so crucial a part in the crisis of July–August 1914 (see p. 00).

See Document 34

Conclusion: the house that Bismarck built

Initially the Bismarckian constitution represented a viable compromise, even if, as Wolfgang Mommsen argued, a 'skirted compromise'[42] between the conflicting demands of Prussia, the liberals and the individual states. However, it was a compromise that had no built-in flexibility, and by the 1880s it had become a straitjacket that distorted the constitutional development of Germany. As long as Bismarck remained in power, the German constitution had some coherence, but with his dismissal and the often farcical attempts by the Kaiser to implement personal rule, the Reich became what Wehler has called 'a polyocracy of rival centres of power'.[43] The *Reichstag*, the Crown, the bureaucracy, the army and the pressure groups all competed for power and, in effect, created a deadlock that paralysed the system. Bismarck's constitutional legacy was thus one of chaos rather than of authoritarianism.

Skirted compromise: a compromise that avoids the main problems

Could Germany have escaped from the Bismarckian straitjacket without the traumatic experiences of a lost war? Margaret Anderson suggests that without the war the Bismarckian system would in the end have evolved into a parliamentary regime: 'the jump need not have been violent. Perhaps the death of the Kaiser at eighty-three would have speeded a regime change – in 1941 – analogous to Spain's at the death of Franco at the same age in 1975.'[44] That is, however, 'virtual history' again! War in fact did intervene and German history took a different course . To what extent the *Kaiserreich* was ultimately responsible for the outbreak of that war is examined in the next chapter.

7 German Foreign Policy, 1871–1914

Introduction

It is a paradox that Bismarck, the diplomat, after 1871 is seen by some historians as a great force for peace, who presided with such moderation and flexibility over Germany's new position in Europe that he deserves the posthumous grant of the Nobel Peace Prize. Whereas Bismarck, the politician, is pilloried as the man who launched Germany on its unhappy *Sonderweg*. William Langer, in his classic book, *European Alliances and Alignments, 1871–90*, argues that 'no other statesman of his standing had ever before shown the same great moderation and sound political sense of the possible and desirable'. Yet was Bismarck, the diplomat, really such a paragon of virtue after 1871? Bruce Waller, for instance, has pointed out that Langer's views on German foreign policy 'were strongly coloured by the effort to take a fair-minded view after the excesses' of the propaganda of the Great War. Waller, on the contrary, points out that Bismarck 'created and preserved tension' by encouraging rivalry in the colonies and the Balkans and argues that at times 'Bismarck's actions would have led to war had it not been for the good sense of other European statesmen.'[1] Could it be argued that Bismarck set Germany on a collision path with its neighbours? He did take the key decision to ally with Austria, but unlike his successors he attempted to maintain some sort of alliance with Russia. In 1914 the world was, of course, very different from in 1890: public opinion was more jingoistic, although Bismarck had helped stoke those particular fires, and German strength had grown to a point where it provoked growing resentment in London, but it does seem unlikely that a statesman of Bismarck's calibre would have alienated Britain, France and Russia at the same time, as his successors had by 1914.

> After 1867 and the new settlement with the Hungarians (*Ausgleich*), officially Austria became Austria–Hungary, but in most books is still referred to as Austria

Key issues

- What were the aims of Bismarck's foreign policy in the 1870s?
- What were the consequences of the Eastern crisis, 1875–78?
- How contradictory was Bismarck's alliance system, 1879–90?
- Why did Bismarck create a German colonial empire?
- Why did Caprivi's 'New Course' in foreign policy fail?
- What were the motives behind Bülow's *Weltpolitik*?
- Why did Germany increasingly become isolated after 1904?
- Why did Germany go to war in 1914?

The new Bismarckian foreign policy, 1871–79

1871 was a major turning-point in Bismarck's foreign policy: between 1862 and 1871 Bismarck had created a new Europe, and now, like Metternich in 1815, he needed peace to preserve it.   The unification of Germany had marked a decisive shift in the balance of power in Europe. In Britain, Disraeli went so far as to argue in the House of Commons: 'This war represents the German revolution, a greater political event than the French revolution of the last century.'[2] Although the military and diplomatic balance had shifted from Paris to Berlin, the new German Reich was still a 'delicate compromise',[3] which could be destroyed by a hostile European coalition. Bismarck's priority was therefore to convince the great powers that Germany was a satiated power with no further territorial ambitions.

Bismarck's aims remained constant even though the diplomatic situation changed:

- He wished to give priority to domestic consolidation, while maintaining Germany's dominant position in Europe. It was of overriding importance to avoid the creation of a hostile alliance against the Reich.

- He needed therefore to isolate France, which had been humiliated by defeat and the loss of Alsace-Lorraine, or possibly appease it in areas where its policy represented no threat to Germany.
- He wished to see Austria–Hungary survive as a great power and act as a bulwark against Russian expansion into the Balkans.
- Good relations with Russia were 'the key to everything',[4] as it was both a potential ally of France and also the main rival of Austria–Hungary in the Balkans.

See Document 35

The League of the Three Emperors

The League of the Three Emperors is often seen as a deliberate attempt by Bismarck to isolate France, but it was initially a way of defusing mutual Austro-Russian distrust. The tsar was determined to prevent Austria from exploiting its increasingly good relations with Berlin to the detriment of Russia, and Bismarck was able skilfully to paper over the differences between the two powers in talks which culminated in the League of the Three Emperors in 1873. It was in many ways 'an empty frame',[5] but for the time being it enabled Bismarck to avoid making a choice between Russia and Austria.

The Three Emperors' League was negotiated on 6 June 1873 at Schönbrunn when the emperors of Germany, Austria–Hungary and Russia agreed to 'consult together' in the event of a crisis and 'to impose the maintenance of peace in Europe against all attempts to destroy it from whatever quarter they come'.[6] If joint military action were needed, a fresh agreement would have to be concluded

The league's inadequacies were quickly revealed by a sudden crisis which blew up with France in 1875. Bismarck had become sufficiently concerned by France's economic and military recovery to make a serious diplomatic misjudgment. He inspired a bellicose leader in the *Berliner Post*, on 8 April, entitled *Is War in Sight?*, which seemed to indicate that Germany was about to attack France. This impression was further strengthened when the German ambassador at St Petersburg began publicly to defend the idea of a preventive war against France. Bismarck was probably bluffing, but the reaction of Britain and Russia indicated the underlying changes in the European balance of power brought about by German unification. Both powers made it clear to Bismarck that they did not want to see the destruction of France. Bismarck rapidly managed to reassure them that he had no intention of attacking France and the crisis blew over, but the incident underlined the potential weakness of Germany's position in Europe and showed that the threat of further German expansion in Europe at the expense of France would eventually create the hostile coalition which Bismarck feared so much.

The eastern crisis, 1875–78

The league was subjected to a more testing challenge when Turkish power in the Balkans was undermined by a chain of events, which started in July 1875 with uprisings in Bosnia and Herzegovina. This threatened to create a power vacuum that both Austria and Russia would compete to fill. Bismarck attempted to mediate between Russia and Austria, while avoiding giving Russia the decisive backing the tsar requested. Initially this seemed to work, and Russia and Austria drew up plans for the peaceful partition of the Balkans. At Budapest in March 1877 Austria actually agreed to Russian military intervention at the price of acquiring Bosnia and Herzegovina, but once the Russians reached Constantinople eight months later the Russian government unilaterally negotiated at San Stefano a settlement with the Turks, which ignored the Budapest treaty. Britain reacted by sending a naval task force to the Straits, and, in an attempt to defuse what had become a dangerous international crisis, the powers appealed to Bismarck to summon a congress in Berlin to devise a compromise.

> In Bosnia and Herzegovina a predominantly Christian peasantry, many of whom were still serfs, were oppressively controlled by Muslim landowners. Thus social divisions coincided with religious and ethnic ones

Bismarck in his role as 'honest broker' dominated the Berlin negotiations. Yet, however hard he tried to be neutral, the very fact that he presided over a congress that stripped Russia of many of its gains from the Turkish war made the Russians bitterly resentful of Germany's 'false friendship'.[7] Under Bismarck's skilful chairmanship, the congress managed to find at least temporary solutions to some of the intractable problems of the Eastern question. The large Bulgaria, which the Russians arbitrarily recognized at San Stefano, was broken up into three parts in an effort to minimize Russian influence, while Austria was given the right to occupy, but not annex, Bosnia and Herzegovina. Although the Russians did make some gains, the congress was generally viewed in Russia as 'a European coalition against Russia under the leadership of Prince Bismarck'.[8]

Bismarck's alliance system

The Austro-German Dual Alliance, 1879

One consequence of the Berlin Congress was the dissolution of the Three Emperors' League. Initially Bismarck attempted to revive it, but Russia's resentment at his chairmanship of the congress made this an impossibility, and he began in November 1878 to work towards a defensive alliance with Austria–Hungary. Over the next twelve months Russo-German relations continued to deteriorate. On the international commissions set up to carry out the decisions of the Berlin Congress, the German representatives usually co-operated closely with their British and Austrian counterparts, and in July 1879 the German government's decision to levy tariffs on grain imports damaged Russia's trade with Germany (see p. 113). Wilhelm I wished to remain loyal to the tsar, who in August warned him 'of the sad consequences [of Bismarck's policies] to our good neighbourly relations by embittering our two nations against each other'.[9] Only by threatening to resign did Bismarck persuade him to agree to the Austrian alliance, which was at last signed on 7 October 1879. Its terms were:

- Should one power be attacked by Russia, the other would come to its rescue with 'the whole war strength' of its empire.
- If either empire was attacked by a third power, the other would adopt a neutral but friendly attitude.
- The treaty was to last five years but could be renewed.
- It was secret, but in the event of another major crisis with Russia its details would be leaked to the tsar to discourage him from taking any further action.

The Dual Alliance was a 'landmark in European History'.[10] In 1854 Bismarck had accused the Prussian government of 'tying the trim . . . Prussian frigate to the worm eaten old Austrian galleon'. Had he in fact done exactly this in 1879? Helmut Böhme and Lothar Gall argue that Bismarck intended to create a large central European bloc (*Mitteleuropa*) which would be able to compete with the Russian and British empires.[11] On the other hand, Bismarck was also convinced that it was in Germany's interests for Austria to survive as a great power to block Russian expansion in the Balkans. Up to a point the Dual Alliance tied Germany to Vienna, but it also gave Berlin considerable influence over Austrian foreign policy, which would in a real crisis enable Bismarck to ensure that the Austrians did not provoke an unnecessary war with Russia.

By 1914 it is, however, arguable that Bismarck's reservations of 1854 were proved more right than wrong. See pp. 000–000 and Document 36

The Alliance of the Three Emperors

Even while Bismarck was concluding the Austrian alliance, he was putting out diplomatic feelers to St Petersburg. By the autumn of 1879 the tsar accepted that he had little alternative but to improve Russo-German relations, and sent a mission to Berlin to discuss a possible agreement. This was a diplomatic victory for Bismarck, as it vindicated his argument that an Austro-German alliance would force Russia to adopt a more flexible policy. Bismarck hoped to revive the Three Emperors' League, which would open the way up to better relations between Vienna and St Petersburg and continue to keep France isolated. Little progress could be made until Austria was ready to give up the prospect of co-operation with Britain against Russia, but once Gladstone won the general election of April 1880, British foreign policy became less hawkish and the prospect of an Anglo-Austrian agreement receded. Bismarck was now able to exert pressure on Vienna to respond to Russian demands less negatively, but to square the circle, he also had to mislead the Russians into believing that the Dual Alliance did not automatically guarantee Germany's defence of Austria–Hungary in the event of a Russian attack. The Three Emperors' Alliance was signed on 18 June 1881. The treaty was in the first instance to last three years. The Three Powers agreed that:

- The Straits should be closed to the warships of all nations, which would stop Britain threatening to send its navy into the Black Sea.

- Austria conceded the eventual reunification of Bulgaria, while Russia agreed that at some time in the future Austria should annex Bosnia and Herzegovina.
- If a member of the League went to war with a fourth power, unless it was the Ottoman Empire, the other two powers would remain neutral.
- There were to be no territorial changes to the Ottoman Empire without the agreement of the three signatory powers.

The Triple Alliance, 1882

In retrospect the Alliance of the Three Emperors was 'little more than an armistice',[12] as it provided no long-term solution to Austro-Russian rivalry in the Balkans. Russian foreign policy remained unpredictable. The new tsar, Alexander III, received conflicting advice from the professional diplomats on the one side, who wanted good relations with Germany, and the leading Pan-Slavs, on the other side, who argued that a struggle between the German and Slav races led by Russia was inevitable. Bismarck, alarmed that the Pan-Slavs were beginning to establish contact with Russian sympathizers in the French army and press, attempted to strengthen the Dual Alliance, so that it would deter even the most fanatical Pan-Slav, without, however, discouraging the pro-German party in Russia. Consequently, when Italy, alarmed by the French occupation of Tunis which it regarded as its own sphere of interest, sought in 1882 an alliance with Austria, Bismarck immediately suggested expanding it to a triple alliance, and agreed to the following terms:

> The Pan-Slav movement was formed in 1858 and saw Turkey, Austria and increasingly Germany as Russia's main enemies

- Both the Central Powers were now committed to supporting Italy in the remote chance of an attack from France.
- Italy would assist them only if they were attacked by two other powers (effectively France and Russia).

The real gain for Germany was that Austria was now freed from the threat of an Italian attack on her southern flank should war break out with Russia. Austria's position was further buttressed first by the Serbian alliance in June 1881 and then by the Romanian alliance in 1883, which Germany also joined, thereby turning it into 'a clear defensive alliance against Russia'.[13] Despite this anti-Russian front, Bismarck also successfully persuaded the tsar to renew the Three Emperors' Treaty both by refusing demands at home for further tariff increases on Russian grain imports, and by encouraging German banks to subscribe to Russian loans.

Bismarck's foray into imperialism, 1884–85

In 1884–85 Germany acquired a colonial empire five times the size of the German Reich (see Map 5). This has puzzled historians, since Bismarck had always scornfully dismissed colonies as an expensive luxury for a newly-formed state like Germany comparable to 'a poverty stricken Polish nobleman providing himself with silks and sables when he needed shirts'.[14] Taylor has argued that the colonial annexations of 1884 were an attempt 'to make [Germany] presentable to France [by] provok[ing] a quarrel with England so that Franco-German friendship should have the solid basis of anglo-phobia'. Certainly Bismarck did all he could to exploit French resentment at the British occupation of Egypt which had taken place in 1881. He remarked to the French ambassador in 1880: 'I want you to turn your eyes from Metz and Strasburg by helping you elsewhere.'[15] A Franco-German rapprochement would pay dividends in Europe for Bismarck, and show both Britain and Russia that the mutual hostility of the two countries was not necessarily permanent.

This may well have been *one* of Bismarck's motives, but there were others as well:

- Bismarck was not unresponsive to the cries for help from the North German colonial traders. P. M. Kennedy, for instance, argues that Bismarck's policy was a calculated response to the pressure on German trade in South West Africa and the South Seas.[16]
- Alternatively, there are the arguments that Bismarck's foray into imperialism was determined by domestic politics: he could use the colonial issue to divide the Liberals, as the National Liberal Party and the newly-founded *Kolonialverein* (Colonial League) were pressing for colonies, while the Progressives opposed them. This assessment is given powerful backing by the Foreign Office official, Friedrich von Holstein, who observed that Bismarck's colonialism 'was scarcely more than an election stunt'.[17] Another domestic advantage of colonialism was that it could be exploited to provide an immediate quarrel with the British, once Crown Prince Frederick came to the throne (see p. 116).
- Bismarck, like other European leaders, also realized that an exciting colonial policy with easy conquests could unite the German people behind him and 'legitimize the status quo' of his government. H.-U. Wehler has called this ' manipulated social imperialism'.[18]
- Mary Townsend argued in 1930 that Bismarck was at heart a committed imperialist, who had pursued a policy of 'cautious preparation',[19] but in light of the arguments above this view is hard to sustain.

See p. 107 and Document 20

In the spring of 1884 the German government granted formal protection to German trading stations in South West Africa, the Cameroons, Togoland and New Guinea to forestall British claims to the area (see Map 5). Bismarck took the obvious step of distracting the British by exploiting Anglo-French differences in Egypt, but he also needed French support to ensure that Germany's interests were protected in the Congo and West Africa. Suspicious that the British were using Portugal's weakness to increase their own influence in the Congo, he refused to recognize the Anglo-Portuguese Treaty of February 1884, and with French assistance

The foundation of Germany's colonial empire

Bismarck hoped that the trading companies themselves would be responsible for administering the new colonies, while the Reich would simply provide external protection. In fact, once having intervened in Africa, Bismarck found that he could not run Germany's colonial empire on the cheap. In West and East Africa the chartered companies proved so incompetent that Berlin was landed with responsibility for both internal administration and defence. For instance, the East African Company drove the African population into open revolt in 1888, and was only saved by the dispatch of German troops, while the South West African Company was so inefficient that Berlin had to send out an imperial commissioner to take control. In 1889 the New Guinea Company went bankrupt.

pushed the Portuguese into proposing an international conference, which was held in Berlin in November 1884. By deciding at the congress to set up the Congo Free State, the frontiers of which were to remain open to international commerce, the powers forced Britain to abandon its plans to control the Congo Basin indirectly through Portugal.

The Bismarckian alliance system under pressure

By the spring of 1885 Bismarck's attentions were once more concentrated on Europe. In France the ultra-nationalist General Boulanger had just been appointed war minister, while the eruption of the Bulgarian crisis again plunged the Balkans into turmoil. The crisis, which destroyed the Three Emperors' League and brought Europe close to war, was caused by the unification of Bulgaria with Eastern Roumelia in September 1885 under Prince Alexander, who was determined to liberate the state from Russian influence. Any chance of Austro-Russian co-operation was destroyed by Serbia's pre-emptive attack on the new Bulgaria, which it now regarded as a dangerous rival in the Balkans. When Serbian troops were decisively defeated at Slivnitza, the Austrians threatened to occupy Serbia if the Bulgarians invaded. The Russians retaliated by strengthening their influence in Bulgaria and forcing Alexander to abdicate. Inevitably this revived British and Austrian fears of a Russian occupation of Bulgaria, and the Alliance of the Three Emperors collapsed.

At the Congress of Berlin in 1878 Eastern Roumelia had been created in order to prevent the emergence of a 'big' Bulgaria

Both Austria and Britain looked to Berlin to take the lead against Russia, but Bismarck was determined not to be pushed into confrontation at the very time that Boulanger was urging a war of revenge against Germany. He therefore again adopted a dual strategy towards Russia, whilst isolating France in western Europe. He attempted to persuade both Austria and Russia, whom he described as 'two savage dogs', to divide the Balkans into spheres of influence, while making it clear to Vienna that he would not be dragged into war against Russia. He also

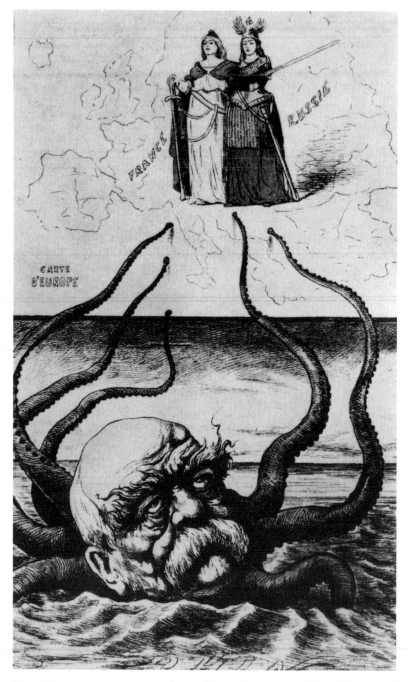

13 A French cartoon commenting on Bismarck's attempts to keep France and Russia apart in the 1880s

Imperial War Museum, no. Q81754

persuaded Britain, Italy and Austria to negotiate the first Mediterranean Agreement in February 1887 with the aim of containing Russia in the Balkans and the Straits. At the same time Bismarck also took steps to isolate France in western Europe. The Triple Alliance was renewed in February 1887 and he encouraged an Italian–Spanish agreement, which was aimed at preventing French colonial expansion in North Africa. By May France was, as Langer observed, 'completely hedged about'.[20]

The Reinsurance Treaty, 18 June 1887

Any improvement in Germany's relations with Russia depended on the outcome of the struggle to influence the tsar, which was bitterly waged between the Pan-Slavs and the traditionally pro-German Russian Foreign Office. Although in March 1887 the tsar rejected Pan-Slav demands for a total break with Germany, he still refused to renew the Three Emperors Treaty, and instead negotiated a new three-year agreement with Berlin, which was signed on 18 June 1887. Its terms were:

- Both empires were pledged to be neutral in a war fought against a third power unless Germany attacked France, or Russia attacked Austria.
- Germany recognized the rights 'historically acquired' by Russia in the Balkans – particularly in Bulgaria.
- Turkey was not to allow the navy of a power hostile to Russia to pass through the Straits. If it did, both Germany and Russia would regard it as an act hostile towards themselves.

Historians and the Reinsurance Treaty

Arguably, to quote Otto Pflanze, 'no treaty concluded by Bismarck has been subjected to greater scrutiny and more controversy'.[21] Ever since the publication of the treaty in 1919, historians have disagreed about whether it contradicted the Dual Alliance with Austria by recognizing Russia's 'right historically acquired' in the Balkans. Pflanze, A. J. P. Taylor and William Langer insist that it did not, as Bismarck had often suggested dividing the Balkans into Austrian and Russian spheres of influence. Yet C. J. Lowe stresses that it 'conflicted with the spirit, if not the letter, of the Dual Alliance of 1879'.[22] In Gall's opinion, 'had it come to the notice of the other side it would have shattered the credibility of German policy, almost certainly brought about the collapse of Bismarck's intricate system of alliances and left Germany largely isolated'.[23] It contradicted the Mediterranean Agreement, the point of which was to deter Russia from expanding into the Balkans. Admittedly Germany did not sign this agreement, but Bismarck had encouraged its negotiation. Historians also argue about the significance of the treaty. To Langer it signified the completion of an 'intricate system of checks and balances which was intended to preserve the peace of Europe' but Taylor regarded it 'at best' as a temporary and not very effective means for dealing with the crisis of 1885–87, a view which is essentially shared by Gall.[24]

The Reinsurance Treaty failed to calm the tension in the Balkans. When Prince Ferdinand of Coburg, who had been born in Vienna and had served with the Austrian army, was elected to the Bulgarian throne in July 1887, the Pan-Slavs whipped up a vitriolic press campaign against Germany, which was accused of secretly supporting Austria. In the autumn it seemed that Russia was about to invade Bulgaria. To stop this, Bismarck applied financial pressure by ordering the *Reichsbank* not to accept Russian bonds as collateral security for loans raised in Germany. This led to a sudden collapse of confidence in Russian credit, and so discouraged Russia from occupying Bulgaria and risking war with Austria. In December Bismarck, again quite contrary to the spirit of the Reinsurance Treaty, further strengthened the position of Austria by persuading Britain and Italy to negotiate a second Mediterranean Agreement aimed at keeping Russia out of Bulgaria and Turkey.

Although these measures deterred the tsar from sending troops into Bulgaria, the Russians did not stop their efforts to undermine Ferdinand. They also looked to Paris for the loans which Berlin was no longer ready to raise. Inevitably this strengthened Franco-Russian relations, but neither side was as yet ready for an alliance. When Wilhelm II came to the throne in June 1888 (see p. 117), and began to urge on Bismarck a British alliance, the tsar belatedly offered to renew the Reinsurance Treaty permanantly, but Bismarck was dismissed in March 1890 before negotiations could begin.

The 'New Course' in foreign policy

After Bismarck's dismissal, German Foreign Office officials advised his successor, General Leo von Caprivi, not to renew the Reinsurance Treaty with Russia. They feared that if details of the treaty leaked out, Russia would blackmail Germany by threatening to reveal its contradictions to Britain and Austria. Caprivi agreed and began to work for a new alliance system or 'New Course', which would associate Britain with Germany's two allies, Italy and Austria, and so hold in check both Russia and France. He was sure that Germany was now strong enough to renounce Bismarck's complicated system of checks and balances and to ally more closely with states with which it seemed to have a common interest. The lapsing of the Reinsurance Treaty was a turning-point in European history and brought to an end the Bismarckian diplomatic system. It led to the Franco-Russian Alliance of 1894, and marked the beginning of a period of increasing international instability which ultimately resulted in the outbreak of the Great War.

Even before the Reinsurance Treaty had officially terminated, the German government had already approached the British government with a proposal to settle any outstanding colonial disagreements. The British drove a hard bargain. In return for Germany giving up its claims to Zanzibar and extensive areas of East Africa, they ceded Heligoland, a strategically important island which dominated the mouths of the Elbe and the Weser rivers (see Maps 4 and 5).

Once it became clear that this *entente coloniale* was not going to lead to Britain joining the Triple Alliance, an increasing volume of criticism, particularly from the colonial pressure groups, began to be directed at Caprivi. His successor, Hohenlohe, whose cousin was the president of the German Colonial Society, realised that public opinion would not let Germany simply opt out of the rush for colonies. Consequently, in 1895 Hohenlohe and Marshall, the state secretary at the Foreign Office, began to focus on building up German influence in South Africa (see Map 5). It was a region with a large number of German immigrants, who had close cultural links with the Boers. German capital had made considerable investments there and a German colony already existed in South West Africa. Marshall hoped to be able to purchase the Portuguese colonies of Mozambique and Angola, and, if possible, turn the Boer republic of Transvaal into a protectorate, thereby creating a solid block of territory under German control.

The economic significance of the Transvaal had been transformed by the discovery of gold there in 1886. Foreign prospectors and adventurers, a large number of whom were British, poured in. Inevitably this posed a challenge to the supremacy of the Boer population, and Paul Krüger, the President of the Transvaal, began to look to Germany for support against the growing pressure from the British in Cape Colony. By the mid-nineties the Germans already dominated the Transvaal economy: they controlled the National Bank, held the whisky and dynamite monopolies, and supplied the state's water. Consequently, when Cecil Rhodes, the Prime Minister of Cape Colony, on his own initiative launched a badly-planned and unsuccessful attempt to overthrow Krüger, the so-called 'Jameson raid', the German government, egged on by the Kaiser, seized the chance to champion the Boers. The Kaiser at first wanted to declare the Transvaal a German protectorate, send military aid to Krüger and then summon a congress in Berlin, which would redraw the map of South Africa, but in the end he was persuaded that, because of British sea power, these were just empty threats. Instead he sent a telegram to Krüger, which congratulated him on having maintained the independence of the Transvaal. However illegal the raid had been, this telegram was a diplomatic blunder. It did much to turn British public opinion against Germany, and failed to win any support from either France or Russia. Yet at the same time it produced an explosion of support for imperialism within Germany.

See Document 37

Imperialism and navalism: the Bülow period, 1897–1909

On December 1897 Bülow announced a new programme of *Weltpolitik*. The motives for this have been the subject of considerable debate by contemporary historians. Mommsen[25] has analysed four main arguments:

See Document 38

Imperialism: a policy aimed at acquiring an empire

Weltpolitik: literally world policy or, in other words, a policy aimed at acquiring a worldwide colonial empire

The Germans seized Kiao-Chow in November 1897; in December 1899 Britain renounced to Germany all its rights over western Samoa

- The semi-Marxist analysis, the best-known exponent of which is George Hallgarten, attributes imperialism to pressure from big business and its insatiable need for markets.
- The Fritz Fischer thesis explicitly argues that Germany was ready to fight an imperialist war to become a great power.
- Eckart Kehr, the brilliant young Weimar historian, and his later disciples, particularly Volker Berghahn and Hans-Ulrich Wehler, argue that imperialism was a defensive strategy employed by the ruling élites to counter democratization.
- A more subtle argument, put forward by John Röhl, is that imperialism was just one element in the way the élites responded to modernization and the emergence of modern mass culture.

Of these four arguments, the Hallgarten approach is the most simplistic. German industry was not so much interested in colonies in Africa but rather in export opportunities in Europe, the Balkans, South America and South Africa. German imperialism was primarily an ideological and political policy. It was a product of the popular belief in the struggle for survival between nations, partly also a reaction to the humiliation over the Krüger telegram and the desire by the government to pursue a popular policy. For Bülow, *Weltpolitik* had much in common with Disraeli's policy of some thirty years earlier. He was convinced that 'only a successful foreign policy can help to reconcile, pacify, rally, unite'.[26] In this sense he was following a policy of social imperialism which would unite the middle classes, the bourgeois parties and the Conservatives behind the government and stop the rise of the SPD. Thus it was not surprising that German colonial policy was erratic and provocative. As Matthew Seligmann and Roderick McLean have written, 'expansion anywhere at any time was always welcome to the German government, whose members kept their eye on every corner of the globe seeking favorable opportunities to obtain territorial trophies that they could present as successes to the German public'.[27] Through its opportunism Germany contrived, at one time or another, to alienate all the great powers, yet as soon as the situation threatened to escalate into a major international incident Germany usually retreated. The total sum of its efforts by 1907 were Kiao-Chow, Britain's share of Samoa and several of the former Spanish islands in the Pacific (See Map 5).

Many of the reasons for the development of *Weltpolitik* also applied to the construction of the German navy. It was a visible symbol of Germany's great power status and a guarantee that it would not suffer further humiliation at Britain's hands. Structuralist historians like Kehr and Berghahn argue that its construction was essentially an attempt to appease leaders of heavy industry and encourage co-operation between the Conservatives and National Liberals against the SPD in the election of 1898. It was certainly popular with heavy industry, but the Conservatives and the agrarians were more sceptical about it. Arguably, its significance in 'the domestic political context' lay in its potential to become, as the Kaiser put it, 'a living embodiment of the unity of the Empire'.[28] In this role it was, up to a point, successful. Unlike the army, which was still Prussian in spirit, it was perceived to be a genuinely national institution.

The launching of the German naval programme in 1898 led to growing tension and an arms race with Britain, which by 1912, in the words of the Austrian foreign minister, had become the 'dominant element of the international situation'.[29] The German government planned to build within 20 years a German fleet of 60 battleships, which was intended for action against the British in the North Sea. This was, however, a long-term aim, but constructing the fleet became an end in its own right for Admiral Tirpitz, the imperial naval secretary. David Kaiser calls him 'a true cold war warrior', who 'continually stressed England's supposed threat to Germany's world position to justify the fleet's existence, while pushing the date of any clash of arms further into the future'.[30]

See Document 39

The odd mixture of weakness and provocation that so marked German foreign policy can be seen during the crucial years of 1904–06, when three major developments took place which radically changed the international situation:

- the Anglo-French *Entente* of 1904, the centrepiece of which was French agreement not to block British plans for financial reform in Egypt, provided Britain recognized France's right to maintain law and order in Morocco;
- the Russo-Japanese war of 1904–05, which resulted in Russia's defeat and withdrawal from China, opened the way up to the Anglo-Rusian colonial *entente* of 1907;
- the French attempt to occupy Morocco in 1905 as a result of agreement with Britain.

Entente: understanding or friendship between two states

Concerned that the *Entente Cordiale* was the first step in an Anglo-French–Russian realignment against Germany, Bülow decided to challenge the right of the French to control Morocco. Germany had a strong case because, according to the Madrid Convention of 1880, it should also

Alfred von Tirpitz, 1849–1930

He joined the Prussian navy in 1865, and by the 1890s he had become a leading advocate of building up a German fleet which could challenge the British in their own home waters. His intention was to create a fleet of 60 capital ships which would be able to force the British to make major colonial concessions. He hoped to build the fleet in stages, but this tactic failed once Britain responded by increasing the size of its own fleet. By 1914 Tirpitz realized that the German fleet was too weak to challenge the British and therefore agreed to the building of submarines. In 1916 he was dismissed. After the war he became a militant anti-Republican and supported plans for a right-wing dictatorship.

have been consulted about Morocco's future. Bülow was sure that neither Britain nor Russia, which had not only been defeated by the Japanese, but also faced growing internal unrest, would support the French. He was optimistically convinced that both the Dual Alliance and the Anglo-French *Entente* would be destroyed, that a new Russo-German alliance would emerge and that France would consequently be forced to come to terms with Germany without the risk of war. Thus when in early 1905 the French government ignored all warnings from Berlin and sent a mission to Fez with instructions to start reforming the Moroccan administration, the Germans demanded a conference on the future of Morocco. Initially Berlin gained a significant diplomatic success: the French cabinet agreed and, bowing to massive German pressure, Delcassé, the foreign minister, resigned in June 1905. Then in July the Kaiser and Tsar Nicholas II met at Björkö and signed a defensive alliance which would operate against any power in Europe. Nicholas was assured that the Moroccan crisis was a 'stepping stone' to better Franco-German relations.

As a result of the 1905 revolution, Russia had become a semi-constitutional monarchy and the Tsar's authority was weakened

Yet these successes were purely temporary, and by April 1906 Germany had suffered a crushing defeat. Berlin failed to break up the Franco-Russian alliance, as the Russian government overruled the tsar and refused to abandon it, and in November 1905 let the Björkö agreement lapse. The *Entente* was significantly strengthened when the British government came down firmly on the side of the French, and even authorized secret military staff talks between the British and French armies on the subject of sending an expeditionary force to France in the event of war with Germany. When the Moroccan conference opened at Algeciras in January 1906, Germany secured the backing of only Austria and Morocco. The other nine states agreed that France had a special interest in Morocco, although Germany did win the concession that the powers should enjoy equal economic rights within Morocco. All in all, Berlin suffered a major diplomatic setback. By insisting on a conference and defending the independence of Morocco, the German government had excluded the possibility of negotiating a separate deal with France.

See Document 40

For his last three years in power, Bülow continued to pay lip-service to *Weltpolitik*, but he became increasingly anxious to slow down the tempo of naval construction and find some sort of compromise with Britain. The financial burden of naval rearmament weighed ever more heavily on the Reich's finances, but public opinion and the agitation of the Navy League, as well as Tirpitz's determination to press on with the production of at least three battleships a year to counter Britain's new Dreadnought 'super' battleships, ensured that no progress could be made. In Morocco Bülow was more successful when he negotiated an economic agreement with France in February 1909. By this, Germany recognized France's special political interests in Morocco as long as both countries were able to share equally in its economic development. Only in the Bosnian crisis did he win what David Kaiser calls 'a cheap diplomatic success',[31] when he unconditionally supported the Austrian annexation of Bosnia–Herzegovina and forced Russia to back down.

The Bosnian crisis 1908–09

The Russians proposed a deal with Austria whereby their warships would be able to pass through the Straits while this right would still be denied to the other powers. In exchange, Austria would annex Bosnia and Herzegovina, which it had administered since 1878 (see p. 129). This was agreed to informally in September, although A. P. Izvolsky, the Russian foreign minister, later claimed that it was understood by both parties that the decision would have to be confirmed by a European conference, but this was never put down on paper. The Austrians duly annexed Bosnia–Herzegovina in October, while the Russians found little international support for their plans at the Straits. In both Russia and Serbia, which eventually hoped to make these provinces part of a Greater Serb state, there were strong protests and even demands for war against Austria. Izvolsky proposed a conference of the great powers, but the Austrians immediately vetoed this proposal, as it feared a repetition of what had happened at Algeciras, where Germany had been heavily outvoted. What made the crisis so dangerous was that Austria, which had the unconditional backing of Germany, was ready to fight Serbia even if she were supported by Russia. Bülow had given Aehrenthal a 'blank cheque', when he informed him on October 30: 'I shall regard whatever decision you come to as the appropriate one.'[32] His intention was to isolate Russia and break up the Franco-Russian alliance. The Russians received backing from neither the French, who were busy negotiating the Moroccan Agreement with Germany, nor the British. Russian attempts to persuade the Germans to mediate were ruthlessly brushed aside and the Russian government had no option but to accept the annexation, especially as it was not ready to fight a war. The crisis seriously damaged Russia's relations with Germany and Austria, and made co-operation in the Balkans much more difficult, whilst at the same time bringing Russia and Serbia together. D. C. B. Lieven argues that German behaviour during the Bosnian crisis 'exerted a real influence over the way in which the Russian government handled the crisis of July 1914'.[33]

Bethmann Hollweg and the coming of war

Historians have been inclined to play down the significance of Bethmann Hollweg's thinking on foreign policy partly because he rose within the ranks of the Prussian home civil service. Yet he did have strong views on the foreign policy Germany should follow. Unlike Bülow, for whom *Weltpolitik* was essentially a policy of 'spin', Bethmann Hollweg reverted to the concept of creating a compact empire in central Africa and Asia Minor. He hoped that he could achieve this through agreement with Britain, but he was going to drive a hard bargain: he would only limit the size of the German fleet if Britain was prepared to remain neutral in a continental war.

This renewed determination of the German government to 'take its place in the sun' was shown in the second Moroccan crisis in 1911. The German foreign minister, Kiderlen-Wächter, believed that if enough pressure was exerted on Paris, it would cede the French Congo to Berlin, which in turn would enable the German government later to blackmail

The second Moroccan crisis

French troops were sent to occupy Fez in May 1911 to protect the Europeans working there from large-scale rioting. It rapidly became obvious that the French were not going to withdraw and had every intention of turning Morocco into a protectorate. Inevitably this broke the 1906 and 1909 agreements and played into Germany's hands. Kiderlen Wachter warned the French that if they remained in Morocco, Germany would insist on some form of territorial compensation. As they made no response, on July 1 the German government sent the *Panther*, a gunboat, to the south Moroccan port of Agadir.

Brussels into surrendering much of the Belgian Congo too. When Britain strongly objected to these demands, Kiderlen initially considered war, but then, owing to pressure from the Kaiser and Tirpitz, who did not want to risk his fleet at this juncture, a sharp decline in the stock market, and the reluctance of Austria to fight, the German government drew back and accepted a compromise involving an offer of a small slice of the French Congo.

The Moroccan crisis was 'a decisive caesura'. The nationalist pressure groups and the Conservatives bitterly condemned the government for its weakness and 'the idea increasingly took root in German public opinion that Germany had no prospect of realizing her global political ambitions without a major European war'.[34] Added urgency was given to this conclusion by the General Staff's assessment that the military balance of power was shifting against Germany. It was particularly concerned by the expansion of the Russian army and the construction of strategic railways in the western provinces, and predicted ominously that Russia, contrary to the assumptions of the Schlieffen Plan (see p. 144), would be able to mobilize *before* France could be defeated. Bethmann was pessimistically convinced that 'the future belongs to Russia which grows and grows and weighs upon us like a heavier and heavier nightmare'.[35] These assessments made a rapprochement with Britain all the more important, but the informal negotiations with Lord Haldane in Berlin in February 1912 came to nothing because Tirpitz, with the Kaiser's support, refused to slow down the tempo of naval construction unless Britain committed itself to neutrality in the event of a German–French war.

In the autumn of 1912 the Balkan states went to war against Turkey, and by December had virtually driven the Turks out of Europe. The sheer speed and scale of the victory created an acute crisis for the great powers. Austria was now faced with a greatly strengthened Serbia, which had occupied part of Albania and enjoyed the support of Russia. Initially the Kaiser himself was inclined to reject Austrian appeals for help, but on Bethmann's advice he came round to seeing that, in the interests of Germany's own position in Europe, Austria could not be weakened. The crisis deepened on 2 December when Bethmann stated in the *Reichstag* that if the Austrians were attacked by Russia, 'then we would fight for the

See Document 36

The German government indicated through the Anglo-German financier, Sir Ernest Cassel, that the Germans would like to discuss the naval question with a British minister. Haldane, the war minister, who was, anyway, about to visit Germany, was thus sent to begin negotiations

maintenance of our own future and security'.[36] Commenting on this speech two days later, Sir Edward Grey, the British foreign minister, reminded the German ambassador that Britain could not stand back and allow France to be defeated. The Kaiser was infuriated by Grey's message and on 8 December convened a 'war council' which was attended by the army and naval chiefs. The conference agreed that war was ultimately unavoidable, but, at Tirpitz's behest, decided to delay it until the Kiel Canal was finished in the summer of 1914. In the meantime, public opinion was to be prepared for the inevitable hostilities.

The 'war council' of 8 December, 1912

How important was this conference? John Röhl and Fritz Fischer regard it as a key date on the road to war, although Wofgang Mommsen and David Kaiser are more sceptical.[37] As Röhl has commented, 'Historians of all shades of opinion have thus placed themselves in the unusual position of arguing to a certain extent against the sources. For them the evidence . . . is too sharp, too exact, "too good to be true"'.[38] Röhl does show convincingly that, after the conference, steps were taken to prepare Germany for war, such as increasing the size of the army bill, building up gold reserves and laying in food supplies. At the very least, as Matthew Seligmann and Roderick McLean argue, the conference 'is best seen not in terms of a German decision for war, but in terms of a decision against long-term peace'.[39]

By the time Franz Ferdinand was assassinated in Sarajevo, the German government was ready to seize any opportunity to stabilize Germany's position in Europe, even if that entailed war. On 28 June Archduke Franz Ferdinand, the heir to the Austrian throne, and his wife were assassinated at Sarajevo by Gavrilo Princip, who was closely associated with the Serb terrorist group, The Black Hand. The assassination confirmed Austrian suspicions of Serbia, and provided an excuse to eliminate the Serb 'menace'. To succeed, however, Vienna needed German support in case of Russian intervention, and also had to move quickly while the shock of the assassination was still fresh in the minds of the European governments. On 3 July Count Hoyos was sent to Berlin with a letter from the emperor, which openly stated that Austrian policy was to eliminate Serbia as 'a political factor in the Balkans'.[40] After discussions with the Kaiser and Bethmann Hollweg, he got the crucial backing necessary – the so-called 'blank cheque'.

In 1928 Sidney Fay wrote: 'The Kaiser and his advisors on July 5 and 6 were not criminals plotting the Great War; they were simpletons putting "a noose about their necks" and handing the other end of the rope to a stupid and clumsy adventurer, who now felt free to go as far as he liked.'[41] In fact, detailed research by Fritz Fischer, Volker Berghahn and others has now shown that Bethmann Hollweg knew precisely what he was doing and was taking a calculated risk. If decisive action against

Serbia could be kept localized without Russian or French intervention, it was most likely that the south-eastern European states could be realigned behind Germany, the Franco-Russian alliance would collapse and the way to colonial expansion would be opened up. If, as was all too possible, a continental war broke out, it was better that it came sooner rather than later while the balance of forces still favoured Germany.

See Document 36

The chances of avoiding a European war were weakened by the length of time the Austrians took to draft the ultimatum, which was only sent to Belgrade on 23 July. The crucial part of the ultimatum insisted that Serbia should, under the supervision of Austrian officials, implement a whole series of anti-terrorist measures. When Belgrade rejected this, Vienna broke off diplomatic relations and on 28 July declared war on Serbia. The initial reaction of the great powers to the Austrian ultimatum was conciliatory. The Kaiser reversed his bellicose position and decided that an Austrian diplomatic rather than military triumph over Serbia would be sufficient. On 27 July the British put forward a plan for a conference of ambassadors to meet in London to discuss the crisis. This was welcomed by the Italians and the French, but the Germans, by now aware of the threatening scale of the crisis, argued that direct Austro-Russian talks would be more effective, but they did nothing to facilitate these. For Berlin the priority was, as Bethmann Hollweg told his ambassador in Vienna, 'solely one of finding a way to realise Austria's desired aim, that of cutting the vital chord of Greater Serbia propaganda without it at the same time bringing on a world war, and if the latter cannot be avoided in the end, of improving the conditions under which we have to wage it where possible'.[42]

Possibly, given more time, war could have been avoided, but in both Germany and Russia the military planners were desperate to mobilize their forces before hostilities broke out. Once the Austrians declared war on Serbia and began to bombard Belgrade, the Russian government issued orders for a partial mobilization of the army on 28 July. Forty-eight hours later this was changed to full mobilization, despite the initial hesitation of the tsar and a personal appeal from the Kaiser. Given the Schlieffen Plan, which depended on defeating the French *before* the

---

The debate on the Schlieffen Plan

Up to 1905 the German army kept open the option of attacking Russia first, in the event of a two-front war. Despite the Schlieffen Plan, this option was still kept open right up to April 1913, and theoretically could still have been put into operation a year later. Consequently, the American historians, Marc Trachtenberg and Dennis Showalter argue that Germany did in fact have military options in 1914, and was not the prisoner of a strategic timetable. On the other hand, Annika Mombauer argues strongly that the army had no intention of abandoning the Schlieffen Plan and supports the traditional argument that in practice the German government was the prisoner of a military timetable.[43]

Russian army was fully ready, Germany had no alternative but to act quickly. On 31 July it sent an ultimatum to Russia warning its government that unless mobilization was halted within 12 hours, Germany would fully mobilize its armed forces. Berlin assumed that France would immediately support Russia, *but* if the unexpected happened and France decided to remain neutral, the German ambassador in Paris was instructed to demand the surrender of the two fortresses of Toul and Verdun to Germany as a pledge of its good faith. The Russians attempted unsuccessfully to convince the Germans that their mobilization plans did not mean war, while the French government firmly informed Berlin that it would 'act in accordance to her interests'.[44]

The countdown to war had started:

- On 1 August both France and Russia ordered full mobilization.
- At 7 o'clock that evening Germany declared war on Russia.
- On 2 August an ultimatum was sent to Brussels declaring that, as Germany had 'accurate' knowledge that France was planning to occupy Belgium, it demanded the right of free passage for its troops through Belgian territory.
- The Belgians rejected this ultimatum, and on 3 August the Germans declared war on France.
- On 4 August the Germans invaded Belgium, an action which led to a British ultimatum and declaration of war.

Conclusion: was war inevitable?

The emergence of Germany as a great military and economic power was indeed a threat to the more established states like Britain, France and Russia. Paul Schroeder has argued that 'The search for the fundamental cause of World War I is futile . . . A different question may help: not why World War 1? but why not?'[45]

If this is the case, why then did war break out in 1914 and not earlier? Was it really inevitable that Germany and Austria should be confronted by the Triple *Entente*? Up to the end of the nineteenth century, war between Britain and Russia or France seemed much more likely, yet ultimately these states managed to compose their differences. It can be argued that the developing power of Germany brought about this 'diplomatic revolution'. Certainly the growth of the German fleet antagonized Britain, as German support for Austria in the Balkans did Russia. German policy seemed at times calculated to alienate all its neighbours, as the two Moroccan and Bosnian crises showed. This, of course, strengthened the Triple Entente and made Germany more dependent on its one remaining ally, Austria–Hungary. Within Germany there was a widespread feeling – even in the SPD – that the military balance was tilting against it, and a general acceptance by 1914 that war was inevitable. It was primarily not the SPD's triumphs in the 1912 elections that persuaded Bethmann to risk war, although this certainly frightened the Conservatives. In the final analysis, Bethmann saw the July crisis as a window of opportunity. If it could successfully be resolved to Austria's advantage without the *Entente* coming to the assistance of Russia, then Germany's position in Europe would be greatly strengthened, the Franco-Russian alliance ruptured, and the way would be open to future colonial expansion. If the *Entente* stood by Russia, then war 'was better now rather than later'.[46] Ironically, in retrospect it can be seen that time was really with, rather than against, Germany. There is no evidence that Germany was actually weakening *vis-à-vis* Russia, and her peaceful economic penetration of Europe, South America and the British Empire was visibly growing. With patience, diplomatic skill and some luck, the Great World War could have been avoided without a German 'surrender'.

See Document 38

8 *Germany at War, 1914–18*

TIMELINE

1914	*Aug.*	All parties in the *Reichstag* vote for war credits
		Battle of Tannenberg
	Sept.	Battle of the Marne
1915		Deadlock on the Western Front
1916		Battles of Verdun, Somme and Jutland
	Aug.	Hindenburg appointed chief of general staff and Ludendorff, quartermaster general
1917	*Feb.*	Russian Revolution
	April	USA declares war on Germany
		Kaiser announces post-war reform of Prussian electoral system
	July	Bethmann Hollweg replaced as chancellor by Michaelis, who in turn is replaced by Hertling in December
	Oct.	Bolshevik revolution in Russia
1918	*Jan.*	Strikes break out in Berlin
	Mar.	Treaty of Brest–Litovsk
	Mar.–Apr.	German offensive on the Western Front
	29 Sept.	German high command calls for an armistice
		Hertling replaced by Prince Max von Baden
	3–4 Oct.	Berlin's first armistice note to President Wilson
	28 Oct.	Wilhelm concedes parliamentary constitution
		Naval mutiny at Wilhemshaven
	3 Nov.	Austria signs armistice
	11 Nov.	Armistice signed between Germany and allies

Introduction

The spirit of unity and the great wave of patriotism that engulfed the nation when war broke in August 1914 is legendary, and was nostalgically recalled in the Weimar Republic. All the parties, including the SPD, voted for war credits, and a political truce (*Burgfrieden*) was announced by the Kaiser in the famous words: 'I no longer recognize parties; I recognize only Germans.'[1]

See Document 41

However, this spirit of 1914 was not as universal as later myths would have it. Local histories have indicated that it was also accompanied by deep feelings of anxiety, while many in the Labour movement only reluctantly accepted their party's endorsement of the war as a necessary defence against the ultra-reactionary tsarist Russia.

The 'spirit of 1914' was a powerful emotion that temporarily hid the bitter divisions in German society and inevitably meant different things to different classes. To the Protestant élite it was a powerful confirmation of Germany's distinctive constitution and route to modernization. To them it indicated 'that the prevailing semi-constitutional system in Germany, if stabilized and ideologically revitalized, was especially well fitted for dealing with the major problems of society and, in particular, that it would serve to keep the working class in its subordinate position within the social structure'.[2] This view was hardly shared by the working classes themselves; to them 'the spirit of 1914' raised expectations of further political and social reform and a new practical spirit of equality. As the war dragged on, disillusion set in and the hopes that it had raised 'took on an aura of an elusive fantasy, a painful reminder of the idealism that had reigned in the first hour'.[3]

Key issues

- How effective was the German war economy?
- How was the war financed?
- What was the impact of the war on the German people?
- Why was the question of war aims so divisive?
- To what extent had the *Burgfriede* broken down by 1917?
- To what extent did Hindenburg and Ludendorff create a dictatorship?
- Why had Germany effectively lost the war by September 1918?

The problem of food and raw materials

By the early autumn of 1914 the strategic character of the war had become clear. In the east, as the Battle of Tannenberg had shown, the Russians could be defeated, while in the west the Anglo-French counter-attack across the Marne and the subsequent German retreat to the Aisne marked the beginning of a deadly, static war of attrition. The failure of the Schlieffen Plan left the Germans at a serious disadvantage in both the east and the west as they had to man fronts of over 400 miles in length, which sucked in huge amounts of troops and material.

Germany, like its adversaries, had to adapt its economy and society to the demands of an industrial war, but this was made more difficult by the fragmentation of its adminstration between federal, state and local institutions. The Prussian Law of Siege, which came into operation at the outbreak of war, gave executive power to local corps commanders, who were directly responsible to the Kaiser, but their districts did not correspond with the existing state and regional governments. This led to the proliferation of committees and bureaucracy, which became a 'nightmare'.[4]

The most immediate challenge to the German war effort came from the British blockade, which threatened to strangle the German economy by intercepting imports of vital raw materials. That this threat was averted was largely the work of Walther Rathenau, under whose initial chairmanship the Prussian War Office set up the War Materials Section (KRA). In co-operation with the industrialists, this office formed war materials corporations, the task of which was to buy or requisition all

14 The Kaiser's speech at the opening of the Reichstag on 4 August 1914 made the headlines in this Berlin newspaper. The Kaiser made his famous statement that he recognized 'no more political parties – just Germans'

Berliner Lokal-Anzeiger, 4 August 1914, front page

Walther Rathenau, 1867–1922

Son of Emil Rathenau, the founder of AEG, Walther Rathenau was a polymath, who was not only one of Germany's leading businessmen, but also wrote essays and books on philosophy and the current state of Germany. He had reported on the situation in German South West Africa in 1907, advised both Bülow and Bethmann Hollweg, and had been considered as a possible Reich secretary of state. After he left the KRA in 1915, thanks partly to his own lecture on the subject, he became a national hero, and for the remainder of the war his books on the future of Germany and of the economy became bestsellers. However, because he advocated a semi-socialist or, perhaps more accurately, a 'national socialist' economic model, he also made many enemies and attracted bitter anti-Semitic attacks. He became known as 'Jesus in morning dress'. By November 1918, since he had urged Germany to fight on to the bitter end in the hope of gaining better peace terms, he was rejected by the SPD, and it was not until 1921 that he entered the Wirth government as minister for reconstruction. He then became the foreign minister in January 1922, but was murdered in June by right-wing assassins (see p. 178).

available raw materials both in Germany and the occupied areas and then distribute them to the war industries. The German war economy developed within what Roger Chickering has called a 'hybrid institutional framework'.[5] The 200 war materials corporations that were eventually created were financed by the government and organized the production of armaments and equipment for the armed forces. Some participants, like Rathenau himself and his colleague, Wichard von Moellendorf, believed that these were creating the basis for a unique German post-war 'national socialism' in which industry and government would co-operate closely. The munitions industry was one of the great triumphs of the German war effort, and right up to October 1918, despite the blockade, the German army never went short of munitions. In blunting the impact of the British blockade, the work of German scientists was crucial. Fritz Haber and Robert Bosch, for instance, devised a process for nitrogen fixation which made German munitions production independent of imported nitrates. Similarly, German chemists also invented synthetic cellulose, which replaced imported cotton in the munitions industry.

The ability of the German government to distribute food was not nearly as effective. While it is true that nobody actually died *directly* of starvation in the Reich during the war, 'undernourishment became a mass phenomenon, a festering source of demoralization, discontent and domestic strife'.[6] The British blockade and the Russian ban on grain exports led to an immediate decline of some 25 per cent in German food production, which was exacerbated by the voracious demands of the army. Responding to the laws of supply and demand, the price of food rose sharply. At first the city governments and the other local authorities attempted to impose price ceilings, but by the end of 1914 it was clear that food would have to be rationed. A start was made with bread when the Imperial Grain Corporation was created, which served as a model for rationing meats, vegetables, fruits, oils and potatoes. In 1916 the War Food Office was set up, but unlike the KRA it lacked the power to override military and civilian food agencies, while itself creating a maze of baffling red tape.

In parts of Germany rationing and distribution were effective, especially in the smaller towns that enjoyed access to the countryside, but it was the big conurbations that suffered most, where bottlenecks on the railways delayed food distribution. For the first two years the good harvests of 1914 and 1915 took the edge off the food shortages, but the cumulative effect of the blockade cannot be exaggerated, as it produced serious shortages in fertilizers, fats and meats, which compounded the shortages of many staple commodities. Although the wealthy could supplement their rations through the black market, it was blue-collar and white-collar workers and their families in the big cities who suffered most (see p. 154).

Blue-collar workers: manual workers **White-collar workers**: office workers

The move to total war

After the costly failure to defeat the French at Verdun, the heavy casualties lost on the Somme and the indecisive naval battle at Jutland, Germany was faced with the choice of either attempting to secure a negotiated peace or an even more ruthless mobilization of men and economic resources – total war in fact. Bethmann Hollweg desired the former and used the failure to take Verdun and the entry of Romania into the war in August to persuade the Kaiser to drop Erich von Falkenhayn, the supreme commander on the Western Front, and replace him with the popular generals von Hindenburg and Ludendorff, who had made so much more progress on the Eastern Front.

By the end of 1916 the Germans had lost 1,500,000 men

The Hindenburg Plan

Bethmann gambled that Hindenburg's charisma would make a negotiated peace for the German people acceptable. Here, however, he miscalculated, as the new military leaders had no intention of advising the Kaiser to end the war. On the contrary they took immediate steps to prosecute the war more vigorously:

- The age of conscription was lowered to 18, which had the effect of increasing the number of conscripts for 1917 to 300,000.
- Ludendorff proclaimed the total mobilization of the German economy for war and demanded immense increases in munitions and weapons.
- The Supreme War office (*Kriegsamt*) under General Groener was set up to oversee and to organize the whole war economy.
- By the Auxiliary Service Law, every fit man in Germany between the ages of 17 and 60 was to be conscripted for war work, if he was not already in the armed forces.

Field Marshal Paul von Hindenburg (1847–1934) and General Erich von Ludendorff (1865–1937)

Hindenburg was the living symbol of the Prussian military class. He was born in 1847 and decorated for his efforts in the war of 1870. He retired in 1911 as a commander of an army corps. In 1914 he was recalled and given command of the eastern front. His chief of staff, Erich von Ludendorff, was a brilliant, bourgeois staff officer, who had been head of the Operations Section of the General Staff and had been the driving force behind the massive expansion in the German army just before the war. After his success in destroying the Liège fortress in August 1914, he was appointed Hindenburg's chief of staff. Together they formed a remarkable team. Ludendorff's organizational skills complemented Hindenburg's enormous popularity. After the epic Battle of Tannenberg, Hindenburg's prestige in Germany was immense, and he became the symbol of German determination to win the war. Already by the end of 1914 a Hindenburg cult had come into existence and everywhere large wooden statues of him were put up. Funds for the war effort were raised by encouraging admirers to purchase nails to hammer into the statue. Hindenburg's fame soon grew to such an extent that the Kaiser himself became jealous. It was the legacy of this fame that he was elected President of the Weimar Republic in 1925 (see p. 201).

- To ensure mass support for these aims, the German Fatherland Party was set up with the intention of mobilizing the people in favour of a victorious peace.

The Hindenburg Plan failed to meet its targets. In practice the creation of the *Kriegsamt* compounded bureaucratic confusion, and its attempts to close down non-essential industries led 'to the mobilization of an army of advocates',[7] who harried it at every level. By early 1917 it was clear the quotas were not being met. Despite desperate efforts to use every bit of scrap iron, German industry was producing less steel in February 1917 than it had in July 1916. Neither did it have much success in mobilizing extra labour, if only because it had already been deployed. To meet this shortfall, over 100,000 Belgians were deported into the Reich and 600,000 Poles were either persuaded or forced to work on German farms. Ultimately the Hindenburg Plan was unsustainable. It was, to quote Gerald Feldman, 'the triumph not of imagination, but of fantasy . . . In his pursuit of an ill-conceived total mobilization for the attainment of irrational goals, Ludendorff undermined the strength of the army, promoted economic instability, created administrative chaos, and set loose an orgy of interest politics.'[8]

Compare this to the much more ambitious labour-deportation programmes carried out in the Second World War. See pp. 259–61

Financing the war

'Every gun, shell, sandbag, cartridge box, horseshoe, belt buckle and boot nail carried a price tag',[9] which had to be paid for by the federal government, whose budget had increased by the end of the war more than ten times since July 1914. State and local government also had to shoulder the enormous costs involved in supporting the families of soldiers at the front, subsidizing rations for the poor, paying the salaries of the newly-expanded army of bureaucrats, while at the same time continuing to pay the salaries of those officials who had been called up. Both central and local government were thus confronted with the urgent problem of how to raise sufficient funds to cover their escalating costs. The options were either to tax or to borrow. The federal government was loath to introduce direct taxation, although the states and communes did in fact levy direct taxes on property and income. Karl Helfferich, the minister for finance, was convinced that direct taxation would be both divisive and bad for morale, and it was not until 1916 that a federal value-added tax, which was aimed at the war profiteers, was introduced, but this was in practice easily evaded. Consequently by 1916 taxation only covered about 15 per cent of the direct costs of the war.

The German government, therefore, had little option but to borrow. As it had no access to the global financial markets, it had to raise the money at home through *Kriegsanleihen* (the sale of war bonds). Nine issues of these were put on the market at a rate of 5 per cent. They proved to be very popular and were purchased by both individuals and institutions in great numbers. By the end of the war nearly a hundred billion marks had been raised through the *Kriegsanleihen*. Yet this only covered two thirds of federal costs and, of course, the interest would ultimately still have to be paid. In the event of victory the defeated enemy would be presented with this bill, but in the meantime there was no alternative but to print money. At local level the federal government set up loan bureaux, which could lend money to the states and local government agencies, and even to private borrowers, on more generous terms than the banks. They were also allowed to print their own notes, which had the legal status of money. 'These policies conjured paper money out of nowhere'[10] and led to escalating inflation, which became one of the defining experiences of the German home front. It resulted in the German people themselves paying for the war and made great inroads into their savings. A war bond, for instance, which was bought in August 1914 at 1000 marks was, four years later, worth in current prices a mere 300 marks. Inflation on this scale was inevitably a source of widespread anxiety on the home front.

Winners and losers

The war affected every German, but on the home front its impact was diverse and created both winners and losers. It brought about a fundamental restructuring of the German economy. The heavy industries, particularly the chemical industry, underwent immense expansion, while the consumer industries were slimmed down or in some cases even closed, unless they could become contractors or subcontractors for war materials. In Wesel, for instance, by the winter of 1916–17 about half the small businesses and workshops had to shut down as a result of the Hindenburg Programme. Inevitably then, it was those Germans who worked for or supplied the large war industries who were best placed to survive the war in good shape.

In many ways the war consolidated class divisions in Germany. It weakened the middle classes, enriched the employers in the war industries and made the working classes more cohesive. Workers switched jobs frequently and the differentials between skilled and unskilled workers and male and female workers narrowed. In the war industries workers' wages steadily increased in relation to the rest of the population, even though this did not exempt them from the effects of inflation and food shortages. The Hindenburg Plan had also extended an embryonic form 'of social partnership'[11] to the unions, which gave them real influence over the drafting of legislation dealing with wages and prices. When the Auxiliary Service Law was submitted to the Reichstag, the SPD successfully extracted from the government significant concessions for the trade unions. Their representatives were now to sit on the committees in each district which were to administer labour mobilization, and it was agreed that in all factories of more than fifty workers joint committees of labour and management would deal with disputes over wages and conditions.

The most vulnerable sector in the war economy were the non-unionized white-collar employees, who were on fixed salaries which were steadily eroded by inflation and whose financial position, in comparison to that of the workers, steadily declined. The professional classes, academics, higher civil servants, journalists and lawyers all experienced a marked decline in their standard of living. Throughout the middle classes inflation created a feeling of insecurity, and towards the end of the war white-collar employees were beginning to organize and even to strike. The financial destruction of these classes was completed by the hyperinflation of 1923 (see p. 183), but 'the seeds of the social crisis' were already planted by 1917.[12]

Women and the family

Traditionally the war has been seen as the real beginning of female emancipation in Germany. German women inevitably experienced the war differently from men. The official assumption was still that women belonged in the 'private sphere' and thus were not legally mobilized by the Auxiliary Service Law of 1916. In reality it was only the more prosperous middle-class women who could afford to remain in the 'private sphere'. Working-class women, despite being recipients of public welfare to compensate them for the absence of their husbands at the front, had little option but to seek employment, as they had to take responsibility not just for running the home, but also for earning sufficient money to pay for essentials to enable their families to survive. By October 1918 more than a third of the total workforce was female. Women quitted jobs in domestic service or lower-paid jobs in textiles or food processing for

For comparisons with the role of women in the Second World War, see p. 261

work on the assembly lines in the armaments industries. In Krupp's factories, for instance, women made up over 40 per cent of the work-force. The wage differentials between the sexes narrowed and women became politicized by joining trade unions. In 1918 they formed 25 per cent of the Socialist unions' membership. Many middle-class women were compelled to work in clerical or secretarial positions in order that their families might survive financially. Upper middle-class women, whose servants could wait in the food queues on their behalf, gravitated to charitable organizations. Through the voluntary National Women's Service they began to organize soup kitchens, child care centres, organizations for collecting second-hand clothes, etc., and began to experience real responsibility and authority in the public sphere for the first time.

For the majority of children the war entailed neglect and the long absences of their mothers, who were involved in war work. Large numbers of children grew up in fatherless households. The younger children were often looked after by siblings or in day-care centres. Like the rest of the population they suffered from varying degrees of malnutrition, and, according to one contemporary estimate, nearly 40 per cent suffered from rickets. As a result of the requisitioning of schools, the call-up of teachers, the shortage of coal which led to the closing of schools during cold weather in winter, and the employment of children at harvest time, education was interrupted and perfunctory. Hundreds of thousands of older children were also given pre-military training in paramilitary organizations. In their teens most working-class children were already at work full-time in the factories. The disorientation of German youth led to a dramatic rise in juvenile crime and truancy. In Cologne this increased from 15 to 48 per cent in the first three years of the war. Attempts were made to control the behaviour of young workers by imposing curfews, banning them from cinemas and forcing them to deposit the major part of their wages in saving accounts.

For comparison with the even greater disruption to education and family life in the period 1942–45 see pp. 261–2

War aims and domestic politics, August 1914–August 1916

For the first two years of the war Bethmann Hollweg managed to preserve a rather precarious domestic peace. As part of the *Burgfrieden*, party strife in the *Reichstag* ceased. In a special enabling act it delegated its legislative powers to the *Bundesrat*, which now assumed the power to promulgate legislation. Although the *Reichstag* still maintained the right to review legislation, its importance was marginalized for the first half of the war.

Bethmann Hollweg's efforts to preserve the *Burgfrieden*

The key to domestic peace was to preserve the *Burgfrieden* and not to allow the potentially divisive issues of post-war domestic reform and war

Was there a sexual revolution?

It was an accepted part of war that soldiers, even if they were married, should have access to prostitutes. Their infidelity was considered much less shocking than female promiscuity on the home front. The latter challenged the 'supportive bond that ordered relations between home and the battlefront'.[13] Major transit centres like Düsseldorf saw prostitution develop on a large scale. The degree of promiscuity amongst middle-class, married woman is impossible to determine, but it was the subject of cartoons, jokes and many a serious article in the newspapers and magazines.

aims to stir up public controversy. It was vital to keep the SPD behind the war effort. It had willingly voted for war credits in August 1914 because it was convinced that Germany was fighting a war of survival and not of conquest. Apart from a few members on the right of the party, it was implacably opposed to annexations. All the other parties on the other hand, including the Centre and the Progressives, initially advocated a policy of annexation. The Pan-Germans, the Nationalist pressure groups and the right-wing parties all supported ambitious plans of annexation in both western and eastern Europe and hoped that the realisation of these demands would distract the people from demands for domestic reform.

Subjected to these conflicting pressures, Bethmann attempted to avoid committing himself to a definite programme for as long as possible. For the first two years of the war he managed to keep the *Burgfrieden* intact. Popular support was still widespread for the war, and, except in the *Reichstag*, censorship, which was under the control of the deputy commanding generals, prevented any public criticism. Both the Protestant and Catholic churches supported the war effort and the tiny German Peace Society was hounded by the authorities.

There was somewhat more opposition to the war amongst the socialist working classes in such traditional radical centres as Bremen, Brunswick,

Bethmann Hollweg and Germany's war aims

Fritz Fischer, with particular reference to the September Memorandum that was drafted by Bethmann's secretary, Kurt Riezler, and called for extensive annexations in France and Belgium, argues that the chancellor was in fact no less expansionist than the Pan-Germans. Now, however, the consensus of argument is that it was only a provisional draft – more 'consideration' than 'decision'.[14] Bethmann's biographer, Konrad Jarausch, stresses that he had 'no plans but only *ad hoc* ideas which could be influenced through changes in the fortune of arms'.[15] Bethmann never renounced the September Programme, and his flexibility did not therefore entirely exclude an annexationist programme if domestic politics so dictated, although his main aim, according to Craig, was the establishment of 'a German *Mitteleuropa* surrounded by willing vassal states'.[16]

Berlin, Düsseldorf and Leipzig. In December 1915, 20 SPD deputies actually voted against war credits, and by the summer of 1916 the *Burgfrieden* was coming under increasing pressure. For the first time since the war had begun, 1 May, Labour Day, was marked by demonstrations in Berlin. When Karl Liebknecht was sentenced by a military court in June to four years in jail for his anti-war campaign, a series of strikes broke out in Berlin, Essen and other industrial centres. These were a turning-point in the history of the opposition to the war because they were the beginning of the purely political strikes which had the potential to paralyse the war economy. On the other hand, the great majority of the SPD continued to support the war because it actually promised considerable political gains for the working classes. It would, they hoped, end the hostility and discrimination which the labour movement had suffered before the war. The need to win the support of organized labour had enabled trade union and party leaders to force the government to make a number of key concessions, such as the legal recognition of trade unions, the establishment of arbitration boards in the larger factories and a role for the unions in the administration of the Auxiliary Service Law in 1916 (see above).

Karl Liebknecht publicly opposed the war as early as December 1914. In 1916 he began to circulate, together with Rosa Luxemburg, a series of anti-war newsletters, the so-called 'Spartacus letters'. He was jailed for anti-war activities in 1916 and was released in October 1918 (see p. 169)

The dismissal of General von Falkenhayn

The longer the war continued, however, the greater the political and domestic strains became. As early as December 1914, Falkenhayn had already conceded that Germany could not win the war outright. The consequences to be drawn from this became a matter of bitter dispute between the generals and the civilian leadership. Bethmann was no Bismarck who had curbed the extravagant ambitions of the generals, but then he was hindered by the increasing weakness of the Kaiser, who was rapidly becoming a mere shadow of himself and lacked the will to arbitrate between the armed forces and the civilians. The power of the generals was greatly strengthened by the lack of an institutional forum where soldiers and ministers could together discuss options and policies. Strategic and political decisions were, therefore, decided in an atmosphere of intrigue and mutual hostility.

Falkenhayn's strategy for ending the war was based on negotiating a moderate peace with Russia after having inflicted a limited defeat on her. He believed that the war itself could only be concluded satisfactorily by convincing Britain that Germany was invincible. He argued, therefore, that Germany should build up her strength in the west and destroy Britain's maritime commerce through an unrestricted U-boat campaign, but this strategy rapidly ran into problems. The submarine campaign had to be called off when it threatened in May 1915, after the sinking of the *Lusitania*, to bring the USA into the war. The reverses suffered at Jutland, Verdun and the Somme, together with Romania's declaration of war, so discredited Falhenhayn's strategy that Bethmann Hollweg was able to persuade the Kaiser to appoint Hindenburg to the supreme command in late August 1916, with Ludendorff as his chief of staff and 'first quarter-

1198 out of the 2000 passengers carried by the *Lusitania*, a Cunard liner, were killed. Many of these were Americans

master', in the hope that their prestige would enable the government to negotiate a peace settlement with the Entente powers on the best possible terms.

The supremacy of Hindenburg and Ludendorff, September 1916–September 1918

From now on the supreme command, or rather, behind the scenes, Ludendorff, became the dominant force in domestic politics. Essentially Ludendorff believed that civilian politicians, and even the Kaiser, were subordinate to the military. His power was based on the charismatic authority which he enjoyed by virtue of his association with Hindenburg. He was a strong advocate of the advantages of a military dictatorship, but the multipolar nature of power in Germany in practice prevented him from creating one, although he became the single most powerful figure in the Reich.

Ludendorff, with Hindenburg's implicit support, dramatically upped the stakes in Germany's war aims. He contemptuously dismissed Bethmann's ambiguities and prevarications, and encouraged the widest fantasies of the nationalists. By forcing the government to announce the creation of an independent Poland in November 1916, he also effectively torpedoed any chance of a negotiated peace with Russia. Then in January 1917 the high command persuaded the Kaiser to agree to renewing unrestricted submarine warfare against Britain, which, far from resulting in a British defeat, brought the USA into the war on the side of the Entente. The constant flood of manifestos from nationalist pressure groups, which, with the full encouragement of the high command, demanded the creation of a German *Mitteleuropa* also contradicted the idea that Germany was fighting a defensive war and polarized the political forces in Germany. Increasingly the right consolidated behind Ludendorff, while the left began to unite behind the demand for a negotiated peace.

The peace resolution and its consequences

The March revolution in Russia had 'an electrifying impact'[17] in Germany and provided a model of how the mounting economic crisis could be exploited to bring about both democratic reform and the end of the war. In April 1917, when a cut in the bread rations led to massive strikes in Berlin, Leipzig, Brunswick, Halle and Magdeburg, the strikers consciously echoed the cries in Russia for 'bread, land and peace', and formed workers' councils based on the soviets. Within the *Reichstag*, the dissident Socialists who had voted against the war loans and been expelled from the SPD now set up their own party, the Independent German Social Democratic Party (USPD). In the *Reichstag* they could count on 24 members, while, outside parliament, their strength lay in the Ruhr, Berlin and the other industrial cities.

Sidebar notes:

Germany, being a federal state, there were several centres of power

Mitteleuropa: a proposed customs union, the centre of which would be the Austrian and German empires and which would stretch from France to the Middle East

The USPD survived until 1922, when its more moderate members rejoined the SPD, while those on the left joined the Communists

The very existence of the USPD on its left flank put pressure on the majority SPD (or MSPD) to call for a negotiated peace. By 1917 the ideological assumptions of the war had been transformed. Russia, crippled by revolution, was ready to make peace, while democratic America had come into the war on the side of the *Entente*. To appease the SPD and head off their opposition to the war, Bethmann managed to persuade the Kaiser to promise the abolition of the three-class voting system in Prussia (see p. 61) and reform the *Bundesrat* after the war, but his announcement of this on 7 April 1917 was ambiguous and not convincing. Neither were there any signs of concessions to a negotiated peace from Hindenburg and Ludendorff, who, on the contrary, drew up 'a programme of war aims that was more extravagant than anything hitherto envisaged'[18] – the so-called Kreuznach Programme. Bethmann reluctantly accepted this programme, although he did tell the *Bundesrat* that his aim was a peace that would exclude 'any idea of rape' and would leave 'no sting, no trace of resentment'.[19]

Bethmann's desperate attempts to hold the balance between left and right resulted only in a policy of vacillation and ambiguity that alienated both sides and also shook the confidence of the Centre and Liberal parties in him. The leader of the left wing of the Centre, Matthias Erzberger, seized the chance to reveal to the Main Commission of the *Reichstag*, when it met in early July to deliberate on war credits, alarming information which he had received from Colonel Bauer, Ludendorff's political link man. Bauer had told him that Austria was in a desperate situation and that there was mounting evidence that the U-boat war was failing. Erzberger then persuaded the Centre party to join with the MSDP and the Progressives, to form a majority in the *Reichstag*, which on 19 July 1917 passed the 'Peace Resolution'. This challenged the high command by bluntly stating: 'The *Reichstag* strives for a peace of understanding and permanent reconciliation of peoples. Forced territorial acquisitions and political, economic and financial oppressions are irreconcilable with such a peace'. Although the USPD argued that this did not go far enough, it was nevertheless 'a spectacular act of parliamentary defiance'[20] which marked the beginning of a new period of political confrontation and was a major blow to the domestic consensus:

See Document 43

- Ludendorff, backed by the right, immediately demanded Bethmann's dismissal and his replacement with a more pliable Prussian bureaucrat, Georg Michaelis.
- The supreme command of the army (OHL) also launched an intensive programme of patriotic propaganda, both amongst the troops and at home.
- Support for the German Fatherland Party (see p. 152) grew to about a million members by January 1918, while this in turn provoked a counter-organization from the peace groups, the 'People's League for Freedom and Fatherland', with a membership as large as the Fatherland party.

Within the *Reichstag* the supporters of a compromise peace gained in confidence. The *Reichstag*'s budget committee, which continued to meet even when the *Reichstag* was adjourned, now began to acquire the role of 'an executive agency for the broader body'.[21] The three parties, which had supported the peace resolution, liaised with the National Liberals and established a joint consultative committee, and in October 1917 a parliamentary majority successfully passed another resolution calling for the democratic reform of the Prussian suffrage. The high command, in response to these developments, again intervened and had Michaelis sacked, but this time Ludendorff consulted the party leaders and engineered in October 1917 the appointment of Georg von Hertling, a Bavarian aristocrat aged 74, who was a member of the Centre party.

OHL, *Oberste Heeresleitung*: the Supreme Command of the German Army

Hertling was by no means a puppet of the OHL. He appeared to back constitutional reform and even included several of the party leaders in the cabinet, but his appointment did not mean that the OHL was beginning to entertain the idea of a negotiated peace. By January 1918 the *Entente* had been shaken by the successive failures of the Nivelle offensive, Ypres, the Italian defeat at Caporetto and the October revolution in Russia which brought Lenin to power. There seemed, therefore, one last window of opportunity to achieve a moderate peace, but this was firmly rejected by Hindenburg and Ludendorff, who seized the chance of the Russian collapse to dictate the harsh, annexationist peace of Brest-Litovsk. This policy led to a renewal of strikes in Berlin and the other industrial centres in January, but the peace itself was ratified in the *Reichstag* by an overwhelming majority, and indicated that Ludendorff's determination to play for the highest stakes could still be proved right, if it was possible to exploit the temporary weakness of the Allied and associated powers and win a decisive victory in the west.

Brest-Litovsk, March 1918, forced the Russians to surrender Poland, the Baltic provinces, the Ukraine, Finland and the Caucasus

The collapse of the Ludendorff offensive and military defeat

The spring offensive in March 1918 was the OHL's final gamble, but the odds were heavily against its success; the Allied forces were greater and far better supplied, and were in a position to prolong the war for as long as was necessary. Initially the Ludendorff offensive enjoyed some success. Four separate attacks, thanks to local superiority, surprise and good planning, managed to make significant initial gains, but then exhaustion, lack of supplies and the superiority of Allied resources soon thwarted all hopes of the great break-through. The Allied counter-offensive began in the late summer of 1918 with a French attack on the Marne. Throughout August and September the Allied attacks continued, and by late September the Germans were in full retreat. On 29 September Ludendorff informed both Hindenburg and Hertling that the war was lost and that an immediate appeal should be made to President Wilson for an armistice. In an effort to make this appeal more persuasive, he urged the creation of a more representative regime, which would have a

xSee Document

29. September
1 9 1 8
Ilr. 39
27. Jahrgang

Berliner

Einzelpreis
einjchließlich
Teuerungszuschlag
15 Pfg.
ober 24 Heller

Illustrirte Zeitung

Verlag Ullstein & Co, Berlin SW 68

Deutscher Panzerwagen mit zwei Mann der Besatzung im Tankanzug, von denen einer eine Splittermaske trägt.

15 On the very day when General Erich von Ludendorff informed the German government that the army needed an immediate armistice, the readers of *Illustrierte Zeitung* were given the impression that Germany was still invincible. The caption of this picture reads: 'A German tank with its two-man crew in tank uniform, one of whom is wearing a protective splinter mask'

Berliner Illustrierte Zeitung, 29 September 1918, front page

See Document 45

greater impact on Washington than the defeated and discredited OHL and the Hertling government it had put in place.

Conclusion

The German people performed prodigious feats during the Great War and managed to keep a much larger coalition of states at bay for over four years. The total war economy, the strength of German industry and the *Burgfrieden* were all factors which strengthened the German war effort, yet ultimately Germany was locked into conflict with a coalition which it could not destroy. The intervention of Great Britain on 1 August cut Germany off from its overseas trade and access to the American money markets. This ensured that the German people suffered the full rigours of the British blockade, and that the costs of the war could not be eased by foreign loans. Rather than raise the contentious issue of direct taxation, the government preferred to meet the shortfall in its finances by printing money, with disastrously inflationary consequences.

The *Burgfrieden* played a key role in uniting the German people and strengthening the legitimacy of the state, but, as the pressures on the home front intensified, divisions re-emerged. The formation of the USPD in April 1917 and then the Peace Resolution in July created the first major cracks in the *Burgfrieden*. The quasi-Bonapartist dictatorship of Hindenburg and Ludendorff, with its fanatical determination to win a total victory, polarized the political situation and prevented the German government from exploring any possibility of a negotiated peace. For Germany and Europe, the Great War was '*the* great seminal catastrophe'[22] of the twentieth century. Both its immediate and long-term consequences are the theme of the rest of this book.

Part Three

The Weimar Republic and The Third Reich

9 *Revolution and Instability, October 1918–23*

	24 June	Rathenau murdered
	7–14 Aug.	London conference
	Aug.	Inflation accelerates
	14 Sept.	Right wing of USPD merges with SPD
	24 Oct.	Ebert's period as president prolonged by constitutional amendment until 1 July 1925
	14 Nov.	Wirth's government resigns; minority government formed by Cuno
1923	11 Jan.	Occupation of Ruhr by French and Belgian troops
	13 Jan.	Passive resistance starts
	12 Aug.	Fall of Cuno government; Grand Coalition formed by Stresemann
	26 Sept.	Passive resistance ends
	Oct.	Separatist movements in Rhineland and Palatinate
	Late Oct.	SPD–KPD government in Saxony deposed
	3 Nov.	SPD withdraws from Grand Coalition
	8–9 Nov.	Hitler–Ludendorff *putsch*
	15 Nov.	*Rentenmark* introduced at value of 1:1 billion paper marks
	23 Nov.	Fall of Stresemann cabinet, although he remains as foreign minister in bourgeois minority government of W. Marx (Centre, DVP, DDP, BVP) and in subsequent governments up to 1929
	30 Nov.	Reparation Commission appoints international committee of exports to assess Germany's capacity to pay

Introduction

Like armchair strategists, who are so quick to spot mistakes made in the midst of 'the fog of war', historians retrospectively reveal the mistaken assumptions or timidity of politicians. In the 1950s, interpretations of the 'abortive revolution' of 1918–19 were influenced by the Cold War. West German historians, like Karl-Dietrich Erdmann, argued that Ebert and the Majority Socialists (MSPD) had little option but to co-operate with the old élites if Germany was to avoid a Communist revolution and create a parliamentary regime. The mirror image of this view was taken by East German historians, who accused the MSPD leaders and the Independent Socialists (USPD) of betraying the revolution The rise of the New Left in West Germany in the 1960s and 1970s (see p. 341) and the increasing availability of fresh sources made the German workers' movements in the period 1918–20 a popular topic of research. Revisionist historians, such as Francis Carsten, Eberhard Kolb and Susanne Miller, showed that initially the SPD and the moderate members of the USPD had a huge majority in the Workers' and Soldiers' Councils, and argued that Ebert should have taken a tougher line with the army, nationalized the mines immediately and implemented the SPD's programme fully. Only with the failure of Ebert to act more decisively did the radical left gain greater influence from the spring of 1920 onwards.[1] Ebert was, however, in tune with the majority of the German workers, who wanted national elections for a democratic *Reichstag* as soon as possible, and he was able to organize these in early January.

The SPD split in April 1917. See p. 158

Friedrich Ebert, 1871–1925: after 1913 Ebert was co-chairman of the SPD. He led the temporary government during the revolution of 1918–19, and was then appointed the first president of the Weimar Republic

Perhaps his mistake was not to harness more effectively the great reservoir of support for democratic and parliamentary socialism in the Soldiers' and Workers' Councils in the last two months of 1918. His failure enabled the pre-war élites to stage a comeback once the immediate effects of defeat had worn off.

Key issues

- Was there a revolution in October 1918–January 1919?
- What were the main provisions of the Weimar Constitution?
- What was the impact of the Treaty of Versailles on post-war Germany?
- What was the legacy of the war for the republic?
- What was the nature of the threats the republic faced from within, 1919–23?
- What were the aims of German foreign policy, 1920–23?
- What were the consequences of the Ruhr crisis for Germany?

An abortive revolution?

Although on 29 September the panic-stricken Ludendorff had abruptly informed his government that it must to appeal to President Wilson for an immediate armistice and reinforce this move by appointing a more representative cabinet, he was not 'the sole author of "the October revolution"', as Taylor has claimed.[2] Already before his intervention, the interparty committee of the *Reichstag* was pressing for significant constitutional changes. A showdown with the OHL would most likely have occurred even if Ludendorff had not decided to let the political parties assume power and the subsequent responsibility for terminating the lost war. The new chancellor, Prince Max von Baden, had been recommended by Conrad Haussmann, the leader of the Progressive party, on the assumption that he combined democratic ideas with the necessary social prestige needed to stand up to the army. Once the news of the armistice appeal became public, the demand for peace 'gathered momentum like an avalanche'.[3] When the American replies of 14 and 23 October indicated that President Wilson was in effect demanding the abdication of the Kaiser before negotiations could take place, it became increasingly clear that public opinion would willingly sacrifice the monarch to gain peace.

On 28 October the *Reichstag* approved sweeping measures to prepare the way for the creation of a constitutional parliamentary government. Even at this stage, the Kaiser and the armed forces showed that they were not ready to subordinate themselves to parliament. The Kaiser fled to the Army GHQ at Spa, while the Admiralty ignored the civil government and ordered the fleet to put out for one last desperate battle against the British. This action was to be the catalyst for the revolution:

Workers' and Soldiers' Councils were modelled on the Russian soviets

- In protest, the sailors at Wilhelmshaven mutinied. When about a thousand of these were arrested, their colleagues organized mass protest meetings, disarmed their officers and formed soviets or councils, which by the evening of 4 November controlled Kiel.
- In the next few days Workers' and Soldiers' Councils were set up in Hamburg, Bremen, Düsseldorf, Leipzig, Frankfurt and Berlin.

See Document 46

- Von Baden hoped at first that this tidal wave of protest could be contained and a constitutional monarchy preserved provided the Kaiser and the crown prince both abdicated. After failure to secure the Kaiser's agreement, he announced the abdication on the afternoon of 9 November without any authorization.
- In the meantime, Ebert demanded that power should be transferred to those who enjoyed the 'full confidence of the people'. On 9 November von Baden handed over power to him.

Ebert's initial plan was to form a coalition government based on the Democrats, MSPD, USPD and Progressives, but this met with strong opposition from the Workers' Councils in Berlin. They demanded that the Workers' and Soldiers' Councils should elect an assembly, that would then appoint a provisional government. To pre-empt this, Ebert negotiated a direct agreement with the USPD to set up a new provisional government in the form of the Council of People's Representatives, consisting of 3 MSPD and 3 USPD delegates.

The most pressing task facing the new government was to negotiate the armistice. The German delegation, headed by Matthias Erzberger, began negotiations on 6 November, and had little option but to agree to the stiff terms dictated by the Allies. Once the agreement was signed on 11 November and the fighting stopped, the Council of People's Representatives turned to domestic politics. Ebert had hoped to preserve the monarchy, though not Wilhelm II, but his hand had been forced by his colleague and co-chairman of the USPD, Philipp Scheidemann, who had, unconsulted, announced a republic to a mass demonstration in the Reichstag square on 9 November. Ebert and the leaders of the Majority Socialists had already achieved their principal aims with the announcement of the October reforms introducing constitutional government. For them, the November 'revolution' was an unnecessary distraction from

---

Armistice terms

On the Western Front these involved the immediate cession of Alsace-Lorraine to France, the withdrawal of the German army from all invaded territories behind a line to the east of a designated neutral zone on the right bank of the Rhine, and the occupation by the Allies of the left bank and of the three bridgeheads of Mainz, Coblenz and Cologne (see Map 6). The Germans were also to surrender large amounts of artillery, heavy equipment and the High Seas Fleet and to abrogate the treaty of Brest-Litovsk.

the main business of dealing with the problems of demobilization, food distribution and preparing for the peace negotiations, all of which needed the help of the traditional military and bureaucratic élites. Ebert regarded the Council as just a caretaker government until a constituent assembly had been elected. The Spartacist Union, led by Karl Liebknecht and Rosa Luxemburg (see p. 157), and the left wing of the USPD wanted, however, a soviet rather than a parliamentary regime in Germany, the replacement of the army by a workers' militia and the nationalization of all medium-sized and large farms and industries. They hoped that an executive council appointed by an assembly elected by the Berlin Workers' and Soldiers' Committees would in practice act as the real revolutionary government, but their lack of political skills enabled the SPD and moderate USPD members to outmanoeuvre them on the Council. In an effort to put pressure on the moderates, the Spartacists organized demonstrations and strikes, which merely pushed the SPD further to the right and made them more reliant on the traditional authorities in their efforts to dampen down unrest at home.

On 10 November, General Groener, the quartermaster-general of the army, pledged his loyalty to the Council of People's Representatives, provided that it supported the officer corps' efforts to maintain discipline. Five days later another important step was taken to pacify the home front when the Central Working Association (*Zentralarbeitsgemeinschaft*) agreement covering heavy industry was negotiated between the trade unions and the employers' associations. The employers recognized the unions as the 'authorized representatives of the workers', and agreed to an eight-hour day and the establishment of workers' committees in all firms with a workforce of more than 50. Essentially they were hoping that these concessions would buy off the workers and so avoid the nationalization of their businesses. Heinrich Winkler has characterized this agreement as one 'of mutual benefit between the unions and heavy industry, which in quasi-syndicalist fashion, asserted the primacy of the economy over Workers' Councils, state bureaucracy and a revolutionary government'.[4]

Quasi-syndicalist: syndicalism aimed to establish trade union control over the economy. This agreement conceded an element of worker control to the unions. Hence it was semi-syndicalist

Despite the left-wing Radicals' frequently repeated mantra of 'all power to the Soviets', there was in reality an overwhelming majority in favour of calling a national assembly. On 29 November the Council of People's Representatives announced a new electoral law introducing proportional representation and full female suffrage. The actual date of 19 January for the election was set by the first Congress of Workers' and Soldiers' Councils which met in Berlin from 16–20 December. Ebert and the moderates had won the most important battle, but the majority of the Congress called for the Council not to wait for the elections before introducing such key reforms as the socialization of industry and the creation of a people's militia to replace the regular army.

These demands, of course, ran contrary both to Ebert's assurances to Groener and the Central Working Association agreement. His obvious unwillingness to implement them led to the resignation of the Independent Socialists from the council and the Prussian government.

The extreme left, which embraced the Spartacus Union and the Bremen left-wing Radicals, united to form the Communist party, and then proceeded to launch the doomed uprising in Berlin on 5 January, which has been called the 'revolution's battle of the Marne'.[5] It was ruthlessly repressed by the *Reichswehr* and the newly-formed volunteer militia, the *Freikorps*, which on 15 January murdered the Communist leaders, Karl Liebknecht and Rosa Luxemburg.

The uprising created bitter divisions in the labour movement, which lasted until Hitler created a forced unity with the Nazi Labour Front (see p. 221). On the one hand the leaders of the Majority Socialists tightened their links with the bureaucracy, the army and the bourgeois parties, while the USPD, joined by a considerable number of SPD defectors, who were sickened by the failure of the Ebert government to achieve any major reforms, moved to the left. This was the start of the second phase of the revolution. In the Prussian *Landtag* and local elections of the spring of 1919 the SPD lost considerable support, while the USPD made impressive gains. From January to April there were strikes and uprisings throughout the Reich, and soviet republics were set up in Munich, Bremen, Mülheim and Halle. The brutal measures employed by the *Freikorps*, which waged a war of revenge against the workers, led to an increasing polarization in German society.

Freikorps: Gustav Noske, as minister of defence and with Ebert's support, encouraged the recruitment by former officers of volunteer forces. This appealed to the mass of demobilized young officers and NCOs, who could not fit back into civilian life, as well as students and adventurers. The politics of the *Freikorps* was overwhelmingly monarchist and right-wing

Reichswehr: the German army, a term used up to 1935

The National Assembly

While the SPD and USPD dominated the political agenda in Germany in the weeks before the elections to the National Assembly, the parties of the centre and the right attempted to adapt to the new political climate:

- The former Conservative parties, the small anti-Semitic groups and the right wing of the National Liberals, which was close to heavy industry,

---

The revolution in Munich

The King of Bavaria abdicated on 7 November, and an unstable USPD–SPD coalition government was set up by Kurt Eisner. In the election of January 1919 the USPD lost most of its support. In response to the assassination of Eisner by a Munich university student, Graf Anton von Arco-Valley, a group of USPD members and anarchists declared a 'Council's Republic'. An attempt to crush it with troops failed on 13 April, but played into the hands of the extremists, who, under the leadership of the Communist Eugen Leviné, a veteran of the Russian 1905 revolution, attempted to introduce a Russian-style Soviet Republic. It lasted just over two weeks. It organized a 'red army', but, after bitter fighting which involved atrocities on both sides, it was crushed by *Reichswehr* and *Freikorps* troops. These traumatic events had a lasting impact on public opinion in Bavaria and help explain why it became a bastion of the radical right (see p. 176).

united to form the German National People's party (DNVP). This was both a nationalist party and also represented heavy industry and the landowning classes.

- The Centre party initially tried to break away from its Catholic image (see p. 111) and adopted the name of the Christian People's party in an attempt to become more non-denominational, but the new name failed to catch on. In Bavaria, where Catholic opinion was more right-wing and critical of the republic, the local Centre party broke away and formed the Bavarian People's party (BVP).

- The Progressive party and the left wing of the National Liberals regrouped under the name of German Democratic party (DDP), while the rump of the National Liberals founded the the German People's party under Gustav Stresemann (DVP).

In the elections on 19 January the moderate democratic parties, the SPD, the Centre and the DDP gained a decisive majority. The new National Assembly was convened in Weimar so that its deliberations would not be threatened by the turbulence of Berlin. The SPD, which had gained 38 per cent of the vote, provided both the first president of the Reich, Ebert, and the chancellor, Philipp Scheidemann. The government was based on the SPD, DDP and Centre – the Weimar coalition.

Its first task was to end the transitionary period and draw up the basic structure of the new constitution. Its main institutions, the *Reichstag*, the presidency and the cabinet, as well as a committee to represent the individual states, were confirmed by an interim law, while the Assembly set up the Constitutional Committee to work on the details. Hugo Preuss, a former National Liberal and constitutional expert, who had been appointed minister of the interior, presented it with an initial draft, which envisaged a federal Germany with a strong central government, but over the next six months this was modified and a compromise arrived at between the Reich and the states. The constitutional privileges of Saxony, Bavaria and Württemberg (see p. 85) were abolished and the states, whose ruling families had all been swept away in November 1918, were now called the *Länder*. The upper house, or the *Reichsrat*, lost its veto and became merely an advisory chamber. The executive was at last made responsible to the *Reichstag*, which was to be elected according to proportional representation by universal suffrage. The head of state was the Reich president, who was directly elected by the people for an initial period of seven years, although there was no limit on the times he could stand for re-election. He was in many ways an '*ersatz* emperor'[6], whose powers were designed as a check on the powers of the *Reichstag*. He appointed and then could dismiss the Reich government; he could order a referendum and Article 48 empowered him to proclaim a state of emergency to safeguard public security and order. The constitution also contained a section on individual rights, and the SPD managed to secure articles guaranteeing the socialization of 'suitable' businesses in private hands.

The former Centre party was to have greater success with Adenauer in 1945–47 in broadening its appeal. See p. 279

Proportional representation: the principle wherby parties are represented in parliament in direct proportion to the number of votes they poll

'Ersatz emperor': a substitute emperor

See Document 47

In retrospect it has been argued that the Weimar constitution facilitated the rise to power of the Nazi party. Proportional representation did indeed magnify the influence of the small parties and make the formation of durable coalitions more difficult, while the existence of Article 48 gave wide-ranging powers to the president, which were abused in the period 1930–33 (see p. 210–17). Similarly, the demand for a referendum could easily be exploited to obstruct the democratic process, as it was by the nationalist right during the debate over the Young Plan in 1929 (see p. 209).

The Versailles '*Diktat*'

From November 1918 up to early May 1919 the Germans were living in what Ernst Troeltsch called 'the dreamland of the Armistice period'.[7] The German government initially hoped that by stressing its democratic credentials it would be able to conclude a peace based on the 14 Points. Its overriding aim was to protect the potential of the German economy so that the way was left clear for a renaissance of German economic power. There was no intention of paying the Allies an indemnity, even though it was conceded that the cost of rebuilding the devastated areas of Belgium and France would have to be met. As for territorial concessions, the cession of Alsace-Lorraine to France was accepted, as were limited annexations by the new state of Poland, but these were to be balanced by the inclusion of Austria and the other German-speaking areas of the former Habsburg Empire in the Reich. Finally, it was assumed that the new democratic Reich would play a key role in the League of Nations and would remain a great power.

When the German delegation was summoned to Paris on 7 May to be presented with the draft terms of the treaty, it received a rude shock:

- The demand for reparations had been greatly inflated by the British proposal for including family allowances and pensions for the wounded.
- Upper Silesia and most of the provinces of West Prussia and Posen were awarded to Poland; only in Marienwerder was there to be a plebiscite. Danzig was to become a free city, under the protection of the League of Nations, and northern Schleswig was to be returned to Denmark.
- In the west, besides Alsace-Lorraine reverting to France, Eupen and Malmedy were to be ceded to Belgium, while the Saar was to be put under the administration of the League of Nations for 15 years, after which there would be a plebiscite. The Rhineland was to be occupied for a period of 15 years by Allied troops.

See Map 6

- Germany would lose all her colonies and foreign investments, as well as most of her merchant navy.
- The German army was to be cut down to 100,000 men, its navy to a mere 15,000, while the general staff was to be disbanded. Tanks, aircraft, submarines and poison gas were all forbidden.

The Germans were allowed only 14 days to consider these terms. Initially there was unanimous agreement that they were unacceptable. The Foreign Office attempted to force a revision by arguing that the 14 Points and the German–American exchange of notes in October 1918 had the legal status of a treaty and that Germany was not alone in starting the war. On 16 June, when the German delegation was handed the final version of the treaty, the only appreciable concession which the Allies made was the decision to hold a plebiscite in Upper Silesia. The treaty met with a storm of protest in Germany and triggered a political crisis splitting the cabinet and leading to the resignation of Scheidemann, but, given Germany's military weakness, the new chancellor, Gustav Bauer, had no option but accept it.

See Documents
51.1, 51.2 and 50

Karl-Dietrich Erdmann observed that the treaty was 'too severe, since Germany could do no other, from the first step onwards, than try to shake it off; too lenient, because Germany was not so far weakened as to be deprived of the hope and possibility of either extricating herself from the treaty or tearing it up'.[8] It was a harsh treaty, which directly affected millions of Germans in the Rhineland, Upper Silesia and West Prussia, yet it was not the Carthaginian peace that contemporaries accused it of being. Despite reparations, the loss of 13 per cent of her territory and the consequent handing over of 6 million Germans to alien regimes, Germany's great power potential remained. Given time and skill, as Stresemann was to show (see pp. 187–9), revision was possible.

Carthaginian peace: the peace of revenge and destruction which the Romans imposed on Carthage

Post-war politics, 1919–23

The legacy of the war

Few would disagree with Wolfgang Mommsen that 'the seedbed of extremist nationalism and the eventual rise to power of the National Socialists was a set of social and economic factors that had their origins in the Great World War'.[9] The legacy of the war created immense problems for the new republic:

- Total war had grossly distorted the German economy. Armament production inflated the heavy industrial sector and accelerated the pre-1914 trend toward industrial concentration, while the British blockade ruined the German export trade, which led to a massive restructuring of industry to the detriment of the consumer and craft industries.
- The government was burdened with a massive public debt of 250.7 billion marks by November 1918, which was exacerbated by welfare payments to war invalids and widows, and reparations.
- As most of the war expenditure had been financed by loans, bonds and the printing of money, inflation gathered pace. Prices had risen by 250

SOUVENIR—XMAS 1919

Photographic house and camera
repairing works

AUG. LANG
Mechanician of precision
COLOGNE
KL. NEUGASSE 9/11

Always bargains in **second-hand** binoculars
Zeiss - Goertz, Voigtländer and Leitz etc.

SAVE
TIME — TROUBLE — MONEY

BY BUYING YOUR

CUTLERY
IN COLOGNE. WE HAVE

RAZORS, POCKET-
KNIVES, SCISSORS,
MANICURE SETS,
KNIVES, FORKS AND
SPOONS, SAFETY-
RAZOR BLADES

AT THE LOWEST PRICES FROM
STOCK IN COLOGNE.

F. ADAMS
GLADBACHERSTRASSE 21

!ARCADIA!

Hohestrasse 79 COLOGNE Brückenstr. 5-9

First - class Confectioners
Shop and Wine Restaurant

OWN pastry   First-class cooking
Best wines   Beer in decanters

ORCHESTRA

Tables may be reserved
by telephone A 5444

Officers and civilians only

Christian Krug
COLOGNE
Breitestrasse 52 Telephone A8882
Theatre wardrobes etc. for
hire. Great choice in gent-
lemen's and ladies dresses.
We buy and hire out.

NÜCHEL&HILLEBRECHT
COLOGNE, Glockengasse, Telephone A5566
Corner Kreuzgasse   Close Schauspielhaus

UNIFORM MAKERS
MILITARY OUTFITS

Manufacture of all Uniforms
for the Army of Occupation.
First-class References.

46

16 German shopkeepers made the best of a bad job and set out to sell to the British occupying forces
by advertising the British military newspaper, the *Cologne Post*

Cologne Post, Souvenir Number, Christmas 1919, p. 46

per cent during the war, and this was only a taste of what was to come. The war bonds into which many patriotic Germans had poured their savings (see p. 153) were to be valueless by 1923.

• The war polarized society into winners and losers: apart from the owners of the war industries – about a hundred and twenty thousand people – who made immense fortunes, those who gained most were the skilled workers in the war industries, while the middle classes were the greatest losers. Civil servants, white-collar workers, small businessmen and craftsmen all saw their status eroded, and their savings, which many had invested in war loans, destroyed. Inevitably this increased the sense of bitterness felt about Germany's defeat and the Versailles settlement, and made this group susceptible to the siren voices of the nationalist right.

• Politically the First World War had left a longing to re-create the exhilarating experience of the spirit of 1914, which contrasted so favourably with the divisive politics of the Weimar Republic. The appointment of Hindenburg and Ludendorff in 1916 had also set a precedent for a plebiscitary dictatorship imposed on Germany by the high command.

Threats from within, 1920–22

Successive governments were confronted by a series of political economic and social problems which appeared insoluble. Not only were they under enormous pressure from the French, who were determined to exploit the peace treaty to weaken or even dismember Germany, but the republic was threatened from within by both the extreme left and the extreme right. By December 1919 the USPD had committed itself to establishing the dictatorship of the proletariat, while in the Ruhr a large number of miners were joining syndicalist organizations and were ready to take direct action against the capitalists and the 'class enemy'. In January 1920 labour unrest on the railways and the coalfields, and a mass demonstration culminating in an attack on the *Reichstag* prompted the government to declare a state of emergency, which temporarily brought the situation under control.

The government viewed the left as the major threat to the republic, yet the assault from the right was potentially far more dangerous. 1919 had witnessed a polarization which had caused many white-collar workers and members of the *Mittelstand* to move from the centre to the right. Students too had embraced a new, hard-line, nationalist ethos, while right-wing papers and pamphlets maintained a constant barrage of agitation against the 'shameful peace' and the 'stab in the back' myth. This attitude was fully shared by many academics, teachers, Protestant priests and members of the judiciary. The latter, holding posts from which they could not be constitutionally dismissed, often dispensed a highly politicized form of justice. Leading Weimar politicians became the target of constant verbal abuse. Matthias Erzberger, for instance, was singled out for particularly bitter attacks because, as finance minister, he was the

The 'stab in the back' myth: this pungent term originated in a statement made to the Investigation Committee of the National Assembly on 18 November 1919 by Hindenburg. The term was immediately taken up by the right, but also found considerable support across the political spectrum amongst those who could not come to terms with Germany's military defeat. By 'stab in the back' it was implied that the strikes and mutinies of October–November 1918 had forced the high command into negotiating an armistice.

pivotal politician who held the coalition together. He particularly annoyed the right when he introduced a series of new taxes on war profits, capital gains and inherited wealth, and asserted the Reich's financial authority over the *Länder*. He was immediately accused by Helfferich, the DNVP leader, of putting his own financial interests first. Erzberger brought a libel action against him, but the judge argued that much of the accusation was factually correct, and he was left with little option but to resign.

Ludendorff was not content just to harry the Weimar regime. In July 1919 he had, with Wolfgang Kapp, a founder member of the Fatherland party (see p. 152), and in close contact with General Lüttwitz, the commander of the *Reichswehr* in central and eastern Germany, set up the National Association with the intention of overthrowing the republic. Their opportunity came when the government, under pressure from the Allies, began to disband the *Freikorps*. Kapp and Lüttwitz seized the chance to exploit their members' alarm at the imminent prospects of unemployment. On 10 March Lüttwitz presented Ebert with demands for his resignation and the retention of the *Freikorps*. When the government dismissed him, the Ehrhardt *Marine Brigade* occupied Berlin and proclaimed Kapp chancellor. General Reinhardt, the *Reichswehr* commander-in-chief, was ready to crush the *putsch*, but, as none of his generals would agree to supply the necessary troops, the government fled first to Dresden and then to Stuttgart. A spontaneous and nation-wide general strike by the trade unions called Kapp's bluff, and on 18 March both Kapp and Lüttwitz fled to Sweden. The *putsch* was successful only in Bavaria, where the *Reichswehr* commanders were able to force the government to resign, replacing it with a right-wing regime which became a 'focus of order'. Bavaria rapidly became 'an Eldorado for extreme right-wing organizations and the leading personalities of militant right-wing radicalism'.[10] It was there that Hitler joined the DAP, which was soon to transform into the Nazi party (NSDAP) (see p. 184).

The unions hoped that the defeat of the *putsch* would lead to a purge of hostile right-wing elements in the army and administration, an accelerated socialization programme and the formation of a new, more left-wing government, but the Ruhr uprising in April effectively prevented the regime from moving decisively against its enemies. As in the winter of 1919–20, *Reichswehr* and *Freikorps* troops, who had not yet been disbanded, were again needed to restore order and to defeat the 'Red Army' in the Ruhr.

In the wake of the defeat of these upheavals, the government brought forward to early June the date of the first election to be held under the new constitution. The results were a disaster for the Weimar coalition. Disillusionment on both the right and the left led to heavy losses for the SPD and DDP, while the USPD and the right-wing DVP and DNVP chalked up impressive gains. The original Weimar coalition parties could now command only 205 seats out of 459. The immediate prospects for stabilizing the regime were complicated by the SPD's decision not to

Reichswehr: the new German army formed after the defeat of 1918

See Document 50

See Document 51.2

The Ruhr uprising

Over the winter of 1919–20 a growing desire for direct action had been developing in the Ruhr. The Kapp *putsch* acted as a catalyst for this. In mid-March 1920 fighting broke out in the eastern Ruhr when workers suspected that *Freikorp* troops were moving to crush the syndicalist movement. 'Overnight', as Wolfgang Mommsen has written, 'the mass strike of Ruhr workers against Kapp and Lüttwitz was transformed into a movement of open insurrection, directed simultaneously against the counter-revolutionary activities of suspect *Reichswehr* units and the policies of the national government, and accompanied by somewhat ill-concerted "wildcat" acts of socialization'.[11] The revolt was supported by about 80,000 men and led by a loosely co-ordinated group of Workers' Councils. Initially it inflicted some sharp defeats on the *Reichswehr*. Carl Severing, the Prussian minister of the interior, representing the Majority Social Democrats and trade union leaders, managed to divide the insurgents by accepting some of their demands – the so called 'eight points'. In April the rump of the 'Red Army' was ruthlessly crushed and some 5000 insurgents sought refuge in the British Rhineland Zone.

participate in the government. After three weeks of negotiations a minority DVP–Centre coalition was formed by the Centre politician, Konstantin Fehrenbach. The SPD, which became 'a kind of cross between a government party and an opposition one',[12] 'tolerated' the administration but avoided accepting political responsibility for its decisions.

Until 1924 domestic politics were dominated by the problems connected with the execution of the Treaty of Versailles. The bitter wrangles with the Allies over reparation payments gave successive governments every excuse to delay stabilizing the currency. Accelerating inflation made it more difficult for the Reparation Commission to estimate the amount Germany could pay, but this was not the only reason why the Weimar governments did not grasp the nettle of currency stabilization. The explosive internal situation ensured that no party was ready to risk a policy of financial cuts and retrenchment, which would simultaneously increase unemployment and cut welfare benefits. The growing strength of the Communist party, with which the left wing of the USPD had amalgamated in October 1920, was evidence that, despite the defeat of the Ruhr uprising, left-wing militancy was far from dead. In the spring of 1921 insurrections broke out in Merseburg, Halle and Mansfeld, although they were defeated within a few days by paramilitary police.

The protracted struggle with the Allies over the execution of the peace terms inflamed the radical right. Patriotic leagues and secret societies were formed as successors to the *Freikorps*, which had been disbanded under the pressure from the *Entente*. Some of these developed into terrorist groups which assassinated separatists and informers who had assisted the Allied occupying forces. They also conducted a campaign to eliminate prominent socialists and politicians of the Weimar coalition, who had appeased the *Entente* powers. In the summer of 1921 both Karl Gareis, the USPD leader, and Matthias Erzberger were murdered, and in June 1922 Walther Rathenau (see p. 150), the foreign minister, was assassinated because he was attempting to pursue a policy of co-operation with the Entente in the hope of persuading them to revise the Treaty of Versailles (see pp. 180–2).

Rathenau's murder created an enormous sensation and momentarily rallied support to the republic. A Law for the Protection of the Republic was passed, despite opposition from the DNVP, the BVP and the KPD, which enabled the government to prohibit extremist organizations, but again its effectiveness was limited by the reluctance of the judiciary to ban right-wing organizations and by the refusal of the Bavarian government to implement it. Given the political polarization in Germany, the government also decided to delay the elections for the presidency until the summer of 1925. Attempts to strengthen the coalition by bringing in the DVP led, however, to the withdrawal of the SPD, and the subsequent collapse of Wirth's second administration in November 1922. A new and much more right-wing administration was formed by Wilhelm Cuno, the head of the Hamburg–America shipping line, who packed the cabinet with non-party experts.

Joseph Wirth, 1879–1956: Wirth had been a mathematics teacher in Baden. He was on the left wing of the Centre party, and was a passionate democrat and republican. He was chancellor from May 1921– November 1922 and pursued a policy of fulfilment, that is of attempting to carry out the Treaty of Versailles

See Document 48

The struggle for survival: foreign policy, 1919–22

Germany's foreign policy aims after the signature of the Treaty of Versailles were summarized by Hermann Müller, the foreign minister, in the Reichstag in July 1919:

- Germany was committed to renouncing the use of military force and reaching an understanding with the *Entente* powers;
- Where possible it would fulfil the treaty, but it would also direct all of its energies towards its peaceful revision.

In practice, however, German foreign policy had little room for manoeuvre. The Reich was, in these early-post-war years, 'more an object of policy by the *Entente*'[13] than an independent force in its own right. German foreign policy therefore oscillated between despairing opposition and more constructive attempts to modify the treaty. The international situation was made much more difficult by the refusal of the American Senate to ratify the Treaty of Versailles, although the USA did sign its own agreement with Berlin, terminating hostilities. America withdrew from all the arrangements made for carrying out the treaty and the proposed Anglo–American military guarantee of France never came into force. For Germany there consequently appeared to be two main possibilities for achieving treaty revision: one was to exploit Anglo–French differences in the hope that this would weaken the united front of the *Entente* and lead to concessions to Germany; the other policy, favoured by the army, influential diplomats and some industrialists, was to come to an understanding with the USSR, which would strengthen Berlin's hand against the *Entente*, but this was a dangerous strategy, which ran the risk of contaminating Germany with Bolshevism.

The issue of drawing up a list of alleged German war criminals to be handed over to Allied courts provided Berlin with the first successful opportunity to play Britain and France off against each other. Through discreet contacts with British officials on the Inter-Allied Military Control Commissions (IAMCCs), which were beginning to monitor German disarmament measures, the government was able to convince the British government that the depth of feeling against this demand was so great that it would hinder the smooth execution of the peace. The British government accepted this, and successfully persuaded the French to moderate their demands and agree to any such trials being carried out by German courts.

Those who favoured a Russian alliance were encouraged in August 1920 by dramatic developments in the Polish–Soviet war, when the Russian advance on Warsaw threatened to transform the situation in Europe. The prospect of the collapse of Poland and the subsequent option of revising Poland's western frontiers with Soviet backing caused immense excitement in Germany, but the government cautiously declared its strict neutrality. Whether this would have held in the event of a Soviet victory is hard to say, but the Battle of Warsaw on 16 August, where the Russians were routed, effectively blocked the immediate possibility of German–Soviet co-operation and 'preserved for the *Entente* the dominant voice in European stabilization'.[14] Consequently, throughout the winter and spring of 1920–21 German policy essentially remained dependent on the decisions of the *Entente* on reparations, the disarmament question and the plebiscite in Upper Silesia. Of these three, reparation was by far the most crucial. The British aimed to fix the global sum as quickly as possible in the hope that once Germany knew the full sum of her debts she would be able to raise credit in America and begin payments. The French government was also playing with the idea of coming to an agreement with Berlin, which would effectively turn Germany economically into a junior partner. The upshot of this thinking was the Seydoux Plan, which could have enabled Germany to pay a large part of her reparation bill in industrial and plant deliveries, but it was rejected by both Britain and Germany at the Brussels Conference at the end of 1920. The German government noted that France had still not given up the right to take sanctions and that no exact figure had been given regarding the total reparations it would have to pay or deliver. Besides, there was also considerable opposition from the German industrialists, who feared the French might exploit the treaty to dominate German heavy industry.

At the Paris Conference in January 1921 the Allies at last agreed on a provisional figure of 226,000 billion gold marks to be paid over a period of 42 years. This caused an outcry in Germany and was immediately

In early 1920 the Poles invaded the Ukraine

rejected by the German government, which produced its own figures a month later. These amounted to a modest overall payment of 30 billion gold marks, which was also conditional upon the retention of Upper Silesia. The offer was so obviously inadequate that the *Entente* occupied Düsseldorf, Duisburg and Ruhrort. As one German official conceded to a British officer on the IAMCC, Berlin had made a 'tremendous mistake in allowing France the opportunity of putting herself in the right'.[15] As a final gamble before the Reparation Commission came up with fresh figures on 1 May, Walther Simons, the German foreign minister, appealed to America and produced a payments plan, which, had it been produced earlier, might have been acceptable, but the Americans at this stage still refused to be drawn into the reparation conflict. At the end of April the Reparation Commission finally completed its study of Germany's financial liabilities under the Treaty of Versailles and fixed the German debt at 132 billion gold marks, which was considerably less than the amount provisionally fixed in Paris in January. The amount was accepted by the Allied leaders, who on 5 May dispatched an ultimatum to Berlin giving the Germans a week to accept the new payment schedule, after which the Ruhr would be occupied.

In Berlin the Fehrenbach government resigned, and a new more broadly-based administration led by Joseph Wirth was formed on 10 May. Wirth, assisted by Walther Rathenau, his minister for reconstruction, was determined to pursue a policy of negotiation rather than

---

Were reparations set too high?

The debt of 132 billion gold marks was divided into three sets of bonds: A, B and C. The last series was worth 82 billion gold marks, and would not be issued until German exports had made a recovery. Effectively this raised a large question mark over whether in reality they would ever be issued at all, as the British had no wish to see a massive boom in the German export trade. Thus, effectively, the German debt was set at 50 billion gold marks. Was even this sum payable? Given the state of German finances in 1921, it still presented immense problems. The only way Germany could pay in gold equivalent was to purchase foreign currencies, but as the value of the mark declined, this became increasingly expensive. The debt of 50 billion gold marks could, for example, only be raised by selling the sum of 750 billion paper marks on the foreign exchange. However, there were ways of paying this sum. The French were ready to consider the transfer of industrial shares to their ownership, although this was opposed by the British, who did not wish to see the French have an important say in German heavy industry. Many German industrialists and bankers such as the DNVP leader, Helfferich and the industrialist, Stinnes, argued that reparations were the root cause of inflation, but in fact if the German government grasped the nettle of stabilizing the currency, increasing taxation and deflating domestic demand, this would theoretically have freed resources for an export drive and made the transfer of reparations funds possible. The short-term problem, however, was that the world recession, tariffs and import quotas prevented such a favourable scenario.[16]

confrontation and to co-operate closely with the British in the hope that Lloyd George would be able to ensure that Upper Silesia remained German. For the next six months the Silesian issue dominated German politics. In the plebiscite in April 1921 a majority in the industrial area and 60 per cent of the total vote had opted for Germany. To pre-empt any move to restore the industrial region to Germany, an armed revolt broke out, led by the Polish nationalist, Wojciech Korfanty. His forces, covertly supported by the French, quickly established themselves along the so-called Korfanty line some eighty kilometres to the west of Kattowitz (see Map 6). German self-defence forces backed by volunteers then moved into Silesia and attacked the insurgents. The British bitterly condemned the Korfanty uprising, but had been unable to secure any major concessions from the French, and in August agreed to have the whole Upper Silesian question transferred to the League of Nations where the French contrived to secure a decision, which ultimately gave the key industrial triangle to the Poles. The policy of closer co-operation with Britain had failed to save Upper Silesia, and Wirth resigned in protest, although he returned to power four days later.

> Many of the volunteers were members of the *Freikorps* who had gone 'underground' to defy the Allied ban on paramilitary groups

By the autumn of 1921 Wirth's policy of fulfilment was also running into considerable difficulties. On 31 August the first instalment of reparations had been paid punctually, but, as the government, like its predecessors, still shied away from stabilizing the currency, cutting expenditure and imposing new taxes, it was becoming ever clearer that Germany would not be able to pay the second instalment punctually. In the short term, Wirth and Rathenau, who became foreign minister in January 1922, sought a moratorium from the *Entente*. Both wanted to play for time until America was ready to take part in a general reparation and inter-Allied debt settlement. In the meantime the government was determined to exploit the economic advantages of inflation, which ensured that German exports were much cheaper than their rivals, and escape from isolation and subservience to the *Entente* by establishing economic and clandestine military contacts with Russia.

> **Moratorium**: a temporary suspension of debt payments

Rathenau also pursued initiatives in both Paris and London, which could, given time, have led to a solution to the reparation crisis. He attempted to revive a version of the Seydoux Plan when he signed the Wiesbaden Accords with Loucheur on 6 October, which would have increased the amount of reparations delivered in kind and envisaged 'direct Franco–German cooperation as the core of western European reconstruction',[17] but opposition from both French and German industrialists prevented their implementation. He was also sympathetic to Lloyd George's plan for the formation of a European consortium to rebuild the Russian economy, although he wanted it to involve central and south-eastern Europe too. Yet when the European powers met to discuss it at Genoa in April 1922, Rathenau's decision to sign the unilateral Rapallo Agreement with the USSR, effectively torpedoed the conference. This, temporarily at least, alienated Lloyd George and intensified mistrust in Paris, where Raymond Poincaré, who was convinced that

The Rapallo Agreement

Both Russia and Germany had some reason to fear marginalization at Genoa. The Soviets were suspicious that the Western powers and Germany would gang up against them, while Germany was apprehensive that they would come to an understanding with Russia, which would permit the Soviet regime to claim reparations. The Germans consequently responded to Soviet initiatives and signed the Treaty of Rapallo. By this treaty both powers mutually renounced any claims to reparations, and agreed to normalize trading relations and enter into full diplomatic relations. In many ways it was a triumph for the Soviet government, which managed to divide its enemies, but for Germany it brought little immediate gain. Arguably it signalled that Germany was not totally isolated, but it intensified the suspicions of Poincaré and did little to defuse the growing crisis over reparations.

only the threat to occupy the Ruhr would force the Germans to pay reparations, had recently come to power. Rathenau was assassinated in June before he was able to repair the diplomatic damage caused by Rapallo.

In July 1922 the Germans requested a two-year moratorium on reparation payments, but Poincaré, faced with no financial concessions on French debts from either Britain or America, insisted that the price of a moratorium would have to be the expropriation by the Reparation Commission of the state-owned mines in the Ruhr and the dyestuff industry. Despite British opposition, he seized the chance to implement his policy when, in early January 1923, the Reparation Commission declared Germany to be in default on deliveries of timber and coal. On 9 January French and Belgian engineers, protected by five French and one Belgian division, began to take control of the Ruhr industries.

The Ruhr occupation, 1923

The immediate impact of the Ruhr occupation was to unite the German nation. For a few months the spirit of 1914 seemed to return. The government suspended all reparation payments and instructed the population of the Ruhr to go on strike and refuse to work for the French. In the short term these passive resistance tactics worked. In the first half of 1923 less coal and coke was delivered than in the last ten days of 1922. Essentially the plan was to convince the French that their policy would fail, but this policy put enormous pressure on the German economy. To subsidize the strikers and compensate for the lost tax revenues from the Ruhr, the government printed money. The value of the mark continued to sink rapidly, and by August it was worthless.

This completed the impoverishment of the large number of the middle classes dependent on fixed incomes, war bonds and insurance annuities. By August it was clear that, although France's international position was weakening, Germany could no longer maintain the passive resistance

Dollar quotations for the mark, 1914–23	
July 1914	4.2
Jan. 1919	8.9
Jan. 1920	64.8
July 1920	39.5
Jan. 1921	64.9
Jan. 1922	493.2
Jan. 1923	17,972.0
July 1923	353,412.0
Aug. 1923	4,620,455.0
Sept. 1923	98,860,000.0
Oct. 1923	4,200,000,000,000.0

Source: G. Craig, *Germany, 1866–1945*, Oxford, Oxford University Press, 1978, p. 450.

See Document 52

campaign. The Cuno government resigned and a 'grand coalition' of the SPD, DDP and DVP was formed, with Stresemann as chancellor. He called off passive resistance on 26 September, but his attempt to gain the necessary powers to get the economy moving again by asking the *Reichstag* to agree to an enabling act, was at first thwarted by the SPD, who feared that it would lead to an extension of the eight-hour day for the workers. Their refusal led to the temporary collapse of the Grand Coalition on 3 October. This was reconstructed once the SPD was reassured that the eight-hour day would only be extended in exceptional circumstances when the good of the country clearly demanded it. The enabling bill was then approved by the *Reichstag* a week later. In November the minister of finance, Hans Luther, replaced the devalued Reichsmark with the new temporary currency, the *Rentenmark*, which was backed by mortgage bonds based on the assets of industry and agriculture, and in August 1924 was succeeded by the new Reichsmark.

See Document 47

Gustav Stresemann, 1878–1929

Stresemann was the most prominent liberal politician in the Weimar Republic. He started his business career as a promoter of industrial interests in Saxony and entered the *Reichstag* as a National Liberal member in 1903. During the war he was an ardent supporter of the extreme war aims of the Pan-German League. After the war he founded the DVP, and he voted against the new republican Weimar constitution in 1919. Gradually, however, he came to accept the republic, and publicly backed it after Rathenau's assassination in 1922. He was chancellor from August to November 1923 and foreign minister continuously from August 1923 until his death in October 1929.

Internally the Reich government was faced with subversive threats from both the extreme left and extreme right. The Communists planned a 'German October'. In both Saxony and Thuringia the KPD began to make military preparations for an uprising, but these were thwarted by vigorous central government intervention. In Thuringia the KPD resigned from the *Land* government and the proletarian defence units were disbanded, while the Saxon government was dismissed, and a state commissioner appointed. Only in Hamburg did an uprising of a few hundred Communists take place, but it was speedily crushed.

From the right the government was faced in October with a mutiny in Küstrin by the 'Black *Reichswehr*', a secret reserve army which it had built up in case of war with France, but it was suppressed by regular *Reichswehr* troops. The real centre of right-wing resistance was, however, Bavaria. The right-wing state government was under pressure from patriotic, nationalist and paramilitary associations, which had set up the *Kampfbund* under the patronage of Ludendorff and led by Hitler. This was planning to emulate Mussolini's march on Rome and stage a coup against the Berlin government. When passive resisistance was halted in the Ruhr, the Bavarian government declared a state of emergency and appointed Ritter von Kahr, who was himself a member of the Patriotic Associations, state commissioner. In October local *Reichswehr* troops refused to obey orders coming from the Berlin government. General von Seeckt, the head of the Army Command, who had been entrusted with full executive power under article 48 'to take all measures necessary for the security of the Reich' declined, however, to intervene, but he did warn Kahr and the local *Reichswehr* commander, von Lossow, not to become involved with the extreme nationalism of the local Patriotic Associations. Ultimately these warnings were heeded when they both refused to join the abortive Hitler–Ludendorff *putsch* of 9 November.

After the failure of the Munich *putsch*, the wave of unrest in the Reich subsided, but in the Rhineland and the Ruhr, Stresemann still faced an acute threat from France. Although the costs of the Ruhr occupation had caused a precipitous decline in the value of the franc and Anglo–American pressure had forced Poincaré on 30 November to agree in principle to the setting up of an experts' committee to review the whole question of reparations, the French were determined to impose their will on the Rhineland and Ruhr before that committee met. They signed short-term agreements with the Ruhr industrialists, which they hoped would form the basis of a more permanent settlement, and discussions took place with Louis Hagen and Kurt von Schröder, the Cologne bankers, on the possible establishment of a Rhenish currency. Similarly, every encouragement was given to Rhineland separatists. The Reich had little option but to 'stick it out and wait for America'.[18] Time was, however, against the French. Separatism collapsed as a result of local opposition, and in Britain in January 1924 a pro-German Labour government came into power. By January, when the Experts Committee chaired by the American banker, Charles Dawes, began its work, it was clear that the French would ultimately have to leave the Ruhr.

German October: this is a reference to the second Russian revolution of October 1917 when the Bolsheviks siezed power

Kampfbund: Fighting League

Hitler, the Nazis and the Munich *putsch*

By spring 1923 Hitler had built up the small German Workers' party , which had changed its name to the NSDAP in February 1921, to become one of the largest of the extreme right-wing groups in Bavaria. It was a measure of Hitler's new standing in right-wing Bavarian circles that in September 1923 he became the political leader of the *Kampfbund*, which had been formed to co-ordinate tactics against the republic. The party's paramilitary force, the SA, was integrated into the military wing of the *Bund*, and Hitler was the 'drummer', whose task was to mobilize public opinion to support a *putsch* in Munich, as a preliminary to taking Berlin by force. The new government was to be headed by Ludendorff, although Hitler would also be a member.

To have any chance of success the *Kampfbund* needed the backing of von Kahr and the heads of the Bavarian police and the local *Reichswehr* units, but, after hearing that the *Reichswehr* would not move against the elected government in Berlin, these officials began to have second thoughts. This left Hitler in a dangerous situation. His followers demanded action, but if he delayed too long the right moment would pass. He consequently tried to coerce Kahr by seizing him and his colleagues while they were addressing a public meeting at the *Bürgerbräukeller* on the evening of 8 November. Reluctantly bowing to force, they agreed to support him, but then Hitler, who was called away to deal with a problem involving the seizure of the Engineers' Barracks, left them in charge of Ludendorff. The latter allowed them to go home on receiving their word of honour that they would support Hitler, but the following morning, they ordered the police to break up the planned march into the city centre. A few days later Hitler was arrested. In February 1924 he was given the minimum sentence of five years' imprisonment, with a virtual promise that he would be released early on probation. The publicity the *putsch* received and the subsequent trial turned Hitler into a national figure.

Conclusion

Given the economic and social legacy of the world war, Wolfgang Mommsen argues that 'the fate of the Weimar Republic was, in a sense, sealed from the start'.[19] Clearly the war accelerated the decline of the middle classes and distorted the German economy, but the fact that the Weimar Republic survived the first four turbulent years of its existence shows that its eventual collapse was by no means inevitable. As John Hiden has observed, 'Weimar democracy was more resilient than has often been acknowledged.'[20]

10 *Partial Stabilization, 1924–29*

TIMELINE

1924	13 Feb.	State of emergency ends
	1 Apr.	Hitler sentenced to five years' imprisonment
	19 Aug.	Dawes Plan approved by the *Reichstag*
	7 Dec.	*Reichstag* election
	20 Dec.	Hitler released from jail
1925	15 Jan.	Hans Luther forms bourgeois bloc government with DNVP
	26 Apr.	Hindenburg elected president
	July	Evacuation of the Ruhr begins
	27 Nov.	*Reichstag* approves Locarno Treaties
1926	24 Apr.	German–Soviet Berlin Treaty
	12 May	Luther government resigns over flag dispute
	8 Sept.	Germany joins League of Nations
	17 Dec.	Fall of Marx cabinet
1927	29 Jan.	Marx heads second bourgeois bloc government
	31 Jan.	Inter-Allied Military Control Commission leaves Germany
1928	20 May	*Reichstag* elections
	29 June	Grand Coalition formed
	20 Oct.	Hugenberg becomes leader of DNVP
1929	9 July	Nazis and DNVP jointly oppose Young Plan
	3 Oct.	Death of Stresemann
	24–29 Oct.	US Stock Market crashes

Introduction

The years 1924–30 were a period of 'relative stabilization'. In foreign policy Stresemann went far to normalize Germany's relations with France and Britain, while by 1928 industrial production had just about overtaken the figure for 1913. Domestically, too, the intensity of the quarrels, which at times had bordered on civil war, had abated. Yet this 'stabilization was fragile and superficial'.[1] The structural cracks in the republic were still visible, and, to quote Detlev Peukert, were 'an outward sign of hidden weaknesses that might prove fatal when the structure was next subjected to severe strain'.[2]

Key issues

- To what extent did Stresemann's foreign policy lay the foundations for a German recovery and re-emergence as a great power?
- What were the economic and political consequences of the stabilization of the mark?
- How 'modern' was the Weimar Republic?
- To what extent can the years 1924–29 be seen as a period of economic recovery and political stabilization?

Foreign policy

Both before and during the war Stresemann had been a particularly strident German nationalist, but Germany's post-war humiliations
convinced him that only a policy of rapprochement with France could
open the way up to a restoration of German influence in Europe. This
conversion was not brought about by a fundamental change of attitudes
but rather by the pragmatic recognition of Germany's situation.

Essential to the success of Stresemann's plans was the adoption of the
Dawes Plan, which the Experts Commission, chaired by Charles Dawes,
had produced in April 1924 (see p. 185). The plan was accepted by the
Entente powers, the USA and Germany at the London Conference in
August 1924, and provided the economic context in which his policy of
détente could be conducted. While the plan did not alter the final total of
reparations fixed in 1921, it recommended:

> **Détente**: a state
> of lessened tension
> or growing relax-
> ation between two
> or more states

- An 800-million-mark loan was to be raised privately, mainly in
  America.
- Annual payments were to start gradually and rise at the end of five years
  to their maximum level.
- These payments were to be secured by the revenues of the German railways, customs and taxes, while a committee of foreign experts was to
  sit in Berlin to ensure that the transfer of payments to Allied accounts
  would occur in a way that did not damage the German economy.
- The plan was provisional and was to be renegotiated within ten years.
- In the event of Germany again refusing to pay, a repetition of the
  unilateral Franco-Belgian occupation of the Ruhr in 1923 (see p. 182)
  would be prevented by America sending a representative to sit on the
  Reparation Commission, who would be able to act as an effective brake
  on the French.

As the financing of the plan had constitutional implications,
Stresemann needed the help of the DNVP to gain the two-thirds majority in the *Reichstag* necessary for ratification. Under pressure from the
industrial and agricultural organizations, which were anxious to see it
adopted, about half the DNVP voted for it (see p. 200). The plan gave the
German economy a chance to recover. American capital poured into
Germany and industry was at last able to finance its needs.

With the failure of the Ruhr occupation, the French had little option
but to insist on the strict implementation of the Treaty of Versailles. In
January 1925 they refused to agree to an Allied evacuation of the Cologne
Zone on the grounds that Germany had used the Ruhr crisis to delay
disarmament. To defuse this crisis, Stresemann, with the support of the
British ambassador, Lord D'Abernon, put forward an ambitious plan for
an international guarantee by the European great powers of the territorial status quo in western Europe. These proposals led to the Locarno
Treaty, the key provision of which was a guarantee of the demilitarization

of the Rhineland and the existing frontiers between Germany on the one side, and France and Belgium on the other. The French attempted to extend the guarantees to Germany's eastern borders, but Stresemann agreed only to conclude arbitration treaties with Poland and Czechoslovakia. He hoped that a rapprochement with France would bring about the withdrawal of the Inter-Allied Military Control Commission from Germany, the ending of the occupation of the Rhineland and possibly the return of the *Saarland*. Then, from a position of strength, he intended to negotiate treaty revisions in the east. He secured good relations with the USSR through the Treaty of Berlin, which guaranteed Germany's neutrality if Russia should be at war with any third power, which effectively meant Poland. The new Locarno spirit led to the evacuation of the Cologne Zone in January 1926 and to Germany joining the league nine months later.

See Document 53

Stresemann exploited every available chance to achieve further revision of the Treaty of Versailles. In 1926 at a summit with Briand at Thoiry he offered to pay off a large part of Germany's reparations debts to Belgium and France in return for the evacuation of the Rhineland and the return of the Saar , provided the Americans could be persuaded to underwrite this with a loan to Germany, but the plan had to be shelved when it became clear that potential American subscribers were not interested. A dramatic, comprehensive revision of the treaty was thus not practical politics, but in 1928 the new Müller government (see p. 203) did launch a major initiative to persuade Britain and France to evacuate the Rhineland and to agree to a revision of the Dawes Plan. The American bankers were ready to revise Germany's reparation total downwards, as it was clear that unless this was done, once Berlin had to pay the full annual instalments under the plan, there would be little capital left to service the loans raised since 1924 in America. An independent committee of experts, set up and chaired by the American banker, Owen Young, recommended that the total overall reparation sum should be reduced from 132 billion gold marks to 112 billion, to be paid over the course of 59 years. If Germany accepted this plan, Britain and France were ready to evacuate the Rhineland in 1930. Stresemann accepted these terms at the Hague Conference in August 1929 and French attempts to set up a new Commission of Verification and Conciliation to monitor the demilitarization of the Rhineland were defeated by joint Anglo-German pressure. Stresemann did not live to see the ratification of the Hague Treaty, but the agreement to evacuate the Rhineland made it more palatable to the German people. Nevertheless in December the government was forced by the Nazi and Nationalist right to hold a referendum, which declared that its signature would be an act of high treason. This, however, was easily defeated and the plan became law on 20 January 1930.

With the evacuation of the Rhineland, Germany's restoration as a great European power was virtually complete. Like his successors in the 1950s, Briand came to the conclusion that Germany could only be peacefully contained through some form of European federation. At the tenth meeting of the League of Nations' Assembly in 1929 he outlined a vague scheme for a 'kind of federal link between peoples who are grouped together geographically, like the peoples of Europe'.[3] Stresemann reacted favourably but he was more interested in creating a purely economic union in which Germany could play the key role and bring her economic muscle to play. Nothing, however, was to come of this, as Stresemann's death and the world economic crisis brought the Franco-German rapprochement to a halt.

In the 1950s there were attempts to claim Stresemann as an advocate of European unity and compare him to Konrad Adenauer (see p. 280). It is true that both men realized that a rapprochement with France was fundamental for the success of their foreign policy, but Stresemann was not a European idealist. As Michael-Olaf Maxelon stresses, 'his basic concept . . . was derived from the German aspiration to power before 1914; only 'his strategic methods were adapted to the power situation after 1918'.[4] This can clearly be seen in his Polish policy, which Detlev Peukert argues was very much a missed opportunity. The Treaty of Versailles had left Germany stronger in eastern Europe than before the war. Consequently, if Stresemann had dropped the policy of revision and accepted the frontiers of 1919, Germany would have been in a position 'to offer a zone of security and cooperation similar to that created in the West, and would in all likelihood have assumed the informal role of dominant power in the region, thanks primarily to her economic strength'.[5] On the other hand, the renouncement of any attempt to regain the lands lost in the east would have been intensely unpopular among both the German people and their élites.

> Germany was potentially stronger because the Austrian Empire had collapsed and Russia had lost her Polish territories

Economic recovery?

Concentrating on the slump of 1929–33 and the inflationary period up to 1923, historians have largely overlooked the ongoing crisis caused by the stabilization of the mark in November 1923.[6] Inflation, at any rate up to the autumn of 1922, provided an easy formula which enabled employers to pass on the costs of higher wages and costs to the customer in the form of higher prices. Similarly, it allowed the state to finance its greatly expanded welfare policies. Stabilization, however, confronted both the employers and the state with tight restrictions. The only way that workers' demands for higher wages and the greatly increased demand for welfare benefits and pensions could be met was by an 'economic miracle' on the scale of that experienced by the *Bundesrepublik* after 1949 (see p. 317). This did not, however, happen, and the subsequent industrial militancy and bitterness of those who had lost their life savings in the inflation helped destabilize the Republic. Knut Borchardt[7] has calculated that they could only have been adequately compensated if the per capita national income had increased by about 25 per cent compared to the figure in 1913. In fact, by 1929 it had increased by a mere 6 per cent.

German industrial production, 1913–29

Year	Industrial production
1913	100.0
1919	37.0
1922	70.0
1923	46.0
1924	69.0
1927	100.0
1928	103.8
1929	102.8

Source: Adapted from Knut Borchardt, *Perspectives on Modern German Economic History and Policy*, Cambridge, Cambridge University Press, 1991, pp. 171–2.

After the stabilization of the mark in November 1923 the government was confronted with demands for compensating the millions of creditors, pensioners and small investors who had seen their savings, annuities and government bonds destroyed by inflation, and who also had money which was owed to them paid off in useless paper money. The Supreme Court, in an important decision, decided that the narrow legal argument that a mark remained a mark whether before or after stabilization might be correct legally but was wrong morally, and called on the government to have every individual debt revalued by the courts on the basis of the current economic situation of each debtor and creditor. Clearly such a cumbersome procedure was economically unacceptable to the government. A high revaluation would cost millions of marks, which the economy could not afford, and might well once again trigger inflation. Under cover of the Enabling Act which remained in force from September 1923 until the spring of 1924 (see p. 184), the government issued a decree providing for a 15 per cent revaluation of private debts, with payment postponed until 1932 . When the creditors rejected this, the government, after bitter arguments with their pressure groups, eventually in 1925 agreed to two laws: one set the resettlement of private debts to be paid at between 12.5 and 25 per cent in 1932, while the other regulated the repayment of public debts (for the most part war bonds) at a mere 12.5 per cent of the original value, to be spread over 30 years. The creditors bitterly resented this and saw it as a deliberate betrayal of them by the republic, an issue which the Nazis were later electorally to exploit (see p. 200).

Stabilization also led to the collapse of the Central Working Association of December 1918 and the quasi-corporate agreements between the employers and the unions (see p. 169). Wage disputes became much more bitter as employers and workers fought over whether profits should be distributed mainly in the form of higher wages or else reinvested in industry. The presence of the KPD on the right of the SPD ensured that the free trade unions had to fight bitterly to keep the loyalty of their members. Compulsory state arbitration of strikes, which had been introduced in 1919, also paradoxically worsened the situation by allowing both employers and employees to adopt deeply entrenched antagonistic attitudes, as in the final analysis it was the state that was responsible for arbitration. The employers saw state arbitration as essentially biased in the interests of the workers, who, in a series of wage disputes between 1924 and 1928, had made considerable gains. In an attempt to gain more freedom to run their factories, the employers consequently abandoned the Central Working Association. The modern industries, particularly firms such as Siemens, still attempted to maintain a degree of co-operation with the unions, but their efforts were torpedoed by the leaders of heavy industry, who were determined to turn the clock back to 1913, as far as labour relations, welfare and wages went. Borchardt[8] argues that this conflict was unbridgeable. On the one hand the employers had to cut production and wage costs to survive, while on the other the unions were duty-bound to defend the gains made in 1918–19.

When the Grand Coalition was formed under the SPD chancellor, Hermann Müller, in 1928, the unions became more assertive. In the autumn of 1928 a strike over wages in the Ruhr and Rhine metal industry was settled by state arbitration, which awarded the workers a small increase. The employers ignored the award and locked out about 250,000 metalworkers for nearly two months in an attempt to prevent accelerating wage demands and to destroy the state arbitration mechanism. The majority in the *Reichstag* supported the workers, who were given financial assistance by the state. Eventually the employers accepted a second arbitration, which awarded the employees a minimal shortening of the week and a 4 per cent wage increase. The failure of the employers to gain complete freedom to set their own wage structure persuaded the heavy industrialists that ultimately a more authoritarian government was needed, which would dismantle the welfare state and allow the employers to discipline the workers. This was to determine their attitude in the economic and political crisis of 1930–32 (see p. 214).

To recapture lost markets and to increase profits, industrialists sought to rationalize their plants. Surplus labour was ruthlessly combed out and new technology was introduced, especially in the mining industry where

---

Hermann Müller, 1876–1931

He came from a middle-class background and was elected to the *Reichstag* for the SPD in 1916. He belonged to the right-wing of the party and supported Ebert in 1918–19. He served as foreign minister in the Weimar coalition governments of 1919–20. In the 1920s he was both co-chairman of the SPD and leader of the parliamentary party in the Reichstag. From 1928 to 1930 he was Reich chancellor.

by 1929 one miner in four had lost his job. This led to a steadily increasing pool of structural unemployment, which did not disappear even in the brief spells of economic expansion that occurred in 1925 and 1927–28. To protect markets and to avoid price undercutting by rivals, the large industries also continued their post-war policy of creating cartels, which for investment relied heavily on the government for funds.

Relative industrial stagnation was paralleled by the worldwide agricultural depression, which hit both the east Elbian landowners and the smaller farmers a devastating blow in 1928, and led to a steep fall in grain prices. Already before the depression the great estates in the east were caught in a 'scissors crisis': to sell their goods on the world market they needed to modernize, yet despite receiving state aid (*Osthilfe*) they were unable to do this, and consequently sank deeper into debt. After 1928 only about 50 per cent of the farms in the west and 33 per cent of those in the east were solvent. The agricultural slump affected not only the farmers but the whole of rural society. Anger in the countryside was directed both at the welfare policy of the state, which was perceived to be favouring the urban working classes and at its trade policies, which in practice encouraged the import of foreign food in exchange for the opening up of export markets. In 1928 there were massive peasant protests in Schleswig-Holstein where public officials and buildings were attacked. In Oldenburg some thirty thousand peasants demonstrated with slogans such as 'From the Welfare State to the Work State'. This hostility was to be effectively exploited by the Nazis.

The structural weaknesses of the German economy were very visible in this brief period of stabilization. Essentially the battle to distribute the financial burdens imposed by the lost war and escalating cost of welfare payments fairly between employers and employees, pensioners and the state, and town and country could only be solved in a context of uninterrupted growth, which was impossible after 1929.

A municipal renaissance

In the same way that historians like Geoff Eley and Margaret Anderson have revised the picture of imperial Germany as a repressive and authoritarian state by looking more closely at local history (see pp. 108–9), Benn Liebermann[9] has shown that during the stabilization era the German cities underwent a considerable renaissance. The mayors backed by a cross-party majority were able to attract foreign investment and complete impressive building programmes, modernize the utilities, such as water and gas supplies, and build exhibition halls and airports. The financing of this led inevitably to intense distributional conflicts with industry, which argued that both domestic and foreign money would be better spent on raising productivity.

Welfare, society and culture: the problems of modernization

The war, and the upheavals that came in its wake, accelerated the pace of change and the 'modernization' of German society. Even in times of prosperity and profound peace, the process can be painful and disorientating, but in the aftermath of a lost war and in the midst of deep-seated economic and political crises, the accelerating modernization of German society merely exacerbated the situation and provoked what Detlev Peukert calls the crisis of 'classical modernity'.

Sonderweg: special path taken by Germany, as opposed to the western democracies, leading to the Third Reich

What is the theory of classical modernity?

'Modernization' is a vague and often subjective term. It was conceived initially by Max Weber, the German sociologist, and then elaborated on by American and German social scientists as a means of providing a systematic account of the development of industrial societies. As applied to German history, it has often used developments in western Europe and America as the yardstick for measuring German peculiarities and has tended to reinforce the concept of the *Sonderweg*. Peukert, in his influential study of the Weimar Republic, defines 'modernity' as 'consisting in the process of industrialization, that took off on a large scale around the middle of the nineteenth century, the urbanization that followed in the closing decades of the century and the social and cultural transformations that occurred as the nineteenth century was succeeded by the twentieth'.[10]

The welfare state

One of the characteristics of 'classical modernization', which was already visible in the Wilhelmine era, was the development of a welfare state. The welfare policy of the Weimar Republic 'represented a quantum leap in the evolution of the welfare state in Germany'.[11] The constitution guaranteed a comprehensive welfare state as one of the basic rights of the German population. Inevitably these ambitious, all-embracing targets for meeting the citizens' social needs in turn engendered frictions and problems that are endemic to modern social policy. Increasingly there was the tendency for the 'nanny state' to emerge, as legislation subordinated the individual to what the official mind considered 'normal'. The welfare state also became ever more bureaucratic and expensive to run, with the corollary that taxation rose, and ultimately it failed to deliver what it had so ambitiously promised in 1919.

Youth

The Weimar Republic, like other contemporary modern societies, also had its 'youth problem', which was a 'code name for the breakdown of traditional ties and social controls'.[13] Young people adapted more easily

The Weimar Constitution and welfare

For instance, Article 119 guaranteed 'the maintenance of the purity and health of the family'; Article 155 expressed a commitment to social housing schemes, and Article 165 to co-determination by means of works councils; Articles 161–63 committed the Reich to expanding its social insurance scheme; and Article 163 contained the ambitious claim that 'Every German shall be given the opportunity to earn his living through productive work. If no suitable opportunity for work can be found, the means necessary for his livelihood will be provided.'[12]

to city life and the new Americanized urban culture. For the Weimar politicians and bureaucrats, the key to solving the 'youth problem' was essentially control. The Reich Youth Welfare Law of 1922 established both a welfare service for dealing with 'deviants' and a youth service whose task was to encourage parents to give their children an upbringing which would ensure both physical and social fitness. While the Republic had considerable success in setting up youth clubs and organizations, it was unable to earn the loyalty and respect of the younger generation. It was seen, to quote Joseph Goebbels (see p. 221), as an 'old men's republic' paralysed by bureaucratic red tape,[14] and was assailed by the youth movements on both the left and the right. These two groups, although relatively small in numbers, did much to propagate the cult of the new youth, which was free of Wilhelmine hypocrisy and pioneering new lifestyles. There were, too, the *wilde Cliquen*, which were made up of rebellious, nonconformist, mainly working-class males who, like their successors in the 1930s and 1950s (see pp. 325 and 335), alarmed the middle-class establishment by deliberately ignoring social norms and rules. The contempt of many of the young for the Republic was exacerbated by youth unemployment, particularly in the years 1930–33. Paradoxically, the Weimar Republic 'gave young people a new prominence, but at the same time threatened them with marginalization'.[15]

Wilde Cliquen: wild gangs

See Document 54

Women

Women were given formal equality by the Weimar Republic. They voted for the first time in a national election in January 1919 and nearly 10 per cent of the deputies in the National Assembly were female. However, they had little impact on economic, fiscal and foreign policy, which was still a male preserve. Regardless of party orientation, they tended to concentrate on 'motherly politics',[16] which were aimed at women and the family. The overall number of women working in Germany in 1925 was 35.6 per cent as compared to 31.2 per cent in 1907, yet this total masked a decline of women at work in domestic service and on the land, and an increase in female white-collar workers and industrial workers. In higher education the proportion of women students studying at university rose to 16 per cent in the winter of 1931–2.

The popular image of the new German woman, which appeared in magazines, newspapers, advertisements and films, was far from reality. It was arguably a male projection which focused largely on the young, single, female, office workers, earning their money by day in the typing pools and 'frittering away the night dancing the Charleston or watching UFA and Hollywood films'.[17] Inevitably this image attracted a considerable backlash. Some of the more conservative observers of both sexes attributed the decline in the population to 'the "boundless egoism" of women who were betraying their natural vocation and striving for greater personal freedom and independence'.[18] Yet in reality the roles of women did not change very much. Both left and right believed that a woman's real place was still at home with her family. It had, however, become acceptable that until women married they should enjoy an 'intermediary stage of personal independence'.[19] Unless women were married to farmers, restaurateurs or shopkeepers, the assumption was still that they would, after a few years of independence, stop working, marry, stay at home and dedicate themselves to house and family. The emergence of the nuclear family with an average of two children, as a result of improved and cheaper contraception and the increase in 'domestic mechanization', did not make women's work any easier. Smaller families and the simplification of housework merely meant that they had more time to devote to the needs of their husbands and children.

UFA: *Universum Film Aktiengesellschaft –* Universal Film Company, whose origins go back to the military film units of 1916

The decline in the birth-rate led to a considerable debate about population policy. On the one hand there were those who fulminated about *Völkertod*, the dying out of the population, and the harmful effects of contraception and abortions, while others, including Social Democrats, advocated a 'qualitative population policy',[20] which involved the rearing of healthy babies and children. How this was to be done was debatable. The mildly left-wing Professor Alfred Grotjahn advocated, for instance, sterilization of 'unsuitable mothers'.[21] There was, however, a consensus that the quality of the German race needed to be improved, and in 1926 the Prussian Ministry of Welfare set up marriage advice centres, whose task was to examine and advise on the 'racial hygiene' of engaged couples.

Despite the exaggerated publicity about the modern young woman, who worked and allegedly led a hedonistic life, the image of the mother and dedicated wife still remained supreme. By 1930, for instance, the American concept of Mother's Day had become widely accepted. There was general agreement that women in the final analysis would have to be 'dutiful, selfless, conciliatory members of an idealized *Volksgemeinschaft*'.[22]

Volksgemeinschaft: 'people's community'

The old and the new Germany

As in the 1950s, 'Americanism' became a 'catchword for untramelled modernity',[23] which involved efficiency, rationality and above all pros-

It could also be argued that what many contemporaries took for 'Americanism' in fact had its roots in European, particularly German, social and economic developments

perity through mass production and consumerism (see p. 325). To many, Americanism was also a means of escaping the bitter feuds, class divisions and self-destruction of the old continent. During the short period of apparent prosperity between 1925 and 1929, Weimar took on some of the characteristics of American society. Mass consumption of high-tech goods such as cars, telephones and radios began to increase. The new 40-hour week and statutory holidays created the context for the development of mass leisure. Boxing, cycle races, football, etc., all attracted vast audiences, which the development of the radio enabled millions to follow. Similarly, the growth of the cinemas and the popularity of dance halls facilitated mass participation.

It was above all the great cities which were in the vanguard of modernism. Under the influence of the Bauhaus architects, new avant-garde suburbs as well as large public buildings were constructed. The big cities, particularly Berlin, which by 1920 was the third largest city in the world after New York and London, became 'the quintessential modern habitat',[24] where all the restraints of convention and small, stifling communities could be ignored. Yet because of this the city also came to symbolize isolation, alienation and rootlessness, particularly to the traditionalists and the rural population.

Over the course of the decade the accelerating modernization process inevitably began to erode the old social political groupings of the *Kaiserreich*:

August Bebel: one of the founders of the SPD and subsequent leader of the party until 1913

See Document 54

- Before 1914 the Social Democratic movement was seen as a state within a state with its own 'Kaiser' – August Bebel. Although its clubs and institutions continued to proliferate after 1919, the formation of the KPD divided and weakened the workers' movement and attracted a growing number of younger workers, as did the Nazi SA after 1930.
- Like the SPD, Catholicism remained a political and social force. Its heartland was still the small towns and rural communities in southern Germany and the industrial areas of the Rhineland, but the ending of official discrimination against Catholicism and the rise of more secular attitudes freed liberated Catholics to vote for parties other than the Centre party. By 1933, except in Bavaria, only 40 per cent of all Catholics in Germany voted for the Centre.
- The *Mittelstand*, too, was becoming fragmented. The small shopkeepers, self-employed craftsmen and, above all, the peasantry were hit hard by the convulsions of 1914–23 and felt their existence challenged by urbanism, department stores, organized labour and the cartels. The white-collar workers, on the other hand, were, as Peukert has put it, 'largely a *tabula rasa* on which the effects of the process of modernization were being particularly vividly imprinted'.[25] They were at home in the big city and benefited from mass consumerism, but once their prospects for upward mobility were destroyed by the great economic crisis of 1929–33, they began to vote for the Nazi party.

Tabula rasa: blank page

The Jews and the ethnic minorities

By Article 113 of its constitution the Weimar Republic was committed to respecting the rights of minorities. Thus, with the exception of the gypsies, the state itself did not discriminate against the Jews, the Poles or any of the other small number of minorities within its frontiers.

The Germans Jews were predominantly urban, middle-class and professional, and played a prominent role in Weimar culture and, to a lesser extent, in politics. Increasingly they were becoming assimilated into the German population, a fact which accounted for the overall decline in the numbers of the Jewish community in Germany between 1919 and 1933. An exception to this trend were the *Ostjuden*, who came in as migrant workers from the ghettos of eastern Europe. Inevitably their alien appearance and vulnerability fuelled anti-Semitic attacks and prejudice. In the *Scheunenviertel*, the eastern European Jewish quarter in Berlin, a crowd of 30,000 people attacked the Jews in November 1923. Up to a point the incident anticipated *Reichskristallnacht* on 9/10 November 1938 (see p. 243), but the crucial difference was that in 1923 the police cleared the mobs from the streets. The established Jewish community also suffered attacks from such anti-Semitic organizations as the Pan-German League and the Nazi party, which called for the disenfranchisement and expulsion of the Jews, while anti-Semitic prejudice was rife in the universities, the DNVP and the Centre party.

The incident was similar to, but on a larger scale than, the riots in Neustettin, 1881 and Xanten, 1891 (see p. 102)

The post-war plebiscites had cut down on the number of minorities within the Reich, but along the Polish and Danish borders there were still pockets of Poles and Danes in Reich territory. Altogether there were nearly 900,000 Poles in Germany, but many of these, particularly in the Ruhr, were well on the way to being assimilated. Polish immigration into Germany during the Weimar Republic almost dried up, although the great estates in the east still needed to recruit seasonal labour from Poland. The Poles were not popular, but the government was bound by Article 113 of the Weimar constitution to allow the establishment of Polish schools in the Ruhr and the eastern borderlands.

The gypsies, however, continued to experience continued official discrimination because they were seen as nothing more than a host of itinerant beggars. Wherever possible they were corralled into specially appointed campsites, and in Prussia, Hessen and Bavaria gypsies over the age of 16 could be sent to the workhouse if they could not prove that they had a regular job.

Weimar culture

Weimar culture, which was heavily subsidized by the state, became the symbol of what we understand by modernity. Through art, architecture, music and literature it sought to explore every aspect of modernity. The roots of much of it, of course, went back to before the war. Expressionism in painting, literature and theatre, modern architecture, psychoanalysis

Expressionism is
the term used
to describe
developments in
German literature,
art, theatre, film
and music during
the period
1909–25

Didactic:
intending to
instruct

See Document 55

and the physics of relativity had all made important breakthroughs before 1914 (see pp. 104–5), but it was only in the 1920s that they really began to affect the public's consciousness and attitudes. In every sphere of the arts there was the desire to experiment and start afresh. As Gordon Craig has so succinctly put it, 'the great caesura of war gaped between them and a past whose institutions, traditions and values had been smashed beyond repair'.[26]

Expressionist theatre was didactic and, through stark stage sets and a variety of new techniques such as film strips and newspaper montage, 'the gospel of social revolution'[27] was propagated. Reinhard Goering in *Seeschlacht* (*Sea Battle*) and Fritz von Unruh in *Heinrich aus Andernach* (*Henry from Andernach*), for instance, urged an end to war and nationalism, while other dramatists like Ernst Toller and Georg Kaiser worked for the liberation of the masses from poverty and capitalism. In music, Paul Hindemith composed string quartets and songs based on expressionist poetry and jazz, and Arnold Schoenberg pioneered the 12-tone scale and atonal music. On a more popular level, Kurt Weill wrote the music for Brecht's *Dreigroschenoper* (*The Threepenny Opera*) and *Mahagonny*. In the mid-1920s the *Neue Sachlichkeit*, or New Objectivity Movement, was launched by writers such as Joseph Roth, Hermann Kesten and Erich Kästner, and painters like Otto Dix and Georg Grosz. Their aim was not only to expose the hypocrisies and frailties of the time, but also to come to terms with the express-train tempo of modern life. Visually and in the sphere of design the greatest force for modernity was the *Bauhaus*, which was established in 1919 by Walther Gropius in Weimar with the aim of setting up a new school of art, architecture and design to 'break down the arrogant barrier between craftsman and artist', in order to bring about a new unity between architecture and art and to 'conceive the new building of the future'.[28] In co-operation with skilled craftsmen and expressionist painters, such as Lyonel Feininger and Paul Klee, the Bauhaus revolutionized the design of everything from cutlery, china and lamps to new housing estates in Germany.

The great majority of artists and writers felt a profound alienation from the Republic and were bitterly critical of the compromises that men like Ebert and Stresemann had to make to stabilize the political situation. Ernst Toller's play *Hoppla Wir Leben* (*Whoops, We Live!*) portrays, for instance, a revolutionary who suffers a breakdown and goes into an asylum for eight years. On his release he bitterly discovers that the worst of the old regime has survived and his old comrades have surrendered their ideals. The Republic was also bitterly attacked in often similar language by the writers of the radical right. Moeller van den Bruck urged the replacement of decadent capitalist liberalism by a regime, which he did not describe in detail but called the 'Third Reich'. His ideas were enthusiastically received by right-wing radicals, and inspired Spengler to produce his *Decline of the West*. Oswald Spengler and Moeller van den Bruck influenced a whole generation of radical conservative writers like Ernst Jünger, who ennobled war and the experience of combat and despised the pacifism of the new Republic.

Party politics, 1924–29

In this middle period of the Republic's history, continued political structural weaknesses prevented the development of a stable parliamentary
democracy. The possibility of constructing a secure coalition, which
could command a majority in the *Reichstag*, rested effectively on either
forming a grand coalition stretching from the SPD to the DVP or on a
Centre, DVP and DNVP bloc. The problem, however, was that disagreements on economic and social questions between the SPD and the bourgeois parties made the former difficult to sustain, while foreign-policy
differences bedevilled relations between the DNVP and its two major
possible coalition partners. This instability was compounded by divisions
within the parties. Frequently the backbenchers would not support the
political line taken by their leaders in the cabinet, which led to a situation
which Gustav Stolper, a member of the DDP, described as creating a
'coalition of ministers, not a coalition of parties . . . there are no government parties, only opposition parties'.[29]

The parties, which had never had to share governmental responsibility
in Imperial Germany, had difficulties in coming to terms with their new
role in a parliamentary democracy. The SPD made an attempt to become
a more broad-based people's party with its Görlitz Programme of 1921,
but this was effectively abandoned when it reunited with the USPD a year
later, and in 1925 it reverted to an essentially Marxist position, as defined
by its Heidelberg Programme. Thus, until it re-entered government in
1928, it offered its support to the bourgeois coalitions only on particular
issues, one of these being Stresemann's foreign policy. The DNVP was
similarly split between ideology and pragmatism. It hated parliamentary
democracy, yet twice between 1925 and 1927 it briefly joined a coalition
'so that it could gain a bigger share of the economic cake',[30] but in 1928,
with the election of Hugenberg as party leader, it returned to its opposition to the democratic system.

The most consistent supporters of the Weimar system were the Centre
and Liberal parties . The Centre was a pivotal force in every government
from 1919 to 1931, but towards the end of the 1920s it began to move to
the right, which made co-operation with the SPD all the more difficult.
The former Liberal parties, the DDP and DVP, on the other hand, in the
six years up to 1930 suffered an increasing erosion of their core support as
a result of the rise of the special-interest parties. In the election of May
1924 these parties gained 10 per cent of the vote, while the Nazis won 6
per cent. In the second election of 1924 the Nazi vote collapsed to 3 per
cent, but the middle-class voters did not return to their traditional parties.
On the contrary, throughout the second half of the 1920s 'the DDP and
DVP were confronted by a bewildering array of *Interessenparteien*, each
contending for a segment of the already splintered middle-class vote'.[31] In
the 1928 election the special-interest parties attracted 14 per cent of the
vote, which overtook the combined total of the DDP and DVP, and nearly
equalled the DNVP's share of the vote. As yet the middle-class vote was

See Document 49

Key party
abbreviations used
in this section:

BVP: Bavarian
People's Party
(Catholic)
DDP: German
Democratic Party
(liberal)
DNVP: German
National People's
Party (nationalist)
DVP: German
People's Party
(liberal)
SPD: Social
Democratic Party
(socialist)
USPD:
Independent Social
Democratic Party
(socialist)

**Marxist
position**:
a belief in the
inevitability of class
conflict and the
collapse of
capitalism

not going to the Nazis, but there is no doubt that the destabilization of traditional middle-class voting patterns facilitated the rise of the NSDAP after 1928. Childers stresses that 'if the ultimate collapse of the Weimar party system is to be analyzed effectively, that analysis must begin not with the severe economic contractions of the early thirties but with the inflation and stabilization crises of the mid-twenties'.[32]

The deep divisions between the parties, the rise of the new interest groups and a system of proportional representation that allowed even the smallest party representation inevitably led to a long string of short-lived and unstable coalition governments. A brief factual analysis of these is necessary to help explain the fragility of parliamentary democracy in Germany, and how by 1930 there was an increasing desire for stability, even if this meant a more authoritarian government.

Stresemann's Grand Coalition comprising the SPD, DDP, DVP and Centre, which had been formed in August 1923, was gravely weakened by the SPD's resignation on 2 November. The party was bitterly critical of the way Stresemann had allowed *Reichswehr* troops to occupy Dresden and had also deposed Wilhelm Zeger, the Saxon minister-president, while refusing to take a similarly tough stance against the Bavarians (see p. 184). Three weeks later it combined with the Nationalists to defeat the government in the *Reichstag*. Prophetically, President Ebert told his party: 'The reasons why you have felled the Chancellor will be forgotten in six weeks, but you will feel the effects of your stupidity for the next ten years.'[33] A fragile Centre–Liberal administration was formed by the Centre leader, Wilhelm Marx. It continued to maintain the state of emergency declared by Stresemann (see p. 183) until March 1924 when the *Reichstag*'s refusal to approve its prolongation led to Marx's resignation and elections in May. These, held while the impact of the Ruhr crisis and hyperinflation were still fresh in the memory of the voters, significantly weakened the DDP and DVP and the SPD, while strengthening both the extreme right and extreme left. Marx's best option now was to create a Centre, DVP and DNVP coalition, but in the end he had to settle for another minority administration, as the DNVP was still formally opposed to the ratification of the Dawes Plan, which was the government's overriding priority. Because of the constitutional implications of the plan for the ownership of the state railways (see p. 187), Marx needed a two-thirds majority to ratify it. He had the backing of the SPD, but still needed the support of at least some DNVP deputies. After immense pressure not only from the government but also from such right-wing pressure groups as the Reich Association of German Industry and the *Landbund* (Land League), which was anxious to see the adoption of the plan and the subsequent flow of American money into Germany, the DNVP leadership reluctantly agreed to allow its members a free vote, and the plan was approved. Marx then hoped to strengthen his government by bringing the DNVP into the coalition, but was unable to overcome the reluctance of the DDP and considerable elements in his own party to work with it.

Wilhelm Marx, 1863–1946: Marx was a lawyer, who became head of the Supreme Court of Appeals in Berlin in 1922. He sat in the *Reichstag*, 1910–1918 and 1920–33, and led the Centre party, 1922–28. He was chancellor four times and stood for the presidency in 1925

According to the Weimar Constitution all legislation with constitutional implications had to be approved by a two-thirds majority

In an attempt to create a more co-operative *Reichstag*, he once again requested its dissolution and fresh elections.

The election of 7 December 1924 was held in a calmer political and economic atmosphere. Thanks to the acceptance of the Dawes Plan, the German economy was beginning to revive. The extreme right and left vote declined, and the SPD again became the largest party in the *Reichstag*. It was possible either to form a grand coalition with the SPD or a bourgeois bloc stretching from the Centre to the DNVP. The latter alternative was the option preferred by Stresemann and the DVP, who felt that the DNVP would be easier to work with over fiscal policy than the SPD. To facilitate this, Stresemann made it clear that Marx would have to resign. President Ebert then appointed Hans Luther, the former non-party finance minister to form an 'above party' cabinet in which members of the DNVP, DVP, Centre party and BVP could serve without formally committing their parties to support it. Within a year, however, it broke up, when the DNVP refused to vote in October 1925 for the Locarno Treaties, and Luther resigned in December.

After nearly eight weeks of negotiations, Luther formed his second government on 19 January 1926, based this time on the Centre, DVP and DDP. An alternative to this would have been a grand coalition based on the parties which had voted for the Locarno Treaties–the SPD, Centre, DVP, DDP and BVP, but this foundered once again on the DVP's refusal to work with the SPD and the latter's reluctance to enter government. The SPD was unwilling to enter government both because it feared that the KPD would exploit its co-operation with the bourgeois parties at a time of rising unemployment and also because it was disillusioned with its last time in government in the Stresemann administration of August to November 1923 (see p. 183). A new factor operating against extending a government leftwards was the election of Hindenburg as president in April 1925. This effectively ensured that the influence of the president

Hans Luther, 1879–1962: a trained lawyer, who was Mayor of Essen, 1918–22 and minister of finance, October 1923–January 1925

Hindenburg's election to the presidency in April 1925

Ebert died in February 1925, shortly before his extended time as president was due to finish. The president was elected directly by the people. In the first ballot the winner needed an absolute majority, in the second a simple majority was sufficient. In the first ballot in March there were seven candidates: Karl Jarres (DNVP and DVP) won 10.4 million votes, Otto Braun (SPD) won 7.8 million and Wilhelm Marx (Centre) came third with 3.9 million. In the second ballot the Weimar parties rallied behind Marx, which forced the right to look for a popular figure in the great wartime hero, Hindenburg. On April 26 he won by a small majority of 900,000, largely because he attracted BVP voters and the working-class vote was split by the KPD. Politically Hindenburg's election was a serious blow for the Republic. Although he respected the letter of the constitution, his presidency marked a slow but definite shift towards presidential power. His general aim was to exclude the SPD from government, if at all possible, whilst including the DNVP.

would now be mobilized, where possible, against the inclusion of the SPD in a coalition.

In May 1926 Luther's second cabinet collapsed as a result of the defeat by a combination of the left-wing parties and the DDP of the 'flag decree', which would have allowed German embassies abroad to fly the old imperial flag. Any immediate reconstruction of a more right-wing governing coalition to include the DNVP was blocked by the DNVP's implacable opposition to Germany joining the league, while a more left-wing coalition was also impossible because the SPD supported, together with the KPD, the proposal for a referendum on the question of expropriating the former royal houses of the German states. This was strongly opposed by the bourgeois parties. Consequently, as a 'mere stop gap',[34] virtually the same cabinet was resurrected within days, with only a very few changes under the chancellorship of Marx, on the assumption that once Germany joined the league and the referendum on the princes' estates was held, these issues would be solved and the way would be clear for either the SPD or DNVP to join the coalition.

In November Marx attempted to strengthen his government by co-operating more closely with the SPD, even though this met with suspicion from the DVP. Despite its hostility to the government's defence policy, the SPD was ready to join a grand coalition, but only if the Marx cabinet first resigned. When the cabinet rejected this, the SPD retaliated by moving a successful vote of no confidence on 17 December against the government, which ensured its resignation. The DNVP also voted against the government, as they hoped that its defeat would open up the way for their participation in a more right-wing administration.

During the next two weeks intensive interparty negotiations took place. Hindenburg, working through General Schleicher put pressure on the Centre party to reject proposals for a grand coalition, and instead to work with the DNVP and DVP to form a government. If this proved impossible, Schleicher advised Hindenburg to go ahead and 'appoint a government in which he had confidence without consulting the parties or paying attention to their wishes', and then 'with the order for dissolution ready to hand, give the government every constitutional opportunity to get a majority in parliament'.[35] Here then was a dress rehearsal for the presidential intervention in 1930–33 (see pp. 210–17). This time, however, the Centre and the BVP agreed to a coalition with the DVP and DNVP, as the DNVP had come round to accept the policy of Locarno and Germany's membership of the League.

This fragile alliance managed to survive for a year, partly because foreign-policy issues did not become acute and also because the DNVP was ready to make some limited concessions over the introduction of unemployment insurance. But by the end of 1927 it was becoming increasingly difficult to reconcile the contradictory interests of the parties forming the coalition. In February 1928, for instance, as a result of opposition led by the DVP, the Centre party's Schools Bill, which would have allowed denominational schools in *Länder* where they had previously not

The referendum took place on 20 June 1926 and was rejected, but support for the left-wing parties rose by 3.5 million compared to the previous election

The SPD was highly critical of the *Reichswehr's* relations with the Red Army, which was enabling it to test weapons secretly in the USSR

General Schleicher: 1882–1934: he served on the General Staff during the Great War and was political adviser to General Groener during the revolution of 1918. He then worked under General von Seeckt at the Ministry of Defence, where he played a leading role in planning German rearmament. By 1929, as a result of his close friendship with Hindenburg, he became a dominant influence in the Republic

existed, was defeated. The Centre withdrew from the coalition and demanded a dissolution of the *Reichstag* and fresh elections.

The subsequent elections led to a swing to the left as well as a flow of votes from the DNVP, the Centre, the DDP and DVP to the new 'interest parties'. As the SPD had emerged greatly strengthened from the elections, and was ready to enter government, Hindenburg could not avoid entrusting Hermann Müller, the chairman of the parliamentary party, with the formation of a new administration. Since there were influential groups in both the Centre and the DVP, which did not want a grand coalition, Muller initially formed a 'cabinet of personalities' and only in January 1929 did this formally become the Grand Coalition backed by the SPD, Centre, DDP and DVP. The main task facing the Müller Cabinet was to negotiate the Young Plan and the Allied evacuation of the Rhineland. Once the referendum approving it was won, the coalition's stock of common purpose was exhausted'.[36] Its break-up in March 1930, which was to have such catastrophic consequences, is dealt with in the next chapter.

See Document 49

An alliance of Nationalists and Nazis was able to secure sufficient support to force the government to submit the Young Plan to a referendum. On 29 December only 13.8 per cent of the population voted against it

Conclusion

On a national basis it is hard to disagree with Kolb's assessment quoted earlier that the political stabilization of the Weimar Republic during this period was at best 'fragile and superficial'.[37] It never really won the loyalty of the German people, and was attacked by the both the right and the left. The breakneck pace of modernization which occurred during the twenties both disturbed and alienated significant groups. By 1929 there was already significant support for a *Volksgemeinschaft*, where traditional rural and family values were protected and incessant cultural experimentation was replaced by cultural conservatism. Yet to the avant-garde artists and many young people it was a bourgeois, conventional, 'old man's republic'.

Economically, the Weimar Republic was burdened by the economic legacy of a lost war and by the heavy costs of running a welfare state. To maintain these payments the economy would have to enjoy a long period of sustained growth, but to make any appreciable cuts in them would alienate the working classes and provoke a major political crisis. Partly as a result of the system of proportional representation, which maximized the impact of the small parties, but also because of the division in the left-wing vote between the KPD and the SPD, and the inability of the larger parties to work together in a coalition, the Weimar system could not deliver a stable government. On the other hand, as a corrective to this pessimistic picture of the 'history of failure',[38] it is important to remember that the situation in Prussia and the large cities was more stable. The city governments with the backing of both left- and right-wing parties had embarked on impressive recovery programmes (see p. 192). Prussia, which after all comprised three-fifths of the Reich, was ruled by a stable

SPD, Centre and DDP coalition, which Otto Braun, its minister-president, called the 'guarantor of the continued existence of the German Republic'.[39]

11 *The Change of Regime: The Collapse of Weimar and the Formation and Consolidation of the Third Reich, 1930–34*

Introduction

In 1955 Karl-Dietrich Erdmann observed that 'all research into the history of the Weimar Republic is necessarily governed, whether expressly or otherwise, by the question as to the causes of its collapse'.[1] Given the horrors that Hitler unleashed upon the world, it is hard not to avoid this perspective. The breakdown of the Weimar Republic and the seizure of power by Hitler was not just a change of regime but a revolution that was to destroy the German Reich and drag Europe down with it.

While interpretations have varied widely over the last seventy-odd years, there is a consensus that Hitler's success can only be explained within the context of a complex range of causes:

1 the nature of the Weimar Constitution with the ambiguous role of the presidency and the multiparty system that could rarely deliver a strong government;
2 the inability of the German economy to deliver prosperity, which in turn prevented the republic from creating an effective welfare state that could at least have integrated large sections of its population into the new regime;
3 the legacy of Imperial Germany and the hostility of the élite to parliamentary democracy and the republic;
4 the impact of the war and inflation on the middle classes, the decline of the Liberal parties and rise of the *Interessenparteien*, the single interest parties, composed of those who had lost out in the inflation;
5 nationalism and the hatred of Versailles;
6 the charismatic appeal of Hitler;
7 the reaction against modernism and the yearning for security;
8 the impact of the world depression of 1930–33, which Robert Boyce has called the 'third global catastrophe'[2] of the twentieth century;
9 the role of key figures like Hindenburg, Brüning, Schleicher and Papen.

This was the context that made Hitler's take-over of power possible, but it was still individual decisions that made this possibility a reality.

Key issues

- The organization, growth and structure of the Nazi party, 1924–29; how ready for power was the party by 1929–30?
- Why did the Grand Coalition break up in March 1930?
- Did the Brüning administration mark the death of Weimar or was it the republic's last chance of survival?
- Why did Brüning fall in May 1932?

- Why could neither Papen nor Schleicher stabilize the situation in Germany in 1932?
- How inevitable was Hitler's appointment as chancellor?
- Why was the Nationalist–Conservative majority unable to restrain Hitler in the period, January 1933–August 1934?
- How did Hitler strengthen his position during this period?
- Why did Hitler have to prevent a 'second revolution'?
- How true is to say that the Nazi takeover of power was not completed until August 1934?

Hitler and the Nazi party, 1925–30

When Hitler was released from prison in December 1924, he had learnt from the failure of the Munich *putsch* that for the foreseeable future he would have to campaign constitutionally and achieve regime change through what he was later to call a 'legal revolution'.

See Document 56

With the lifting of the ban on the Nazi party in Bavaria in January 1925, he rapidly rebuilt the party with himself in the position of charismatic leader. The *Führer* cult helped integrate the oddly-sorted groups with conflicting interests, which composed the party, into some sort of coherent whole. Over the next four years the essential nature of the party was determined until its dissolution in 1945. The organization of the NSDAP became institutionalized through party bureaucrats in Munich, such as Rudolf Hess, who protected Hitler's charismatic image without posing any threat to his power. Hitler only intervened in issues that involved his supreme authority. The NSDAP was controlled from its party offices in Munich, and each level was subordinate to the one above it. On a national basis the party was divided into thirty-five *Gaue*, or regions, each controlled by a *Gauleiter*. Below these were the local branches, which were run by a cadre of activists. This seemingly logical pattern was threatened, however, by the determination, which was encouraged by Hitler, of the organizations affiliated to the party – the SA, the Hitler Youth, the Nazi Teachers' Association, etc. – to see themselves as responsible to *him* alone rather than being firmly integrated into the party system.

Charismatic leader: one who can inspire his followers with fanatical loyalty and devotion

Cadre: a core unit, which can serve later as a basis for mass expansion

Hitler never officially revised the party's 1920 programme, but in practice he toned down its economic radicalism to win over new supporters. A better guide to his first principles can be found *in Mein Kampf*, even though it is not a precise blueprint for the future. Page after page shows that for Hitler the world was a battlefield where the 'Aryan' races clashed with the apparently scheming and 'evil' agents of world Jewry. His identification of the Jews with Russian Bolshevism, while far from original, had, to quote Ernst Nolte, an 'explosive political effect',[3] and enabled his ideas to reach a wider middle-class public, which was deeply alarmed by the prospect of a Communist revolution in Germany. Hitler's whole

For the first time in Russian history Jews became prominent in public life during the Bolshevik Revolution. Hence to its opponents, the Whites, the revolution was often seen as Jewish-inspired

See Document 57

Adolf Hitler, 1889–1945

Hitler was born in Braunau am Inn, Upper Austria. In *Mein Kampf* he claimed that he had experienced a poverty-stricken childhood, but in fact his father, Alois, an Austrian customs official, earned sufficient to keep his family. It is true that Alois was a rigid disciplinarian, lacking humour and often violent towards his son, and that his mother reacted by being over-protective. Inevitably this had an impact on Hitler's character, on which psycho-historians have only been able to speculate. In 1905 Hitler left school without any academic qualifications, and failed to gain a place at the Academy of Fine Arts in Vienna. Up to 1914 he had no regular employment, and lived the life of an increasingly impoverished drifter, first in Vienna and then in Munich. In the former city he enthusiastically absorbed contemporary Social Darwinist, *völkisch* and racist thinking and closely studied the tactics of the Austrian Social Democrats, the Pan-German Nationalists and the Christian Social Party. He was particularly interested in how the latter party was able to attract support from those who felt their existence threatened.

In August 1914 he volunteered to join a Bavarian regiment. Instead of being repatriated to his native Austria, his request was instantly granted. He fought for the next four years with considerable personal bravery and was awarded the Iron Cross (First Class). In 1918 he was wounded in a British gas attack, but nevertheless rejoined his regiment in Munich in late November. In the summer of 1919 his skills as an agitator were recognized and he was employed to counter the impact of communist, socialist and pacifist propaganda amongst the troops. He joined the German Workers' Party, which was later renamed the *Nationalsozialistische Deutsche Arbeiterpartei*, of which he became chairman in July 1921. Its 25-point programme was nationalist, anti-Semitic and anti-capitalist in character. It was also committed to taking over agricultural land in the national interest.

Hitler was imprisoned in Landsberg fortress after the failure of the Munich *putsch* in November 1923 (see p. 184), where he dictated *Mein Kampf* as a political testament to his secretary, Rudolf Hess, who was later to become deputy leader of the party. He was released from prison in December 1924.

See Document 57

programme for the regeneration of Germany depended on creating a racially pure state, which would be demographically strengthened by the colonization of western Russia by German farmers.

Although up to 1927 the Nazi party, following the example of Italian Fascism, attempted to dominate the cities, the party's core supporters remained the *Mittelstand*, which had been impoverished by the war, the agricultural depression and above all by the inflation. Much of the NSDAP's success after 1930 was a result of its ability to win the majority of the *Mittelstand*'s votes, which had previously gone to the single-interest parties, *Interessenparteien*, (see p. 109) votes. In the winter of 1927–28, with the start of the agricultural depression, Hitler abandoned the Urban Plan and began to campaign more intensively in the countryside. Despite his determination not to alter the 1920 programme, he moderated the emphasis on land confiscation in Point 17. Although this policy change was too late to help the Nazi party much in the 1928 elections, its potential effectiveness was illustrated by the fact that in some rural areas in north–west Germany, such as Schleswig-Holstein, the Nazis gained over 10 per cent of the vote.

The Depression and the fall of the Müller government

The Wall Street Crash in October 1929 marked the onset of the world depression, which hit Germany particularly hard because its economy depended on short-term credits from America. Over the next three years the impact of the slump was devastating. By 1932 the production of capital goods had sunk to half its 1913 level, wages dropped to 87 per cent of their 1928 level, and unemployment rose to 5.1 million by September 1932. Inevitably, a depression on this scale affected every section of the economy, and a frightening loss of security 'penetrated every area of German society',[4] which encouraged extremist parties on both the right and left. Unemployment hit the age group 18–30 particularly hard, and by 1933 some of these had been unemployed for as long as five years. Many sought relief from this debilitating experience by joining the para-military organizations of either the right or the left – the SA, the SPD's *Reichsbanner* or the KPD's *Rotfront*.

See Document 54

The initial stages of the depression acted 'as a trigger to the abandonment of a political system which had already lost its legitimacy'.[5] Already by the end of 1929 the Grand Coalition was beginning to unravel. SPD backbenchers had voted against their own chancellor in protest against a cabinet decision to build a battle cruiser. In December 1929 Chancellor Müller had great difficulty in securing support for an emergency budget covering the state's deficit. Once the Young Plan referendum had been won (see p. 188), the differences in the cabinet over financing the unemployment insurance system came to a head. The SPD argued that there should be no cut in benefits, while the DVP called for reductions. At the same time, German industry was beginning a concerted campaign against the whole principle of social welfare, the costs of which were

By the German insurance law of July 1927, all workers were entitled to financial relief as long as they were willing to work and were unemployed through no fault of their own. Insurance contributions were limited to 3 per cent of wages and contributed equally by employer and employee. Financially, it was calculated, this would be sufficient to provide relief for about 800,000, with reserves for a further 600,000

The number of unemployed (millions), January 1929–33

Year	Unemployed
1929	2.850
1930	3.218
1931	4.887
1932	6.042
1933	6.014

Source: Adapted from B. Gebhardt, *Handbuch der deutschen Geschichte*, vol. 4, ed., K. D. Erdmann, Stuttgart, Union Verlag, 1959, p. 352.

already spiralling as a result of the onset of the depression. A compromise was offered by the Centre party, which would have delayed a decision on the crucial issue of reform until the autumn, but under the influence of the trade unions this was rejected by the SPD, and the cabinet decided to resign on 27 March. Later, Rudolf Hilferding, the left-wing SPD deputy, bitterly criticized the trade unions and SPD backbenchers for being 'ready to let German democracy and the German Republic go to the devil . . . over the question of thirty pfennigs for the unemployed'.[6] In hindsight he had a point, as the demise of the Grand Coalition fatally weakened German democracy, but nevertheless at stake was the major issue of whether or not unemployment benefits should be cut.

When Chancellor Müller resigned, President Hindenburg seized the chance to appoint Heinrich Brüning, the leader of the Centre party in the *Reichstag*. Hindenburg and his advisers, particularly General Schleicher, the head of the Ministerial Bureau in the Defence Ministry, had been waiting to replace Müller with a more authoritarian and 'anti-Marxist' chancellor. He had already in January 1930 discussed with Count Westarp, the chairman of the DNVP parliamentary party, the possibility of appointing a presidential cabinet.

Presidential cabinet: a cabinet appointed by the president and independent of the *Reichstag*

The Brüning cabinets, March 1930–May 1932

Brüning's role in the destruction of the Republic is a matter of considerable controversy. Contemporaries were divided as to whether his chancellorship marked, in the words of Arthur Rosenberg, the 'death of the Weimar Republic', or whether, on the contrary, Brüning represented its last hope. Friedrich Meinecke, for instance, observed in 1946 that 'the path to the abyss' only began with Brüning's fall.[7] Similar debates continue to reverberate. Werner Conze[8] echoed Meinecke with his arguments that Brüning was intending to create a presidential constitution (along the lines, perhaps, of the later French Fifth Republic), which had been made inevitable by the collapse of coalition politics, and that only *after* his dismissal did Germany's slide towards dictatorship accelerate. Bracher, however, both in his classic study on *The Dissolution of the Republic* and in later works, does not hesitate to attribute considerable

Heinrich Brüning, 1885–1970

After serving in the First World War, Brüning became an official in the Christian Trade Union Movement, and in 1924 a Centre party deputy in the *Reichstag*. In 1929 he became the parliamentary leader of the party. He rapidly gained a reputation for his expertise in economic and financial matters, and moved the Centre party back to a more right-wing position. Personally he was a monarchist and somewhat sceptical about parliamentary democracy.

blame to Brüning for the dissolution of the Republic. He stresses that 'Brüning's solution occurred at a time when parliamentary majorities were still possible.' Hans Mommsen is equally critical, even though he gives full weight to the structural complexities facing Brüning, and unequivocally argues that '[b]reaking the spirit of the constitution and replacing it with formal legalism was his doing'.[9]

Until the late 1970s there was a widespread consensus that Brüning's savagely deflationary policy was avoidable, and, whatever his political aims, this greatly facilitated the rise of the Nazi party. Yet Knut Borchardt has questioned this orthodoxy and argued that, as there was no realistic alternative to deflation, 'we can only study this tragedy and . . . abstain from engaging in over-presumptuous criticisms'.[10] In his posthumous autobiography,[11] Brüning claimed that he was a revisionist who was determined to end reparation payments and achieve military equality with the *Entente* powers. This, however, may well have represented a later rationalization of what seemed to contemporaries an increasingly confused set of policies.

See Document 58

Brüning's first cabinet formed on 28 March was supported by the Centre, the DDP and DVP. From the start he made it clear that if his government were defeated, he would request a dissolution of the *Reichstag* and govern with emergency decrees. His first finance bill achieved a narrow majority, but the second one, involving increased taxes, deflationary cuts in welfare expenditure and 'an emergency contribution' from those on fixed incomes, was defeated in July. When further attempts to promulgate it by resorting to Article 48 were rejected as unconstitutional by the *Reichstag*, it was promptly dissolved and a general election was held on 14 September. This was a decision of 'breathtaking irresponsibility',[12] which allowed the Nazi party to become a major political force, and began, to quote Gerhard Schulz, 'the permanent violation of the constitutional system by the dictatorial power of the *Reichspräsident*'.[13] In the subsequent electoral campaign the Nazi party exploited the growing insecurity of the voters with consummate skill. Their main theme was that only Hitler could unite the people, whom parliamentary democracy had demoralized and split into competing egotistical interest groups, into a new national community. Whole regions were saturated with Nazi canvassers and electoral meetings, while Hitler himself held major speeches in the large cities. The results on 14 September were 'a political earthquake',[14] when the NSDAP increased its seats from 12 to 107, and became the second largest party in the *Reichstag*.

See Document 47

See Documents 49 and 59

Brüning at first hoped to gain the passive support of the NSDAP for his government in the *Reichstag*, and even proposed that 'in all *Land* parliaments where it was arithmetically possible, the NSDAP and the Centre might combine to form a government',[15] but Hitler rejected this as he was unwilling to call off his strident demands for the immediate cancellation of reparations. Brüning was equally unsuccessful with the DNVP, but in the end was saved by the SPD, which agreed to 'tolerate' his cabinet, partly to keep Hitler from the chancellorship, but also to keep

Blick auf den Sitzungssaal des Reichstags, den der Abgeordnete Herold eröffnet
Auf den Bänken der Nationalsozialisten sitzen die Abgeordneten ausnahmslos in den in Preußen verbotenen
Braunhemden mit der Hakenkreuz-Armbinde

17 The meeting of the new *Reichstag*, 13 October 1930. The Nazi delegates are sitting on the far right, as viewed from the podium

Tempo, 14 October 1930, p. 2

Where did the Nazi votes come from?

In 1930 6.5 million or 18.3 per cent of the electorate voted for the Nazis and this increased to 37.3 per cent in July 1932. The sharp increase in the electoral turnout in 1930 and 1932 and the large number of first-time voters, who came onto the electoral roll between May 1928 and July 1932, benefited the Nazis. Mass unemployment, Hitler's pledges to create work, and the glamour of the SA attracted many young, male voters. The Nazi vote was further increased by voters moving over from the smaller, middle-class single-interest parties (see p. 190). By 1930 the NSDAP had constructed a web of middle-class organizations, which were able to attract peasants, self-employed businessmen, clerical workers, students, and women, as well as many members of the professions. Although statistics indicate that the NSDAP did best in the predominantly Protestant and rural districts of northern Germany, and was not as effective in the Catholic areas and cities, it did nevertheless attract votes from all sections of society. As Jürgen Falter has shown,[16] about 40 per cent of Nazi voters were workers, as were 60 per cent of the SA. In contrast to the SPD, which became increasingly associated with Brüning's deflationary policy, the Nazis promised to provide work-creation projects and offered the prospect of creating a new classless national community.

intact its coalition with the Centre in Prussia. As long as he enjoyed both the toleration of the SPD and the support of Hindenburg, Brüning was now able to embark on what Eberhard Kolb has called the 'silent constitutional changeover'.[17] Over the next two years parliamentary democracy in Germany was progressively weakened. The number of emergency decrees rose from 5 in 1930 to 66 in 1932, and Brüning increasingly bypassed the *Reichstag* either by consulting party and pressure group leaders directly or by using the *Reichsrat* as a substitute for the legislature, as had been the case in the war (see p. 155).

His priority was to use the misery of the Depression to persuade the Western powers to scrap reparations. At the same time, he was hoping to lay the foundations for a future economic recovery by cutting back on welfare costs. To appease the right, he also backed Foreign Office plans for a customs union with Austria, which, he argued, would give Germany 'an adequate natural area of living space'.[18] Inevitably this provoked sharp protests from France, and when Germany was plunged into a major banking crisis in July 1931, the French vetoed every proposal for an emergency loan until Germany not only renounced the customs union but also gave up attempts to revise reparations for at least five years. Brüning responded by suspending reparation payments until further notice. Although this caused a massive flight of capital from Germany, the severity of the banking crisis persuaded the American president, Hoover, to force the French into agreeing to declare a moratorium on reparation payments for a year. At great cost, Brüning was now near to achieving one of his main aims. He was able to convince a committee of financial experts specially convened under the provisions of the Young Plan that Germany would not be able to make any payments, even after the expiry of the moratorium. The committee then suggested that both reparations and inter-Allied debts should be cancelled, a proposal that was effectively adopted at the Lausanne Conference in June 1932.

Brüning was not able to exploit this dearly-bought success, as he was dismissed from office by Hindenburg on 29 May 1932, when, as he claimed, he was 'within a hundred yards short of the goal'.[19] Why then was he so abruptly removed?

The banking crisis of July 1931

The banking crisis was triggered by the failure of the *Kreditanstalt* in Vienna in July 1931. The German banks, which had since the inflation of 1923 only small capital reserves, were immediately put under pressure by their customers, who, alarmed by the repercussions of the collapse of the *Kreditanstalt*, started withdrawing their deposits. On 13 July the *Darmstädter und Nationalbank* (DANAT) had to stop all payments. On 14 and 15 July all the other German banks also closed, and when they reopened, customers could only withdraw small sums. The Government was forced to come to the rescue with a sum of one billion marks.

1 The depth and intensity of the depression inevitably caused his government to lose popular support. His deflationary policies of reducing the salaries of the civil servants, freezing wage levels and making unemployment payments ever more difficult to secure inevitably alienated both the *Mittelstand* and the workers. These policies were so unpopular that Brüning became known as the 'Hunger Chancellor'. When he travelled on a train, the window blinds of his carriage were permanently drawn to stop crowds catching sight of him and hurling stones.

2 Both the DNVP and the Nazis were bitterly opposed to him. On 11 October 1931, just before the meeting of the *Reichstag*, they had held a joint rally at Bad Harzburg to demonstrate their hostility to the government. His continued co-operation with the SPD and quasi-constitutional regime made him a suspect figure in their eyes, and a few days later only the SPD saved him from losing a vote of no confidence in the *Reichstag*. This dependence on the SPD also alienated the Ruhr industrialists. In January 1932 it was significant that Hitler was invited to speak to their representatives at the Industry Club in Düsseldorf.

3 Brüning could survive as long as he had Hindenburg's backing, but this too was beginning to be eroded. He lost much of his trust when he was unable to gain a majority in the *Reichstag* for a constitutional amendment prolonging Hindenburg's term in office without another election. Ironically, in this election Hindenburg emerged as the candidate of the constitutional parties and was opposed in the second ballot solely by Hitler as the representative of the Nationalist Right, who gained 36.8 per cent of the vote. By the spring of 1932 Hindenburg was being advised by General Schleicher (see p. 202) to drop Brüning, on the grounds that his dependence on the SPD alienated the very groups his administration was supposed to protect, while his foreign policy had failed.

The immediate causes of Brüning's dismissal were the ban on the SA on 13 April 1932 as a result of growing evidence that it was planning a *coup d'état* against the state, and government proposals for dividing up the bankrupt estates in the east for peasant settlement. These were immediately pounced on by the east Elbian landowners as 'agrarian bolshevism'. Schleicher, who had secretly negotiated with Ernst Röhm (see p. 222), the leader of the SA, an agreement that in the event of war the SA would come under the command of the *Reichswehr*, argued that the SA ban would deprive the *Reichswehr* of a potential military reserve force. In reality, however, he was working to prepare the way for Hitler's membership of a nationalist coalition led by Franz von Papen, a right-wing member of the Centre party in the Prussian *Landtag*, which would replace the Republic with an authoritarian regime backed by the *Reichswehr*. Hitler responded to these overtures with caution, as he was determined not to enter a coalition in a subordinate position. He was

Franz von Papen, 1879–1969

Von Papen was a career officer, who joined the General Staff in 1911 and then became a military attaché in Washington. He was recalled from this post because the US government suspected him of contacts with German spies. In 1919 he was elected to the Prussian *Landtag* and represented the right wing of the Centre party. He also owned the majority of shares in the Catholic paper, the *Germania*. After serving as chancellor, May–November 1931, and then vice-chancellor under Hitler, 1933–34, Papen served as ambassador to Austria, 1934–38, and then to Turkey, 1939–44. He was acquitted by the Nuremburg war crimes tribunal in 1946, but sentenced to eight years' hard labour by a German de-Nazification court, although he was released in 1949.

convinced that the Nazis were capable of winning an overall majority in an election and consequently initially agreed to support Papen, provided that the SA ban was lifted and a general election was held within weeks. Hindenburg and Strasser accepted these conditions and on 29 May Brüning was then dismissed and the government entrusted to von Papen.

The von Papen and Schleicher cabinets, June 1932–January 1933

The election took place on 31 July and resulted in the Nazi party gaining 230 seats, but it was still well short of an overall majority, even though it was the largest party in the *Reichstag*. Papen himself could only rely on the 37 members of the DNVP. Hitler demanded the right to form a new government, but suffered a major political setback on 13 August, when Hindenburg only offered him the vice-chancellorship in Papen's cabinet. The next month was a confused period. There was talk of a Centre–Nazi coalition, and a Nazi, Hermann Göring (see p. 217), with the support of

The *coup d'état* against Prussia

The SPD–Centre government was deposed on 20 July. The Reich chancellor assumed the post of minister-president, while a Reich commissioner took over the Ministry of the Interior. This crippled the SPD, and deprived them of 'their last bastion'.[20] The Prussian police now came under the direct control of the Reich. Why did the SPD not offer any resistance against this illegal act? The odds were stacked against them: the *Reichswehr* was ready to intervene; with huge numbers unemployed there was little chance of a general strike succeeding; and the two left-wing parties were bitterly divided. The KPD viewed the SPD as 'social fascists' who had backed Brüning and were their main 'class' enemy, as they were ready to co-operate with the bourgeois parties rather than overthrow the system. The consequence of the coup was that the SPD now lost its influence in German politics and became marginalized.

the Centre was elected president (speaker) of the *Reichstag*. Papen had already deposed the Prussian government in July, and had ambitious plans for dissolving the *Reichstag* and delaying elections until he had drawn up a new constitution which, with a restricted franchise and a non-elected upper chamber, would drastically reduce the powers of the legislature. However, the timing of his plans went wrong when he was compelled on 12 September to dissolve the *Reichstag* prematurely after an overwhelming vote of no confidence in his government. At first he was determined not to set a date for a new election, but retreated when the Centre and the NSDAP threatened to use Article 59 to indict him for violating the constitution.

The elections of 6 November were another blow for the Nazis. As a result of increasing disenchantment with Hitler, who appeared to be unable to win power, the Nazis actually lost 2 million voters and their number of seats fell to 196. The ominous signs that Nazi power was ebbing still did not persuade Hitler to serve in a Papen cabinet. Initially Papen was ready to use the army to dissolve the *Reichstag* and to suppress the parties and then have a new authoritarian constitution endorsed, either through a plebiscite or a specially elected national assembly. Schleicher, who was now minister of defence, opposed this course as he feared that it would lead to civil war. As an alternative he was convinced that he could win over Hitler, or at the very least persuade Gregor Strasser and some sixty Nazi deputies to back the government. Hindenburg was initially ready to back von Papen, but when Schleicher made it clear to him that the *Reichswehr* did not support the chancellor, he had little option but to dismiss him and appoint Schleicher the new chancellor on 2 December.

The following day Schleicher offered Gregor Strasser the posts of vice-chancellor and minister-president of Prussia. This plunged the Nazi party into crisis. Hitler immediately vetoed Schleicher's proposal, and when Strasser then resigned in protest, Hitler was only able to prevent a split in the party by appealing successfully to the loyalty of the *Reichstag* deputies, *Gauleiter* and regional inspectors to their *Führer*. While the Nazi party was in turmoil, Schleicher attempted to persuade both the SPD and the trade unions to support his government through a package of economic reforms and work-creation projects. This alarmed both the industrialists and the east Elbian landowners and made them more ready to contemplate an alliance with the Nazis, even though they appeared to be on their way to 'the rubbish pile of history'.[21]

Papen, smarting at being outmanoeuvred by Schleicher, was anxious to do a deal with Hitler, and as early as 10 December, had put out feelers via the Cologne banker, Kurt von Schröder, with whom Hitler was also in contact. On 4 January Schröder managed to arrange a meeting between Hitler and Papen. Initially Hitler appeared to be ready to accept office in a Papen cabinet, provided that he controlled the defence and interior ministries. Over the next two weeks Hitler's position was strengthened by the electoral success in the *Land* election of Lippe, where

Gregor Strasser, 1892–1934, came from a lower middle-class background in Bavaria. He joined the Nazi party in 1922 and believed passionately in a 'German or National socialism'. In 1928 he played a key role in improving the party's organization. He was murdered in the 'Night of the Long Knives' (see p. 223)

the NSDAP won 39.5 per cent of the vote, and by the increasing difficulties facing the government. Schleicher had failed to win over either the SPD or the unions and also had infuriated the east Elbian landowners by not increasing tariff duties on imported food. In mid-January Hindenburg finally came round to instructing Papen 'personally and in strict confidence'[22] to explore the possibility of forming a government with the Nazis. On 28 January Schleicher resigned after Hindenburg neither gave him permission to dissolve the *Reichstag* nor granted his request for unlimited emergency powers. Hitler was now able successfully to demand the chancellorship for himself and the ministries of the interior in both the Reich and Prussia for Dr Wilhelm Frick and Hermann Göring respectively. Papen believed that by appointing reliable conservative figures to the other nine posts, he would be able to contain Hitler and the other two Nazis in the cabinet. On the evening of 28 January this arrangement was accepted by Hindenburg and the new Hitler cabinet was sworn in on 30 January.

Hitler's appointment as chancellor could have been avoided. Support for the Nazi party was, to quote Michael Burleigh, 'a mile wide, but beyond a hard-core of fanatics, only an inch deep',[23] and by the autumn of 1932 was already declining. Yet his appointment did have a certain political logic about it: the Weimar Republic was irreparably damaged by 1932 and the traditional élites were not strong enough to set up an authoritarian regime themselves. If they were to seize power, they had no alternative but to work with Hitler. The electoral reverses that the NSDAP had suffered in November also encouraged them to hope that the Nazis could be more easily exploited as lobby fodder.

The failure to contain Hitler

When von Papen wrote his memoirs in the early 1950s, he argued that his 'own and Schleicher's cabinets and Hitler's government were only part of a logical sequence of events'.[24] Up to a point this was true. Hitler inherited a situation where rule by decree was the norm and the possibility of

Gestapo: the state secret police

Herman Göring, 1893–1946

Göring was a Bavarian whose father was a consular official. In the Great War he joined the air force and became commander of the famous *Richthofen* squadron. He joined the Nazi party and became head of the SA in 1922. He was elected a Nazi *Reichstag* deputy in 1928 and in 1932 the president (speaker) of the *Reichstag*. As Prussian minister of the interior in Hitler's cabinet in 1933, he organized the *Gestapo* and set up the first concentration camps. During the Third Reich he held several key posts. He built up the German air force and was put in charge of the Four Year Plan in 1936 (see p. 234). He was sentenced to death as a war criminal at Nuremberg, but managed to commit suicide before his execution.

a coup against the Weimar Republic was increasingly canvassed by both the DNVP and the *Reichswehr*. There was considerable common ground between Hitler's aims and those of his coalition partners. They, too, wanted an authoritarian constitution and the restoration of German power. Initially, therefore, it seemed quite feasible, in view of the overwhelming non-Nazi majority in the cabinet, that Papen's rash boast that within two months 'we will have pushed Hitler so far into a corner that he'll squeak' was a realistic assessment,[25] but it ignored the dynamism of the Nazi movement and Hitler's own determination to outflank his conservative 'minders'.

The election of 5 March 1933

Hitler's immediate aim, shared by his cabinet, was to eliminate the remaining powers of the *Reichstag*. He thus turned down the offer of a pact with the Centre party, which would have given him a majority in the *Reichstag* and easily gained the cabinet's consent for yet another election. The only opposition was from Alfred Hugenberg, the new minister of economics, who supported a dissolution but feared the increased power that an election might give Hitler. In the subsequent campaign Hitler cleverly exploited the nation's desire for unity and recovery, and stressed the total failure of the 'November parties' by implication associating his allies in the cabinet with them. He cleverly reassured those who feared the revolutionary potential of the Nazis by pledging to 'take under its firm protection Christianity as the basis of our morality and the family as the nucleus of our nation and state'. He also promised both to assist agriculture and to launch 'a massive and comprehensive attack on unemployment'.[26]

See Document 47

Exploiting the scope that Article 48 gave the chancellor the government in early February granted itself the necessary powers to forbid political meetings and to ban opposition newspapers. The abolition of the Prussian government (see p. 215) also ensured that Hermann Göring, as Prussian minister of the interior, could control the Prussian police and reinforce them with auxiliary SA men. It was, however, the *Reichstag* fire that provided Hitler with an ideal chance to exploit the fears of a Communist uprising, which the Nazis had so assiduously spread, and immediately to promulgate the Decree for the Protection of People and State, which not only gave the central government the powers arbitrarily to order the arrest of individuals, censor the post and have private houses searched, but also to dismiss *Land* governments if they refused to implement the necessary 'measures for the restoration of public security'. This decree gave Hitler enormous powers and has been described as 'a kind of *coup d'état*'.[28] Yet when the German people voted on 5 March 1933, the Nazis won only 43.9 per cent of the votes and to claim a majority had to rely on their alliance with the DNVP, which was supported by a mere 8 per cent of the electorate.

The *Reichstag* fire: The fire was so opportune that contemporaries were convinced that the Nazis started it, but it is probable that the former Dutch Communist, Marinus van der Lubbe, was to blame. But more important than who actually started the fire is the fact that, 'by instantly taking advantage of the fire the Nazis made the deed their own'[27]

18   Hitler in 1936

Imperial War Museum, no. HU5239

The Enabling Act

The election results released a new burst of revolutionary and terrorist activities which amounted to a 'revolution from below'. The SA became, in effect, a revolutionary force, which dealt not only with the Communists, but also destroyed both potential and actual political opposition to the Hitler government. This wave of violence that swept through

Revolution from below: a revolution that is driven by the grass-roots of the party rather than being dictated from above

Germany was not, however, without its dangers for Hitler. It constantly threatened to spiral out of control and alienate both Hitler's coalition partners and the Reich President, whose support at this stage was still vital. He thus made repeated appeals, which were not totally successful, to end the gratuitous violence against individuals and particularly the 'obstruction or disturbance of business life'.[29] To reassure his coalition partners, Hitler invited the Crown Prince, the military establishment of the *ancien régime* and the President to a brilliantly orchestrated ceremony at the *Garnisonskirche* in Potsdam where he pledged allegiance to the traditions and values of the past and skilfully reawakened memories of the unity of August 1914. Two days later the *Reichstag* sat in the Kroll Opera House to debate the Enabling bill, the intention of which was to approve the transfer of full legislative and executive powers to the chancellor for a four-year period. Initially it was drafted on the basis of previous Weimar emergency laws, but its scope was dramatically widened by the introduction of clauses which gave the cabinet full powers to introduce budgets and to change the constitution independently of the *Reichstag*. Since it involved a change in the constitution, the government had first to secure a two-thirds majority. Although the majority of the KPD deputies and twelve of the SPD members had already been arrested, the approval of the bill was only made possible when the Centre party, reassured by Hitler's promises to protect the rights and privileges of the Catholic Church, and believing that it would also be able to influence Hitler 'from the inside', as it had successive Weimar administrations since 1919, decided to vote for the bill. Hitler sought to reassure the bourgeois parties that the *Reichstag* and *Reichsrat*, the presidency, and the *Länder* would not be permanently weakened, but also made it quite clear that if he did not gain the necessary majority, he was nevertheless 'prepared to go ahead in face of the refusal and the hostilities which will result from that refusal'.[30] The Opera House was encircled by the SS, while inside the SA lined the corridors. The bill was passed by 444 votes to 94 with only the SPD opposing it. The Enabling Act was of crucial importance as it preserved the façade of the legal revolution and removed any doubts the civil service or the judiciary had as to the legality of the Nazi takeover.

Garnisonskirche: the military church in Potsdam

On 14 July Hitler signed the Concordat with the Papacy which conceded the Catholic Church religious and administrative freedom

Gleichschaltung and the creation of the one-party state

The Enabling Act decisively strengthened Hitler's position in the cabinet because the signature of the president was no longer required for decrees or legislation. As early as 22 April, according to Joseph Goebbels, 'the Führer's authority in the Cabinet is absolute'.[31] Empowered by the Enabling Act, strengthened by the SA and enjoying considerable support from public opinion, Hitler was able, through the process of co-ordination or *Gleichschaltung* to create a one-party centralized Reich by early 1934. The key stages in this process were:

Gleichschaltung: originally an electrical term meaning synchronization

1 The *Länder* lost what remained of their traditional independence.

Joseph Goebbels, 1897–1945

Goebbels was one of the few leading Nazis who had studied at university and gained a Ph.D. He failed to become a journalist and was initially secretary to a nationalist politician and joined the Nazi party in 1925. He became the *Gauleiter* of the North Rhine district and secretary to Gregor Stasser and in November 1926 *Gauleiter* of Berlin, and set up the newspaper, *Der Angriff*. Two years later he was put in charge of party propaganda, and played a major role in projecting the message of the Nazi party throughout the Reich, 1930–32. In March 1933 he became minister for popular enlightenment and propaganda. In July 1944 he was appointed Reich trustee for total war, and in April 1945, shortly after Hitler's suicide, he and his wife also committed suicide after first killing their children.

Through a mixture of 'revolutionary pressure from below and action from above',[32] their legislatures were brought into line with the new National Socialist regime, a process which had already started before the enabling bill was passed. In those states which the Nazis did not already control, the police forces were initially taken over by newly-appointed commissioners, then the *Länder* diets were reconstituted to reflect the ratio of the parties in the *Reichstag*, and finally Reich governors, who were usually the local *Gauleiter*, were appointed with the necessary powers to dismiss unco-operative ministers and to draw up their own legislative programmes. In the Prussian provinces *Gauleiter* were also appointed *Oberpräsidenten* (senior administrative officials). The *Länder* diets were dissolved in January 1934, and the state governments were subordinated to the Reich government.

2 In the course of the summer of 1933 all parties, associations and private armies were either abolished or taken over by the Nazis. The *Stahlhelm*, the right-wing ex-soldiers' league which was closely linked to the DNVP, was, for instance, incorporated into the SA. On 2 May the SA and SS occupied trade union offices throughout Germany, and from then on all workers were enrolled in the new German Labour Front (DAF). On 22 June the SPD was banned, while the Law against the New Formation of Parties of 14 July confirmed the dissolution of the political parties and made the Nazi party the only legal party in Germany. Employers' associations were amalgamated and formed into the Reich Chamber of German Industry, and in January 1934 the Reich Economic Chamber was set up, but business men were able to manage their own affairs and were not subordinated to party zealots.

3 Nazi direction of education, the media and culture was quickly achieved. Goebbels, as minister of propaganda, controlled broadcasting and ensured a uniform news coverage in the press. In September 1933 the Reich Chamber of Culture was set up. All 'intellectual workers' were compelled to join. Teaching organizations were also affiliated to the National Socialist Teachers' Organization.

The defeat of the 'Second Revolution'

By July of 1933, far from being pushed into a corner, Hitler had created a single-party monopoly and a centralized governmental dictatorship. Yet the ambiguities and apparent compromises of the 'legal revolution' of 1933 still left von Papen and Hindenburg in office, and the 'conservative bearers of state',[33] the bureaucratic, military and big business élites, intact. Indeed, Hitler needed their help if he was going to revive the economy and rearm Germany. They were, however, increasingly resented by the SA and the radical wing of the party, which had hoped that the seizure of power would entail a clean break with the *ancien régime*. Hitler's most dangerous critic was Ernst Röhm, who, as chief of staff of the SA, controlled a potentially revolutionary force of some two and a half million men.

See Document 60

Once Hitler had declared an end to the 'legal revolution' in July 1933, the SA increasingly became an 'embarrassing legacy of the years of struggle'.[34] Röhm still hoped for a second and more radical Nazi revolution, which would achieve the more socialist aspects of the Nazi programme. Above all he wanted to turn the SA into the basis for a new mass army. It was this that threatened the *Reichswehr*'s role and led to its growing rivalry with the SA. Hitler had already shown that he wished to retain the *Reichswehr*, when in January 1934 he decided in principle on the reintroduction of traditional military conscription. However, what made the problem increasingly urgent by the spring of 1934 was the imminent question of the succession to the presidency, which was posed by Hindenburg's ill health and great age. It was more than likely that the generals would attempt to block Hitler's own ambitions to succeed him if they perceived the SA still to be threatening their role in rebuilding Germany's armed forces. For Hitler there was a real danger that the army and the conservative élites might, after Hindenburg's death, demand a monarchist restoration, which was their last chance of imposing some control on the Nazi regime. There were already reservations in national-conservative circles about having brought Hitler to power, and the hope

Ernst Röhm, 1887–1934

Röhm, whose father was a Bavarian civil servant, had a distinguished war record as a captain in the Bavarian army. In the immediate post-war period he remained an army staff officer, and played a crucial role in liaising with the Bavarian paramilitary groups, especially the Nazis, which he joined in 1923. The next five years were a period of failure: he was not elected to the *Reichstag* in 1924, bitterly disagreed with Hitler over the future shape of the SA, and faced the danger of prosecution for a number of homosexual affairs. In 1928 he emigrated to Bolivia as a military instructor, but was called back by Hitler to become chief of staff of the SA. Over the next three years Röhm played a crucial role in the Nazi assumption of power. The SA was reorganized and expanded into a mass organization.

that a crisis over the SA might enable them to establish an authoritarian government under their own control. Edgar Jung, a leading right-wing intellectual and Papen's speech writer, observed: 'We are partly responsible that this fellow has come to power [and] we must get rid of him again.'[35] However, as long as Hitler could control the SA, the *Reichswehr* would not support a restoration, as both General von Blomberg, the defence minister, and General Freiherr von Fritsch, the new commander-in-chief of the army, as well as many junior officers, were convinced that Hitler was the right man to rearm Germany.

From March 1934 onwards Hitler, egged on by Göring, Himmler and Hess, who desired to eliminate a dangerous rival to their own ambitions within the party, ' moved erratically and with spells of doubt and indecision towards a show-down with the SA'.[36] On 17 June Hitler received a sharp rebuke from Papen in a sensational speech delivered at Marburg University. The latter warned against the consequences of a second revolution and went on to criticize the growing *Führer* cult. 'Never again in the Third Reich', as Ian Kershaw has observed, 'was such striking criticism at the heart of the regime to come from such a prominent figure.'[37] When Hitler visited the president at his estate at Neudeck on 21 June, he was left in no doubt about the threat facing him, as he was informed by Blomberg that if he failed to control the SA, Hindenburg would hand over power to the army.

Consequently, if his regime was to survive, Hitler now had little choice but to destroy Röhm, but he was also determined to eliminate his leading critics on the right as well. In the subsequent 'Night of the Long Knives' not only the SA leaders, but the two conservative monarchists in Papen's office, Herbert von Bose and Edgar Jung, as well as other political enemies of Hitler, including Schleicher and Gregor Strasser, were all murdered. Police files indicate that at least eighty-five people were liquidated, while according to the 'white book', which was published in Paris by German émigrés, the number was as high as 401.

Following the elimination of Röhm, Hitler was able to consolidate his power without difficulty. Papen was dismissed and was lucky to escape with his life. When Hindenburg died on 1 August, there was no opposition from the army to Hitler combining the offices of chancellor and president – a step which was confirmed by plebiscite on 19 August. As head of state, Hitler became the supreme commander of the armed forces, which now swore an oath of loyalty voluntarily to him. He had survived a crisis which could have led to civil war and the end of the Nazi regime. He had succeeded in eliminating the threat from the SA without becoming the prisoner of the conservative élites.

Conclusion

Bracher argued that a 'combination of inevitability and chance'[38] led to the Nazi dictatorship. The Weimar Republic, beset by deep-seated structural political and economic problems was losing its political legitimacy in the eyes of a large number of Germans by late 1929. Hindenburg and his advisers were already weighing up the possibility of returning to a more authoritarian structure based on the Bismarckian constitution. In that sense it was possible that the Weimar Republic would in any event have been replaced with a more authoritarian regime. The onset of the world depression in 1930 and the rise of the Nazi party as a mass movement of protest injected a new dynamic into German politics and made the dissolution of the republic much more likely. It offered the possibility of a realignment of the forces on the right and held out the prospect to the Nationalist–Conservative right of mass backing for their plans for an authoritarian presidential regime. Over the period 1930–32 a *de facto* presidential regime was set up and the Prussian government, the bastion of social democracy, destroyed. When it was initially appointed, the Hitler government seemed, as Papen later claimed, to be merely a logical development of the politics of the previous three years. In that sense it had an air of inevitability about it, but the Nazi party was essentially a fragile party of protest and appeared already to be in decline in January 1933. Chance, luck and personalities also played into Hitler's hands. Was it, for instance, inevitable that the Grand Coalition should collapse in March 1930, or that Gregor Strasser should have obeyed Hitler's veto to join Schleicher's cabinet? Similarly what would have happened if Hindenburg had not at last agreed to appoint Hitler as chancellor?

12 *The Third Reich, 1933–39*

Introduction

The Third Reich is the subject of intense historical debate. Arguments still rage about the structure of the Nazi state and its foreign, economic and racial policies. Auschwitz and the Holocaust have made it very difficult for historians to 'historicize', or normalize, the Hitler regime and assess dispassionately the social and economic impact of the Hitler years on German history after 1945. The current debate on the Third Reich and modernization has opened up fresh perspectives, which are helpful in assessing its legacy to the Federal Republic. Rainer Zitelmann and Michael Prinz, for instance, have argued that the Nazi Labour Front (see p. 239) not only began to bring about 'the modernisation of leisure'[1] through the introduction of mass tourism for the German workers, but during the war drafted ambitious plans for a comprehensive post-war welfare state. It remains, however, difficult to reconcile this enlightened aspect of the Nazi regime with its barbaric racial policies. Modernization, of course, does not always have to be equated with the development of pluralism and democracy. As Detlev Peukert has reminded us, the paradoxical association of the concepts of 'normality and modernity' with 'fascist barbarism' in the Third Reich raises fundamental questions about the 'pathologies and seismic fractures within modernity itself, and about the implicit destructive tendencies of industrial class society'.[2]

When studying the Third Reich and the degree of support Hitler received, we need to bear in mind Martin Broszat's advice that we should not always study history backwards.[3] Those who at first supported

Auschwitz was built near Oswiecim in Polish Upper Silesia. About one million European Jews were gassed there, and after the war its name came to symbolize Nazi terror and brutality

Nazism could not foresee how the Third Reich would develop. The aims of both the élites and a majority of Germans overlapped with the initial stages of Nazi policy. Hitler's destruction of the Versailles Treaty and the provision of full employment were achievements which had universal backing. The atomization of society through *Gleischaltung* (see p. 220), as well as the terror apparatus of the *Gestapo* and SS made opposition on any large scale very difficult to achieve.

Gestapo:
*Geheime
Staatspolizei* (secret
state police) estab-
lished originally by
Göring in Prussia in
1933

SS: *Schutzstaffeln*
(guard unit)
founded originally
in 1925 to protect
leading Nazis

Key issues

- How was Nazi Germany governed and was Hitler a 'weak dictator' ?
- How did Hitler manage to create full employment and to what extent was the German economy prepared for a long war?
- Was the *Volksgemeinschaft* anything more than propaganda?
- To what extent can the Third Reich be called a 'racial state'?

The political structure of the Third Reich

The Third Reich was characterized by rival hierarchies and centres of power as well the lack of a clear command structure. It is possible to distinguish the following distinct centres of power, although there was some overlap between them:

- the central government with its traditional ministries and civil service;
- the emergence of the SS state under Himmler by the end of the 1930s;
- the single-party monopoly of the Nazi party;
- the charismatic dictatorship of Hitler.

Central government

When Hitler came to power he had no detailed plans for creating a specifically Nazi state as such. Although the Reich cabinet became increasingly less relevant after the passing of the Enabling Act, right up to the winter of 1937–38 seven important ministries of state were still in the hands of Conservative–Nationalist ministers. Only in December 1935 did Blomberg, the war minister, for instance, permit his civil servants to join the NSDAP, and Frick, the Nazi minister of the interior, was equally anxious to exclude the party from meddling in his ministry. Overall, the weakening of the traditional federal structure of the Reich strengthened the central ministries. The bureaucracy escaped a radical restructuring, although, by the Law for the Restoration of the Professional Civil Service, it was purged of potential enemies to the regime and of Jews, unless they had fought in the war. It was not until February 1939 that party member-ship become an essential condition for any new entrant.

Parallel to, but virtually independent of, the traditional ministries there grew up a series of hybrid Reich organizations, which combined both party and state responsibilities. Their leaders were prominent Nazis, who were responsible to the *Führer*. Fritz Todt, Hitler's road-building expert, was given the necessary powers to implement the *Autobahn* programme. As Inspector General for German Roads, his office formed 'an element of direct *Führer* authority . . . alongside the normal state government and administration'.[4] Another characteristic of the Nazi government was the accumulation of ministries and influential positions by individual Nazi leaders. In May 1933 Göring was appointed Reich Aviation Minister, while still retaining the Prussian Minister–Presidency and Ministry of the Interior. Then in 1936 he was put in charge of the new Four Year Plan (see p. 00).

The SS state

Heinrich Himmler, by building up the SS into a 'state within a state', also created an independent sphere of authority, which was accountable theoretically only to Hitler. This sprawling SS empire was the most important of the Supreme Reich authorities, and, like so many National Socialist organizations, created a large number of new offices which, in Broszat's words, 'tended repeatedly to generate new positions having a "direct" relationship with Hitler and to encourage these in turn to strive for a separate existence, like some permanent process of cell division'.[5]

The SS had been formed in 1925 as a small force to protect the leading Nazis. Under Himmler, who became its head in 1929, it took charge of the party's intelligence and espionage section. As a reward for its loyalty to Hitler in 1934 during the confrontation with Röhm (see pp. 222–3), it was made independent of the SA and given responsibility for running the concentration camps, for which task the notorious Death's Head Units (*Totenkopfverbände*) were formed. In February 1936, despite opposition

---

Heinrich Himmler, 1900–45

Himmler was the son of a Bavarian secondary school teacher. For a short time after the Great War he was a poultry farmer in Bavaria. He was an avid reader of anti-Semitic literature, and long before he joined the Nazi party had become a fanatical believer in German racial superiority. He took part in the Munich *putsch*, but did not join the Nazi party until 1926. In 1929 he was made head of the SS. In 1933 he was appointed chief of police in Bavaria and by 1936 had consolidated his grip on the whole police apparatus in Germany. In 1939 he became Commissar for the Consolidation of German Nationhood (RKFDV), which gave him a virtual monopoly over Nazi racial and extermination policy in the occupied areas. Hitler appointed him minister of the interior in 1943, but his bungled attempt to end the war in April 1945 by using contacts in Stockholm led to Hitler ordering his arrest. He was captured by British troops in May, but committed suicide before he could be tried by the Nuremberg tribunal.

from Frick, Himmler was effectively given control over the political police, the *Gestapo*, and was able to fuse it with the SD, the Security Service of the SS. His appointment as Chief of the German Police in June 1936 enabled him to command both the SS and the Reich police forces. Himmler's power potential was further increased by the formation of a small number of armed regiments, the *Waffen SS*, based on the SS squads which had operated together with the SA as a 'revolutionary strike force' in the early months of the takeover of power.

The party

Alte Kämpfer:
Nazi veterans who
joined the party
before 1923

In the spring of 1933 the role of the NSDAP in the new Nazi Germany was far from clear. Röhm and many of the *alte Kämpfer* passionately believed that there should be a radical social and political revolution, but this view was not shared by Goebbels, Göring, Himmler and Frick, who had created for themselves formidable empires within the existing state. Whether the NSDAP should become a cadre party, which would train the future leaders of the regime, or merely a large depoliticized mass movement, that could be used both to mobilize the masses and also for propaganda purposes, was also a matter of debate. In the summer of 1933 Hitler had played with the idea of creating a National Socialist Senate along the lines of the Fascist Grand Council in Italy, but he rapidly dropped the idea for fear that it might undermine his own position. In July 1933 he cryptically stated that the 'party had now become the state' and that all power lay with the Reich government.[6] Its role in practice, as Hitler made clear at the *Gauleiter* conference on 2 February, was to carry out propaganda activities and indoctrination on behalf of the government's measures and in general 'to support the government in every way'.[7] Yet Hitler also needed it to counter-balance the bureaucracy and thus he could not allow the party to decline into a mere propaganda organization. At Nuremberg in September 1935 he reminded the civil service that 'whatever can be solved by the state will be solved through the state, but any problem which the state through its essential character is unable to solve will be solved by means of the movement'.[8]

In general, until 1938 party influence within the government remained relatively weak. While in some ministries there was a personal union of party and state, Nazi ministers, especially Wilhelm Frick at the Ministry of the Interior, often objected vigorously to party attempts to interfere in their departments. As long as the wishes of the *Führer,* as far as they could be ascertained, were not ignored, it was usually possible to contain the party's meddling, and civil servants quickly learned to see 'the party as a rival but not necessarily as an invincible one',[9] and party and state appeared to settle down to an uneasy coexistence .

Yet in the winter of 1937–38 Nazi influence began to increase. Ribbentrop was appointed to the Foreign Ministry specifically to weaken the influence of the career diplomats. In February 1938 the independence of the military was also seriously impaired when Hitler sacked both

General Fritsch, the Commander-in-Chief, for allegations that he was a homosexual, and the Defence Minister, Blomberg, for marrying a former prostitute. The Defence Ministry was replaced by the new High Command of German Armed Forces (OKW), which was directly responsible to Hitler. The *Anschluss* of Austria and then the annexation of the Sudetenland and Bohemia (see pp. 249–52) also strengthened the influence of the party, as the newly-appointed commissioners were able to implement Nazi policy without any of the interference from the judiciary or the bureaucracy which they had experienced in the old Reich.

The role of Hitler

Only Hitler could mediate between the mass of competing agencies of which the Third Reich was composed. Theoretically Hitler was omnipotent. As *Führer* he was 'supreme legislator, supreme administrator and supreme judge', as well as being 'the leader of the Party, the Army and the People'.[10] The cabinet seldom met after 1934, the *Reichstag* was a rubber-stamp and Hitler had combined the presidency with the chancellorship. Paradoxically, however, Hitler did not play a significant part in the day-to-day running of the government. He has been described as a 'remote umpire handing down decisions from on high',[11] but even this arguably exaggerates his role in government. He disliked making decisions and usually preferred to let events take their course rather than intervene. At most he might announce vague declarations of intent which did not transmute into clear directives. Often his ministers had no communication with him at all, especially when he was in his isolated chalet in the Berghof in Bavaria. Thus officials frequently had little option but to interpret Hitler's intentions themselves, often drawing contradictory conclusions. Werner Willikens, the state secretary in the Prussian Agriculture Ministry, accurately described this Byzantine process of interpreting Hitler's will as 'working towards the *Führer*'.

See Documents 61 and 62

Intentionalists: those historians such as Karl Dietrich Bracher, Klaus Hildebrand and Eberhard Jäckel, who are convinced that developments in the Third Reich were the result of Hitler's intentions

While historians agree that the administration of the Third Reich was chaotic and deeply divided by personal and institutional rivalries, the reasons for this are still sharply debated. The intentionalists, such as Bracher, argue that Hitler *intentionally* employed a policy of divide and rule to protect his own position, while structuralists insist that this chaos was the *result* of Hitler's unstable, charismatic rule,[12] rather than his *intention*.

Was this chaos at the centre of the Nazi regime a sign that Hitler was really a 'weak dictator'? In Hans Mommsen's frequently quoted words, Hitler was 'reluctant to take decisions, often uncertain, concerned only to maintain his own prestige and personal authority, and strongly subject to the influence of his environment – in fact, in many ways, a weak dictator'.[13] There is, however, little evidence that Hitler ever desired a different system. On the contrary, his charisma depended on distancing himself from the mundane day-to-day decisions of government. In reality, of course, although Hitler was theoretically omnipotent, he was not immune to the pressure from events. Party members, for instance, put

Structuralists: historians like Martin Broszat and Hans Mommsen who place more emphasis on the political, economic and social structure of the regime than on personalities

19   'The charismatic Führer'. The front page of the supplement to *12 Uhr Blatt* celebrating Hitler's 50th birthday, 20 April 1939

Sonderbeilage 12 Uhr Blatt, 20 April 1939, front page

him under pressure to intensify the persecution of the Jews (see p. 243), and there were also, of course, difficult economic problems, such as the worsening balance of payments deficits. On the other hand, by 1938 he had broken most potential centres of opposition to his regime. In determining foreign policy and rearmament, in which he was particularly interested, he had been able successfully to implement his policies.

Arguably, his 'weakness', if that is the really the right word, lay in the fundamental instability of the regime he had created.

An economic miracle?

In January 1933 the Hitler government was confronted with formidable economic problems:

- The German economy was practically bankrupt and the official unemployment rate was well over 6 million, and possibly as high as 8 or 9 million.
- Industrial production had declined to the levels of the 1890s, while the volume of German trade had sunk by 50 per cent.
- Agriculture was burdened with debt and was uncompetitive internationally.

Hitler had no detailed plans for dealing with the economic crisis, but, if the Nazi regime was to survive, unemployment had to sink dramatically and industrial production to rise sharply.

Engineering an economic recovery

The new government, in the words of the Ministry of Labour, applied 'a multitude of inter-related measures'.[14] Some of these were policies which Papen and Schleicher had cautiously begun to experiment with. Rearmament, which is traditionally seen as 'kick-starting' the German recovery, was only one of the reasons for its rapid revival; there were others:

- As many young people as possible were removed from the labour market and were employed temporarily by such organizations as the Voluntary Labour Service or the Land Service, and by 1935, with the reintroduction of conscription, a million young people were annually absorbed for two years by the *Reichswehr*.
- The length of the working week was cut, and many women were squeezed out of the labour market with the carrot of the marriage loan, which was only available to newly-married couples on condition that the wife stayed at home.
- The Law for Reducing Unemployment pumped a billion Reichsmarks into public works schemes such as road and canal building. Government subsidies were also provided for house construction.
- The motor industry was also aided by tax concessions, which dramatically improved sales and helped the component industries.

At the same time Hitler took great care to assure the business community that there would be no 'wild experiments'.[15] Schacht, the *Reichsbank*

Hjalmar Schacht, 1877–1970

Schacht was a leading banker in the inter-war years. In 1923 he was appointed president of the *Reichsbank*, where he was responsible for halting hyperinflation and introducing the *Rentenmark* currency (see p. 183). He resigned in 1930 in protest against the Young Plan. As a German nationalist, he supported a coalition with Hitler and in 1933 was reappointed to the *Reichsbank*, and then in September 1934 became economics minister. As a result of disagreements over the economic consequences of rearmament, he resigned in 1937 and was dismissed from the *Reichsbank* in 1939. He remained a minister without portfolio until 1944, when he was put in a concentration camp on the suspicion that he was involved in the 20 July plot to kill Hitler. He was tried at Nuremberg by the Allies but acquitted.

president, was given responsibility for ensuring that job creation schemes did not lead to inflation, a task that was made easier by the dissolution of the trade unions and fixing of wage rates at 1932 levels. While employers' associations did not completely escape co-ordination (see p. 221), businessmen were given considerable leeway to manage their own affairs.

See Document 60

20 Carrying their shovels as if they were guns, men of the German labour service march in military formation past their saluting leader in the Zeppelin stadium, Nuremberg, 1937

Imperial War Museum, no. NYP68056

The number of unemployed (millions), January 1934–39

1934	3.773
1935	2.974
1936	2.520
1937	1.853
1938	1.052
1939	0.302

Source: Adapted from: B. Gebhardt, *Handbuch der deutschen Geschichte*, Vol. 4, ed. K. D. Erdmann, Stuttgart, Union Verlag, 1959, p. 352.

Also, despite all the earlier rhetoric, few concessions were made to the *Mittelstand*'s demands for abolishing the department stores or controlling the great trusts. On the contrary, 'the fighting organizations of the industrial middle classes' were dissolved and the steady growth in cartels proceeded unchecked. Helped by the upturn in the economic cycle, Nazi efforts to revive the economy were remarkably successful. By the summer of 1934 unemployment had come down to 2.5 million, although it then stubbornly remained stuck at that level until conscription and rearmament caused its decline to accelerate in 1936, and by 1938 virtually full employment was achieved.

As serious as the unemployment problem was the plight of agriculture (see p. 208). In the summer of 1933 the Reich Food Estate was set up, which assumed responsibility for all aspects of food production and marketing. Initially a combination of higher tariffs, tax cuts, favourable interest rates and guaranteed prices helped boost the agrarian economy. In 1938–39 productivity was 25 per cent higher than ten years earlier, and Germany was 83 per cent self-sufficient. On the other hand, by 1935 price controls on food began to operate against the agricultural interest. Since they were intended to stop rises in the cost of living, they prevented farmers from profiting from the growing demand for foodstuffs. Consequently, the profit margins of agriculture remained relatively low and rural labourers continued to migrate to the towns (see p. 238).

The economics of rearmament and the Four Year Plan, 1933–36

In order to finance rearmament at the same time as huge work-creation projects were being implemented, in the summer of 1933 Schacht devised the brilliant device of 'Mefo bills', which were of crucial assistance in initially raising the necessary funds. Yet, even so, the progress of German rearmament was constantly threatened by recurring balance of payments crises as the revival of the economy led to a rapid rise in imports. To pay for the imports needed for rearmament, Schacht, who became econom-

Mefo bills

Government agencies initially paid industries, which received military contracts, with credit notes, or 'Mefo bills'. These were issued by four large private companies and two government ministries under the name of the *Metall-Forschungs AG* (Metal Research Co., abbreviated to *Mefo*). On receipt of the *Mefo* bills the *Reichsbank* paid cash, and so ensured that companies were promptly reimbursed. As the bills were valid for a five-year period, the government also raised large sums of money by offering them at 4 per cent per annum on the money market and also by forcing banks to invest 30 per cent of their deposits in them.

ics minister in 1934, introduced the New Plan, which set up strict controls for the government regulation of imports and currency exchange. He also managed to negotiate a series of bilateral trade agreements with the Balkan and South American states by which German purchases were paid for in Reichsmarks. These in turn were used by these countries to purchase German goods and to invest in the construction of plants, which would later produce goods required for the German war economy. His efforts, however, had only minimal success and the gathering pace of rearmament and economic recovery continued to suck in an ever-growing volume of imports. In December when the Defence Ministry demanded the doubling of copper imports, Schacht argued that the necessary foreign exchange to pay for this did not exist and that from now on rearmament would have to be paid for by increasing the volume of exports.

Hitler, however, refused to allow economic arguments to slow down the rearmament programme. First of all in April 1936 he began to marginalize Schacht by appointing Göring commissioner of raw materials and currency, and then in August, in a memorandum which is 'one of the basic documents of the Third Reich',[16] launched the Four Year Plan, for the execution of which Göring was responsible. By increasing production and encouraging the use of substitutes for imported raw materials, its aim was to make Germany as independent as possible of imports and to be ready for war by 1940. Richard Overy argues that it marked 'the

How the Four Year Plan worked

The core of the Four Year Plan was to increase production in synthetic rubber, fuel oil and iron ore. Large plants were built for the production of synthetic rubber and oil and the *Reichswerke*, the Hermann Göring Steelworks, were constructed at Watenstedt-Salzgitter to exploit local low-grade ores. In 1938 they took over the running of the major Austrian iron, steel and machinery companies, and, six months later, the Škoda works in the Sudetenland. While massive increases in production were achieved, the Plan failed to meet its targets, particularly in synthetic fuel, and consequently imports continued to be a drain on Germany's currency reserves.

point at which the armed forces' conception of recovery of defensive strength gave way to Hitler's conception of large-scale preparations for aggressive imperialism over which the armed forces were to have less and less say'.[17] During the winter of 1936–7 Göring effectively took over responsibility for rearmament from the Ministries of Economics and Defence, forcing Schacht to resign in November.

In 1959 Klein challenged the accepted view that Germany had been preparing for total war, and argued that, despite the Four Year Plan, the 'scale of Germany's economic mobilization for war was quite modest'.[18] He stressed that consumer goods output had in fact increased by over 30 per cent between 1936 and 1939. A. J. P. Taylor used this to support his claim that Hitler had no plans for a major war, while Milward insisted that he envisaged only a series of brief *Blitzkriege* that would not overstrain the German economy.[19] The Klein-Milward thesis became something of a 'new orthodoxy' in the 1960s and 1970s, but 20 years later Richard Overy effectively challenged its assumptions, and conclusively showed that the Four Year Plan really was 'a decisive step towards preparing Germany for total mobilization', which provided the vital economic base for the later expansion of the armaments industries. Overall, according to Overy, 'consumption as a share of national income declined from 71 per cent in 1928 to 58 per cent in 1938' and between 1936 and 1939 armaments and preparations for war absorbed over 60 per cent of all capital investments made. This is not to say that Hitler would not have welcomed a brief war, but in May 1939, as he warned his generals, ' the government must . . . also prepare for a war of from ten to fifteen years duration'.[20]

A growing economic crisis?

Rearmament at this pace did, of course, create economic problems. There were production bottlenecks and interservice rivalry for scarce resources, as well as labour shortages and a constant lack of sufficient foreign exchange to pay for imports. There was also an increasing danger of inflation as the bank-note circulation trebled between 1933 and 1939. Tim Mason argued that Hitler was forced into war in 1939 'because of domestic pressures and constraints which were economic in origin and also expressed themselves in acute social and political tension'.[21] The German economy certainly faced problems, but the situation in the summer of 1939 was more under control than it had been a few months earlier. Walther Funk, who succeeded Schacht as economics minister, had launched the New Finance Plan, by which businesses with state armaments contracts would receive 40 per cent of their payments in tax certificates, a certain proportion of which could only be cashed in after three years. Labour shortages were being met by recruiting foreign workers from southern and central Europe, the introduction of labour conscription, and large-scale industrial retraining programmes. By 1939 the German economy was second only to America's and less vulnerable to global pressures than either the French or British. Not surprisingly, Overy insists that '"crisis" is an inappropriate characterization of the German economy in the months before the war'.[22] Yet there were signs of growing inflationary trends and an increasing shortage of resources with which to meet the escalating demands of the rearmament programme. Although it was the diplomatic rather than economic factors that determined the actual outbreak of the war in 1939, it is never-theless argued by Kershaw that 'the mounting economic problems fed into the military and strategic pressures for expansion'.[23]

The *Volksgemeinschaft*

The *Volksgemeinschaft*, or 'People's Community', was not a new concept. It was inspired by the 'spirit of 1914', which had temporarily enthused the Germans at the beginning of the Great War (see p. 147). With the divisiveness of post-war politics and the painful impact of moderniza-tion, the concept had lost none of its appeal during the Weimar Republic. The Nazi *Volksgemeinschaft* superficially appeared to respond to these yearnings for unity, stability and 'the normal order of things', but funda-mentally for Hitler the ultimate aim of the *Volksgemeinschaft* was to inculcate a new mentality and ethos into the German people that would turn it into a 'fighting community' ready for war. It was this ultimate aim that rendered the nature of the *Volksgemeinschaft* paradoxical: Nazi ideology, with its stress on land settlement, the peasant, the artisan and the role of women in the family, appeared to imply that the Nazis would attempt to introduce an anti-modernist social revolution aimed at unscrambling modern industrial society, yet in practice, with large-scale rearmament and total war, Nazism became a modernizing force, which effectively destroyed all that remained of the old Germany for ever.

Fostering the spirit of the *Volksgemeinschaft*: propaganda and education

The Propaganda Ministry under Goebbels was set up on 13 March 1933 'to transform the very spirit itself to the extent that people and things are brought into a new relationship with one another'.[24] In achieving this, the new medium of the radio played a major role. Regional radio stations, which had previously been under the control of the *Länder*, were amalgamated into the Reich Radio Company, whose director liaised closely with Goebbels. Cheap radios were mass-produced and great efforts were made by specially appointed local radio wardens to encour-age the Germans to buy them and to tune in to the programmes.

The Propaganda Ministry also devised strict guidelines for the arts, as it was vital that the public should be fed a suitable cultural diet which did not challenge Nazi ideology. Although modern design survived in indus-trial and consumer products, experiments in modern art forms were

Nazi schools and the Hitler Youth

The Nazis created a small number of special schools and institutions which were entrusted with the task of producing the future elite of Germany. By 1939, 21 *Napolas* (National Political Educational Establishments), the Adolf Hitler schools, and four *Ordensburgen* had been set up. These instutions were supposed to educate a new Nazi élite, but the *Napolas* attracted very few members of the professional classes, who continued to regard the grammar schools and universities as the best way to influential and well-paid careers. Ultimately, students from the *Napolas* would go on to the *Ordensburgen*, which were intended to be the finishing schools for the future Nazi élite.

expressly condemned, while in literature novels on such topics as war and the early days of the Nazi movement were the approved subjects. Hitler as an 'artist manqué'[25] regarded modern art as 'degenerate' and favoured pastoral scenes or depictions of great battles. Goebbels did, however, recognize the importance of light and largely apolitical popular entertainment in the cinema and on the radio. Only a quarter of the films produced between 1933 and 1934, for example, had an overtly political content. The others were comedies, thrillers, love stories and musicals.

Although, outwardly, the traditional structure of the German educational system remained in place, educational syllabuses were changed to reflect the demands of Nazi ideology. In schools the curriculum was revised to give more teaching time to history, biology and German as the three subjects which lent themselves to exploitation by Nazi propaganda, and in September 1933 a new subject, 'racial science', was introduced as a compulsory element in the timetable. However, the most effective instrument for influencing young people was the Hitler Youth. By 1936, 60 per cent of all young people in Germany were members, and increasing pressure on the Catholic Church led to the dissolution of its own youth organizations in 1939, the year in which service in the Hitler Youth became compulsory. Its activities and sense of belonging undoubtedly attracted many young people. Christa Wolf, who was later one of East Germany's leading authors, recalled in a semi-autobiographical novel how at first it seemed to offer 'the promise of a loftier life'.[26] By the late 1930s, however, it had become a large bureaucratic organization with

The organization of the Hitler Youth

Between the ages of 10 and 14, boys belonged to the *Jungvolk* and from 14 to 18 to the Hitler Youth, where their time was taken up by a mixture of sport, war games and indoctrination. For girls of 10–14 there was the *Jungmädel* and then from 14–18 the *Bund deutscher Mädchen* (German Girls' League), where the emphasis was on physical fitness and the teaching of traditional female domestic skills. To quote Claudia Koonz, they 'prepared girls for a lifetime in the second sex'.[27]

increasingly elderly leaders. Compulsory membership also meant that it had to absorb numerous bored and resentful teenagers. Not surprisingly, it began to experience 'a growing crisis',[28] which during the war years erupted in places into open youth rebellion (see pp. 265–6).

The peasantry

David Schoenbaum argued that support for the peasantry, together with anti-Semitism, was 'one of the few consistent premises of Nazi life'.[29] Certainly the Reich Entailed Farm Law of September 1933 guaranteed the small farmer's security of tenure by declaring that farms between 7.5 and 125 hectares were to remain the permanent property of the original peasant owners, while the regime lost no opportunity to portray the peasantry as 'responsible carriers of German society renewing its strength from blood and soil'.[30] Nevertheless, once the economy started to expand, the government could not halt the renewed flight from the land. The rural population reacted to poor housing, bad pay and the gruelling nature of unmechanized farm work by migrating to the cities. Consequently, the pace of urbanization and modernization speeded up and Germany, despite Nazi rhetoric about the idyllic rural life, increasingly continued to develop into an advanced industrial society.

Women and the family

See Document 63

The primary importance of women to the Nazis was their role as child-bearers and homemakers. To train women for motherhood and marriage, the regime set up two women's organizations, the National Socialist Womanhood and the German Women's Enterprise. Initially it attempted to persuade young women to leave work by making motherhood an attractive financial alternative by offering loans, tax-relief schemes and family allowances. However, the government did accept that women would continue to work in industry once the economy recovered. A women's section was formed within the German Labour Front in July 1934 under Gertrud Scholtz-Klinik, and women were recruited to work in many of the new plants which were built under the Four Year Plan. By May 1939, 12.7 million women were in employment and comprised 37 per cent of the German workforce. Increasingly, women also joined the professions in greater numbers, even though in 1933 they had been dismissed from the higher ranks of the civil service, and medical and legal professions. For instance, the total of female doctors actually increased from 5 per cent in 1930 to 7.6 per cent in 1939. The *Völkische Beobachter* conceded in 1937 that 'today we can no longer do without the woman doctor, lawyer, economist and teacher in our professional life'.[31]

The Nazi concept of the family was contradictory. On the one hand the family was the 'germ cell'[32] of the nation, yet as a small oasis of privacy it was also subject to some distrust by the regime. Parental control over children was threatened by the government's racial laws and eugenic policies (see p. 241) and by the growing pressure for children to join the Hitler Youth. According to Claudia Koonz, Nazi family policy was 'deeply revolutionary because it aimed at the creation of a family unit that was not a defence against public invasion as much as the gateway to intervention'.[33] In reality the Nazi priority was not so much the family as the procreation of healthy 'Aryan' children. Hitler himself observed that 'it must be considered reprehensible conduct to refrain from giving healthy children to the nation'.[34] This led both to banning abortion in May 1933 and to some improvement in the status of unmarried mothers, even though public opinion and the party itself was conservative on this issue.

Lebensborn: Spring of Life

Himmler and the *Lebensborn* homes

The unmarried mother's greatest defender was Himmler, who argued that she should be 'raised to her proper place in the community, since she is during and after her pregnancy, not a married or an unmarried woman but a mother'.[35] As long as single-parent children were 'racially and hereditarily valuable', he was ready to protect them through a 'legal guardianship'. He opened the *Lebensborn* homes for pregnant and nursing mothers whose children had been fathered by SS men and 'other racially valuable Germans'.[36]

The workers

A key myth of the *Volksgemeinschaft* was Hitler's claim to have 'broken with a world of prejudices' and created equality between the 'workers of the brain and fist'.[37] Hitler claimed to have liberated the workers from their unpatriotic Marxist leaders and to have given them a more respected place in society. The workers were corralled into the Labour Front, while their employers were officially called 'plant leaders'. Elected Councils of Trust were set up in all factories where there were more than twenty workers, but, after 1935, elections were abruptly discontinued because the workers were electing what the regime considered to be politically 'unreliable' candidates. Theoretically these councils could take an employer to a Court of Social Honour as long as they had the support of the local labour trustee, an official appointed by the Ministry of Labour, but this only rarely happened. Between 1934 and 1936 there were only 616 cases out of a workforce of well over 20 million.

See Documents 64 and 65

Politically the Labour Front could not afford to be just an instrument of control. It also had to be seen to be putting into operation what Hitler called 'socialism of the deed'. To achieve this it set up two organizations, which owed much to the experiments in welfare capitalism in the 1920s. The first one, the 'Beauty of Work' scheme, headed by Albert Speer, attempted to persuade employers to make their factories a more humane environment by improving the lighting and installing swimming baths, showers and canteens. By 1939 nearly 70,000 companies had agreed to

---

Albert Speer, 1905–81

Speer was the son of a well-known architect and was won over to the Nazis when he attended one of Hitler's rallies in 1931. He joined the party and in 1934 became the 'party architect', and for the next eight years designed grandiose buildings for the new Germany. In 1942 he was appointed armaments minister. In 1946 he was sentenced to 20 years' imprisonment at Nuremberg. Later he published his diary and wrote his memoirs, in which he bitterly criticized the Third Reich.

See Document 59

---

implement these improvements. The second one, the Front's leisure organization, 'Strength Through Joy' (KDF), was primarily, as its head, Robert Ley, observed, an attempt to dispel boredom, as from it 'sprang stupid, heretical, yes, in the end criminal ideas'.[38] It organized concerts and plays for the workers and arranged a number of subsidized cruises or holidays in the German countryside. By 1938 both the hotel industry and much of the passenger traffic of the *Reichsbahn* were becoming economically dependent on the KDF's holiday plans.

Reichsbahn: the national railways

One of the most popular policies of the KDF was the *Volkswagen* (VW) project. The work started on building the VW in the summer of 1938. The workers were offered a savings scheme which in theory would eventually enable them to purchase the car. However, unlike conventional hire-purchase agreements, the VW would only be delivered after the final payment had been made. By 1940, 300,000 people had already signed up, to the scheme although the war halted production and the cars were never produced.

Volkswagen: people's car

Full employment, which Franz Neumann called Hitler's 'sole gift to the masses',[39] gave the workers a growing economic power which they were beginning to exploit. In 1936 absenteeism and go-slows increased, and a series of lightning strikes compelled the regime to take steps to control the situation. Workers who broke their contracts with their employers to move on to fresh jobs were threatened with the confiscation of their work books, without which they could not be employed. In June 1938, in an effort to stop employers from poaching labour from each other, the trustees of labour were given the power to determine uniform wage levels in key industries. Labour conscription was also introduced, which could channel workers towards particular industries. Ultimately, as a final deterrent, there loomed the terror of the Gestapo and 'the camps of education for work', which were almost as brutal as the concentration camps. None of these measures stopped wages from rising in the armaments industries, where the workers, either individually or in small groups, managed to exploit the novel situation of full employment by gaining concessions from the employers, which Detlev Peukert called a 'sort of "do-it-yourself" wage system'.[40]

How integrated were the workers into the *Volksgemeinschaft*? Were they incarcerated 'in a great convict prison', to quote the former SPD trade union leader, Wilhelm Leuschner,[41] or did they in fact share at least some of the values of the *Volksgemeinschaft*? While a working-class culture did manage to survive in the Third Reich, there was nevertheless 'some penetration of Nazi values'.[42] Younger workers, especially, for whom the Hitler Youth had provided new chances, took advantage of retraining possibilities and transferred to more skilled jobs. Material benefits like longer holidays and low heating and lighting costs certainly appeased the workers, but many also could not help admiring Hitler for his foreign policy successes. As oral history projects have revealed, in the immediate post-war period of turmoil many workers looked back nostalgically on the years 1934–39 as a period of 'work, adequate nourishment, KDF and the absence of disarray'.[43]

See Document 65

Race and eugenics

The National Community was to be composed of a racially homogeneous 'Aryan' people, whose health and racial purity were at all costs to be preserved. A series of laws increasingly discriminated against those Germans who were judged to be of 'lesser racial value', banning them, for instance, from receiving any of the financial privileges given to those with large families, and, after October 1935, all prospective marriage partners had to have a fitness certificate. Euthanasia was a logical development of this policy. At first, beginning in the winter of 1938–39, it was practised on children with 'congenital deformities', and then a few months later it was extended to adults, although attempts were made to keep it secret. It was temporarily halted when it became public knowledge and was condemned by the Bishop of Münster in August 1941 (see p. 266), but soon recommenced and was widened to embrace foreign workers judged to be suffering from incurable physical illnesses, racially 'inferior' babies of eastern European women working in the Reich, terminally-sick inmates from the German prisons and sometimes *Wehrmacht* soldiers suffering from incurable shellshock.

The *Reichswehr* changed its name to the *Wehrmacht* in 1935

As the Nazis believed that criminal and 'asocial' behaviour as well as sexual deviancy were determined by genetic factors, they were convinced that individuals suffering from these perceived 'disorders' had to be sterilized for the good of society. The law of November 1933 against dangerous habitual criminals, for example, introduced the principle of compulsory castration for certain types of sexual offenders, and increasingly both punishments and the treatment of prison inmates were determined by biological–racial criteria.

The 'asocials' were people, such as tramps and the homeless, who did not conform to accepted social behaviour

The non-Jewish racial minorities

The sterilization laws were extended to cover the small number of mixed-race children fathered by French African soldiers during the Rhineland occupation. The Nazi regime inherited from the Weimar Republic a legacy of hostile policies towards the Sinti and Roma (gypsies). In 1935 the SS financed a research unit in the Ministry of Health, which decided that 90 per cent of the Sinti and Roma were of mixed race, and were therefore likely to be of a criminal and 'asocial' predisposition, and should as a consequence be sterilized. In September 1939 Himmler started to deport the 30,000 gypsies in the Reich to occupied Poland. Initially only a small number were transported, but from December 1942 onwards the programme gathered pace and by 1945 only a few hundred had escaped being sent to Auschwitz.

Unlike the Weimar Republic, the Third Reich was not committed by its constitution to guaranteeing civil rights to its Slav minorities. Initially, however, the existence of German minorities in Poland and Czechoslovakia compelled the Nazi government to adopt a relatively tolerant policy towards the Sorbs for fear of retaliation, but once Czechoslovakia was dismembered and Poland occupied (see pp. 252), both the leaders of the Sorb and of the Polish communities were arrested and sent to concentration camps. Himmler intended to move the Sorbs to occupied Poland, as they were viewed as 'the same racial and human type'[44] as the Poles, but his energies were absorbed by dealing with the far larger number of Jews, and he was never able to implement these plans for the small Sorb population.

See Document 48

The Jews

When Hitler first came to power, he did not issue any policy directives on the Jewish question. Initially, only independent action by the SA against individual Jews and their property, which threatened to damage his government's reputation, forced Hitler to attempt to channel the violence into a boycott of Jewish shops on 1 April, but this was rapidly halted when it was sharply criticized both at home and abroad. Hitler then sought to appease the party by expelling the Jews from the Civil

The intentionalist–structuralist debate

The intentionalists, particularly Lucy Dawidowicz, Klaus Hildebrand and Karl Dietrich Bracher, argue that Hitler from the beginning *intended* the mass-murder of the Jews, even though he could not implement this straightaway. Structuralist scholars, such as Martin Broszat, Hans Mommsen and Karl Schleunes, while not disputing Hitler's anti-Semitism, locate the ultimate cause of the Holocaust in the disjointed and chaotic way in which Nazi Germany was governed. They argue that the bureaucracy and the Nazi leaders competed with each other in formulating anti-Semitic policies, which led to ever more radical policies being implemented. Understandably, the intentionalists are highly critical of what they regard as attempts to depersonalize the responsibility of what ultimately led to the Holocaust. Dawidowicz, indeed, regards such an approach as initiating a new 'cycle of apologetics' in German history.[45]

See Documents 66 and 67

Service, the universities and journalism. Over the next two years economic and political realities forced the Nazi government to discourage overt racial violence against the Jewish community, but in the summer of 1935 Hitler again responded to fresh acts of anti-Semitic violence by attempting to placate party activists. On 15 September he announced at Nuremberg the notorious 'Law for the Protection of German Blood', forbidding marriage or sexual intercourse between Jews and German gentiles, and the Reich Citizenship Law, which deprived Jews of their German citizenship. However, both laws disappointed many of the Nazi zealots, who suspected that Hitler had accepted the advice from his civil servants rather than from the party.

By the spring of 1938 the party activists were again demanding ever more radical measures against the Jews, while Göring, as commissioner of the Four Year Plan (see p. 234), was urging their rapid economic expropriation. The triumphalist mood caused by the *Anschluss* of Austria and the growing threat of war with Czechoslovakia also contributed to the clamour for further action against the Jews. A whole raft of anti-Semitic decrees were promulgated, which involved not only measures forcing Jews to adopt specifically Jewish forenames but also having their wealth and property registered as a preliminary for expropriation by the state.

The turning-point in the treatment of the Jews was the *Reichskristallnacht* riots of November 1938. In the aftermath of the riots the Jews were made to pay a collective fine of 1.25 billion marks. Individual Jews were forced out of jobs in the retail trade, skilled labour and management. In April 1939 the remainder of their wealth was seized, and they were banned from public places, such as theatres and beaches. The small number of Jewish children who were still pupils in state schools were expelled. Reinhard Heydrich, the chief of the security police and the SD, was given responsibility for organizing the emigration of the remaining 214,000 Jews in Germany, but paradoxically Göring's ruthless expropriation policies had made Jewish emigration more difficult to achieve, since foreign states were reluctant to accept refugees without any financial means of support.

Reichskristallnacht

The cause of this pogrom was the assassination of Ernst von Rath, a junior diplomat in the German embassy in Paris, by Herschl Grynszpan, a 17-year-old student, whose parents, together with 17,000 other Jews of Polish descent, had recently been expelled from Germany. As the Polish government refused to admit them, they were forced to camp on the no-man's-land between the Polish and German frontiers. Goebbels, apparently with the tacit approval of Hitler, organized 'spontaneous' attacks on synagogues and Jewish-owned businesses. Some 25 million marks' worth of damage was done and probably as many as a hundred Jews were killed, while nearly thirty thousand were put into concentration camps.

Martin Bormann, 1900–45

Before serving with the artillery in the Great War, Bormann worked on a farm. After the war he was recruited by the *Freikorps* and was imprisoned for a political murder in 1924. He joined the Nazi party in 1927, and after 1933 became deputy to Rudolf Hess. He also managed the Adolf Hitler Fund of German Business. He replaced Hess when the latter flew to Scotland in 1941 and became director of the party chancellery. As he was always at Hitler's side, he amassed enormous powers and controlled access to the Führer. He was killed in May 1945 trying to escape from Berlin.

See Document 61

Although, on 12 November 1938, Hitler had, it seems, informed Göring both verbally through his chief of staff, Martin Bormann, and by phone that 'the Jewish question [should] be now once and for all co-ordinated and solved one way or another',[46] he did not publicly associate himself with the series of anti-Semitic policies initiated in the aftermath of *Reichskristallnacht*. Twice, however, in January 1939 he was quite clear about the future fate of the Jews. He told the Czech foreign minister of his intention to 'destroy the Jews',[47] and soon afterwards made his chilling prophecy in the *Reichstag* that the outbreak of war would lead to the 'annihilation of the Jewish race in Europe'.

See Document 66

The intentionalists interpret these threats as evidence of Hitler's ultimate aims, but the structuralists remain unconvinced. They warn historians against taking Hitler's words too literally. Hans Mommsen, for example, argues that Hitler 'considered the "Jewish question" from a visionary political perspective that did not reflect the real situation',[48] and is convinced that Hitler was invoking a ritual hatred of the Jews, rather than spelling out precise plans for their murder. While these horrific threats were not a blueprint for the Holocaust, it is difficult not to see them as expressions of intent, however vague they might be. As Lucy Dawidowicz pointed out about one of Hitler's earlier speeches, 'in the post-Auschwitz world' his words carry a 'staggering freight'.[49]

Conclusion

In January 1933 the new Hitler government was greeted with a widespread feeling that it was, as Golo Mann remarked, 'historically right',[50] and that its time had come. The majority of Germans were ready to make allowances in the spring of 1933 for what they assumed to be at the time the casual and short-lived brutalities of the SA, provided Hitler could deliver on his promises to create a new deal and provide work. His attempts to create an inclusive nation, where membership was defined by race rather than class, has been brilliantly characterized by Schoenbaum as a 'verbal social revolution'.[51] Nazi propaganda put great emphasis on the equality of all Germans. In many ways this was an illusion as big business, the Junkers and the bourgeoisie still survived. Nevertheless, Hitler did manage to create a fragile consensus and a feeling of hope and even of moderate prosperity. Of course, this was underpinned by terror against dissidents and had only been achieved by the destruction of the pluralist state. Overall, the public perception of Hitler was that he was restoring 'law and order' to Germany and was the architect of a great national revival and 'economic miracle'.

Pluralist state: a state in which there are different parties, pressure groups – in fact a diversity of forces

Yet the paradox of the Third Reich was that behind the facade of efficiency and unity it was what Neumann has called a 'Behemoth' or 'a non-state, a chaos, a situation of lawlessness, disorder and anarchy'.[52] What was it that prevented its collapse from internal contradictions and conflicting agencies? Certainly the SS and the *Gestapo* played a vital role in protecting the regime, but then so did the long line of Hitler's successes up to 1941. He had achieved more than the wildest dreams of any revisionist in the Weimar Republic, and in 1940 was probably the most popular chancellor Germany has ever had!

13 Expansion, War and Defeat

TIMELINE

1933	Oct.	Germany withdraws from the Disarmament Conference and the League of Nations
1934	July	Abortive coup in Vienna
1935	Jan.	Saar plebiscite
	June	Anglo–German naval pact
	Oct.	Italy invades Abyssinia
1936	7 Mar.	Military reoccupation of the Rhineland
	July	Start of Spanish Civil War
	Oct.	Rome–Berlin Axis
	Nov.	Anti-Comintern Pact
1937	5 Nov.	Meeting at Reich Chancellery recorded by Colonel Hossbach
1938	Mar.	Anschluss of Austria
	1–10 Oct.	Occupation of the Sudetenland
1939	15 Mar.	Occupation of Bohemia
	1 Sept.	Invasion of Poland
	3 Sept.	Britain and France declare war on Germany
1940	9 Apr.	Invasion of Denmark and Norway
	10 May	Offensive against the West begins
	10 June	Italy declares war on France and Britain
	22 June	Franco-German armistice.
1941	6 Feb.	German troops sent to North Africa
	May	Martin Bormann becomes director of the party chancellery
	22 June	Operation Barbarossa
	2 Oct.–5 Dec.	Battle for Moscow
	7 Dec.	Pearl Harbour
	11 Dec.	Germany and Italy declare war on America
1942	20 Jan.	Wannsee Conference
	8 Feb.	Speer becomes armaments minister
	22 Apr.	'Central Planning' established to allocate raw materials and energy supplies
	Aug.	Over 200,000 Jews gassed in Chelmno, Treblinka and Belzec
1943	Jan.	Casablanca Conference: Britain and USA demand unconditional surrender
	27 Jan.	Decree concerning the registration of men and women for Reich defence tasks
	31 Jan.	Germans surrender at Stalingrad
	24–30 July	Allied air raid on Hamburg kills 30,000 people
	8 Sept.	German troops occupy northern Italy
	20 Aug.	Himmler appointed interior minister
1944	Jan.	Gestapo breaks up the Kreisau Circle
	27 Jan.	Soviet forces retake Leningrad
	6 June	D-Day landings
	20 July	The abortive bomb plot to kill Hitler
1945	25 Apr.	American and Soviet troops meet on the Elbe
	30 Apr.	Hitler's suicide. Doenitz becomes Reich president
	7–8 May	Unconditional surrender of the German armed forces
	23 May	Dissolution of Doenitz regime by Allies

Introduction

In the same way that there is a 'twisted road to Auschwitz',[1] so too is there a 'twisted road' to the outbreak of the Second World War in September 1939. A. J. P. Taylor has argued that Hitler had no particular policy and was in fact just pursuing a pragmatic policy of making Germany 'the greatest power in Europe from her natural weight'.[2] Hans Mommsen, too, has doubts about whether Hitler's foreign policy really consisted of unchanging priorities and is convinced that, like his anti-Semitic policy, it was determined more by economic pressures, opportunism and expectations from within the Nazi party. Inevitably these interpretations, which play down Hitler's intentions, are strongly opposed by protagonists of the Programme School, such as Andreas Hillgruber and Klaus Hildebrand, who argue that Hitler's foreign policy was formulated as early as the mid-1920s and consisted of two distinct phases – the continental phase involving the defeat of France and the USSR and then a global phase ending in the defeat of the USA and the British Empire and the establishment of global German hegemony.[3] The reason why Nazi foreign policy generates such controversy is because Hitler's actions were often, at least in the short term, contradictory and opportunist. Nevertheless, his obsession with the need for *Lebensraum* in western Russia is a constant thread that runs through his speeches to generals, officials, businessmen and journalists. As Alan Bullock has argued, Hitler combined 'consistency of aim with complete opportunism in methods and tactics'.[4] There is no doubt that after 1936 Germany was rearming in depth, and in May 1939 Hitler explicitly told his generals that they 'must prepare for a war from ten to fifteen years duration'[5] (see p. 235).

> The Programme School is intentionalist and believes that Hitler had a definite programme

Key issues

- How opportunistic was Hitler's foreign policy in the period 1933–39?
- Why did Hitler attack the USSR in June 1941 while the British Empire was still undefeated?
- How did Nazi Germany control its continental empire, 1940–44?
- How do the structuralists and intentionalists differ in their interpretations of the Holocaust? Is either interpretation unambiguously correct?
- Why did the war years witness a marked increase in the power of the party and the SS?
- How effective was the German war economy and how important was foreign labour to its functioning?
- How did the war affect the lives of the German people?
- In what ways was Speer correct to call the Doenitz regime the 'last stage of the Third Reich'?
- How useful is the concept of *Resistenz* in assessing the opposition to Nazism in the Third Reich?
- Why did the German opposition fail to overthrow Nazism?

The road to war, 1933–39

During his first three years in power Hitler had to tread carefully. It was obvious, as a senior official in the Foreign Office told him, that 'in judging the situation we should never overlook the fact that no kind of rearmament in the next few years could give us military security . . . we shall for a long time yet be hopelessly inferior to France'.[6] Thus Hitler's room for manoeuvre was initially very limited. Nevertheless he did take several initiatives during the period 1933–35:

- He withdrew from the League of Nations in October 1933.
- He signed a ten-year non-aggression pact with Poland, which breached the French alliance system in eastern Europe, and he did nothing to stop an attempted coup by Austrian Nazis in Vienna in July 1934.
- In March 1935 he took another risk, when he announced the introduction of conscription.

The introduction of conscription did, however, have potentially more serious consequences. It led to a meeting of the British, Italian and French heads of government at Stresa, who issued a joint statement stressing their determination to maintain the peace settlements. Hitler was, however, easily able to break up the unity of the 'Stresa Front', when Britain, without consulting either Italy or France, accepted his offer of a bilateral naval pact, which limited the German navy to 35 per cent of the Royal Navy.

The League had declared Italy an aggressor, and Britain and France after their failure to negotiate a compromise agreement reluctantly supported the League's policy of limited sanctions

Mussolini's attack on Abyssinia in October 1935 and the Anglo-French decision to impose sanctions on Italy gave Hitler the opportunity to remilitarize the Rhineland. To avoid isolation and possible defeat, Mussolini had little option but to assure him of Italian support for this move. Using the pretext of the ratification of the Franco-Soviet treaty of 27 February 1936, Hitler reoccupied the Rhineland, despite the reservations of his generals and diplomats, with a weak military force, without any opposition from either France or Britain. This was, to quote William Carr, 'a real turning point in the inter-war years, which marked the beginning of a shift in the balance of power away from Paris and back to Berlin'.[7] It robbed France of its main strategic advantage over Germany and showed with painful clarity that neither Britain nor France was ready to defend the Locarno settlement and the Treaty of Versailles.

The rise of Hitler had led to a rapprochement between France and the USSR. The introduction of conscription led to the signature of the Franco-Russian pact in May 1935

Although Germany's military weakness prevented Hitler from taking any major initiatives for the next two years, he gave limited military assistance to General Franco, the Spanish Nationalist leader, in his uprising against the Republican government. This was partly because Hitler feared a Communist takeover in Spain, but the civil war in Spain also helped divert the attention of the great powers from Germany and central Europe. The German–Italian October Protocols, and the Anti-Comintern Pact of November 1936 with Japan, which Italy joined a year later, were two further propaganda coups that pointed in the direction of

October Protocols were called the Rome–Berlin Axis by Mussolini in a speech in Milan on 1 November 1936. They were only a loosely-worded understanding for collaboration a 'new globe spanning alliance'[8] which threatened the democracies in every theatre, even though at the moment those agreements lacked any substance. By the end of 1937 Germany's military and diplomatic position had improved dramatically, and the Four Year Plan was well under way (see p. 234). At a meeting at the Reich chancellery on 5 November attended by his military chiefs, Hermann Göring and Constantin von Neurath, the foreign minister, Hitler reviewed foreign policy options for the next seven years. He informed the assembled generals and ministers that Germany's 'problem of space' had to be solved by 1943–45, but that if the right opportunities, such as a political crisis in France or an Italian–French war, presented themselves, Czechoslovakia could be destroyed as early as 1938.

Anti-Comintern Pact: this was aimed against the Comintern – the Communist International set up by Lenin in 1919

Historians and the Hossbach Memorandum

The memorandum was used by the prosecution during the Nuremberg war crimes trials in 1946 (see p. 276) to show that Hitler had a precise blueprint for war. Taylor, however, in 1961 showed that not only was it written some five days after the meeting by Hitler's adjutant, Colonel Hossbach, but that it is a fragment of a copy that has disappeared. He argued that it was essentially concerned with the allocation of raw materials rather than foreign policy and that Hitler's exposition was for the most part 'day dreaming unrelated to what followed in real life'. While historians agree that the memorandum was hardly a blueprint for action, the consensus of research still favours W. Carr's views that Hitler was warning his generals that 'a more adventurous and dangerous policy was imminent'.[9]

The opportunities to annex Austria and then to destroy Czechoslovakia arose both more quickly and in a different form from that foreseen in Hitler's exposition of 5 November. It was Schuschnigg, the Austrian chancellor, who was the unwitting catalyst for the *Anschluss*. In an attempt in February to reach some agreement that would have controlled the activities of the Austrian Nazis, he provided Hitler with an opportunity to dictate a series of conditions which would have turned Austria into a German satellite. It was then Schuschnigg's attempt on 9 March to regain a measure of independence by asking his countrymen to vote in a referendum for a 'free and German, independent and social, Christian and united Austria' that pushed Hitler three days later into sending troops across the frontier. Faced with an enthusiastic reception from the crowd at Linz, Hitler quickly abandoned his original idea of appointing a satellite government under the Austrian Nazi, Seyss-Inquart, and instead incorporated Austria into the Reich.

See Document 67 and Map 7

In an agreement with Austria in July 1936, Germany recognized Austrian independence, while Vienna promised to pursue a German-orientated foreign policy and appoint two pro-German conservatives to the cabinet, but in practice Nazi agitation continued

The *Anschluss* was a 'watershed for Hitler and the Third Reich'.[10] French and British passivity convinced him that his plans for creating a Greater German Reich were now within his grasp, but before he could do that he would have to liquidate Czechoslovakia, whose strategic position, well-equipped army and efficient armaments industry made it a considerable threat to Germany's southern flank. Its potential strength, however, was undermined by ethnic tensions between the Czechs and Slovaks, and the existence of 3 million Sudeten Germans who wished to join the Reich.

Two weeks after the *Anschluss* Hitler instructed Henlein, the Sudeten German leader, to formulate demands for Sudeten self-government, which in reality could not be granted without breaking up the Czech state. In May the Czech government, mistaking German manoeuvres near the borders for preparations for an invasion, mobilized its army. When Britain, France and Russia informed Hitler that they would not tolerate such an attack, he announced his innocence, but the incident confirmed his suspicions of the Czech state, and led him to set 1 October as the deadline for 'smashing' it. For the rest of the summer Hitler continued both to encourage Sudeten separatism and to stir up similar demands among the Hungarian and Polish minorities in Czechoslovakia so that Poland and Hungary would support the destruction of the Czech state.

On 12 September Hitler's campaign entered a new stage, when his demand for immediate self-determination for the Sudeten Germans provoked increasing unrest in the Sudetenland and led to the subsequent intervention of Neville Chamberlain, the British prime minister, who flew to see Hitler three times between 15 and 29 September:

- At Berchtesgaden on 15 September Hitler initially agreed to Chamberlain's proposals for sending an international commission to the Sudetenland to arrange for ceding to Germany all areas which contained a German population of over 50 per cent.
- By the time Chamberlain had secured French and Czech agreement to this and returned for the second conference at Bad Godesberg on 22 September, Hitler had decided to reject the intervention of an international commission and demanded the immediate German occupation of the Sudetenland, which the following day he only reluctantly postponed to 1 October.
- The weight of evidence suggests that Hitler was ready for war. His calculation was that the Czechs would reject his terms and be abandoned by the Western powers, who would give Germany a free hand to destroy the state. But in the face of partial British and French mobilization and the lack of enthusiasm of his generals and Mussolini for war, 'the unthinkable happened'.[11]
- Hitler accepted Mussolini's offer of mediation and on 29 September at the Munich Conference Hitler agreed to an international guarantee of rump Czechoslovakia while German forces would be permitted to occupy the Sudetenland in stages between 1 and 10 October 1938.

See Map 7

For Hitler the conference was a diplomatic defeat, which cheated him of Czechoslovakia and also provided evidence that Britain, despite its willingness to appease, would not allow Germany a completely free hand

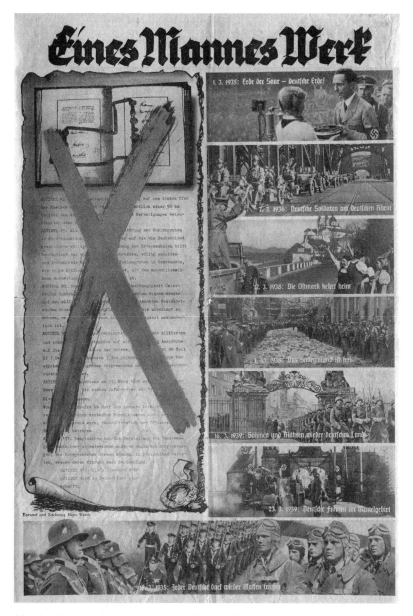

21 In the supplement to mark Hitler's 50th birthday the *12 Uhr Blatt* attributes the destruction of the Treaty of Versailles, 1933–39, to Hitler alone. The heading reads: 'One man's work'

Sonderbeilage 12 Uhr Blatt, 20 April 1939, p. 6

in eastern Europe. Consequently on 21 October 1938 he ordered the army to draw up new plans for the destruction of Czechoslovakia. His chance came when the tensions between the Slovaks and the Czechs, which he had done so much to provoke, came to a head in March 1939.

He was able to force the Czech President, Hacha, to agree to the German occupation of Prague and the creation of an independent Slovakia, which became a German protectorate.

The occupation of Prague, which was followed shortly afterwards by the annexation of Memel, persuaded the British and French governments to guarantee the independence of Poland. As German diplomatic attempts over the course of the winter to persuade Poland to agree to the restoration of Danzig and the Corridor to German rule in return for eventual gains in the Ukraine had failed, the guarantee convinced Hitler that he would have to destroy Poland, and, perhaps fight Britain and France as well, if he were to continue with his expansionary policy. As early as 3 April, orders were issued to the army to prepare for an invasion of Poland by 1 September at the latest.

Both the Western powers and Germany, recognizing that the key to the coming conflict lay in Moscow, began negotiations with Stalin. The subsequent Nazi–Soviet Non-Aggression Treaty of 23 August was an enormous success for Hitler, as it secured Stalin's benevolent neutrality in return for territorial concessions in eastern Europe and deprived Britain and France of the only alliance which could have stopped Poland's defeat. When the Western powers unexpectedly responded to this treaty by ratifying their treaties of guarantee with Poland, Hitler postponed the attack and made several unsuccessful attempts to separate Britain and Poland by offering Britain an alliance and a guarantee of its empire. Once these attempts failed, Hitler gave the order for war on 31 August. Taylor argues that the war began because Hitler launched 'on 29 August a diplomatic manoeuvre [aimed at persuading the British to force the Poles to make concessions] which he ought to have launched on 28 August'.[12] Possibly, given more time, he might have separated Britain and Poland, but he did not want a compromise settlement with the Poles. At most he was hoping to manoeuvre them into a position where their 'stubbornness' could be blamed for causing the war.

The invasion of Russia, June 1941

Between September 1939 and June 1940 Hitler achieved a series of staggering successes. Poland was defeated within a month, while by the following June France was suing for an armistice, and British troops had been driven from the continent. Hitler had assumed that Britain would terminate hostilities. When it did not, he half-heartedly pursued a number of options ranging from an invasion of southern England to military collaboration with Nationalist Spain and Vichyite France against the British Empire.

His real priority, however, was the destruction of the USSR. Already by August 1940 a growing number of troops were being sent eastwards, and on 18 December he made the crucial decision to attack Russia in the spring of 1941. Hitler tried to convince his generals that the defeat of the

Soviet Union would also lead to the defeat of Britain, but if Britain's See Document 68
defeat had really been his first priority, he would surely have concentrated on the naval war and on attacking Britain in the Mediterranean
with adequate forces. It is therefore more accurate to say that the defeat
of Britain was only a 'subsidiary aim of the Russian offensive'.[13] While
Stalin had exploited the Nazi–Soviet Pact to strengthen the Russian position in eastern Europe, he was still supplying Germany with raw materials and food, and there was no evidence that he was planning war in the
near future. The decision to attack Russia at that juncture can only be
understood in the context of Nazi ideology. Hitler's belief in his mission
to destroy Bolshevism and to provide *Lebensraum* was the real reason for
the invasion. He had planned the operation carefully, and, as Bullock
emphasizes, 'of all decisions it is the one which most clearly bears his own
personal stamp, the culmination (as he saw it) of his career'.[14] The attack
was launched on 22 June 1941 after German forces had first pushed the
British out of Greece and overthrown the anglophile administration in
Yugoslavia.

Germany's European empire, 1939–44

By the summer of 1942, apart from a few neutral enclaves, the Nazi See Map 7
empire stretched from the Pyrenees to the Caucasus. In Norway, Holland
and Denmark the Germans attempted to rule through the existing
administrative machinery. Northern France and Belgium were run by
German military governments, as they were in the front line in the war
against Britain, while the rest of France was administered from Vichy by
its own quasi-Fascist regime under Marshal Pétain. In western Europe
there was some attempt to disguise German intentions under the veneer
of idealistic talk about a united anti-Bolshevik Europe, in which, according to Otto Dietrich, Germany's press chief, there would be 'equal
chances for all'.[15] The meeting of the Anti-Comintern Pact in Berlin in
1941 was even described as 'the first European Congress', and was celebrated by a specially composed 'Song of Europe'. The reality of course
was different. Both men and women were conscripted and sent to work
in Germany (see pp. 259–61). Against the French franc the value of the
Reichsmark was set at an extortionate rate and no payments were to be
made for French imports until after the war. The French banking system
was increasingly controlled by the Germans , and mixed Franco-German
companies were set up, in which the Germans held a majority of shares.
In 1943 an attempt was made by Albert Speer, the German armaments
minister, and his opposite number in Vichy, Jean Bichelonne, to integrate French industry into a European economy dominated by Germany.
In exchange for the ending of labour conscription in Germany for French
workers, France would produce consumer goods for the German market,
thereby allowing German factories to concentrate completely on war
production. The plan, however, was bitterly opposed by Fritz Sauckel, the

By the end of
1941 the war had
become global.
When Japan
attacked the US
fleet at Pearl
Harbor, Hitler
declared war on
the USA in the
hope that this
would encourage
the Japanese to tie
down the British
and US forces in
the Far East

Reich plenipotentiary for labour mobilization, and subsequently dropped.

In eastern Europe German plans were far more ambitious. Not only was the territory, which had been lost at Versailles reannexed, but what was left of Poland was placed under German administration (the *Generalgouvernement*), and when the USSR was invaded, three large new territories, Bialystok, Ostland and Ukraine, were formed and placed under German control. Although the economies of the occupied areas in eastern Europe were ruthlessly exploited and millions sent back to Germany for forced labour, Hitler's primary aim was eventually to build up a German population of 250 million in western Russia over the course of about eighty years, while Himmler had similar ambitions for resettling the whole of Poland with Germans. Inevitably this would entail the 'ethnic cleansing' of the existing population. A start was made by either shooting the Polish élites or sending them to concentration camps, while the population was divided into groups according to race, and the great mass of the Poles were forced out of the inner cities, forbidden to speak Polish in public and debarred from cinemas, theatres and libraries.

In preparation for the Russian campaign, four SS *Einsatzgruppen*, each numbering between 500 and 1000 men were formed to prepare the way for 'the political and administrative organization' of the occupied areas. In practice this meant, as one of their number later testified at Nuremberg, 'putting to death all racially and politically undesirable elements among the prisoners'[16] – Soviet officials, gypsies, Jews and the so-called 'second class Asiatics'. Shortly after the invasion, the RKFDV (Commissariat for the Strengthening of the German Race) began work on the General Plan East, which envisaged within 25 years an initial settlement of the Ukraine and Volga regions with a series of frontier marches or settlements populated by SS war veterans. A start was made in the Hegewald in the Ukraine, but the defeat at Stalingrad put a stop to any further settlements.

Between 140,000 and 580,000 Soviet officials or 'Bolsheviks' were shot. By 1943 about 2.2 million Jews were also murdered. The lot of the majority of Russian prisoners of war was equally horrific. They were imprisoned in camps behind the front and fed with minimal rations. By 1945 57.5 per cent had died in captivity

The Holocaust

The resettlement of millions of people according to racial criteria and the systematic attempts to eliminate the Russian and Polish élites was the context in which the liquidation of nearly six million Jews took place. With the conquest of Poland, between two and three million Jews fell into Hitler's power. There were a further three million Jews in Russia and half a million in occupied territory in western Europe. The horror of the Holocaust renders it a particularly difficult subject for dispassionate historical analysis. The structuralist view that the Holocaust was the result of muddle and improvization, rather than a consequence of clear planning, is criticized by Lucy Dawidowicz as a 'mechanistic interpretation' of Nazi Germany, which eliminates personal blame.[17] On the other hand, the intentionalists' understandable emphasis on the unique horror of the Holocaust can also inhibit efforts to analyse the events that led to it historically.

So far it has proved impossible to trace accurately when and by whom the decision was taken to launch the Holocaust, as there is no clear documentary link between Hitler and the murder of the Jews in the death camps. Intentionalist historians argue that the decision was made once war had broken out in September 1939, but the structuralists remain sceptical. Many have been puzzled by how 'evolutionary' or 'improvised'[19] Nazi anti-Jewish policy was in reality. Until June 1941 emigration continued to remain official policy, and after the French defeat in June 1940 there were plans for resettling the European Jewish population in the French colony of Madagascar, but these had to be shelved once it was clear that Britain would not make peace, as the British navy continued to control the Indian Ocean. Consequently the RKFVD took the decision to concentrate the Polish Jews, who had been expelled from the newly annexed territories, in ghettos in occupied Poland. Although this caused immense logistical problems, as it coincided with the military build-up for the invasion of Russia, Hitler refused to stop the deportation programme and rejected any suggestion that the Jews in Reich territory should be employed in the local war industries.

Plans for resettling Jews in Madagascar and Siberia

Plans for 'resettlement' in Madagascar, or later in Siberia, were not really an alternative to extermination. As Hermann Graml has pointed out, the Nazi authorities assumed that the great majority of Jews would die in Madagascar from disease, and consequently mass murder would be 'given the appearance of a natural process'.[20] It is significant that Philipp Bouhler, who had been in charge of the euthanasia programme in Germany (see p. 241), was the designated governor of Madagascar.

The invasion of Soviet Russia in June 1941 was a turning-point in Nazi policy towards the Jews. It was a war of extermination against 'Jewish Bolshevism' in which by the spring of 1942 well over a million Jews, who were not members of the Communist party, had been murdered. These massacres marked a new and more deadly threshold in Nazi policy. The structuralists argue that it was the successful Red Army counter-attack in December 1941 which was the crucial factor leading to the Holocaust.[21] Not only did the continuation of the war rule out Siberia as a possible area for Jewish 'resettlement', but it created severe logistical problems in Poland and occupied Russia, which would be further exacerbated by bringing more Jews into the area. This is why Broszat argues that the Holocaust was a '"way out" of a blind alley into which the National Socialists had manoeuvred themselves'.[22] The intentionalists respond that Broszat reduces the Holocaust to an accidental consequence of the military situation in eastern Europe. Dawidowicz, for example, argues that Hitler 'implemented his plan in stages, seizing whatever opportunities offered themselves to advance its execution'.[23] The combination of short-term opportunism with long-term intentions in Hitler's planning strategy has already been emphasized by Bullock in relation to his foreign policy (see p. 247), but the lack of evidence showing Hitler's precise involvement in the decision-making on the Holocaust makes it impossible for historians to trace his exact role in these terrible events.

However, it is clear that by late 1941 there were so many schemes being worked on for the extermination of the Jews that it is more than likely that 'a green light was coming from the highest level'.[24] At the very least, it must have been obvious to senior Nazis and their officials that Hitler supported such policies. Arguably, this was sufficient to inspire them to 'work towards the *Führer*' (see p. 229) and ensure that his wishes would be carried out. In January 1942, at the Wannsee conference in Berlin, plans were drawn up for rounding up the Jews throughout Europe and conscripting them into labour gangs in eastern Europe, where it was assumed that 'a large number will drop out through natural elimination'. The remainder would then be 'dealt with accordingly'.[25] Extermination camps were constructed in 1942 at Belzec, Sobibor and Treblinka, and gas chambers were built at Maydanek and Auschwitz. Nearly six million Jews had been murdered by 1945.

See Document 62

See Documents 57 and 66

The increasing influence of the party and the SS

From June 1941 until November 1944 Hitler was rarely in Berlin and was isolated from all contacts in his headquarters in East Prussia and the Ukraine. As supreme commander of the army, he took on an immense workload, leaving him little time for matters affecting the home front. The Reich government became ever more dysfunctional, despite repeated attempts by ministers to create an effective executive. The Ministerial Council for the Defence of the Reich, which was set up in August 1939, ceased to meet after November 1939, and Hitler consistently opposed the emergence of any committee with real executive powers that might eventually be used to challenge him. He vetoed attempts by Heinrich Lammers, the head of the Reich chancellery, to reintroduce regular cabinet meetings and even disapproved of ministers meeting unofficially. Decisions could still be achieved by going straight to Hitler, but increasingly access was controlled by Martin Bormann (see p. 244) as chief of the party chancellery at the *Führer* headquarters. Essentially the regime was incapable of being reformed, as it 'was both the inexorable product of Hitler's personalized rule and the guarantee of his power'.[26]

As with the French revolutionaries in 1791–92, the war was seen by many of the party activists to be 'a great school of public virtue' in which the restrictive compromises of 1933 could at last be swept away. Both the SS and the party made considerable inroads into the authority of the state. The SS, indeed, threatened to develop into a 'collateral state', which could undermine and dissolve the existing state institutions:[27]

- As commissioner for consolidating German nationhood (RKFDV), Himmler was given responsibility for the resettlement of ethnic Germans and eliminating 'the harmful influences of such alien parts of the population as constitute a danger to the Reich and the German community'[28] in the occupied and incorporated territories.
- The control of the concentration camps enabled the SS to use prison labour in its industrial undertakings, which in 1944 consisted of about a hundred and fifty firms ranging from quarrying to the manufacture of armaments and textiles.
- By 1944 the *Waffen-SS* consisted of 35 divisions.
- Himmler also controlled key military and civil positions: he was appointed Reich minister of the interior in 1943, commander of the reserve army in 1944, and then in quick succession commander-in-chief of the Rhine army group in December 1944 and of the Vistula army group in January 1945. Yet, paradoxically, while his power grew in the Reich, his influence on Hitler was undermined by Bormann at the *Führer* headquarters.

The war increased the party's responsibilities at every level. On it fell the task of maintaining the morale of the civilian population. The *Gauleiter* were appointed Reich defence commissioners in September 1939, and in the event of an emergency, such as an invasion, were to take complete charge of the civil authorities within their *Gaue*. These became the key administrative units within the Reich, on which the citizen's militia, the *Volkssturm*, was based when it was created in the autumn of 1944. In the occupied and newly annexed territories in the east the party was able to assert its authority. The new *Gaue* were not encumbered with the administrative legacies of the pre-1933 period, which in the old Reich forced the party administrators to share power with the traditional bureaucracy. In new territories the Reich commissioners were first and foremost party functionaries, whose task was not to create an efficient administration but to carry out the ideology of the Nazi movement.

The war also sharpened the party's ambition to achieve the social and racial revolution which had been denied it in the 1930s. Supported by Bormann who, in a circular in June 1941 to the *Gauleiter*, bluntly stated that Christianity was incompatible with National Socialism, a vicious campaign was launched by the NSDAP against the Churches. Christian publications were seized, while the welfare activities of the Catholic nuns were now carried out by 'the brown sisters', a Nazi organization, and feast days, which were traditionally celebrated as holidays, were simply moved to the nearest Sunday, so as to avoid any interruption in the war effort. Confronted by popular opposition, particularly from the Catholics, Hitler stopped the campaign within the old Reich, but in the newly annexed territories it continued unchecked. In the *Reichsgau*

Wartheland (the newly incorporated area of the West Prussian province of Posen – see map 7), for example, 94 per cent of the churches in the dioceses of Posen–Gnesen were closed down and 11 per cent of the clergy murdered. As Kershaw has observed, this 'clearly showed the face of the future',[29] and, if Germany had emerged from the war victorious, the Churches would almost certainly have faced renewed persecution.

In many other spheres the war also enabled the party to extend its social, cultural and political influence, as the following examples indicate:

- The evacuation of city children to the countryside, where they were without their parents, to escape the bombing increased both the responsibilities of the Hitler Youth leaders and their opportunities for exposing children to Nazi ideology.
- What remained of the independence of the judiciary was fatally undermined when in April 1942 a *Reichstag* 'resolution' gave Hitler complete power to remove from office 'judges, who clearly fail to recognize the mood of the hour'.[30] This enabled the party to interfere directly in the legal process.
- After Stalingrad, Nazi influence within the army increased. By the end of 1943 party officials took part in the selection and training of new officers; after the 20 July plot (see p. 268) the Nazi salute replaced the traditional military salute. Goebbels also set up a special post-office box address, to which any soldier in the ranks could write if he felt that his officers were not sufficiently loyal to the regime.

The war economy

When Allied economic experts analysed the records of the German war economy in 1945, it seemed to them that the German economy had not been mobilized for a total war until 1942. These findings led to the *Blitzkrieg* thesis. This is best summed up by Alan Milward who described the *Blitzkrieg* as a 'system of warfare best suited to the character and institutions of Hitler's Germany',[31] as it did not involve full mobilization of all economic resources, which would have strained the loyalties of the civilian population at a time when it was far from enthusiastic about the war. Much emphasis has been placed on the fact that Britain in 1940 and 1941 outperformed Germany in the mass production of weapons, but Richard Overy has convincingly argued that this was not because of a lack of German investment but rather because of structural problems in the German war economy. The timing of the outbreak of the war had wrong-footed Hitler, since much of the initial spending on rearmament had been invested in military infrastructure projects, such as barracks and airfields, rather than weapons. Many of the smaller and medium-sized German armament firms were reluctant to introduce modern, mass-production techniques, while the *Reichswehr* preferred quality rather than quantity of armaments, all of which considerably slowed up the tempo of production.

In 1940, for instance, Germany spent about $6,000 million on armaments, while Britain spent only $3,500 million, yet the latter managed to produce over 50 per cent more aircraft, 100 per cent more vehicles and nearly as many tanks as did Germany

Albert Speer and the total war economy

By the winter of 1941 it was clear that these problems could only be overcome through mass production and rationalization of the war economy. A start had been made by Fritz Todt, but he was killed in a plane crash in February 1942. His successor was Albert Speer, the party architect, (see p. 240) who had the decisive advantage of having direct access to Hitler. He could thus override objections from the armed forces simply by appealing to Hitler. Over the next two years he was to achieve a 'production miracle'.[32] In April 1942 the Central Planning Board was set up, which allocated the supply of raw materials to each sector of the economy. Speer was even able to take away from the armed forces their fiercely protected right to design their own weapons. He also encouraged industrialists to apply new scientific management techniques, to rationalize production, maximize plant capacities and standardize designs. Employers were helped in this process by the employment of foreign workers and POWs who were subject to harsh discipline and could not oppose the new production methods, as some German workers still attempted to do.

Although Speer achieved an impressive increase in armaments production, which, despite the Allied bombing campaign, peaked in 1943–44, he was nevertheless, to quote Gordon Craig, 'denied the right to go beyond the limit of what rationalization could accomplish'.[33] His efforts were undermined by the autonomy of both the *Gauleiter* and the SS, whose economic resources he was unable to exploit (see p. 257). In the end, too, the Allied strategic bombing campaign also disrupted production by interrupting supplies, forcing factories to evacuate and demoralizing the workers.

The labour problem

Although, in September 1939, females already composed 37.4 per cent of the total labour force, the Reich Labour Ministry in the spring of 1940 urged the introduction of comprehensive female conscription, but the unpopularity of this measure both at home and with married soldiers on the front caused the party leadership to have second thoughts. Initially, Polish labour and then, after the defeat of France in June 1940, French prisoners of war were made available for German industry and agriculture. Proposals to use Russian workers were at first opposed by many Nazis, including Himmler, for both racial and security reasons, but Speer, with the support of Hitler, overcame these objections. The party was reassured by the appointment of Fritz Sauckel, a trusted and loyal Nazi, who was commissioner for the military district of Cassel, to the post of plenipotentiary for labour mobilization. His task involved both organizing the large-scale recruitment of foreign labour into Germany, and then ensuring that this workforce was effectively exploited and disciplined.

Erhält ab 11.5.43 keine Lebensmittelkarte

Der Grenzübertritt ist nur unter Vorlage eines gültigen Passes (Paßersatz-papiers) und eines gültigen Sichtvermerks zur Ausreise und Wiedereinreise gestattet. Der Urlaubsschein ist mitzuführen und bis zur Beendigung der Urlaubsreise sorgfältig aufzubewahren.

Anspr.: 14.5.43 - 13.11.43

Urlaubsschein

AEintr.:14.5.42

LEAVE PASS

Der Holländer　Jan Hendrik O v e r v l i e t
(Vor- und Zuname)

aus　A m s t e r d a m　Holland
(Heimatland, Heimatort)

geb. am　8.10. 1919 , beschäftigt als　Elekriker

ist vom　11.5.43　bis　23.5.43　nach

Amsterdam　beurlaubt.
(Urlaubsort)

Grund des Urlaubs: 2. Familienheimfahrt und Tarifurlaub
(Familienheimfahrt, Krankheitsurlaub, Heimaturlaub, besondere Anlässe usw.)

Der Urlauber hat Arbeiterrückfahrkarte bis Amsterdam erhalten.

Der Urlauber ist über die für die Mitnahme von Geldmitteln in deutscher bzw. der betreffenden ausländischen Währung geltenden Bestimmungen unterrichtet worden.

Der Urlauber ist verpflichtet, nach Beendigung des Urlaubs die Arbeit in unserem Betrieb wieder aufzunehmen. Der Arbeiter ist in Deutschland bei der

Betr.-Krankenk. d. verein. Siemenswerke Krankenkasse

— Bezirksknappschaft — in Berlin - Siemensstadt versichert.

LGW Fabrikgruppe IX Sonderaufgaben

Luftfahrtgerätewerk Hakenfelde
Gesellschaft mit beschränkter Haftung

Ber. Spandau, den 12. April 1943

(Firmenstempel und Unterschrift)

Bescheinigung des Arbeitsamts

Berlin

Der Erteilung des Sichtvermerks zur einmaligen Aus- und Wiedereinreise wird zugestimmt.

, den　194

(Stempel)

I. A.:

(Unterschrift)

150000. 2. 43. C/0590

22　A heavily stamped leave pass for a Dutch electrical worker travelling from Berlin to Amsterdam. This indicates the relatively favourable conditions under which western as opposed to eastern European and Italian workers (after 1943) were employed in the Third Reich during the Second World War

In response to the ever-increasing demand for German troops on the eastern front, which inevitably ensured that many workers needed at home were called up, Hitler announced at the end of January 1943 that all males between 16 and 65, who were not in the armed forces, and all females between 17 and 45 were to register for war work. In fact, only about 900,000 women were called up, as mothers with young children, and wives of the self-employed, were exempt. Reich commissioners were also given the power to close all non-essential trades and businesses and allocate their workers to the war industries. This spelt ruin for the small independent artisans, who had in 1933 been amongst Hitler's most enthusiastic supporters. The employers of the large armament industries, however, preferred foreign workers, whom they could discipline and often ruthlessly exploit. By the end of 1944 there were over seven million foreign workers in Germany. The west European workers, particularly the Flemish-speaking Belgians and the French, were treated well, but the Poles, the Russians and the Italians operated in conditions which were little better than slave labour. German society, with a workforce increasingly stratified by race, began to show, in Ulrich Herbert's words, the characteristics of a 'quasi-colonial social order'.[34]

Once Italy had defected from the Axis side in September 1943, the Germans occupied most of Italy and effectively treated it as a conquered country

Michael Burleigh and Wolfgang Wippermann have argued that the huge influx of foreign labour 'made the German working class more or less passive accomplices in Nazi racial policy',[35] as it became ever more closely involved in the whole machinery of surveillance and repression in the factories. In general, however, the majority of German workers, preoccupied with their own problems, showed little concern for the fate of the foreign workers. As Ulrich Herbert has observed, 'the foreigners were simply there, as much part of wartime life as ration cards or air raid shelters . . . Their own privileged position as Germans *vis-à-vis* these workers was likewise nothing exceptional, certainly no cause for misgiving.'[36]

The struggle for survival: the German people, 1942–45

Up to 1944 the German population received adequate rations – an '*Existenzminimum*', below which living standards were not allowed to fall. Basic food rations were between 7 and 15 per cent above the minimum calorific standard. Workers in heavy industry received generous food allowances, which often provided better diets than they had experienced in peacetime. Soldiers' families, who had suffered particularly in the Great War (see p. 155), received special ration coupons for food and rent. Nevertheless, the longer the war lasted the greater the burden that fell on the home front, particularly on women, many of whom had both to work and look after their families in the absence of their husbands in the armed forces. This inevitably changed their lives by giving them a new responsibility and independence and often produced acute tension when their husbands returned on leave hoping to find their home life untouched by war. Loneliness, separation from their husbands and children, if they were evacuated, and, the ever-present threat of death from the bombs also led to a greater sexual promiscuity.

See Document 69

The war also intensified the burden on the peasantry, who became increasingly alienated from the Nazi regime. In practice, despite the Nazi propaganda about blood and soil (see p. 238), their interests were being sacrificed to the urban majority. As Jill Stephenson has stressed, the 'problems which had dogged small-scale agriculture for decades were intensified in the abnormal circumstances of a second twentieth century war'.[37] The peasantry were burdened with endless regulations and red tape aimed at setting sowing and harvesting targets. The government also requisitioned their horses and called up their sons. The wives of small farmers were particularly severely hit by the war. In the words of a military report from Nuremberg in 1942, 'a peasant wife whose husband is at the front . . . has not a single quiet minute from 4 in the morning until 9 at night'.[38] Many farms did, of course, have Polish or French workers, but they too could create problems, especially when fraternization with Germans, which was strictly forbidden, took place.

The longer the war lasted, the more German society increasingly resembled a ' kind of kicked-in anthill'.[39] As early as 1940, perhaps as many as two million children were moved out from the cities in the north and the west. As the bombing intensified in 1943–44 a further 9 million women, children and elderly men were moved or fled to the countryside, where mass migration on this scale caused severe problems. Many urban refugees disliked what they considered the tedium of rural life, and as the *Regierungspräsident* of Upper Bavaria observed, while 'a majority of the local women are working . . . the evacuees just try to make life for themselves as comfortable as possible'.[40]

In 1944 refugees from eastern Germany started to join the evacuees. In the autumn of 1944 Soviet troops occupied East Prussia. An indication of what awaited many east Germans was seen in the raping, mutilation and murdering of women and children in the small East Prussian village of Nemmersdorf. To avoid this horrendous fate, about five million civilians from East Prussia, the Warthegau, Danzig, Pomerania, Silesia and eastern Brandenburg from October 1944 to January 1945 'trekked' into the interior of the Reich.

The end of the Third Reich

The end of the war was already in sight by the autumn of 1944. Oil supplies had been drastically reduced and transport facilities disrupted throughout the Reich by Allied bombing raids. The Allied advance into occupied territories and the increasing reluctance of the neutral states to export raw materials to Germany also exacerbated the acute economic difficulties and shortages on the home front. Once the Red Army gained control of the industrial areas of Silesia in January 1945, and British troops occupied the Ruhr in April 1945, the German war economy ground to a halt. Hitler committed suicide on 30 April 1945 in his bunker in Berlin after nominating Admiral Doenitz president of the Reich with Goebbels as his chancellor and Bormann as party minister. Both Göring and Himmler were passed over because they had been rash enough to

---

Regierungs-präsident: district president

In 1969 an analysis by the federal archives in Bonn came to the conclusion that at least 600,000 of these refugees died and a further 2.2 million cases were 'unresolved'[41]

Hitler had ordered Himmler's arrest because he had requested Swedish mediation to end the war with the Western powers, while Göring, had sent him a telegram on 23 April in which he informed him that unless he heard to the contrary before 10 o'clock that evening he would act according to the decree of 29 June 1941, which made him the *Führer's* successor

23   View of the Brandenburger Tor, Berlin, March 1945

Presse- und Informationsamt der Bundesregierung, no. 46748

take independent action on the assumption that Hitler was already dead or incapacitated.

Goebbels and Bormann immediately attempted to negotiate a cease-fire with the Soviets. When this failed, Goebbels and his wife committed suicide on 1 May after first killing their children, while Bormann was killed attempting to flee Berlin. Doenitz, who was in Schleswig-Holstein, meanwhile broadcast to the Reich the news that Hitler had died in combat 'at his post in the Reich Chancellery, while fighting to the last breath against Bolshevism'.[42] He intended to conclude a separate armistice with the Western Powers, which would allow him to continue the war long enough on the eastern front to enable as many German troops as possible to retreat westwards and evade surrendering to the Soviet forces . He formed a Nazi–Nationalist cabinet and was determined to maintain an authoritarian state, purged of only the worst Nazi abuses. For a very short time Himmler was left in charge of security, but on 6 May he was dismissed and most of the SS officers were arrested by the *Wehrmacht*. He committed suicide on 23 May after being arrested by the British.

Doenitz avoided formally capitulating to the Allies until 8 May, which allowed nearly three million German troops to escape being taken prisoner by the Russians. The Third Reich survived for two more weeks, as

For a long time it was thought that Bormann had escaped, but his skeleton was unearthed on a building site in 1972

Doenitz persuaded the British and American occupying forces that his administration was still temporarily needed to help with the growing problems of hunger, disease, refugees and the threat of Communism, but his position became increasingly untenable, as he wished to preserve 'the most beautiful and best that National Socialism has given us – the unity of the racial community'.[43] He also openly criticized the denazification policies of the Western Allies for destroying those 'quiet, decent citizens',[44] who stood between Germany and Communism. On 23 May 1945 he and his cabinet were at last arrested, and on 5 June the Allies became the sovereign rulers of occupied Germany.

The other Germany: the German opposition, 1933–45

In 1945, when the appalling consequences of the Hitler regime, not just for Germany but for Europe as a whole, were obvious, attention inevitably focused on the German opposition. Although it is true that Hitler himself was popular for most of the time and that under his leadership there had been a renaissance of German power, there was nevertheless a hard core of opposition to the Nazi regime. Only a relatively small number of outstandingly courageous Germans joined the active opposition, but there were a great many more who rejected certain elements of National Socialism and indulged in relatively minor acts of civil disobedience such as refusing to give the 'Heil Hitler' salute or hanging out a church banner rather than a swastika flag. In the 'Bavaria Project' on 'Resistance and Persecution in Bavaria' historians have shown how grass-roots opposition in fact 'block[ed] or partially restrict[ed] Nazism's societal penetration'.[45] This analysis has led to the use of the controversial concept of *Resistenz*, a medical term, which here means immunity to Nazi ideology. It helps the historian understand that grey area between resistance to and acceptance of the regime in which so many Germans existed.

According to *Gestapo* statistics, in 1939 there were 27,367 German political prisoners

The Churches

The concept of *Resistenz* is particularly useful when assessing the opposition from the Churches. The Churches had both the organization and the ideology to oppose the Third Reich, but, composed for the most part of ordinary Germans, they could not in practice divorce themselves from the climate of the times. Consequently, most priests, like their parishioners, approved of much of Hitler's foreign policy and anti-bolshevism, while amongst both the clergy and laity in the Catholic and Protestant Churches, despite many honourable exceptions, there was, to say the least, no root-and-branch opposition to the regime's anti-Semitism. Only in matters that affected their independence were the Churches ready seriously to oppose Hitler. Thus Martin Niemöller was able to form the Confessional Church in 1933–34 and effectively defeated attempts to

Hitler and the Protestant Churches

Hitler had hoped to group the Protestant Churches into one *Reichskirche* (Reich Church) under an elected Reich bishop, in order to facilitate their political control. The election of his nominee, Bishop Otto Müller, an ex-military chaplain and fanatical Nazi, was met with strong opposition within the Protestant Churches, spearheaded by Martin Niemöller, the pastor of the Berlin parish of Dahlem. Initially Müller responded by intimidation which led to Niemöller setting up the Confessional Church in October 1934. Eventually Hitler withdrew his support from Müller and created a Ministry of Church Affairs, but this too failed to co-ordinate the Protestant Churches. These were now divided into three main groups: the 'German Christians' under Müller, the Confessional Church and the mainstream Church establishment, which attempted to co-operate with the Nazis while safeguarding its independence.

absorb the Protestant Churches into a new uniform Nazi *Reichskirche*. The Catholic bishops also waged a stubborn, but ultimately unsuccessful battle to prevent the absorption of Catholic youth groups into the Hitler Youth.

The Catholic Church was effective in criticizing the regime openly only when it enjoyed public support. In August 1941 Bishop Galen of Münster, responded to widespread public concern by launching a bitter attack on the Nazi euthanasia programme (see p. 241), which forced Hitler, albeit temporarily, to suspend it. The Churches were more cautious about criticizing Nazi racial policy. Pope Pius's condemnation of Hitler's violations of the Concordat (see p. 220) and his racial policy in the encyclical of 1937, *With Burning Concern*, was an exception to the general policy of tolerating the regime. In 1941, as Jews were already being deported to Poland and murdered in Russia, the Church was careful to complain only about the fate of 'non-Aryan' Catholics or of Jews married to Catholics. The Confessing Church was equally careful, although in October 1943 it did address a pastoral letter to all its congregations, in which it unambiguously announced that 'terms like "eradication", "liquidation" or "unfit to live" are not known in the law of God'.[46] As institutions, it was inevitable that both Churches should react cautiously, as they had to be responsive to public opinion, the political situation and above all think of their own self-preservation. On the other hand, many individual Protestant and Catholic priests, such as Dietrich Bonhoeffer and Alfred Delp, felt no such inhibitions and did not hesitate to condemn Hitler, as is testified by the death of several hundred clergy in Buchenwald.

Encyclical: papal letter sent to all Roman Catholic bishops

Dietrich Bonhoeffer, 1906–45: a Protestant pastor and member of the Confessing Church. He was arrested in 1943 and hanged in April 1945. Alfred Delp, 1900–45: a Jesuit, who was a member of the Kreisau Circle (see p. 267) and was arrested in July 1944 and hanged after torture in February 1945

After the war the Americans calculated that 300–400 Protestant clergy died, while the number of Catholics was 800, although some of these would have come from occupied Poland

Youth rebellion

The concept of *Resistenz* is again helpful in understanding the relationship of youth subcultures to the Nazi regime. The activities of the 'swing

The White Rose group

The White Rose group was the most politicized of the youth groups. It was primarily based in Munich, and was led by the philosophy and psychology professor, Kurt Huber, and five Munich students, amongst whom Hans and Sophie Scholl played a key role. Inspired by Christianity and the philosophy of the great German idealists, Goethe, Kant and Schiller, in 1942–43 they distributed a series of cyclostyled anti-Nazi leaflets in Munich, which were aimed at the professional middle classes and their fellow students in Munich. In February 1943 they were arrested, tried and executed.

movement', which was popular amongst students, were apolitical but the liking of its adherents for jazz, American dances like the jitterbug, American and British fashions, and above all their acceptance of Jews and half-Jews in their groups challenged the social norms of the *Volksgemeinschaft* and led Himmler to threaten their 'ringleaders' with incarceration in the concentrations camps.[47] The 'Edelweiss Pirates', groups of young teenage workers, which were located mainly in the Ruhr and Rhineland cities and emerged at the end of the 1930s as a reaction against regimentation in the Hitler Youth and the factories, were for the most part also apolitical. Their activities were limited to boycotting, as far as possible, Hitler Youth activities, but some groups did physically attack Hitler Youth patrols, and distribute Communist leaflets or Allied propaganda sheets, which they had found during their excursions to the countryside. In Cologne–Ehrenfeld in 1944 an 'Edelweiss Pirates' gang worked closely with an underground group which assisted *Wehrmacht* deserters, escaped prisoners of war and foreign workers. It attacked military installations and even managed to kill the head of the Cologne *Gestapo* before it was broken up.

The left-wing opposition

Convinced Socialists and Communists had an ideology which psychologically prepared them to oppose Nazism but, unlike the Churches, their organizational structure had been destroyed with the dissolution of the political parties and the trade unions abroad. They had therefore to operate from underground or abroad. The left-wing opposition consisted of three main groups:

1 The SPD established its party headquarters first in Prague and then in Paris, and up to 1939 managed to smuggle illegal literature across the frontiers.
2 The Communists had more success than the SPD in developing an underground movement, which the *Gestapo* was never able completely to eliminate. In 1935 they were ordered by Stalin to negotiate a united front with the SPD against Fascism, but years of mistrust and hostility

between the two parties was impossible to overcome. The KPD remained a tool of the Kremlin, and with the signature of the Nazi–Soviet Pact in August 1939 (see p. 252), it was given the contradictory instructions of supporting Hitler's foreign policy, while opposing his domestic policy.

3 There were, too, several smaller groups which aimed to unify the left in Germany and avoid the divisions of the Weimar years. The *Roter Stosstrupp* (Red Assault Party) hoped to create a new socialist society once the Third Reich had collapsed, while *Neu Beginnen* (New Start) believed that only by close co-operation between the best elements in the KPD and SPD could Hitler be opposed effectively and a democratic socialist society be built after the war.

The left-wing opposition potentially had a large constituency of support, but it could not mobilize it. This was partly because the Nazis had destroyed its structures, but also because the regime had shown itself able to deliver full employment, a tolerable standard of living and, for the most part, a popular foreign policy. It was not surprising therefore that several leading SPD members began to look to the army as the only effective opposition to Hitler.

The Conservative élites and the Kreisau Circle

The members of the Conservative-Nationalist opposition were prominent individuals or 'notables', such as Erwin Planck, Papen's former state secretary, Carl Goerdeler, price commissioner, 1934–35, and Lord Mayor of Leipzig, and General Beck, army chief of staff until 1938. They provided potentially the most effective resistance to Hitler, as they could work within the system to destroy Nazism. Initially the notables had supported or at least tolerated Hitler, but the Sudeten crisis (see p. 250) led many of them to conclude that he would plunge Germany into a war that it could not win. In the summer of 1938 plans were drawn up by Erich Kordt, chief of the ministerial bureau in the Foreign Office, and Generals Beck, Witzleben and Oster to have Hitler arrested, to have martial law declared and to hold elections for a constituent assembly, but the Munich settlement destroyed what, to say the least, was 'a most promising attempt to overthrow Hitler'.[48] In the autumn of 1939 another plan for assassinating Hitler by placing a bomb in the Reich chancellery was halted at the last minute, when Hitler cancelled plans for a western offensive.

With the formation of the Kreisau Circle in 1941, the non-Communist opposition in Germany for the first time had a forum where it could discuss plans for the future of post-war Germany across the political divide. The circle, which was composed of Social Democrats, both Protestant and Catholic priests, civil servants and *Wehrmacht* officers, met at Kreisau, the Silesian estate of Count Helmuth James von Moltke and became the 'think tank' of the opposition until it was broken up by the *Gestapo* in January 1944.

Martial law: the declaration of military government and the suspension of civilian law

James von Moltke, 1907–45, was the grand-nephew of Field Marshal Helmuth von Moltke (see p. 77). His mother was an English South-African. He had studied law in Britain and practised in Berlin

How reactionary was the Conservative opposition?

It should come as no surprise that the foreign policy of the Conservative–National opposition automatically assumed that Germany should retain most of what it had acquired up to October 1939. Hermann Graml has argued that it was based on 'seductive visions of a German Reich of medieval proportions' and Prussian and conservative in character.[49] In a memorandum in January 1941 Goerdeler proposed the return of Germany's colonies and the creation of a confederation of free European states under German leadership. The Kreisau Circle was more committed to a European federation with a European parliament and cabinet. The domestic policies of the Conservative opposition, as Ian Kershaw has pointed out, 'were essentially oligarchic and authoritarian, resting heavily on corporatist and neo-conservative notions advanced in the Weimar Republic, envisaging self-governing communities, limited electoral rights and the renewal of Christian values'.[50]

20 July 1944

General Olbricht was the Chief of Staff of the home army

There were cells of opposition in both the Army Group Centre on the Russian front and in General Olbricht's headquarters in Berlin which in 1943 planned a series of assassination attempts against Hitler, but each one, as a consequence of 'a barely credible succession of trivial incidents',[51] failed. In early 1944 Operation Valkyrie, a plan both to assassinate Hitler and stage a military *coup d'état* by mobilizing the reserve army was drawn up by Colonel Claus Schenk von Stauffenberg. After Hitler's assassination, martial law would be declared, a provisional government including Conservative, Centre, Social Democrat and non-party representatives formed, and peace negotiations immediately opened with the West. Stauffenberg's appointment as chief of staff to General Fromm, the commander-in-chief of the home army, gave him access to Hitler's headquarters, where, after two unsuccessful attempts on 6 and 15 July, he was able to plant a bomb on July 20.

Stauffenberg, 1907–44, was wounded in Africa and appointed staff officer in Berlin in 1943. He was executed within hours of the 20 July plot failing

Colonel Brandt was a staff officer present at the conference on 20 July

The tragic consequences of 20 July 1944 are well-known. In a sense the coup failed because 'Colonel Brandt kicked Stauffenberg's briefcase to the wrong side of the oak support of the conference table',[52] but the plotters also left 'too many loose ends . . . dangling'.[53] They failed to put the communications centre at the *Führer* headquarters out of action, immediately to seize the radio stations in Berlin and to arrest party and SS leaders. As soon as it became known that Hitler was still alive, the conspirators lost the initiative, and the armies both in Germany and France refused to co-operate. The consequences of its failure was the elimination of most of the German opposition, as Hitler ordered the arrest of more than 7000 people, 5000 of whom were executed by April 1945.

Conclusion

Given that Germany's position in January 1945 was far worse than in October 1918, why were there no strikes and revolts as there had been in November 1918? In reality, of course, there is little comparison between the twilight periods of the two wars. Unlike the *Kaiserreich* in 1918, the Third Reich was a totalitarian regime, which was able to use terror and repression to control the home front. The opposition also lacked a focus: unlike 1918, there were no unions or socialist parties, and the cohesion of the workforce had been diluted by the conscription of so many workers and their replacement by women, foreign slave labourers and teenagers. In the final analysis there was no alternative but to fight on. In 1918 President Wilson envisaged a regime change in Germany but not unconditional surrender. President Roosevelt, on the other hand, demanded an unconditional surrender, and military occupation as a prelude to a regime change. In the east the brutal reputation of the Red Army inspired the population with fear and gave them reason to fight to the end. Paradoxically the Allied bombing campaign also strengthened support for the regime. Not only did it fail to break German morale, but the daily struggle to survive arguably took people's minds off political issues. However, with the advance of Allied troops into Germany in April 1945, there was a sudden resurgence of political activity. Former members of the SPD and KPD who had been released from the concentration camps, together with local supporters, set up anti-Fascist committees in the large cities, which in most cases the Allied forces rapidly disbanded.

Part Four
Partition and Reunification, 1945–90

14 *Occupation and Division, 1945–49*

Introduction

As the Allies advanced into the Reich they witnessed scenes of 'indescribable, impenetrable chaos'.[1] To the west of Berlin nearly every town with a population of over 50,000 had been destroyed by British and American bombers. In Cologne, for instance, 72 per cent of the buildings were destroyed, while in Berlin the number was a high as 75 per cent. The railways had been paralysed by Allied bombing, and the main roads were blocked with long columns of refugees. It was no wonder that the Germans called it *Stunde null* (the year zero). Yet paradoxically, amidst this destruction and misery, the preconditions for a German economic and political revival already existed. A surprising amount of industrial machinery had survived the bombing. In May 1945, compared to Britain, Germany still possessed double the number of machine tools. Even before the war had ended, in reaction to the stifling autarky of the Third Reich some businessmen were also considering a return to a more liberal economy and had clandestinely made contact with free-market economists such as Ludwig Erhard, the future economics minister of the FRG.

See Document 70

The lost war also unleashed a social revolution that accelerated the modernization of German society:

- The influence of the great east Elbian Junker landowners had been eliminated by the death of many of the traditional officer class on the eastern front and the liquidation of their estates, and often their families too, by the advancing Red Army.
- The urban evacuees from the bombed-out cities and the 12 million German expellees from East Prussia, Pomerania, Lower Silesia and the Sudetenland finally destroyed the traditional structure and isolation of rural and small-town Germany (see page 262).[2]

Key issues

- How different were the policies of the four occupying powers?
- Was the Allied occupation of Germany a 'missed opportunity' for radical economic, social and political reform?
- Was the division of Germany inevitable?
- To what extent did the founding fathers of the FRG draw on the Weimar constitution?
- Was the founding of the GDR a temporary expedient in response to the formation of the FRG?

The great powers and the future of Germany

Henry J. Morgenthau was the US treasury secretary, 1934–45

Germany surrendered unconditionally on 8 May, and with the demise of the Doenitz regime two weeks later (see p. 264), government effectively passed into the hands of the Allied commanders-in-chief. Germany was divided into the four zones agreed upon at the Yalta Conference in February 1945 (see Maps 8 and 9), and each occupying power was also given a zone in Berlin, but, beyond that, Britain, France, the USA and the USSR had no clear plans for the future of the former Reich. The British and Americans had wavered between the extremes of the Morgenthau Plan which would have reduced Germany to a deindustrialized backwater, and a cautious acceptance of a future Germany based on a loose federal constitution. Stalin too had initially agreed that the Allies should eliminate 'forever' Germany's 'ability to function as a single state',[3] but by the spring of 1945 he had accepted the possibility of a united but disarmed and neutral Germany. Whether he believed that it would be Communist is not clear, but the USSR's most immediate aim was for reparations to rebuild its shattered economy. At this stage it was the French who were the most determined opponents of German unity, and their overriding aim was to create an independent Rhineland and a Ruhr under international control. Whatever the shape of the future Germany

24 The *Trümmerfrauen* (female rubble-clearers) at work, 1946. In Berlin alone 60,000 women were employed clearing rubble and salvaging bricks and other building materials without any mechanical assistance

Presse- und Informationsamt der Bundesregierung, no. 10581

would be, it had been agreed at Yalta that Poland would be compensated for the land lost to the Soviet Union by the Nazi–Soviet Pact in 1939 by the annexation of German territory on its western borders.

By the time the Allies met at Potsdam, they could only paper over the growing differences between themselves on how Germany should be treated:

- There was a consensus on the need to enforce the 'four ds' – denazification, demilitarization, decartelization and democratization, but no real agreement on how this should in practice be carried out.
- The Allies agreed to the eventual restoration of a united, but decentralized Germany, but 'for the time being' there was to be no German government, although central departments or ministries were to be set up for finance, transport, communications, foreign trade and industry.
- The great powers confirmed that Germany should pay reparations of $20 billion, half of which should go to Russia, but failed to come to an agreement on how, and over what length of time this should be paid. A compromise was accepted which would enable the USSR and the Western powers to extract reparations from their own zones, although Britain and America would allocate 10 per cent of these to the USSR, and a further 15 per cent in exchange for food and raw materials from the Soviet Zone. The failure to devise an overall reparation policy did

not bode well for the future of Germany. Molotov, the Soviet foreign minister, was quick to ask what: 'if reparations were not treated as a whole . . . would happen to overall treatment of economic matters?'[4]

- Britain and America protested strongly over the delineation of Poland's western frontiers where, contrary to their wishes but with Soviet support, the Poles had been allowed to annex German territory right up to the western branch of the river Neisse, rather than to the eastern branch as had initially been agreed to by Britain and the USA (see Map 8). By July 1945 the Poles were already expelling the Germans from Silesia and the Oder–Neisse region.

See Documents 71 and 72

Germany under military government, 1945–47

The four allied commanders on the Control Council in Berlin were supposed to apply the Potsdam guidelines to their joint administration of Germany, but as their governments increasingly could not agree on the country's future, each occupying power began to implement the Potsdam agreements in its own way and to reform German institutions and society according to its own standards.

Denazification and re-education

Twenty-two Nazi leaders, twelve of whom were sentenced to death, were tried by the international military tribunal at Nuremberg for conspiracy against peace and crimes against humanity. At a lower level in each zone, denazification was implemented with varying degrees of thoroughness. The Russians, convinced that Nazism was a product of German capitalism, removed not only Nazi officials, teachers and industrialists but also changed the whole economic structure of their zone. Thus the estates of big landowners, which were seen as breeding grounds for reactionaries, were broken up and the larger factories nationalized. The Americans pursued denazification initially with a fanatical zeal, and by December 1945 had arrested nearly double the number detained by the British. Denazification, however, rapidly encountered major problems throughout Germany, as administrative and managerial personnel were removed from key positions and often replaced with incompetents. After a major coalmining disaster in the Ruhr in 1946, for instance, the British decided to tolerate ex-Nazis in key management posts as long as they could produce the coal. In October 1946 the Control Council divided the Germans into five categories ranging from major offenders to non-offenders and handed over the responsibility for their denazification to German tribunals working under Allied supervision Although this was a necessary step towards restoring self-government in Germany, the ruling by the German courts that all Germans seeking employment in official positions should have written statements confirmed by oath (affidavits) attesting to their good character was all too easily abused. As the Cold

25   A German soldier returning to Berlin from a Yugoslav prisoner-of-war camp,
June 1946

Presse- und Informationsamt der Bundesregierung, no. 111569

War intensified, denazification became an irrelevance and by early
1948 the four occupying powers had each declared the process to be
at an end.

See Document 73

As the Potsdam Agreement had decreed that all traces of militarism
and National Socialism were to be eliminated in order to prepare the way
for the development of democracy, denazification was accompanied by
ambitious attempts to reform the German education system. Nazi teachers were purged, old textbooks withdrawn and new teachers hastily
trained. Again it was in the Russian Zone that the most radical reforms
were implemented. Comprehensive schooling was introduced, although
for the time being a selective sixth form was preserved for those going on
to higher education. Universities were forced to practise positive discrimination in favour of the children of workers and peasants. The Western
powers on the other hand failed to change the basic structure of the
German education system, and both universities and the *Gymnasien*
(grammar schools) managed to survive the occupation virtually
unscathed.

Democratization and decentralization

The occupying powers were committed by the Potsdam Agreement both to decentralizing the political structure of Germany and to making local government more democratic. The Allied decision to break up Prussia in February 1947 allowed the non-Prussian states in western Germany at last to escape Prussian domination and cleared the way for the creation of a more balanced federal system. In the British Zone three new states, Schleswig-Holstein, Lower Saxony and North Rhine–Westphalia were created out of the former Prussian territory. The boundaries of the French and American Zones had been drawn up without regard to the historic borders of the south German *Länder*. Most of Bavaria was included in the American Zone, but the Zone's western regions, as one American official observed, were 'made up of such an assortment of legs, arms, fingers, ears and other stray pieces of dismembered body that one could hardly believe one's eyesight'.[5] Out of these fragments the Americans created Hesse and Württemberg-Baden, while the French, faced with a similar problem, joined together Baden and Württemberg–Hohenzollern. The Russians formed five new *Länder* in July 1945: Saxony, Mecklenburg, Saxony–Anhalt, Thuringia and Brandenburg.

> Only in 1952 was the *Land* of Baden–Württemberg created

Each power had a different approach to reconstructing the German local government system. The British created a Central Economic Office, which was run by German officials subject to military government instructions, and treated their zone as a unified whole. The French, on the other hand, who wished to encourage separatism and hoped eventually to annex the Saar, had no co-ordinating body above the *Land* level. Both the French and the British believed, however, that political power should be conceded only gradually from the bottom upwards to the Germans, and it was not until the autumn of 1946 that municipal elections were held in both zones. The Americans, inspired by their own political traditions of federalism, rapidly restored the *Länder* governments in their zone. By the end of 1946 democratically elected *Länder* legislatures had met in Munich, Wiesbaden and Stuttgart, but it was not until May 1947 that similar elections were held in the British and French Zones. The Russians set up governments in their *Länder* as early as July 1945, but they also formed what could have been the nucleus of either a central German or a Soviet zonal administration when they created eleven central zonal ministries. Initially, however, these had only symbolic value, as according to an American observer, they 'had only fragmentary information'[6] about the economic situation in the provinces and had no power to influence them.

The revival of politics

The Russians allowed the formation of German political parties in their zone as early as June 1945, probably hoping that they would be able to use them as a means of projecting their own influence throughout Germany. The Americans hastily followed suit in August, the British a month later and the French not until December 1945. In all four zones similar party groupings emerged, consisting of the Communists (KPD), the Socialists (SPD), the Christian Democrats (CDU) and the Liberals (LDPD).

German Party leaders and activists were determined not to recreate the divisive politics of the Weimar Republic, which had done much to let the Nazis seize power in 1933 (see pp. 209–17). They therefore attempted to make their parties as inclusive as possible. The Christian Democratic Union aimed to appeal to both south German and Rhineland Catholics as well as north German Protestants. It was, as a French newspaper commented, 'socialist and radical in Berlin, clerical and conservative in Cologne and reactionary in Hamburg and counter-revolutionary and particularist in Munich'.[7] Kurt Schumacher, the leader of the SPD in the British Zone, believed the new party would fall apart, but he underestimated the political skills of Konrad Adenauer, who, after being dismissed by the British from the post of *Oberbürgermeister* of Cologne, rapidly emerged as the most powerful man in the CDU.

Despite its poor showing in 1932, liberalism as a political force also revived spontaneously in 1945. It appealed to those who disliked the CDU's close links with the Catholic Church, but who wanted a capitalist rather than a socialist economy. In 1947 a united Liberal party, the DDP, was founded at Eisenach under the joint chairmanship of Theodor Heuss and Wilhelm Külz, the Liberal leaders in the Western and Soviet zones. The DDP collapsed, however, when Külz supported the German People's Congress , which was convened by the East German Socialist Unity party in Berlin in December 1947 (see p. 287). The Liberal rump in West Germany then set up the broadly based Free Democratic party under the chairmanship of Heuss, which appealed to both supporters of the old right-wing National Liberal party and the more left-wing Democratic party.

Initially the mood amongst the workers in both the Soviet and Western zones was for 'the organisational unity of the German working class',[8] but Stalin at first rejected this demand, hoping that the KPD would by itself be able to dominate the anti-Fascist bloc of parties in the Soviet Zone. By the autumn this policy was failing. The KPD and its leaders were seen as 'bullies and stooges'[9] of the Russians, and the SPD, as the larger party, represented a potential challenge to Soviet authority, especially with the emergence in the British Zone of Schumacher, who was bitterly hostile to co-operation with the Communists. Belatedly Stalin decided on the forced amalgamation of both parties. In February 1946, after several months of bribery and intimidation, the Central Executive of the SPD in the Soviet Zone voted for a new united party, the Socialist Unity Party of Germany, the SED, which was modelled on the Russian Communist party.

The democratic credibility of the vote was implicitly challenged when Wilhelm Pieck, the chairman of the KPD, agreed to submit the decision

Initially Stalin's policy in eastern Europe was to create a coalition or bloc of 'anti-Fascist' parties. In the Soviet Zone in Germany this consisted of the CDU, KPD, SPD and LDPD

See Document 74

Konrad Adenauer, 1876–1967, and Kurt Schumacher, 1895–1952

Adenauer was elected Lord Mayor of Cologne in 1917, but was dismissed by the Nazis in 1933. In the aftermath of the 20 July conspiracy he was briefly arrested, although innocent of involvement. The Americans reappointed him lord mayor, but he was dismissed again by the British for discussing with the French the possibility of setting up an independent Rhineland state. This freed him to take part in politics, and at the age of 70 he became the leader of the CDU in the British Zone. He was a pragmatist, who believed that party programmes were essentially 'instruments' for winning elections. Although he himself was convinced that 'with the word socialism we win five people and twenty run away',[10] he agreed in 1947 to compromise with the Christian–Socialist wing of the CDU and accept the Ahlen Programme, which advocated the nationalization of heavy industry and the major banks. This prevented a divisive row with Jacob Kaiser, the leader of the CDU in the Soviet Zone, who saw the party as 'a bridge between East and West',[11] and enabled Adenauer to concentrate his efforts on building up the party's organization in the Western zones. With the intensification of the Cold War and Kaiser's flight to the West in December 1947, Adenauer was able to steer the CDU away from socialism in the direction of the market economy (see p. 317). In August 1949 he was elected the first chancellor of the *Bundesrepublik*, a post he held until October 1963.

Schumacher was first elected as an SPD candidate to the *Reichstag* in 1930, where he was a strong opponent of both the Communists and the Nazis. In 1933 he was arrested and interned in Dachau concentration camp, and released ten years later. In 1945 he rebuilt the SPD in the Western zones, but refused to accept the merger of the SPD in the Soviet Zone with the KPD. He failed however to modernize the SPD, which remained encumbered with the out-of-date Heidelberg Programme of 1924 (see p. 199). He supported the creation of a separate West German state and believed that it would act as a magnet to attract the GDR, provided that it implemented social democratic reforms. He thus bitterly accused Adenauer of supporting big business and of working too closely with the Western Allies. He was consequently opposed to the European Coal and Steel Community and the Pleven Plan (see p. 296).

Wilhelm Pieck joined the KPD in 1919 and during the Third Reich was in exile in France and the USSR. He returned to Germany with the Red Army. From 1949–60 he was president of the GDR

to a referendum of both SPD and KPD party members in Berlin on 31 March. In East Berlin the Russians were able to close down the polling stations half an hour after they had opened, but in Western zones of the city the voting continued and only 18 per cent of the SPD members approved of the amalgamation. This rejection was, however, qualified by a second vote. In response to the question of whether they supported 'an alliance . . . which will guarantee continued cooperation and exclude fraternal strife',[12] 62 per cent of the membership agreed. The SPD's amalgamation with the KPD destroyed the claims of the SPD to be the strongest political party in Germany, and it was reduced to a rump party, with its electoral base in the industrialized areas in the British Zone.

The trade unions

At Potsdam the Germans were given the right to form trade unions, but the implementation of this was again left to the occupying powers. The Americans and the French encouraged the Germans to reconstruct the movement from the grass-roots upwards, but it was in the more industrialized Soviet and British Zones that the future patterns of German trade unionism were to be created. The Russians backed the idea of a centralized unitary trade union movement, because they hoped that the SED would be able to exploit it to exercise a decisive influence throughout Germany. Consequently the Free German Trade Union Association (FDGB) was formed in the Soviet Zone in February 1946 as a single trade union representing all German workers. In the British Zone trade unionists at first also wanted a centralized organization, as it would avoid the divisions and weaknesses of the Weimar period. Hans Böckler, the future Chairman of the German Trade Unions Federation (DGB), put forward plans for a united general union, but the scheme was criticized by the military government and its British trade union advisors, who feared that this would both maximize Communist influence, and discourage members from actively participating. Böckler was persuaded to accept instead a scheme whereby independent unions were grouped together into an overall federation. In August 1947 the trade union movements in the American and British zones were fused, and were joined by those in the French Zone in December. At first there was considerable contact between trade unionists in the western and eastern zones but the onset of the Cold War made a united German trade union movement impossible to bring about.

The economy

According to the Potsdam Agreement the Allies were committed to developing 'common policies' covering disarmament, decartelization, and land reform, and to maintaining a common currency and transport system as well as 'import and export programmes for Germany as a whole'. In reality the economies of the four zones were at first virtually sealed off from each other. The manufacturing industries in the Soviet Zone, for example, had no access to their markets in western Germany and goods could only be exported to western Europe if they were paid for in dollars, which no European country could afford. Coal production in the Ruhr in 1946 was running at a third of its 1936 daily average, and Germany's main food-producing areas in the east, Pomerania and East and West Prussia, had been ceded to Poland. Food shortages were the single greatest cause of misery during the occupation, and it was not until the currency reform of 1948 that rations approaching 2000 calories per day were available.

The Reichsmark currency, thanks to the ravages of war-time inflation, was almost valueless, and if the Allied powers had not continued the

Third Reich's policy of freezing pay and prices, Germany would have been overwhelmed by hyperinflation As long as the introduction of a new currency was delayed by Allied disagreements on the future of Germany, there were two distinct economies in Germany: one was 'the official economy, grinding along on the basis of rations, production plans and quotas',[13] while the other, the economy of barter or the 'black market', was the standard means by which individuals obtained food, and factories their raw materials.

Black market:
illegal traffic in
officially rationed
or very scarce
commodities

In March 1946 the four occupying powers published the 'Plan for Reparations and the Level of the Post-War German Economy', which aimed to reduce post-war production to the level of 1932, but it was never implemented, since the Allies were unable to reach any agreement on the future of Germany as a political or economic entity. Both the Russians and French ruthlessly exploited their zones in the interests of their home economies. By 1949 the Russians had probably extracted the $10 billion reparations they had claimed at Potsdam. The Soviet authorities also siphoned off reparations from current production by converting factories which had previously been privately owned into SAGs or Soviet limited companies, which by the end of 1946 produced some 30 per cent of the zone's industrial output.

The four powers also failed to agree on a common policy for land reform and the restructuring of German industry. The most radical steps were undertaken in the Soviet Zone where by 1948 both the key industries had been nationalized and the large estates and farms divided up. The British also attempted to break up and then nationalize the component parts of the great industrial trusts in the Ruhr, but nationalization was halted by the formation of the Bizone (see p. 285) in January 1947, which gave America an effective veto over economic policy in the British Zone. The Americans were determined that decartelization should only take place within the overall context of a capitalist economy, and the whole problem was consequently left to the new West German government to solve later (see p. 317).

By the end of 1947, in the absence of any effective central control, Germany was already divided into two distinct economic zones: the American-controlled, capitalist Western Germany and the Soviet-dominated, socialist East. There were some signs of economic recovery in the Anglo-American Bizone. Production climbed up to half the 1936 level and manufacturers were beginning to rebuild their plants, accumulating stocks of raw materials in preparation for an economic upturn. The Russians only began to develop a comprehensive economic strategy for the reconstruction of their zone in June 1947, when, in response to the Bizone, they set up the German Economic Commission to administer the economy of their zone (see p. 286). To increase production, the SMAD (Soviet Military Administration) also attempted to mobilize the workforce. By Order 234, which 'amounted to a full blown transfer of Soviet style labour relations to East Germany',[14] key factories were allocated special deliveries of food, and efforts were made to improve their working conditions by the introduction of welfare provisions such as crèches and medical clinics. People's Control Committees were set up to stop thefts on the factory floor, and workers were to be paid piece-rates. Order 234 started, according to Jeffrey Kopstein, the crucial process in East Germany of 'refashioning the factory as a social and political as opposed to purely economic institution'[15] (see p. 334).

Was the occupation a missed opportunity?

The question, as far as the Western zones were concerned, was a matter of heated discussion, particularly in the 1960s and 1970s. Lutz Niethammer has, for instance, shown that the number of ex-Nazis in the *Länder* administration in the American Zone was greater than the numbers of Nazi party members employed in it before the war. He argued that denazification was a superficial process that permitted a large number of ex-Nazis to regain their positions 'with a fresh white waist-coat'.[16] There were similar arguments about the failure to change the education system. David Welch, for instance, speaks for many when he says that a major opportunity 'to break with the past was lost'. Other historians (E. Schmidt) regret the failed attempts to reform the civil service or the total and speedy abolition of cartels (Abelshauser).[17] It is all too true that many ex-Nazis did return to power and influence, but they did so in a society in which the appeal of Nazism had been shattered through defeat, and where as a result of the Nuremberg trials the history of Nazi atrocities had become well-known. The failure to reform the universities certainly fuelled the student unrest of the 1960s, but they did not become the reserve of the nationalist right as they did during the Weimar Republic. The ambitious reform programmes of the Western powers were curtailed by the Cold War and the resulting swing to the bourgeois right throughout Western Europe in the early 1950s. The Western powers did try to depoliticize the civil service by banning civil servants from standing for election, but this was reversed later by Adenauer, and anti-trust legislation had to wait until 1957. However, in the Soviet Zone, there really was a fundamental social and political revolution (see Chapter 15).

The decision to set up a West German state

In the 1950s there was little doubt in the West that the blame for starting the Cold War and the partition of Germany lay squarely with the USSR. Yet an analysis of the events leading up to the division shows that the Western powers 'repeatedly took initiatives to which Soviet measures came largely as a response'.[18] Of course it is true that events such as the ruthless suppression of opposition in Poland and the shotgun marriage of the SPD–KPD (see p. 279) bred an atmosphere of fear in the West, but it is, nevertheless, arguable that Western leaders overreacted and precip-

Cold War: this term is used to describe relations between the West and the Soviet bloc between 1947 (if not earlier) and 1989. It means a state of extreme tension stopping just short of war, and ideological hostility

itated the division of Germany. In the crucial period 1946–48 the British and the Americans took the following actions:

- In March 1946, reparation payments to the USSR were halted.
- The Anglo-American Bizone was set up in January 1947.
- The Marshall Plan was announced in June. When the Organization for European Economic Co-operation was set up in April 1948 to co-ordinate the distribution of ERP (Marshall Aid) funds, both Bizonia and the French Zone were also represented on it.
- The agreement to form a West German state was taken in the London six-power conference in early June 1948.
- The Deutschmark currency was introduced into West Germany on 20 June 1948.

The failure to agree on a joint reparation policy at the Potsdam Conference was already a step towards partition. In May 1946 the USSR refused to accept an interzonal import–export plan proposed by General Clay, the American military governor, as it would have involved waiting until the German economy had recovered sufficiently to finance its own essential imports of food and raw materials. Clay responded by announcing that no further reparation deliveries would be made from the American Zone until German economic unity was restored. Shortly afterwards at the Paris conference of foreign ministers James Byrnes, the American Secretary of State, repeated this message, but he also offered to integrate the American zone economically with all four or any one of the other zones in an effort to bring about German economic unity on terms acceptable to Washington. Only the British, faced with spending some $320 million per year on their zone, accepted. On 6 September American policy on the future of Germany became clearer still when Byrnes announced at Stuttgart that there should be no delays to economic reconstruction and that more power should be handed over to the Germans to run their own affairs. The economic merger of the British and American Zones to form Bizonia on 1 January 1947 marked the beginning of this process (see Map 8).

The Council of Ministers of the four occupying powers met regularly to discuss Germany and other post-war matters

Recent research[19] has emphasized how the weakness of the British economy acted as a catalyst for the division of Germany. Ernest Bevin, the British foreign secretary, was convinced that Stalin would only consent to a united Germany if he believed that the Communists could seize power. He argued, therefore, that it was imperative to set up, as a temporary holding operation, an independent and economically self-supporting West German state. At the Moscow foreign ministers' conference the British persuaded the Americans to drop a proposal which would have enabled the Russians to have received reparations from the current production in the Ruhr, in favour of going ahead with rebuilding West Germany as an interim measure. To implement this decision, production in the Western Zones was now permitted to rise to the 1936 level and the administrative structure of the Bizone was made more effective.

The Bizone

In 1948 all the offices of the Bizone were centralized at Frankfurt. To these were now added an Economic Council, made up of 52 members who were chosen by the *Land* assemblies, and an Executive Committee, composed of the directors of the bizonal administrative agencies. This had the powers, subject to overall Anglo-American approval, to promulgate laws on economic matters and to ensure that they were carried out. It could also appoint and remove the executive directors of the Bizonal Economic Agencies.

The composition of the Economic Council reflected the composition of the *Land* parliaments: the SPD and the CDU combined with its sister party in Bavaria, the Christian Social Union (CSU), were each given 20 seats. The remaining 12 seats were distributed amongst the smaller parties, most of which, with the exception of the KPD, were more inclined towards the CDU than the SPD. A glimpse of the politics of the future West German state can already be seen in the struggle over the appointments of the senior officials who would run the five administrative offices of the Bizone. When the SPD group failed to secure its preferred candidates, it retired into opposition, and the council's business was carried out by the other parties led by the CDU–CSU, the so-called Frankfurt Coalition. In retrospect the Bizone was, to quote Theodor Eschenburg, the 'germ cell and prefiguration of the later FRG'.[20]

When the London foreign ministers' conference met in November, partition seem[ed] to be in the air',[21] as General Robertson, the British military governor, observed. The conference ended in deadlock. The USSR accused the Western Allies of breaking the Potsdam Treaty, while the latter rejected proposals from Moscow for setting up a central German government on the grounds that this would merely facilitate the spread of Communism throughout Germany. As soon as the conference broke up, Bevin and Marshall took the following crucial decisions:

- As an interim measure, Bizonia would have to be strengthened by the inclusion of the French Zone.
- Failing agreement with the Soviets on a single German currency, the Western Zones would have to be given a new currency.
- At the least, an interim West German state would have to be created. Bevin stressed that the option for free elections for an all-German government should be left open 'so that any irredentist German movement should be based on the west rather than the east'. In other words, West Germany would, it was hoped, ultimately act as a 'magnet' for the Eastern Zone, rather than the other way round.[22]

Irredentist: demanding the restoration to a country of land originally belonging to it

The Czech Communists used their control of the trade unions and police on 22 February to seize power in Prague. Elections were held on 30 May on the basis of a single National Front list, which committed all the parties to supporting a manifesto approved by Moscow

To implement this, Britain, France, the USA and the Benelux states met again in London from February to early June. A note of urgency was given to the proceedings by the Communist seizure of power in Czechoslovakia at the end of February. French co-operation was assured by an agreement allowing the Saar to be integrated into the French economy. On 2 June plans were announced for setting up a West

---

Currency reform in the Western Zones and the Soviet Zone, June 1948

1 In the West the reform consisted of the following measures:
  • The Deutschmark (DM) was introduced to replace the Reichsmark. Every West German was immediately allowed to change 40 marks at a 1:1 rate and then two months later they could exchange a further 20. Businesses were given an allowance of 60 DM per worker towards their wage costs.
  • Wages, salaries, pensions and share dividends were protected and converted into DM at the rate of 1:1. The tough measures aimed at cutting down the volume of notes in circulation hurt the small saver as opposed to owners of shares or real estate. Those who had money on deposit in the banks had to exchange the old currency for the new at a ratio of 100 Reichsmarks to DM 6.50.
  • The banks were granted generous deposits of DM which enabled them to extend credit to business and industry.
  • The Western Allies protected the new currency by making the *Bank Deutscher Länder* into an independent central bank with responsibility for managing the currency. They also laid down that public authorities must not run up debts unless they were covered by current income.
2 The introduction of the East German Mark on 23 June penalized the remaining independent industrialists and businessmen in the Soviet Zone. Their financial assets were converted at a rate varying from 3 to 10 Reichsmarks to one East Mark, while the financial assets of the state-owned factories (VEBs), *Land* governments, trade unions and the SED was converted at the rate of 1:1. Effectively the currency reform was exploited by the Russians to ensure a partial confiscation of all investments and savings still in the private sector.

German state. On 20 June a new currency, the Deutschmark, was introduced into Bizonia and the French Zone, and three days later into Berlin. This measure, as Christoph Klessmann observed, touched 'the main nerve affecting any form of national unity'.[23]

The Soviet Response, 1946–49

For Stalin the division of Germany was a defeat. Not only would partition make it much more difficult for the USSR to influence German politics at a national level, but it would also ensure that the massive economic potential of the Ruhr would be harnessed by the West. When it became increasingly clear in 1947 that America and Britain were pushing hard for a revived German economy within an international capitalist system, and if that was not achievable then at least a temporary partition of Germany, Stalin began to move cautiously to strengthen the Soviet Zone by setting up the German Economic Commission in June 1947. Its task was to co-ordinate economic policy and, with the assistance of the SMAD, to draw

26 West Berliners marvel at the goods on display in the shop windows after the introduction of the *Deutschmark* in June 1948

Presse- und Informationsamt der Bundesregierung, no. 29088

up a zonal economic plan. The Commission was composed of the heads of the zone's ministries and the chairmen of the zonal federation of the trade unions (FDGB) and the farmers' association (VdgB), both of which were controlled by the SED. As with the Bizone, it can in retrospect be called the 'germ cell' of a future German state, the GDR, although the Russians played down its political and economic significance by emphasising that it was firmly under control of the Soviet military government.

To counter the decision to create a West German state, the Russians tried to play on the reservations many West Germans inevitably had about the impending partition of their country. Walther Ulbricht, the First Secretary of the SED, called two *Volkscongresse* (the German People's Congresses) for Unity and Just Peace. Their task was to mobilize public opinion right across Germany against partition. The first congress met in early December 1947 in Berlin. Roughly a third of those attending came from the West, but they were mainly delegates from the KPD strongholds in the Ruhr. In March the second congress met and set out to evoke the revolutionary spirit of 1848 (see Chapter 3). It elected a German People's Council (*Volksrat)* of 400 delegates to prepare for a referendum on German unity and to draw up an all-German constitution, which could also serve temporarily as the basis for an East German constitution. In May Wilhelm Pieck, the chairman of the SED, told its leadership cadres that once a West German state was created, the Soviet Zone would inevitably have to 'develop its own independent state structure'. It was immaterial whether the Western powers 'tore Germany apart . . . a month earlier or a month later. The important thing was to be prepared for every eventuality.'[24]

On 23 June the Russians responded to the currency reform in the West by introducing the new East Mark in the Soviet Zone (see p. 286), and then, under the pretence of preventing devalued Reichsmarks from flooding into their zone, they imposed a blockade on West Berlin (see Map 9), which lasted until 12 May 1949, in a gamble to stop the creation of a West German state. The rail and road links to the West were cut and the supply of electricity from East Berlin to the Western sectors was halted (see Map 9). The blockade rapidly became a struggle which America and its allies could not afford to lose if their plans for the construction of a West German state were to be realized. The immediate response of the Western Allies was the airlift which, contrary to expectations, managed to supply West Berlin with food and fuel throughout the very mild winter of 1948–49. The Western Allies also discussed with the Russians the option of allowing the East Mark to become the sole currency for the whole of Berlin, subject only to the control of a four-power financial commission, but the talks broke down once it became obvious that Moscow's primary aim was still to drive the Western powers from Berlin and to force them to abandon their plans for a West German state. Consequently, in spite of efforts by the United Nations to mediate, the blockade continued until 9 May 1949, when Stalin at last realized that it had failed. For Soviet policy its consequences were a disaster: it not only facilitated the integration of the Western Zones into an American-dominated Western Europe but it also ensured that the Western part of Berlin would eventually became an economic, political and social outpost of West Germany.

The birth of the two Germanies

The constitutions for the two German states were drawn up against the threatening background of the Berlin crisis. The East and West German political élites had in common a 'deep distrust of the common man'.[25] In the West this took the form of creating a complex constitutional system of checks and balances, which would ensure stability and consensus. In the East, despite references to the power of the 'people', it took the form of creating a one-party dictatorship. Neither set of politicians were free agents, as their constitutions had to be approved of by their respective occupying powers. The West German politicians were, however, in a stronger position than their counterparts in the SED, as there was a broad consensus both on the left and on the right in support of a democratic constitution, and they were skilfully able to exploit the differences between Britain, France and America to achieve concessions. The SED leaders, on the other hand, were dependent on Stalin for their survival, and it was always possible that a change of policy in Moscow could still consign their constitution to the dustbin.

The Federal Republic

The first draft of the constitution was drawn up by a committee of constitutional experts and then analysed in depth by the Parliamentary Council, which was elected by the *Länder* parliaments. The CDU–CSU and the SPD each had 27 seats, but on social and economic questions the former could count on the backing of the five Liberals (FDP) and the smaller parties, while the SPD could only sometimes rely on the support of the two KPD members. The SPD made a serious tactical mistake when it decided to accept Adenauer's nomination as president of the Parliamentary Council in return for allowing Carlo Schmid to chair the main committee. Adenauer was able to exploit this position to turn himself into a national figure, which was to be much to his advantage in the election campaign of August 1949.

In Peter Pulzer's words, the founding fathers of the Bonn constitution (the Basic Law) were 'burnt children who knew what fire was like. Their vision was one of disaster-avoidance, not a new heaven and a new earth.'[26] The Basic Law was a 'hybrid' or 'mixture of Weimar traditionalism and a determination to reform'.[27] The Parliamentary Council inevitably drew on the Weimar model (see p. 171), but it was also determined to improve it. The intention of Article 67, for example, was to prevent a repetition of the unstable coalition governments of the Weimar period by laying down that a chancellor could only be forced to resign if there was already a majority in the lower house (*Bundestag*) for his successor. Similarly, according to Article 68 the president could only call an election before the statutory end of a parliament, provided the *Bundestag* after 21 days had failed to choose a new chancellor. There were to be no referenda, except on local matters, and the president was not to be directly elected by the people but chosen by the Federal Convention, a body made up of an equal number of *Bundestag* and *Länder* representatives (Article 54). In the first 19 articles of the constitution, basic human rights such as freedom of conscience and speech and the right to property were guaranteed, and provision was made for setting up a federal constitutional court to interpret the constitution. The Basic Law was essentially a compromise and, unlike the Weimar constitution, did not seek to define the future socio-economic shape of the state. Article 6, which committed the state to protecting 'marriage and family', was welcomed by the Churches, but no special protection was afforded to denominational schools, while the trade unions were disappointed that there was no mention of co-determination or nationalization of key industries (see p. 319). One of the most controversial issues debated by

Carlo Schmid, 1896–1979, was half-French. After fighting in the German army in the Great War he studied law and became a judge in 1931. From 1940 to 1944 he was in the German military administration in France and Belgium, and then became head of the German administration in Württemberg–Hohenzollern under the French. In 1947 he joined the SPD and was elected to its executive. He was an ardent supporter of Franco-German reconciliation

Bundestag literally means the federal assembly. The term *Bund* (federation) was used to stress the decentralized structure of the new FRG

the Parliamentary Council was the powers of the *Bundesrat,* the upper house. Neither Adenauer nor the SPD wanted a strong *Bundesrat* which would be able to veto bills coming up from the *Bundestag.* On the other hand, the CDU did not want an upper house in which the majority of delegations would be appointed by the predominantly SPD *Länder* governments. In the end a compromise was reached whereby the *Länder* were represented in the *Bundesrat* by delegates selected by the *Land* governments on the basis of their population. As most of the smaller *Länder* were SPD-controlled, this would ensure that they would be balanced by the larger, predominantly CDU–CSU *Länder* like Bavaria.

When the Parliamentary Council presented the final draft of the Basic Law to the military governors for their approval, changes were demanded in two areas: initially at any rate, West Berlin was not to be part of the federation, and the federal nature of the constitution was to be reinforced by giving the *Länder* greater fiscal powers. On 8 May the Parliamentary Council finally approved the amended Basic Law and two days later it decided that the provisional seat of government should be Bonn. With the exception of Bavaria, the *Länder* legislatures ratified the Basic Law, but even the Bavarians were arguably 'whisper[ing] "yes" in the same breath as shouting "no"',[28] as they consented in a second vote to accept the law as long as two-thirds of the *Länder* had already approved it.

See Document 75 and Map 8

The date for the general election was fixed for 14 August. Fifty per cent of the deputies were to be elected by a direct constituency vote, while the rest were to be selected from party lists compiled on the basis of the *Länder*. There was also a 5 per cent 'barrier clause' under which a party had to win 5 per cent of the total votes in order to win any seats in the *Bundestag*. The campaign was dominated by Schumacher and Adenauer, who made the main theme of his campaign a crusade against 'the birth of a Socialist economy'.[29] He was helped by his alliance with Erhard, the economics director of the Bizone, whose social market economic policies (see pp. 316–17) were apparently beginning to show some signs of success. Adenauer also benefited from Schumacher's ill-judged attack on the Catholic Church as the 'fifth occupying power', which inevitably irritated many moderate Catholic voters. The CDU–CSU with 139 seats just managed to beat the SPD, which won 131 seats, while the FDP gained 52. When the *Bundestag* met in September, Adenauer was elected the first chancellor of the Federal Republic (FRG), supported by an FDP–CDU–CSU coalition. Many of his party would have preferred a grand coalition with the SPD, but Schumacher's insistence that he would only consider it if the SPD controlled the Economics Ministry effectively ruled that option out.

The German Democratic Republic

As long as there was still the chance of a restoration of four-power control and the eventual creation of a neutral German state potentially friendly to the USSR, the Russians were reluctant to set up an independent East German state. Once the Berlin blockade had failed, however, Stalin had little option but to agree to this. During the spring and summer of 1949 the SED leadership pursued three interrelated aims:

- To create a National Front out of the *Volkskongress*, which would enable the SED to pose as the 'champion of national unity' in contrast to the "splitters"[30] in the West.
- To set up a Communist East German state which would guarantee their own continuance in power, whilst attracting Communists in West Germany.
- To persuade SMAD to allow them greater independence. This would, they hoped, 'lift the burden of guilt by association – for the rape, plunder, repression and economic exploitation by Soviet forces',[31] which had acted to the party's detriment since 1945.

The *Volksrat* (see p. 287) in March 1949 approved the constitution of the future German Democratic Republic (GDR). Although its constitution appeared to be not so different from the Basic Law, in reality it was a 'make-believe constitution',[32] which attempted to camouflage a one-party dictatorship. Its citizens were theoretically guaranteed the fundamental democratic rights of freedom of speech and freedom of the press, and the right to strike and even to emigrate. Superficially the parliament was not dissimilar to the model adopted in the FRG. The *Volkskammer* (People's Chamber) was elected for four years under a system of proportional representation, while the upper house, the Chamber of States, was a watered-down version of the *Bundesrat*.

In May, elections for a third *Volkskongress* (people's congress) were held. The voters were presented with a single list of candidates representing the mass organizations (trade unions, etc.) and the bloc parties, which included the Soviet Zone Christian Democrats (CDUD) and the Liberal Democrats (LDPD). The leaders of these parties still believed that by forming an electoral bloc with the SED they would act as a bridge to their sister parties in the FRG. The voters were also asked whether they were 'for or against German unity and a just peace treaty'. This was, as they knew, in reality an appeal to support the creation of an East German state. Despite a massive propaganda campaign and considerable manipulation of the voting results, it was impossible to hide the fact that a third of the electorate had voted against the proposals, which was enough to convince the SED leadership that elections to the *Volkskammer* needed to be delayed for at least a year.

Stalin did not give his final consent to setting up the East German state until the outcome of August elections in West Germany had made it clear that no compromise was possible with the Western powers. On 7 October the *Volkskongress* proclaimed the formation of the German Democratic Republic (GDR) (see Map 8) as 'a powerful bulwark in the struggle for the accomplishment of the National Front of Democratic Germany'.[33] The SMAD was replaced by the Soviet Control Commission, and most of its responsibilities were transferred to the GDR. For the time being the *Volksrat* became the provisional parliament, and a government headed by Otto Grotewohl and Walther Ulbricht was formed on 12 October (see p. 326). Although Stalin might still have entertained the possibility of sacrificing the GDR for the reunification of a neutral Germany, Gerhart Eisler, the director of the information department of the Economic Commission remarked prophetically at a meeting on 4 October that 'once we have set up a government, we will never give it up, neither through elections or other methods'. Ulbricht then added 'A few still have not understood this.'[34]

Conclusion

At the time, the division of Germany seemed inevitable. Yet for Stalin the creation of the FRG was a major defeat, which left the Ruhr and most of Germany in the hands of the Western Allies. The GDR has been described by Willy Loth as Stalin's 'unwanted child',[35] and its creation was essentially a response to the policies of the Western Allies. However, whether partition could have been avoided is open to debate. In theory some sort of neutral Germany could perhaps have been created, but the Western Allies were not alone in distrusting Stalin's motives. The record of rapine and pillage committed by the Red Army in 1945 was, in the eyes of the West Germans, a major deterrent to risking a neutral Germany, which would be vulnerable to a Soviet takeover. The divisions between the former allies were also reflected amongst the German political élites. In June 1947 the minister–presidents of the German *Länder* in the four

---

The GDR leadership: Walther Ulbricht, 1893–1973, and Otto Grotewohl, 1894–1964

Ulbricht initially trained as a cabinetmaker. After fighting in the Great War, he joined the Spartacus League and then the KPD. He was a member of the *Reichstag*, 1928–33, and fled to Moscow on Hitler's rise to power. There he was secretary of the KPD's Politbureau in exile and co-founder of the National Committee for a Free Germany in 1943. In 1946 he became the first secretary of the SED. When the GDR was founded, Ulbricht exercised the real power on the basis of his role in the SED. From 1960 to 1973 he was chairman of the GDR's State Council.

Otto Grotewohl joined the SPD in 1912, and when he returned from the war in 1918 joined the USPD. He went into the *Reichstag* as an SPD deputy in 1925 and worked in the SPD underground, 1933–38. In 1945 he was chairman of the Central Council of the SPD and played a key role in the merger of the SPD and KPD in 1946. As minister–president of the GDR he was effectively a figurehead.

zones of occupation met in Munich to discuss national unity, but the conference rapidly ended in stalemate as the East Germans proposed a strongly centralized model of government, which the West Germans feared would lead to Soviet domination.

15 *The Cold War and the Two Germanies, 1950–88*

TIMELINE

1949	*22 Nov.*	Petersberg Treaty
1950	*25 June*	Outbreak of Korean War
	9 Aug.	FRG constitution extended to West Berlin
	8 Sept.	GDR joins Comecon
1951	*15 Apr.*	European Coal and Steel Community replaces Ruhr Authority
1952	*10 Mar.*	Stalin's note proposing a united but neutral Germany
	26 May	General Treaty signed in Bonn
	27 May	EDC Treaty signed in Paris
1953	*5 Mar.*	Stalin's death
	16–18 June	Strikes and disturbances in GDR
1954	*26 Feb.*	Basic Law amended to permit creation of *Bundeswehr*
	31 Aug.	French Assembly rejects EDC
	19–23 Oct.	London Conference agrees to FRG's sovereignty and membership of NATO
1955	*5 May*	FRG becomes a sovereign state
	9 May	FRG joins NATO
	14 May	Warsaw Pact set up
	9–13 Sept.	Adenauer's Moscow visit
	20 Sept.	USSR recognizes GDR's sovereignty
	22 Sept.	Hallstein Doctrine announced
1956	*23 Oct.–4 Nov.*	Hungarian uprising crushed
1957	*25 Mar.*	Treaty of Rome signed creating EEC
1958	*27 Nov.*	Khruschev issues Berlin ultimatum.
1961	*13 Aug.*	Border between East and West Berlin closed. Start of construction of Berlin Wall
1963	*22 Jan.*	The Elysée Treaty
1968	*21 Aug.*	Warsaw Pact intervenes in Czechoslovakia
1970	*19 Mar.*	Stoph–Brandt meeting at Erfurt
	12 Aug.	FRG–USSR Treaty signed in Moscow
	7 Dec.	FRG–Polish Treaty signed
1971	*3 Sept.*	Four-Power agreement on Berlin
1972	*21 Dec.*	Basic Treaty signed between FRG and GDR
1973	*11 Dec.*	Prague Treaty between FRG and Czechoslovakia
1975	*1 Aug.*	Helsinki Declaration
1979	*14 Dec.*	NATO's 'twin track' decision
1980	*13 Dec.*	Martial law declared in Poland
1985	*11 Mar.*	Gorbachev becomes general secretary of Communist party of USSR
1987	*7–11 Sept.*	Honecker visits FRG

Introduction

The two German states were the products of the Cold War, and from the beginning were bitter rivals, each intent on reuniting the whole of

Germany in its image. The Federal Republic traced its origins to the Bismarckian Reich and, as such, claimed the former German territory beyond the Oder–Neisse line, while the GDR argued that, unlike its rival in the West, it had made a true break with the past. As a result of the 'popular revolution', which purged the Soviet Zone of Nazism in the immediate post-war years, it alone could claim the moral high ground and represent the new Germany. Its historical mission was to create a united German workers' state purged of both capitalism and the considerable remnants of Nazism.

In the early fifties both states were *de facto* protectorates of the occupying powers. In West Germany the Occupation Statute, which the new West German state had to sign with its former occupiers in 1949, gave the Allied high commissioners extensive rights to control foreign policy, approve domestic legislation and intervene whenever they felt that these rights might be threatened. Similarly in the GDR, the Soviet Control Commission was in reality a 'parallel government'[1] which was possessed of even wider powers. Both states were integrated at varying speeds into the opposing economic, political and military systems of their occupiers. The Cold War and the division of Europe created the parameters within which the two states conducted their foreign policies and attempted to come to terms with the consequences of the lost war.

Key issues

- Why did Adenauer attach so much importance to Western integration?
- To what extent did this intensify what Christoph Klessmann calls the 'reactive mechanism' of the Cold War?
- How effective was the Hallstein Doctrine?
- Why was the position of the GDR so vulnerable during the period 1949–61?
- What was the diplomatic significance of the construction of the Berlin Wall?
- Why did the GDR initially view Bonn's switch to *Ostpolitik* with considerable suspicion?
- What were the aims of *Ostpolitik* and how successful was it?
- What did the GDR gain from *Ostpolitik*?
- How did the FRG avoid a contradiction between its *Ostpolitik* and Western integration?

Adenauer and Western integration, 1949–54

For Adenauer Western integration was the 'great hope of the 1950s'[2] because it offered the dual prospect of close co-operation with the Western European democracies and security within an Atlantic community dominated by the USA. In time it would also become a means for revising the occupation statute and securing greater independence for the FRG. Integration was also supported by Washington, for whom it was not only the means for containing Soviet Russia, but also a way of preventing the re-emergence of a strong, belligerent Germany.

Adenauer cleverly exploited the situation created by the Cold War to achieve an ever-closer integration of the FRG into western Europe. His first foreign policy success came with the Petersberg Agreement in November 1949. This permitted the FRG 'to re-enter the international sphere'[3] by joining the Council of Europe and the OEEC as an independent state, to open consulates in other countries and to have a seat on the board of the International Authority of the Ruhr. Adenauer had already floated ideas for joint Franco-German ownership of the Ruhr, and was therefore receptive to Schuman's plan for the pooling of the European coal and steel industries under supranational control to create a European Coal and Steel Community (ECSC), which would replace the International Authority of the Ruhr. He understood only too well that this plan was also a means for ensuring that France retained more influence over the Ruhr than its economic strength warranted, yet to him these concessions were worth making. By preventing Franco-German economic rivalry, the ECSC treaty of 18 April 1951 broke the long tradition of Franco-German hostility, and 'fulfilled many of the functions of a peace treaty'[4] between the two powers.

Adenauer also believed that European integration could solve the difficult question of German rearmament. As early as the spring of 1950, he was urging the creation of an armed security police and a West German military component to 'an international legion'.[5] The outbreak of the Korean War in June led to increasing demands for a West German defence contribution, to which the French responded with the proposal for a European Defence Community (the Pleven Plan) in which West German troops would be firmly subordinated to a European Defence Commission. Adenauer immediately grasped that he could use German rearmament as a means of persuading the Western powers to abolish the occupation statute and grant sovereignty to the FRG.

In May 1952 both the EDC Treaty and the General Treaty were signed. By the latter agreement the Western powers consented to abolish the occupation statute and recognize the sovereignty of the Federal Republic. They also pledged to work for a reunified, democratic Germany modelled on the existing FRG and anchored firmly in the growing western European community. As the Western powers still maintained their rights to negotiate, at some future date, a peace treaty with a united Germany, the question of the eastern frontiers was left open. This complex web of treaties completely unravelled when France refused to ratify the EDC Treaty on 30 August 1954. By guaranteeing to keep the size of the West German army to what had been agreed in the EDC Treaty and by voluntarily renouncing nuclear weapons, Adenauer ensured that a new General Treaty was rapidly negotiated in October.

France, weakened by its defeat in Indochina, did not oppose the FRG's entry into NATO in May 1955. The Western Allies repeated their commitment to work towards a united federal Germany integrated into the European community, but until that happened units of their troops would still be based in the FRG, and Berlin would remain under four-power control (see Map 9).

Hans-Peter Schwarz has argued that the 1955 treaties compare favourably with the Vienna Settlement of 1815 (see pp. 12–14). A new, stable West European state system had been created, which was to survive virtually unchanged up to 1990, but this success was paid for by Germany. Although, in theory, the door was kept open for reunification, in practice the integration of the FRG into NATO, the ECSC and the Council of Europe made this unity impossible to achieve in the foreseeable future. To use Klessmann's phrase, Western integration intensified 'the reactive mechanism'[6] of the Cold War, which led to the GDR's ever-deeper integration into the Soviet bloc. This was the danger Kurt Schumacher was referring to when he committed the SPD in 1950 to opposing any agreement that did not 'leave open and even strengthen the possibilities of German unity'.[7] Adenauer's Westpolitik had the support of most West Germans, but it was, in Hermann Graml's words, 'constantly subjected to furious detailed criticism and anxious attempts to apply the brakes',[8] because it cemented the division of Germany into two states.

See Document 76

Soviet efforts to halt the FRG's integration into the West

Moscow and the GDR tried to exploit this fear of the consequences of Western integration to halt West German rearmament. From the autumn of 1950 through to the spring of 1952 the Russians and the GDR leadership proposed a series of initiatives aimed at achieving a united but neutral Germany. How far these initiatives were genuine offers or just attempts to slow down Western integration and to destabilize the Adenauer regime is a matter of heated historical debate. The most controversial of these initiatives was launched by Stalin in March 1952 when he proposed an independent Germany and free national elections

The Politbureau or Political Bureau was the executive committee of the SED, which was modelled on the Politbureau of the USSR

The GDR and German unity

The GDR Politbureau was divided over how unity could be achieved. In the autumn of 1950 Ulbricht, who could only envisage German unity if it resulted in the creation of a Stalinist Germany, was isolated, while Otto Grotwohl, supported by other 'liberals' like Rudolph Herrnstadt and Anton Ackermann, were ready to explore different roads to unity. Herrnstadt even told the Central Committee of the SED in October that his colleagues should not think that 'the coming unified democratic Germany would simply be an enlarged copy of the present GDR'.[9]

supervised by a commission of the four former occupying powers. Germany would have to accept permanent neutrality, but would be spared reparations and be free to form any government its people voted for. It would even be allowed to have a small army. In Hans-Peter Schwarz's words a 'certain mythology'[10] grew up around the history of this note, as it did with 'the stab in the back' myth of 1918 (see p. 175). There was a strong body of West German opinion, led by Schumacher, Jakob Kaiser, the minister for all German affairs, and Paul Sethe, the influential editor of the *Frankfurter Allgemeine* newspaper, that was convinced that Adenauer should have been more responsive to Stalin's initiative. This view has been supported more recently by Rolf Steininger and Willy Loth, although rejected strongly by other historians such as Hans-Peter Schwarz and Gerhard Wettig.[11] Neither Adenauer nor the Western powers, however, were ready to jeopardize all that had so far been achieved in integrating the FRG economically and militarily into the West. Adenauer was also sceptical as to whether Stalin would risk the potential domino effect which self-determination for the GDR would have on the other Soviet satellites in eastern Europe. Consequently the Soviet initiative was never seriously taken up.

After Stalin's death in March 1953, the question of German unity was again raised by Winston Churchill, who proposed a four-power summit to discuss the question, while Lavrentii Beria, the deputy Soviet prime minister, was actually considering abandoning the GDR to the West for $10 billion, provided that it resulted in a neutral and peaceful, reunited Germany. However, the riots in East Germany in June (see p. 330) and Beria's subsequent fall, as well as American and West German reluctance to open the Pandora's box of German unity, just at a time when the consolidation of western Europe was taking place, ensured that the Big Four summit did not take place until July 1955 in Geneva. By this time the Federal Republic had been recognized as a sovereign state and joined NATO, while the GDR's membership of the new Warsaw Pact, which had been created to counter NATO, was imminent. Khrushchev effectively ruled out unification by observing that Russia would not tolerate any threat to the 'political and social achievements' of the GDR, and two months later recognized its sovereignty.

The FRG as a European power, 1955–58

Relations with the Western powers

Adenauer's foreign policy was based on Western integration, the core of which was Franco-German co-operation and a close alliance with the USA. He viewed the 1957 Treaty of Rome, which set up the EEC, as an event which was equal in importance to the unification of Germany in 1871. His American and European policies worked well as long as the Americans were ready to commit a large number of troops to Europe and make no concessions to the USSR about the status of the GDR or Berlin. Once America started in 1957 to adopt a more flexible policy towards the USSR and consider cutting its garrison in Germany, Adenauer drew closer to France. The incipient Franco-German *entente* survived the coming to power of General de Gaulle in 1958, and strengthened during the acute crisis over Berlin, 1959–61, even though both statesmen had fundamentally different visions of Europe, as de Gaulle wanted only a very loose confederation of states completely independent of America. Their complex political relationship has been characterized as a 'masked conflict' or a 'senile friendship based on a misunderstanding'.[12]

> **Entente**: understanding or friendship between two states

Relations with the GDR and the USSR

In September 1955 Adenauer visited Moscow and agreed to the exchange of ambassadors in return for the repatriation of the remaining German prisoners of war. He was, however, determined that this should not lead to a diplomatic recognition of the GDR, and thus announced in the *Bundestag* on 22 September what became known as the Hallstein Doctrine. He stated that Bonn would treat the recognition by the GDR of any state other than the USSR as an unfriendly act which would result in the termination of diplomatic relations. Financial assistance and development aid for the new states in Asia and Africa was also made strictly dependent on their non-recognition of East Germany. However, the longer the division of Germany lasted, the more this policy began to be seen as a quixotic attempt to 'overcome the status quo by ignoring it'.[13] It cut the GDR off from the Western and developing worlds, but at the price of further integrating it into the Soviet bloc. By 1957, officials like Herbert Blankenhorn, the FRG's representative to NATO, and Karl Pfleiderer, the West German ambassador to Yugoslavia, were beginning to anticipate the thinking of ten years later (see pp. 302–5) and argue that the recognition of the GDR and closer economic links with the other satellite states would 'slowly draw them step by step into the direction of the West and as a consequence towards liberty'.[14]

> **Hallstein Doctrine**: This was named after Professor Hallstein, the state secretary in the Bonn Foreign Ministry, 1951–57

The Berlin crisis, 1958–61

The main challenge to the existence of the GDR stemmed from the 'miraculous' economic recovery of the FRG (see p. 317). The bright lights and prosperity of West Germany inevitably attracted many of the GDR's younger and more ambitious citizens through the still-open frontier in Berlin – a situation which both the West German and American governments did everything to encourage. Between 1945 and 1961 altogether about one-sixth of the whole East German population had fled westwards through the hole in the Iron Curtain in Berlin. A dramatic improvement in the standard of living would stem this exodus, but to achieve this it was first of all necessary to stop the brain drain of skilled workers and professionals to the FRG (see p. 318). This would, however, entail forcing the Western Allies to change the status of West Berlin.

Khrushchev, the first secretary of the Soviet Communist party, was at first cautious when urged by the East Germans to do this, but by the autumn of 1958 he was increasingly confident that the USSR was strong enough to force the USA into revising the status of West Berlin and even possibly into signing peace treaties with the two German states. By putting pressure on West Berlin, he believed he could easily squeeze concessions from the Western Allies without the risk of war. As he earthily observed, 'Berlin is the testicles of the West . . . every time I want to make the West scream I squeeze on Berlin.'[15]

The first Berlin crisis was 1948–49. See p. 288

The second Berlin crisis began on 10 November 1958, when Khrushchev called for a peace treaty with the two German states. On 27 November he issued a six-month ultimatum, demanding the demilitarization of West Berlin, the withdrawal of Western troops, and its change of status into a 'free city'. If the Western Allies refused to sign a peace treaty with the two German states, Khrushchev threatened to conclude a peace treaty with the GDR alone and to recognize its sovereignty over East Berlin, which was still nominally under four-power control. This would enable it to control access to West Berlin and interfere with traffic using the corridors from the FRG. The Western Allies would thus have to deal with East German rather than Russian officials, and so in effect be compelled to recognize the GDR, which would shatter the Hallstein Doctrine.

The Globke Plan: according to this plan drawn up by Hans Globke, the state secretary in the chancellery, the FRG and GDR would recognize each other's sovereignty, and Berlin would become a free city. A referendum on unification would be held within five years, and if there was a majority for reunification, free elections would follow for a parliament representing a united Germany. The plan was a development of an earlier proposal made in the spring of 1958 for the neutralization of the GDR along the lines of the Austrian settlement of 1955

Although the Western Allies rejected the ultimatum, they agreed that a foreign ministers' conference should meet in Geneva in the summer of 1959. Adenauer viewed with growing alarm London's and Washington's evident desire for compromise, and in an attempt to avert damaging concessions, launched the Globke Plan, which combined proposals for both a provisional and a comprehensive solution to the German problem.

The deepening crisis, however, ensured that neither this plan nor a revised version of it in 1960 were ever discussed. At Geneva no agreement was secured and over the next two years Khrushchev successfully kept up the pressure. Officially the Western powers continued to demand free all-German elections, but plans for creating a nuclear-free zone in Central Europe, recognizing Poland's western frontiers and the GDR, were also seriously considered. Adenauer, meanwhile, was desperate to stop any of these plans from reducing the FRG to a neutral, third-class state, but in May 1960 when the Paris conference was due to open, he had no idea what President Eisenhower and Harold Macmillan, the British prime minister, might be about to propose. It was therefore, for him at least, 'a gift from heaven',[16] when Khrushchev used the shooting down of an American spy plane over Russia as an excuse to walk out of the summit meeting, and wait until a new American president was elected in the autumn.

On 5 May 1960 a Soviet anti-aircraft missile shot down an American U-2 spy plane over the Urals

Until the autumn of 1960 it was Khrushchev who orchestrated the Berlin crisis, and Ulbricht was only a minor player, but, faced with the flood of refugees to the West in 1960–61, Ulbricht began to press Khrushchev to sign a separate peace treaty with the GDR, at one point sharply commenting: 'You only *talk* about a peace treaty, but don't *do* anything about it.'[17] Although John Kennedy, the new American president who had been elected in November 1960, was tougher than Khrushchev had expected, Washington's response did indicate a possible solution to the Berlin problem. While Kennedy strengthened American forces in Europe, he also urged negotiation on the whole German question and pointedly stressed in a television broadcast on 25 July 1961 that the West was mainly interested in free access to West Berlin rather than to Berlin as a whole. Hitherto Khrushchev had rejected the possibility of closing off the East Berlin frontier, as he had aimed at detaching West Berlin from the FRG rather than cutting it off from East Germany. However, the growing unrest in the GDR caused by the forced collectivization of agriculture, which in turn increased the number of refugees (see p. 333) to the West, persuaded him to agree to Ulbricht's demands for closing off East Berlin from the West. This decision was confirmed at a meeting of the Warsaw Pact states in Moscow on 3–5 August 1961, and in the early morning of 13 August the operation was efficiently and swiftly carried out (see p. 333).

See Document 77 and Map 9

The construction of the Berlin Wall marked a turning-point in the German question:

- The United States and its allies, by tolerating it, in effect acknowledged the GDR's right to exist.
- The Wall both consolidated the GDR and ensured that the Soviet Union retained responsibility for maintaining international access to West Berlin.
- The existence of the GDR was assured for the foreseeable future, and ultimately there would be little option for Bonn but to recognize it and seek, in the words of Egon Bahr, the SPD politician and father of *Ostpolitik*, 'change through rapprochement'.[18]

Ostpolitik: the 'eastern' policy of the FRG towards the GDR and the Eastern Bloc after 1969

The desire of Britain and America for a détente with the USSR, which was obvious throughout the Berlin crisis, persuaded Adenauer to strengthen his links with Gaullist France. He consequently supported de Gaulle's dramatic veto of Britain's application to join the EEC in January 1963, and on 23 January signed the Franco-German Treaty of Friendship (Elysée Treaty). When this treaty was debated in the *Bundestag*, a preamble was added which emphasized that it did not mark a shift in the FRG's foreign policy, which was hostile to Britain and America. Nevertheless, Adenauer's pro-French policy marked the beginning of bitter divisions in the CDU–CSU between the Atlanticists, like Ludwig Erhard and Gerhard Schröder, who looked primarily to Washington and wanted Britain in the EEC, and the Gaullists like Franz Joseph Strauss and Adenauer himself, who now looked to Paris and ultimately wanted an integrated western Europe independent of the USA.

Détente: A state of lessened tension or growing relaxation between two states

27   The Berlin Wall being constructed at the Harzer Strasse, 18 August 1961

Presse- und Informationsamt der Bundesregierung, no. 60479

The development of *Ostpolitik*, 1963–69

The Berlin crisis of 1958–61 had made it clear that the United States accepted the status quo and was ready to give a greater priority to a *détente* in Europe than to German unification. The West Germans, as Willy Brandt was later to put it, 'lost certain illusions that had outlived the hopes underlying them'.[19] Thus gradually during the 1960s Bonn began the slow and painful process of jettisoning the Hallstein Doctrine and rethinking its policy towards the GDR and the Soviet bloc.

28 Konrad Adenauer (left) and Charles de Gaulle embrace after signing the Franco-German Treaty of Friendship, Paris, 22 January 1963

Presse- und Informationsamt der Bundesregierung, no. 131178/EN

The first tentative signs of a new approach from Bonn were visible as early as June 1962, when the Adenauer government tried unsuccessfully to use the decision to renew inter-German trade and the granting of credits to force the GDR to allow West Berliners access to East Berlin. Then, in December 1963, Willy Brandt, as mayor of West Berlin, seized the initiative and negotiated directly with East Berlin. By agreeing to refer to it as the 'GDR capital', he secured for 18 days the right of West Berliners to visit their relatives across the Wall. Later these arrangements were extended to cover public holidays up to Whitsun 1966. They were a good example of the policy of 'small steps',[20] which Brandt had been urging Bonn to take in order to alleviate the plight of the East Germans.

Ostpolitik began to take a more definite shape when the Grand Coalition under Kurt Kiesinger was formed in December 1966, with Willy Brandt as foreign secretary (see p. 340). In his first few months in

---

Willy Brandt, 1913–92

During the Third Reich Brandt worked in the SPD resistance movement in Norway. He returned to Berlin in 1946. From 1957 to 1966 he was mayor of West Berlin. He was a charismatic figure and was compared to America's J. F. Kennedy. He led the SPD election campaigns of 1961 and 1965, but failed to win sufficient seats to put his party in power. In 1966, when the SPD joined the Grand Coalition, he became foreign minister and began to work towards a better understanding with the GDR. In 1969 he became chancellor and was able to pursue a more vigorous policy of *Ostpolitik*.

See Document 78

power, Kiesinger made several statements defining the scope of the new policy. The old references to the East Zone from the Adenauer era were replaced by the more cryptic references to 'the other part of Germany', and he stressed that by encouraging 'human, economic and cultural relations' he wished 'to bridge the gulfs and not deepen them'.[21] In April 1967 Kiesinger presented the GDR with several practical proposals for improving inter-German trade, communications and contacts between relatives cut off by the division of Germany. This was supplemented by an open letter from the SPD to the 7th Party Congress of the SED suggesting talks between the two parties.

At first these initiatives were brushed aside by the SED. Ulbricht went out of his way to dismiss compromise and to argue that unity was only possible between two socialist Germanies. However, to avoid isolation in the Soviet bloc, where there was a considerable desire for détente, the GDR had to go through the motions of following up Bonn's proposals. In May, Willi Stoph, the prime minister, demanded the opening up of normal diplomatic relations between the two states. When Kiesinger replied by suggesting setting up a joint committee of officials to make proposals for facilitating contacts between the populations of the two states, he immediately met 'a wall of maximum demands' in a second letter which insisted upon the recognition of West Berlin as 'a separate political entity', as well as a treaty between the 'two sovereign German states'.[22]

Warsaw Pact troops invaded Czechoslovakia to replace the Dubcek government, whose reforms were undermining the Eastern bloc. In November Brezhnev defended the invasion by stressing that any threat to socialism in a Warsaw Pact country was a threat to all its allies

The 'Prague Spring', the liberalization process initiated by Alexander Dubcek on Czechoslovakia, was perceived by East Berlin as an object lesson on the dangers of making too many domestic concessions. In West Germany, on the other hand, Soviet intervention in Czechoslovakia in August 1968 and then the promulgation of the Brezhnev Doctrine were seen by many on the right wing of the CDU–CSU to prove the bankruptcy of *Ostpolitik* and led to demands for a return to the Cold-War policies of the Adenauer days. Brandt, however, refused to discontinue *Ostpolitik* and argued that the USSR would be ready to make concessions now that it had firmly re-established its control in Eastern Europe.

See Document 78

After his election victory of September 1969 (see p. 344), Brandt was in a position to implement *Ostpolitik* more fully. Together with his foreign minister, Walther Scheel, the party chairman of the FDP, he embarked upon negotiating a complex set of interlocking treaties which were to mark a major turning-point in relations between Bonn and Moscow and between the two Germanies themselves. On one level Brandt's policy was primarily a matter of coming to terms with the realities of 1945, or as he put it in his famous television speech from Moscow in August 1970, 'the political situation as it exists in Europe'.[23] This, of course, involved the *de facto* recognition of the East German regime, although his whole strategy, by defusing the tense situation between the two states, was also aimed at leaving the door ajar for future unification.

Ostpolitik was not conducted in a vacuum. Brandt was anxious to reassure the Western powers that he had no intention of reviving the

Rapallopolitik of the Weimar Republic and was thus adamant that the FRG did not intended to weaken 'its Adenauerian anchoring in the West'.[24] He told Brezhnev repeatedly that Bonn was committed to membership of NATO and the European Community. In the course of 1970–72 five sets of intricate and interdependent agreements were negotiated: the treaties between the FRG, the USSR, Poland, Czechoslovakia and the GDR and then the four-power agreement on Berlin.

In 1922 the Weimar Republic signed the Treaty of Rapallo with the USSR to gain an element of independence from the Western powers, Britain and France (see p. 182)

The Moscow, Warsaw and Prague Treaties, 1970–73

The key to a successful *Ostpolitik* lay in an improvement in relations between Bonn and Moscow. The FRG's signature of the Nuclear Non-Proliferation Treaty in November 1969, its readiness to increase technological and economic links with Russia and its willingness to support a European security conference, which Moscow hoped would confirm its post-war hegemony in eastern Europe, were all preliminary concessions made with that aim in mind. Against a background of fierce opposition from the CDU press, the Moscow Treaty, which was 'the foundation stone of *Ostpolitik*',[25] was signed on 12 August by Brandt and Brezhnev. Both the USSR and the FRG declared that they had no territorial claims against any other state. The FRG recognized the 'non-violability' of Poland's western frontier and of its frontier with the GDR. In a second part of the treaty the FRG committed itself to negotiating treaties with Poland, the GDR and Czechoslovakia. While Bonn still did not officially recognize the GDR, it agreed to abandon the Hallstein Doctrine and accept that both Germanies would eventually become members of the United Nations.

The side note reads:

The Non-Proliferation Treaty, which aimed to prevent the further spread of nuclear weapons, was signed by the USA and the USSR in July 1968

The Russians had in effect gained West German recognition of their central European empire, yet this recognition was not unconditional. The West Germans also presented Brezhnev with a 'letter on German unity' which stressed the FRG's right to work towards a state of peace in Europe in which 'the German people regains its unity in free self-determination'.[26] Similarly, the term 'inviolable' – as applied to the Oder–Neisse line and the inner German frontier – rather than the preferred Soviet word 'immutable', arguably kept the door open for a later peaceful revision of the frontiers. Finally, the ratification of the treaty was made dependent on a four-power agreement over Berlin.

Negotiations with the Poles ran parallel to the Moscow talks, but were loaded with a greater emotional freight. The Poles were uneasy that their frontiers were in effect recognized over their heads by the FRG and the USSR in the Moscow negotiations. There were, too, disagreements about the legality of the expulsion of the Germans from Upper Silesia and elsewhere in 1945 (see p. 276), and about the number of ethnic Germans still in Poland. Nevertheless, by December 1970 the negotiations were at last completed. Both states recognized that they had no territorial demands on each other and that the Oder–Neisse line was 'inviolable'. Trade and financial assistance from Bonn was to be increased, while the ethnic

Germans still within Poland were to be allowed to emigrate to the FRG.

When Brandt flew into Warsaw to sign the treaty, he visited the site of the former ghetto and, as a gesture of atonement for Germany's wartime crimes, went down on his knees in front of the memorial to the Jews who had been murdered there by the Nazis. This deeply symbolic act was viewed with mixed feelings at home, as indeed was the whole Warsaw Treaty, since it was felt that Brandt had ceded too much for too little, particularly when it later became clear that the Poles were only issuing a limited number of exit visas to the ethnic Germans.

The negotiations between the FRG and Czechoslovakia started in October 1970 but dragged on until June 1973 when the Treaty of Prague was signed, although it took the *Bundestag* another year to ratify it. Besides guaranteeing existing frontiers and renouncing the use of force, it also made the Munich Treaty of 1938 (see p. 250) 'void' whilst safeguarding the retrospective validity, as far as it concerned such matters as marriages or wills, of German law in the Sudetenland during the period 1938–45. Czechoslovakia also agreed to allow the emigration of any Czechs with German citizenship – some 10,000 in all.

Four-power negotiations over Berlin, 1970–71

The quadripartite Berlin negotiations in effect made the Western Allies the 'guarantors of *Ostpolitik*'.[27] This involvement of the Western powers strengthened Brandt's negotiating position *vis-à-vis* both the Russians and the East Germans. It also reassured NATO that *Ostpolitik* would not lead to a weakening of the FRG's links with the West and a return to the *Rapallopolitik* of the 1920s. In February 1970, in response to an earlier Western note of August 1969 requesting discussions on the thorny problem of access to West Berlin (see Map 9), the Russians agreed to quadripartite discussions on Berlin. The Western Allies wanted a settlement, underwritten by the USSR, which would finally confirm West Berlin's links with the FRG and guarantee its freedom of access to the West (see Map 9). At first the Russians were anxious to avoid making too many concessions, but their desire for a general European security conference and their reluctance to alienate President Nixon, at a time when he was planning to visit China, made them more ready to make concessions over Berlin. The agreement, signed on 3 September 1971, was a 'milestone in the history of divided Berlin and divided Germany'.[28] The Soviets conceded three vital principles:

The Chinese government was highly critical of the Soviet policy of *détente* and relations had deteriorated to the point where armed clashes had occurred along the Sino-Soviet border

- unimpeded traffic between West Berlin and the FRG;
- the recognition of West Berlin's ties with the FRG;
- the right for West Berliners to visit East Berlin 'under conditions comparable to those applying to other persons entering these areas'.[29]

In return, the Western powers agreed that the Western sectors of Berlin were not legally part of the FRG (even if in practice they had been since

West Berlin adopted the Basic Law in 1950), and that consequently Bonn should avoid holding provocative federal ceremonies, such as the election of the president of the FRG, there.

The Basic Treaty

A settlement with the GDR was the ' last and most important part of the *Ostpolitik* treaties',[30] and could only be achieved after the Moscow Treaty and the quadripartite agreement on Berlin. Brandt offered the GDR 'negotiations at government level' in his first formal policy statement to the new *Bundestag* on 28 October 1969. The leadership of the SED was divided in its approach. Ulbricht was now more inclined to explore the possibilities of a rapprochement with Brandt than the rest of the Politbureau, and was, as he said in Moscow in August 1970, quite convinced that a treaty with the FRG was 'a means to move forwards large numbers of Social Democratic members' who 'are supporters of capitalism, but also against the Vietnam War'.[31] Honecker, who was being groomed to take over from Ulbricht (see p. 357), and Stoph were more cautious and were acutely aware of the possible threat to the stability of the GDR of an open-ended agreement with Bonn. Even Brezhnev, despite his desire for a general European *détente* was fearful that inter-German relations might take on a momentum of their own and wrench East Germany out of the Soviet orbit. Thus the initial contacts between the two German states were characterized by extreme caution on the side of the GDR. Nevertheless, in March, as a result of Soviet pressure, Stoph invited Brandt to Erfurt. The meeting showed the potential dangers of *Ostpolitik* for the GDR as the immense enthusiasm of the crowds for Willy Brandt threatened to escalate out of the control of the police and gave the FRG an easy propaganda victory. Stoph insisted rigidly on full diplomatic recognition of the GDR by the FRG. Although Brandt could not concede this, he did tell Stoph that '[n]o one must try to subject the other to overweening influence. I have not come here to demand the liquidation of any ties of the GDR or of any social order.'[32] Nevertheless, despite this concession, the only agreed joint statement the two heads of state could make was the mutual declaration that 'war would never again originate from German soil'. Two months later Stoph and Brandt again met at Kassel just inside the West German border. As the East German delegation had been firmly instructed by Brezhnev to avoid the question of inter-German ties, and to concentrate on scoring propaganda points, the talks were inconclusive and both sides agreed to a pause for reflection before further meetings. In July Brezhnev stressed in discussions with Honecker the solid advantages of the treaty with the FRG for the GDR in that '[i]ts frontiers, its existence will be confirmed for all the world to see'. Nevertheless, he warned him that Brandt was aiming at the 'Social Democratisation' of the GDR and added: 'It . . . must not come to a process of rapprochement between the FRG and the GDR . . . Concentrate everything on the all-sided strengthening of the GDR, as you call it.'[33]

29 Willy Brandt on his knees before the memorial to the Warsaw Ghetto, Warsaw, 7 December 1970

Presse- und Informationsamt der Bundesregierung, no. 33028

The negotiations between the two German states started in November 1970. Initially little progress was made, but the deadlock was broken once the draft of the Four-Power Berlin Treaty was in place in September 1971. For it to be completed and signed, a series of technical agreements on transit traffic, the rights of West Berliners to visit East Berlin and postal communications had to be negotiated and included in the treaty. Once this was achieved, the two states moved on to negotiate the crucial Basic Treaty, which was only signed in December 1972. In it the FRG recognized the GDR as an equal and sovereign state. The FRG did, however, stress that it still considered the people of the GDR to have a common German citizenship and, in a 'Letter concerning German unity' which it presented to East Berlin, it repeated its determination to work for German reunification. Despite intense opposition from the CDU (see p. 346), the Basic Treaty was ratified in May 1973. The existence of the two Germanies now seemed to be a permanent international fact, and both states joined the United Nations in 1973.

Ostpolitik in practice, 1973–88

In May 1974 the two German states set up what the FRG insisted on calling 'permanent representations' in each other's capital. Pointedly, the West German representative, Gunter Gaus, reported back to the chancellor, while his East German opposite number, Michael Kohl, formally reported like any other diplomat to the GDR foreign minister. As Chancellor Helmut Kohl was to observe ten years later, the task of *Ostpolitik* was an attempt 'to ease the painful consequences of the division of our fatherland [and] to strengthen the consciousness of belonging together among all Germans, to preserve what unites and to create new commonalities between them'.[34] Up to the autumn of 1989 most West Germans believed that the inner German frontier would survive for generations. Bonn thus exploited every contact and exchange, whether financial, political, social or sporting, with the GDR to create a whole web of close links or 'interdependences'. On the other hand, Bonn stopped well short of destabilizing the GDR, as it feared that this would trigger Russian intervention and end the benign consequences of *Ostpolitik*. The East German regime reacted defensively to this 'aggression in felt slippers',[35] as Otto Winzer, its foreign minister, had so perceptively phrased it as early as 1963, by attempting to fence itself off from the West. It declared itself to be a separate 'socialist nation' permanently allied to the USSR. West German visitors were reported on by the security police, transit routes were strictly controlled and the case-histories of the East Germans who applied to travel to the West were investigated with particular care.

Helmut Kohl was chancellor, 1982–1998. See p. 352

Viewed from Bonn, could *Ostpolitik* be called a success? It certainly had, in the words of a *Bundestag resolution* of 1987, 'directly useful results for the people'.[36] Transit links between East and West Germany were modernized with the help of West German subsidies, postal deliveries were improved and telephone calls from the FRG to the GDR climbed from half a million in 1969 to 40 million in 1988. Similarly, personal visits from West to East rose from one million a year in 1969 to eight million in the mid-Seventies. Each visitor had to pay the sum of 13 Deutschmarks a day, which was doubled in October 1980. At the total cost of some 3.5 million Deutschmarks Bonn was also able to buy the freedom of 34,000 political prisoners and facilitate the reuniting of some 250,000 families.

For the GDR the main advantages of *Ostpolitik* were economic. The steady flow of Deutschmarks eastwards was supplemented by generous credits, which enabled the GDR to import vital industrial goods from West Germany. In 1983–84 bank loans of nearly two billion Deutschmarks were negotiated by Franz Joseph Strauss, which saved the GDR from a possibly terminal economic crisis, and did much to restore its economic credibility. Altogether, from 1972 to 1989, some 14 billion Deutschmarks were transferred at state level from Bonn to the GDR. Inevitably this led to a growing financial dependency on West Germany. The two key East German financial link men with Bonn, Alexander

Schalk-Golodkowski and Gerhard Schürer were convinced by 1988 that only some sort of confederation with the FRG could save the GDR from bankruptcy. This would appear to vindicate *Ostpolitik* and helps to explain the collapse of the GDR in 1989, but these credits were not used by Bonn primarily as a tool to bring down the regime. Rather they were a means to stabilize it and to prevent a dramatic collapse, which might lead to a repetition of the traumatic events of 1953 or 1961 and the end of *Ostpolitik*. Certainly up to 1988–89 the assumption was that the Brezhnev doctrine still applied and that Russia would intervene to stop the disintegration of the GDR. Nevertheless, some concessions were demanded for this great flow of credit. In 1984, for example, Strauss extracted from the GDR further alleviations on inter-German travel, and the dismantling of minefields and automatic shooting devices along the frontier.

Schmidt was chancellor 1974–82

Chancellor Helmut Schmidt consciously used *Ostpolitik*, as he wrote later in his memoirs, 'to increase the self-respect of Erich Honecker, Ulbricht's successor, in the international context and reduce the inferiority complexes of the GDR leadership'.[37] Once the CDU–CSU returned to power, Kohl continued this policy. In September 1987 Honecker paid a highly successful state visit to Bonn and right up to 1989 a regular stream of FRG politicians visited East Berlin and were photographed shaking Honecker's hand. One or two critical voices argued that the FRG had allowed the GDR to gain the initiative in *Ostpolitik*, but the consensus of opinion in the governing coalition, the bureaucracy and the SPD was that only 'stabilization' would give the GDR the self-confidence to liberalize.

The FRG between East and West

By the mid-1970s the FRG was, as Schmidt observed, 'in the eyes of the world de facto economically the second world power of the West'[38] and was the fourth largest contributor to the budget of the United Nations.

Hans-Dietrich Genscher was leader of the FDP, 1974–85, and foreign minister, 1974–92

As a major power the FRG faced a potentially serious dilemma. On the one hand it was enmeshed in NATO and the European Community, while on the other it was committed through *Ostpolitik* to a policy of détente with the USSR, the GDR and the other Russian satellites. Any serious East-West confrontation would destroy *Ostpolitik* and force Bonn back to the rigidities of the Adenauer era. Schmidt and his foreign minister, Hans-Dietrich Genscher, consequently worked hard to encourage détente and East–West links through NATO, the EC, the United Nations, the G7 and the many other international organizations that existed in the 1970s.

The EEC fused with the ECSC and EURATOM to form the EC (European Community) in May 1967. The G7 or Group of 7 was composed of the seven states with the world's leading economies

At the Conference on Security and Co-operation, which met at Helsinki, 1973–75, Genscher and Schmidt in alliance with Henry Kissinger, the American secretary of state, managed to defeat the USSR's intention of negotiating what would in effect have been a peace treaty permanently guaranteeing the status quo in eastern Europe. However, they did enthusiastically support the commitment to human rights and the vague-sounding provisions for peaceful co-operation in a variety of areas such as science, the environment, trade and energy which were incorporated in the Helsinki Final Act, as they saw these as the building blocks of détente.

By 1977 the FRG's delicate balance between Western integration and *Ostpolitik* began to come under severe pressure when it became evident that Russia had embarked on a large-scale programme for building a new generation of middle-range nuclear missiles, the SS-20s, which were a direct threat to western Europe. Schmidt played a key role in convincing the NATO leaders in 1979 to adopt the controversial 'two track proposal', which he hoped would salvage the policy of détente by committing NATO to deploying intermediate Pershing II and cruise missiles in Europe in 1983, only if reductions could not first be satisfactorily negotiated with Moscow. However, as a result of the Soviet invasion of Afghanistan in December 1979 and then the eruption of the Solidarity movement in Poland in August 1980, no such agreement was possible.

Brezhnev sent 100,000 troops into Afghanistan to defend a Marxist regime, which had recently seized power

What the West German political establishment now feared most appeared to be about to happen: namely that hostility between the two superpowers would make *Ostpolitik* unworkable. In increasingly desperate attempts by Bonn to escape from this dilemma, *Ostpolitik* began to degenerate into an open appeasement of Moscow and the eastern European regimes. Bonn did not join London and Washington in criticizing the Russian invasion of Afghanistan or the Polish government's reaction to Solidarity. Indeed no less a person than Willy Brandt actually condemned Solidarity for threatening the stability of the Polish regime. When martial law was declared by the Polish government in Poland in December 1981, Schmidt again went out of his way to avoid censuring it. He was unwilling to sacrifice what had already been achieved in *Ostpolitik* for the sake of the Poles. Nevertheless, he did ask Honecker to use his influence in Moscow to moderate Soviet policy arguing that 'in truth . . . both German states have great weight . . . we have a right to throw this weight into the scales'.[39] Ultimately the FRG was left with no option but to deploy the Pershing and cruise missiles in November 1983, although Kohl, Schmidt's successor, took great care to minimize the impact of this action on *Ostpolitik* (see p. 352).

In August 1980, strikes organized by the Solidarity movement paralysed the Danzig shipyards and then spread throughout Poland giving rise to the fear that Soviet troops would invade to crush it

The foreign policy of the GDR, 1973–87

By 1984 132 states had recognized the GDR's sovereignty. Legal recognition enabled it to play a role in international politics through UNESCO and the UN where in the early 1980s it served for a two-year spell as a non-permanent member of the Security Council. It also participated in the Helsinki Conference in 1975 as a fully independent state and signed the Final Act, which was something of a Trojan horse, as it encouraged

See Document 79

dissidents within the GDR to demand greater civil rights (see p. 360). As an ally of the USSR, the GDR began to play an increasingly influential role in advising and assisting the revolutionary Marxist parties emerging in the African states of Angola, Ethiopia, Mozambique and Guinea-Bissau in the 1970s. In return for economic concessions, the GDR provided military and technical experts. By 1980 some 2700 East German military personnel were serving in Africa. The GDR also sent food and equipment to North Vietnam and field hospitals for Russian troops to Afghanistan.

The contradictions between the growing dependence of the GDR on financial credits from Bonn and loyalty to Moscow did not emerge until 1989. For most of the Honecker era, membership of the Warsaw Pact and close co-operation with Moscow remained the bedrock of the GDR's foreign policy. In October 1975, for instance, it signed a 25-year treaty of friendship, co-operation and mutual assistance with the USSR, and in 1980–81 Honecker was a strong advocate of military intervention in Poland to crush the Solidarity movement. Yet, like Schmidt and Kohl, he also attempted to insulate inter-German relations from the effects of growing Russian–American tension, and he kept open the lines of communication with Bonn, even though Moscow vetoed his plans for a summit with Kohl until 1987.

Conclusion

The legacy of Hitler's war tore the German Reich apart. In the new confrontation between Communism and capitalism, the front line in Europe ran through Germany. The partition of Germany favoured the Western powers. On the one side the FRG contained the great industrial complex of the Ruhr and two-thirds of the population of post-war Germany, while on the other the GDR was a small rump cut off from its economic links with the West and faced with the wrenching task of reorientating its economy towards the East. The basic parameters of the FRG's foreign policy were set in the Adenauer era. Integration into a Western bloc protected by American military strength would not only provide a reliable defence against the USSR, but would also create a prosperity which would in time like a magnet draw the GDR out of the Soviet axis. The policy of the GDR was a mirror image of that of the FRG. To defeat the magnet-like pull of the FRG and to stand any chance of appealing over the head of the Bonn government to the German people as a whole, it had to create a dynamic economy which would give the GDR a legitimacy it otherwise lacked. The only way the GDR could break out of the vicious circle caused by the flight of its skilled workers westwards into the FRG was to persuade Khrushchev to have the frontier with West Berlin sealed off.

Once this occurred in August 1961, the GDR gained a certain immunity from the pull of the West. The period of détente, or 'the long peace',[40] which in essence was based on an overestimation by the West of the power and durability of the Soviet bloc, led to the abandonment of the Hallstein Doctrine and the decision by Kiesinger and Brandt to bring about what Egon Bahr called 'change through rapprochement'[41] with the help of *Ostpolitik*. The signature of the Basic Treaty was a turning-point in the relations between the two Germanies. Within their respective blocs both the FRG and the GDR played increasingly important economic, military and political roles. The FRG never tried, as did the Weimar Republic, to balance between Russia and the West. Through NATO and the EC it was clearly anchored in the West, even if its chancellors worked hard to persuade Washington and the other Western capitals to keep open their lines of communication with the East. Neither did *Ostpolitik* end the Franco-German axis within the EC. On the contrary, it deepened and took on 'the character of a well established marriage in which quarrels would be expected but not taken as disastrous'.[42] Nothing, however, had changed the essential vulnerability of the GDR, whose very existence in the last resort still depended on Russian bayonets, as the events of 1989–90 were to show (see p. 366), even though most West Germans up to the autumn of 1989 still believed that the inner German frontier would survive for generations. In the end both Adenauer's magnet theory and *Ostpolitik* were vindicated by events.

16 *Domestic Developments in the Two German States, 1949–63*

Introduction

Both German states shared a common heritage and traced their roots back to the Bismarckian Reich. Both had the difficult task of coming to terms with their Nazi past and they were both confronted with the challenge of integrating the expellees from the east, reviving their economies and reshaping their welfare system. Their responses to these challenges, however, were so different that Hartmut Kaelble observed that 'apart from the language and the history up to 1945'[1] the two Germanies had very little in common by 1990. By the end of the 1950s they had already developed radically different social, political and educational systems.

THE FRG

Adenauer's initial survival, 1949–53

By the mid-fifties West Germany had made such an impressive recovery that Adenauer was already being proclaimed a statesman of European and indeed world stature. Yet in the winter of 1949–50 the FRG was beset with apparently intractable economic problems and the failure of his government seemed imminent. It was by no means clear that Adenauer possessed sufficient power to govern effectively. The Occupation Statute (see p. 296) ensured that ultimate responsibility for foreign policy, security, the export trade and the Ruhr still lay with the Western Allies. The increased powers of the *Länder*, whose minister–presidents were, as Hinrich Kopf, the minister of Lower Saxony observed, determined not 'to sing the Horst-Wessel song and to say yes'[2] appeared to be a formidable brake on a strong central government. The situation in the *Bundestag* initially also seemed similar to that in the *Reichstag* during the Weimar Republic. Despite the electoral law prohibiting parties from claiming seats in the *Bundestag* unless they had won at least 5 per cent of the total votes cast, there were still 12 parties represented in parliament. Some of these, like the BP (Bavarian Party) or the SSW (South Schleswig Voters League), represented regional or group interests or were parties of protest. The CDU itself was a fragile structure which could easily have fractured, and it was only in 1950 that its leadership began to build up an effective national party organization. There was, too, the challenge of how to integrate the 9.5 million refugees and expellees from the former territories in the east, which was 'ticking like a time bomb in the framework of the fledgling state'.[3]

How then did Adenauer manage to survive and consolidate the FRG so effectively? There are a number of factors which help explain this:

- He was able to attract support from a diverse cross-section of West Germans: Catholics and Protestants who wished to rebuild Germany as a Christian community; the supporters of the social market economy; many younger voters and politicians who supported European integration; and finally those, many of whom were expellees, who hated the USSR and still hoped for the return of the eastern territories.

- He also possessed a superb political machine in the chancellor's office which was run by Hans Globke. This carefully monitored developments within the party and vetted senior appointments to the civil service in order to ensure that only politically reliable men occupied the key posts.

- He was helped by the failure of the SPD under Kurt Schumacher, whose bitter criticism of the market economy alienated many potential supporters; Schumacher gambled on its collapse, but once its success and durability became clear, the SPD had nothing to offer.

- Above all, Adenauer was helped by the Cold War, which ensured that the Western powers urgently needed the support of the FRG (see Chapter 15). Soviet intervention in the GDR to quell the riots of June 1953 increased the distrust of the USSR in the FRG and acted as an endorsement of Adenauer's policy of Western integration.

- House-building programmes offered the West Germans the eventual prospect of a flat of their own, while the expellees and economic casualties of war were helped by the Equalization of Burdens Law (see p. 320).

In 1953 a combination of these factors helped Adenauer win a decisive electoral victory, which showed that neither Western integration nor the social market economy could easily be reversed.

Hans Globke, 1898–1973, had drafted the Nuremberg race laws of 1935 and became state secretary in the West German chancellery, 1953–63

See Document 80

The social market economy and the 'economic miracle'

In the 1950s economic growth in the FRG was outstanding, yet in the winter of 1949–50 there were few signs of this development. After the short inflationary boom in the second part of 1948 triggered by the

Ludwig Erhard and the social market economy

The social market economy became the 'brand name'[4] for the economic system of West Germany. It was seen as a 'third way' between a completely free market and a state-controlled socialist economy, which increasingly existed in the GDR. The concept originated in the 1930s and its aim, in Nicholl's words, was 'to wed free price mechanism and market competition to a socially responsible policy'.[5] The state had to enforce fair competition, prohibit the formation of cartels and stimulate the economy when necessary. Initially as economics director of Bizonia and then as economics minister under Adenauer, Erhard attempted to put these ideas into practice. Inevitably he had to make many compromises. In agriculture, for instance, its principles were never applied, as Adenauer, for reasons of social cohesion and electoral politics, continued a policy of subsidies and protection, which was virtually unchanged since the Third Reich. Similarly it was not until 1957 that anti-cartel legislation was introduced.

currency reform (see p. 286) and Erhard's decision to lift price controls, the economy cooled in the winter of 1948–49. Industrial production grew again by an overall 24 per cent in the following year , but in the winter of 1949–50 economic recovery began to falter. Unemployment was over two million, prices were rising and industry faced serious bottlenecks in supply. It seemed as if Erhard's aim of creating a free market economy had already failed. Criticism was growing not only in the SPD and the unions but also within Adenauer's cabinet and among the Allied high commissioners. Although Erhard did announce a small work-creation programme, he refused to be panicked into emergency measures, and his approach initially seemed to be vindicated when the outbreak of the Korean War in June 1950 led to a sharp rise in industrial production. Yet by early 1951 the economy was faced with a serious balance of payments deficit caused by the cost of imported raw materials. Ironically, Erhard was put under pressure by the Americans, the champions of the free market, to control raw materials to ensure that heavy industry would have priority. The SPD assumed that the market economy had failed, but Erhard skilfully avoided state intervention by delegating to the industrialists the task of allocating raw materials through their own associations to the manufacturing industries. By the autumn of 1951 the global economic boom caused by the Korean War began to work in favour of the FRG. There was a huge demand for machine tools, steel and high-tech exports, which West German industry was in a strong position to meet.

As Overy has observed, the German economic miracle was 'not a miracle in the sense that defied explanation':[6]

- Liberalization of world trade, coupled with the cheap price of raw materials and a tight monetary policy carried out by the Federal Central Bank, *Die Bank der Deutschen Länder*, ensured that manufacturers made their profits in the export market.

Die Bank der Deutschen Länder was renamed the Bundesbank in 1957

- Unlike its competitors, the FRG was also initially spared the huge expense of rearmament, although from 1952 onwards the government began to put aside money in a contingency fund in preparation for setting up the new German army.
- The Marshall Plan funds were relatively modest, but did help buy vital equipment and expand the capacity of the iron and coal industries. Arguably the Plan's real significance was the stability and confidence it provided by indicating the degree of American commitment to western European reconstruction and defence against Communism.
- The German workforce was also skilled and well-educated, and constantly boosted by the flow of predominantly young and highly-skilled refugees from the GDR. Between 1950 and 1962 some 3.6 million people had fled from the GDR to the FRG. To quote Alan Kramer, it was 'not the Marshall Plan and its contribution of $1.5 billion spread over four years, but Stalin's – and Stalinism's – annual gift of DM 2.6 billion worth of trained labour that provided the greatest capital input to the West German economy'.[7]

Unlike Weimar, the FRG had no crippling burden of reparations. In 1952 Adenauer agreed to repay the Marshall Plan credits and the pre-war loans raised under the Dawes Plan (see p. 187). Israel was also awarded a sum of DM 3 billion

The first half of the 1950s was a golden age for the West German economy. It enjoyed a rapid and sustained growth. In 1955 the gross domestic product grew by 12 per cent. In the spring of 1956 inflation rose to 2 per cent, and the central bank increased the discount rate, much to

Productivity in the FRG, 1951–59

(1950 = 100)

Year	All industry	Mining	Basic production and goods	Investment goods	Consumer goods	Food and stimulants
1951	109.6	107.2	108.0	113.8	107.2	109.7
1952	114.2	112.4	110.8	121.4	109.6	114.9
1953	122.1	114.8	118.9	124.6	119.7	129.5
1954	129.2	118.6	128.0	134.2	125.3	132.9
1955	138.3	126.9	138.0	145.0	132.2	140.5
1956	144.5	132.1	144.7	150.5	139.3	145.4
1957	155.1	138.9	157.4	158.9	150.3	166.1
1958	163.1	145.4	166.9	167.3	155.7	166.1
1959	179.8	158.1	186.1	180.5	167.9	174.5

Note: Productivity as defined by output per man-hour. Figures exclude electricity power generation and the construction industry.

Source: A. Kramer, *The West German Economy*, Oxford and New York, Berg, 1991, p. 206.

the irritation of Adenauer, who feared that it might damage his chances of being re-elected in 1957. In 1958 there was a small recession in which the GDP rose by a mere 4.4 per cent. The bank then eased its monetary controls and 1960 witnessed another boom year in which the economy grew by an annual rate of 8.6 per cent. Only gradually in the early sixties could it be seen that 'the miracle years of growth had passed'.[8]

The spectacular economic achievements of the social market economy did much to defuse labour unrest, but social peace was also a 'pre-condition'[9] of its success. In the early 1950s there was considerable potential for labour unrest as profit margins far outstripped wages. In 1951 over a million working days were lost in strikes, but the actual wage claims were moderate and did not erode industrial profits, which continued to be reinvested in modernization projects. One reason for this relative moderation was that Adenauer, when confronted by the threat of strikes in the Ruhr, conceded, against the wishes of the FDP and many in his own party, the principle of co-determination to the iron, steel and coal unions. In 1952 the Works Constitution Law was passed, which extended workers' consultative councils throughout industry. This did not go as far as the workers wanted, but within the context of rising prosperity the councils did create a framework for relatively peaceful labour relations. With the exception of a three-week engineering strike in Bavaria in 1954 the first really significant wage push occurred in 1960, by which time the population was becoming more accustomed to prosperity .

> **Co-determination (*Mitbestimmung*)**: a system that aims to create harmonious relations between employers and employees by setting up a series of collaborative institutions

Social integration

The economic recovery also made it easier to integrate the expellees and defuse their growing bitterness, the potential dangers of which were shown in 1950 when the 'Bloc of Expellees and Disenfranchised', whose three leaders were all former Nazis, won 23.4 per cent of the vote in Schleswig-Holstein. The most immediate need of not only the expellees but also the majority of Germans was housing. As a result of the war, about 25 per cent of the housing stock had been destroyed. The Construction Law of April 1950 permitted central government to make generous grants to the cities and the *Länder* for large-scale building projects, and by 1957 well over four million dwelling units had been built.

> See Documents 70 and 71

To ensure that the financial consequences of defeat were more fairly shared, the Adenauer cabinet proposed in 1952 the Equalization of Burdens bill. Its intention was to compensate the expellees and those who had lost all their property as a result of the war at the expense of those who had been more fortunate. The SPD hoped for a 'second Basic Law'[10] as Erich Ollenhauer, Schumacher's successor, expressed it, which would create a more just and equal society, while the CDU and FDP tried to minimize its implications for private property. Eventually a compromise was achieved, which played a major part in satisfying and integrating the

30   A Mercedes-Cabrio on the production line in the Daimler-Benz works, Stuttgart, May 1956

Presse- und Informationsamt der Bundesregierung, no. 3560/1

expellees and other financial casualities of the war into the new West German state.

The apparently unstoppable rise in GDP also enabled Adenauer to reform the provisions for old-age pensions in 1957. Instead of adopting

---

The Equalization of Burdens Act, 1953

Klessmann calls it the 'greatest tax on wealth in the history of Germany':[11]

- There was to be a levy on 50 per cent of the wealth of all real assets, that is land, buildings and capital goods, within West German territory, as measured by the values current on 21 June 1948.
- The tax would be paid over 30 years and would be redistributed in the form of grants and pensions to the recipients after their claims had been carefully sifted by special committees.

However, as the value of property and land had increased rapidly in the fifties and sixties as a consequence of economic growth and inflation, 'an originally daring venture became a quite marginal affair'.[12] Nevertheless, by 1978 110.4 billion Deutschmarks had been redistributed.

31   A German family enjoying the fruits of the economic miracle, November 1960
Presse- und Informationsamt der Bundesregierung, no. 9077/4

a system modelled on the principle of the social market economy, which would have encouraged individuals to take out private pensions, Adenauer introduced index-linked state pensions accompanied by a large one-off rise of 60–75 per cent which was naturally very popular and contributed to his victory in the 1957 General Election.

The *Bundeswehr* (Citizen's Army)

Historically army–state relations have been one of the most intractable problems in German political history (see pp. 124–5 and 176). Initially, when the scheme for a new army as part of the European Defence Community was drawn up under the Pleven Plan in 1952 (see p. 296), public opinion was sceptical, and the SPD opposition would almost certainly have prevented Adenauer from obtaining the necessary two-thirds majority to amend the Basic Law to permit the creation of a West German army. The protracted delay caused by the French failure to ratify the plan enabled the government not only to win round public opinion, but also to consider how the new army should best be integrated into a democratic German society. The German soldier was no longer to be an automaton obeying orders instantly, but rather a 'citizen in uniform' who was to think for himself and willingly defend the democratic values of his society. A cross-party majority in the *Bundestag* also insisted on appointing a parliamentary special commissioner with the right to investigate affairs and a personnel advisory committee to review the appointment of senior officers. The necessary changes to the Basic Law were made in March 1956 with the support of most of the SPD. Unlike the *Reichswehr* in the Weimar Republic, the *Bundeswehr* as an institution was completely integrated into the democratic state and played only a 'marginal role'[13] in its politics.

Triumph and decline: the Adenauer regime, 1953–63

See Document 80

In 1957, after four more years of increasing prosperity, the CDU–CSU won an absolute majority of 50.2 per cent of the vote. The chancellor, with his call for no experiments, had caught the mood of the time. At the age of 81 Adenauer was at the height of his political power, but gradually over the next four years his formidable political skills began to desert him, and his own party, the FDP and the West German people became increasingly impatient for his retirement. An early indication of how the Adenauer regime might eventually come to an end was afforded by the crisis in the governing coalition in the winter of 1955–56. The FDP split and the majority led by Thomas Dehler, who was critical of Adenauer's rigid policy towards the USSR and the GDR, withdrew from the coalition, and began to consider working with the SPD, which did indeed happen in North Rhine–Westphalia. In Hans-Peter Schwarz's view, 'irrevocable forces were let loose by this event . . . which ventured into new directions, and gained a majority in the late 1960s'.[14]

Adenauer was essentially an authoritarian figure cast in a Bismarckian mould, impatient of parliament and the *Länder*. By the end of the fifties this cavalier attitude began to alienate public opinion. In 1959, for example, he considered becoming president of the FRG when Theodor Heuss retired, believing that it would enable him still to dominate politics. When he discovered that the constitution would not permit this, he rapidly backtracked and pushed the nondescript agriculture minister, Heinrich Lübke, into the post.

For the first time since 1952, Adenauer also faced the challenge of an effective and modernized SPD. In reaction to its defeat in 1957, the party at last came to terms with the Adenauer–Erhard revolution. In the Godesberg Programme of 1959 it embraced much of Erhard's philosophy. In a famous formula coined by Professor Schiller (see p. 345), the SPD would aim for 'as much competition as possible' with 'as much planning as necessary'.[15] In June 1960 the party moved on to embrace Western integration and NATO, and in August it chose Willy Brandt, the young and charismatic Mayor of West Berlin (see p. 303), as the chancellor candidate to challenge Adenauer.

The 1961 election campaign was dominated by the closure of the frontier between East and West Berlin on 13 August. Adenauer made a serious mistake when he appeared to play down this momentous event and delayed his visit to West Berlin until 22 August. This allowed Brandt to accuse him of indifference towards West Berlin and indeed the whole question of German unity. Nevertheless, despite losing their overall majority in the election, the CDU–CSU still retained 46 per cent of the vote, while the SPD increased its percentage by only 4.4 per cent. It was the FDP which did best by increasing its share of the poll from 7.7 per cent to 12.8 per cent, which enabled it to hold the balance between the CDU and SPD. Adenauer managed to negotiate a coalition with the FDP and survive for two more years, but he had first to appease Ludwig Erhard, the leading contender for his position, by promising that he would step down before the next election and fend off the demand by Erich Mende, the leader of the FDP, for his immediate resignation by holding exploratory talks with the SPD on the possibility of forming a grand coalition without the Liberals.

See Documents 77 and 80

The event that finally made retirement inevitable was the *Spiegel* affair. In October 1962 *Der Spiegel*, the news magazine, published a confidential report on the inefficiencies of the *Bundeswehr*.

The minister of defence, Franz-Josef Strauss, who, as a high-profile politician, was frequently criticized by *Der Spiegel*, was persuaded by his civil servants that the article was treasonable and that the editors, Rudolf Augstein and Conrad Ahlers, should be arrested. This heavy reaction, with police raids in the middle of the night, awakened memories of the Third Reich and provoked a strong public reaction. The press was highly critical, the intelligentsia strongly supported Augstein and there were student demonstrations and sit-ins at several universities. Adenauer badly misjudged the situation when he launched a bitter attack against Augstein in the *Bundestag* on 7 November, claiming that the country faced an 'abyss of treason'.

Der Spiegel, which was launched in 1947, was a news magazine modelled on the American *Time* magazine. It had a circulation of over half a million and a readership of five million

See Document 81

Franz-Josef Strauss, 1915–88

Strauss was one of the most controversial figures in West German politics. His father was a butcher, but Franz-Josef's intellectual brilliance won him a place at the *Maximilianeum* in Munich, a special school for gifted students. After a brief period as a prisoner of war, he played an increasingly important part in post-war Bavarian politics and was a founder member of the CSU. In 1948 he was elected to the Economic Council of the Bizone and in 1949 to the *Bundestag*. After serving as minister for special tasks and nuclear energy, he was appointed defence minister in 1957. Although after his resignation in 1962 he returned to office as finance minister in 1966 in the Grand Coalition (see p. 340), he never succeeded in becoming chancellor of the FRG because his nationalism and his apparently extreme anti-Communism frightened off the majority of electors in a period of détente and *Ostpolitik* (see pp. 302–13). He was chairman of the CSU, 1961–88.

He could probably have ridden out the storm, if the Free Democrats had not resigned from the cabinet in protest against the failure of the Defence Ministry to consult the FDP Minister of Justice, Wolfgang Stammberger, before acting against Augstein. Adenauer once again began negotiations with the SPD for a grand coalition. This had its effect and brought the FDP back into government, subject to two conditions: Strauss would have to resign and Adenauer himself would have to retire by October 1963.

The *Spiegel* affair was a major event in modern German political history. For the first time a government had been compelled constitutionally to concede defeat over the question of civil liberties. Adenauer never recovered from this setback. His popularity dropped dramatically, and in March 1963 the CDU lost the Rhineland Palatinate *Land* election. At last, on 22 April, he recognized Erhard as his successor and he resigned six months later. He did, however, retain the chairmanship of the CDU, a position which he used unsparingly to criticize Erhard.

FRG: reconstruction or modernization?

The Adenauer era was full of paradoxes.[16] On the one hand it witnessed accelerated economic and social change, which created an upwardly mobile society. Farming, for instance, was mechanized and lost half its workforce by 1960. On the other hand the fifties also witnessed the survival of many of the pre-war élites in the churches, the universities and big business. The one élite that was destroyed by the war was the old Prussian ruling class (see p. 274), whose traditional place in the bureaucracy was filled mostly by southern and western German middle-class officials.

The role of women illustrates the uneasy balance between change and restoration that epitomizes the Adenauer period. Women had played a vital role as both breadwinners and mothers in the immediate post-war period when so many men were still POWs. They were granted full equality in the Basic Law and the government was committed to amend the anachronistic Wilhelmine Civil Code by 1953, but in practice the cabinet was in no hurry to carry out this pledge. By the early 1950s it was clear that the immediate post-war period had in fact 'only disrupted, not transformed' the position of women.[17] Indeed, according to the revised Civil Service Law of 1950 the government had the power to dismiss women from state employment, provided that their husbands earned sufficient money to support the family. Only slowly under pressure from the Federal Court did the situation begin to change, but the expectation was still 'that a woman should marry, raise a family and build her life around the private sphere'.[18] Yet, paradoxically, as a result of the war there were a large number of single women who had no marriage prospects and therefore had to develop a new and independent lifestyle. 'Unwittingly', as Eva Kolinsky observed, 'the non-married women of the lost generation were trailblazers of change.'[19]

See Document 82

The degree to which West German society became 'Americanized' in the 1950s is debatable. Ralph Willett sees the occupation as 'the prologue to a more developed Americanization. Chewing gum and Lucky Strikes whose packaging alone symbolized the beautiful new world of modernity, were harbingers of MacDonalds, corporation skyscrapers and nuclear missiles'.[20] Yet initially most West Germans were still constrained by a shortage of money, long working hours and poor living conditions. Only towards the end of the decade did a real breakthrough take place into the 'consumer age', when the West Germans began to spend on cars, new furniture and holidays, and to follow American fashion styles.

Popular attitudes in the FRG in the early fifties also reveal a 'striking and elusive mixture of restoration and new tones and accents'.[21] On the one hand, society was characterized by a studded indifference to politics, a pessimistic view of the future and a strong desire to lead a private life – the *ohne mich* attitude.

Hitler was still quite widely admired and many Germans rejected the responsibility of their country for the war. There was also a deep cultural conservativism, which was strengthened by the leading role of the Catholic Church. This led to tighter film censorship and in the early 1950s to the production of *Heimat* films, which propagated the message that the Germans themselves were also the victims of Nazism. The emergence of rock and roll and *die Halbstarken*, or teddy boys, whom some journalists compared to the SA, triggered a major cultural battle about what Uta Poiger has called 'the complicated process of reconstructing Germanness'.[22] This led to the paradox that while the West German conservative élites supported the integration of the FRG into a Western world dominated by the USA, they were scornful of popular American culture.

On the other hand, there was a refreshingly new openness and desire for social harmony. Among the population there was considerable demand for foreign films, recipes and literature. Hemingway, for example, was one of the most popular authors in Germany in the early 1950s. The Adenauer era was a period of psychological and spiritual reconstruction. The West Germans wished to adapt to a modern and more liberal society the message and experience of the Nazi *Volksgemeinschaft*, which had preached, even if it did not practise, social equality (see pp. 236–41). Ironically, so Mark Rosen argues, the Germans pursued a 'reverse *Sonderweg*'[23] in the 1950s, as a more modern and classless society than their western European neighbours.

Ohne mich literally means 'without me' and summed up the wish of many Germans in the 1950s not to become involved in politics

THE GDR, 1949–61

Democratic centralism: the dictatorship of the SED

The Communists
were Pieck,
Ulbricht, Merker
and Dahlem and
the former SPD
members were
Grotewohl, Meier
and Friedrich
Ebert, the son
of the former
president of the
Weimar Republic

The model for the SED, the ruling party of the GDR, was the Communist party of the Soviet Union. Just before its first party conference in January 1949 it set up that 'classic model of the executive committee of the Communist Party, the Politbureau',[24] on which sat four former Communists and three former Social Democrats. Under the chairmanship of Ulbricht a small secretariat was also formed both to prepare the agenda of the Politbureau and to ensure that its decisions were carried out after they had been given what was usually an automatic endorsement by the Central Committee, which was composed of 80 members elected at the party congress. These three organs were able to control the party, the mass organizations, such as the trade unions, and the Free German Youth Movement, as well as the state bureaucracy. A pyramid-like structure was thus created in which the chain of command ran from the top to the bottom and extended right across the GDR so that all subordinate party committees and groups at whatever level received their orders from the committee immediately above them.

See Document 74

The government of the GDR had been formed on 12 October 1949. Theoretically it was a coalition under Otto Grotewohl (see p. 292) in which the SED shared power with the CDUD and LDPD, but the five key posts of the Interior, Education, Planning, Justice and Industry were firmly in the hands of the SED. Optimistically the two bourgeois parties believed that they would win the coming election with a landslide, but under Soviet pressure they agreed to delay it for a year, which enabled the SED to consolidate its position. In the hysterical atmosphere produced by the outbreak of the Korean War, witch hunts were carried out by the Party Control Commission against alleged 'Titoists' and other dissident socialists. It rapidly became 'more dangerous to be a former member of the SPD than an active Nazi'.[25] The authority of the state was strengthened by the creation in December 1949 of the Supreme Court and the Department of Public Prosecutions and in February 1950 by the Ministry of State Security, the *Stasi*, which was accountable to the Politbureau. Its duty was to detect all internal opposition to the SED regime and to engage in espionage.

In 1947 Joseph
Tito, the Yugoslav
Communist
dictator, refused to
tow the party line
from Moscow
and pursued an
independent
foreign policy

Through a process reminiscent of the Nazi *Gleischaltung* in the years 1933–34 (see p. 220) the SED was able to turn the mass organizations and the bourgeois parties into 'conveyor belts' for the transmission of SED policy. Pressure was also exerted on the two bourgeois bloc parties, the CDU and LDP, to purge their more dissident elements. By the autumn of 1950 they joined the National Front, an inclusive organization which had been set up by the *Volkskongress* movement (see p. 291) to act as a comprehensive all-German organization representing all the parties and organizations interested in national unity – albeit a unity on the SED's terms. The Front was entrusted with drawing up the single unified lists of

32   Parade of the Free German Youth (FDJ), Berlin, 4 July 1952

Press- und Informationsamt der Bundesregierung, no. 892/32

candidates all offering the same policies which were to be presented to the voters in the elections on 15 October. The election was the final stage of what Willy Loth has called 'a *coup d'état*'[26] against the constitution of the GDR. The party claimed that 99.72 per cent of the voters had voted for the unity list. The dominant position of the SED was camouflaged by the composition of the elected *Volkskammer*. It won outright only 25 per cent of the vote, but thanks to the 30 per cent gained by the mass organizations and a further 7.5 per cent each secured by the Peasants party (DBD) and the National Democratic party of Germany (NDPD), which were both led by ex-Communists, there was never any chance of the two bourgeois parties being in a position to veto policy. In 1952 the powers of democratic centralism were further strengthened when all five of the *Länder* in the GDR were abolished and replaced by 14 counties (*Bezirke*).

Building a socialist economy, 1948–52

Economic recovery was delayed both by the Stalinist policies of the SED and by the continued Russian demands for reparations. As late as 1950 some 25 per cent of the industrial goods produced in the GDR went to the USSR as reparations. Since the GDR was cut off from Western investment and the supplies of Ruhr coal and steel on which its industries were dependent before the war, it was forced into a 'search for domestic raw materials [which] at times, according to Rainer Karlsch, reached the irrational'.[27] The Cold War inevitably tightened the GDR's economic links with the Soviet bloc. In September 1950 it joined COMECON, and by 1951 76 per cent of its trade was with the Socialist bloc.

By splitting up the larger farms, post-war land reform had seriously weakened the agricultural sector (see p. 276). Yields continued to be hit by a lack of fertilizers, and an acute shortage of livestock led to shortages in milk, cheese and meat. Inevitably these shortages drastically depressed the standard of living and the productivity of its workers. In 1950 wages had sunk to 71 per cent of their 1936 level, while meat and fat consumption were a mere 50 per cent of their 1934–38 level. Both to consolidate its position and to plan production targets, investment and distribution, the government needed to control the economy. By 1950 it was well on the way to doing this. The *VEBs*, together with the *SAGs*, accounted for some 76 per cent of the total industrial production, while the banking and insurance sectors were completely in the state's hands. Independent retail trade faced fierce competition from the HOs, and both the surviving larger farms and independent artisans were harried by punitive taxation. Production targets were ambitious. The Five Year Plan, which was based on the Soviet model, was launched in 1950, and aimed at doubling the output of 1936, while living standards were 'to exceed significantly the pre-war level'.[28] Its main targets were the metallurgical and machine-building sectors, which were to expand by 153.6 per cent and 114.8 per cent respectively.

In reality these targets could only be met by neglecting the consumer industries and keeping wages at a permanently low level. Butter, milk and sugar were still rationed. Pensions were kept to a minimum and the house-building programme remained at a markedly more modest level than in the *Bundesrepublik*. The expellees, too, were given far less generous compensation than those in the FRG. The workers were alternatively repressed and bribed by the party. Co-determination 'in the managing of the economy' was, so they were told, realized 'through the democratic organs of the state'.[29] Only if they exceeded the production norms set for their plant were they awarded bonuses.

COMECON, the Council for Mutual Economic Aid, had been set up in Moscow in 1949 in response to the Marshall Plan

VEB: *Volkseigener Betrieb* or nationalized enterprise; **SAG**: *Sowjetischer Aktiengesellschaft* or Soviet limited company, which produced goods for the USSR as part of East Germany's reparations, 1946–53

HO: *Staatliche Handelsorganisation*, (state trade organisations) ran a whole range of shops

The expellees in the GDR

The three and a quarter million expellees from the German eastern territories formed a diverse group of skilled artisans, agricultural labourers and even former members of the Prussian landed gentry. By the law of 8 September 1950 they were given some financial assistance to buy tools and household furniture and promised priority in housing, but after that the state assumed that the increasing demand for labour and the expansion of heavy industry would integrate them into the GDR. The term 'worker–settler' was dropped, and the expellee problem was officially deemed to have been solved.

Following the Russian example, the activist movement was introduced in 1948, and Adolf Hennecke, a 51 year-old coal miner from Zwickau, was carefully groomed to exceed his norm of coal mined during one shift by at least 250 per cent. When he achieved this by 387 per cent, he was turned into a popular hero.

The Five Year Plan initially achieved some impressive successes in the production of iron, steel and chemicals. Raw steel production was, for example, already double that of 1936, and on the basis of these statistics at its party conference in July 1952 the SED leadership decided, despite Soviet reservations, to accelerate the planned construction of Socialism and to overcome the 'last traces of capitalist thought'.[30] The speed with which Ulbricht moved must be seen in the context of the international situation. The future of the GDR, as the Stalin note of March 1952 (see pp. 297–8) indicated, was by no means assured. Ulbricht hoped that the socialization of the GDR along Stalinist lines would make reunification impossible except on the SED's terms. Klaus Schroeder has described this policy as 'a disguised opposition to the keeping open of the German question by the Soviet Union'.[31]

> In the 1930s the Stakhanov movement in the USSR aimed at raising the production of labour. The feats of Alexei Stakhanov, who, under specially favourable conditions, achieved spectacular production results were used to justify raising the production targets of the other workers

> See Document 83

17 June 1953: riot or popular revolt?

By 1953 Ulbricht had managed to unite almost the whole of the East German people against his regime by the ruthlessness with which he had attempted to impose a Soviet pattern of socialism on a highly developed, capitalist, industrial society. The farmers resented the low prices they received for their crops and the fines they were forced to pay if they were late with their food deliveries. The remaining independent businessmen and artisans were also worried about whether their livelihoods would be nationalized by the state. The workers, too, resented the low wages, high taxation and rising food prices which were necessary to pay for the creation of the new armed frontier force. Tension was further heightened by the arrest of the leading politicians in the bloc parties, the LDPD and CDU. Not surprisingly, the number of refugees fleeing to the West, despite the construction of a five-mile-deep restricted zone along the frontier, increased to almost half a million in the first six months of 1953. In February 1953 the situation was so charged that the bishops of the Evangelical Church in the GDR warned the government to take note 'of the distress which threatened to lead to a catastrophe of major proportions'.[32]

After Stalin's death in March 1953, Ulbricht came under pressure from the new Soviet leadership, which desired a détente with the West, to modify his policies. In early June the SED leaders were summoned to Moscow and told that unless they halted all moves towards collectivization, encouraged independent businessmen and stopped the persecution of the Churches, there would be a 'catastrophe'.[33] As Willy Loth argues,[34] Soviet policy needs to be seen within the context of Beria's proposals

> Karl Hamman, the LDPD minister for trade, and Georg Dertinger, the CDUD foreign minister, were both arrested

> There was no immediate heir to Stalin. The key members of the new Soviet leadership were Malenkov, Bulganin, Beria and Khrushchev, who by 1957 became the dominant leader

33   Demonstrators on the Potsdamer Platz flee from approaching Soviet tanks, 17 June 1953
Presse- und Informationsamt der Bundesregierung, no. 65142/8#

See Document 83

for the future of the GDR (see p. 298). The Russians, however, had omitted to make one vital change: they did not order Ulbricht to cancel his May directive increasing the work norms for the workers by 10 per cent.

Ulbricht's refusal to rescind this led to growing unrest. On 16 June a demonstration of building workers marched first to the trade union headquarters and then to the House of Ministries to demand the abolition of the norms. Failing to obtain instant concessions, the workers began to call for a general strike and the production of more consumer goods, the restoration of works councils and the lifting of the ban on the SPD. In the meantime a wave of spontaneous and unco-ordinated strikes and demonstrations had erupted across the whole of the GDR. There was intense anger directed at the regime. Crowds collected outside prisons, and state and party offices and called for the resignation of the government, but only in Görlitz and Bitterfeld were efforts made to set up democratic local governments. Elsewhere there were no plans to control radio stations and transport networks or to seize arms. By 18 June, Soviet military intervention and the immediate withdrawal of the work norms restored order, although sporadic strikes, protests and demonstrations fanned by American radio transmissions from West Berlin continued for the next few weeks.

The nature of the events of 16–17 June

The events of 16–17 June were interpreted very differently in the two Germanies. In the GDR they were seen as a Fascist *putsch* manipulated by the West, while in the FRG the riots were regarded as a popular uprising against Stalinist tyranny. In 1965 Arnulf Baring modified this latter view by arguing that the revolt went through three brief phases:

- initially it was a demand for lower work quotas and food prices;
- on the afternoon of 17 June it was 'transformed into a popular revolt';
- this rapidly petered out, not so much as a result of Soviet intervention but because of a lack of leaders and a programme.

Christoph Klessmann argues that it was 'undoubtedly a workers' uprising'. On the other hand it was also partly, as Armin Mitter and Stefan Wolle stress, a forerunner of the events of 1989 (see pp. 364–7).[35] There were demands for lifting the frontier, free elections and the resignation of the government. Yet both these explanations are simplifications of complex events. The GDR was a deeply fractured society, and many of those who demonstrated on 16 and 17 June had their own separate agendas. More recently Gareth Pritchard[36] has argued that it was a complex mixture of factors: a recrudescence of Nazism, a youth revolt, a struggle for westernization, and a violent but last spasm of the German socialist tradition.

The quelling of the riots by Soviet troops illustrated only too clearly that 'the power of the SED rested on Russian bayonets'.[37] The SED party leadership was determined to prevent a repetition of these traumatic events. It immediately arrested some six thousand people, who were held in conditions reminiscent of 'the torture chambers of the SA . . . during the Hitler period',[38] and thousands were purged from the SED, the trade unions and the bloc parties. The *Stasi* was reformed and put more effectively under the control of the party, and had from then on to compile daily reports, which would be processed by information groups in each county administration (*Bezirksverwaltung*). Under Soviet supervision, the police and the paramilitary plant defence groups were re-equipped and made more effective. However, the Russians also insisted on the regime making considerable concessions: pensions were increased, more consumer goods were to be produced and food prices lowered. As a gesture of goodwill, the USSR also agreed to return the last 33 SAGs to German ownership.

Ulbricht's survival against the odds, 1953–57

Any chances of radical change in the aftermath of these events was, however, destroyed when Ulbricht managed to rout his critics in the Politbureau. On 7 July 1953 he had only two supporters, Erich Honecker and Hermann Matern, but the majority were unwilling to strike without

Beria was made the scapegoat for the course of events in the GDR

explicit Kremlin backing, which after Beria's fall on 29 June was not given. It was indeed 'a turning point at which GDR history failed to turn'.[39] On 18 July Wilhelm Zaisser, Rudolph Herenstadt and Max Fechner, who had dared to defend the workers' right to strike, were expelled from the Central Committee. At the 4th Party Congress Ulbricht was re-elected first secretary, and in the national election of October 1954 he was able once again to present the voters with a single list of candidates. In the new government 20 of the 28 ministers belonged to the SED. Both Ulbricht and the party, it seemed, had recovered from the events of June 1953.

In June 1956 Polish factory workers in Posen rioted in protest against their working conditions, and the revolt had to be crushed by armed force

Two years later Ulbricht faced another challenge when Khrushchev's dramatic revelation of Stalin's crimes at the 20th party congress in Moscow in February 1956 plunged the Communist world into crisis. Within the GDR this caused growing criticism of the SED's leadership. There was considerable support for the uprising in Posen in June. In August and September a series of strikes broke out in the GDR. The Hungarian uprising at the end of October led to further unrest in the large industrial cities and the universities. As one miner in Saxony observed, it seemed that 'a small spark would be sufficient to begin an uprising amongst us'.[40] Nevertheless, a repetition of 17 June was avoided partly by political and economic concessions such as a cut in the working day and the release of 20,000 political prisoners, but also by the effective deployment of factory defence forces. The brutal defeat of the Hungarian revolt by Soviet troops in November also acted as a powerful deterrent to the population of the GDR.

In the summer of 1956 the new Communist leadership in Hungary began to make political concessions. By the autumn these had led to an ever-growing demand for more democratization. By the end of October Hungary was threatening to pull out of the Warsaw Pact. To stop this, Russian troops were sent in on 4 November to restore a pro-Soviet regime

The events of 1956 were 'a flashpoint that failed to ignite'.[41] There had been plans in Moscow to replace Ulbricht with a more moderate figure, a 'German Gomulka', who would adopt a reformist programme. In early 1956 Karl Schirdewan was actually being 'groomed'[42] by Moscow as Ulbricht's replacement, but the revolts in Poland and Hungary distracted the Soviet leadership at the critical moment, and simultaneously Ulbricht's value to the USSR was greatly increased by the loyalty of the GDR during these crises. This reprieve gave him the necessary freedom to defeat his reformist rivals. One group led by Wolfgang Harich was arrested in early 1957 and, by skilfully exploiting the divisions amongst his other opponents, Ulbricht managed to make a clean sweep of the rest by the summer of 1958.

Failure to catch up with the FRG

By 1955 the standard of living in the GDR was the highest in the COMECON. Wages, too, had risen rapidly since 1953, yet the availability of food and consumer goods still lagged far behind the FRG. With the launch of the second Five Year Plan in 1958, Ulbricht stated that the 'main economic task' was to overtake the FRG 'within a few years . . . in per capita consumption of all important food items and consumer goods'.[43] The GDR had little option, as he expressed it, but 'to square off'[44] against the FRG. Only by rivalling the FRG's prosperity could it defeat the magnet-like pull of its economy and effectively challenge the Hallstein Doctrine (see p. 299).

Initially it seemed as if Ulbricht's gamble would succeed In 1958–59 the GDR's economy grew by almost 12 per cent per annum. In 1959, to co-ordinate the GDR's economy more closely with the other COMECON states, the second Five Year Plan was replaced by a Seven Year Plan with an emphasis on energy, chemicals and electrical engineering. By 1965 industrial production was planned to increase by 188 per cent and consumer production by 177 per cent. In December 1959, in order to lay the basis for a more efficient agricultural sector which could outproduce the FRG, the decision was also taken to complete the process of collec- tivization.

However, these targets were, as Christoph Klessmann has put it, 'aiming for the stars'.[45] High labour costs in the GDR, poor-quality work, the lack of foreign exchange and the domination by the Western powers of the global economy all indicated that the GDR would fall ever further behind the FRG.

Collectivization: the replacement of private farms by co-operatives and state-run farms

The immediate economic impact of collectivization was disastrous. There were severe teething troubles: yields plummeted and serious shortages in bread, butter and meat were reported. There was conse- quently a huge increase in the number of refugees fleeing westwards through the open frontier in Berlin. In 1960 199,000 fled, and in the six months up to January 1961 a further 103,000. By June 1961 the *Stasi* was also reporting increasing unrest in the factories. Ulbricht, however, refused to make any concessions. Possibly, as Dietrich Staritz and Klessmann[46] have argued, he was consciously intending to exploit the mounting economic crisis to push Khrushchev into agreeing to close the inner Berlin frontier, but it is more likely that the party accelerated the pace of collectivization because socialization in the countryside was proceeding more slowly than in the rest of the economy – at the end of 1959 only 43 per cent of the agricultural sector was collectivized.

The torrent of refugees did, however, make the Berlin Wall inevitable, if the GDR was not to collapse. Once permission was given for the closure of the frontier at the meeting of the Warsaw Pact states on 3–5 August 1961 (see p. 301), Erich Honecker, the minister in charge of security, carried out operations efficiently and swiftly in the early hours of 13 August. At first much of 'the anti-Fascist protective wall' consisted of barbed wire, but this was quickly replaced by a more permanent concrete structure, the notorious Berlin Wall. Although it was bitterly resented in the GDR, the security forces prevented any widespread protests. This day, 13 August, was a major turning-point in the history of the GDR and the party loyalists came to regard it as the 'secret foundation day of the GDR'.[47]

The socialist '*Volksgemeinschaft*'

The SED was determined to build a new workers' and peasants' state in which capitalism, the 'seedbed' of Fascism, would for ever be eliminated from East German society. There was no partial restoration as in the FRG. Instead 'almost the whole of the old society'[48] was deconstructed over the decade 1950–60. Only in the Church and the medical profession did the traditional bourgeoisie manage to retain its influence.

The key posts in both party and state were occupied by former KPD members, who had gained their political experience in the Weimar Republic. Below them a new élite had hastily to be trained, amongst the generation of workers' and peasants' children who had joined the Free German Youth (FDJ) in 1945, to fill the posts in the mass organizations, the schools and the nationalized industries. Shaped by their experiences in the Hitler Youth and traumatized by the end of the war, 'a minority, although probably a large minority'[49] accepted the offer of re-education at special workers' and peasants' faculties and 'bonded' enthusiastically with the new regime to build what they hoped would be a modern, class-less industrial society.

What was the nature of this new German state they created? Klessmann has described it as 'a contradiction-ridden socialist experiment conceived as an alternative to the FRG and accepted as such by a small loyal minority'.[50] Unlike Poland, Hungary or the other eastern European states, it was not a nation–state. It was only a fragment of a nation and locked into permanent competition with the other German state, the FRG. Claus Offe has argued that the GDR possessed only an economic identity and represented 'a pure . . . form of a socialist economic society'.[51] The factory became the context for socializing the adult population. It provided routine medical care, and organized cultural and social activities and even shopping facilities.

Legally women enjoyed complete equality with men in this new workers' and peasants' state. By the Law on the Protection of the Mother and the Child in 1950 it was clearly stated that 'Marriage does not lead to any restrictions or narrowing down of a woman's rights.'[52] Through the provision of factory crèches and after-school supervision of children, they were actively encouraged to work. In reality most women occupied the lowest-paid and unskilled jobs, as they lacked the right qualifications. They suffered under 'the bondage of a double burden'[53] because they still had the role of looking after the children and the home.

Education, literature, art and the mass media were all employed in helping to create a new working-class and socialist mass identity. Schools and universities became institutions primarily concerned with producing a steady supply of qualified workers, technicians and managers for industry and agriculture, and with the indoctrination of their students into Marxism–Leninism. In 1959 a single, comprehensive, ten-class higher school with a uniform curriculum was introduced, in which science and technical subjects played the major part. The universities were set similar goals and their staff were subjected to close supervision. The main inspiration for the arts and literature was socialist realism. Cultural activities were controlled by the state and were viewed as 'a force of production that would help to raise labour productivity'.[54] Jazz and much of Western literature and modern art were dismissed, as they had been in the Third Reich, as both decadent and irrelevant.

Opposition and dissent

Although some of the GDR's policies were beneficial, such as the provision of full employment and assistance for working women, nevertheless, 'a lot of people', as Mary Fulbrook has observed, 'did not like the GDR'.[55] The riots of 16–17 June 1953 were the most dramatic example of opposition to SED rule until September–October 1989, but there was a considerable amount of low-key *Resistenz* to party policies right up to 1989, particularly from workers, who disliked the intrusive nature of party demands. There was grumbling about pay levels, working conditions and production quotas, which sometimes led to brief strikes. Former SPD members, older people, who could not accept the division of Germany, and members of the traditional professions, particularly doctors, formed 'pockets of immunity to the Party'.[56] In the rural areas in the 1950s there were still some remnants of Nazism. Swastikas and graffiti were sometimes scrawled on walls, but, more often than not, this was the work of school students, and was rather the desire to shock the authorities than evidence of a Nazi revival.

Resistenz is best translated as 'immunity' to an ideology. See p. 264

Like the FRG, the GDR also had its youth problem. There were occasional political protests particularly at the universities during the Hungarian revolt of 1956. East German youth was also influenced by American fashions in clothing, music and films. In the late 1950s rock and roll fan clubs sprang up, and there were disturbances in East Berlin and the other larger cities. Idolization of Elvis Presley went hand in hand with what one *Stasi* report described as 'depraved ravings against leading comrades'.[57]

It was, however, the Protestant Church that provided the most effective opposition to the totalitarian claims of SED Germany, as it possessed a coherent anti-Marxist philosophy. It represented an alien body in the GDR, and, as in the Third Reich, was capable of considerable *Resistenz* to the regime (see p. 264). The Protestant Church was not, however, a united monolithic body, but a group of eight loosely-connected regional Churches, some of which had close links with the Protestant Churches in West Germany. It was, therefore, subject to constant harassment from the regime. Although Ulbricht's initial confrontation with the Church, in which he attempted to destroy its youth organizations, was halted as a result of Soviet pressure in June 1953 (see p. 329), the SED nevertheless continued to try to marginalize the Church's influence:

In 1948 the Confessing Church, which had been created in 1934 to resist Hitler's attempts to create a German Nazi Church, was replaced by the United German Evangelical Church, which included both East and West German members

Jugendweihe was the secular, socialist version of the Christian ceremony of confirmation. It marked the coming to maturity of young people in a socialist community

- In 1954 it introduced the *Jugendweihe*, as an alternative to confirmation, and put considerable pressure on parents to participate.
- It also sought to divide the pro-western and strongly anti-GDR supporters of Otto Dibelius, one of the founders of the Confessing Church in 1934 and the Bishop of Berlin Brandenburg, from those pastors who were more prepared to compromise with the regime.

In 1958 the intensifying Cold War enabled the SED to weaken the links of East German Protestants with their brethren in the West. When the West German Evangelical Church decided to provide military chaplains for the *Bundeswehr,* the East German Churches had little option but to distance themselves from the decision. In July 1958 this led to a truce between Church and State. On the one hand the party managed to negotiate an agreement whereby the Church consented to 'respect the development towards socialism and contribute to the peaceful construction of the life of the community', but on the other hand, in return for this concession, the state had to concede that 'every citizen enjoys full freedom of belief and conscience'.[58] This enabled the Church to continue both to provide a rival ideology to Communism and to run a wide range of social organizations that were not under the SED's control. Ultimately, in the 1980s, these were to play an important part in the downfall of the regime (see p. 360).

Conclusion: the two Germanies: a comparison

Between 1949 and 1961 Germany was increasingly divided into two states integrated into mutually hostile blocs. On the one side, to quote T. A. Schwartz, 'the FRG in its early years of existence was effectively a part of the American political, economic and military system, more like a state such as California or Illinois than an independent nation',[59] while, on the other, the GDR became ever more closely enmeshed in a socialist eastern Europe dominated by the USSR. Thus two different and competing systems grew up. The 1950s was a decade of reconstruction for both Germanies. In the FRG this took the form of an export-orientated social market economy within the overall framework of Western integration and liberal democracy, but in the GDR it was a time of enforced socialism and massive state investment in heavy industry carried out according to the Soviet pattern within the context of COMECON and the Warsaw Pact

The experiences of the German people in the two states rapidly diverged. In the GDR the Churches were marginalized and at times persecuted, while in the FRG the Roman Catholic Church, in particular, exercised considerable influence through the CDU on both the government and the people. In the GDR there was legal equality for women, who were urgently needed in the workforce, even though in practice this equality was not a reality, but not even this theoretical legal equality had been achieved in West Germany, where married women were still encouraged to devote themselves exclusively to the family. In both states traditional rural life was revolutionized: farming was mechanized in the West and the numbers working on the land halved by 1960; in the East, collectivization swept away the independent small farmer. The experiences of the middle and professional classes could not have been more contrasting. In the FRG, a dynamic, upwardly mobile society was created and the bourgeois élites survived in business, law, the teaching professions and local government, while, in the GDR, only in medicine and the Church did the pre-war bourgeoisie enjoy a significance presence.

17 *The Decades of Challenge: The Two Germanies, 1963–88*

Introduction

For both Germanies the 1960s were a decade of considerable change, which some historians argue amounted to 'a second foundation' or 'refoundation'[1] of the two states. Both states, in almost a 'looking glass symmetry',[2] relaxed the dogmas and orthodoxies of the fifties. In the GDR the construction of the Berlin Wall created a situation where the whole population was in effect under 'house arrest'.[3] It no longer had the option of flight to the West and thus had grudgingly to come to terms with the party and state as best it could. Ulbricht, now assured of the survival of the GDR, was able to introduce a series of reforms which partially modernized its economic, legal and social structure.

In the FRG, too, there was a similar process of modernization. The legal code was liberalized and the welfare state expanded, but starting with the *Spiegel* affair of 1962 (see p. 323) there was also what has been described as a 'cultural and political revolution'.[4] The decade witnessed a rapid growth in political activism, agitation and public debate, which challenged the 'collective amnesia'[5] of the 1950s. In East Germany, given the ubiquity of the *Stasi*, political protest was isolated and unco-ordinated. Nevertheless, by the 1980s there were, as in the FRG, environmentalist, civil rights and homosexual self-help groups, although on a much smaller scale until the autumn of 1989.

A turning-point in the history of both states was the dramatic hike in oil prices by OPEC in 1973 and the inflationary crisis caused in part by America's inability to balance her budget in the wake of the Vietnam War. To survive, industrial economies were faced with a decade of 'wrenching re-orientation'.[6] The FRG was strong enough to adapt to the challenging demands of the global economy, while the long-term failure of the GDR – and indeed of the whole of COMECON – to restructure and to adapt its industries was ultimately to be one of the most crucial reasons for its collapse in 1989–90.

OPEC:
Organization of
Petroleum
Exporting
Countries

Key issues

- Why did Erhard fail as chancellor?
- What did the Grand Coalition achieve?
- What was the nature of the cultural revolution in the FRG in the 1960s?
- What did Schmidt and Brandt achieve? How different were the problems both faced?
- How serious a problem was terrorism in the FRG?
- Why did the SPD lose its grip on power in 1982?
- How multiracial had the FRG become by the 1980s?
- Why did the FRG become a 'two-thirds society' in the 1980s?
- Were the Kohl–Genscher governments a 'conservative counter-revolution'?
- To what extent were the 1960s for both Germanies a period of 'refoundation'?
- How successful were Ulbricht's attempts to transform the GDR in the 1960s?
- To what extent did Honecker manage to stabilize the GDR?
- How popular was the GDR with its own citizens in the 1970s and 1980s?
- Was the collapse of the GDR inevitable?
- How far had the two Germanies grown apart by 1988?

THE FRG, 1963–89

The Erhard government

Arguably by 1963 the FRG was a secure, prosperous and democratic state integrated into western Europe. Yet in the eyes of many, especially in the generation which came of age in the early sixties in the FRG, West German democracy was still on probation. Its stability was yet to be challenged by the combination of a major economic and political crisis. In the mid-sixties, however, it did have to face its 'first acid test',[7] when growing economic problems coincided with the end of 17 years of predominantly CDU–CSU rule and the emergence of strident political extremism on both the far right and far left.

Although in retrospect the Erhard coalition seems to be a brief post-script to the long Adenauer era, initially there seemed to be no reason why it should collapse so rapidly. Economic growth improved sharply in 1964, and in the election of September 1965 the CDU–CSU won 47.6 per cent of the vote, which was its second most impressive victory since 1949. In his first policy statement to the new *Bundestag*, Erhard dramatically announced that the post-war era was 'at an end'. He ambitiously attempted to launch a new programme for a 'shaped' or 'fully formed' society (*formierte Gesellschaft*) that would build on the achievements of the social market economy, yet at the same time persuade pressure groups such as the trade unions and professional and industrial associa-tions to moderate their selfish interests and co-operate with each other for the common good of society. This concept made little impact, even though it did pinpoint one of the main problems of contemporary democracy .

Of far more immediate concern to both the government and the people was the state of the economy. By early 1966 inflation was creeping up to a rate of 4 per cent per annum and public spending had been increasing more than government revenues since 1961. By 1965 the budget deficit had risen to 1.4 per cent of the GDP. Wages, too, had been increasing more rapidly than labour productivity. Not surprisingly, after the election the government's first priority was to fight inflation by squeezing domestic demand. The *Bundesbank* did this so effectively that it slowed down the domestic economy to the point of recession. Politically the consequences of this for Erhard were disastrous. His repu-tation for economic invincibility was severely damaged and in July 1966 the CDU lost the Rhineland–Westphalian *Land* election. The coalition was also divided on how to deal with the budget deficit. The CDU–CSU proposed extra taxes, while the FDP wanted cuts in expenditure. The last straw for the FDP was Erhard's failure to persuade the Americans to accept cuts in Bonn's financial contributions towards the cost of station-ing US troops in West Germany. The FDP's resignation from the coali-tion on 27 October led to Erhard's replacement as leader of the CDU–CSU by Kurt Kiesinger, who then rapidly negotiated a coalition with the SPD to the exclusion of the FDP.

Kurt Kiesinger had joined the Nazi party in 1933, and was elected to the *Bundestag*, 1949–58, after which he became minister–president of Baden–Württemberg

The Grand Coalition, 1966–69

The formation of the Grand Coalition marked a controversial period in the politics of the FRG. It gave the SPD the chance to gain political cred-ibility and finally break with the Schumacher legacy of opposition by accepting the responsibilities of government, while the CDU saw membership as a chance to consolidate its position and remove the stranglehold of the Liberals on government. To many West Germans the Grand Coalition communicated a reassuring sense of unity in the face of the growing problems confronting the FRG, but others, particularly students and the left-wing intelligentsia, were appalled by the fact that the only parliamentary opposition to the new government was provided by the small FDP. To them it seemed as if the FRG was teetering on the edge of becoming a one-party state. The writer, Günter Grass, warned that 'the youth of our country will turn to left and right wing extremism'.[8]

The Grand Coalition became a target for extremism, but it did not cause this extremism by itself. On the right the rise of the National Democratic party of Germany, which bitterly criticized 'the so called pluralist society' and campaigned for a strong, nationalist Germany independent of NATO and the West, was primarily a product of the recession. On the left some of the more radical members of the Social Democratic Students Federation set up in December 1966 'the extraparliamentary opposition' (APO) in reaction to the formation of the Grand Coalition. Ever since the *Spiegel* affair there had been a growth in left-wing political activism, agitation and public debate that had challenged the political amnesia of the 1950s, but arguably the real motor for student unrest was the overcrowded, outdated and authoritarian nature of the German universities, which had hardly changed since the late nineteenth century. The unrest developed into 'the greatest trauma of the entire history of the Federal Republic',[9] and reached its peak at Easter 1968 when Rudi Dutschke, a leading member of APO, was shot and wounded by a right-wing assassin. This led to the most serious rioting in Germany since 1932, with demonstrations in 27 cities.

It was against this background, which could so easily have led to an authoritarian backlash, that the government pursued its policies for

The NPD (*Nationaldemokratische Partei Deutschlands*) was formed in 1964, but was already in decline by the late 1960s

Rudi Dutschke, 1940–79, initially made his name in a Berlin group called Subversive Action, which organized several demonstrations against the Vietnam War and the state visit of the Shah of Iran, 1966

The cultural revolution

Politically this was led by the three Hamburg-based papers: *Der Spiegel, Die Zeit* and *Der Stern*. They enthusiastically backed *Ostpolitik* and were increasingly anti-American and more sympathetic towards the USSR. The majority of the literary and academic intelligentsia moved sharply to the left and became highly critical of the *Bundesrepublik* and of conservative institutions generally. This mood was fuelled by such works as Fritz Fischer's *Griff Nach der Weltmacht* (see p. 138), Rolf Hochhuth's play *Der Stellvertreter*, which virtually accused Pope Pius XII of complicity in the Holocaust, and Karl Jaspers's *Wohin treibt die Bundesrepublik?* Jaspers argued vehemently that the FRG was about to develop into an authoritarian regime. The Eichmann trial of 1960 in Israel and the Auschwitz trial of 1963–65 of 16 former SS men and one prisoner overseer in Frankfurt refocused attention on Nazi crimes at a time when Ludwig Erhard and Franz-Josef Strauss were attempting to declare the end of the post-war era. Until the early 1980s the left dominated the political debate, and it was scarcely 'respectable' for any educated person to vote for the CDU!

34   The 'International Vietnam Congress' at the *Technische Universität*, West Berlin, 18 January 1968. Rudi Dutschke, a leading student militant, is addressing the Congress

Presse- und Informationsamt der Bundesregierung, no. 132252/EN

These books were published in English: F. Fischer, *Germany's Aims in the First World War*; R. Hochhuth, *The Deputy*; K. Jaspers, *The Future of Germany*

Keynesianism: The econonomic theory based on the work of the British economist, John Maynard Keynes, who advocated state investment and public works at times of economic recession (demand management) to avoid unemployment (see Document 58)

stabilizing the economy, updating the constitutional structure of the state and beginning the difficult process of rethinking the FRG's foreign policy (see p. 303). All in all it is fair to say that 'the Grand Coalition managed to set Germany back on track in the most difficult circumstances'.[10] The economics minister, the SPD Karl Schiller, and the CSU finance minister, Strauss, although temperamentally very different, formed a strong team which was able to restore confidence in the economy. In June 1967, when the recession was at its trough, the *Bundestag* passed the Stabilization Law which set up a legal framework to enable the government to steer the economy in times of slump by raising credits, altering income and business taxes, and building up reserve funds for public investment. These measures, which were inspired by the determination to avoid a repetition of the economic crisis of 1930–33, were widely praised as the '"Magna Carta" of Keynesianism in a market economy', although criticized by others as 'corporate gradualism'.[11] They did, however, restore confidence. By 1969 the GDP grew by 5.6 per cent and inflation dropped to 1.5 per cent.

The Grand Coalition's commitment to more intervention in the economy inevitably involved some encroachment by the central govern-

ment on the financial powers of the *Länder*. In June 1967 Article 109 of
the Basic Law was changed so that the *Länder* governments would be
forced to take account of the condition of the national economy as a
whole when planning their budgets. Two years later further changes were
made to the Basic Law, facilitating financial co-operation between the
Länder and central government in such areas as higher education, agriculture and structural improvements to the regional economy. These
reforms inevitably strengthened the power of the central government,
but the constitutional position of the *Länder* in the *Bundesrat* still made
it difficult for Bonn to coerce them against their will.

| See Document 58 |

  Another constitutional measure of importance was the enactment of
the Emergency Laws. In 1949 when the Basic Law was drawn up (see
p. 289), these powers were still exercised by the high commissioners of
the occupying powers. Clearly the Basic Law needed to be amended so
that the FRG could protect itself in the event of war or civil unrest.
Inevitably, the very concept of an Emergency Law awoke old memories
and fears of the notorious Article 48 of the Weimar Constitution, which
had helped Hitler to power. A campaign group was set up called
'Emergency of Democracy' which gained support not only from the
APO, but also from a considerable number of FDP and SPD voters.
Nevertheless, in spite of strident opposition, the law was passed in May
1968 and provision was made for an elected committee of 22 *Bundestag*
members and one representative from each *Land* in the *Bundesrat* to have
the power to issue decrees if two-thirds of the committee agreed that
parliament could no longer function effectively.

| See Document 47 |

  There was also discussion between the SPD and CDU–CSU about
dropping proportional representation and creating a first-past-the-post
voting system similar to the British system. The initial attractions of this
to them was that it would deny the small Liberal party the role of king-
maker in the formation of governments and thus enable a single party to
gain a sufficiently large majority to form a stable government by itself.
When a public opinion survey in January 1968 showed that the
CDU–CSU would gain a large majority through this electoral system, the
SPD quickly changed its mind.

  By 1969 cracks were beginning to appear in the coalition. Voting for
the new president (speaker) of the *Bundestag* in February and then for the
federal president was divided along party lines. Willy Brandt, the SPD's
chancellor candidate (see p. 303), despite the cautious attitude of many
of his colleagues, decided in September before the general election to go
for the option of an SPD–FDP coalition. The election was by no means a
foregone conclusion. Kiesinger was more popular than Brandt, but the
SPD did have some important advantages. Schiller made much of the
success of his economic policy, and showed that the SPD could be trusted
with the economy, while Brandt and Gustav Heinemann, who had been
elected federal president, managed to mobilize nearly all but the most
extreme left-wing intellectuals, journalists and opinion-formers behind
the SPD. In a hard-fought election campaign, the SPD and FDP won

Gustav Heinemann, 1899–1976

Heinemann initially served in the Adenauer cabinet, 1949–50, as minister of the interior, but resigned in 1950 and then withdrew from the CDU in protest against rearmament and Adenauer's policy of Western integration, which to him appeared to rule out the possibility of German reunification. He moved over to the SPD in 1957 and in 1966 became minister of justice. From 1969 to 1974 he was the president of the FRG. His political outlook was formed when he was a member of the Confessing Church (see p. 000) and he was convinced that the FRG should conduct a dialogue with the GDR and eastern Europe. As president he also advocated tolerance and understanding of the views of the New Left and APO.

between them 48.5 per cent (the FDP only 5.8 per cent) of the vote, while the CDU–CSU gained 46.1 per cent. Brandt and Walther Scheel, the leader of the FDP, then managed to convince their parties of the viability of a social–liberal coalition, and on 21 October 1969 Brandt was elected chancellor by the *Bundestag* with a narrow majority of 251 to 249.

See Document 80

Willy Brandt as chancellor, 1969–74

The first Brandt administration

The SPD–FDP coalition enabled Brandt in October 1969 to become the first SPD chancellor since 1930. Brandt's rhetoric and charismatic style of leadership awakened expectations which he was unable to satisfy, except in the area of *Ostpolitik* (see pp. 305–8). In his first speech as chancellor in the *Bundestag* he declared confidently 'we do not stand at the end of our democracy. We are only at the beginning', and then he made his famous invocation 'to dare more democracy'.[12] He announced a whole range of prospective reforms in taxation, welfare and law, all aimed at creating a fairer and more democratic society. Over the next four years he succeeded in expanding the provisions of the welfare state:

See Document 78

- The Pension Reform Act of 1972 made the rights to a pension less dependent on past financial contributions.
- The effectiveness of Health and Accident Insurance was improved, and family and unemployment allowances raised.
- The criminal law was modernized and made more humane.
- In particular, efforts were made to remove the inferior status of women. Abortion was made easier to obtain, although it was not until 1977 that the concept of guilt in divorce was swept away and replaced by the term 'irreparable breakdown'.
- Some attempt was made to reform the educational system. In 1971 the Educational Support Law provided grants for students from the lower income groups and after prolonged controversy some of the *Länder* introduced comprehensive schools.

- Equally controversial were the SPD's attempts to expand the role of workers' councils originally set up by the Adenauer government. These were bitterly contested and only in 1979 after a decision by the Federal Constitutional Court did the law take effect.
- Censorship was relaxed, as were laws against homosexuality.

Inevitably these welfare measures and social reforms drove up government spending at the very time when inflationary pressures, largely caused by the dramatic weakening of the American dollar and the collapse of the fixed exchange rates created by the Bretton Woods Agreement in 1944 (see p. 347), were increasing, and needed to be countered by cuts in both personal and public expenditure. The strong Deutschmark, which in the opinion of most economists was ripe for revaluation, tempted speculators to change millions of American dollars into West German marks. This enabled banks to grant loans to individuals and businesses on easy terms, which only further fuelled inflation. Both Finance Minister Möller and his successor, Karl Schiller, urged spending cuts, which were stubbornly opposed by the left wing of the SPD and the powerful and ambitious minister of defence, Helmut Schmidt (see p. 347). It was only when Schiller resigned in June 1972 that Schmidt, who then took over the combined Ministry of Finance and Economics, ruthlessly pushed through the very cuts he had opposed earlier.

This law created supervisory bodies in each company with more than 2000 employees, composed of equal numbers of representatives of employers and employees. However, in the case of deadlock, the chairman, who was elected by the shareholders and owners, had the casting vote

Terrorism

The wave of terrorism that swept through the FRG from 1970 to 1972 forced the government in one crucial area to revert to authoritarian policies more reminiscent of the Adenauer era at the height of the Cold War than the new era of democracy announced by Brandt in 1969. There were in 1971 some 392 extreme left-wing organizations with a total membership of 67,000, ranging from the reconstituted Communist party (KDP) to groups of urban terrorists, who represented the hard core of the radical student movement of the 1960s. The most well-known of these was the Baader-Meinhof group. Its aim was, through arson and assassination of state officials, particularly judges, to inspire 'the intimidated masses'[13] to liberate themselves from capitalist oppression. The potential danger for Brandt in all this lay in the increasing polarization of public opinion on the issue of urban terrorism. At a time when he was in the midst of negotiations over *Ostpolitik*, he could not afford to be accused of being soft on terrorism. He therefore carefully distanced his party from the extreme left, and in January 1972, together with the minister-presidents of the *Länder*, issued the so-called 'extremist directive', which reminded the authorities responsible for recruiting state employees that loyalty to the Basic Law was essential. Secret surveillance of the terrorists was authorized and a reorganization and co-ordination of the *Länder*

The KPD was banned in 1956. See also Document 84

police forces carried out. These measures were vindicated when Ulrike Meinhof and Andreas Baader were arrested in June 1972 after bomb attacks on the offices of Springer Press in Hamburg and on the head-quarters of the American army in Heidelberg. In September, terrorism returned to the FRG when the Olympic Games in Munich were the scene of an Arab terrorist attack which killed 11 Israelis and one German policeman.

The election of November 1972 and Brandt's second administration

A vote of 'constructive no confidence' was a vote of no confidence which actually designated a successor to the chancellor (see p. 289)

Brandt's *Ostpolitik* came in for fierce criticism at home, and thus the 'extremist directive' must be seen as partly a response to the criticism of those like Gerhard Schröder (see p. 301), who accused the Brandt–Scheel government of a 'fatal drift to the Left'.[14] Brandt's government only survived the vote of constructive no confidence in April 1972 on its *Ostpolitik*, which was tabled by the CDU–CSU, by a mere two votes. These, it later emerged, were won over by bribery. Three weeks after the Basic Treaty was ratified in May 1973, Bavaria applied unsuccessfully to the Federal Constitutional Court to have it declared incompatible with the Basic Law of 1949. By the summer of 1972 defections from both the SPD and FDP had eroded the government's slender majority in the *Bundestag*. The SPD's difficulties were further increased by a severe defeat in the Baden–Württemberg *Land* election. Nevertheless, while the SPD itself was unpopular, Brandt and *Ostpolitik* were not. Thus he was ready to risk a general election which would in effect become a referendum on his handling of *Ostpolitik*.

In the constitution of the Weimar Republic there had been provision in these circum-stances for demanding a refer-endum, but the founding fathers of the Bonn Republic, mistrustful of the 'common man', had not revived this in the new constitution (see pp. 000 and 000). Instead, the only way of challenging a government deci-sion was the cumbersome route of going to the Federal Constitutional Court in Karlsruhe

Through 'a somewhat dubious manoeuvre'[15] he managed to contrive to lose a vote of no confidence in the *Bundestag* in September, which opened the way up for an election on 19 November. Brandt fought a quasi-presidential campaign in which, as one of his biographers observed, he 'reached new heights of charismatic leadership'.[16] The SPD gained 3 million new votes, the great majority coming from first-time voters, and achieved the greatest victory in its history.

According to the constitution, elec-tions were normally held at fixed intervals. However, as a result of his defeat both the opposi-tion and the governing coalition recommended to the president that there should be fresh elections

Despite this success, Brandt failed to dominate his second administra-tion. Immediately after his electoral victory he underwent an operation for laryngitis. In his absence Schmidt and Herbert Wehner, the deputy party chairman, appointed the new cabinet without consulting him. When Brandt came out of hospital, he became increasingly remote and indecisive. Within the SPD divisions between the right and left intensi-fied. At the party conference in March 1973 the left, which drew its support mainly from the Young Socialists, the SPD youth movement, strengthened its grip on the party directorate, where it won 28 of the 34 seats.

Brandt's problems were compounded first by the continued specula-tive conversion of billions of dollars into Deutschmarks, and then by the hike in oil prices in November 1973. From January to March 1973 the

West German money supply was swamped by the inflow of 27.8 billion dollars. Only when the Deutschmark left the Bretton Woods system in March and its relation to the dollar was left to the market, was the *Bundesbank* able to implement a tight counter-inflationary policy. In October the effectiveness of this policy was destroyed by the decision of the Arab states, organized in OPEC, to triple the price of oil in the winter of 1973–4. Consequently, the FRG had to spend some 17 billion more marks on oil imports in 1974 than in 1973, thereby giving further impetus to inflation. The situation was exacerbated by trade-union militancy. In January 1974, for instance, the union of public employees went on strike, forcing the *Länder* to negotiate an 11 per cent wages increase. By the spring of 1974 the economists were forecasting 8 per cent inflation and high unemployment.

> In 1944 at Bretton Woods, USA, 44 states agreed to the creation of fixed rates of exchange between currencies after the war. In 1949 the Deutschmark accepted the Bretton Woods system

Just at the very time when decisive leadership was required, it was becoming obvious to the electorate that Brandt could not provide it. Consequently the SPD rapidly began to lose support. In March it even lost control of Hamburg, a traditionally left-wing stronghold. The final straw for Brandt was the revelation that his personal assistant, Günter Guillaume, was an East German agent and a member of the *Stasi*. In the marked absence of any support from the leading members of his party he resigned and was replaced by the ambitious Schmidt.

The Schmidt era, 1974–82

Schmidt was a very different man from Brandt. He was an abrasive realist who often spoke contemptuously of the more Utopian ideas of the left wing of his party. He was essentially a man of action or *Macher*, as he was called. To the silent majority in the FRG his decisiveness was a welcome change to Brandt's dithering, but within the SPD his pragmatism was to lead to serious problems. Between 1969 and 1972 the membership of the SPD had increased by 22.5 per cent, a considerable percentage of which had initially been members of the APO. The social composition of these new members was predominantly middle-class and their politics were

---

Helmut Schmidt, 1918–

At the end of the war Schmidt joined the SPD in Hamburg and in 1953, after holding various posts in the city's government, was voted into the *Bundestag*, where he became an expert on defence and security matters. He was also a major proponent of modernization within the SPD and influenced the Godesberg Programme of 1959 (see p. 322). After a spell back in local government in Hamburg, he returned to the *Bundestag* in 1965 and was appointed leader of the SPD parliamentary group, 1967–69. He was defence minister, 1969–72 and finance minister, 1972–74. As chancellor, 1974–1982, he emerged as a pragmatic but forceful leader who did much to strengthen West Germany's international reputation.

significantly more radical than the traditional blue-collar supporters of the SPD. Thus increasingly in the contentious areas of the economy and defence Schmidt's policies were subjected to a growing volume of criticism from them. By 1980, as Peter Pulzer observed, 'in many respects the West German divide between Left and Right now ran not between the parties but down the middle of the SPD'.[17]

See Document 85

Economic problems

The most difficult problem facing Schmidt right up to his resignation in 1982 was the economic consequences of the oil price rises. By 1975 unemployment had increased to one million and the GDP fallen by 1.6 per cent. The left wing of the SPD wanted the government to spend its way out of the recession, but Schmidt cautiously pursued a policy of moderate expenditure cuts and reductions in tax concessions. He was determined that the FRG should pay for the increased price of oil through exports and thus was strongly opposed to protectionism in the Western world. To prevent this he adopted a three-pronged strategy. He threw the formidable weight of the FRG behind successive measures for achieving exchange-rate stability. In 1978, together with the French President, Giscard d'Estaing, he took the lead in devising the European Monetary System in which members of the EC would co-ordinate their monetary and fiscal systems. He also worked hard to strengthen such international economic institutions as the International Monetary Fund and the World Bank and played a key part in the economic summits of the G7 (see p. 310). Under Schmidt it was quite clear, to quote Lothar Kettenacker, that 'West Germany was no longer the proverbial political dwarf and economic giant, but a fully accepted player on the global field.'[18]

The International Monetary Fund and the World Bank were set up at the Bretton Woods Conference in 1944

By 1978 the West German economy appeared to be well on the way to recovery. At the Bonn Economic Summit, Schmidt agreed that the FRG should act as a locomotive for the world economy and reflate its economy by the equivalent of 1 per cent of the GNP, provided that the Americans brought their own inflation under control. In the short term these measures seemed to work. In 1979 the GDP grew to 4.2 per cent and unemployment fell to below a million, but OPEC's second drastic price hike in the aftermath of the Iranian revolution in 1979–80 caused the price of oil to rise by 45 per cent for two consecutive years and plunged the FRG back into recession by late 1980.

Despite these recurring economic crises, throughout this period the majority of the population grew steadily more wealthy. Wages increased while the working week shrank and holiday entitlement grew. Mass tourism, as one sociologist observed, by encouraging 'spontaneity, mobility, the capacity for enjoyment and an interest in new experiences replaced the old values of order, thrift and self-discipline associated with the work ethic'.[19] Only in the 1980s when unemployment rose to over two million did the FRG become a ' two-thirds society',[20] a phrase used to describe the existence of an intractable rump of unemployed who were effectively excluded from the consumer society. Overrepresented in this underclass were the foreign workers living in Germany, who numbered some 4.5 million by 1981.

Party politics, 1974–82

Schmidt remained in office during this period only by virtue of a difficult balancing act between an ever more leftwards-inclined SPD and an increasingly more conservative FDP. Walther Scheel, who had been elected federal president in May 1974, was replaced by the more right-wing Hans-Dietrich Genscher, a friend of the new leader of the CDU, Helmut Kohl (see p. 352). Genscher would have preferred to work with the CDU, but for the time being the hostility of Strauss's CSU to the whole concept of *Ostpolitik* made this an impossibility. The situation was exacerbated by demands on the left of the SPD for economic reflation, while the FDP urged financial retrenchment and moved towards a more monetarist approach to the economy. In March 1976 it was uncertain whether the FDP would remain in the coalition. In Lower Saxony, for example, it was already negotiating a coalition with the CDU. For the

> Monetarism was a shift away from the Keynesian priorities of reducing unemployment to the belief that it was the government's main duty to control inflation and balance the budget

---

Foreign workers in the FRG

The West German government only began to import foreign workers on a large scale once immigration from the GDR dried up. Whereas before 1914 Germany had looked to eastern Europe for a source of extra labour (see p. 99), as a result of the Cold War employers were now forced to recruit in Greece, Turkey, Italy, North Africa, Spain and Portugal. In the early 1960s the government signed a number of labour-importation treaties with these states. During the rest of the decade immigration rose dramatically. By 1973 there were 2,595,000 foreign workers in the FRG, the majority of whom came from Turkey. As with the Poles some eighty years earlier, these workers were imported into West Germany 'as fodder to fuel economic growth'.[21] They were to come to Germany as '*Gastarbeiter*' (guest workers) and were not eligible for German citizenship.

During the recession of 1973 the West German government banned all further recruitment, but the number of foreigners nevertheless continued to increase, largely as a result of the immigration of dependents. Gradually the migrant workers developed 'mature ethnic groupings resembling the Polish community in the Ruhr before the First World War'[22] with their own newspapers and cultural clubs. The Turks and other Muslims also set up their own mosques. In 1987 Duisburg, for instance, had 30 mosques, while in the early 1990s 1200 Muslim parishes had been created in the whole of reunified Germany.

Most of the German population was ambivalent about the *Gastarbeiter*. Right into the 1970s there was relatively little social contact between the host community and the immigrants, and by the 1980s immigrants were becoming targets for the small racist groups that were beginning to emerge. On the other hand, a degree of assimilation had also taken place. In 1990 some 9.6 per cent of all marriages in Germany were 'mixed'.

time being, however, Schmidt was saved by the divisions within the CDU–CSU. Kohl was ready to accept *Ostpolitik* and work with the FDP, but Strauss and Hans Filbinger, the CDU minister-president of Baden–Württemberg, were still bitterly opposed to it and saw the FDP as 'the stirrup holder for the Social Democrats'.[23] In the *Bundestag* elections of October 1976 the distrust of Strauss amongst northern CDU voters and the FDP was a powerful factor which brought about the narrow CDU–CSU defeat. The Schmidt–Genscher coalition just managed to survive with a two-vote majority.

See Document 80

Schmidt's decisive but pragmatic leadership was another reason why the SPD–FDP coalition managed to struggle on until 1982. His genius for crisis management was fully displayed in 1977, when he refused to capitulate to blackmail by the 'Red Army Group' in the Mogadishu incident.

Schmidt's handling of this crisis enhanced his appeal to the electorate, but, as the 1980 election approached, he was again helped by the divisions in the CDU–CSU and the rivalry between Strauss and Kohl, which culminated in Strauss replacing Kohl as chancellor candidate. In the election campaign Strauss almost certainly 'frightened away more voters than he attracted'[24] and, consequently, while the CDU lost 4 per cent of its vote, the SDP's share remained stable and the FDP gained 10.6 per cent, its best result since 1961. The defeat of the CDU finally ended Strauss's hope of the chancellorship, and Kohl once again took over the leadership of the party.

See Document 80

Schmidt's position, however, remained precarious. Much of his party opposed the monetarist policy of the economics minister, the FDP Count Otto Lamsdorff, while the left wing of the SPD was implacably hostile to his twin-track policy on nuclear missiles (see p. 311). Politically the SPD also faced a growing challenge when the hundreds of citizen-initiative groups, which had sprung up during the 1970s to campaign against the government on such environmental issues as the building of nuclear

---

Schmidt and the Mogadishu incident

After assassinating the federal attorney-general and the director of the Dresdner Bank, the 'Red Army Group' kidnapped Hans-Martin Schleyer, the president of the Federal Association of German Industry, and demanded, in exchange for his release, the freeing of 11 terrorists from prison. Schmidt personally took control of the situation and insisted that there could be no deal. His resolution was tested on 13 October when an Arab terrorist group in close contact with the 'Red Army Group' hijacked a Lufthansa Boeing 737. After murdering the pilot in Aden, they flew the plane on to Mogadishu in Somalia. Schmidt rejected an exchange of the passengers for the terrorists and, after receiving permission from the Somali government, dispatched a force of élite West German border guards who successfully rescued the passengers on 17 October. Although this decisive action did not prevent the murder of the unfortunate Schleyer, it was nevertheless a severe defeat for the terrorists, which strengthened rather than weakened public confidence in the democratic institutions of the FRG.

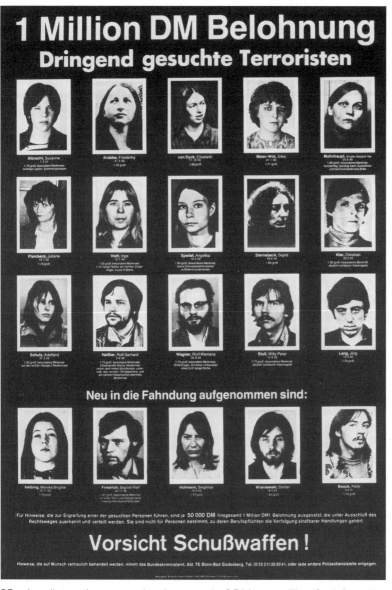

35 A police notice announcing the reward of DM one million for information leading to the arrest of leading members of the Red Army Group (REAF), 1977

Presse- und Informationsamt der Bundesregierung, no. 106899

power stations or airport runways, finally coalesced into a general umbrella organization known as the Green party in 1980. They now had the potential to attract many of the middle-class voters who had voted for the SPD in 1969 and 1972. By the summer of 1982 the FDP was beginning to move towards a coalition with Kohl. In a pre-emptive strike, Schmidt forced the FDP to resign from the coalition on 17 September.

His hopes of a dissolution of parliament and a general election were dashed when, on 1 October, Kohl won a vote of constructive no confidence in the *Bundestag* and was able to form a coalition with Genscher. A surprise SPD victory in the Hesse elections in late September had persuaded both Genscher and Kohl not to run the risk of holding an early election which might see the return of the SPD, supported, perhaps, by the Greens.

A Conservative counter-revolution: the Kohl–Genscher governments, 1982–89

In his inaugural speech to the *Bundestag*, Kohl promised a rigorous economic programme of cuts, deregulation and encouragement to entrepreneurs. More ambiguously, he also stressed the need for 'spiritual moral change'[25] which was interpreted by some observers to mean a return to the ideas of the Adenauer era. He did, after all, declare himself to be Adenauer's spiritual grandson. In reality, however, he was a cautious and pragmatic chancellor, who did much to preserve the legacy of his predecessors.

Kohl's immediate task on becoming chancellor was to consolidate his own position. Like Brandt in 1972 he engineered the loss of a no-confidence vote to force an early election in March 1983, which he fought on the basis of a programme for economic stabilization and the implementation of NATO's twin-track decision (see p. 311). The continuation of *Ostpolitik* was guaranteed by the inclusion of the FDP in the coalition. The SPD was in no position to defeat Kohl. Although its new chancellor candidate, Hans Jochen Vogel, was a moderate in the mould of Schmidt, his party was badly split on the issue of missile deployment in the FRG, and, by ruling out a coalition with the Greens, he had rejected in advance the only route whereby the SPD could at that stage have returned to power. Predictably, the election was a disaster for the SPD, whose share of the vote declined to the level of 1959. The CDU, on the other hand, gained its best result since 1957, while the FDP just cleared the 5 per cent hurdle with a mere 6.5 per cent of the vote. The Greens

Helmut Kohl, 1930–

In 1947 Kohl joined the youth wing of the CDU; he was elected to the *Landtag* of the Rhineland–Palatinate in 1959 and ten years later became the state's minister–president. In 1972 Kohl was elected chairman of the federal CDU and in 1976 was the chancellor candidate in the national election. Although in 1980 Straus replaced him as chancellor candidate, he retained the chairmanship of the CDU, and thus was in a strong position to form a government in 1982. Kohl presided over the reunification of Germany in 1990 and remained chancellor until 1998.

36 Helmut Schmidt (right) congratulates his successor, Helmut Kohl, on winning the vote of no confidence, 30 September 1982

Presse- und Informationsamt der Bundesregierung, no. 63874/11a

managed to win sufficient votes to gain representation in the *Bundestag* for the first time.

See Document 80

The government was only moderately successful in its attempt to return to the principles of the social market economy. It introduced a programme for tax cuts phased over seven years and tried to keep annual budget increases down to 3 per cent, but nevertheless it could not prevent a rise in welfare spending and industrial subsidies. Confronted with mass unemployment, it enacted measures to make the labour market more flexible, and to encourage retraining and early retirement, but in 1987 the number out of work was still over 2.2 million. In 1983 the economy had started to recover. With the collapse in oil prices in the mid-1980s the terms of global trade began once more to favour the FRG. Inflation fell from 6.2 per cent in 1981 to 0.6 per cent in 1986. For the next five years the FRG was able to build a large trade surplus which was annually worth more than 5 per cent of the GDP. It was this economic power that was to facilitate German unity in 1989–90 (see Chapter 18).

The stubborn persistence of unemployment, which remained at over two million for most of the decade, undoubtedly damaged the mid-term popularity of the government. In addition, Kohl's competence as party

'Party donations affair': over a long period of time considerable financial donations from industry had been made secretly and illegally to all three political parties. In 1984 the FDP finance minister, Count Lambsdorff, resigned when it was discovered that he had exempted the Flick Corporation from large tax payments after financial donations had been made to the FDP

leader was put in question by the continued bitter feuding between Strauss and the FDP. Within the CSU itself there were internal divisions caused both by Strauss's arrogant leadership and his extraordinary volte-face over *Ostpolitik* when, after years of hostility to *Ostpolitik* and Communism, he was instrumental in negotiating financial credits to the GDR (see p. 309). Two CSU members split off in 1983 to form the new right-wing Republican party, which in 1989 achieved considerable success in the West Berlin *Land* elections. Both the FDP and the CDU were also deeply involved in the 'party donations affair'. As chairman of the CDU, Kohl was inevitably caught up in the ramifications of this scandal, although he was not legally culpable. In the eyes of many voters the Bitburg affair also raised serious questions about his judgement. Kohl had planned to stage a symbolic gesture of reconciliation on the 40th anniversary of the end of the Second World War in a small military cemetery at Bitburg during President Reagan's state visit to Germany. When it was discovered that SS troops were buried there, Kohl, despite considerable international pressure, stubbornly persisted with the ceremony.

The debate on German national identity and the Nazi past

The Bitburg affair needs to be understood within the context of the debates on German identity and the German past, particularly the Holocaust. In the late 1970s and early 1980s a consensus was emerging that the FRG did not owe total loyalty to the USA, and had interests of its own which it was legitimate to pursue. Accompanying this growing self-confidence was the recurring question about the responsibility of the German people for the Holocaust. The debate erupted again when Kohl stated on a visit to Israel in January 1984 that by the 'grace of late birth'[26] his generation was not directly guilty. The fortieth anniversary of the end of the Second World War fuelled the debate further, and in 1986–87 it became the focus of a major and often bitter historical debate (*Historikerstreit*). Andreas Hillgruber in two essays appeared to compare the consequences and suffering of the destruction of the Reich in 1944–45 with the Holocaust, while Ernst Nolte, in an even more controversial article in the *Frankfurter Allgemeine Zeitung*, which was entitled 'A Past that Will Not Go Away', argued that the massacre of the Armenians by the Turks in 1915 and the Kulaks by the Soviets in 1929 were as iniquitous as the Holocaust and that consequently the Germans should not be accused of a unique crime.

Both historians were accused by the left of moral relativism and trivialization of the Holocaust.[27] Many on the left, such as the social philosopher, Jurgen Habermass, and Rudolf Augstein, the editor of the *Spiegel*, were convinced that these arguments were part of a conservative counter-revolution.

In the *Länder* elections the SPD was able to exploit the unpopularity of the government, but when it came to the General Election of January 1987 it was again defeated. It attempted in vain to attract the Green vote by committing itself to the 'ecologization of production and consumption',[28] but this merely exposed it to taunts from the CDU of being opposed to progress. The ruling coalition's campaign, however, was again seriously weakened by bitter in-fighting between the CSU and FDP. The vote of the CDU–CSU fell back to 44.3 per cent while the FDP rose to 9.1 per cent.

See Document 80

The party splits in the governing coalition deepened over the next two years. Right at the beginning of the new parliament there were bitter disageements over the legislative programme for the new parliament, and 15 members of the coalition withheld their vote when Kohl was elected chancellor by the *Bundestag*. In the *Länder* elections the CDU–CSU suffered a series of devasting defeats which accumulatively weakened Kohl's authority in Bonn. By the autumn of 1989 it seemed that Kohl's days as chancellor were numbered, but he was 'thrown a much needed lifeline'[29] by the collapse of the GDR.

In 1915 and 1916 the Turks had massacred and deported the majority of the Armenian population in Asia Minor. In 1929, during the collectivization programme, Stalin deported the expropriated Kulaks (independent farmers) to Siberia, where a large number died

THE GDR, 1961–89

Partial modernization, 1961–70

As for the Federal Republic, the 1960s were a watershed for the GDR. Ulbricht was convinced in 1961 that the closing of the inter-German border gave the GDR for the first time a chance to compete equally with the FRG. His aim, he stated, 'was to improve the material and cultural living conditions of our people, so that we clearly prove our superiority over West Germany and also over other capitalist countries'.[30] To achieve this, however, he had radically to modernize the cumbersome economic and planning structure of the fifties. Thus he and the new, more technocratically-minded members of the Politbureau, like Erich Apel and Günter Mittag, enthusiastically embraced the ideas of Yevsei Lieberman, the Russian economist, who advocated both ceding more independence to management and the introduction of the principle of profitability. To implement this, the 'New Economic System' for planning and managing the economy was announced in July 1963. A key position was held by the 82 Associations of Nationalized Enterprises (VVB) which were given a considerable latitude in carrying out proposals put forward by the National Planning Commission. Significantly, workers' wages were linked to profits in an attempt to boost production.

The New Economic System depended on the support, or at least co-operation, of the population. Thus there had to be a considerable change of emphasis in the control techniques practised by the party, and, to achieve this, Ulbricht underwent something of a metamorphosis into a 'liberal'. Rather than the overt use of terror there was a more subtle attempt to win over the population or at least neutralize discontent. These reforms, of course, stopped well short of allowing any genuine democracy to develop. Wolfgang Berger, one of the economic reformers of the sixties, recalled in 1992 that their 'aim was . . . to develop and improve the existing mechanisms, to stress the democratic in democratic centralism'.[31] The mass organisations did however, undergo a degree of liberalization. The Trade Union Federation (FDGB) was encouraged to defend more actively the interests of the workers, even though it was never allowed to develop into an independent trade union movement, as all the key positions in the union still lay in the hands of the SED. There was also a more sensitive attempt to appeal to young people. The Free German Youth (FDJ) temporarily lost its monopoly as a youth organization, and had, for a time, to compete with the unions and student clubs to attract young East Germans.

The constitutional and legal structure of the GDR was also partially modernized. The new legal code significantly liberalized the old Prussian legal system, which had remained the basis of East German law in many areas. On the other hand, the definition of crimes against the state was widened to include 'anti-state agitation', which was so loosely defined that it could be applied to almost any criticism of the regime. Increasingly the SED based its power on what Peter Ludz has called a form of 'consultative authoritarianism'[32] rather than Stalinist terror. In the local elections of October 1965, for instance, voters were allowed to reject individual candidates on the single list, although in practice only two candidates failed to be elected. There was also an element of public consultation when the new constitution was drafted, which in its final form was submitted to a referendum in April 1968. Freedom of conscience and religion were theoretically conceded as were many other civil rights, but the position of the SED as the ruling party was confirmed and thus declarations on the freedom of the media and on parliamentary sovereignty were mere travesties of the truth.

By the end of the decade it was clear that Ulbricht's gamble had failed. The hostile reaction of the population to the invasion of Czechoslovakia by Warsaw Pact troops in August 1968 (see p. 304), in which the GDR played a limited supporting role, revealed that under the surface there was still a deep resentment of the regime that the largely cosmetic social and political reforms had not obliterated. There were refusals in factories to sign party petitions backing the invasion, while in some towns groups of youths staged illegal gatherings and chanted such slogans as 'We want our freedom'.[33] In places the West German flag was flown; elsewhere Nazi songs were sung and at one FDJ campsite near Rostock a picture of Hitler was displayed.

See Document 86

Neither was there much chance that an East German economic miracle might mollify the population. The New Economic System had been only partially successful: initially production did increase, the living standards of the population rose and more consumer goods became available, but by 1969 East German productivity was again falling in comparison with that of the FRG. In a desperate attempt to reverse this trend, Ulbricht and the economic reformers invested vast sums, which had not originally been budgeted for, in introducing automation into the metalworking industries. This merely led to cuts in the consumer goods available for the population and reinforced popular discontent. Within the Politbureau, Honecker managed to mobilize sufficient support to compel Ulbricht in September 1970 to abandon the New Economic System. The association of similar reforms in Czechoslovakia (see p. 304) with political liberalization persuade Brezhnev and 'conservatives' in the GDR like Honecker to veto any further economic liberalization. Ulbricht remained in office as a mere figurehead and had impotently to stand aside while a more modest Five Year Plan was drafted. In April 1971 he was ordered to resign by Brezhnev, who was irritated by his insistence that the highly-developed nature of German socialism made the GDR the equal of the USSR. Two months later Honecker, who replaced him, abandoned his reforms completely. Ulbricht lingered on as 'honorary chairman of the SED' until his death on 1 August 1973.

Could Ulbricht's economic reforms have saved the GDR? Charles Maier[34] argues that if they had remained in place they would have 'eventually unleashed forces for pluralism', but they would also have enabled the GDR to develop a much more flexible economy, which could have withstood more effectively the shocks of the oil price rises in the 1970s and early 1980s. Honecker's economic policy failed catastrophically in 1989, but this does not mean that the continuation of Ulbricht's New Economic System would necessarily have saved the GDR. It was, after all, visibly failing in 1968–70. Harold James[35] has pointed out that in Hungary and Poland experimentation with semi-liberal economic policies did continue, but failed to prevent economic collapse. The GDR had a stronger economy than both those states, but even so it was also severely handicapped by deficient raw material reserves, an acute shortage of foreign exchange with which to purchase Western technology and its economic dependence on Russia. An inevitable consequence of this weakness was the mediocre quality of its industrial research, caused by poor equipment and low budgets.

The Unity of Social and Economic Policy, 1971–89

Honecker replaced the New Economic System with the much more cautious concept of the Unity of Social and Economic Policy. Central decision-making and controls were reintroduced without any serious attempt to analyse the underlying economic problems. Rising economic production was to finance social reform. In reality this meant that an expensive social welfare policy was to be pursued at the cost of industrial investment, which might ultimately have produced goods that could have been internationally competitive. Retrospectively Gerhard Schürer, the head of the Planning Commission, believed that this decision to subsidize overgenerous welfare provision was the fatal flaw in the GDR's economic policy. In 1991 he observed that 'that was when the switches were set. From then on the train travelled millimeter by millimeter in the wrong direction. It travelled away from the realities of the GDR.'[36] Social

---

Erich Honecker, 1912–94

Honecker was born in the Saar as the son of a miner. He joined the Communist youth organization in 1926 and, after attending a course in Moscow, became one of its leaders in 1930. He was arrested by the Nazis in 1935 and only freed in 1945. He was put in charge of building up the Free Communist Youth (FDJ) until 1955, and then, after a further year in the USSR, he returned to become minister for security. In this role he was responsible for planning and building the Berlin Wall in 1961. In the 1960s he was the 'crown prince' to Ulbricht, whom he replaced in 1971. When the GDR collapsed, legal proceedings were started against him, but in 1993 they were halted on the grounds of his ill health and he was allowed to join his wife in Chile.

---

expenditure rose by 90 per cent between 1971 and 1979, while national income increased by just 46 per cent.

Honecker's retreat to the orthodox policies of centralized planning ensured that a top-heavy system of bureaucratic control prevented the East German economy from reacting quickly to the economic challenges of the 1970s – the destabilization of the international monetary system and the dramatic rise in oil prices. Nor was the flexibility of East German industry helped by the socialization of the remaining small, independent enterprises. Errors and missed opportunities, as Charles Maier has commented, 'accumulated throughout that decade and emerged spectacularly during the 1980's'.[37] In January 1980 a belated attempt was made to streamline East German industry when the main branches of industry were organized into *Kombinate*, which embraced all the main factories in a particular industrial sector, but these, too, were in their turn subjected to the dead weight of bureaucracy, as their decisions were closely scrutinized by a Workers' and Peasants' Inspectorate.

The GDR's economy like West Germany's was severely hit by the sudden rise in the prices of oil and raw materials in 1973. Although the USSR did not immediately charge market prices for its oil exports to the COMECON states, the rapid rise in world prices for hydrocarbons and chemicals inevitably led to a worsening of the GDR's balance of payments, since the price of imports rose more steeply than the price of exports. Over the period 1972–75, for example, import prices rose by 34 per cent, whereas export prices increased by only 17 per cent. In turn, this sharp deterioration in the terms of trade led to the GDR increasing its foreign debt, particularly with the Western states. Honecker's failure to achieve solvency was to be one of the main reasons for the collapse of the GDR in 1989. As early as November 1973, he responded to pessimistic forecasts about the growth of debt up to 1980 by ordering, ostrich-like, all further work on such projections to cease. Again in May 1978 the Council of Ministers blocked attempts by the State Planning Commission to get to grips with the balance of payments problem on the grounds that it would irreparably damage the Unity of Economic and

Social Policy. West German loans in 1983 and 1984 (see p. 309) temporarily saved the GDR from bankruptcy, but by November 1987 the debt to the West had risen to 38.5 billion Valuta marks. The financial situation was made much worse in the early eighties by the failure of an ambitious attempt to develop a viable computer industry, which had cost the GDR nearly 14 billion marks. The economic outlook was so grim that it is not surprising that in September 1987 the *Stasi* was already reporting that economic problems and shortages were discrediting the regime.[38]

Valuta mark: the currency used for foreign trade by the GDR, which was roughly equivalent to the Deutschmark in value

The 'niche society'

While Honecker's economic policy proved in the long term to be fatal for the GDR, it did enable him for a time to neutralize opposition and create a social peace of sorts. Günter Gaus, the first West German permanent representative in East Berlin, coined the concept of the GDR as a 'niche society' where people withdrew into private retreats, such as the family, circles of friends or the pursuit of hobbies, 'so that a good man with his family and among friends can water his potted flowers, wash his car, play skat, have conversations, celebrate holidays'.[39] The corollary of this was that party control of the public sphere was at least grudgingly tolerated.

The concept of a 'niche society' was immediately seized upon by the West and became an overworked cliché used to explain the apparent acceptance of the regime by the population. The *Stasi* files show that in reality 'the evidence of workers unrest and the splutterings of revolt is far greater than ever imagined'.[40] Mary Fulbrook indeed questions whether there was ever 'a "golden age" in the GDR when the subordinate masses were genuinely content to leave politics to a well meaning but powerful élite'.[41] However, for a time Honecker did in the early to mid-seventies create at least the illusion of stability and an acceptance of the regime by the population. By the 1970s almost the whole population participated in the mass party organization. Diplomatic recognition by the West made the GDR an international fact of life. The vast majority of East Germans had little option but grudgingly to come to terms with the party. Acceptance of the regime was, of course, also assisted by Honecker's social reforms, a greater toleration initially towards writers, artists and

Honecker's cultural policy

Up to the mid-seventies there was something of a honeymoon with the cultural intelligentsia. The novelist, Ulrich Plenzdorf, was able to write, for instance, about 'a socialist drop-out'[42] who suffered from having to fulfil industrial norms and pressures to conform. There was also a spate of books about the difficulties experienced by women in the GDR. However, in 1976 the honeymoon came to an abrupt end when the folk-singer Wolf Biermann was deprived of his passport whilst on a tour in the FRG.

intellectuals, and the production of more consumer goods, such as fridges, washing machines and cars. The strength of the regime seemed confirmed in March 1978 when the Protestant Churches recognized that they had to work within a socialist society and in return received a 'precarious and partial negotiated autonomy'.[43]

Growing opposition

Some of the factors that gave the regime this illusion of permanence began, by the end of the 1970s, to develop the potential for undermining it. *Ostpolitik* and the implications for human rights of the Helsinki Accords (see pp. 310–11) increased popular demand for closer contact with the West and a more liberal regime. The March agreement of 1978 had sought to exploit the Church 'as an indirect means of controlling dissent'.[44] Thus, astonishingly frank discussions could take place, provided that they occurred on Church premises and within the context of a gathering or prayer meeting presided over by a priest who, it was understood, would keep a tight control of the situation and ensure discretion.

In the late seventies and early eighties under the protection of the Church it was perhaps inevitable that incipient political activism should take root. Initially a network of small peace groups grew up. These were critical both of NATO's deployment of missiles in West Germany and of the GDR's introduction of military education into the school curriculum, as well as of the Soviet invasion of Afghanistan. In June 1985, at the Peace Workshop in East Berlin, the possibility of setting up a GDR-wide seminar on human rights was first mooted, and in the autumn two campaign groups were founded, *Gegenstimmen* (Counter-voices) and *Initiative Frieden und Menschenrechte* (Initiative for Peace and Human Rights). The latter group functioned independently of the Church and attempted to exploit Gorbachev's more liberal approach to put pressure on Honecker for change. In 1986 the Peace Workshop attracted some 1300 participants and was banned the following year by the *Stasi*. The mid-eighties also saw the rise of the environmentalist movement for which the disaster at the Russian nuclear power station in Chernobyl in 1986 acted as a catalyst. The *Stasi* managed with some success to sow dissension among the environmentalists and split the movement, but the subsequent burgeoning of small groups in fact only served to fuel public debate.

In 1987 there briefly seemed to be some hope that the GDR would follow Gorbachev's example and embark upon a policy of liberalization. Before his state visit to West Germany, Honecker allowed a dramatic increase in the issue of visas for those who wished to see relatives and friends in the FRG. The celebrations marking the 750th anniversary of the foundation of Berlin also deliberately fostered 'the view of the GDR as a forward-looking, progressive and increasingly tolerant society'.[45] On

---

See Documents 78 and 79

Events in the USSR, 1985–88: In 1985 the 54-year-old Mikhail Gorbachev came to power as general secretary. He was determined to reform the Soviet economy. To do this he realized that the financial drain caused by the arms race and the war in Afghanistan would have to be stopped and that both Soviet society and the economy would have to be modernized. He therefore pursed the policies of *perestroika* (restructuring the economy) and of *glasnost* (more openness in politics) and sought to end the Cold War

the Olaf Palme peace march of September 1987, for example, the unoffi-
cial peace movements were allowed to participate alongside official
representatives of the GDR. Yet by the late autumn there were signs that
the government was reverting to a policy of confrontation. In November
1987 the *Stasi* raided the Environmental Library in Berlin, seized the
printing presses and made several arrests. In January 1988 large numbers
of demonstrators who sought to infiltrate the annual Luxemburg–
Liebknecht parade were also arrested. Over the next twelve months
Honecker continued to clamp down on all expressions of dissident views.
He even censored the Soviet magazine *Sputnik*, as it was uncomfortably
full of Gorbachev's ideas on *perestroika* and *glasnost*. He failed, however,
to stamp out the activities of the dissidents. In May 1989, for example,
dissident groups monitored the local elections and exposed the massive
vote-rigging in favour of the SED.

> **Luxemburg–Liebknecht Parade**: This was held in honour of Rosa Luxemburg and Karl Liebknecht, who were murdered by *Freikorps* troops in January 1919 (see p. 170)

Up to this point the great mass of the population still remained quies-
cent, but in the course of the summer of 1989, with the opening of the
Hungarian frontiers to Austria this was to change.

Conclusion: a tale of two Germanies

Despite gloomy predictions in the early 1960s that the West Germans
were merely 'fair weather democrats',[46] the constitution of the FRG relatively easily withstood the minor recession of 1966–67, the student riots
of 1968, the subsequent outbreak of terrorism, and the major economic
crises caused by the steep rise in oil prices in 1973 and 1979. Indeed, with
the development of numerous citizen initiatives and the Green movement at the end of the 1970s the FRG was arguably well on the way to
becoming a more participatory democracy. The pessimistic forecast of
Karl Jaspers (see p. 341) could not have been further from the truth.

Behind the barrier of the Wall the GDR was able to achieve a stability
of sorts. Ulbricht, hitherto 'the keeper of the holy grail of Marxism–
Leninism',[47] began to dismantle the rigidly centralized economic structure of the Stalinist economy and to create a more flexible economy in
which the profit motive acted as an important spur. Eventually these
reforms would have 'unleashed forces for pluralism',[48] which would in all
probability have destabilized the GDR politically. In that sense
Honecker's return to orthodoxy, coupled with more generous welfare
policies, was at least a short-term act of preservation, even though in the
longer term it prevented the East German economy from responding
more flexibly to the new post-Keynesian demands of the world economy
after 1973.

The collapse of the GDR in 1989 has inevitably focused the attention
of contemporary historians on its obvious structural weaknesses, yet
arguably a more challenging area of research is the 'astonishing fact' that
the GDR 'none the less existed for 40 years'.[49] Some historians see its
history as a 'Decline and Fall in Stages' (to quote the title of Mitter and

Wolle's book – *Untergang auf Raten*)[50] from 1953 onwards, but this interpretation ignores the fact that there was in fact 'a rise and fall, from the baseline of 1953 to a period of comparative tranquility in the early 1970s'.[51] Only from the mid-1970s onwards was this gradually undermined by economic problems and the 'increasing permeability of the GDR towards the West'[52] as a consequence of *Ostpolitik* and the Helsinki Agreements. In the end, however, it was the weakening of Russia's will to hold the GDR that signalled its demise.

18 Reunification and After

TIMELINE

1989	2 May	Hungary dismantles barbed-wire barriers on border with Austria
	10–11 Sept.	Hungary allows GDR citizens to cross frontier to Austria
	7 Oct.	Gorbachev visits GDR for 40th anniversary
	9 Oct.	70,000 demonstrate against SED regime in Leipzig
	18 Oct.	Honecker replaced by Krenz
	9 Nov.	Berlin Wall breached
	13 Nov.	Modrow becomes prime minister of GDR
1990	19 Jan.	Former *Stasi* offices stormed
	12–14 Feb.	Two-Plus-Four Formula announced at Ottawa
	18 Mar.	GDR election gives 'Conservative alliance' majority
	1 July	Monetary, economic and social union between FRG and GDR
	31 Aug.	Unification Treaty signed
	11–12 Sept.	Two-Plus-Four Treaty signed in Moscow
	3 Oct.	GDR joins FRG: Germany reunified
1991	Jan.–Mar.	First Gulf War
		Three million East Germans unemployed or on short-time work
1992–93		Post-reunification recession
		Massive increase in asylum seekers entering Germany
1994	Oct.	General election: CDU–CSU–FDP coalition retains power
	12 July	Federal Court rules that German troops can be deployed in multilateral operations outside Nato
1996	Jan.	Kohl's 50-point plan for reform of the economy
1998	Sept.	General election: Red–Green electoral victory
1999	Mar.	Oscar Lafontaine resigns as finance minister
	Mar.–June	Kosovo war
	Nov.	CDU funding scandal is revealed
	Dec.	Germany agrees to participate in European Rapid Reaction Force
2000	Apr.	3.99 million Germans unemployed (9.8 per cent)
2001	11 Sept.	Terrorist attacks in New York and Washington
2002	Jan.	Deutschmark replaced by Euro
	Sept.	General election: SPD–Green coalition just hangs on to power
2003	Mar.–Apr.	Second Gulf War

Introduction

However inevitable it might seem in retrospect, the collapse of the GDR was not foreseen in Moscow, Bonn or any other Western capital. German unification was not, as proponents of *Ostpolitik* envisaged, a gradual knitting together of the two states but rather a sudden 'hurtling and hurling together sanctioned by great power negotiations'.[1] Without the radical political and economic changes that swept through eastern Europe in the late eighties, German unity would have been inconceivable. Russia, weakened by military stalemate in Afghanistan and the flare-up of ethnic conflicts within its borders, and virtually bankrupt, was no longer in a position to enforce the Brezhnev Doctrine (see p. 304). Gorbachev thus had little option but to wind up the Cold War, seek Western credits and try to rejuvenate the Soviet economy by the partial introduction of market principles. By early autumn 1989 both Poland and Hungary had virtually ceased to be members of the Soviet bloc.

Key issues

- What were the immediate causes of the collapse of the GDR?
- What persuaded Kohl to abandon the gradualist approach to German unity?
- How did Kohl achieve unity with international consent?
- Why did the territories of the former GDR suffer economically from unity?
- What was the impact of unity on the German economy as a whole?
- Was reunification the main cause of German economic weakness in the 1990s?
- What political impact did reunification have on the politics of the FRG?
- To what extent did a new German foreign policy emerge in the 1990s?

The collapse of the GDR

To survive the enormous changes sweeping through eastern Europe in the late summer and autumn of 1989, the GDR needed to win the loyalty of its own people. Whilst there was some support amongst intellectuals for an independent and more democratic East German state which could pioneer a 'third way', avoiding both capitalism and the post-Stalinist dictatorship of the SED, events were to show in 1990 that the over-whelming desire of the population was for unity with the FRG as the surest way of guaranteeing the rule of law and (so it was hoped) prosperity. Throughout 1988–89 West Germany had continued to exercise its magnet-like attraction on the East Germans. In 1988 nearly two and a half million GDR citizens received visas to visit the FRG, and in the period from November 1988 to September 1989 over 86,000 requests for permanent emigration were granted. Not surprisingly then, it was the emigration issue that was to be the catalyst to the terminal crisis of the GDR.

On 2 May 1989 Hungary began to dismantle the barbed wire along its frontiers with Austria, thereby providing a potential escape route to the West. Toward the end of July thousands of East Germans travelled to Hungary, ostensibly on holiday. By 7 August, 200 had broken into the gardens of the West German embassy in Budapest and were camping there in an attempt to force Bonn to intervene on their behalf with the Hungarian and Austrian authorities and so facilitate their emigration to Austria and thence to the FRG. On 11 September the Austrians agreed to

Developments in Poland and Hungary, 1988–89

As early as January 1989 the Polish Communist party decided to recognize the Solidarity movement (see p. 311), which had been officially banned in the autumn of 1982. This concession, which was not opposed by Gorbachev, led to the 'round table' negotiations between the government, Church and Solidarity, that were influential in speeding up the pace of change throughout the eastern bloc. It was agreed that Solidarity could contest the elections of June 1989, although the Communist party still reserved 60 per cent of the seats in the lower house. In August, however, as a result of the growing popularity of Solidarity, which won most of the seats available to it, a new Solidarity-led government was formed, in which the Communists had only two members. Significantly, Gorbachev made it clear that the USSR would not intervene to prop up an unpopular Communist regime. In Hungary modernizing Communists seized control of the party in early 1989 and committed it to recognizing the emerging non-Communist parties and to removing the fortifications and alarm systems along the Austrian border. As early as March 1989 Gorbachev declared that he would not interfere in Hungarian domestic politics. In June 'round table' talks began between the government and the opposition groups. In October a new temporary democratic constitution was adopted and free parliamentary elections were held in March and April 1990.

accept them and they began to pour across the frontier. In the meantime more GDR refugees similarly besieged the West German mission in East Berlin and the embassies in Prague and Warsaw. By early September, 3500 East Germans were encamped in the embassy grounds in Prague.

Unwilling to force a confrontation on the eve of the celebration of the 40th anniversary of the founding of the GDR, Honecker responded to pressure from the West German and Czech governments to grant them exit visas to the West, but he insisted that they would have to travel back through the GDR to West Germany in sealed trains, after which the Czech–GDR frontier would be closed. There was no chance of keeping these events secret from the rest of the population of the GDR whose televisions were nightly turned on to news programmes from the West German television stations. Once the route the trains were taking to the West German frontier became known, large crowds attempted to storm Dresden station in the hope of somehow boarding them. For the first time since 1961, the crippling prospect of mass emigration again faced the GDR government.

This much-publicized exodus was a turning-point for the protest movement within the GDR. Paradoxically, the sudden opportunity to emigrate prompted the formation of new and stronger opposition movements amongst those who were determined to stay and press for democratic reforms at home. The government's hesitant and unsure handling of the crisis had lifted the 'taboo on open debate; private grumbles could no longer be isolated, ignored, denied'.[2] There was the sudden perception that protest really might effect change. In the vanguard of this were small reform groups, which over the previous few years had been meeting under the protection of the Evangelical Church (see p. 360). In the early autumn of 1989 they began to reorganize themselves into political organizations such as the *New Forum, The Social Democratic Initiative, Democracy Now, Democratic Awakening*, etc., and work for political change.

The crisis escalated significantly on 24 September when a mass demonstration took place at Leipzig. Since 1982 there had been regular Monday evening services in the *Nikolaikirche* dedicated to praying for peace. When these resumed in early September 1989 at the time of the annual international Leipzig trade fair, they attracted increasingly large numbers. On 25 September tens of thousands of demonstrators paraded peacefully through the city singing protest songs and shouting out such slogans as 'We are the people' and 'We are staying here' (implying that they would push for reform at home rather than escape to the FRG). In retrospect it can be seen that the 'fate of the East German regime was decided on the Leipzig Ring'[3] on four successive Monday evenings between 25 September and 16 October. Although there were clashes between the police and demonstrators, particularly on 2 October, the crucial factor was that the regime did not dare use force on a large scale to clear the streets, as the Chinese had in Tiananmen Square earlier in the year. Once the police permitted the Leipzig demonstrators to march into the inner city on 9 October they set a precedent that was followed all over the GDR in the coming weeks.

Nikolaikirche: St Nicholas's Church

The reasons for non-intervention are complex. The demonstrators were disciplined and non-violent, and the Politbureau was deeply divided about what approach to take and unsure of the loyalty of the factory defence groups and the young conscript policemen. Above all, in the climate of reform initiated by Gorbachev, it is doubtful whether any such intervention would have been successful. When Gorbachev visited East Berlin on 6–7 October to celebrate the 40th anniversary of the GDR, he pointedly supported reform, remarking cryptically that 'life punishes late comers'.

On 17 and 18 October the frustration in the Politbureau with Honecker's stubborn refusal to reform and come to grips with the crisis sweeping the GDR led to a ' palace revolution' and his replacement by Egon Krenz, the former head of security and youth affairs. The Krenz regime, which lasted for barely a month, was nothing but a 'brief interregnum'.[4] He grandly announced a policy of change or *Wende*, but in reality his concessions were all designed to protect the SED's monopoly of power. There were, for instance, to be elections on the basis of the constitution, which of course could only result in confirming the leading role of the SED. At local level, however, the SED leaders were already beginning to negotiate with Church leaders.

In the absence of any effective restraints by the police or the army, the crowds of demonstrators in the cities continued to grow. On 4 November half a million congregated in Alexanderplatz in East Berlin to demand further reform and the right to travel. Two days later a proposal was made by the Krenz government to issue permits for travel on up to 30

37 GDR refugees in the grounds of the West German embassy, Prague, 1 October 1989

Presse- und Informationsamt der Bundesregierung, no. 132197/EN

days a year, but this was rejected by the *Volkskammer* as insufficient. On 9 November a more sweeping concession was made, which gave to all GDR citizens with a passport the right to an exit visa valid for any frontier crossing including Berlin. Initially this was supposed to take effect from the morning of 10 November, but it was announced prematurely to a press conference on the evening of the 9 November, and at 11 p.m. the border guards facing a crowd of 20,000 opened up the crossing points. The breaching of the Berlin Wall became the symbol of the revolutions

Volkskammer: the lower house of parliament

that ended Communist power in eastern Europe, even though Krenz hoped that it would be an act of damage limitation and win back support for the government and party. His hopes were proved wrong. All over the GDR local party leaders came under attack and were forced to resign. Those who remained were forced onto the defensive by the revelations of party incompetence and corruption.

On 13 November the *Volkskammer*, which was still dominated by the SED, charged Hans Modrow, the Dresden party secretary, with the formation of a new government. Modrow, who had never been trusted by Honecker, was seen as a reformer and modernizer. Although, in his opening speech to the *Volkskammer,* he recognized the role of the people in the 'democratic renewal' of the GDR, the government was still unelected and dominated by the SED. Consequently, it was unable to appease the new opposition groups, and even within the *Volkskammer* the old bloc parties, the CDUD and LDPD (see p. 291) began to reconstitute themselves as genuine democratic parties.

To contain the revolution, the Modrow government agreed on 22 November to an initiative first put forward by the Church for a dialogue with the opposition groups. The model taken was the Polish 'round table' meetings where Solidarity delegates had negotiated with the Warsaw government (see p. 365). Between 7 December and 12 March 1990 there were 16 (East German) 'round table' meetings, which, in the absence of elections, 'became the repository of whatever legitimacy existed'.[5] At the first meeting Modrow conceded that free elections should take place on 6 May 1990.

In January the major bone of contention between the government and opposition groups was the future of the former Ministry for State Security, *the Stasi*, which in December had undergone a metamorphosis into the Office for National Security. Modrow believed it still had a role in defending the state from subversion from within, while the opposition groups were adamant that it should be dissolved. Faced with the threatened resignation of the bloc parties from his coalition and the boycott of the 'round table' meetings by the opposition groups, he agreed on 11 January to its dissolution. Two days later the authority of his government received another blow when a protest demonstration escalated out of control. Angry crowds invaded the old *Stasi* headquarters in the *Normannenstrasse* and began to ransack the files. They could only be restrained by the personal intervention of Modrow and the leaders of the New Forum (see p. 360).

By mid-January Modrow was faced with problems on all sides:

- heavy emigration westwards showed no signs of stopping;
- demoralization of the SED was continuing apace;
- within the *Volkskammer* the bloc parties were reluctant to be associated with the SED or, as it was now called, the Party of Democratic Socialism (PDS).

38 The Berlin Wall, 10 November 1989, after its opening the evening before

Presse- und Informationsamt der Bundesregierung, no. 1131364/EN

39 On 11 November 1989 citizens of the GDR were able to drive unimpeded through the Helmstedt/Marienborn checkpoint. Here we can see a convoy of East German Trabants

Presse- und Informationsamt der Bundesregierung, no. 116932

Once he agreed to advance the date for the election from 6 May to 18 March 1990, Modrow was able in early February to construct a 'government of national responsibility' which included the main opposition parties and groups. The March elections, which reduced the PDS vote to 16.4 per cent and gave the CDU 40.8 per cent of the vote, marked the end of Communism in the GDR and made unification a virtual certainty. As Konrad Jarausch observed, 'the overwhelming vote for quick union with the Federal Republic provided irrefutable domestic and international legitimation for the unification drive'.[6]

Reunification: Kohl seizes the initiative

In the autumn of 1989 the Kohl government in Bonn had no idea that the gathering crisis in the GDR was terminal. At the end of October Kohl wished Krenz 'success' with his reforms and, very much in the tradition of *Ostpolitik*, declared that Bonn wanted 'a calm sensible development'.[7] This measured response was, however, overtaken by the sheer pace of change in the GDR. The growing demand for unity, the flood of refugees westwards and the visible disintegration of the GDR ultimately forced Kohl into pursuing a more active policy for German unity. Still, even by 28 November in his 10-point programme he was envisaging a confederate structure that would only slowly and in the distant future lead to full unity. Then, just before Christmas, he visited the GDR where the enthusiastic reaction of the crowd in Dresden left him in little doubt of the strength of feeling for national unity.

Lothar de Maizière (1940–) joined the CDUD as a young man, but refused any party job until November 1989. As a lawyer, he made a speciality of defending Christians who were in trouble with the GDR authorities, although the *Spiegel* was later to accuse him of being a *Stasi* informer

Under pressure from public opinion and the accelerating disintegration of the GDR, Modrow, too, moved closer to advocating unity. On 1 February, in a document entitled 'For Germany, one Fatherland', he conceded that the 'union of the two German states [was] moving onto the agenda'.[8] He then went on to outline plans for an economic, currency and transport union, which would gradually evolve by way of a confederation into a united neutral German federation. Kohl rejected the proposal for neutrality outright because the continued membership of Germany in NATO was essential to win the support of the Western powers for unification, and he was now ready to force the pace of both political and economic currency union. The success of the East German CDU in the election of 18 March and the formulation of a coalition government led by the CDU leader Lothar de Maizière made the realization of Kohl's plans much easier. By the end of April the two German leaders agreed in principle on a monetary and economic union to begin on 1 July.

It was crucial to gain the agreement of the USSR, America and Germany's main western European allies, Britain and France, to German unity. However, only Russia and America had the power to stop it. Thus the real negotiations were between Bonn, Moscow and Washington. At first Gorbachev was opposed to the liquidation of the GDR, and in

December 1989 he told his Central Committee that he would 'see to it that no harm comes to the GDR'.[9] Yet by the end of January his support for it was ebbing rapidly. On 10 February he informed Kohl in Moscow that the Germans themselves should decide on the question of German unity, although he was still reluctant to agree to a united Germany's membership of NATO. Nevertheless, the way to unity now seemed clear. At Ottawa four days later, President Bush also gave the green light and outlined a formula for proceeding with the negotiations, the Two-Plus-Four talks, which would bring together both the two Germanies and the four former occupying powers, who still had residual rights in Berlin. In a series of negotiations in Bonn, Berlin and Paris in the summer of 1990, German unity was brokered, and on 12 September the Two-Plus-Four Treaty was signed in Moscow. It was in effect a peace treaty legally ending the Second World War. It terminated the remaining rights of the former occupying powers in Germany and committed Germany to recognizing the Oder–Neisse border with Poland. Residual Russian opposition to German unity and the membership of a united Germany in NATO had been overcome by generous West German loans, which Gorbachev hoped would facilitate the modernization of the Russian economy. 'This was', as Garton-Ash has observed, '*Realpolitik* in a highly civilized form with the telephone and cheque book instead of blood and iron, but it was *Realpolitik* all the same.'[10] Any incipient opposition in the West, particularly in London and Paris, was stilled by Kohl's insistence on Germany's continued membership of NATO and the incorporation of East Germany into the European Community.

From April to October the de Maizière government presided over the liquidation of the GDR. Parallel to the Two-Plus-Four Talks, the two Germanies negotiated the terms of their reunification. The State Treaty on Monetary, Social and Economic Union was concluded on 18 May. The introduction of the Deutschmark at midnight on 1 July was in effect 'the third major German monetary reform of the century',[11] but unlike those of 1923/4 or 1948 (see p. 190 and 286), the monetary assets of those affected were strengthened rather than sacrificed.

- wages and pensions were converted at the rate of one East mark to one DM;
- savings above 4000 marks for those between 14 and 59 years old were converted at the rate of 50 pfennigs to one East mark;
- for citizens over the age of 59 this limit was raised to 6000 East marks.

Negotiations for political unity began on 6 July. The negotiators faced the challenge of uniting 'two incompatible legal systems and meshing opposing political cultures'.[12] Although de Maizière and his spokesman in the negotiations, Günter Krause, tried hard to argue that the new unified Germany should be a genuine mix of both the former GDR and the FRG, in practice the overwhelming power of Bonn ensured that essentially the treaty, which was signed on 31 August 1990, incorporated the GDR into the FRG. In Article 23 of the Basic Law, which had been used to integrate the Saar territories into the FRG in 1957, there was a simple mechanism for unity. It provided for the automatic extension of the Basic Law to any other regions of Germany joining the FRG. The political structure of the new Germany was 'simply the Federal republic writ large'.[13] Thus the former *Länder* in the GDR were to be reconstituted and given representation in the *Bundesrat*, while 144 new members representing the East Germans would take up their seats in the *Bundestag* in Bonn. At midnight on 2 October 1990 a united Germany came into existence.

It had been intended in 1948 that the Saar would remain an autonomous territory economically fused to France, but when the population voted for union with the GDR in 1955, the French raised no objections to it becoming the eighth *Land* of the FRG. See also Document 87

The economic legacy of unification

In the heady days of the summer of 1990 it was assumed that unification would be quick and painless and that the East German *Länder* would rapidly undergo an economic miracle, as West Germany had done in the early 1950s. However the reality was very different. An opinion poll, which was taken in the summer of 1991 showed that a large majority on each side believed that 'only since unification has it become evident how different Eastern and Western Germany are'.[14] The West Germans began to resent the economic burdens imposed by reunification, while the East Germans saw themselves as only second-class citizens. It became increasingly clear that a much longer time than originally envisaged would be necessary to integrate East Germany economically and to some extent politically into the old FRG. There are hardly any precedents for the situation which faced post-unification Germany except perhaps, as Rolf Steininger has argued, the situation in the United States at the end of the Civil War.[15]

It was above all economic difficulties that hindered a smooth fusion of the two Germanies. The hastily negotiated state treaty which began to operate on 1 July 1990 sought to merge two fundamentally different economic systems – a semi-autarchic, centrally planned socialist economy on the one hand with a capitalist, free trading global economy on the other. The treaty laid down that the former GDR had to accept:

Autarchic:
self-sufficient

- the relevant economic, social and labour laws;
- a monetary and banking system regulated by the *Bundesbank;*
- a currency union of 1:1 for all wage-earners and current financial transactions;
- the break-up and privatization of the state monopolies (*Kombinate*) by the especially established *Treuhandanstalt* (THA), which was set up in March.

Treuhandanstalt:
state holding trust

The economy of the old GDR was granted no interim period before being confronted by the full rigour of West German and EC competition. Not surprisingly, the effect of this was devasting. By 1992 whole swathes of

East Germany were virtually deindustrialized, and it had become an area of long-term structural unemployment resembling the *mezzogiorno* (Southern Italy). Could this have been avoided? The speed of unification was, of course, determined by political considerations. Amongst the economists there were a few who believed that the 'shock therapy' of immediate unification would work wonders, but the majority were more cautious and were in favour of a more gradual process of economic integration, with parallel currencies based on a realistic exchange rate. In retrospect it is clear that the government made a series of false calculations:

- It set the exchange rate for the East mark against the DM at too high a rate, which resulted in making most of the former GDR's production uneconomic.
- Wage harmonization with West Germany in 1996 dealt a mortal blow to profitability because, as a result of the lower productivity in the East, wage costs soared to over 70 per cent above those in the West.
- Enterprises were initially disposed of far too quickly by the THA at knock-down prices and before they had a chance to rationalize.

Inevitably, the collapse of the East German economy led to widespread bitterness against the Kohl government. In the spring of 1991, when 3 million East Germans were either on short time or unemployed, in Leipzig and other major cities there were large demonstrations directed against the Bonn government. This led to an immediate massive increase in subsidies, grants and financial assistance for retraining.

From mid-1992 to January 1993 East Germany suffered a further disastrous 'double dip slump'.[16] By the time the upturn started in late 1994, the remaining industries in East Germany supplied only 12 per cent of local demand compared to 70 per cent in 1989, and unemployment affected 25 per cent of the workforce. The output of the service industries was now 50 per cent higher than that of the manufacturing sector. However, alongside the old rust heaps of obsolescent heavy industry there was a modest growth in new high-tech industries. Siemens, for instance, built a 4.2 billion microchip plant in Dresden, while Opel and Volkswagen opened new plants in the former GDR. Above all, the construction industry, assisted by 33 billion Deutschmarks' worth of tax allowances, did much to kick-start East German economic growth during the period 1994–96. East Germany was again particularly hard hit by the down-turn in the economy between 1997 and 1998. The slow-down was exacerbated by the ending of building subsidies. Overall growth was also significantly lower than that in the West. Thus East Germany by the end of the century remained a poor relation to the core territories of the old FRG, and dependent on tax breaks and grants to fuel economic expansion.

Economically, reunification was a heavy burden for the West Germans and has led to the development of a dual economy in the new Germany. Briefly it seemed that unification would cost the West Germans very little, and in the December 1990 election Kohl promised that taxes would not be increased. However, the temporary boom it triggered in the West rapidly led to inflationary overheating, which caused the *Bundesbank* sharply to raise its interest rates to an all-time high, which did much to deepen the recession of 1992–93. Belatedly Kohl then imposed 'one-off' surcharges of 7.5 per cent on each individual's tax bill in 1991–92 and again in January 1995. This went only a fraction of the way to funding the huge costs of regional assistance to the East. Christopher Flockton has calculated that in 1993 alone DM 235 billion were transferred to the former GDR.[17] Inevitably this added an immense burden to the FRG's public finances and in 1994 its debt was equivalent to 58 per cent of its GDP and had overshot the Maastricht guidelines by a massive 60 per cent in 1995.

Guidelines were agreed upon at Maastricht in 1990 for the convergence of the core EU economies in preparation for the single currency

The depth of the recession of 1992–93 led to an agonizing reappraisal of the German economy. On the one hand it had performed impressively at the end of the 1980s, while on the other it was burdened by the highest production costs in the world, the shortest working week and a whole raft of restrictive environmental legislation. Free-market economists advocated privatization, the cutting of red tape and a whole range of other measures aimed at making the German economy more competitive. Under pressure from the EC, steps were taken to privatize the railways, Lufthansa and the *Bundespost*. German industry also did much to reduce wage and production costs in 1992–93. The fact that the export industries helped drag Germany out of recession in 1993–94 indicated that considerable progress was made in regaining international competitiveness, but then growth again slowed with the recession of 1995–96 and the onset of a prolonged economic crisis in 1998.

The Maastricht Treaty and the preparations for introducing the single currency also made structural reforms in the German economy even more urgent. In January 1996 Kohl introduced the 50-Point Plan, which set out to reform the tax, pension and health systems and remove a considerable amount of red tape, but its proposals failed to pass the SPD-dominated *Bundesrat*. Initially the new SPD–Green administration, which was elected in 1998, attempted to reverse the Kohl reforms and embarked on a programme that was essentially redistributive in nature rather than aimed at making the economy more competitive. However, with the resignation of the left-wing finance minister, Oskar Lafontaine, the government began to pursue a less punitive approach towards business and in 2000 drew up a five-year programme for cutting taxes on both business and income, but by 2002 this had little impact on Germany's increasingly serious economic position, which Graf Lambsdorff, the former FDP economics minister, compared to the 'British sickness' of the 1970s.[18]

Politics after 1990

German reunification certainly shook the party structure of the old FRG, but in the 1990s it did not fundamentally alter it. The two large federal parties, the SPD and CDU–CSU, remained dominant, although in 1998 the Greens replaced the FDP as the pivotal party which could make or break coalitions. In 1990 both the CDU and FDP linked up with their GDR counterparts, the former bloc parties (see p. 291), which had since November 1989 once again become democratic parties. In the election of 1990 the CDU became temporarily the largest party in the East, while the FDP won more voters there than in the West. Although in the winter of 1989–90, the eastern SPD was founded and merged with its western counterpart, it polled only 23.6 per cent of the votes in the new *Länder* largely because until August 1989 it had supported Modrow's attempts to create a third way in the GDR between old-style socialism and West German capitalism. The Greens were the only party not to merge with their eastern counterparts and both groups fought separate election campaigns. Only in 1993 did a united Green alliance emerge. The PDS (formerly the SED), helped by the fact that the 5 per cent electoral law (see p. 290) was applied separately to East and West Germany, managed to win a base of 17 seats in the *Bundestag*, and therefore succeeded in preserving 'a grass roots presence across the new *Länder*'.[19]

See Document 87

In 1990 Kohl was able to capitalize on his success in unifying Germany to win an impressive electoral victory. For similar reasons the FDP, by concentrating on Genscher's role in unification, was able to win its largest share of the vote since 1949. However, support for both government parties rapidly began to evaporate with the escalating problems in eastern Germany and the downturn in the economy in 1991–92. The massive increase in asylum seekers entering Germany in 1991–92 also led to criticism of the government, and a marked increase in racial incidents. Right across the new *Länder*, CDU support declined to the 20 per cent level, and the revival of the far-right Republican party chalked up significant successes in the Baden–Württemberg regional elections in 1992.

Kohl was 'down but not out'[20] by early 1994, but in the October election he made a surprising come-back partly because of the up-turn in the economy and his success in amending the constitution so as to make the entry of asylum seekers more difficult. The CDU–CSU lost ground in the new *Länder* but managed to hold its core support in the old FRG. While the SPD made some gains in the East, it was the PDS that won most of the protest votes, and in the West the Greens made a strong recovery.

The 1998 election initially appeared to be 'a watershed event'.[21] The SPD, benefiting from the renewed economic downturn, at last managed to attract the majority of working-class votes in the East, while the CDU declined by a further 11 per cent there. The parties of the extreme right had a negligible impact, but the PDS and the Greens managed to consolidate their position. The new chancellor, Gerhard Schröder, formed a Red–Green coalition, and embarked on a radical programme of redistributive taxation, abandoning nuclear power and giving immigrants the right to dual citizenship. However, within a year, in the absence of any marked improvement in the economy, public opinion began to turn rightwards again. In Hesse a CDU–FDP government replaced a local

Red–Green coalition and Schröder rapidly began to jettison his left-wing programme, which led to the resignation of his finance minister, Oskar Lafontaine. Yet, as the results of the European elections and four regional elections indicated, the Red–Green coalition continued to lose support. This momentarily slowed in the winter of 1999–2000 when the news of another major funding scandal, which closely involved Kohl, plunged the CDU once again into crisis.

In the Schleswig-Holstein regional elections in February 2000 the SPD actually increased its vote, but by April it was already clear that the CDU was recovering under its new national leader, Angela Merkel, who was not only the first woman but also the first politician from the GDR to head one of Germany's major parties. Right up to August 2002 the defeat of the Red–Green coalition by the CDU–CSU seemed a forgone conclusion. However, the wooden style of its chancellor candidate, Edmund Stoiber, and Schröder's quick response to those who had suffered in the disastrous floods in central Germany as well as the public's fear of being dragged by America into a war with Iraq, enabled the government coalition to regain the initiative and to retain power with a reduced majority of just nine. Nevertheless, the economic and political problems faced by the new Red–Green administration were so formidable that in the immediate aftermath of the 2002 election many political observers were already questioning whether the coalition would survive for any length of time.

Kohl admitted to receiving large amounts of money secretly from businessmen and industrialists throughout the 1990s

In August 2002 after torrential rain the Elbe overflowed and flooded Dresden and the surrounding countryside

A new foreign policy

Unlike 1870 Germany was reunited in 1990 peacefully at the cost of no other state's territorial integrity. Nor, really, did reunification trigger a blaze of triumphalism. Essentially the priorities of the new Germany's foreign policy still lay with NATO and the EC–EU. As over the preceding four decades, European integration remained, 'an integral part of the FRG's *raison d'état*'.[22] For modern Germany, power is still equated with economic strength and prosperity rather than the size of its armed forces. Nevertheless, the end of the Cold War had radically changed the context in which the FRG conducted its foreign policy. Europe was no longer divided into two apparently stable blocs, as it was between 1962 and 1989. Germany now bordered a zone of potential instability and chaos and was faced, like her Western allies, with a very different international and security environment:

- Russia still remained a great power, but with an ageing nuclear arsenal, while many of the former Soviet states were politically unstable and themselves possessed nuclear weapons.
- The ethnic–national conflicts between the states in ex-Yugloslavia threatened to destabilize the Balkans and send further waves of asylum seekers to Germany.
- Germany, like the rest of the developed world, was also threatened by

state-sponsored terrorism and the flood of economic immigrants from Africa and Asia.

Rather than acting unilaterally, the German government's response to these dangers was to support and develop a dense network of overlapping multilateral institutions: NATO, the Council of Europe, the Council of Baltic Sea Co-operation, the Schengen Group and the European Union. NATO remained the 'bedrock' of Germany's foreign policy, and its government pressed hard to extend it eastwards. For instance in 1991 a US–German initiative for regular consultations between NATO, Russia, and the Baltic and eastern European states was accepted at the NATO summit in Rome. To defuse its neighbours' residual fears of a united Germany, the German government has also constantly stressed the importance of widening and deepening the European Union. At Maastricht not only did it agree to a monetary union with a common currency, the Euro, which came into force in January 2002, but also to a common foreign and security policy. Thus, in co-operation with France, Germany became the prime mover in creating the Eurocorps, a small multinational task force of 35,000 troops. Kohl also sought to build a bridge between the defence roles of NATO and the EU by creating 'a combined joint defence force' under the WEU but within NATO.

> The Council of Baltic Sea Co-operation was set up in 1992. To it belong all the Nordic and Baltic states. In March 1995 seven European Union countries agreed at Schengen to end border checkpoints and controls. These became known as the Schengen Group

As the most powerful state at the heart of Europe, Germany inevitably struggled to reconcile potentially contradictory agendas. The special relationship with Paris at times conflicted with its traditionally close relations with Washington, while the desire to extend the EU to the eastern European states was a potential cause of friction with Russia. To square the circle, the German government sought both to create a mutilateral framework for its foreign policy, and, within this, to construct a series of 'smaller diplomatic groupings which fall into an "institutional grey zone" between unilateralism and mutilateralism'.[23] On the one hand Germany tried to develop the Organization for Security and Co-operation in Europe which, in its original form, was set up after the 1975 Helsinki Conference (see p. 310) to act as a forum for discussing pan-European problems with the eastern states. On the other hand Germany joined a number of much smaller groupings such as the five-power Contact Group to co-ordinate policy in the Balkans, and also agreed with Denmark and Poland to form a joint army corps.

In the post-Cold-War world, Germany has also had to face up to demands for its participation in peace-keeping missions, which have involved increasing military commitments. The *Bundeswehr* was prevented from playing a part in the Gulf War both by the strength of public opinion and by the Basic Law which prevented the deployment of German troops outside the NATO area. In July 1994 the Constitutional Court removed this restriction, stipulating, however, that German forces could only be used within the context of a peace-keeping multilateral organization. This then made possible the sending of a contingent of German troops to Somalia, the dispatch of ground troops to Bosnia, participation in the war in Kosovo in 1999, and in 2002 assisting British and American forces in Afghanistan. Opposition within the Red–Green coalition was overcome by the argument of the foreign minister, Joschka Fischer, that 'it took a foreign army to free Auschwitz'.[24] Nevertheless, Fischer was adamant that troops should be used only if diplomatic efforts for a settlement had been exhausted. This same caution was visible when Schröder refused to join the USA, Britain, Poland and Spain in the second Iraq war of March–April 2003. This policy, temporarily at least, ruptured the traditional German 'special relationship' with Washington.

Conclusion: the Berlin Republic

With reunification and then the symbolic move of the government to the former capital of Berlin in September 1999, the long post-war period in German history was well and truly at an end. Although in 1990 there was considerable anxiety amongst Germany's neighbours about the political consequences of German reunification, the new Berlin Republic, far from dominating Europe, has suffered from a series of major economic problems resulting not only from unification but an increasing overregulation of the labour market and the economy. Unification has not led to a significant increase in German nationalism. The new Germany remains one of the most pacifist nations in Europe and intensely distrustful even of apparently just wars against dictators as obviously evil as Saddam Hussein of Iraq. Politically the Germans of the early twenty-first century are profoundly different from their forebears of a hundred years earlier.

Part Five

Assessment

19 *Is There a German* Sonderweg?

Given the disastrous developments in German history in the first part of the twentieth century, which engulfed the world in two major wars, it is not surprising that both German and non-German historians alike are preoccupied by the question of what went wrong in the course of German history. When and why did Germany embark on the fatal *Sonderweg* which led to the horrors of the Third Reich and Auschwitz?

Up to a point all states and cultures have their own defining characteristics which make them unique. Unlike the British Isles, the Iberian or Italian Peninsulas or even France, Germany lacks any clear-cut geographical borders. The survival of the Holy Roman Empire gave German civilization a certain universalism, which inspired nationalists like Friedrich Jahn in the early nineteenth century to argue that a future German state should include the Dutch, the Flemings, the Danes and the Swiss, as well as the Austrians and the Prussians. In practice, however, the international situation has always determined at any given moment what shape the great German core of Europe should take. It was Napoleon and the French revolutionary wars which destroyed the Holy Roman Empire. Similarly it was the balance of forces in Europe in 1815 and the fears of revolutionary nationalism, which still left Austria as one of the great powers and led to the creation in 1815 of that '*Zwitterding*' (hermaphrodite), the German Confederation.

Could the Confederation have evolved into a *grossdeutsch* German federal state? In its early years the odds were against this happening. The formation of a German state was against the interests of Austria as a great European power with territories in Italy, in eastern Europe and along the Adriatic. The creation of the middle-sized states, the 'third Germany', also added a further barrier to the formation of a united German state. However, if the 1848 revolts really had led to the collapse of the Austrian Empire, some sort of *Grossdeutschland* would probably have emerged, but the Austrian revival in the winter of 1848–49 ensured that, as far as national unity went, 1848 was a 'turning point that did not turn'. Yet the attempt to realize a Prussian-dominated *Kleindeutschland* through the Radowitz Plan and the successful opposition to this by Austria and the South German states was a dress rehearsal for the dramatic events that led to the creation of Prussian Germany in 1866–71.

To the great majority of historians between 1871 and 1945 both in the Reich and abroad, it seemed that Germany, far from pursuing a *Sonderweg* in 1870, had at last become a nation–state and had joined the mainstream of European development. Only after 1918, and even more so after 1945, was the nature of the Bismarckian Reich seen as increasingly reactionary and diverging from the Western liberal model. To structuralist historians like Hans-Ulrich Wehler and Wolfgang

Mommsen, the unstable Bonapartist system created by Bismarck, which was aimed at protecting the Prussian monarchy and the conservative élites, prevented the political modernization of the German state, and consequently impelled Germany on its *Sonderweg*. While Bismarck did create a constitution that could not easily accommodate change, it is not easy to argue that the Second Reich as a whole was reactionary. In many areas it was an exemplary modern society with, for example, excellent education, welfare and legal systems.

For Germany, as indeed for Europe, the First World War was the catastrophe that opened the way up for both the Bolshevik revolution and the rise of Fascism. To what extent is Germany responsible for this catastrophe? While there were certainly nationalist and ultra-conservative advocates of a short preventive war to restore the popularity of the Bismarckian settlement, it was Bethmann Hollweg's assessment of the threatening international situation that led him into the fatal decision to support Austria. Given the extraordinary success of the German economy and its justified claims to be a world power, strained relations with its neighbours were from time to time unavoidable, but German policy, partly through its own incoherence, provoked the formation of hostile blocs against it. These alliances would in time, however, have loosened and perhaps even have unravelled. In retrospect it can all too easily be argued that Germany's mistakes were to overrate the Russian threat, to put too much emphasis on the need for a colonial empire and to alienate Britain by building a battle fleet for use in the North Sea, but to many, though not all, Germans, this was not apparent at the time.

The impact of the war was a disaster for Germany. Despite the initial *Burgfriede* it was deeply divisive and the longer it lasted the more economically ruinous it became. Defeat led to democratization and accelerated modernization, but within the worst possible context. The bitter struggle with France over the execution of the treaty prolonged the immediate post-war dislocation until 1924. If the Weimar Republic had enjoyed a fraction of the economic prosperity and political stability of the *Bundesrepublik* in the 1950s, it would slowly have been able to reconcile and integrate its domestic enemies into a more democratic society. Conceivably, later constitutional reforms might have strengthened the executive and Weimar might have evolved into a presidential republic along the lines of the later French Fifth Republic of 1958, but there would surely have been no Third Reich.

In 1958 de Gaulle strengthened the executive in France by making the presidency the focal point of the constitution

Hitler was able to rise to power within the context of the political, economic and social crisis of the early thirties. The Nazi combination of *völkisch*, authoritarian and nationalist ideas provided a solution for both the dispossessed middle classes and the traditional élites. It promised both 'restoration' and a 'new deal' without destroying the actual structure of society in the way Bolshevism had in Russia. Nazism was a charismatic and pseudo-religious movement which, as Peuckert has stressed, was 'the combined outcome of the experience of crisis, the yearning for security and the desire for aggression, all merged into a breathless dynamism that latched on to whatever was the next immediate event: the next election campaign, the next mass demonstration, the next brawl'.[1]

By far the most difficult task facing historians is to explain convincingly how Hitler's unstable charismatic dictatorship was able to establish such a grip on Germany that it could lead it to destruction in 1945. It helps here to remember Martin Broszat's[2] advice that history should not always be studied backwards. Obviously those who at first supported Hitler could not foresee how the Third Reich would develop. The aims of both the élites and the majority of the German people overlapped with the initial stages of Nazi policy. Hitler's destruction of the Treaty of Versailles and provision of full employment were achievements which had overwhelming popular backing. The Nazi 'economic miracle' and, up to a point, the *Volksgemeinschaft* appeased the working classes, despite longer working hours and wage controls. The atomization of society through the destruction of the trade unions, pressure groups and the political parties as well as the terror apparatus of the Gestapo and SS also made opposition on any large scale very difficult to achieve.

Hitler's legacy to Germany was its occupation by the four victorious powers and then its division into two mutually hostile states in the subsequent Cold War. Once again it was outside forces that imposed a new order on Germany. Western Germany under the protection of the USA became a prosperous liberal state, while East Germany became integrated into the Soviet system. With the building of the Berlin Wall and Bonn's abandonment of the Hallstein Doctrine for *Ostpolitik* this division seemed permanent. As a consequence of the 'cultural revolution' of the 1960s and 1970s West Germany evolved into an open-minded social democratic society, which ceaselessly reproached itself for the crimes of the Nazi past. In the GDR a certain degree of stability also appeared to have been achieved in the early seventies, but by 1989 changes in the international balance of power again paved the way for the reorganization of Germany. Once it was clear that the USSR lacked both the strength and the will to prop up East Germany, reunification became possible in 1990.

In both London and Paris it was feared that the new united Germany would, as in the past, be a colossus dominating Europe, but its first decade of existence did not witness any triumphalism or flexing of muscles. On the contrary, the German economy stagnated alarmingly. The Berlin Republic appeared to be the Bonn Republic writ large. It still favoured European integration and was deeply reluctant to participate in military ventures unless their peace-keeping purposes were self-evident. If Germany is still pursuing a *Sonderweg*, it is, as Mark Rosen[3] has observed, a 'reverse *Sonderweg*', which makes Germany, in spite of all its blemishes, in so many ways a more liberal, peaceful and open state than many of its neighbours.

Part Six

Documents

I Growing opposition to the French, 1793

Professor Bartholomäus Fischenich expresses his increasing dislike of the French in a letter to the poet and playwright, Fredrich von Schiller, March 1793.

If the French advance further and reach here (Bonn), then I shall probably go away for I am most dissatisfied with the way they are behaving and would not be able to refrain from saying so publicly. I cannot bear it that they should propagate their ideas by force and that they should be unfaithful to their own principles. They inveigh against compulsion in matters of religion and yet they use armed force to make their citizens take oaths of loyalty and they propagate their liberty with fire and the sword.

Source: T. C. W. Blanning, *The French Revolution in Germany. Occupation and Resistance in the Rhineland, 1792–1802*, Oxford, Oxford University Press, 1983, p. 264.

2 An extract from Fichte's lecture to the German nation

Fichte delivered these lectures (Reden) *in the amphitheatre of the Berlin Academy, where they were enthusiastically received in the winter of 1807–08 just after the French had reduced Prussia to a rump state. In this extract Fichte argues that the Germans can only triumph over their enemies – and provide a beacon of hope to Europe – by staying true to their native genius and philosophy.*

It depends on you whether you will be . . . the end of an unworthy race . . . or the beginning . . . of a new age glorious beyond your dreams . . . remember that you are the last in whose power this great transformation lies.

Since affairs stand thus you will not overcome them with material weapons; your spirit alone must rise against them. The greater fate is yours to found the empire of the spirit and of reason and to destroy crude physical force as the ruler of the world. . . .

The old world with its splendor and greatness as well as its defects has sunk. . . . If that which has been expressed in these *Reden* is true, then of all peoples you are the one in whom the germ of human perfection most clearly lies and to whom the vanguard in its development has been assigned. If this quality in you is ruined, all hope of salvation for the entire human race in the depths of its evil will be destroyed. . . . There is no alternative; if you sink, entire humanity sinks with you, devoid of hope of future resurrection.

Source: E. N. Anderson, *Nationalism and the Cultural Crisis in Prussia, 1806–1815*, New York, Octagon Books, 1976, p. 59.

3 Karl Freiherr vom-und-zum Stein's assessment of the constitution of the German Confederation, 24 June 1815

Optimistically he hoped that pressure from the princes and public opinion would in time modify it.

Every man who loves his fatherland and who wishes it good fortune and fame, is called on to investigate whether the contents of this document meet the expectations of the nation. . . .

One can only expect so defective a constitution to have a very weak influence on the public well being of Germany and one must hope that the despotic clauses of the constitution, which several meetings (*Cabinette*) of the German leaders were unable to delete, will in time through public opinion, the freedom of the press and the example of several princes, especially in Prussia, who wish to grant their subjects a wise and beneficent constitution, be repealed

Source: E. Huber, *Dokumente zur Deutschen Verfassungstheorie, vol. 1, 1803–1850*, Stuttgart, Kohlhammer, 1961, p. 562. (Translated by the author.)

4 Arminius Riemann's speech at the Wartburg Festival, 1817

Riemann was a member of the Burschenschaft in Jena. His speech is shot through with bitter disillusionment about how the realization of German unity had been frustrated. Only Archduke Charles of Weimar had carried out his promise to grant a constitution by 1817.

Four long years have flowed by since [the battle of Leipzig] ; the German people had built up lovely hopes. THEY HAVE ALL BEEN FRUSTRATED. Everything has turned out differently from what we expected. Much that is great and splendid, that could and should have happened, has not taken place; many holy and noble feelings have been treated with mockery and derision. Of all the Princes of Germany, only one has honoured his given word, that one in whose free land we are celebrating the festival of the Battle.

Source: H. Schulze, *The Course of German Nationalism. From Frederick the Great to Bismarck, 1763–1867*. Cambridge, Cambridge University Press, 1991, p. 122. (Translated by Sarah Hanbury-Tenison.)

5 An extract from Karl Follen's *Fundamental Concepts for a German Reich Constitution*

Karl Follen was a lawyer and lecturer at Jena university and the most radical of the early nationalists. To his group belonged Karl Sand, the assassin of Kotzebue.

1. The Germans are a people, that is they have the same physical and spiritual characteristics; to this can be added the same language, the

same historical memories, the same religion. To the German people belong: the Swiss, the inhabitants of Alsace and the Friesians, etc.

2 . . . To preserve and foster this national unity the tribes are for ever unified in a single whole.

3 The Reich is a union of all Germans . . . Germans see in their people their humanity and in their fatherland, their earth.

4 All German have the same rights. Nowhere do privileges exist. Their rights and laws are established by a majority after all have voted. All the power of the bureaucracy rests on the people's sole sovereign power. . . .

5 Through elected representatives the people exercise legislative power.

6 Schooling is organized on a national basis; it ensures that all classes in the state receive the same education and that the division between townsman and peasant disappears.

Source: R. Müller, W. Hardtwig and H. Hinze (eds), *Deutsche Geschichte in Quellen und Darstellungen*, vol. 7, 1815–17, Stuttgart, Reclam, 1997, pp. 247–9. (Translated by the author.)

6 Friedrich von Gentz defends the Karlsbad decrees

Friedrich von Gentz (1764–1832) was one of Metternich's key advisers. In this extract he welcomes the decisions of the German ministers, who after a six month conference announced the Karlsbad Decrees.

It is already clear from the facts (which have until now been only revealed piecemeal, and are surely not exhausted) about the whole sequence of disturbances, that an exceptionally large number of unruly heads, part seducers and part seduced, have participated in the extravagant plans for a radical transformation of Germany, according to first one, then another idiotic model. This would certainly not have been the case if the last few years had not witnessed the prevalence of opinion that Germany viewed as an integral state and in her federal condition, basically only exists in name, has no real means of supporting herself, is liable any day to disintegrate and, in a word, is a blank slate on which anyone can write and sketch anything that the genius of caprice (which is called Freedom) might suggest. It is above all through the latest Federal Decrees, but especially through the establishment of this Commission that this madness, although not quite eradicated, has yet been visibly shattered.

Source: H. Schulze, *The Course of German Nationalism. From Frederick the Great to Bismarck, 1763–1867*, Cambridge, Cambridge University Press, 1991, p. 124. (Translated by Sarah Hanbury-Tenison.)

7 The Hambach Festival

Johann Wirth, the editor of Die Tribune, *appeals at the* Hambacher Fest, *27 May 1832, for an alliance of patriots to spread the gospel of nationalism and unity.*

[If only] the purest, most able, and courageous patriots could agree . . . if only twenty such men, bound together by a common cause and led by a man they trusted . . . tirelessly pursued their mission . . . then the great work must succeed and the forces of treason would sink into the dust before the power of patriotic love and the omnipotence of public opinion.

Source: J. Sheehan, *German History, 1770–1886*, Oxford, Oxford University Press, 1987, p. 611.

8 Bavaria and the Confederation

The British ambassador in Frankfurt, Thomas Cartwright, sent this dispatch to the Foreign Office in London on 25 June 1832, an extract of which is published below.

Bavaria and the constitutional states have been unwilling to recognize in the Diet the arbitrary right of interfering beyond a given point in their internal affairs, and Austria will not be mending matters by carrying through the Diet by a simple majority a string of resolutions to increase that arbitrary power which those states already view with jealousy. If she does resort to such a course, the dissenting states will assuredly not feel themselves bound by articles to which they refuse to accede. . . . The Diet therefore will not find affairs advanced one iota by the adoption of any measures to which Bavaria and the other constitutional states are not parties; on the contrary the difficulties of its actual position will only be aggravated.

Source: G. S. Warner, *Bavaria in the German Confederation*, London, Fairleigh Dickenson/London University Press, 1977, pp. 234–5.

9 The problems of inner German trade

The Union of Merchants in a petition drawn up by the political economist, Friedrich List (1789–1846), in 1819 complained about the large numbers of customs barriers.

[They] cripple trade and produce the same effect as ligatures which prevent the free circulation of the blood. The merchants trading between Hamburg and Austria, or Berlin and Switzerland must traverse ten states, must learn ten customs tariffs, must pay ten successive transit dues. Anyone who is so unfortunate as to live on the boundary line between three or four states spends his days among hostile tax gathers and customs house officials. He is a man without a country.

Source: W. O. Henderson, *The* Zollverein, Cambridge, Cambridge University Press, 1939, p. 23.

10 Agreement between the Prussian and the Bavarian–Württemberg customs unions

Friedrich von Motz, the Prussian minister of finance, explains the signifi-
cance of the commercial treaty between the Prussian Customs Union and the
Bavarian–Württemberg Union in a circular note sent to the Prussian
ministries in Europe on 18 August 1829.

It is not a customs union such as that formerly made between Bavaria
and Württemberg and later between Prussia and Hesse-Darmstadt. It is
characterised not so much by the establishment of a common tariff
organisation as by close cooperation in administering and collecting
customs duties. . . . It is a commercial treaty but of a far more comprehensive nature than any other of its kind. . . . The states, which have
signed the treaty have agreed first to secure uniformity in customs
administration, secondly, to treat in the same way as their own produce
that imported from the territory of another party to the agreement, and
thirdly, to place each other's subjects on the same footing as their own as
regards the carrying on of business and also to make all communications
and other facilities for trade and commerce reciprocally available and to
make use of them as cheaply as possible. An attempt has been made to
remove, as far as trade and commerce are concerned, the frontiers dividing the various states from each other. In so far as this object has not been
completely attained by the present treaty, efforts will be made to
approach ever more closely to it at the annual conferences which it has
been agreed to hold.

Source: W. O. Henderson, *The* Zollverein, Cambridge, Cambridge University Press, 1939, pp. 90–1.

11 Austria and the renegotiation of the *Zollverein*, 1851–52

An extract from an undated and unsigned memorandum from winter
1851–52 in the Vienna Haushof und Staatsarchiv.

This Customs union is a matter of life and death to Austria. She will push
it forward with greater energy than anything else and will not blench even
at concessions on the purely political field in order to promote it.

Source: H. Böhme, (ed.), *The Foundation of the German Empire*, Oxford, Oxford University Press, 1971, p.
70.

12 Impoverishment of the weavers in Silesia

Wilhelm Wolf, who later worked with Marx and Engels, described the plight
of the weavers in Silesia in the early 1840s.

Devoid of all means the weaver had to buy his yarn from the manufacturer and then supply him with the finished cotton. As the yarn was bought by payment in the form of an advance on his wares the weaver was in the hands of the manufacturer . . . I have often met these poor during the winter, in terrible weather, hungry and freezing, carrying their finished cotton many miles to the manufacturer. At home wife and children were waiting for the return of the father; for a day and a half they had eaten nothing other than potato soup. The weaver was shocked by the low offer made for his product, but there was no mercy . . . he took what was offered to him and returned full of despair to his family.

Source: H. W. Koch, *A History of Prussia*, London, Longman, 1978, p. 230.

13 A negative view of the 1848 revolutions

A. J. P.Taylor wrote The Course of German History *at the end of the Second World War. His negative view of the consequences of the 1848 revolutions reflects the period it was written in.*

1848 was the decisive year of German, and so European history: it recapitulated Germany's past and anticipated Germany's future. Echoes of the Holy Roman Empire merged into a prelude of the Nazi 'New Order'; the doctrines of Rousseau and the doctrines of Marx, the shade of Luther and the shadow of Hitler jostled each other in bewildering succession. Never has there been a revolution so inspired by a limitless faith; never has a revolution so discredited the power of ideas in its result. The success of the revolution discredited conservative ideas; and the failure of the revolution discredited liberal ideas. After it, nothing remained but the idea of Force, and this idea stood at the helm of German history from then on. For the first time since 1521, the German people stepped on to the centre of the German stage only to miss their cues once more. German history reached its turning point and failed to turn. This was the fateful essence of 1848.

Source: A. J. P. Taylor, *The Course of German History*, London, Methuen, 1961, p. 69.

14 The demands of the peasantry

In 1850 a correspondent made the following observation in the Gegenwart.

On the subject of ancient rights, the peasants have inherited a very communist conception of forest property. They don't need sermons on modern theories of property to come up with the idea that property should be generally distributed. When the popular movement broke out in 1848, and this idea immediately went through the whole of the Nassau peasantry, it was based *far less on revolutionary than on conservative inclinations*; they wanted to reestablish a convention which has existed since ancient times with respect to the wood, and if need be, to extend it to cover a number of other things too.

Source: W. Siemann, *The German Revolution of 1848–49*, New York, St Martin's Press, 1998. p. 182.

15 The reaction to the riots in Berlin of 18–19 March 1848

The report of the Landrat *of the Calau Kreis in Brandenburg to the* Oberpräsident *of the Potsdam Province, 31 March 1848.*

The absence of any post from Berlin on 19 March created the greatest stress amongst the people here in Calau and the vicinity . . . as there was no doubt that in Berlin the most serious events must have taken place. On the evening of the 19th more precise information became available from local inhabitants who had left Berlin on the morning of the 19th, and there was great consternation as a result of the lamentably bloody clash between the army and the citizens [of Berlin]. . . . The excitement died down, however, when the proclamation of his Majesty the King became known and the people trusted him absolutely. On the 21st both here and in Vetschau gatherings were organized to express sympathy for the wounded and for the relatives of those killed in Berlin. A large number of the inhabitants of Calau went to Berlin in order to attend the funeral of the fallen. On 22nd memorial services were held in Calau and Lubbenau and on 25th in Senftenburg, where – in Senftenburg – officials and citizens in formal address met in front of the *Rathaus* and accompanied by school students, teachers and the clergy processed into the church with a flag with the German colours [black red yellow]. After the service they moved to the market place where from a platform appropriate speeches were held and a collection made for the widows and orphans of those who fell in Berlin on 18 and 19 March. Then the meeting broke up peacefully. . . . To be prepared for all possible occurrences in Calau for the protection of people and property a *Bürgerwehr* (home guard) has been formed and its leaders elected. At the moment it is not carrying out patrol and guard duties, as this is at present unnecessary. Only drill is taking place.

Source: G. Falk (ed.), *Die Revolution, 1848–49 in Brandenburg. Eine Quellenversammlung*, Frankfurt am Main and Berlin, Lang, 1998, pp. 89–90. (Translated by the author.)

16 An extract from Wilhelm Jordan's speech on 24 July 1848

Wilhelm Jordan, a delegate from East Prussia, who had begun his career as a Radical Liberal, made this speech in the Frankfurt parliament in response to a proposal by 16 left-wing delegates to recognize the independence of Poland.

I say that the policy that is presented to us: Give Poland her freedom whatever it might cost, is a short sighted, self-forgetting policy, a policy of weakness, a policy of fear, a policy of cowardliness. It is high time for us, finally to wake up out of that bemused self-forgetfulness, in which we enthuse about all the other nationalities, while we ourselves still lie in shameful bondage and are trampled upon by the whole world - to wake up to a healthy national egoism [*Volksegoismus*] in order to state clearly what the well being and honour of the fatherland requires. . . .

If we wish to be absolutely honest, then we must not only give Posen back, but half Germany. . . .

The superiority of the German tribes over the Slavonic peoples, with the possible exception of the Russians is a fact, which must strike every unbiased observer. Against such – I would like to say – natural historical facts, a decree in harmony with cosmopolitan justice won't get anywhere. That is a proposition, which is as real for us as the globe itself (laughter from the left and centre).

Source: R. Müller, W. Hardtwig and H. Hinze (eds), *Deutsche Geschichte in Quellen und Darstellungen*, vol. 7, Stuttgart, Reclam, 1997, pp. 298–9. (Translated by the author.)

17 The situation in October 1848

H. B. Oppenheim, the editor of the Reform *wrote perceptively in this paper on 5 October.*

the Frankfurt central state is floating in the air, and the basis of our reality, the place of our choice for our battles lies elsewhere. As certain as it is that German unity is to be founded only on and by freedom, just as certain is it that the victory or failure of democracy will be decided in the individual states and – as most recent events have shown clearly enough, in the German states of the first rank, in their capitals, in Vienna or Berlin. Dynasties do not fall before paper storms that have been flung at Frankfurt – but they waver before the hammer blows of social democracy in Berlin and Vienna. If Prussia goes backward, German freedom is lost, but if democracy is victorious in Berlin, it is victorious for all Germany.

Source: J. Davis Randers-Pehrson (ed.), *Germans and the Revolution of 1848–1849*, New York and Washington, Peter Lang, 1999, p. 427.

18 King Frederick William rejects the imperial crown

In a letter dated 13 December 1848 the king informs his friend Count Bunsen, the Prussian ambassador in Berne, who had advised him to accept it, why this was impossible.

You say (literally as Herr von Gagern said to me on 26 and 27 of last month): 'You want consent of the princes; well and good, you shall have it'.

But my dearest friend, therein lies the rub: I want neither the Princes' consent to THE election, nor THE throne. Do you understand the words I have marked?

I will cast light over them for you as briefly and brightly as possible. The crown is actually no crown. The crown which a Hohenzollern could accept IF the circumstances COULD make this possible, is not one which an Assembly, which, although constituted by princely consent is riddled with the seeds of revolution, MAKES . . . , but one which bears God's mark, which makes HIM on whom it is set after being annointed with holy Chrism, 'by the Grace of God', because and how it made more than thirty-four princes into Kings of the Germans by the Grace of God and always keeps company with the last ones of that ancient line. The crown which the Ottonians, the Hohenstaufens and the Habsburgs have worn, a Hohenzollern can of course wear; it honours him superabundantly with the glitter of a thousand years. The one, however, which you unfortunately mean, dishonours superabundantly with its carrion reek of the 1848 revolution, the absurdest, the stupidest and the worst, if not, God be praised, also the most evil thing of this century.

Source: H. Schulze, *The Course of German Nationalism. From Frederick the Great to Bismarck, 1763–1867*. Cambridge, Cambridge University Press, 1991 pp. 139–40. (Translated by Sarah Hanbury-Tenison.)

19 Bismarck gives his support to the Olmütz proclamation

Bismarck spoke in support of the proclamation in the upper house of the Prussian Landtag, *3 December 1850*

What kind of a war is this? Not an expedition of isolated regiments to Schleswig or Baden, not a military promenade through troubled provinces, but a major war against two of the three great continental powers, whilst the third mobilizes on our frontier, eager for conquest and well aware that in Cologne there is treasure to be found that could end the French revolution and give their rulers the French Imperial crown. . . . Why do large states go to war nowadays? The only sound basis for a large state, and this is what distinguishes it from a small state, is state egoism and not romanticism, and it is not worthy of a great state to fight for something that is not in its own interest. Show me therefore, Gentlemen, an objective worthy of war, and I will agree with you.

Source: W. Medlicott and D. Coveney (eds), *Bismarck and Europe*, London, Arnold, 1971, pp. 16–17.

20 Hans-Ulrich Wehler on Bismarck's Bonapartism

For a comparative typology of forms of political rule, which can accommodate the constitutional reality of imperial Germany, the concept of Bonapartism is particularly useful. Its explanatory value in illuminating the social function of political authority is to be found in its peculiar combination of charismatic plebiscitary and traditionalist elements, all of which were also clearly in evidence in Germany. Deriving from the regime of Napoleon III . . . Bonapartism is best understood as an authoritarian government which first appeared in a relatively early phase of industrialization when the pre-industrial elites were still able to demonstrate their strength; the bourgeoisie was making rapid advances, while simultaneously threatened below by the workers movement – foreshadowed by the 'red spectre' of the revolutionary years of 1848 to 1849. . . . The bourgeoisie was being strongly moved by fear of social upheaval into accommodating itself with the forces of tradition. . . . In the light of such a specific constellation of forces, often viewed as an open-ended state of suspension, extraordinary opportunities could open up for a charismatic politician to carry out a policy of stabilization on behalf of the ruling classes by the use of certain devices appropriate to the times.

Source: H.-U. Wehler, *The German Empire, 1871–1918*, Leamington Spa and Dover, NH, Berg, 1985, p. 57.

21 The link between the economy and national unity

The Bremer Handelsblatt *was one of the more prominent liberal newspapers in North Germany, and, in a leading article on 11 July 1857, it stressed the imperative of economic unity.*

Whoever looks at the situation without prejudice and fear will recognize immediately the intimate connection, especially in Germany, of the national political problem, this Alpha and Omega of German politics. The commerce and transportation of a country have in spite of the egoism among individuals a common aspect. They demand one law, one defence abroad. This need has been satisfied in all other countries which we may mention, but not in Germany. A common code of commercial law is now slowly struggling to life; a common legislation is a pious wish, and abroad we all enjoy the same right, defencelessness.

Source: E. N. Anderson, *The Social and Political Conflict in Prussia, 1858–1864*, Nebraska, University of Nebraska Press, 1954, p. 149.

22 Bismarck predicts war with Austria

As the Prussian minister in Frankfurt, Bismarck was able to follow Austrian policy closely. In April 1856 he sent the following assessment to Otto von Manteuffel and Leopold von Gerlach.

Because of the policy of Vienna, Germany is clearly too small for us both; as long as an honourable arrangement concerning the influence of each cannot be included and carried out, we will both plough the same furrow, and Austria will remain the only state to whom we can lose or from whom we can permanently gain. . . . For a thousand years intermittently – and since Charles V, every century – German dualism has regularly adjusted the reciprocal relations [of the powers] by a thorough internal war; and in this century also no other means can set the clock of evolution at the right hour. . . . In the not too distant future we shall have to fight for our existence against Austria . . . and it is not within our power to avoid that, since the course of events in Germany has no other solution.

Source: G. Craig, *The Politics of The Prussian Army, 1640–1945*, Oxford, Oxford University Press, 1955, p. 160.

23 Bismarck's 'blood and iron' speech

On 29 September 1862 Bismarck addressed the Budget Commission of the Prussian Landtag.

Germany does not look to Prussia's liberalism, but to its power: Bavaria, Württemberg, Baden can indulge in liberalism, but no one will expect them to undertake Prussia's role; Prussia must gather and consolidate her strength in readiness for the favourable moment, which has already been missed several times; Prussia's boundaries according to the Vienna treaties are not favourable to a healthy political life; not by means of speeches and majority verdicts will the great decisions be made – that was the great mistake of 1848 and 1849, but by blood and iron.

Source: D. G. Williamson, *Bismarck and Germany, 1862–1890*, London, Longman, 1998 (2nd edn), p. 97.

24 The Treaty of Prague, 23 August 1886

Article I. [Proclaims a new era of peace and friendship between Prussia and Austria]
Article II. [Austria agreed to concede Venetia to Italy.]
Article III. [All prisoners of war to be freed as soon as possible.]
Article IV. His majesty the Emperor of Austria acknowledges the dissolution of the Germanic Confederation, as hitherto constituted, and gives his consent to a new organization of Germany without the participation of the Imperial Austrian state. His Majesty likewise promises to recognize the more restricted Federal relations, which His Majesty the King of Prussia will establish to the north of the line of the Main; and he declares his concurrence in the formation of an Association of German States situated to the south of that line, whose national connection with the North German Confederation is reserved for further arrangement between the parties, and which will have an independent national existence.
Article V. His Majesty the Emperor of Austria transfers to His Majesty the King of Prussia all the rights, which he acquired by the Vienna Treaty of

Peace of 30 October 1864 over the Duchies of Holstein and Schleswig, with the condition that the populations of the Northern Districts of Schleswig shall be ceded to Denmark if, by a free vote they express a wish to be united to Denmark.

Article XI. His Majesty the Emperor of Austria undertakes to pay His Majesty of Prussia the sum of 40,000 Prussian thalers, to cover part of the expenses, which Prussia has been put to by the war.

Source: E. Hertslet, *The Map of Europe by Treaty*, vol. 3, London, Butterworth's, 1875–91, pp. 1720–6.

25 Heinrich von Treitschke on German unity, December 1870

Heinrich von Treitschke (1834–96), historian and National Liberal delegate in the Reichstag, *was critical of the concessions that Bismarck had to make to Bavarian particularism in November 1870, but conceded that there was no alternative.*

(7 December 1870). . . . We have never had any illusions that the inclusion of the south at the present moment would be anything but the greatest sacrifice that the north has ever made for the German cause. . . . But such a cornucopia of particularistic concessions as are contained in the treaty with Bavaria exceeds our worst fears. . . .

It cost me a bitter struggle before I recognized that in spite of all this, the *Reichstag* has no mandate to reject the Bavarian treaty. Our justified resentment must yield to a higher duty, to the faith that we must keep with our south German compatriots. . . .

If the noble ideas of the war prevail in peacetime too, the German state can exist and grow despite its loose institutions.

Source: W. M. Simon, *Germany in the Age of Bismarck*, London, Allen and Unwin, 1968, p. 139.

26 The experience of workers in the *Kaiserreich*

1) *The following is an extract from a letter written by Max Lotz (1876–?), a coalminer in the Ruhr, to Adolf Levenstein, a factory foreman and amateur sociologist. Lotz was the illegitimate son of a Jewish tenor and a variety show actress. Here Lotz complains about how his employer, who in this case is the Prussian state as he works in a nationalized mine, has increased its demands on its employees.*

Every car holds fourteen bushels, so I may state that the Prussian state has the honour (along with Haniel, Stinnes, Thyssen and accomplices) of having introduced the largest cars anywhere in the Ruhr area. In fact in recent weeks they have tried (and as I write this, they have almost completely accomplished it) to force on us a whole new line of cars, which, according to our calculations, hold five to six shovelfuls more than the old size. Of course the piecework rate for both kinds of cars is the same, so we don't have much good to say about the new cars.

Source: A. Kelly (ed.), *The German Worker*, Berkeley, CA and London, University of California Press, 1987, p. 330.

2) *Doris Vierbeck (1869–?) worked as a cook in a wealthy Hamburg household. She came to Hamburg from rural Holstein in 1888.*

If the bell rang once, it was for me, twice was for the maid; and three short rings meant the manservant was wanted. When they rang for me, I was allowed first to ask at the speaking tube what they wanted; the maid and the manservant had to rush right upstairs, and often just for a trifle. At the speaking tube I had to say, 'what do you wish?' That's what the ladies wanted. If there was no answer, I had to run upstairs. Now frequently I had something on the stove that couldn't be left for long. At the very least I had to take it off to make sure it wouldn't boil over or burn because the conferences upstairs could drag on. But this took too long for the ladies, so they rang loud and long, and when possible a third time, before I got upstairs. 'My God, where have you been?' – that was the usual beginning. My apologies were not accepted. 'Empty excuses' they called them. It often happened that they'd send me many times a day for no reason at all. Then they'd say scornfully as I left, 'see how fast you can get away!' And so they drove us pointlessly to exhaustion.

Sources: A. Kelly (ed.), *The German Worker*, Berkeley, CA and London, University of California Press, 1987, p. 140.

27 The Jewish question

Walther Rathenau, the son of Emil Rathenau , the founder of the electrical comapany, AEG, was, as a Jew, acutely sensitive to the atmosphere of anti-Semitism in Germany at the turn of the century. He wrote in an article in Die Zukunft, *30 March 1897, about the Jewish problem.*

[It] buzzes through the classrooms and university lecture halls; it runs through the streets and examines the names of the shops; it makes a noise in the office and giggles down the back stairs; it nests in the seats of the railway carriages and presides over the bars; it swaggers on the parade ground and knocks on the doors of the courts.

Source: Höre, Israel, *Die Zukunft*, 6 June 1897, p. 455.

28 Kaiser Wilhelm II's views on art

When opening the Siegesallee (Victory Avenue) in Berlin in 1901, the Kaiser delivered the following attack on modern art.

Sculpture, has remained, in large part unsullied by the so called modern trends and tendencies, and still holds the commanding heights. Preserve it thus. . . . Art that disregards the laws and limits I have described is no longer art; it is factory work, trade. . . . Whoever . . . departs from the laws of beauty, and from the feeling for aesthetic harmony that each man senses within his own breast . . . is sinning against the original well springs of art. . . . If, as so often happens nowadays, art merely makes misery look more loathsome than it is already, then it is sinning against the German people.

Source: W. Mommsen, *Imperial Germany, 1867–1918*, London, Arnold, 1995, p. 132.

29 A Protestant, nationalist view of the *Kulturkampf*

In 1874 the liberal, Protestant historian, Heinrich von Sybel supported the Kulturkampf *as a political necessity.*

A party with branches all over Europe, strongly disciplined and unconditionally subject to orders of the Pope, has been doing everything it can for six years to prevent the advance of Prussia and the unity of Germany. Immediately after the German victory the German members of this party constituted themselves into a parliamentary party in order, as their manifestos openly proclaimed, to defend the interests of the Pope, this same Pope whose servants and agents everywhere are fighting with passionate bitterness against the German cause. . . . It was politically wise to take little notice of this clerical hostility before the French army was defeated; but after France had been overwhelmed it was an urgent duty of the state to render the internal enemy of our national cause harmless. There has never been a juster defensive struggle.

Source: W. M. Simon, *Germany in the Age of Bismarck*, London, Allen and Unwin, 1968, pp. 171–2.

30 Extracts from the Anti-Socialist Law, 1878

1 Societies which aim at the overthrow of the existing political or social order through democratic, socialistic or communistic endeavours are to be prohibited.

This applies also to societies in which democratic, socialistic or communistic endeavours aiming at the overthrow of the existing political or social order are manifested in a manner dangerous to the public peace, and particularly to the harmony among the classes of the population.
    Associations of every kind are the same as societies . . .

4 The police are empowered:
1 To attend all sessions and meetings of [a] society.
2 To call and conduct membership asssemblies
3 To inspect the books, papers and cash assets, as well as to demand information about the affairs of [a] society.

4 To forbid the carrying out of resolutions which are apt to further the endeavours in 1, paragraph 2.
5 To transfer to qualified persons the duties of the officers or other leading organs of society. To take charge and manage funds . . .
6 Whoever knowingly, or after public notice is given, acts in contravention of these regulations, or of the decisions based thereon, is to be punished by a fine not exceeding one thousand marks, or with arrest or imprisonment not exceeding six months.

Source: V. L. Lidtke, *The Outlawed Party – Social Democracy in Germany, 1878–1890*, Princeton, Princeton University Press, 1966, pp. 339–48.

31 Kaiser Wilhelm II's approach to politics

In his memoirs the former Chancellor Hohenlohe recorded the following discussion about the German navy with the Kaiser in March 1897.

He enumerated the ships we have and the ones we would need in order to survive a war . . . he would have to find the means, and if the *Reichstag* didn't approve this, he would nevertheless carry on building and present the *Reichstag* with the bill later. Public opinion didn't concern him. He knew that people didn't love him, and cursed him; but that wouldn't deter him. I then reminded the Emperor of the difference between Prussia and the Empire; said that in Prussia he had old rights which continued to exist, so far as the Prussian constitution had not limited [them]. In the Empire the Emperor had only the rights which the *Reichstag* conceded to him. The Emperor interjected 'the Emperor hardly has any rights', which I attempted to refute. Besides this was quite unimportant, said H.M: the South German democratic states didn't worry him. He had 18 army corps and would make short work of the South Germans.

Source: I. Porter and I. Armour, *Imperial Germany, 1890–1918*, London, Longman, 1991, pp. 72–3.

32 The Pan-German League

This was founded in 1894 with the intention of protecting German interests throughout the world. Its aims were expressed in its handbook.

1 The Pan-German League strives for the invigoration of German national feeling, especially the awakening and cultivation of the consciousness of racial and cultural belonging of all sections of the German people.
2 This task means that the Pan-German League undertakes:
   a) the preservation of German nationality in Europe and beyond and its support in areas where it is threatened;
   b) a solution to the cultural, educational and school questions in favour of German nationals;

c) to fight with all its might, whatever hinders our national development;

d) an energetic policy for German interests throughout the world, especially a continuation of German colonialism towards practical results.

Source: P. Panayi, *Ethnic Minorities in Nineteenth and Twentieth Century Germany*, Longman, Harlow, 2000, p. 79.

33 A report of an interview with the Kaiser in the *Daily Telegraph*, 27 October 1908

While staying at Colonel Stuart Wortley's house in England. the Kaiser informed his host of all he had allegedly done for Britain. Stuart Wortley used this as a basis for an interview with the Kaiser, *which was published in the* Daily Telegraph *after it had been sent to Berlin for approval. Bülow failed to read it and to realise the anger it would cause in Germany.*

In your Black Week, when disaster followed disaster, I received a letter from my revered grandmother, which showed that her health and peace of mind were being undermined by grief and anxiety. Instantly I wrote her a sympathetic answer, but I did more than that! I told my *aides-de-camp* to draw up the most accurate statement in their power of the numbers and positions of both armies, as they stood at that period. I worked on these figures to the best of my ability, drawing up a plan of campaign, which I submitted to the criticism of my staff; then I sent it to England, where in Windsor Castle it awaits the impartial verdict of history. And let me remark on an extraordinary coincidence – my plan almost exactly corresponded with that which Lord Roberts ultimately adopted and carried through to the successful end. And now I ask you – is not this the behaviour of a man who wishes England well? Let England give a fair answer.

Source: E. Ludwig, *Kaiser Wilhelm II*, London and New York, Putnam's, 1926, p. 341.

34 Conservative foreboding

In January 1896 Arthur von Posadowsky-Wehner expressed the following fear.

Germany is becoming more and more an industrial state. Thereby that part of the population is strengthened upon which the Crown cannot depend – the population of the great towns and industrial districts, whereas the agricultural population provided the real support for the monarchy. If things went on as present, then the monarchy would either pass over to a republican system or, as in England, become a sort of sham monarchy.

Source: V. Berghahn, *Germany and the Approach of War in 1914*, London, Macmillan, 1973, p. 18.

35 Bismarck's 'nightmare' of an enemy coalition

Bismarck's Kissingen Memorandum of 15 June 1877 is a valuable guide to his diplomatic strategy and ceaseless efforts to hinder the formation of a hostile coalition against Germany.

A French newspaper said of me recently that I had a 'coalition nightmare'; this kind of nightmare will long (and perhaps always) be a legitimate one for a German minister. Coalitions can be formed against us, based on the western powers with the addition of Austria, even more dangerous perhaps on a Russo-Austrian-French basis; great intimacy between two of the last named powers would always offer the third of them a means of exerting very effective pressure on us. In our anxiety about these eventualities, I would regard as desirable results of the eastern crisis (not immediately, but in the course of years): 1. gravitation of Russian and Austrian interests and mutual rivalries towards the east; 2. Russia to be obliged to take up a strong defensive position in the East and on its coasts, and to need our alliance; 3. for England and Russia a satisfactory status quo, which would give them the same interests in keeping what they hold as we have; 4. separation of England, on account of Egypt and the Mediterranean, from France, which remains hostile to us; 5. relations between Russia and Austria which would make it difficult for them to launch against us the anti-German conspiracy to which centralist or clerical elements in Austria might be somewhat inclined.

Source: W. Medlicott and K. Coveney (eds), *Bismarck and Europe*, London, Arnold, 1971, pp. 102–3.

36 Bethmann Hollweg and July 1914

As the Chancellor's secretary, Kurt Riezler was in position to understand his master's thinking during the crisis of July 1914. The following are extracts from his diary.

7 July 1914

The secret information which he [Bethmann] imparts to me conveys a disturbing picture. He regards the Anglo-Russian negotiations over a naval convention . . . very seriously, last link in the chain. . . .

The Chancellor talks of difficult decisions. Murder of Francis Ferdinand. Official Serbia involved. Austria wants to bestir herself. Message of Francis Joseph to the Emperor enquiring about *casus foederis*. Our old dilemma in every Austrian move in the Balkans. If we encourage them, they will say we pushed them into it; if we try to dissuade them, then we are supposed to have left them in the lurch. Then they turn to the western powers whose arms are open, and we lose our last halfway reliable ally. This time it's worse than 1912; for this time Austria is on the defensive against the subversive activities of Serbia and Russia. A move against Serbia can lead to world war. The Chancellor expects a war, however it turns out, to lead to an overthrow of the whole existing order. . . . The future belongs to Russia, which grows and grows and weighs upon us like a heavier and heavier nightmare.

8 July 1914
If war comes from the East, so that we would come to Austria–Hungary's aid rather than Austria–Hungary coming to ours, we have a chance of winning it. If war does not come, if the Tsar does not want it or if an alarmed France advises peace, then we still have the prospect of manoeuvring the *Entente* apart over this move.

Source: I. Porter and I. Armour, *Imperial Germany*, London, Longman, 1991, pp. 99–100.

37 The Krüger telegram

This was drafted in early January by the German Foreign Office and represented an effort to tone down the Kaiser's warlike intentions.

I wish to express my sincere congratulations that you and your people without asking the help of friendly powers, have succeeded in restoring peace through your own actions against armed bands, which broke into your country as disturbers of the peace, and in preserving the independence of your country against attack from without.

Source: A. Palmer, *The Kaiser*, London, Weidenfeld and Nicolson, 1979, p. 77.

38 Hugo Stinnes's advice: the gradual approach

In 1911 Hugo Stinnes made the following observation to Heinrich Class, the leader of the Pan German League.

Give us three or more years of peaceful progress, and Germany will be the undisputed master of Europe. The French are lagging behind us; they are a nation of small rentiers. And the English dislike hard work and lack the mettle for new ventures. Apart from them, there is no one in Europe to compete with us. Three or four years of peace, then, and I assure you that Germany will secretly come to dominate Europe

Source: W. J. Mommsen, *Imperial Germany, 1867–1918*, London, Arnold, 1995, p. 91.

39 Anglo-German naval rivalry

This extract is from a note compiled by an official in the Reich Navy Office in February 1900.

the enlargement of the British fleet cannot proceed at the same rate as ours because the size of their fleet requires considerably larger replacements. . . .The inferiority in tonnage which our battle fleet will continue to have *vis a vis* Britain's in 1920, shall be compensated for by particularly good training of our personnel and better tactical manoeuvrability of large battle formations.

Source: V. Berghahn, *Germany and the Approach of War in 1914*, London, Macmillan, p. 38.

40 Hazards of war

In October 1908 the Crown Prince was critical of Bülow's relatively accommodating attitude towards France in Morocco. Bülow made the following reply.

Unless our honor is engaged, we should always ask ourselves what is to be expected from a war. No war in Europe can bring us much. There would be nothing for us to gain in the conquest of any fresh Slav or French territory. If we annex small countries to the Empire we shall only strengthen those centrifugal elements which, alas, are never wanting in Germany.

In 1866 and 1870 there was a great prize to be won. Today that is no longer the case. Above all, we ought never to forget that nowadays no war can be declared unless a whole people is convinced that such a war is necessary and just. A war, lightly provoked, even it were fought successfully, would have a bad effect on the country; while if it ended in defeat it might entail the fall of the dynasty.

Source: D. Kaiser, 'Germany and the Origins of the First World War', *Journal of Modern History*, vol. 55, pp. 455–6.

41 The *Burgfrieden*

On 4 August Hugo Haase read the following statement on behalf of the SPD.

We stand today before the brutal fact of war and the terrible threat of enemy invasion. The decision to be made is not whether to take sides for or against the war but rather on the means necessary for the defence of our country . . . our heartiest best wishes go out to our brethren, irrespective of party affiliations, who are called to the colours. . . . Much if not all would be lost to our people and its future independence in the event of a victory of Russian despotism. . . . We therefore shall act in accordance with what we have already emphasized: we shall not abandon the fatherland in its hour of danger. . . . We condemn . . . every path of annexation.

Source: K. S. Pinson, *Modern Germany*, New York and London, Macmillan, p. 314.

42 *Mitteleuropa*

In the late August of 1914 war aims and programmes were drafted by industrialists, generals and government departments. On 28 August the Pan-German League drew up the following plan for a German-dominated Central Europe, which had a considerable input into Bethmann Hollweg's September Programme.

Central Europe . . . together with those regions which the German Reich and Austria Hungary will win as a result of victory, will form a large economic area. . . . This core will gradually . . . and without pressure from the core states bring about integration with the Netherlands, Switzerland, the three Scandinavian states, Finland, Italy, Romania and Bulgaria. If one includes the colonies and neighbouring territories of these states, an enormous economic area will come into existence, which will be able to defend and assert its economic independence against any other.

Source: F. Fischer, *Griff nach der Weltmacht*, Düsseldorf, Droste, 1964, p. 120. (Translated by the author.)

43 The Peace Resolution, 19 July 1917

As on 4 August 1914, the German people, on the threshold of the fourth year of the war, stand behind the words of the speech from the throne: 'we are not driven by a desire for conquest!' Germany took up arms only for the defence of its freedom and independence and for the preservation of its territorial integrity.

The *Reichstag* strives for a peace of understanding and lasting reconciliation of nations. Such a peace is not in keeping with forcible annexations of territory or forcible measures of political, economic or financial character.

The *Reichstag* also rejects all plans which would result in economic isolation and hostility among nations after the war. The freedom of the seas must be made secure. Only economic peace will prepare the ground for the friendly living together of the nations.

The *Reichstag* will actively support the creation of international judicial organizations.

So long as the enemy governments will not agree to such a peace . . . the German people will stand together as one.

Source: K. S. Pinson, *Modern Germany*, New York and London, Macmillan, p. 334.

44 The deteriorating morale of the German army

Rudolph Binding, a staff officer, and later a writer, wrote the following in his diary on 28 March 1918 at the height of the German spring offensive on the Western Front.

Today the advance of our infantry suddenly stopped near Albert. Nobody could understand why. Our airmen had reported no enemy between Albert and Amiens. The enemy's guns were only firing now and again on the very edge of affairs. Our way seemed entirely clear. I jumped into a car with orders to find out what was causing the stoppage in front. . . .

As soon as I got near [to Albert] I began to see curious sights. Strange figures, who looked very little like soldiers, and certainly showed no sign of advancing, were making their way back . . . there were men driving cows before them on a line; others who carried a hen under one arm and a box of note papers under the other. Men carrying a bottle of wine under their arm and another open in their hand.

Source: J. Terraine, *The First World War*, London, Macmillan, 1984, p. 165.

45 Hindenburg concedes defeat

On 3 October 1918 Hindenburg wrote the following to the imperial chancellor.

The Supreme Command continues to hold to its demand expressed on September 29 of this year that a request for an armistice should be sent to our enemies immediately. As a result of the collapse of the Macedonian Front, the consequent weakening of the reserves on our western front, and the impossibility of making good the very severe losses which we have suffered in the last few days, there is, as far as it is humanly possible to judge, no further chance of forcing a peace on the enemy. Our adversaries are continually bringing up fresh reserves.

Source: A. Rosenberg, *Imperial Germany. The Birth of the German Republic*, New York, Oxford University Press (paperback), 1970, p. 245.

46 The November revolution

The War Ministry sums up the situation in a report to the government dated 8 November, 1918.

9 A.M. serious riots in Magdeburg
1 P.M. In Seventh Army Corps Reserve District rioting threatened
5 P.M. Halle and Leipzig Red. Evening: Düsseldorf, Halstein, Osnabrück, Lauenburg Red; Magdeburg, Stuttgart, Oldenburg, Brunswick and Cologne all Red
7.10 P.M. General Officer Commanding Eighteenth Army Corps Reserve at Frankfurt deposed.

Source: R. M. Watt, *The Kings Depart*, London, Weidenfeld and Nicolson, 1968, p. 186.

47 Article 48

The key emergency powers which enabled the issue of legislation by presidential decree were contained in paragraph 2 of the Weimar Constitution

II.   If a *Land* does not fulfill the responsibilities assigned to it under the constitution or laws of the R*eich*, the *Reich* President can take the appropriate measures to restore law and order with the assistance of the armed forces.

      In the event of a serious disturbance or threat to law and order, the *Reich* President may take the necessary measures for restoring law and order, intervening if necessary with armed forces. To achieve this he may temporarily suspend either completely or partially the basic rights in Articles 114, 115, 117, 118, 123, 124 and 153.

III. The *Reich* President is bound to report immediately to the *Reichstag* all measures taken under paragraphs 1 and 2 of this article. The measures are to be rescinded on the request of the *Reichstag*.

Source: W. Michalka and G. Niedhart, *Die Ungeliebte Republik. Dokumente zur Innen-und Aussenpolitik Weimars 1918–1933*, Munich, 1980, p. 62. (Translated by the author.)

48 The Germans on the wrong side of the new frontiers

A German government proclamation issued on the date of the coming into force of the Treaty of Versailles on 10 January 1920.

The unfavourable result of the war has surrendered us defenceless to the mercy of our adversaries, and imposes upon us great sacrifices under the name of peace. The hardest, however, which is forced upon us is the surrender of German districts in the east, west and north. Thousands of our fellow Germans must submit to the rule of foreign states without the possibility of asserting their right of self-determination.

. . . In this dark hour, let us appreciate the treasure which remains our common property, and which no outside power can take away from us.

Together we keep the language, which our mother taught us, together with the realm of thought, of speech, of ideas, in which the greatest minds of our people have striven to express the highest and noblest ideas of German civilization. By all the fibres of our being, by our love and by our whole life we remain united.

Everything that is in our power to preserve your mother tongue, your German individuality, the intimate spiritual connection with your home country will be done. Just as before, whenever we had a possibility to negotiate, we made it our secret task to preserve your vital national rights in spite of your separation. . . .

For centuries it has been the fate of the German people that many Germans outside the German Empire had to submit to the rule of foreign powers. But wherever their colonies existed, even in the midst of foreign nations, they have retained their German individuality and the spiritual union with the mother country through the hardest times, and the power of their national civilization has sent its rays over vast expanses. Their work shall be an example to you for the difficult task which a hard fate imposes upon you.

Source: Documents on British Foreign Policy, First Series, vol. IX, London, HMSO, 1960, pp. 17–18.

49 National election results in the Weimar Republic in percentages

Date	NSDAP	DNVP	DVP	Centre/ BVP	DDP	SPD	USPD	KPD	Others
19.1.19	–	10.3	4.4	19.7	18.6	37.9	7.6	–	1.5
6.6.20	–	14.9	13.9	17.6	8.3	21.6	17.9	2.1	3.7
4.5.24	6.5	19.5	9.2	16.6	5.7	20.5	1.1	12.6	8.3
7.12.24	3.0	20.5	10.1	17.3	6.3	26.0	–	9.0	7.8
20.5.28	2.6	14.2	8.7	15.2	4.9	29.8	–	10.6	14.0
14.9.30	18.3	7.0	4.9	14.8	3.8	24.5	–	13.1	13.6
31.7.32	37.3	5.9	1.2	15.7	1.0	21.6	–	14.3	3.0
6.11.32	33.1	6.5	1.8	15.0	1.0	20.4	–	16.9	5.3
5.3.33	43.9	8.0	1.1	13.7	0.9	18.3	–	12.3	1.08

Source: T. Childers, 'Inflation, Stabilization and Political Realignment in Germany, 1924 to 1928, in G. D. Feldman et al., *The German Inflation Reconsidered*, Berlin, de Gruyter, 1982, p. 430.

50 Hitler in Munich in 1920

Hans Frank, a Nazi lawyer and later governor-general of German-occupied Poland, recalled the impression Hitler made on him when he first heard him speak in January 1920 in Munich.

I was strongly impressed straight away. It was totally different from what was otherwise to be heard in meetings. His method was completely clear and simple. He took the overwhelmingly dominant topic of the day, the Versailles *Diktat*, and posed the question of all questions: What now German people? What's the true situation? What alone is now possible? He spoke for over two-and-a half hours, often interrupted by frenetic torrents of applause – and one could have listened to him for much, much longer. Everything came from the heart, and he struck a chord with all of us . . . he uttered what was in the consciousness of all those present and linked general experiences to clear understanding and the common wishes of those who were suffering and hoping for a programme. In the matter itself he was certainly not original . . . but he was the one called to act as spokesman of the people . . . he concealed nothing . . . of the horror, the distress, the despair facing Germany. But not only that. He showed a way, the only way left to ruined people in history, that of the grim new beginning from the most profound depths through courage, faith, readiness for action, hard work, and devotion to a great, shining, common goal . . . he placed before the Almighty in the most serious and solemn exhortation the salvation of the honour of the German soldier and worker as his life task. . . .When he finished, the applause would not die down. . . . From this evening onwards . . . I was convinced that if one man could do it, Hitler alone would be capable of mastering Germany's fate.

Source: I. Kershaw, *Hitler, 1889–1936: Hubris*, London, Allen Lane, 1998: pp. 148–9.

51 Reaction to the Treaty of Versailles

1) *The German government accompanied the signature of the treaty with the following statement.*

Surrendering to superior force but without retracting its opinion regarding the unheard of injustice of the peace conditions, the government of the German Republic declares its readiness to accept and sign the peace conditions imposed by the Allied and Associated governments.

Source: D. Williamson, *War and Peace*, London, Hodder, 1994, p. 38.

2) *The Pan German* Deutsche Zeitung *published the following on its front page on 28 June.*

Vengeance! German nation! Today in the Hall of Mirrors of Versailles the disgraceful treaty is being signed. Do not forget it! In the place where, in the glorious year of 1871, the German empire in all its glory had its origin, today German honour is being carried to its grave. Do not forget it! The German people will, with unceasing labour, press forward to reconquer the place among the nations to which it is entitled. Then will come vengeance for the shame of 1919.

Source: K. S. Pinson, *Modern Germany*, New York and London, Macmillan, p. 398.

52 The impact of the inflation

This memoir by a professional woman dependent on her salary for her existence, indicates the devasting impact of hyperinflation.

May I give you some recollection of my own situation at that time? As soon as I received my salary, I rushed out to buy the daily necessities. My daily salary, as editor of the periodical, *Social Praxis*, was just enough to buy one loaf of bread and a small piece of cheese or some oatmeal. On one occasion I had to refuse to give a lecture at a Berlin city college because I could not be assured that my fee would cover the subway fare to my classroom, and it was too far to walk. On another occasion, a private lesson I gave to the wife of a farmer was paid somewhat better – by one loaf of bread for the hour.

Source: J. Hiden, *The Weimar Republic*, London, Longman, 1974, p. 86.

53 Stresemann's strategy for revising the Treaty of Versailles

Stresemann wrote to the German ex-crown prince on 7 September 1925.

[T]here are three great tasks that confront German foreign policy in the more immediate future. In the first place the solution of the Reparation question in a sense tolerable for Germany, and the assurance of peace, which is essential for the recovery of our strength. Secondly the protection of the Germans abroad, those 10 to 12 millions of our kindred who now live under a foreign yoke in foreign lands. The third great task is the readjustment of our eastern frontiers; the recovery of Danzig, the Polish frontier, and a correction of the frontier of Upper Silesia.

D. Williamson, *War and Peace*, London, Hodder, 1994, p. 61.

54 An SA convert

A British tourist, Patrick Lee Fermor, met a young German worker who had just left the KPD for the NSDAP.

[The walls of his room] were covered with flags, posters, slogans and emblems. His SA uniform hung neatly ironed on a hanger. He explained these cult objects with a fetishist zest, saving up till the last the centrepiece of his collection. It was an automatic pistol. . . . When I said that it must be rather claustrophobic with all that stuff on the walls, he laughed and sat down on the bed, and said: 'Mensch! You should have seen it last year! You would have laughed! Then it was all red flags, stars, hammers and sickles, pictures of Lenin and Stalin and Workers of the World Unite! I used to punch the heads of anyone singing the Horst Wessel Lied! . . . Then suddenly, when Hitler came to power, I understood it was all nonsense and lies. I realized Adolf was the man for me, All of a sudden!' 'Had a lot of people done the same, then?' [Fermor asked] 'Millions! I tell you, I was astonished how easily they all changed sides!'

Source: M. Burleigh, *The Third Reich*, London and Basingstoke, Macmillan, 2000, pp. 132–3.

55 Culture and modernity

H. Reiser made the following observation in a perceptive review in the periodical, Die Schöne Literatur.

But what if [artistic] form – that is, all known and familiar forms – has become a lie, because the present age, as a cultural epoch, has no form – creates no forms other than steel structures, machines and other technical marvels? What if the present age, both in its material externals and in spiritual, cultural and artistic terms, is itself a formless disintegrated mishmash – if it is as God-foresaken and futile as any age has ever been? . . . Who can doubt that a casualty of this age will want to vent his cries of despair? Anyone can read Mörike [the poet, 1804–75]. But in this age of cinema, radio and Stinnes, he will have to hoodwink himself if he is going to find Mörike the perfect answer. He will have to pretend that the express-train tempo of modern life is a post-chaise canter, that the stink of petrol is like rose petals, and that a stock exchange wizard has a fairy tale heart of gold.

Source: D. Peuckert, *The Weimar Republic. The Crisis of Classical Modernity*, Harmondsworth, Penguin, 1991, p. 168.

56 Working within the constitution

In September 1930 three young army officers stationed in Ulm were accused of working for the Nazi party and so breaking military regulations which banned soldiers from supporting revolutionary parties . They were put on trial before the Supreme Court at Leipzig. When Hitler was called as a witness , he stressed how he aimed to achieve a 'legal' revolution.

The National socialist movement will try to achieve its aim with constitutional means in the state. The constitution prescribes my methods, not the aim. In this constitutional way we shall try to gain decisive majorities in the legislative bodies so that the moment we succeed we can give the state the form that corresponds to our ideas.

The chairman of the court summed up the statement to the effect that the setting up of the Third Reich was being worked for in a constitutional way.

Source: J. Noakes and G. Pridham (eds), *Nazism 1919–1945*, vol. 1, *The Rise to Power, 1919–1934*, Exeter, Exeter University Press, 1998, p. 90.

57 Hitler on the Jews in *Mein Kampf*

To Hitler 'the Jew' was the most deadly enemy of ' the Aryan', whose ultimate intention was global domination. In Chapter 11 of Mein Kampf *Hitler argued that the Jews had found in Marxism the ideal weapon for destroying the German state.*

In the organised mass of Marxism he has found the weapon which lets him dispense with democracy and in its stead allows him to subjugate and govern the peoples with a dictatorial and brutal fist.

He worked systematically for revolutionisation in a twofold sense: economic and political. Around peoples who offer too violent a resistance to attack from within he weaves a net of enemies, thanks to his international influence, incites them to war, and finally, if necessary, plants the flag of revolution on the very battlefields.

In economics he undermines the states until the social enterprises, which have become unprofitable are taken from the state and subjected to his financial control.

In the political field he refuses the state the means for its self-preservation, destroys the foundations of all national self maintenance and defence, destroys faith in the leadership, scoffs at its history and past, and drags everything that is truly great into the gutter.

Culturally he contaminates art, literature, the theatre, makes a mockery of natural feeling, overthrows all concepts of beauty and sublimity, of the noble and the good, and instead drags men down into the sphere of his own base nature.

. . . Now begins the great last revolution. In gaining political power the Jew casts off the few cloaks that he still wears. The democratic people's Jew becomes the blood Jew and tyrant over peoples. In a few years he tries to exterminate the national intelligentsia and by robbing the peoples of their natural leadership makes them ripe for the slave's lot of permanent subjugation.

The most frightful example of this kind is offered by Russia where he killed or starved about thirty million people with positively fanatical savagery, in part amid inhuman tortures, in order to give a gang of Jewish journalists and stock exchange bandits domination over a great people.

Source: Hitler, *Mein Kampf*, with an introduction by D. C. Watt, London, Hutchinson, 1974, pp. 295–6.

58 Could the impact of the Great Depression of 1930–33 on Germany have been mitigated?

Knut Borchardt argued in a seminal study that in reality little could have been done to avert the economic course of events.

With the depression begins a new epoch in the history of capitalist or market economies. From this point so called *Globalsteuering* (macro-economic policy) became the duty of the state. In particular the goal of a high level of employment, not to say full employment, received practically the status of a constitutional requirement. This is one of the most important consequences of the Great Depression. . . . But for the Germans, the consequences went even further. In their country there was something additional that allowed the economic crisis to become an event of exceptional significance: the collapse of the Weimar Republic and the rise to power of National Socialism. Among the answers to the question, 'How was this possible? How was Hitler possible? it is usual to refer to the great depression.

In this regard, it is easy to see the question has often been posed as to whether the crisis could have been avoided if only politicians had more insight or more competence [Borchardt, however, rejects these arguments]. . . .

That an expansionary economic policy actually did assist the subsequent upturn after 1932 is explicable in part because a readjustment and especially a massive lowering of costs, actually did occur during the depression. Previously there had been no such solution to Germany's economic problem. For in Germany the real problem of the Great Depression was its pre-history and the subsequent restraints that followed from that pre-history. . . . We can only study this tragedy and we should abstain from engaging in over presumptuous criticism.

K. Borchardt, *Perspectives on Modern German Economic History and Policy*, Cambridge, Cambridge University Press, 1991, pp. 143 and 161.

59 Hitler as Saviour

In his memoirs, Albert Speer recalls the hope and optimism that Hitler radiated in the dark days of 1930–32. In 1931 Speer heard him speak for the first time.

Here it seemed to me was hope. Here were new ideals, a new understanding, new tasks. . . . The perils of Communism, which seemed inexorably on the way, could be checked, Hitler persuaded us, and instead of hopeless unemployment, Germany could move toward economic recovery. He had mentioned the Jewish problem only peripherally. But such remarks did not worry me, although I was not an anti-Semite; rather I had Jewish friends from my school days and university days, like virtually everyone else. . . . It must have been during these months that my mother saw an S.A. parade in the streets of Heidelberg. The sight of discipline in a time of chaos, the impression of energy in an atmosphere of universal hopelessness, seems to have won her over also.

Source: A. Speer, *Inside the Third Reich*, London, Weidenfeld and Nicolson, 1970, pp. 16–18.

60 Hitler's speech to the *Reichsstatthälter* (Reich Governors), 6 July 1933

It was vital to prevent interference by the party and the SA threatening economic recovery and alienating the army, big business and the bureaucracy. Hitler had no wish for a showdown with the old élites at this point, as this would only delay rearmament and economic recovery. Consequently he made the following speech to the Reichsstatthälter *on 6 July.*

The revolution is not a permanent state of affairs, and it must not be allowed to develop into such a state. The stream of revolution released must be guided into the safe channel of evolution . . . we must therefore not dismiss a businessman if he is a good businessman, even if he is not yet a National Socialist; and especially not if the National Socialist, who is to take his place knows nothing about business. In business ability must be the only authoritative standard . . .

History will not judge us according to whether we have removed and imprisoned the largest number of economists, but according to whether we have succeeded in providing work. . . . The ideas of the programme do not oblige us to act like fools and upset everything, but to realize our trains of thought wisely and carefully. In the long run our political power will be all the more secure, the more we succeed in underpinning it economically. The *Reichsstatthälter* must therefore see to it that no organization or Party Offices assume the functions of government, dismiss individuals and make appointments to offices, to do which the Reich Government alone – and in regard to business the Reich Minister of Economics – is competent.

Source: N. Baynes (ed.), *Hitler's Speeches, 1922–39, Vol.1*, Oxford, Oxford University Press, 1942, pp. 865–6.

61 The difficulties of obtaining a decision from Hitler

Carl Schmitt, a leading constitutional lawyer, and the diplomat, Ernst von Weizsäcker, recalled after the war the difficulties of obtaining a decision from Hitler.

Ministers . . . might for months on end and even for years, have no opportunity of speaking to Hitler. . . . Ministerial skill consisted in making the most of a favourable hour or minute when Hitler made a decision, this often taking the form of a remark thrown out casually, which then went its way as an 'order of the Führer'.

Source: J. Noakes and G. Pridham (eds), *Nazism 1919–1945*, vol. 2, *State, Economy and Society*, 1933–1939, Exeter, Exeter University Press, 1984, p. 197.

62 Working towards the Führer

The state secretary in the Prussian Agricultural Ministry, Werner Willikens, in a speech on 21 February 1934 to representatives from the agricultural ministries in the federal states, advised them on the art of interpreting the will of the Fuhrer when no precise guidelines were given by him.

Everyone with opportunity to observe it knows that the Führer can only with great difficulty order from above everything that he intends to carry out sooner or later. On the contrary, until now everyone has best worked in his place in the new Germany if, so to speak, he works towards the Führer. . . .

Very often, and in many places, it has been that individuals, already in previous years, have waited for commands and orders. Unfortunately, that will probably also be so in the future. Rather, however, it is the duty of every single person to attempt, in the spirit of the *Führer*, to work towards him. Anyone making mistakes, will come to notice it soon enough. But the one who works correctly towards the *Führer* along his lines and towards his aim will in future as previously have the finest reward of one day suddenly attaining legal confirmation of his work.

Source: I. Kershaw, *Hitler 1889–1936: Hubris*, London, Allen Lane, 1998, p. 529.

63 The role of women in Nazi Germany

On 8 September 1934 Hitler summed up for the National Socialist Women's Section the Nazi view of the role of women in society.

If one says that man's world is the State, his struggle, his readiness to devote his powers to the service of the community, one might be tempted to say that the world of woman is a smaller world. For her world is her husband, her family, her children and her house. But where would the greater world be if there were no one to care for the small world? . . . Providence has entrusted to women the cares of that world which is peculiarly her own. . . .

Every child that a woman brings into the world is a battle, a battle waged for the existence of her people.

Source: N. Baynes (ed.), *Hitler's Speeches*, Vol. I, Oxford, Oxford University Press, 1942, pp. 528–9.

64 Social equality in the *Volksgemeinschaft*

In a speech made in Berlin on 1 May 1937 Hitler claimed to have created a new equality in Germany.

We in Germany have really broken with a world of prejudices. I leave myself out of account. I, too, am a child of the people; I do not trace my line from any castle: I come from the workshop. Neither was I a general: I was simply a soldier, as were millions of others. It is something wonderful that amongst us an unknown from the army of the millions of German people – of workers and of soldiers – could rise to be head of the Reich and of the nation. By my side stand Germans from all walks of life who today are amongst the leaders of the nation: men who once were workers on the land are now governing German states in the name of the Reich. . . . It is true that men who came from the bourgeoisie and former aristocrats have their place in this Movement. But to us it matters nothing whence they come if only they can work to the profit of our people. That is the decisive test. We have not broken down classes in order to set new ones in their place: we have broken down classes to make way for the German people as a whole.

Source: N. Baynes (ed.), *Hitler's Speeches*, vol. I , Oxford, Oxford University Press, 1942, pp. 620–1.

65 Recalling the Third Reich

The universities of Essen and Hagen in the 1980s conducted an oral history project on the Life, History and Social Culture of the Ruhr, 1930–1960. *It consisted of some two hundred interviews. Extracts from an interview with Ernst Bromberg, a retired fitter are quoted below. Bromberg stressed that he had no time to participate in Nazi politics.*

Yes well obviously, if you were on piece work, you didn't have any time to make speeches, you got up in the morning when you had to, you didn't overstretch your break periods – because after all – the money was tempting. . . . I didn't worry any more about the Nazis, put it that way, apart from my Labour Front contribution, I just didn't have anything to do with the Nazis, you know – anyway I was tied up with my Protestant clubs all week, you know. . . . Nothing really changed there.

Source: Ulrich Herbert, 'Good Times, Bad Times: Memories of the Third Reich', in R. Bessel (ed.), *Life in the Third Reich*, Oxford, Oxford University Press. 1987, p. 99.

66 Hitler threatens the Jews with annihilation

In a speech to the Reichstag *on 30 January 1939 Hitler promised the annihilation of the Jews should war break out.*

Today I will once more be a prophet: If the international Jewish financiers in and outside Europe should succeed in plunging the nations into a world war, then the result will not be bolshevization of the earth and thus the victory of Jewry, but the annihilation of the Jewish race in Europe!

Source: N. Baynes (ed.), *Hitler's Speeches* vol. I, Oxford, Oxford University Press, 1942, p. 741.

67 The Hossbach Memorandum

Hitler summoned a meeting of his key ministers and service chiefs on 5 November 1937. He informed them that what he had to say was the product of intense deliberation and should be regarded as his 'last will and testament'. Five days later minutes of the meeting were compiled by Hitler's adjutant, Colonel Hossbach. In 1946 what survived from these minutes was accepted by the Nuremberg tribunal as a 'blueprint' of Hitler's intentions to wage war.

The aim of German policy was to make secure and to preserve the racial community and to enlarge it. It was therefore a question of space [*Lebensraum*]. . . . The question for Germany was: Where could she achieve the greatest gain at the lowest cost? German policy had to reckon with two hate inspired antagonists, Britain and France, to whom a German colossus in the centre of Europe was a thorn in the flesh . . . Germany's problem could only be solved by the use of force . . . If the resort to force with its attendant risks is accepted . . . there then remains still to be answered the questions 'When'? and 'How'? In this matter there were three contingencies to be dealt with.

Contingency 1: Period 1943–5

After that date only a change for the worse, from our point of view, could be expected . . . Our relative strength would decrease in relation to the rearmament which would then have been carried out by the rest of the world. If we did not act by 1943–5 any year could, owing to lack of reserves, produce the food crisis . . . and this must be regarded as a 'waning point of the regime'. . . . If the *Führer* was still living, it was his unalterable determination to solve Germany's problem of space by 1943–5 at the latest . . .

Contingency 2

If internal strife in France should develop into such a domestic crisis as to absorb the French army completely and render it incapable of use for war against Germany, then the time for acting against the Czechs would have come.

Contingency 3

If France should be so embroiled in war with another state that she could not 'proceed' against Germany. For the improvement of our politico-military position our first objective, in the event of our being embroiled in war, must be to overthrow Czechoslovakia and Austria simultaneously in order to remove the threat to our flank in any possible operation against the West.

Source: *Documents on German Foreign Policy, Series D*, vol.1, London, HMSO, 1957–1966, pp. 29–38.

68 Hitler issues the order to prepare for war against the USSR, July 1941

General Halder recorded Hitler's assessment of the military and diplomatic situation at a military conference on 31 July 1940. To defeat Britain and keep America out of the war he argued, Russia would have to be invaded.

Führer:

(a) Stresses his scepticism regarding technical feasibility [of an invasion of Britain]; however satisfied with results produced by Navy.

(b) Emphasizes weather factor.

(c) Discusses enemy resources for counteraction.

(d) In the event that invasion does not take place, our action must be directed to eliminate all factors that let England hope for a change in the situation. To all intents and purposes the war is won. . . . Submarine and air warfare may bring about a final decision, but this may be one or two years off. Britain's hope lies in Russia and the United States. If Russia drops out of the picture, America too is lost for Britain, because elimination of Russia would tremendously increase Japan's power in the Far East.

Russia is the Far Eastern sword of Britain and the United States pointed at Japan. . . .

With Russia smashed, Britain's last hope would be shattered. Germany will then be master of Europe and the Balkans. Decision: Russia's destruction must therefore be made part of this struggle. Spring 1941. The sooner Russia is crushed, the better. Attack achieves its purpose only if Russian state can be shattered to its roots with one blow . . . Holding part of the country alone will not do. Standing still for the following winter would be perilous. So it is better to wait a little longer but with resolute determination to eliminate Russia.

Source: J. Noakes and G. Pridham (eds), *Nazism 1919–1945* vol. 3, *Foreign Policy, War and Extermination*, Exeter, Exeter University Press, 1991, p. 790.

69 The impact of the war on the family

By the autumn of 1943 the war was taking its toll on family life as the follow-ing extracts from an SD report of 18 November 1943 indicate.

Many women are also concerned that the stability of their marriages and the mutual understanding of their partners is beginning to suffer from the lengthy war. The separation which, with short breaks, has now been going on for years, the transformation in their circumstances through total war and in addition, the heavy demands which are nowadays made on every individual are changing people and filling their lives. When on leave, the front-line soldier often no longer shows any understanding for his family's domestic circumstances, which are governed by the war, and remains indifferent to the many daily cares of the home front. This often produces an increasing *distance between the married couple*. Thus wives often point out that having looked forward to being together again during their husband's leave, the occasion is spoilt by frequent rows caused by mutual tensions. That even happens in marriages which were previously models of harmony . . . .

The *splitting up of families* without the possibility of making visits with all the accompanying problems is in the long run felt to be an intolera-ble burden both by men but in particular by women . . . . Above all, the married men say that their family is the only compensation they have for their heavy work load. One shouldn't take away from them the only thing that makes life worth living. But the wives are no less subjected to a heavy mental burden because they want to live in their own homes, to look after them and to care for their husbands and children . . . the majority of the evacuated women and children are accommodated in small villages and rural parishes under the most primitive conditions. They have to cook in the same kitchens with their hosts, which often gives cause for conflict, since people look into each other's pots and get jealous if the other family has something better to eat. In a number of cases there can be no question of family life since sometimes not all children can be accommodated with their mother in the same house, and furthermore often the only living room that is available has to be shared with the host family.

Source: J. Noakes (ed.), *Nazism, 1919–1945*, vol. 4. *The German Home Front in World War II*, Exeter, Exeter University Press, 1998, pp. 360–2

70 Western Germany in 1945

An extract from the diary of Sir William Strang, political adviser to the military government, 1–6 July 1945.

villages and small towns off the main roads quite intact: towns and villages at important communication points badly smashed. Larger centres like Münster or Osnabrück, half or three-quarters devastated; industrial cities like Dortmund almost totally in ruins, except round the outer fringes. The population more healthy looking, better dressed, and showing less sign of strain than one would have expected, even in the more heavily damaged urban areas. The official ration is low, but in the country it is at present supplemented from stocks and garden produce. The position in the large towns is difficult, and the workers certainly do not receive enough to sustain heavy labour. . . . Roads still lead in and out of Dortmund (though it is like threading a maze to find one's way about them), and where those roads meet the life of the community continues to spring and begins to reorganise itself. I asked whether [the commander of the military government detatchment at Dortmund] thought that Dortmund would ever be re-built. He said certainly, sooner or later. The city authorities were already thinking ahead and actively debating alternative schemes: he himself had been brought into consultation.

Source: Sir William Strang (political adviser to the military governor of the British Zone), *Diary of a Tour Through the British Zone, 1–6 July 1945*, Public Record Office, London, FO 371 46933.

71 The situation in Breslau, July 1945

Father Paul Peikert, a Catholic priest, described the situation in Breslau under Soviet–Polish occupation in a letter to a colleague.

Already now 300 to 400 people die in Breslau a day, that is 10,000 to 12,000 people a month.

Now the same methods of extermination are applied to us as we applied to other peoples, only with the one outward appearance of humanity that the Russians and the Poles do not murder senselessly as did our *Waffen SS* and *Gestapo* in the occupied territory to the horror of the whole world. But if one considers the intention, it amounts to the same thing.

Source: S. Siebel-Achenbach, *Lower Silesia from Nazi Germany to Communist Poland, 1942–1949*, London, Macmillan, 1994, p. 127.

72 The political principles of the Potsdam Agreement, 2 August 1945

1. In accordance with the Agreement on Control Machinery in Germany, supreme authority in Germany is exercised, on instructions from their respective governments, by the Commanders-in-Chief of the armed forces of the United States of America, the United Kingdom, the Union of Soviet Socialist Republics, and the French Republic, each in his own zone of occupation, and also jointly, in matters affecting Germany as a whole, in their capacity as members of the Control Council. . . .
2. So far as is practicable, there shall be uniformity of treatment of the German population throughout Germany.
3. The purposes of the occupation of Germany by which the Control Council shall be guided are:
   I.   The complete disarmament and demilitarisation of Germany and the elimination or control of all German industry that could be used for military production . . .
   II.   To convince the German people that they have suffered a total military defeat and that they cannot escape responsibility for what they have brought upon themselves, since their own ruthless warfare and the fanatical Nazi resistance have destroyed the German economy and made chaos and suffering inevitable.
   III. To destroy the National Socialist Party and its affiliated and supervised organisation, to dissolve all Nazi institutions, to ensure that they are not revived in any form, and to prevent all Nazi and militarist activity or propaganda.
   IV.   To prepare for the eventual reconstruction of German political life on a democratic basis and for eventual peaceful co-operation in international life by Germany . . .
9. The administration of affairs in Germany should be directed towards the decentralisation of political structure and the development of local responsibility. To this end . . .
   IV.   For the time being no central German government shall be established. Notwithstanding this, however, certain essential central German administrative departments headed by State Secretaries, shall be established, particularly in the fields of

finance, transport, communications, foreign trade, and industry. Such departments will act under the direction of the Control Council.

Source: R. Morgan (ed.), *The Unsettled Peace*, London, BBC, 1974, pp. 63–4.

73 Denazification in the American Zone

General Clay, the military governor of the American Zone, in a communication to the War Department in Washington sums up the problems caused by large-scale denazification.

15 December 1946

On my return to Germany I find that as a result of my talk with the Laenderrat [*sic*] [Council of States] there has been a vigorous upswing in execution of the denazification program. However, it has become apparent that due to the large number of people chargeable under the law (estimated at approximately three million) the administrative difficulties will require at least two years and perhaps longer for full completion of the program. Obviously, political stability in Germany cannot be obtained fully until the program is completed. Therefore, it appears most desirable to reduce the numbers chargeable under the law, emphasising that this reduction is to permit German administration to concentrate on the punishment of active Nazis who were or are in places of prominence in German life.

Source: J. E. Smith (ed.), *The Papers of General Lucius Clay: Germany, 1945–49*, vol. 1, Bloomington, Indiana University Press, 1974, p. 265.

74 The SED as a Marxist party

An extract from the resolution of the 1st party conference, 28 January 1949.

The characteristics of a party of the new type are:

The Marxist–Leninist party is the conscious vanguard of the working class. That is, it must be a workers' party which primarily has in its ranks the best elements of the working class, who are constantly heightening their class consciousness. The party can only fulfil its role as the vanguard of the proletariat if it has mastered Marxist–Leninist theory, which gives it insight into the laws of development of society. Therefore the first task in the development of the SED into a party of the new type is the political and ideological education of the membership and particularly of the office-bearers in the spirit of Marxism–Leninism.

The role of the party as vanguard of the working class is realised in the day-to-day strategic guidance of party activity. This makes it possible to direct all aspects of party activity in the areas of government, economy, and cultural life. To achieve this it is necessary to form a collective strategic party leadership by electing a Political Bureau (Politburo). . . .

The Marxist–Leninist party is founded on the principle of democratic centralism. This means strictest adherence to the principle that leading bodies and officers are subject to election and that those elected are accountable to the membership. This internal party democracy is the basis for the tight party discipline which arises from members' socialist consciousness. Party resolutions are binding on all party members, particularly for those party members active in parliaments, governments, administrative bodies, and in the leadership of the mass organisations.

Democratic centralism means the development of criticism and self-criticism within the party and supervision to ensure that resolutions are rigorously carried out by the leadership and by members.

Toleration of factions and groupings within the party is not consistent with its Marxist–Leninist character.

Source: J. Thomanek and J. Mellis (eds), *Politics, Society and Government in the GDR: Basic Documents*, Oxford and New York, Berg, 1988, pp. 48–9.

75 The Basic Law, 23 May 1949

Preamble:
The German people in the *Länder* of Baden, Bavaria, Bremen, Hamburg, Hesse, Lower Saxony, North-Rhine Westfalia, Rhineland–Palatinate, Schleswig-Holstein, Württemberg-Baden, and Württemberg–Hohenzollern, conscious of its responsibility before God and man, animated by the resolve to preserve its national and political unity, and to serve the peace of the world as an equal partner in a united Europe, desiring to give a new order to political life for a transitional period, has enacted, by virtue of its constituent power, this basic law of the FRG. It has also acted on behalf of those Germans to whom participation was denied.

The entire German people is called on to achieve by free self-determination the unity and freedom of Germany . . .

Article 20: (1) The FRG is a democratic and social federal state.

Article 21: (1) The parties participate in the shaping of the political will of the people. Their foundation is free, their inner structure must correspond to democratic principles, they have to account for the source of their funds in public.

Article 23: For the time being, this basic law applies in the territory of the *Länder* [mentioned above in the preamble] In other parts of Germany, it shall be put into force on their accession. . . .

Article 116: (1) This Basic Law understands as German, except for other legal stipulations, whoever has German citizenship or whoever lived as a refugee or expellee of German ethnic origin or as his spouse or descendant on the territory of the German Empire on 31 December 1937.

Source: K. Jarausch and V. von Gransow (eds), *Uniting Germany. Documents and Debates*, Oxford and Providence, Berg, 1994, pp. 6–7.

76 Adenauer and Western integration

Sir Ivone Kirkpatrick, the permanent under-secretary of state at the Foreign Office in London, wrote an account of the following conversation with the West German ambassador, Herbert Blankenhorn in December 1955.

The German ambassador told me yesterday that he wished to make a particularly confidential communication to me on this subject. I would recollect that I had told him on my return from Geneva that I had come to the conclusion that we might eventually have to be more elastic than the Americans were prepared to be and that we might have to move to a position in which we declared that, provided Germany was unified by means of free elections and provided that unified German Government had freedom in domestic and foreign affairs, we should sign any reasonable security treaty with the Russians.

The Ambassador told me that he had discussed this possibility very confidentially with the Chancellor. Dr Adenauer wished me to know that he would deprecate reaching this position. The bald reason was that Dr Adenauer had no confidence in the German people. He was terrified that when he disappeared from the scene a future German Government might do a deal with Russia at the German expense. Consequently he felt that the integration of Western Germany with the West was more important than the unification of Germany. He wished us to know that he would bend all his energies towards achieving this in the time which was left to him, and he hoped that we would do all in our power to sustain him in this task.

Source: R. Steininger, *The German Question, the Stalin Note of 1952 and the Problem of Reunification*, New York, Columbia University Press, 1990, pp. 118–19.

77 Adenauer's message to the East Germans

After the closing of the frontier in Berlin on 13 August 1961, Adenauer made a speech before a special session of the Bundestag *on 18 August.*

Let me finally say a few words to the inhabitants of the Eastern sector of Berlin and the Soviet zone of Germany. Your sorrow and suffering are our sorrow and suffering. In your particularly difficult situation you were able at least to derive some comfort from the thought that, if your lot should become quite unbearable, you could mend it by fleeing. Now it looks as if you had been deprived of this comfort, too. I request you with all my heart: do not abandon all hope of a better future for yourselves and your children. We are convinced that the Free World, and particularly we here, shall some day be successful in our efforts to obtain freedom for you. The right to self-determination will continue in its victorious march throughout the world and will not halt at the boundary of the Soviet zone. Believe me, the day will come when you will be united with us in freedom. We do not stand alone in the world; justice is on our side, and so are all the nations who love freedom.

Source: W. Heidelmeyer and V. von Gransow, *Documents on Berlin, 1943–63*, Munich, Oldenbourg Verlag, 1963, p. 288.

78 Willy Brandt on *Ostpolitik*

In January 1970 Brandt outlined in the Bundestag *the philosophy behind his foreign policy.*

Some 25 years after the unconditional surrender of the Hitler Reich the concept of the nation forms the tie in divided Germany. In the concept of the nation, historical reality and political will are combined. The word 'nation' encompasses and means more than common language and culture, more than state and social system. The word 'nation' is based on the continuous feeling of belonging together held by a people of a nation.

Nobody can deny the fact that in this sense there is and will be one German nation as far as we can think ahead. . . . We must . . . have a historical and political perspective . . . if we confirm the demand for self-determination for the whole German people. History which has divided Germany through its own faults – at any rate not without its faults – will decide when and how this demand can be implemented. Yet as long as the Germans muster the political will not to abandon this demand the hope remains that later generations will live in one Germany in whose political system the Germans in their entirety can cooperate.

The national components will also have their place in a European peace settlement. We have, however, a long and tedious way to go to reach self-determination for the Germans. . . . The length of this road must not prevent us from arriving at a regulated coexistence between the two states in Germany. . . . What matters is the German contributions in an international situation in which, to quote President Nixon, a transition from confrontation to cooperation will occur.

Source: D. Bark and D. Gress, *A History of West Germany*, vol. 2, Oxford, Blackwell, 1993, p. 167.

79 *Ostpolitik* and the Helsinki Final Act viewed through East German eyes

The first secretary of the SED in the Schwerin district wrote to Honecker on 19 June 1978 about the attitude of the public to the whole process of détente with the West.

[It can be] sensed . . . that many citizens have difficulty in the correct evaluation of the specifics of our policies in the interests of peace . . . in this connection the influence of the class enemy is not without effect.

It is still clear that every step toward normal international legal relations between states leads to illusions with respect to the Federal Republic of Germany, for example, concerning travel there or other such matters.

Here we see that the enemy is still, despite all, using his manifold organizational influences to target citizens, at least as far as problems concerning holiday travel or a sense of nationalism – if only occasionally – is concerned.

Source: M. Fulbrook, *Anatomy of a Dictatorship*, Oxford, Oxford University Press, p. 146.

80 Election results, FRG, 1949–87, Germany, 1990–2002

Year	CDU–CSU	SPD	FDP	KPD	DRP	Greens
1949	31.0	29.2	11.9	5.7	1.8	–
1953	45.2	28.8	9.5	2.2	1.1	–
1957	50.2	31.8	7.7	–	1.0	–
1961	45.3	36.2	12.8	–	0.8	–
					NPD	
1965	47.6	39.3	9.5		2.0	–
1969	46.1	39.3	5.8		4.3	–
1972	44.9	45.8	8.4		0.6	–
1976	48.6	42.6	7.9		0.3	–
1980	44.5	42.9	10.6		0.2	1.5
1983	48.8	38.2	6.9		0.2	5.6
1987	44.3	37.0	9.1		0.6	8.3
				PDS	Republicans	
1990	43.8	33.5	11.0	2.4	2.1	5.1
1994	41.4	36.4	6.9	4.4	1.9	7.2
1998	35.1	40.9	6.2	5.1	6.0	6.7
2002	38.5	38.5	7.4	4.0	1.0	8.6

Source: *Statistisches Bundesamt*, Wiesbaden, Germany.

81 The *Spiegel* Affair

Sebastian Haffner, a leading West German journalist, made the following observation on the affair in the Süddeutsche Zeitung, *in November 1962.*

What is usually referred to as 'the accompanying circumstances of the *Spiegel* affair' is in reality the affair itself. The fateful question for Germany which is being raised at this time is not whether the *Spiegel* has – in some articles that may be weeks or months old – crossed the uncertain and flexible limit that distinguishes legitimate public information on defence matters from treason. Let the lawyers calmly decide that point for themselves. The question is whether the Federal Republic of Germany is still a free and constitutional democracy, or whether it has become possible to transform it overnight by some sort of *coup d'état* based on fear and arbitrary power.

D. Bark and D. Gress, *A History of West Germany*, vol. I, Oxford, Blackwell, 1991, p. 505.

82 The position of women in post-war Germany

Walther von Hollander writing in the woman's magazine, Constanza, *in 1948 describes the tensions between men and women in immediate post-war Germany.*

I know a great many women who try everything in their power to make sure that their husband does not notice the helpless and humiliating position in which he finds himself. In addition to the worries where the daily bread will come from and to the efforts of providing something resembling civilised living, women find the strength to encourage their husbands and to put up with his passivity and weakness. But the situation really becomes intolerable when the helpless man then acts like a domestic tyrant. A powerless tyrant – a disgusting type. And however many excuses one may find for his behaviour in the adverse circumstances of our times, his demands simply are too much for the woman who is already stretched beyond her physical and emotional strength.

Source: E. Kolinsky, *Women in Contemporary Germany. Life, Work and Politics* (2nd edn), Oxford and New York, Berg, 1991, pp. 29–30.

83 Soviet criticism of Ulbricht's policy, 2 June 1953

When Ulbricht, Oelssner and Grotewohl visited Moscow on 2 June they were given the following document by the Soviet Leadership.

The pursuit of a wrong political line in the German Democratic Republic has produced a most unsatisfactory political and economic situation. There are signs of bitter dissatisfaction – among broad masses of the population, including the workers, the farmers, and the intellectuals – with the political and economic policies of the GDR. The most conspicuous feature of this dissatisfaction is the mass flight of East German residents to West Germany. From January 1951 through April 1953, 447,000 people have fled alone. Working people make up a substantial number of the defectors. An analysis of the social composition of defectors reveals the following: 18,000 workers; 9,000 medium and small farmers, skilled workers, and retirees; 17,000 white-collar workers and intellectuals; and 24,000 housewives. It is striking that 2,718 members and candidates of the SED and 2,619 members of the FDJ were among the defectors to West Germany in the first four months of 1953.

It should be recognised that the main cause of this situation is the false course adopted during the Second Party Conference of the SED – and approved by the Central Committee of the Communist Party of the Soviet Union – accelerating the pace of the construction of socialism in East Germany, without the necessary domestic and foreign policy preconditions.

Source: V. Ingimundarson, 'Cold War Misperceptions: The Communist and Western responses to the East German Refugee Crisis in 1953', *Journal of Contemporary History*, vol. 29, 1994, p. 473.

84 The Red Army Faction

Horst Mahler, founder of the Berlin Socialist Lawyers Collective and member of the RAF, was arrested in October 1972. When brought to trial, he made the following declaration to the court.

You charge me with conspiracy. . . . But you yourself, the gang of General Motors, Ford, Aramco, General Electric, ITT, Siemens, AEG, Flick, Quandt, BASF, Springer, Unilever, United Front, and certain others . . . are the most monstrous criminal association in history. To destroy this with all necessary and obtainable means is a necessity of life for more than 3 billion people. . . . The imperialist system, which presents hell on earth to ever increasing portions of humanity, may only be defeated by the action of armed people and not by incantations, moral appeals, and parliamentary trifling. The Red Army Faction has taken up the idea of arming the people.

Source: J. Becker, *Hitler's Children. The Story of the Baader-Meinhof Terrorist Gang*, London, Pickwick, 1989, p. 249.

85 The leftward drift of the SPD in the 1970s

In his book, People and Politics, *Willy Brandt described the changes taking place in the SPD in the 1970s.*

[The SPD's] membership was being restratified by a process of sociological change corresponding to the growth of the so-called service society. Its internal climate was also being modified by an influx of young and restless recruits. Within a single decade transformation and expansion had accounted for the remarkable fact that only one-third of the membership was 'old', while two-thirds were new recruits, very many of them academics and white collar workers. The successful assimilation of this greatly altered body of support was not a foregone conclusion. Many feared – and others hoped – that a substantial left-wing group would diverge from the mainstream of the party.

Source: W. Brandt, *People and Politics*, Boston, Little, Brown and Co., 1978, p. 438.

86 Reaction of the population of the GDR to the invasion of Czechoslovakia by Warsaw Pact troops, August 1968

In early September the East German trade union movement, the FDGB, conducted a survey of public opinion, of which the following is an extract.

– increased daubing of swastikas, SS runes, graffiti in toilets, factories, on buildings and squares.
Mostly this graffiti consists of slogans such as 'long live Dubcek – freedom for Czechoslovakia
– Russians and Germans get out of Czechoslovakia – It is just like thirty years ago'. . . .
– provocative expressions and incitements against our state, against the Soviet Union and leading personalities (particularly against Comrade Walter Ulbricht). For example four youths in the *Zentrum Warenhaus* Erfurt described Soviet soldiers as pigs and pig Russians.

Source: M. Fulbrook, *Anatomy of a Dictatorship. Inside the GDR, 1949–89*, Oxford, Oxford University Press, 1995, p. 197.

87 The decision on German unity

The Bundestag *welcomes the vote by the GDR Volkskammer to join the GDR on 23 August 1990.*

In a government declaration before the *Bundestag* on Thursday, Chancellor Helmut Kohl called the decision of the *Volkskammer* that the scope of the Basic law be expanded to include the area of the GDR . . . a 'memorable event in German history'. 'Today is a day of joy for all Germans. Wednesday 3 October 1990, will be a date of reunification. It will be a great day in the history of the people . . .'.

Deputy SPD chairman, Oskar Lafontaine, also welcomed the *Volkskammer* resolution as representing a foundation upon which the people of East Germany would be able to live their lives in freedom. Lafontaine reminded listeners that political unification was a prerequisite for 'real unity' – namely, the establishment of uniform living standards throughout Germany. At the same time he referred to Carlo Schmidt's demand for a European nation, and spoke out for a new national concept that could be realized in a United States of Europe. . . .

The Chancellor particularly acknowledged the contribution of his predecessor Konrad Adenauer, to the presently completed unification of Germany. What Adenauer described in his memoirs is finally being achieved, said Kohl.

Source: K. Jarausch and V. von Gransow, *Uniting Germany. Documents and Debates, 1944–1993*, Oxford and Providence, Berg, 1994, pp. 180–1.

Notes and References

Chapter 1

1   B. Simms, *The Struggle for Mastery in Germany* (London and Basingstoke, St Martin's Press) 1998, p. 1.

2   J. J. Sheehan, 'What is German History? Reflections on the Role of the *Nation* in German History and Historiography', in *Journal of Modern History*, vol. 53, March 1981, p. 1.

3   Ibid., p. 6.

4   D. Blackbourn, *Germany, 1780–1918* (London, Fontana, 1997) p. 13.

5   J. Sheehan, *German History, 1770–1866* (Oxford, Oxford University Press, 1989) p. 14.

6   Ibid., p. 23.

7   A. J. P. Taylor, *The Course of German History* (Methuen, 1961) p. 3.

8   Sheehan, 'What is German History?', p. 8.

9   Ibid., p. 9.

10   Blackbourn, *Germany, 1780–1918*, p. 7.

11   Ibid., p. 19.

12   T. Nipperdey, *Germany from Napoleon to Bismarck, 1800–1866* (Princeton, Princeton University Press, 1996) p. 38.

13   Sheehan, *German History*, p. 294.

14   Blackbourn, *Germany, 1780–1918*, p. 84.

15   Sheehan, *German History*, p. 249.

16   Ibid., p. 260.

17   Nipperdey, *Germany from Napoleon to Bismarck*, p. 62.

18   Ibid., p. 68.

19   Sheehan, *German History*, p. 386.

20   J. Whalley, 'The German Lands before 1815', in M. Fulbrook (ed), *German History since 1800* (London, Arnold, 1997) p. 32.

21   Sheehan, *German History*, p. 398.

22   Nipperdey, *Germany from Napoleon to Bismarck*, p. 82.

Chapter 2

1   W. D. Grüner, 'Die deutschen Einzelstaaten und der deutsche Bund', in A. Kraus (ed.), *Land Reich, Stamm und Nation* (Munich, Beck, 1984) p. 20.

2   P. W. Schroeder quoted in Sheehan, *German History*, p. 410; W. Conze, *Staat und Gesellschaft im deutschen Vormärz 1815–1848* (Stuttgart, Klett, 1962); W. D. Grüner, 'Die Deutschen Einzelstaaten'; E. Krahe, 'The German Confederation and the Central European Order', *American Historical Association Meeting* (Washington, 1955).

3   E. R. Huber, *Deutsche Verfassungsgeschichte*, vol. 1 (Stuttgart, Kohlhammer, 1957) p. 746.

4   Sheehan, *German History*, p. 409.

5   Ibid., pp. 408–9.

6   G. S. Werner, *Bavaria and the German Confederation, 1820–1848* (London,

Associated University Press, 1977) p. 33.

7   Ibid., p. 143.

8   Ibid., p. 150.

9   C. Clark, 'Germany, 1915–1848: Restoration or Pre-March?', in Fulbrook
      (ed.), *German History since 1800*, p. 44.

10   B. Simms, *Struggle for Mastery*, pp. 116–17.

11   Ibid., p. 115.

12   Ibid., p. 115.

13   W. Henderson, *The Zollverein* (Cambridge, Cambridge University Press,
      1939) p. 25.

14   Nipperdey, *Germany from Napoleon to Bismarck*, p. 317.

15   Henderson, *Zollverein*, p. 53.

16   Ibid., p. 53.

17   H.-U. Wehler, *Deutsche Gesellschaftsgeschichte, 1815–1845/48* (Munich, Beck,
      1996) p. 131.

18   H.-J. Voth, 'The Prussian Zollverein and the Bid for Economic Superiority',
      in P. G. Dwyer (ed.), *Modern Prussian History, 1830–1947* (Harlow, Pearson,
      2001) p. 110.

19   H. Böhme, Deutschlands Weg zur Grossmacht (Cologne, Kiepenhauer und
      Witsch, 1966). Sheehan, *German History*, p. 503.

20   Huber, *Deutsche Verfassungsgeschichte*, vol. 2, p. 298.

21   Nipperdey, *Germany from Napoleon to Bismarck*, p. 316.

22   Ibid., p. 281.

23   See T. Stamm-Kuhlmann, 'Restoration Prussia', in Dwyer, *Modern Prussian
      History*, p. 57.

24   Nipperdey, *Germany from Napoleon to Bismarck*, p. 243.

25   Ibid., p. 293.

26   L. Lee, 'Liberal Constitutionalism as Administrative Reform: The Baden
      Constitution of 1818', in *Central European History*, vol. 8/2, 1975, p. 112.

27   Sheehan, *German History*, p. 588.

28   Nipperdey, *Germany from Napoleon to Bismarck*, p. 254.

29   Ibid., p. 344.

30   Wehler, *Deutsche Gesellschaftsgeschichte*, p. 397.

31   Nipperdey, *Germany from Napoleon to Bismarck*, p. 244.

32   Ibid., p. 335.

33   Ibid., p. 336.

34   Ibid., p. 340.

35   Blackbourn, *Germany 1780–1918*, p. 107.

36   M. Kitchen, *The Political Economy of Germany* (London, Croom Helm, 1978)
      p. 12.

37   Wehler, *Deutsche Gesellschaftsgeschichte*, p. 68.

38   Ibid., pp. 133–4; W. G. Hoffmann, 'The Take-Off in Germany', in W.
      Rostow (ed.), *The Economics of Take-off into Sustained Growth* (London,
      Macmillan, 1974) pp. 95–118; H. Mottek, *Wirtschaftsgeschichte Deutschlands*,
      vol. 2 (East Berlin, Deutscher Verlag der Wissenschaft, 1978) pp. 56–8.

39   Henderson, *Zollverein*, p. 337.

40   Voth, *Prussian Zollverein*, p. 121. See also statistics on p. 115.

41   Sheehan, *German History*, p. 503.

42   See U. Frevert, *Women in German History. From Bourgeois Emancipation to
      Sexual Liberation* (Berg, Oxford, 1989) p. 71.

43   Nipperdey, *Germany from Napoleon to Bismarck*, p. 154.

44   Blackbourn, *Germany 1780–1918*, p. 91.
45   Ibid., p. 91.

Chapter 3

1   A. J. P. Taylor, *The Course of German History*, p. 69.
2   V. Valentin, *Geschichte der deutschen Revolution von 1848–1849*, 2 vols (new edition) (Hemsbach, Beltz, 1998).
3   See, for instance, W. Siemann, *The German Revolution of 1848–49* (London, Macmillan, 1998) pp. 218–23; Wehler, *Deutsche Gesellschaftsgeschichte*, p. 779.
4   Sheehan, *German History*, p. 657.
5   H.-J. Hahn, for instance, concedes that 'he is unable to furnish a clear set of causes to explain the year of European revolutions in 1848'! Hans-Joachim Hahn, *The 1848 Revolutions in German-speaking Europe* (Harlow, Pearson, 2001) Introd., xi.
6   Simms, *Struggle for Mastery*, p. 171.
7   Sheehan, *German History*, p. 636.
8   Ibid., p. 636.
9   W. Carr, *Schleswig-Holstein, 1815–48*, (Manchester, Manchester University Press, 1963) p. 255.
10   Siemann, *German Revolution of 1848–49*, p. 47.
11   Simms, *Struggle for Mastery*, p. 168.
12   Wehler, *Deutsche Gesellschaftsgeschichte*, pp. 642–3.
13   Siemann, *German Revolution of 1848–49*, p. 57.
14   Sheehan, *German History*, p. 671.
15   Siemann, *German Revolution of 1848–49*, p. 71.
16   Ibid., p. 75.
17   Ibid., p. 76.
18   Sheehan, *German History*, p. 676.
19   Hahn, *1848 Revolutions*, p. 139.
20   Nipperdey, *Germany from Napoleon to Bismarck*, p. 547.
21   Siemann, *German Revolution of 1848–49*, p. 144.
22   Ibid., p. 143.
23   Ibid., p. 146.
24   Nipperdey, *Germany from Napoleon to Bismarck*, p. 583.
25   Sheehan, *German History*, p. 691.
26   Wehler, *Deutsche Gesellschaftsgeschichte*, p. 772.
27   Carr, *A History of Germany, 1815–1990* (London, Arnold, 1991) p. 64.
28   Nipperdey, *Germany from Napoleon to Bismarck*, p. 637.
29   Sheehan, *German History*, p. 733.
30   See statistics in J. Breuilly, 'Revolution to Unification', in J. Breuilly (ed.), *19th-Century Germany* (London, Arnold, 2001) p. 140.
31   Sheehan, *German History*, p. 747.
32   H. W. Koch, *A History of Prussia* (London, Longman, 1978) p. 245.

Chapter 4

1   Nipperdey, *Germany from Napoleon to Bismarck*, p. 643.

2   J. Sheehan, *German History*, p. 876.

3   O. Pflanze, *Bismarck and the Development of Germany*, vol. 1 (second edition) (Princeton, Princeton University Press, 1990) p. 168.

4   F. Stern, *Gold and Iron: Bismarck, Bleichroder and the Building of the German Empire* (London, Allen and Unwin, 1977) p. 52.

5   C. Grant Robertson, *Bismarck* (London, Constable, 1918) p. 128.

6   F. Stern, *Gold and Iron*, p. 23.

7   L. Gall, *Bismarck, The White Revolutionary*, vol. 1 (London, Allen and Unwin, 1986) p. 258.

8   Pflanze, *Bismarck and the Development of Germany*, vol. 1, p. 202.

9   Nipperdey, *Germany from Napoleon to Bismarck*, p. 627.

10 W. E. Mosse, *The European Powers and the German Question, 1848–71* (Cambridge, Cambridge University Press, 1958) p. 253.

11 A. J. P. Taylor, *Bismarck, The Man and the Statesman* (London, Hamish Hamilton (Arrow Books)) p. 75.

12 Pflanze, *Bismarck and the Development of Germany*, vol. 1, p. 254.

13 Gall, *Bismarck, The White Revolutionary*, vol. 1, p. 258.

14 Nipperdey, *Germany from Napoleon to Bismarck*, p. 636.

15 H.-J. Voth, *Prussian Zollverein*, p. 124.

16 Pflanze, *Bismarck and the Development of Germany*, vol. 1, p. 258.

17 Grant Robertson, *Bismarck*, p. 234 and Taylor, *Bismarck*, p. 98.

18 Pflanze, *Bismarck and the Development of Germany*, vol. 1, p. 345.

19 Gall, *Bismarck, The White Revolutionary*, vol. 1, pp. 314–5.

20 Taylor, *Bismarck*, p. 102.

21 Mosse, *European Powers*, p. 263.

22 G. A. Craig, *Germany, 1866–1945* (Oxford, Oxford University Press, 1978) p. 19.

23 Taylor, *Bismarck*, p. 115.

24 S. W. Halperin, 'The Origins of the Franco-Prussian War Revisited: Bismarck and the Hohenzollern Candidature for the Spanish Throne', in *Journal of Modern History*, vol. 45, 1, 1973, p. 85.

25 Ibid., p. 91.

26 M. Howard, *The Franco–Prussian War* (London, Rupert Hart Davis, 1962) p. 388.

27 See Taylor, *Bismarck*, p. 129; T. Hamerow, *The Social Foundations of German Unification*, vol. 2 (Princeton, Princeton University Press, 1972) p. 417.

28 J. Breuilly, 'Revolution to Unification', p, 155.

29 B. Simms, *Struggle for Mastery*, pp. 108–9.

30 J. Breuilly, 'Revolution to Unification', p. 140.

Chapter 5

1   K. S. Pinson, *Modern Germany* (London, Macmillan, 1966) p. 219.

2   H. Rosenberg, 'Political and Social Consequences of the Great Depression of 1873–1896 in Central Europe', in *Economic History Review*, vol. 13, 1943, p. 64.

3   H.-U. Wehler, *The German Empire, 1871–1918*, Leamington Spa and Dover, NH, 1985) p. 49.

4   D. Blackbourn, *Germany 1780–1918*, p. 344.

5   Ibid., p. 341.

6   Ibid., p. 361.
7   D. Blackbourn and G. Eley, *The Peculiarities of German History* (Oxford, Oxford University Press, 1984) p. 223.
8   Ibid., p. 241.
9   M. Kitchen, *Political Economy of Germany*, p. 247.
10   M. L. Anderson, *Windthorst. A Political Biography* (Oxford, Oxford University Press, 1981) p. 197.
11   V. R. Berghahn, *Imperial Germany, 1871–1914*, Providence, RI and Oxford, Berghahn Press, 1994) p. 101.
12   P. Panayi, *Ethnic Minorities in Nineteenth and Twentieth Century Germany* (London, Pearson, 2000) p. 102.
13   Pflanze, *Bismarck and the Development of Germany*, vol. 3, p. 206
14   Panayi, *Ethnic Minorities*, p. 101.
15   Ibid., pp. 82 and 85.
16   Ibid., p. 87.
17   R. S. Levy, *The Downfall of the Anti-Semitic Political Parties in Imperial Germany* (New Haven, CT and London, 1975) p. 154–5 quoted in ibid., p. 85.
18   Rathenau, 'Hore Israel', in *Zukunft*, 6.3, 1897, p. 454.
19   Berghahn, *Imperial Germany*, p. 77.
20   Ibid., p. 136.
21   Quoted in ibid., p. 133.
22   W. Mommsen, *Imperial Germany, 1867–1918, Politics, Culture and Society in an Authoritarian State* (London, Arnold, 1995) p. 132.
23   Ibid., p. 134.
24   Craig, *Germany, 1866–1945*, p. 36.
25   Mommsen, *Imperial Germany*, p. 102.

Chapter 6

1   Important books in this debate are: M. Rauh, *Die Parlamentarisierung des deutschen Reiches* (Düsseldorf, Droste, 1977); F. Fischer, *Germany's Aims in the First World War* (London, Chatto and Windus, 1967); H.-U. Wehler, *The German Empire*; T. Nipperdey, *Deutsche Geschichte, 1866–1918*, vol. 2 (Munich, Beck, 1992); D. Blackbourn and G. Eley, *Peculiarities of German History*; V. Berghahn, *Germany and the Approach to War in 1914* (London, Macmillan, 1973).
2   G. Eley, 'Bismarckian Germany', in G. Martel (ed.), *Modern Germany Reconsidered, 1870–1945* (London, Routledge, 1992) p. 26.
3   Mommsen, *Imperial Germany*, p. 134.
4   M. Seligmann and R. R. McLean, *Germany From Reich To Republic, 1871–1918* (London, Macmillan, 2000) pp. 17–18.
5   Ibid., p. 18.
6   J. Röhl, *Germany without Bismarck* (London, Batsford, 1967) p. 22.
7   Pflanze, *Bismarck and the Development of Germany*, vol. 2, p. 155.
8   Quoted in Wehler, *German Empire*, p. 53.
9   Mommsen, *Imperial Germany*, p. 49.
10   Taylor, *Bismarck*, p. 160.
11   Gall, *Bismarck, The White Revolutionary*, vol. 2, p. 11.
12   Blackbourn, *Germany 1780–1918*, p. 262.

13   Anderson, *Windthorst*, p. 182.
14   J. Sheehan, *German Liberalism in the Nineteenth Century* (London, Methuen, 1982) pp. 143–4.
15   Seligmann and McLean, *Germany from Reich to Republic*, p. 32.
16   Anderson, *Windthorst*, p. 233.
17   Eley, 'Bismarckian Germany', p. 3; Böhme, *Deutschlands Weg*.
18   Quoted in Stern, *Gold and Iron*, p. 207.
19   Gall, *Bismarck, The White Revolutionary*, vol. 2, p. 135.
20   E. Kraehe, 'Review Article on Otto Pflanze's Trilogy', in *Central European History*, vol. 23, no. 4, 1990, p. 376.
21   H.-U. Wehler, 'Bismarck's Imperialism, 1862–1890', in *Past and Present*, vol. 48, 1970, p. 147.
22   Pflanze, *Bismarck and the Development of Germany*, vol. 3. p. 350.
23   Taylor, *Bismarck*, p. 202.
24   Seligmann and McLean, *Germany from Reich to Republic*, p. 36.
25   Ibid., p. 55.
26   Ibid., p. 61.
27   J. Sperber, *The Kaiser's Voters. Electors and Elections in Imperial Germany* (Cambridge, Cambridge University Press, 1997).
28   M. Anderson, *Practicing Democracy* (Princeton, Princeton University Press, 2000), p. 191.
29   Seligmann and McLean, *Germany from Reich to Republic*, p. 91.
30   Anderson, *Practicing Democracy*, p. 429.
31   Wehler, *German Empire*, p. 62.
32   Seligmann and McLean, *Germany from Reich to Republic*, p. 78.
33   Mommsen, *Imperial Germany*, p. 150; J. Röhl, *The Kaiser and his Court. Wilhelm II and the Government of Germany* (Cambridge, Cambridge University Press, 1994); K. A. Lerman, *The Chancellor as Courtier. Bernhard von Bülow and the Government of Germany, 1900–1909* (Cambridge, Cambridge University Press, 1990).
34   Craig, *Germany, 1866–1945*, p. 262.
35   Seligmann and McLean, *Germany from Reich to Republic*, p. 93.
36   Ibid., p. 93.
37   Craig, *Germany, 1866–1945*, p. 273.
38   Mommsen, *Imperial Germany*, p. 151.
39   Ibid., p. 151.
40   Ibid., p. 156.
41   W. Carr, *History of Germany, 1815–1990*, p. 185.
42   See Mommsen, *Imperial Germany*, p. 34.
43   Wehler, *German Empire*, p. 62.
44   Anderson, *Practicing Democracy*, p. 437.

Chapter 7

1   W. Langer, *European Alliances and Alignments, 1871–1890* (New York, Knopf, 2nd edn, 1962), pp. 503–4; B. Waller, *Bismarck* (Oxford, Blackwell, 2nd edn, 1997), pp. 52–3. See also B. Waller, *Bismarck at the Crossroads* (London, Athlone Press, 1974) p. 254.
2   Quoted in J. Röhl (ed.), *From Bismarck to Hitler* (London, Longman, 1970) p. 23.

3   L. Geiss, *German Foreign Policy, 1871–1914* (London, Routledge, 1976) p. 12.

4   Seligmann and McLean, *Germany from Reich to Republic*, p. 40.

5   Geiss, *German Foreign Policy*, p. 30.

6   W. Medlicott and D. Coveney (eds), *Bismarck and Europe* (London, Edward Arnold, 1971) p. 86.

7   N. Rich, *Great Power Diplomacy, 1814–1914* (New York, McGraw-Hill, 1992) p. 227.

8   Craig, *Germany, 1866–1945*, p. 113.

9   Medlicott and Coveney, *Bismarck and Europe*, p. 114.

10 Craig, *Germany, 1866–1945*, p. 36.

11 Böhme, *Deutschlands Weg*; Gall, *Bismarck, The White Revolutionary*, vol. 2.

12 Medlicott and Coveney, *Bismarck and Europe*, p. 110.

13 A. J. P. Taylor, *The Struggle for Mastery in Europe, 1848–1918* (Oxford, Oxford University Press, 1954) p. 277.

14 M. E. Townsend, *The Rise and Fall of Germany's Colonial Empire* (New York, Macmillan, 1930) p. 160.

15 A. J. P. Taylor, *Germany's First Bid for Colonies* (London, Macmillan, 1938) p. 18 and *Struggle for Mastery*, p. 272.

16 P. Kennedy, 'German Colonial Expansion: Has "the Manipulated Social Imperialism" Been Antedated?', in *Past and Present*, vol. 54, 1972, pp. 134–41.

17 Seligmann and McLean, *Germany from Reich to Republic*, p. 48.

18 See Wehler, 'Bismarck's Imperialism, 1862–1890', pp. 119–55.

19 Townsend, *Rise and Fall of Germany's Colonial Empire*, p. 62.

20 Langer, *European Alliances*, p. 407.

21 Pflanze, *Bismarck and the Development of Germany*, vol. 3, p. 251.

22 Lowe, *The Great Powers, Imperialism and the German Problem, 1865–1925* (London, Routledge, 1994) p. 66.

23 Gall, *Bismarck, The White Revolutionary*, vol 2, p. 153.

24 Langer, *European Alliances*, p. 425; Taylor, *Struggle for Mastery*, p. 318; Gall, *Bismarck, The White Revolutionary*, p. 153.

25 See Mommsen, *Imperial Germany*, pp. 166–7. The key works are: W. Hallgarten, *Imperialismus vor 1914*, 2 vols (Munich, Beck, 1963); Fritz Fischer, *Griff nach der Weltmacht, 1914–1918*, (Düsseldorf, Droste, 1964); V. Berghahn, *Germany and the Approach of War in 1914* (London and Basingstoke, Macmillan, 1973); Röhl, *Germany without Bismarck*; Röhl, *The Kaiser and his Court*.

26 Quoted in Mommsen, *Imperial Germany*, p. 81.

27 Seligmann and McLean, *Germany from Reich to Republic*, p. 125.

28 Ibid., p. 128.

29 Lowe, *Great Powers*, p. 153.

30 D. Kaiser, ' Germany and the Origins of the First World War', in *Journal of Modern History*', vol. 55, p. 457.

31 Ibid., p. 455.

32 Quoted in Taylor, *Struggle for Mastery*, p. 453.

33 D. C. B. Lieven, *Russia and the Origins of the First World War* (London, Macmillan, 1993) p. 37.

34 W. Mommsen, 'The Topos of Inevitable War in Germany in the Decade before 1914', in V. R. Berghahn and M. Kitchen (eds), *Germany in the Age of Total War* (London, Croom Helm, 1981) p. 32.

35 Seligmann and McLean, *Germany from Reich to Republic*, p. 144.

36 J. Röhl, *Kaiser and his Court*, p. 170.

37   See particularly Kaiser, 'Germany and the Origins of the First World War',
     p. 466.
38   Röhl, *Kaiser and his Court*, p. 166.
39   Seligmann and McLean, *Germany from Reich to Republic*, p. 146.
40   Rich, *Great Powers' Diplomacy*, p. 442.
41   Quoted in S. R. Williamson, 'Austria Hungary Opts for War', in H. H.
     Herwig (ed.), *The Outbreak of World War I* (Boston and New York,
     Houghton Mifflin, 1997) p. 64.
42   Rich, *Great Powers Diplomacy*, p. 452.
43   See Seligmann and McLean, *Germany from Reich to Republic*, pp. 148–51.
44   Rich, *Great Powers Diplomacy*, p. 460.
45   Paul W. Schroeder, 'World War 1 as Galloping Gertie', in Herwig, *Outbreak
     of World War I*, p. 144.
46   Kaiser, 'Germany and the Origins of the First World War', p. 467.

Chapter 8

1   Quoted in Craig, *Germany 1866–1945*, p. 60.
2   Mommsen, *Imperial Germany, 1867–1918*, p. 210.
3   R. Chickering, *Imperial Germany and the Great War, 1914–1918* (Cambridge,
     Cambridge University Press, 1998) p. 17.
4   Ibid., p. 35.
5   Ibid., p. 39.
6   Ibid., p. 40.
7   Ibid., p. 81.
8   G. Feldmann, *Army Industry and Labour* (Princeton, Princeton University
     Press, 1966) p. 150.
9   Chickering, *Imperial Germany*, p. 103.
10   Ibid., p. 106.
11   Mommsen, *Imperial Germany*, p. 224.
12   Chickering, *Imperial Germany*, p. 113.
13   Ibid., p. 120.
14   Gerhardt Ritter quoted in Craig, *Germany 1866–1945*, p. 365; see also
     Fischer, *Griff nach der Weltmacht*, pp. 113–20.
15   Quoted in Craig, *Germany 1866–1945*, p. 365.
16   Ibid., p. 365.
17   Chickering, *Imperial Germany*, p. 158.
18   Craig, *Germany 1866–1945*, p. 382.
19   Ibid., p. 383.
20   Chickering, *Imperial Germany*, p. 164
21   Ibid., p. 165.
22   G. Kennan, *The Decline of Bismarck's European Order* (Princeton, Princeton
     Uuniversity Press, 1978) p. 3.

Chapter 9

1   K. D. Erdmann, in B. Gebhardt, *Handbuch der deutschen Geschichte'*, vol. 4,
     (Stuttgart, Union Verlag, 1973) pp. 87–91; F. L. Carsten, *Revolution in
     Central Europe, 1918–19* (London, Wildwood House, 1972); S. Miller, *Die

Bürde der Macht. Die deutsche Sozialdemokratie, 1918–1920 (Düsseldorf, Droste, 1978). This debate is explored in E. Kolb, *The Weimar Republic* (London, Routledge, 1992).

2   Taylor, *Course of German History*, p. 206.
3   Kolb, *Weimar Republic*, p. 5.
4   Heinrich Winkler quoted in ibid., p. 14.
5   Kolb, *Weimar Republic*, p. 16.
6   Ibid., p. 19.
7   Ibid., p. 30.
8   Quoted in ibid., p. 33.
9   Mommsen, *Imperial Germany*, p. 232.
10   Kolb, *Weimar Republic*, p. 38.
11   Mommsen, *Imperial Germany*, p. 252.
12   Alfred Kastning quoted in Kolb, *Weimar Republic*, p. 39.
13   P. Krüger, *Die Aussenpolitik der Republik von Weimar*, Darmstadt, Wissenschaftliche Buchgesellschaft, 1985, p. 91.
14   W. A. McDougall, *France's Rhineland Diplomacy, 1914–24* (Princeton, Princeton University Press, 1978) p. 138.
15   Quoted in D. Williamson, *The British in Germany, 1918–30* (New York and Oxford, Berg, 1994) p. 186.
16   See Sally Marks, 'Reparations Re-Considered: A Reminder', in *Central European History* ii, no. 4 (Dec. 1969), pp. 358–60 and C. S. Maier, *Recasting Bourgeois Europe; Stabilization in France, Germany and Italy in the Decade after World War I* (Princeton, Princeton University Press, 1975) pp. 241–2.
17   C. Fink quoted in Williamson, *The British in Germany*, p. 151.
18   Krüger, *Die Aussenpolitik der Republic von Weimar*, p. 227.
19   Mommsen, *Imperial Germany*, p. 231.
20   J. Hiden, *Republican and Fascist Germany* (Harlow, Longman, 1996) p. 43.

Chapter 10

1   Kolb, *Weimar Republic*, p. 66.
2   D. Peukert, *The Weimar Republic: The Crisis of Classical Modernity* (London, Allen Lane, 1991) p. 4.
3   Quoted in D. Williamson, *War and Peace: International Relations, 1914–45* (London, Hodder, 1994) p. 63.
4   M.-O. Maxelon, quoted in Kolb, *Weimar Republic*, p. 175.
5   Peukert, *Weimar*, p. 204.
6   See T. Childers, 'Inflation, Stabilization, and Political Realignment in Germany, 1924 to 1928', in G. D. Feldman (ed.), *The German Inflation Reconsidered: A Preliminary Balance* (Berlin, de Gruyter, 1982) pp. 409–31.
7   K. Borchardt, *Perspectives on Modern German Economic History and Policy* (Cambridge, Cambridge University Press, 1991) p. 171.
8   Ibid., p. 182.
9   B. Liebermann, *From Recovery to Catastrophe* (New York and Oxford, Berghahn, 1998).
10   Peukert, *Weimar*, p. 82.
11   Ibid., p. 130.
12   Ibid., p. 132.
13   Ibid., p. 89.

14 H. Mommsen, *From Weimar to Auschwitz, Essays in German History* (London, Polity Press, 1991) p. 36.

15 Peukert, *Weimar*, p. 95.

16 Frevert, *Women*, p. 170.

17 Peukert, *Weimar*, p. 99.

18 Frevert, *Women*, p. 186.

19 Ibid., p. 185.

20 Ibid., p. 188.

21 Ibid., p. 188.

22 Ibid., p. 203.

23 Peukert, *Weimar*, p. 178.

24 Ibid., p. 181.

25 Ibid., p. 157.

26 Craig, *Germany 1866–1945*, p. 470.

27 Ibid., p. 472.

28 Ibid., p. 473.

29 R. Lepsius, 'From Fragmented Party Democracy to Government by Emergency Decree and National Socialist Take over: Germany', in J. Linz and A. Stepan (eds), *The Breakdown of Democratic Regimes: Europe* (Baltimore and London, Johns Hopkins University Press, 1978) p. 44.

30 Kolb, *Weimar Republic*, p. 69.

31 Childers, *Inflation, Stabilization and Political Realignment*, p. 411.

32 Ibid., p. 413.

33 J. Wright, *Gustav Stresemann* (Oxford, Oxford University Press, 2002) p. 258.

34 Kolb, *Weimar Republic*, p. 75.

35 Ibid., p. 76.

36 Ibid., p. 78.

37 Ibid., p. 66.

38 Michael Stürmer quoted in ibid., p. 66.

39 Hagen Schulze, 'Democratic Prussia in Weimar Germany, 1919–33', in P. Dwyer (ed.), *Moden Prussian History*, p. 214.

Chapter 11

1 Quoted in Kolb, *Weimar Republic*, p. 129.

2 R. Boyce, ' World War, World Depression: Some Economic Origins of the Second World War', in R. Boyce and E. Robertson (eds), *Paths to War* (London, Macmillan, 1989) p. 55.

3 E. Nolte, *Three Faces of Fascism: Action Française, Italian Fascism, National Socialism* (New York, Mentor, 1969) p. 419.

4 Peukert, *Weimar*, p. 252.

5 Ibid., p. 249.

6 Craig, *Germany 1866–1945*, p. 352–3.

7 A. Rosenberg, *History of the German Republic* (London, Methuen, 1936) p. 306 and F. Meinecke, *The German Catastrophe* (Cambridge, MA, Harvard University Press, 1950) p. 70.

8 W. Conze, 'Die Krise des Parteienstaates in Deutschland 1929/30', in *Historische Zeitschrift*, vol. 178, 1954, pp. 47–83.

9 K. Bracher, 'Democracy and Power Vacuum: The Problem of the Party State', in V. R. Berghahn and M. Kitchen (eds), *Germany in the Age of Total*

War (London, Croom Helm, 1981); Mommsen, *From Weimar to Auschwitz*, p. 140.

10   K. Borchardt, *Perspectives*, p. 161.

11   Quoted in Kolb, *Weimar Republic*, p. 118.

12   I. Kershaw, *Hitler*, vol. 1 (London, Arnold, 1998) p. 324.

13   Quoted in Kolb, *Weimar Republic*, p. 113.

14   Kershaw, *Hitler*, vol 1, p. 333.

15   Quoted in Kolb, *Weimar Republic*, p 113.

16   J. W. Falter, 'Die Wähler der NSDAP, 1928–1933: Sozialstruktur und parteipolitische Herkunft', in Michalka (ed.), *Die Nationalsozialistische Machtergreifung* (Padeborn and Munich, Schoning, 1984) pp. 47–59.

17   Ibid., p. 114.

18   Quoted in Williamson, *War and Peace*, p. 86.

19   Kolb, *Weimar Republic*, p. 118.

20   Kolb, *Weimar Republic*, p. 120.

21   D. Orlow, *The History of the Nazi Party*, vol. I, *1919–33* (Newton Abbot, David and Charles, 1971) p. 308.

22   Quoted in Kolb, *Weimar Republic*, p. 124.

23   M. Burleigh, *The Third Reich: A New History* (London, Macmillan, 2000) p. 143.

24   F. von Papen, *Memoirs* (London, Deutsch, 1951) p. 251.

25   Quoted in K. Bracher, *The German Dictatorship* (Harmondsworth, Penguin, 1973) p. 248.

26   Quoted in J. Noakes and G. Pridham (eds), *Nazism*, vol. I (Exeter, Exeter University Press, 1998) p. 132.

27   J. Fest, *Hitler* (Harmondsworth, Penguin, 1977) p. 588.

28   Noakes and Pridham, vol I, *Nazism*, p. 142.

29   Ibid., p. 150.

30   Quoted in A. Bullock, *Hitler. A Study in Tyranny* (Harmondsworth, Penguin, 1962) p. 269.

31   M. Broszat, *The Hitler State* (London, Longman, 1981) p. 281.

32   Ibid., p. 99.

33   Ibid., p. 262.

34   Bullock, *Hitler*, p. 286.

35   Kershaw, *Hitler*, vol. I, p. 508.

36   Craig, *Germany 1866–1945*, p. 588.

37   Kershaw, *Hitler*, vol 1, p. 510.

38   Bracher in Berghahn and Kitchen (eds), *Germany in the Age of Total War*, p. 190.

Chapter 12

1   See M. Roseman, 'National Socialism and Modernisation', in R. Bessel (ed.), *Fascist Italy and Nazi Germany: Comparisons and Contrasts* (Cambridge, Cambridge University Press, 1997) p. 210.

2   D. Peukert, *Inside Nazi Germany* (Harmondsworth, Penguin, 1989) p. 16.

3   M. Broszat, ' A Plea for the Historisation of National Socialism', in P. Baldwin, *Reworking the Past* (Boston, MA, Beacon Press, 1990).

4   Broszat, *Hitler State*, p. 266.

5   Ibid., p. 276.

6   Noakes and Pridham, *Nazism*, vol. 2, p. 171.

7   Ibid., p. 234.

8   Ibid., p. 237.

9   Orlow, *History of the Nazi Party*, vol. 2, pp. 135 and 193.

10 F. Neumann, *Behemoth: The Structure and Practice of National Socialism* (London, Cass, repr., 1967) p. 74.

11 E. Petersen, *The Limits of Hitler's Power* (Oxford, Oxford University Press, 1969) p. 4.

12 See I. Kershaw, *The Nazi Dictatorship, Problems and Perspectives* (London, Arnold, 1993) pp. 60–7.

13 Quoted in K. Hildebrand, *The Third Reich* (London, Routledge, 1984) p. 137.

14 Quoted in R. Overy, *War and Economy in the Third Reich* (Oxford, Oxford University Press, 1995) p. 5.

15 Ibid., p. 56.

16 Noakes and Pridham, *Nazism*, vol. 2, p. 280.

17 Overy, *War and Economy*, p. 186.

18 B. H. Klein, *Germany's Economic Preparations for War* (Cambridge, MA, Harvard University Press, 1959) p. 78.

19 A. J. P. Taylor, *The Origins of the Second World War* (London, Hamish Hamilton, 1961) and A. Milward, *The German Economy at War* (London, Athlone Press, 1965).

20 Overy, *War and Economy*, pp. 185, 192 and 190.

21 T. Mason, 'Intention and Explanation: A Current Controversy about Interpretation in National Socialism', in G. Hirschfeld and L. Kettenacker (eds), *The Führer State: Myths and Realities* (Stuttgart and London, Kletta Cotta/German Historical Institute, 1981) p. 39.

22 Overy, *War and Economy*, p. 223.

23 Kershaw, *Hitler*, vol. 2, p. 163.

24 Quoted in Noakes and Pridham, *Nazism*, vol. 2, p. 397.

25 Ibid., p. 398.

26 Quoted in ibid., p. 193.

27 C. Koonz, *Mothers in the Fatherland* (London, Cape, 1987) p. 196.

28 Peukert, *Inside Nazi Germany*, p. 152.

29 D. Schoenbaum, *Hitler's Social Revolution* (London, Weidenfeld and Nicolson, 1967) p. 161.

30 J. E. Farqharson, *The Plough and the Swastika* (London and Beverley Hills, Sage, 1976) p. 212.

31 J. S. Stephenson, *Women in Nazi Society* (London, Croom Helm, 1975) p. 172.

32 Koonz, *Mothers in the Fatherland*, p. 178.

33 Ibid., p. 180.

34 Stephenson, *Women in Nazi Society*, p. 61.

35 Ibid., p. 64.

36 R. Grünberger, *A Social History of the Third Reich* (Harmondsworth, Penguin, 1974) p. 314.

37 Quoted in N. Baynes, *Hitler's Speeches*, vol. 1 (Oxford, Oxford University Press, 1942) p. 620–1.

38 M. Burleigh, *Third Reich*, p. 250.

39 Neumann, *Behemoth*, p. 431.

40 Peukert, *Inside Nazi Germany*, p. 112.

41 Quoted in Overy, *War and Economy*, p. 224.

42   Kershaw, *Nazi Dictatorship*, p. 145.

43   Ulrich Herbert, 'Good Times, Bad Times; Memories Of The Third Reich', in R. Bessel (ed.), *Life in the Third Reich* (Oxford, Oxford University Press, 1987) p. 97.

44   M. Burleigh and W. Wipperman, *The Racial State: Germany, 1933–45* (Cambridge, Cambridge University Press, 1991) p. 135.

45   L. Dawidowicz, *The War Against the Jews, 1941–45* (Harmondsworth, Penguin, 1986), p. xxvi; K. Hildebrand, *Third Reich*; Bracher, *German Dictatorship*; M. Broszat, 'Hitler and the Genesis of the Final Solution', in H. W. Koch (ed.), *Aspects of the Third Reich* (London, Macmillan, 1985) pp. 390–429; H. Mommsen, 'The Realization of the Unthinkable: The "Final Solution" of the Jewish Question in the Third Reich', in G. Hirschfeld (ed.), *The Policies of Genocide* (London, Allen and Unwin, 1986) pp. 97–144; K. A. Schleunes, *The Twisted Road to Auschwitz* (London, Deutsch, 1972).

46   Quoted in Noakes and Pridham, *Nazism*, vol. 2, p. 588.

47   Dawidowicz, *War Against the Jews*, p. 142.

48   Mommsen, 'Realization of the Unthinkable', p. 112.

49   Dawidowicz, *War Against the Jews*, p. 43.

50   Quoted in R. Gellateley, *The Gestapo and German Society* (Oxford, Oxford University Press, 1990) p. 12.

51   Schoenbaum, *Hitler's Social Revolution*, p. 52.

52   Neumann, *Behemoth*, p. 375.

Chapter 13

1   See ch. 12, note 45.

2   Taylor, *Origins of the Second World War*, p. 68.

3   H. Mommsen, 'National Socialism: Continuity and Change', in W. Laqueur (ed.), *Fascism: A Reader's Guide* (Harmondsworth, Penguin, 1979); K. Hildebrand, *The Foreign Policy of the Third Reich* (London, Batsford, 1973); A. Hillgruber, *Hitlers Strategie, Politik und Kriegsführung, 1940–41* (Frankfurt am Main, Bernard and Graefe, 1965).

4   A. Bullock, 'Hitler and the Origins of the Second Word War', in E. M. Robertson (ed.), *The Origins of the Second World War* (London, Macmillan, 1971) p. 193.

5   Quoted in Overy, *War and Economy*, p. 190.

6   Quoted in Williamson, *War and Peace*, pp. 88–9.

7   W. Carr, *Arms, Autarky and Aggression* (London, Arnold, 1972) p. 126–7.

8   G. Weinberg, *The Foreign Policy of Hitler's Germany*, vol. 1 (Chicago and London, Chicago University Press, 1970) p. 348.

9   Taylor, *Origins of the Second World War*, p. 132; W. Carr, *Arms*, p. 128.

10   Kershaw, *Hitler*, vol. 2, p. 83.

11   Ibid., p. 119.

12   Taylor, *Origins of the Second World War*, p. 131.

13   Hildebrand, *Foreign Policy*, p. 17.

14   Bullock, *Hitler and the Origins*, p. 218.

15   G. Wright, *The Ordeal of Total War* (New York, Harper and Row, 1968) p. 140.

16   H. Bucheim et al., *Anatomy of the SS State* (London, Collins, 1968) p. 60.

17   Dawidowicz, *War Against the Jews*, p. xxvi.

18 M. R. Marrus, 'The History of the Holocaust: A Survey of Recent Literature', in *Journal of Modern History*, vol. 59, no. 1, 1987, p. 115.

19 Ibid., p. 125.

20 H. Graml, *Antisemitism in the Third Reich* (Oxford, Blackwell, 1992) p. 82.

21 Broszat, 'Hitler and the Genesis'; L. Kettenacker, 'Hitler's Final Solution and its Rationalization', in G. Hirschfeld (ed.), *Policies of Genocide*, pp. 73–95; Mommsen, 'Realization of the Unthinkable' in ibid., pp. 97–144.

22 Broszat, 'Hitler and the Genesis', p. 405.

23 Dawidowicz, *War Against the Jews*, Introd., xxxi.

24 Noakes and Pridham, *Nazism*, vol. 3, p. 1136.

25 Ibid., p. 1131.

26 Kershaw, *Hitler*, vol. 2, p. 573.

27 Fest, *Hitler*, p. 180.

28 Broszat, *Hitler State*, p. 319.

29 Kershaw, *Hitler*, vol. 2, p. 428.

30 Quoted in Broszat, *Hitler State*, p. 341.

31 A. Milward, *German Economy*, p. 31.

32 Overy, *War and Economy*, p. 343.

33 Craig, *Germany 1866–1945*, p. 734.

34 U. Herbert, *Hitler's Foreign Workers* (Cambridge, Cambridge University Press, 1997) p. 189.

35 M. Burleigh and W. Wippermann, *Racial State*, p. 235.

36 Herbert, *Hitler's Foreign Workers*, p. 396.

37 J. S. Stephenson, 'Nazism, Modern War and Rural Society in Württemberg, 1939–45', in *Journal of Contemporary History*, vol. 32, no. 3 (1997), p. 347.

38 Overy, *War and Economy*, p. 307.

39 P. Ayçoberry, *The Social History of the Third Reich* (New York, New Press, 1999) p. 231.

40 P. Erker, 'Landbevölkerung und Flüchtingszustrom', in M. Broszat, K-D Henke, and H. Wolle (eds), *Von Stalingrad zur Währungsreform: Zur Sozialgeschichte des Umbruchs in Deutschland* (Munich, Oldenbourg Verlag, 1988) p. 377.

41 Ayçoberry, *Social History*, p. 231.

42 Kershaw, *Hitler*, vol. 2, p. 832.

43 M. Kitchen, *Nazi Germany at War* (London, Longman, 1995) p. 298.

44 Ibid., p. 300.

45 Kershaw, *Nazi Dictatorship*, p. 159.

46 J. Conway, *The Nazi Persecution of the Churches*, 1933–45 (London, Weidenfeld and Nicolson, 1967) p. 266.

47 D. Peukert, *Inside Nazi Germany*, p. 168.

48 P. Hoffmann, *The History of the German Resistance* (London, MacDonald and Jane, 1977) p. 96.

49 H. Graml et al., *The German Resistance to Hitler* (Oxford, Blackwell, 1992) p. 21.

50 Kershaw, *Nazi Dictatorship*, p. 154.

51 H. Rothfels, *The German Opposition to Hitler* (London, Oswald Wolff, 1970) p. 78.

52 T. Prittie, *Germans against Hitler* (London, Hutchinson, 1964) p. 248.

53 Kershaw, *Hitler*, vol. 2, p. 677.

Chapter 14

1   R. Andreas-Friedrich, *Schauplatz Berlin: Tagebuchaufzeichnung, 1945 bis 1948* (Frankfurt am Main, Suhrkamp, 1984) p. 19.

2   A good introduction to the social revolution of 1943–48 is H. James, 'The Prehistory of the Federal Republic', in *Journal of Modern History*, vol. 63, March 1991, pp. 99–115.

3   N. M. Naimark, *The Russians in Germany; A History of the Soviet Zone of Occupation, 1945–9* (Cambridge, MA, Harvard University Press, 1995) p. 9.

4   B. Kuklick, *American Policy and the Division of Germany* (Ithaca, Cornell University, 1977) p. 157.

5   H. Zink, *The United States in Germany, 1944–55* (Westport, CT, Greenwood Press, 1974) p. 177.

6   Naimark, *Russians in Germany*, p. 45.

7   C. Klessmann, *Die doppelte Staatsgründung* (Göttingen, Vandenhoek and Ruprecht, 1988) p. 143.

8   Klessmann, *Die doppelte Staatsgründung*, p. 137.

9   Naimark, *Russians in Germany*, p. 276.

10   Ibid., p. 145.

11   M. McCauley, *The GDR since 1945* (London, Macmillan, 1983) p. 32.

12   Ibid., p. 282.

13   A. Kramer, *The West German Economy* (Oxford and New York, Berg, 1991) p. 125.

14   J. Kopstein, *Economic Decline in East Germany, 1945–89* (Chapel Hill, NC and London, University of North Carolina Press, 1997) p. 23.

15   Ibid., p. 24.

16   L. Niethammer, *Die Mitläuferfabrik: Die Entnazifierung am Beispiel Bayerns* (East Berlin, Dietz Verlag, 1982) p. 13.

17   D. Welch, 'Priming the Pump of German Democracy. British Re-education Policy in Germany after the Second World War', in I. D. Turner (ed.), *Reconstruction in Postwar Germany* (Oxford and New York, Oxford University Press, 1989) pp. 215–38; E. Schmidt, *Die verhinderte Neuordnung, 1945–52* (Hamburg, Europäische Verlagsanstalt, 1970); W. Abelshauser, *Wirtschaftsgeschichte der Bundesrepublik* (Frankfurt am Main, Suhrkamp, 1983).

18   M. Fulbrook, *The Two Germanies, 1945–1990: Problems of Interpretation* (London, Macmillan, 1992) p. 14.

19   See J. Farquharson, ' "The Essential Division". Britain and Germany and the Partition of Germany, 1945–49', in *German History*, vol. 9, no. 1, Feb. 1990, pp. 23–45.

20   T. Eschenburg, *Jahre der Besetzung (1945–9)*, vol 1, *Geschichte der Bundesrepublik Deutschland* (Stuttgart and Wiesbaden, Deutsche Verlags-Anstalt/Brockhaus, 1983) p. 419.

21   D. Williamson, *A Most Diplomatic Diplomatic General. The Life of General Lord Robertson of Oakridge* (London, Brassey's, 1996) p. 114.

22   Ibid., p. 115.

23   Klessmann, *Die doppelte Staatsgründung*, p. 188.

24   S. Suckut, 'Zur Vorgeschichte der DDR-Gründung', in *Studien zur Deutschlandsfrage*, vol. 12 (Berlin, Duncker und Humblot, 1993) pp. 121–2.

25   P. Merkl, *The Origins of the West German Republic* (Oxford, Oxford University Press, 1963) p. 176.

26 P. Pulzer, *German Politics, 1945–1995* (Oxford, Oxford University Press, 1995) p. 47.

27 Eschenburg, *Jahre der Besetzung*, p. 511.

28 Merkl, *Origins of the West German Republic*, p. 160.

29 H.-P., Schwarz, *Konrad Adenauer. A German Politician and Statesman in a Period of War, Revolution and Reconstruction*, vol. 1, Providence and Oxford, Berghahn, 1995) p. 428.

30 Naimark, *Russians in Germany*, p. 58.

31 Ibid., p. 58.

32 Merkl, *Origins of the West German Republic*, p. 75.

33 Naimark, *Russians in Germany*, p. 59.

34 Suckut, 'Zur Vorgeschichte', p. 143.

35 W. Loth, *Stalin's Unwanted Child* (London, Macmillan, 1998).

Chapter 15

1 W. Otto, 'Deutsche Handlungsspielraum und sowjetischer Einfluss', in E. Scherstjanoi (ed.) *Protocoll des Kolloquiums. Die Gründung der DDR* (Berlin, Akademie Verlag, 1993) p. 144.

2 Schwarz, *Adenauer*, vol. I, p. 459.

3 C. Adenauer, *Memoirs* (Weidenfeld and Nicolson, London, 1966) p. 221.

4 D. Bark and D. Gress, *History of West Germany*, vol. I (Oxford, Blackwell, 1993) p. 270.

5 Schwarz, *Adenauer*, vol. I, p. 526.

6 C. Klessmann, *Die Doppelte Staatsgründung*, p. 177.

7 L. J. Erdinger, *Kurt Schumacher* (Stanford, CA, Stanford University Press, 1965) p. 172.

8 W. Benz, (ed.), *Die Bundesrepublik Deutschland*, vol. 1 (Frankfurt, Fischer, 1983) p. 355.

9 P. Grieder, *Tension, Conflict and Opposition in the Leadership of the Socialist Unity Party (SED), 1946–73*, Ph.D. thesis, University of Cambridge (no. D196726), 1995, p. 97.

10 Schwarz, *Adenauer*, vol. I, p. 159.

11 Schwarz, *Adenauer*, vol. I; R. Steininger, *The German Question, the Stalin Note of 1952* and *the Problem of Reunification* (New York, Columbia University Press, 1990); G. Wettig, 'Stalin and German Reunification', in *Historical Journal*, vol. 37, no. 2, 1994, pp. 411–19.

12 C. Klessmann, *Zwei Nationen, eine Nation. Deutsche Geschichte, 1955–70* (Göttingen, Vandenhoeck and Ruprecht, 1988) p. 76.

13 Ibid., p. 85.

14 Schwarz, *Adenauer*, vol. 2, p. 299.

15 J. Gaddis, *We Know Now, Rethinking Cold War History* (Oxford, Oxford University Press, 1997) p. 140.

16 Klessmann, *Zwei Nationen*, p. 89.

17 Gaddis, *We Know Now*, p. 144.

18 Klessmann, Zwei Nationen, p. 93.

19 T. Garton Ash, *In Europe's Name. Germany and the Divided Continent* (London, Cape, 1993) p. 60.

20 B. Marshall, *Willy Brandt: A Political Biography* (London, Macmillan, 1997) p. 44.

21   Bark and Gress, *History of West Germany*, vol. 2, p. 98.
22   H. Jacobsen et al., *Drei Jahrzente Aussenpolitik der DDR* (Munich, Oldenbourg, 1979) pp. 432–3.
23   Garton Ash, *In Europe's Name*, p. 73.
24   Ibid., p. 79.
25   A. J. Nicholls, *The Bonn Republic* (London, Longman, 1997) p. 232.
26   Garton Ash, *In Europe's Name*, p. 71.
27   Marshall, *Willy Brandt*, p. 70.
28   Bark and Gress, *History of West Germany*, vol. 2, p. 194.
29   Ibid., p. 195.
30   Ibid., p. 215.
31   See Grieder, *Tension, Conflict and Opposition*, pp. 312–3.
32   Bark and Gress, *History of West Germany*, vol 2, p. 178.
33   Garton Ash, *In Europe's Name*, p. 78.
34   Ibid., p. 137.
35   Ibid., p. 204.
36   Ibid., p. 139.
37   Ibid., p. 184.
38   Ibid., p. 87.
39   Ibid., p. 167.
40   J. Gaddis, *The Long Peace: Inquiries into the History of the Cold War* (New York and Oxford, Oxford University Press, 1987).
41   Garton Ash, *In Europe's Name*, p. 130.
42   Nicholls, *Bonn Republic*, p. 199.

Chapter 16

1   H. Kaelble, J. Kocka and H. Zwar (eds), *Sozialgeschichte der DDR* (Stuttgart, Klettcotta, 1994) p. 573.
2   H. P. Schwarz, *Die Ära Adenauer*, vol. 2, *Geschichte der Bundesrepublik Deutschland* (Stuttgart and Wiesbaden, Deutsche Verlags-Anstalt/Brockhaus, 1981, 1983) p. 178.
3   Ibid., p. 120.
4   H. Giesch, K. H. Paque and H. Schmieding, *The Fading Miracle* (Cambridge, Cambridge University Press, 1992) p. 31.
5   Nicholls, *Bonn Republic*, p. 60.
6   R. Overy, 'The Economy of the Federal Republic since 1949', in L. Larres, K. and P. Panayi (eds), *The Federal Republic since 1949* (London, Longman, 1996) p. 34.
7   A. Kramer, *West German Economy*, p. 213.
8   Giesch, Paque and Schmieding, *Fading Miracle*, p. 141.
9   P. Pulzer, *German Politics*, p. 63.
10   Klessmann, *Die doppelte Staatsgründung*, p. 242.
11   Ibid., p. 242.
12   Giesch, Paque and Schmieding, *Fading Miracle*, p. 80.
13   Nicholls, *Bonn Republic*, p. 146.
14   Schwarz, *Die Ära Adenauer*, vol. 2, p. 210.
15   Nicholls, *Bonn Republic*, p. 157.
16   See the brief review article by M. Rosen, 'Reconstruction and Modernization.

The Federal Republic and the Fifties, *Bulletin*, vol. XIX, no. 1, May 1997, pp. 5–16, London, German Historical Institute.

17   E. Kolinsky, *Women in Contemporary Germany* (Oxford and New York, Berg, 1992) p. 31.

18   Ibid., p. 79.

19   Ibid., p. 80.

20   R. Willett, *The Americanization of Germany* (London, Routledge, 1989) p. 132.

21   Rosen, 'Reconstruction and Modernization', p. 11.

22   U. Poiger, 'Rebels without a cause', in R. Pommerin (ed.), *The American Impact on Postwar Germany* (Oxford and Providence, RI, Berghahn, 1995) p. 116.

23   Rosen, 'Reconstruction and Modernization', pp. 15–16.

24   D. Staritz, *Geschichte der DDR* (Frankfurt am Main, Suhrkamp, 1985) p. 52.

25   Grieder, *Tension, Conflict and Opposition*, p. 39.

26   Loth, *Stalin's Unwanted Child*, p. 125.

27   Quoted in R. G. Stokes, 'Autarky, Ideology and Technological Lag: The Case of the East German Chemical Industry, 1945–64', in *Central European History*, vol. 208/1, 1995, p. 36.

28   McCauley, *GDR since 1945*, p. 54.

29   Klessmann, *Die doppelte Staatsgründung*, pp. 273–4

30   Staritz, *Gerschichte der DDR*, p. 77.

31   K. Schroeder, *Der SED – Staat* (Munich, Hauser, 1998) p. 116.

32   A. Mitter and S. Wolle, *Untergang auf Raten* (Munich, Bertelsmann Verlag, 1993) p. 45.

33   V. Ingimundarsan, 'Cold War Misperceptions: The Communist and Western Responses to the East German Refugee Crisis in 1953', in *Journal of Contemporary History*, vol. 29, 1994, p. 472.

34   Loth, *Stalin's Unwanted Child*, p. 155.

35   A. Baring, *Uprising in East Germany* (Ithaca, NY, Cornell University Press, 1972) pp. 73–6 ; Mitter and Wolle, *Untergang auf Raten*; Klessmann, *Die doppelte Staatsgründung*, p. 277.

36   See G. Pritchard, *The Making of the GDR* (Manchester, Manchester University Press, 2000).

37   Mitter and Wolle, *Untergang auf Raten*, p. 162.

38   Ibid., p. 107.

39   Grieder, *Tension, Conflict and Opposition*, p. 136.

40   Mitter and Wolle, *Untergang auf Raten*, p. 256.

41   M. Fulbrook, *Anatomy of a Dictatorship. Inside the GDR, 1949–1989* (Oxford, Oxford University Press, 1995) p. 187.

42   Grieder, *Tension, Conflict and Opposition*, p. 211.

43   Klessmann, *Zwei Nationen*, p. 309.

44   Kopstein, *Economic Decline*, p. 43.

45   Klessmann, *Zwei Nationen*, p. 310.

46   See ibid., and Staritz, *Geschichte der DDR*.

47   Staritz, *Geschichte der DDR*, p. 138.

48   Ibid., p. 77.

49   D. Wierling, 'The Hitler Youth Generation in the GDR: Insecurities, Ambitions and Dilemmas', in K. Jarausch (ed.), *Dictatorship as Experience* (New York and Oxford, Berghahn, 1999) p. 308.

50   C. Klessmann, 'Rethinking the Second German Dictatorship' in ibid., p. 370.

51   Quoted in M. Kohli, 'Arbeit, Lebenslauf und soziale Differenzierung', in
      Kaelble, Kocka and Zwar (eds), *Sozialgeschichte der DDR*, p. 39.
52   Quoted in G. Edwards, *GDR Society and Social Institutions* (London,
      Macmillan, 1985) p. 13.
53   Ina Merkel, 'Leitbilder und Lebensweisen von Frauen', in Kaelble, Kocka and
      Zwar, *Sozialgeschichte der DDR*, p. 376.
54   McCauley, *GDR since 1945*, p. 58.
55   Fulbrook, *Anatomy of Dictatorship*, p. 151
56   Ibid., p. 161.
57   Ibid., p. 164.
58   Ibid., p. 101.
59   T. A. Schwartz, *America's Germany. John J. McCloy and the Federal Republic
      of Germany*, Cambridge MA, Harvard University Press, 1991) p. 305.

Chapter 17

1   See Pulzer, *German Politics*, ch. 4 and Staritz, *Geschichte der DDR*, p. 38.
2   C. Maier, *Dissolution. The Crisis of Communism and the End of East Germany*
     (Princeton, Princeton University Press, 1997) p. 89.
3   Fulbrook, *Two Germanies*, p. 19.
4   Bark and Gress, *History of West Germany*, vol. 2, p. 68.
5   Fulbrook, *Two Germanies*, p. 20.
6   Maier, *Dissolution*, p. 90.
7   L. Kettenacker, *Germany since 1945* (Oxford, Oxford University Press. 1997)
     p. 135.
8   Bark and Gress, *History of West Germany*, vol 2, p. 73.
9   Nicholls, *Bonn Republic*, p. 193.
10   Kettenacker, *Germany*, p. 136.
11   Giesch, Paque and Schmieding, *Fading Miracle*, p. 148.
12   Marshall, *Willy Brandt*, p. 66.
13   Ibid., p. 79.
14   Ibid., p. 81.
15   Nicholls, *Bonn Republic*, p. 238.
16   Marshall, *Willy Brandt*, p. 82.
17   Pulzer, *German Politics*, p. 141.
18   Kettenacker, *Germany*, p. 147.
19   Nicholls, *Bonn Republic*, p. 185.
20   Kettenacker, *Germany*, p. 148.
21   Panayi, *Ethnic Minorities*, p. 219.
22   Ibid., p. 224.
23   Nicholls, *Bonn Republic*, p. 254.
24   Ibid., p. 273.
25   K. Larres and P. Panayi (eds), *The Federal Republic of Germany since 1949*,
     p. 123.
26   Quoted in Bark and Gress, *History of West Germany*, vol. 2, p. 424.
27   These are discussed in ibid., pp. 432–7; See also R. Evans, *In Hitler's Shadow*
     (London, Tauris, 1989) for a more detailed coverage.
28   M. Siekmeier and K. Larres, 'Domestic Political Developments II: 1969–90',
     in Larres and Panayi, *The Federal Republic*, p. 132.
29   Ibid., p. 135.

30 J. Roesler, 'The Rise and Fall of the Planned Economy in the German
    Democratic Republic, 1945–89, in *German History*, vol. 9, no. 1, 1991, p. 55.

31 Grieder, *Tension, Conflict and Opposition*, p. 266.

32 Quoted in Klessmann, *Zwei Nationen*, p. 337.

33 Fulbrook, *Anatomy of a Dictatorship*, p. 195.

34 Maier, *Dissolution*, pp. 88–9.

35 H. James, 'The Landscape that did not Blossom, in *Times Literary
    Supplement*, 13 June 1997, p. 5.

36 Quoted in Maier, *Dissolution*, p. 60.

37 Ibid., p. 81.

38 See ibid., pp. 59–107.

39 Ibid., p. 29.

40 Fulbrook, *Anatomy of a Dictatorship*, p. 155.

41 Ibid., p. 141.

42 McCauley, *GDR since 1945*, p. 185.

43 Maier, *Dissolution*, p. 173.

44 Fulbrook, *Anatomy of a Dictatorship*, p. 206.

45 Ibid., p. 235.

46 Fulbrook, *Two Germanies*, p. 73

47 Staritz, *Geschichte der DDR*, p. 195.

48 Maier, *Dissolution*, p. 89.

49 K. C. Lammers, 'The German Democratic Republic as History, in
    Contemporary European History, vol. 6, no. 3, 1997, p 425.

50 A. Mitter and S. Wolle, *Untergang auf Raten*, ch. 16.

51 Fulbrook, *Anatomy of a Dictatorship*, p. 172.

52 Ibid., p. 172.

Chapter 18

1   Garton Ash, *Europe's Name*, p. 343.

2   Fulbrook, *Anatomy of a Dictatorship*, p. 248.

3   Maier, *Dissolution*, p. 139.

4   Ibid., p. 158.

5   Ibid., p. 177.

6   K. Jarausch, *The Rush to German Unity* (Oxford, Oxford University Press,
    1994) p. 117.

7   Garton Ash, *Europe's Name*, p. 346.

8   J. Osmond et al., *German Reunification: A Reference Guide and Commentary*
    (London, Longman, 1992) p. 53.

9   Garton Ash, *Europe's Name*, p. 349.

10 Ibid., p. 354.

11 Maier, *Dissolution*, p. 241.

12 Jarausch, *The Rush to German Unity*, p. 169.

13 W. Patterson and D. Southern, *Governing Germany* (Oxford, Blackwell,
    1991) p. 11.

14 R. Steininger, 'The German Question, 1945–95', in K. Larres (ed.), *Germany
    since Unification* (Basingstoke and London, Palgrave, 2001) p. 27.

15 Ibid., p. 29.

16 C. Flockton, 'The German Economy in the 1990s: On the Road to a Divided
    Polity', in Larres, *Germany since Unification*, p. 76.

17   Ibid., p. 70.
18   Quoted in *Die Zeit*, 26 Sept. 2002, p. 6.
19   W. Chandler, The German Party System since Unification', in Larres, *Germany since Unification*, p. 94.
20   Ibid., p. 95.
21   Chandler and Larres in ibid., p. xxxviii.
22   A. Hyde-Price, 'Germany's Security Policy Dilemmas: NATO, the WEU and the OSCE', in ibid., p. 212.
23   Ibid., p. liii.
24   Ibid., p. lii.

Chapter 19

1   D. Peukert, *Inside Nazi Germany*, p. 42.
2   Broszat, 'A Plea for the Historicisation of National Socialism'
3   See ch. 16, note 23.

Note

In writing Chapters 10, 11 and 12, the author has drawn on information in his book, *The Third Reich* (Harlow, Pearson/Longman, 2002 (3rd edn)). Similarly for Chapters 14, 15 and 16 he has drawn on another of his books, *Germany from Defeat to Partition, 1945–1963* (London, Pearson/Longman, 2001).

Bibliography

This bibliography is an introductory selection of books in English on German history, 1815 to the present.

General histories covering the whole or the greater part of the period

W. Carr, *A History of Germany*, 1815–90, London, Arnold, 4th edn, 1991, is well-written and, within its limits, a comprehensive study of virtually the whole period. M. Fulbrook (ed.), *German History since 1800*, London, Arnold, 1997, contains a series of interesting and stimulating essays by leading historians on various aspects of German history. Many of these essays are repeated in J. Breuilly (ed.), *19th Century Germany. Politics, Culture and Society, 1780–1918*, London, Arnold, 2001. There are several older surveys which are still worth reading, but they only go up as far as 1945 or the early post-war years: G. Mann, *The History of Germany since 1789*, London, Chatto and Windus, 1968; H. Holborn, *A History of Modern Germany, 1648-1945*, 3 vols, London, Eyre and Spottiswoode, 1969, and K. Pinson, *Modern Germany. Its History and Civilization*, New York, Macmillan, 1966. A. J. P. Taylor, *The Course of German History*, London, Hamish Hamilton, 1945, is a provocative book worth reading if only because of its breathtaking generalizations and bias! For the 'long' nineteenth century, D. Blackbourn, *Germany 1780–1918*, London, Fontana, 1997, is a concise survey which is very useful for both social and economic as well as political history, as is V. R. Berghahn, *Modern Germany, Society, Economy and Politics in the Twentieth Century*, Cambridge, Cambridge University Press, 1982. G. Craig, *Germany. 1866–1945*, Oxford, Oxford University Press, 1978, is a highly readable study of the German Reich from its formation to its collapse. International developments are covered by A. J. P. Taylor, *The Struggle for Mastery in Europe, 1848-1918*, Oxford, Oxford University Press, 1954, J. Lowe, *The Great Powers and the German Problem, 1865–1925*, London, Routledge, 1994, N. Rich, *Great Power Diplomacy, 1814–1914*, Columbus, OH, McGraw-Hill, 1992. K. Hildebrand, *German Foreign Policy from Bismarck to Adenauer*, London, Unwin Hyman, 1989, offers a broad sweep of foreign policy. J. J. Sheehan, 'What is German History. Reflections on the Role of the *Nation* in German History and Historiography', in *Journal of Modern History*, vol. 53, March 1981, is a brief but seminal article on the whole question of the German nation and German nationalism.

Thematic works covering more than one period

The development of Prussia is covered by H. W. Koch, *A History of Prussia*, London, Longman, 1978, and by P. G. Dwyer (ed.), *A Modern Prussian History, 1830–1947*, Harlow, Pearson, 2001. G. Craig, *The Politics of the Prussian Army, 1640–1945*, Oxford, 1955, is still well worth reading, as is G. Ritter's classic study, *The Sword and the Sceptre*, Miami, FL, University of Miami Press, 1969. The constitutional background is well covered by H. W. Koch, *A Constitutional History of Germany*, London, Longman, 1984. J. Sheehan, *German Liberalism in the Nineteenth Century*, London, Methuen, 1982, is an invaluable guide to the development of German liberalism up to 1914, as is E. L. Evans, *German Centre Party 1870–1933; A Study in Political Catholicism*, Carbondale, IL, Southern Illinois University Press, 1981, for the Centre party. A. Milward and S. B. Saul, *The Development of the Economies of Continental Europe, 1850–1914*, London, Allen and Unwin, 1977, and C. Trebilcock, *The Industrialization of the Continental Powers, 1870–1914*, London, Longman, 1981, put the growth of the German economy within the European context, while M. Kitchen, *The Political Economy of Germany, 1815–1914*, London, Croom Helm, 1978, is a useful guide to developments in both agriculture and industry in the 19th century. Ute Frevert, *Women in German History*, Oxford, Berg, 1989, is an indispensable study for the history of women in Germany during this period. A good guide to the whole question of ethnic minorities in Germany is Panikos Panayi, *Ethnic Minorities in Nineteenth and Twentieth Century Germany*, Harlow, Pearson, 2000, while a comprehensive study of German nationalism is M. Hughes, *Nationalism and Society, Germany 1800–1945*, London, Arnold, 1988.

1815–71

The two most detailed general studies are T. Nipperdey, *Germany from Napoleon to Bismarck*, Princeton, Princeton University Press, 1996, and J. Sheehan, *German History, 1770–1866*, Oxford, Oxford University Press, 1989, both of which are particularly strong on economic, social and cultural history. H. Schulze, *The Course of German Nationalism. From Frederick the Great to Bismarck 1763–1867* (trans. by S. Hanbury-Tenison), Cambridge, Cambridge University Press, 1991, is a useful collection of primary sources covering this period.

The restoration period, 1815–48

The relations between the German states and the German Confederation are explored in D. Billinger, *Metternich and the German Question*, Newark, DE, University of Delaware Press, 1991. Brendan Simms, *The*

Struggle for Mastery in Germany, 1779–1850, London and Basingstoke, Macmillan, 1998, provides an excellent and concise account of the growing Prussian–Austrian rivalry after 1815. G. S. Werner, *Bavaria and the German Confederation, 1820–1848*, London, Associated University Press, 1977, is a specialized but readable analysis of the fiercely separatist German policies of Bavaria. W. Henderson, *The Zollverein*, Cambridge, Cambridge University Press, 1939, is still the classic work on the *Zollverein* in English. H. J. Voth, 'The Prussian Zollverein and the bid for Economic Superiority', in P. G. Dwyer (ed.), *Modern Prussian History, 1830–1947*, London, Pearson, 2001, pp. 109–25, is a brief but more up-to-date study. L. Lee, 'Liberal Constitutionalism as Administrative Reform: The Baden Constitution of 1818', in *Central European History*, vol. 8, 1, 1975, highlights developments in one of the more liberal south German states.

1848

J. Sperber, *The European Revolutions 1848–1851*, Cambridge, Cambridge University Press, 1994, places the German revolts in their European context, while W. Siemann, *The German Revolution of 1848–49*, Basingstoke and London, Macmillan, 1998, is arguably the best single-volume study of the revolutions in print. H Kahn, *The 1848 Revolutions in German-Speaking Europe*, Harlow, Pearson, 2001, is also a clear and concise study of these complex events. E. Eyck, *The Frankfurt Parliament, 1848–49*, London, Macmillan, 1968, provides very detailed treatment of the Frankfurt parliament. J. Davis Randers-Pehrsen, *Germans and the Revolution of 1848–49*, New York and Washington, Peter Lang, 1999, is also interesting and well worth reading.

The unification of Germany, 1851–70

The political and economic background to unity is well covered in E. Anderson, *The Social and Political Conflict in Prussia, 1858–1864*, Lincoln, University of Nebraska Press, 1954, and T. Hamerow, *The Social Foundations of German Unification*, 2 vols, Princeton, Princeton University Press, 1969–72. The diplomacy of unification is analysed by W. Carr, *The Origins of the Wars of German Unification*, London, Longman, 1991, and W. E. Mosse, *The European Powers and the German Question, 1848–71*, Cambridge, Cambridge University Press, 1958. A. Bucholz, *Moltke and the German Wars, 1864–71*, Basingstoke and London, Palgrave, 2001, is an illuminating study of Moltke's military genius and his conduct of the wars of unification. The Franco-Prussian war is covered by M. Howard, *The Franco-Prussian War*, London, Rupert Hart Davis, 1966[2], and S. W. Halperin, 'The Origins of the Franco-Prussian War Revisited: Bismarck and the Hohenzollern Candidature for the Spanish Throne', *Journal of Modern History*, vol. 45, I, 1973. There are an enormous number of books devoted to the towering figure of Bismarck. The standard biographies in English are O. Pflanze, *Bismarck and the Development of Germany*, 3 vols, Princeton, Princeton University Press, 1990, and L. Gall, *Bismarck, and the German Empire*, 2 vols, London, Allen and Unwin, 1986. A. J. P. Taylor's *Bismarck. The Man and the Statesman*, London, Harnish Hamilton, 1955, has dated but remains a provocative and interesting work. C. Grant Robertson, *Bismarck*, London, Constable, 1918, is still worth reading.

A brief guide through the complexities of the unification and the consolidation of the new Reich is D. G. Williamson, *Bismarck and Germany, 1862–1890*, Harlow, Longman, 1998 (2nd edn). H. Böhme, *Deutschlands Weg zur Grossmacht*, Cologne, Kiepenhauer und Witsch, 1966, is invaluable for the economic dimension to German unity, but for English language readers a very useful selection of the material which Böhme used for this book has been edited and translated: H. Böhme (ed.) (trans. by A. Ramm), *The Foundation of the German Empire*, Oxford, Oxford University Press, 1971. F. Stern, *Gold and Iron, Bleichröder and the Building of the German Empire*, London, Allen and Unwin, 1977, sheds light on the links between politics and high finance during the Bismarck period.

The German Empire, 1871–1918

Concise and very informative is M. Seligmann and R. McLean, *Germany from Reich to Republic, 1871–1918*, Macmillan, Basingstoke and London, 2000. H.-U. Wehler, *The German Empire, 1871*, Leamington Spa and Dover, NH, 1985, is the classic structural study of the empire, while W. J. Mommsen, *Imperial Germany, 1867–1918. Politics, Culture and Society in an Authoritarian State*, London, Arnold, 1995, contains a series of perceptive essays about how the Reich 'modernized' without becoming a constitutional liberal state. V. R. Berghahn, *Imperial Germany, 1871–1914*, Providence, RI and Oxford, Berghahn Press, 1994, is particularly strong on economic and social history; David Blackbourn and G. Eley, *The Peculiarities of German History*, Oxford and New York, Oxford University Press, 1984, is a brilliant attempt to refute the *Sonderweg* theory, as is G. Eley, 'Bismarckian Germany', in G. Martel (ed.), *Modern Germany Reconsidered, 1870–1945*, London, Routledge, 1992. M. Anderson, *Practicing Democracy. Elections and Political Culture in Imperial Germany*, Princeton, Princeton University Press, 2000, and J. Sperber, *The Kaiser's Voters. Electors and Elections in Imperial Germany*, Cambridge, Cambridge University Press, 1997, explore the functioning of universal franchise in the pre-war Reich. G. Schollgen (ed.) *Escape into War? The Foreign Policy of Imperial Germany*, Oxford, Berg, 1990, contains a series of interesting essays on aspects of German foreign policy, 1871–1914, and I. Geiss, *German Foreign Policy, 1871–1914*, London, Routledge, 1976, is a useful survey.

The Bismarckian Reich, 1871–90

For an in-depth political study, O. Pflanze, *Bismarck and the Development of Germany*, vols 2 and 3, Princeton, Princeton University Press, 1990, are invaluable. M. L. Anderson, *Windthorst*, Oxford, Oxford University Press, 1981, is a helpful biography of the leader of the Centre party. V. L. Lidtke, *The Outlawed Party – Social Democracy in Germany, 1878–1890*, Princeton, Princeton University Press, 1966, covers Bismarck's anti-socialist campaign, I. N. Lambi, *Free Trade and Protection in Germany, 1868–1879*, Wiesbaden, Steiner, 1963, is a useful account of the tariff debates in the 1870s, while H. Rosenberg, 'Political and Social Consequences of the Great Depression of 1873–1896 in Central Europe', in *Economic History Review*, vol. 13, 1943, is inevitably dated, but is still a stimulating article. Bismarck is the hero in the classic W. L. Langer, *European Alliances, 1871–1890*, revised edn, New York, A. Knopf, 1951. G. F. Kennan, *The Decline of Bismarck's European Order*, Princeton, Princeton University Press, 1979, and B. Waller, *Bismarck at the Crossroads, the Restoration of German Foreign Policy after the Congress of Berlin*, London, Athlone Press, 1974, explore the complex last decade of Bismarck's diplomacy. M. E. Townsend, *The Rise and Fall of Germany's Colonial Empire*, New York, Macmillan, 1930, is still useful, but of course very dated. P. Kennedy, 'German Colonial Expansion: Has the Manipulated Social Imperialism Been Antedated?', in *Past and Present*, vol. 54, 1972, is still a key introduction to Bismarck's colonial policy. H.-U. Wehler, 'Bismarck's Imperialism, 1862–1890', in *Past and Present*, vol. 48, 1970, is a brilliant case for the social imperialism argument, while A. J. P. Taylor, *Germany's First Bid for Colonies*, London, Macmillan, 1938, argues that Bismarck was pursuing only diplomatic objectives. W. M. Simons (ed.), *Germany in the Age of Bismarck*, London, Allen and Unwin, 1968, T. B. S. Hamerow (ed.), *The Age of Bismarck. Documents and Interpretations*, New York, Harper Row, 1973, and W. N. Medlicott and D. K. Coveney (eds), *Bismarck and Europe*, London, Arnold, 1971, all provide relevant collections of the documents, the latter book concentrating solely on Bismarck's foreign policy. D. G. Williamson, *Bismarck and Germany*, Harlow, Longman, 1998, also contains a selection of documents.

Germany, 1890–1914

For the establishment of Wilhelm II's 'personal rule', J. Röhl, *Germany Without Bismarck. The Crisis of Government in the Second Reich, 1890–1900*, London, Batsford, 1967; J. Röhl, *The Kaiser and his Court*, Cambridge, Cambridge University Press, 1994, J. Röhl and N. Sombart (eds), *Kaiser Wilhelm II, New Interpretations*, Cambridge, Cambridge University Press, 1982, and K. L. Lerman, *The Chancellor as Courtier*, Cambridge, Cambridge University Press, 1990 are key studies. J. Retallack,

Germany in the Age of Kaiser Wilhelm II, Macmillan, Basingstoke and London, 1996, and I. Porter and I. Armour, *Imperial Germany, 1890–1918*, Harlow, Longman, 1991, are a good general account of the period (the latter also includes an interesting selection of documents), while K. Jarausch, *The Enigmatic Chancellor, Bethmann Hollweg and the Hubris of Imperial Germany*, New Haven, CT, 1973, is still the best study of Bethmann's chancellorship, 1909–14. Germany's uneasy relationship with Britain can be followed in M. Kennedy, *The Rise of Anglo-German Antagonism*, London, Allen and Unwin, 1980. A detailed but readable analysis of Germany's road to war can be found in V. R. Berghahn, *Germany and the Approach of War in 1914*, Basingstoke and London, Macmillan, 1973, and F. Fischer, *War of Illlusions: German Policies from 1911 to 1914*, London, Chatto and Windus, 1973. D. Kaiser, 'Germany and the Origins of the First World War', in *Journal of Modern History*, vol. 55, 1983, contrasts the policies of Bülow and Bethmann Hollweg. An important essay also is W. Mommsen, 'The Topos of Inevitable War in Germany in the Decade before 1914', in V. R. Berghahn and M. Kitchen (eds), *Germany in the Age of Total War*, London, 1981. H. H. Herwig (ed.), *The Outbreak of World War I*, Boston and New York, Houghton Mifflin, 1997, provides a good introduction to the debate on the causes of the war. A selection of primary sources can be found in J. C. G. Röhl (ed.), *From Bismarck to Hitler: The Problem of Continuity in German History*, London, Longman, 1970, and I. Geiss, *July 1914: The Outbreak of the First World War. Selected Documents*, New York, Norton, 1968.

1914–18

By far the best overall study is R. Chickering, *Imperial Germany and the Great War, 1914–1918*, Cambridge, Cambridge Univesity Press, 1998. Fritz Fischer's classic, *Germany's Aims in the First World War*, London, Chatto and Windus, 1967, is essential reading. The Hindenburg–Ludendorff semi-dictatorship is covered by M. Kitchen, *The Silent Dictatorship: The Politics of the German High Command, 1916–1918*, London, Batsford, 1976. G. Feldmann, *Army, Industry and Labour*, Princeton, Princeton University Press, 1966, is an important study of the German war economy, while the upheavals of 1918–19 are covered by F. L. Carsten, *Revolution in Central Europe*, London, Wildwood House, 1972, and A. G. Ryder, *The German Revolution of 1918: A Study of German Socialism in War and Revolt*, Cambridge, Cambridge University Press, 1967.

Germany, 1919–45

J. Hiden, *Republican and Fascist Germany*, Harlow, Longman, 1996, approaches the whole period from historiographic and thematic angles.

It also has an excellent bibliography. The four-volume document collection by J. Noakes and G. Pridham, *Nazism, 1919–1945*, vol. I, *The Rise to Power*, vol. II, *State, Economy and Society, 1933–39*, vol. III, *Foreign Policy, War and Racial Extermination*, vol. IV, *Germany at War: The Home Front, 1939–45*, Exeter, Exeter University Press, 1983–98, is an essential companion to students studying this period.

The Weimar Republic

A. Rosenberg, *History of the German Republic*, London, Methuen, 1936, is still well worth reading. A study written from a liberal angle is E. Eyck, *The Weimar Republic*, 2 vols, Cambridge, MA, Harvard University Press, 1962–64. More concise studies are J. Hiden, *The Weimar Republic*, Harlow, Longman, 1974; E. J. Feuchtwanger, *From Weimar to Hitler, 1918–33*, Basingstoke and London, Macmillan, 1993, and A. J. Nicholls, *Weimar and the Rise of Hitler*, Basingstoke and London, Macmillan, 1968. The best by a long way of the short, overall studies is E. Kolb, *The Weimar Republic*, London, Unwin Hyman, 1988, as it has an invaluable section on 'Basic Problems and Trends of Research'. D. Peukert, *The Weimar Republic: The Crisis of Classical Modernity*, London, Allen Lane, 1991, is excellent on the social, economic and cultural background to the years 1919–33. An interesting but brief revisionist article on the problem of reparations is Sally Marks, 'Reparations Re-Considered: A Reminder', in *Central European History* V, no. 4 (Dec. 1969). M. Trachtenberg, *Reparation in World Politics: France and European Economic Diplomacy, 1916–1923*, New York, Columbia University Press, 1980, and B. Kent, *The Spoils of War. The Politics, Economics and Diplomacy of Reparations, 1918–32*, Oxford, Oxford University Press, 1989, are more weighty analyses. C. S. Maier, *Recasting Bourgeois Europe: Stabilization in France, Germany and Italy in the Decade after World War I*, Princeton, Princeton University Press, 1975, contains an interesting study of the German reparation and economic crisis, 1919–23 and the partial stabilization after 1924. A. McDougall, *France's Rhineland Diplomacy, 1914–24*, Princeton, Princeton University Press, 1978 and D. G. Williamson, *The British in Germany, 1918–30*, New York and Oxford, Berg, 1992, provide useful background for Anglo-French policies on Germany. The impact of hyperinflation is covered by E. E. Rowley, *Hyperinflation in Germany: Perceptions of a Process*, Aldershot, Scolar Press, 1994. T. Childers, 'Inflation, Stabilization and Political Realignment in Germany, 1924 to 1928', in G. D. Feldman (ed.), *The German Inflation Reconsidered: A Preliminary Balance*, Berlin, de Gruyter, 1982, analyses its political consequences, while K. Borchardt, *Perspectives on Modern German Economic History and Policy*, Cambridge, Cambridge University Press, 1991, contains two important chapters on the Great Depression and the collapse of Weimar. R. Boyce, 'World War, World Depression: Some Economic Origins of the Second World War', in R. Boyce and E.

Robertson (eds), *Paths to War*, London, Macmillan, 1989, provides a concise global overview of the Depression and its consequences. J. Hiden, *Germany and Europe, 1919–1939*, London, Longman, 1977, and W. Michalka, *German Foreign Policy, 1917–1933*, Leamington Spa, Berg, 1987, are concise surveys of foreign policy. J. Wright, *Gustav Stresemann*, Oxford, Oxford University Press, 2002, is an important new biography of Stresemann, as is W. Patch, *Heinrich Brüning and the Dissolution of the Weimar Republic*, Cambridge, Cambridge University Press, 1998, of Brüning. D. Abraham, *The Collapse of the Weimar Republic. Political Economy and Crisis*, Princeton, Princeton University Press, 1981, and M. Broszat, *Hitler and the Collapse of Weimar Democracy*, Leamington Spa, Berg, 1987, cover the collapse of Weimar, while shorter studies can be found in K. Bracher, 'Geman Democracy and Power Vacuum: The Problem of the Party State', in V. B. Berghahn and M. Kitchen (eds), *Germany in the Age of Total War*, London, Croom Helm, 1981, H. Mommsen, *From Weimar to Auschwitz. Essays in German History*, London, Polity Press, 1991, and R. Lepsius, 'From Fragmented Party Democracy to Government by Emergency Decree and National Socialist Takeover: Germany', in J. Linz and A. Stepan (eds), *The Breakdown of Democratic Regimes*, Baltimore, MD and London, Johns Hopkins University Press, 1978.

Hitler, Nazism and the Third Reich

There is an enormous bibliography on every aspect of the Third Reich. I. Kershaw, *The Nazi Dictatorship, Problems and Perspectives*, London, Arnold, 1993, and K. Hildebrand, *The Third Reich*, London, Routledge, 1984, provide good guides to the complex historiographical problems involved in studying the Third Reich. M. Broszat, 'A Plea for the Historisation of National Socialism', in P. Baldwin (ed.), *Reworking the Past*, Boston, MA, Beacon Press, 1980, explores the problems of placing National Socialism's legacy and its place in the context of German history. Good, overall studies of the Third Reich are K. Bracher, *The German Dictatorship: The Origins, Structure and Consequences of National Socialism*, Penguin, Harmondsworth, 1973; N. Frei, *National Socialist Rule in Germany: The Fürhrer State, 1933–45*, Oxford, Blackwell, 1993, and M. Burleigh, *The Third Reich. A New History*, London, Macmillan, 2001. A briefer introductory study is D. G. Williamson, *The Third Reich* (3rd edn), Harlow, Pearson, 2002. There are a large number of Hitler biographies. A. Bullock, *Hitler. A Study in Tyranny*, Harmondsworth, Penguin, 1962, remains an important classic, but the best and most detailed biography is I. Kershaw, *Hitler* (vol. 1), *1889–1936: Hubris* (vol. 2), *1936–1945: Nemesis*, London, Allen Lane, 1998–2000. A short but perceptive biography is N. Stone, *Hitler*, London, Hodder, 1980. For the administration of the Third Reich, M. Broszat, *The Hitler State. The Foundation and Development of the Internal Structure of the Third Reich*,

London, Longman, 1981, is an indispensable study. H. Mommsen, 'National Socialism: Continuity and Change' in W. Laqueur (ed.), *Fascism: A Reader's Guide*, Harmondsworth, Penguin, 1979, is an interesting short essay on the Nazi regime. D. Orlow, *The History of the Nazi Party* (2 vols), *1919–1945*, Newton Abbot, David & Charles, 1971–73 is a thorough study of the role of the party (including the SS) throughout the Third Reich. The development of the SS state is analysed in H. Buchheim, M. Broszat and H.-A. Jacobsen, *Anatomy of the SS State*, London, Collins, 1968, and R. L. Koehl, *The Black Corps: The Structure and Power Struggles of the Nazi SS*, Madison, WI, University of Wisconsin Press, 1983, while R. Gellateley, *The Gestapo and German Society*, Oxford, Oxford University Press, 1987, is a study of how the Gestapo functioned and of the support it enjoyed from the German public. An informative book on Hitler's role in the Nazi state is E. N. Peterson, *The Limits of Hitler's Power*, Princeton, NJ, Princeton University Press, 1969. For a study of Hitler as an integrative factor in the Third Reich, see I. Kershaw, *The Hitler Myth, Image and Reality in the Third Reich*, Oxford, Oxford University Press, 1987.

The most recent study of the economy is R. J. Overy, *War and Economy in the Third Reich*, Oxford, Oxford University Press, 1995, but B. H. Klein, *Germany's Economic Preparations for War*, Cambridge, MA, Harvard University Press, 1959, and A. S. Milward, *The German Economy at War*, London, Athlone Press, 1965, are still worth reading. The best analysis of Nazi agricultural policy is J. Farquharson, *The Plough and the Swastika. The NSDAP and Agriculture in Germany, 1928–1945*, London, Sage, 1976. The impact of the war on rural society is explored in J. S. Stephenson, 'Nazism, Modern War and Rural Society in Württemberg, 1939–45' in *Journal of Contemporary History*, vol. 32, no. 3, 1997. U. Herbert's *Hitler's Foreign Workers*, Cambridge, Cambridge University Press, 1997, is an interesting study of the role of foreign workers in the wartime economy and how they were treated by the Germans. There are a large number of books on German society during the Third Reich. P. Ayçoberry, *The Social History of the Third Reich*, New York, The New Press, 1999, and R. A. Grünberger, *Social History of the Third Reich*, Harmondsworth, Penguin, 1974, provide comprehensive overviews, while D. Schoenbaum's perceptive *Hitler's Social Revolution*, London, Weidenfeld & Nicolson, 1967, only goes up to 1939. J. S. Stephenson, *Women in German Society*, London, Croom Helm, 1975, and C. Koonz, *Mothers in the Fatherland. Women, the Family and Nazi Politics*, London, Jonathan Cape, 1987, are histories of the role of women in the Third Reich. D. A. Peukert's *Inside Nazi Germany: Conformity, Opposition and Racism in Everyday Life*, Harmondsworth, Penguin, 1989, has some interesting chapters on youth and the workers. M. Roseman, 'Socialism and Modemisation', in R. Bessel (ed.), *Fascist Italy and Nazi Germany. Comparisons and Contrasts*, Cambridge, Cambridge University Press, 1997, deals with the problem of how 'modern' National Socialism was. German Society during the war is covered by M. Kitchen, *Nazi Germany at War*, Longman, Harlow, 1995, and T. Charman, *The German Home Front 1939–1945*, London, Barrie and Jenkins, 1989.

There is again a huge literature on Nazi anti-Semitism and the Holocaust. D. Bankier, 'Hitler and the Policy-making Process on the Jewish Question', in *Holocaust and Genocide Studies*, vol. III, no. I, 1988, and M. R. Marrus, 'The History of the Holocaust: A Survey of Recent Literature', *Journal of Modern History* vol. 59, no. 1, 1987, are helpful introductions to the intentionalist/structuralist debate. M. Burleigh and W. Wippermann, *The Racial State: Germany 1933–45*, Cambridge, Cambridge University Press, 1991, is the best overall account of Hitler's racial and eugenic policies. K. A. Schleunes, *The Twisted Road to Auschwitz. Nazi Policy towards German Jews*, London, Deutsch, 1972, and H. Graml, *Anti-Semitism and its Origins in the Third Reich*, Oxford, Blackwell, 1992, analyse the complex events that led to the Holocaust. L. S. Dawidowicz, *The War against the Jews, 1933–45*, Harmondsworth, Penguin (10th anniversary edn), 1986, trenchantly states the intentionalist case, while M. Broszat, 'Hitler and the Genesis of the Final Solution', in H. W. Koch (ed.), *Aspects of the Third Reich*, London and Basingstoke, Macmillan, 1985, H. Mommsen, 'The Realization of the Unthinkable: The "Final Solution" of the Jewish Question in the Third Reich' and L. Kettenacker, 'Hitler's Final Solution and its Rationalization', both in G. Hirschfield (ed.), *The Policies of Genocide*, London, Allen and Unwin, 1986, argue the structuralist point of view. D. J. Goldhagen, *Hitler's Willing Executioners. Ordinary Germans and the Holocaust*, New York, Abacus, 1997, considers the attitudes of the German people towards the persecution of the Jews.

The best study of German foreign policy in English up to 1939 is G. L. Weinberg, *The Foreign Policy of Hitler's Germany*, vol. 1, *Diplomatic Revolution in Europe, 1933–36*, vol. 2, *Starting World War II 1937–39*, Chicago, University of Chicago Press, 1970–80. W. M. Carr, *Arms, Autarky and Aggression*, London, Edward Arnold, 2nd edn, 1979, is a much shorter account of the years 1933–39, while K. Hildebrand, *The Foreign Policy of the Third Reich*, London, Batsford, 1973, is a brief study of Nazi foreign policy up to 1945 from an intentionalist point of view. A. J. P. Taylor, *The Origins of the Second World War*, London, Hamish Hamilton, 1961, is still worth reading, as are A. Bullock, 'Hitler and the Origins of the Second World War' and T. Mason, 'Some Origins of the Second World War', in E. M. Robertson (ed.), *The Origins of the Second World War*, London, Macmillan, 1971. For Hitler's decision to attack Russia, see G. L. Weinberg, *Germany and the Soviet Union, 1939–41*, Leiden, Brill, 1954, R. Cecil, *Hitler's Decision to Invade Russia*, London, Davis-Poynter, 1975, and E. M. Robertson, 'Hitler Turns from the West to Russia, May–December, 1940', in R. Boyce and E. Robertson (eds), *Paths to War*, London, Macmillan, 1989. G. Wright, *The Ordeal of Total War, 1939–45*, New York, Harper & Row, 1968, and N. Rich, *The Establishment of the New Order*, vol. 2, London, Deutsch, 1973–74, cover German policy in occupied Europe.

Overviews of the German resistance are provided by H. Rothfels, *The German Opposition to Hitler*, London, Oswald Wolff, 1973; T. Prittie, *Germans against Hitler*, London, Hutchinson, 1964; P. Hoffmann, *The History of the German Resistance in Germany*, Montreal, MacDonald and James, 3rd edn, 1996; and H. Graml et al., *The German Resistance to Hitler*, Cambridge, MA, Harvard University Press, revised edn, 1970. J. Conway, *The Nazi Persecution of the Churches, 1933–45*, London, Weidenfeld and Nicolson, 1967, concentrates on relations between the Nazi regime and the Church, while D. C. Clay (ed.), *Contending with Hitler. Varieties of German Resistance in the Third Reich*, Cambridge, MA, Harvard University Press, 1991, is a more comprehensive study, and I. Kershaw in *Popular Opinion and Popular Dissent in the Third Reich: Bavaria, 1933–45*, Oxford, Oxford University Press, 1983, explores the question of *Resistenz*. An introductory article on the legacy of the third Reich is H. James, 'The Preview of the Federal Republic', *Journal of Modern History*, vol. 63, March 1991, pp. 99–115, while H. Winkler, *The Long Shadow of the Reich Weighing upon German History* (the 2001 annual lecture), the German Historical Insititute, London, 2002, discusses this over a longer period of time Hitler's legacy.

Germany, 1945–2000

General histories covering both Germanies

Two informative and concise general histories on post-war Germany, which cover both the FRG and the GDR, are L. Kettenacker, *Germany since 1945*, Oxford, Oxford University Press, 1997, and P. Pulzer, *German Politics 1945–1995*, Oxford, Oxford University Press, 1995. D. G. Williamson, *Germany from Defeat to Partition, 1945–63*, Harlow, Pearson, 2001, covers the formative years of both states and also contains a selection of sources. P. Merkl, *The Origins of the West German Republic*, Oxford, Oxford University Press, 1963, is particularly good on the genesis of the FRG's contribution. How the two states deal with their Nazi past is considered in G. Herf, *Divided Memory: The Nazi Past in the Two Germanys*, Cambridge, MA, Harvard University Press, 1997. M. Fulbrook, *The Two Germanies, 1945–1990: Problems of Interpretation*, London and Basingstoke, Macmillan, 1992, is a brilliant but brief survey of the two German states.

The occupation and division of Germany

There are several books on the zonal policies of the occupying powers: J. Gimbel, *The American Occupation of Germany, 1945–49*, Stanford, CA, Stanford University Press, 1968; B. Kuklick, *American Policy and the Division of Germany*, Ithaca, NY, Cornell University Press, 1977, F. Willis, *The French in Germany, 1945–49*, Stanford, CA, Stanford University

Press, 1962, N. M. Naimark, *The Russians in Germany: A History of the Soviet Zone of Occupation, 1945–49*, Cambridge, MA, Harvard University Press, 1995. British policy is covered by I. D. Turner (ed.), *Reconstruction in Post-war Germany*, Oxford and New York, Berg, 1989, and more briefly in the biography of the British military governor by D. G. Williamson, *A Most Diplomatic Diplomatic General. the Life of General Lord Robertson of Oakridge*, London, Brasseys 1996. For the division of Germany, see W. Loth, *Stalin's Unwanted Child. the Soviet Union, the Germany Question and the Founding of the GDR*, London and Basingstoke, Macmillan, 1998; T. A. Schwartz, *America's Germany. John McCloy and the Federal Republic of Germany*, Cambridge, MA, Harvard University Press, 1991, and J. Farquharson, '"The Essential Division". Britain and the Partition of Germany 1945–1949' *German History*, vol 9, no. 1, 1991 pp. 23–45. J. Gaddis, *We Know Now, Rethinking Cold War History*, Oxford, Oxford University Press, 1997, puts the division of Germany in the overall context of the Cold War. The debate about the Stalin note of March 1952 is covered in R. Steininger, *The German Question, the Stalin Note of 1952 and the Problem of Reunification*, New York, Columbia University Press, 1990, and G. Wettig, 'Stalin and German reunification' *Historical Journal*, vol. 37, no. 2 pp. 411–19, 1994. O. von Ruhm (ed.), *Documents on Germany under Occupation, 1944–55*, Oxford, Oxford University Press, 1955, is a useful collection of source materials on the occupation and the early years of the Cold War.

The FRG: From its origins to 1990

A. Glees, *Reinventing Germany. German Political Development since 1945*, Oxford and Washington, DC, Berg, 1996, and A. Nicholls, *Bonn Republic*, London, Longman, 1997, are good introductions to the Bonn Republic up to 1990. A more detailed two-volume 'blockbuster' is D. Bark and D. Gress, *A History of West Germany*, vol. 1, *From Shadow to Substance, 1945–63*, vol. 2, *Democracy and its Discontents, 1963–1991*, Oxford, Blackwell, 2nd edn, 1991. The biographies and autobiographies of the major politicians are also important sources for understanding the history of the FRG. K. Adenauer, *Memoirs*, London, Weidenfeld and Nicolson, 1966, and the comprehensive two-volume biography, H.-P. Schwarz, *A German Politician and Statesman in a Period of War, Revolution and Reconstruction*, 2 vols (translated), Oxford and Providence, RI; Berghahn, 1995–97 are key sources for the period 1945–63, particularly for foreign policy. There is useful material, particularly on *Ostpolitik*, in B. Marshall, *Willy Brandt, A Political Biography*, Basingstoke and London, Macmillan, 1997, while L. J. Erdinger, *Kurt Schumacher*, Stanford, Stanford University Press, CA, 1965, is helpful for the early post-war years of the SPD. Economic developments up to 1955 are covered by A. Kramer, *The West German Economy*, Oxford and New York, Berg, 1995, H. Giesch, K. H. Paque and H. Schmieding, *The Fading Miracle*, Cambridge, Cambridge University Press, 1992 and R. Overy, 'The Economy of the Federal

Republic since 1949', pp. 3–34 in K. Larres and P. Panikos (eds), *The Federal Republic since 1949*, Harlow, Longman, 1996, cover the picture up to 1990. An informative book on the new West German society is R. G. Moeller (ed.), *West Germany under Construction: Politics, Society and Culture in the Adenauer Era*, Ann Arbor, University of Michigan Press, 1997. The question of the Americanization of German society is discussed in R. Willett, *The Americanization of Germany*, London, Routledge, 1989, R. Pommerin (ed.), *The American Impact on Postwar Germany*, Oxford and Providence, RI, Berghahn, 1995; and M. Rosen, 'Reconstruction and Modernization. The Federal Republic and the Fifties', *Bulletin*, vol XIX, no. 1, May 1997, pp. 5–16, London, German Historical Institute. C. C. Schweitzer (ed.), *Politics and Government in Germany, 1944–1994: Basic Documents*, Oxford and New York, Berg (2nd edn), 1995, contains a useful collection of documents on politics in the FRG.

The GDR

The fall of the GDR in 1990 has inevitably made all the histories of East Germany written before that period out of date, as historians now have access to the East German archives. M. Fulbrook, *Anatomy of a Dictatorship. Inside the GDR, 1949–89*, Oxford, Oxford University Press, 1995, is one of the first books in English to use this new material and it has a useful chapter on the fall of the GDR. G. Pritchard, *The Making of the GDR*, Manchester, Manchester University Press, 2000, covers the early years of the Republic. Some older studies, such as M. McCauley, *The GDR since 1945*, Basingstoke and London, Macmillan, 1983, D. Childs, *The GDR: Moscow's German Ally*, London, Allen and Unwin, 1985, and G. Edwards, *GDR Society and Social Institutions*, London and Basingstoke, Macmillan, 1985, still remain useful for the political, social and economic aspects of the GDR. A. Baring, *Uprising in East Germany*, Ithaca, NY, Cornell University Press, repr. 1972, is well worth reading, but needs to be supplemented by post-1990 work, such as V. Ingimundarsan, 'Cold War Misperceptions: The Communist and Western responses to the East German Refugee Crisis in 1953', *Journal of Contemporary History*, vol. 29, 1994. K. J. Jarausch (ed.), *Dictatorship as Experience*, New York and Oxford, 1999, is an illuminating collection of essays on the socio-cultural history of the GDR, while J. Kopstein, *Economic Decline in East Germany, 1945–89*, Chapel Hill, NC, and London, University of North Carolina Press, 1997, is an interesting study of the GDR's economy. J. Thomaneck and J. Mells, *Politics, Society and Government in the GDR: Basic Documents*, Oxford and New York, Berg, 1989, contains a selection of relevant primary sources.

The Unification of Germany

Ostpolitik and unification are well covered in T. Garton Ash, *In Europe's Name. Germany and the Divided Continent*, London, Cape, 1993. K.

Jarausch, *The Rush to German Unity*, Oxford, Oxford Univerisity Press, 1994, is a readable and comprehensive account of the events leading to unification, while C. Maier, Dissolution. *The Crisis of Communism and the End of East Germany*, Princeton, Princeton University Press, 1997, is particularly good on the economic collapse of the GDR. A good collection of primary sources on unification is K. Jarausch and V. von Gransow (eds), *Uniting Germany. Documents and Debates 1944–93*, Oxford and Providence, RI, Berghahn, 1994.

The Berlin Republic

K. Larres (ed.), *Germany Since Unification. The Development of the Berlin Republic*, London and Basingstoke, Palgrave, 2001, is an informative collection of essays on the political, economic, military and diplomatic developments in the new Germany since 1990.

Glossary and Abbreviations

Anschluss: The incorporation of Austria into Germany, 1938.

APO: Extra-Parliamentary Opposition (*Ausserparlamentarische Opposition*). In December 1966 on the initiative of the radical student leader Rudi Dutschke, the APO was founded in opposition to the Grand Coalition. It had no formal structure and was closely connected to the Socialist Student Federation.

Aryan: Originally a Hindu term meaning a member of the highest caste, which first appeared in Count Gobineau's (1816–82) *Essay on the Inequality of the Races*. It was much used by the Nazis to denote ethnic Germans as opposed to Jews.

Blitzkrieg: A lightning war, which would, to quote Hitler, 'defeat the enemy as quickly as lightning'.

Bloc parties: In July 1945 the Russians created the anti-Fascist bloc of parties in the Soviet Zone. After April 1946 it was dominated by the SED (q.v.).

Bund: The German Confederation, 1815–66.

Bundesrat: Federal Council or upper house of parliament in which the *Länder* (q.v.) are represented in the FRG (q.v.). It was also the name of the upper house in the Second Reich, where the states were represented according to their size and power. Thus Prussia had 17 votes, Bavaria, 6, Saxony and Württemberg 4 each, and the other states from 3 to 1 each.

Bundestag: The lower house of parliament in the FRG (q.v.).

Bundeswehr: The Federal Army of the FRG (q.v.).

Bureaucracy: National and *Land* administrations, the civil service.

CDU: Christian Democratic Union (*Christlich Demokratische Union*).

CDUD: German Christian Democratic Union in the GDR (q.v.) (*Christlich Demokratische Union Deutschlands*).

Centre party: Founded by Ludwig Windthorst (1812–91) to defend Catholic interests in united Germany. From 1893–1907 it was the key party in a Conservative–Centre coalition, and it joined or co-operated with every coalition government in the Weimar Republic up to 1932. It was disbanded in 1933.

Collectivization: The replacement of private farms by LPGs (agricultural production co-operatives) in the GDR (q.v.) between 1952 and 1961.

COMECON: The Council For Mutual Economic Assistance, which was set up by Stalin in response to the European Recovery Programme (Marshall Aid). The GDR (q.v) joined it in 1950.

CSU: Christian Social Union in Bavaria (*Christlich–Soziale Union*). It is allied to the CDU (q.v.).

DAP: German Workers Party (*Deutsche Arbeiterpartei*).

DDP: German Democratic Party (*Deutsche Demokratische Partei*).

DNVP: German National People's Party (*Deutsch-nationale Volks-partei*).

DVP: German Peoples Party (*Deutsche Volkspartei*).

EDC: European Defence Community.

[E]EC: [European] Economic Community of which the FRG (q.v.) was a founding member.

Entente, Anglo-French: Originally an understanding reached by the two powers on colonial issues, but increasingly it became a focus for anti-German collaboration after the first Moroccan crisis.

Entente, Triple: The term applied to the collaboration between Britain, France and Russia, 1907–17.

FDJ: Free German Youth (*Freie Deutsche Jugend*). The youth movement in the GDR (q.v.), founded in 1946. In the 1980s membership was about 2,300,000.

FDP: Free Democratic Party (*Freie Demokratische Partei*).

FRG: Federal Republic of Germany.

Führer: Leader. The term adopted by Hitler to denote his absolute leadership over first the Nazi party and then Germany as a whole.

Gau: A regional division of the Nazi party organization.

Gauleiter: A regional Nazi party leader in charge of a *Gau*.

GDP: Gross Domestic Product.

GDR: German Democratic Republic.

German Labour Front (*Deutsche Arbeitsfront*): This was created in May 1933 and put under the control of Robert Ley to replace the trade unions.

Gleichschaltung: Literally co-ordinating or streamlining; the process of putting everything under Nazi control.

Grossdeutschland: A united Germany which includes the German-speaking regions of the Austrian Empire.

Holy Roman Empire: Originally composed of the German and North Italian territories of Otto I who was crowned emperor by the Pope in 962. From 1273 onwards the Empire was increasingly dominated by the Habsburgs. It was dissolved in 1806 by Napoleon.

Intentionalists: Historians who emphasize the importance of the *individual* and personal *intention* in history. For example, intentionalists, like Andreas Hillgruber, Klaus Hildebrand and Lucy Davidowicz, stress the *intentions* of Hitler and his key role in the formulation of policies, particularly the foreign and racial policies of the Third Reich (q.v. Structuralists).

Junker class: A term used to describe the great east Elbian Prussian landowners. The term originally came from *Jungherr* and denoted the sons of the nobility serving as officer cadets.

Kartell: Cartel or manufacturer's group set up to control and regulate production. Also used to describe an alliance of parties in the Second Reich.

KDF: Strength through Joy (*Kraft durch Freude*). The leisure organization of the German Labour Front (q.v.).

Kleindeutschland: A united Germany without Austria and therefore dominated by Prussia.

Kolonialverein: Colonial Society founded in 1887; it helped create the ideological framework in which German nationalism developed up to 1914. The society remained active during the Weimar period.

KPD: The German Communist Party (Kommistische Partei Deutschlands). Founded in 1919 and banned in 1933; after working underground it was refounded in 1945, and amalgamated with the Soviet Zone SPD (q.v.) in 1946 to create the SED (q.v.).

Kulturkampf: A struggle between cultures. A term used to describe Bismarck's conflict with the Catholic Church, 1881–87.

Land: An individual German state within united Germany. The Reich of 1871 had 25 federal states, the largest being Prussia which covered two-thirds of Germany (q.v. *Bundesrat*).

Landtag: Chamber of deputies at the level of one of the individual German states.

Landwehr: Set up in February 1813 to comprise all men not serving in the regular army. In 1815 the *Landwehr* was reorganized, so that in war it would amalgamate with the regular army, but in time of peace keep its character as a militia. Increasingly the liberals saw it, in Boyen's words, as 'the happy union of the warrior and civilian society'. Hence their dismay at von Roon's reforms in 1860, which reduced its size and down-graded its importance.

Lebensraum: Literally living space, which Hitler hoped to gain for an apparently overpopulated Germany in Russia. This was a key component of his foreign policy.

Mittelstand: Literally 'middle estate'. It denoted what in Britain was called the 'lower middle class': peasants, small businessmen, self-employed artisans and white-collar office workers.

Modernization: According to the German sociologist, Max Weber, and later German and American scholars, this involved first the emergence of a modern capitalist economy and bureaucracy and then a democratic national state (q.v. *Sonderweg*).

Moratorium: A suspension of debt (or reparations) payment.

National Front of Democratic Germany: Formed in 1949 in the GDR (q.v.) to campaign for a united democratic socialist Germany; in reality it was a front for Soviet control of the GDR.

Nationalism: In the course of German history from 1815 until the present, nationalism has taken on several different forms, ranging from a sense of linguistic and cultural identity to the more aggressive ambitions in the *Kaiserreich* to become a world power. Under the Nazis nationalism led to the Holocaust and the extermination policies in eastern Europe.

Nationalverein: The National Union founded in 1858 to agitate for the creation of a *kleindeutsch* (q.v. Germany).

NATO: North Atlantic Treaty Organization set up in 1949. The FRG (q.v.) joined in 1955.

NPD: The right-wing National Democratic Party (*Nationaldemokratische Partei Deutschlands*) was formed in 1964.

NSDAP: The National Socialist German Workers party (*Nationalsozialistische Deutsche Arbeiterpartei*). In February 1920 the small German Workers party changed its name to NSDAP. In July 1921 Hitler was elected chairman. It was banned after the Munich *putsch* but refounded in 1925. On 14 July 1933 it was declared the only legal political party in Germany.

OPEC: Organization of Petroleum Exporting Countries.

Ostpolitik: The eastern policy conducted by the FRG (q.v.) towards the GDR (q.v).

Pan-Germans: Those who believed in the unification of all Germans in Europe. Hence the Pan-German League believed that the 1871 frontiers were only the starting point for the future development of the German state.

PDS: Party of Democratic Socialism (successor to the SED (q.v)).

Politbureau: The Political Bureau of the SED (q.v.). It was based on the Russian model and was the key decision-making body in the GDR (q.v.).

Progressive Liberal Party (*Fortschrittspartei*): Founded in 1861 and underwent several amalgamations with subsequent name changes until 1918, when most of its members joined the DDP (q.v.).

RAF: Red Army Faction (Rote Armee Fraktion). A left-wing extremist group which carried out a campaign of violence in the FRG (q.v.) in the 1970s and 1980s.

Reich: Literally Empire. The first Reich was the Holy Roman Empire (q.v.). The Second Reich was the united *Kleindeutschland* of 1871, while Hitler used the term Third Reich to describe the new Nazi Germany in 1933. This term had come into common usage with the publication of Moeller van den Bruck's book, *Germany's Third Reich* in 1923.

Reichsbank: The German Central Bank, 1875–1945, responsible for currency issue.

Reichsrat: The upper house of the German parliament in which the federal states were represented, 1919–33. It was, unlike the *Bundesrat* (q.v.), which it replaced, in practice subordinated to the democratically elected *Reichstag* (q.v.).

Reichstag: The lower house of the German parliament, 1871–1945.

Reichswehr: The German army, 1919–35. This was then replaced by the term *Wehrmacht*, which also included the air force and navy.

RKFDV: Commissar for the Consolidation of German Nationhood (*Reichskommissar für die Festigung des Deutschen Volksstums*). This position gave Himmler responsibility for 'ethnic cleansing' in eastern Europe.

SA: Nazi storm or assault troops (*Sturmabteilung*). The SA was originally founded in 1921 to protect party meetings. With the elimination of Röhm on 30 June 1934 it effectively lost its power to the SS (q.v.).

SAG: Soviet limited company (*Sowjetische Aktiengesellschaft*). These were set up in the Soviet Zone in January 1946 to produce goods for the USSR as part of the German reparation programme.

SD: Security Service of the SS (*Sicherheitsdienst*) (q.v.).

SED: Socialist Unity Party of Germany (*Sozialistische Partei Deutschlands*).

Septennat: A septennial (i.e. lasting for 7 years) military budget.

SMAD: Soviet military administration in Germany.

Sonderweg: Literally special path. Scholars such as Hans-Ulrich Wehler, using Britain and France as models, have argued that industrialization in Germany was not accompanied by social and political 'modernization' or democratization. Hence Germany took its 'special path'. This is disputed, particularly by D. Blackbourn and G. Eley.

SPD: The German Social Democratic party (*Sozialdemokratische Partei Deutschlands*) was formed through the amalgamation of Ferdinand Lassalle's General German Workers' Union and August Bebel's Union of German Workers' Associations at the unity congress at Gotha in 1875. By 1912 the SPD was the largest party in Germany. It was dissolved by Hitler, but was reformed in 1945 (q.v. SED and USPD).

SS: Literally protection squad (*Schutzstaffel*). It was founded in 1925 to protect the leading Nazis. It played a key role within the Nazi party, when Himmler was put in charge of it in 1929, and then, after 1933, in Nazi Germany. When Himmler established control over the whole police and security systems within the Reich in 1936, its influence was greatly strengthened. Its control of the police and then the occupied territories enabled it to play a dominant role in formulating the racial policy of the third Reich (q.v. *Waffen-SS*).

Stasi: State Security Police (*Staatssicherheitsdienst*) in the GDR (q.v.).

Structuralists: The name given to the school of historians, the most eminent members of which are H. and W. Mommsen, M. Broszat and H.-U. Wehler, who apply a structural analysis to modern German history. When dealing with the Third Reich, they play down the role of the individual and place more emphasis on the German élites and the polycratic nature of the regime (q.v. Intentionalists).

USPD: German Independent Social Democratic Party (*Unabhängige Sozialdemokratische Partei Deutschlands*).

Völkisch: This term can be translated as 'folkish', but there is no real equivalent in English. The *Völkisch* ideology preached the creation and preservation of a traditional Germanic, national and above all racial community. It was anti-Semitic, as the Jews were perceived to be a threat to the traditional Germany, and it formed an important component of the ideology of the Nazi party. (q.v. nationalism).

Volksgemeinschaft: Literally national community. This was to be created by unifying the population primarily on the basis of nationalism (q.v.) and race. By fusing nationalism with some elements of socialism, Hitler hoped to end class conflict and create a new national community.

Volkskammer: Lower house of the GDR parliament (q.v.).

Waffen-SS: Militarized or armed SS. A term first used in 1940. Three SS regiments were created after 1934, which formed the core of the *Waffen-SS* (q.v. SS).

Warsaw Pact: A military alliance of eastern European Communist states set up by the USSR in 1955. The GDR joined in 1956 (q.v).

Zollverein: The German Customs Union formed in 1833 with a membership of 18 states. By 1852 only the two Mecklenburgs, the Hansa cities and Holstein remained outside. The Austrian Empire, however, remained excluded.

Index